BIOGRAPHICAL MEMOIRS OF
FELLOWS OF THE BRITISH ACADEMY
XIII

Biographical Memoirs of
Fellows of the British Academy
XIII

Published for THE BRITISH ACADEMY
by OXFORD UNIVERSITY PRESS

Oxford University Press, Great Clarendon Street, Oxford OX2 6DP

Oxford New York
Auckland Bangkok Bogotá Buenos Aires Cape Town Chennai
Dar es Salaam Delhi Hong Kong Istanbul Karachi Kolkata
Kuala Lumpur Madrid Melbourne Mexico City Mumbai Nairobi
São Paulo Shanghai Singapore Taipei Tokyo Toronto

British Library Cataloguing in Publication Data
Data available

978–0–19–726585–7

Typeset in Times
by New Leaf Design, Scarborough, North Yorkshire
Printed on acid-free paper by
Antony Rowe Limited,
Chippenham, Wiltshire

The Academy is grateful to Professor Ron Johnston, FBA
for his editorial work on this volume

Contents

KENNETH ANDREWS

Kenneth Raymond Andrews
1921–2012

K. R. ANDREWS, known to colleagues as Ken, died on 6 January 2012. He was born in London on 26 August 1921 to Arthur Walter and Marion Gertrude Andrews. He received his schooling at Henry Thornton School, Clapham, and went to King's College University of London in 1939, originally to study languages, but he soon switched to history. After a year he joined the RAF and served in Kenya and the Yemen. He returned to university after the war, graduated with a first in History in 1948, and was then taken on as a research student by C. R. Boxer who supervised his Ph.D. research on 'The economic aspects of Elizabethan privateering'. Ken proceeded briskly and the degree was duly awarded by the University of London in 1951.

After graduation, Ken became a teacher of history at what then was the Ealing Technical College where he catered mainly for A-Level and day release students. Having served this apprenticeship he received an academic position at the University of Liverpool for the short interlude, 1963–4, after which he was appointed in 1964 to a lectureship in the Department of History at the University of Hull to replace Ralph Davis, who had proceeded from there to the chair in Economic History at Leicester. At Hull, Ken advanced quickly from lecturer to senior lecturer and served 1979–88 (part-time 1986–8) as Professor of History. Although a Londoner through and through, and although burdened with a teaching and administrative load much greater than his academic counterparts at better endowed universities in the United Kingdom, Ken Andrews remained attached and loyal to Hull and published his best work from there. He also attracted some research students, including John C. Appleby who followed Ken's lead both in investigating the holdings of the High Court of Admiralty, particularly as these related to Ireland, and in pursuing the history of piracy and outlawry in England.[1] It came as little surprise therefore when Ken announced at his retirement dinner that he intended to remain in Cottingham, having developed a great affection for the landscapes of the East Riding of Yorkshire.

Andrews was brought into the academic stream in 1963 when D. B. Quinn, who then held the Andrew Geddes and John Rankin Chair of Modern History at the University of Liverpool, supported him for a one-year temporary lectureship there. The two were already acquainted since their research interests overlapped, and Quinn had been acting as unofficial mentor to Ken during his years at Ealing. As a historian Andrews was greatly influenced by Quinn not only in his choice of research subject but also in his methodology and mode of communication. Thus where Quinn had launched himself in 1940 as a scholar of English exploration with his two-volume Hakluyt edition on *The Voyages and Colonising Enterprises of Sir Humphrey Gilbert* and followed this up in 1955 with a further two volumes devoted to *The Roanoke Voyages, 1584–1590*, Andrews commenced his publishing career in 1959, while still at Ealing, with a Hakluyt edition on *English Privateering Voyages to the West Indies, 1588–1595*. A Hakluyt sequel followed in 1972 devoted to *The Last Voyages of Drake and Hawkins*. Both master and mature disciple were concerned to compile and annotate the evidence that would justify a reinterpretation of England's encounters with the wider world during the sixteenth and seventeenth centuries. Therefore Andrews's 1978 tribute to his erstwhile mentor, following upon Quinn's retirement from Liverpool, might almost have been a description of his own work; Quinn, he then said, had reconstructed 'the foundations of history ... not by the all-too-fashionable method of thinking up a bright idea and rummaging around for enough evidence to make it plausible, but by applying all the technical resources of research to clarify existing knowledge and supplement it with new, producing thereby a deeper and ultimately truer understanding of the past'.[2] The readiness with which both Quinn and Andrews dedicated themselves to the incremental advancement of knowledge through empirical investigation is surprising given that for

---

[1] J. C. Appleby (ed.), *A Calendar of Material Relating to Ireland from the High Court of Admiralty Examinations, 1536–1641* (Dublin, 1992); J. C. Appleby and P. Dalton (eds.), *Outlaws in Medieval and Early Modern England: Crime, Government and Society, c.1066–c.1600* (London, 2009).

[2] K. R. Andrews, N. P. Canny and P. E. H. Hair, 'David Beers Quinn', Preface to K. R. Andrews, N. P. Canny and P. E. H. Hair (eds.), *The Westward Enterprise; English Activities in Ireland, the Atlantic and America, 1480–1650* (Liverpool, 1978), p. viii; as the coordinator of this jointly authored appraisal of Quinn I can testify that these were Andrews's words.

long periods of their careers each was committed to Marxism, in practice as well as ideologically. Quinn satisfied what he would have seen as his vocational responsibility when, in 1947, he published his short volume *Raleigh and the British Empire* in the Home University Library imprint; a series designed by scholars-of-the-left to reach people who had not enjoyed the opportunity to attend university. Andrews followed Quinn's example in 1967 with his lively and opinionated *Drake's Voyages* which was reissued in 1970 in a Panther edition directed at the general public.

For their mainstream work, however, each persisted with the meticulous collection of fresh evidence, possibly because investigation into the origins of Britain's overseas empire had been previously studied closely by a sequence of scholars who had exulted in the achievements of the great English mariners of early modern times and who had reached a broad audience at a time when the history of empire was both popular and academically fashionable. Andrews, like Quinn, appreciated that these earlier interpretations could be superseded only if it could be shown that the evidence on which they were based was deficient in one or several respects. Quinn and Andrews each showed respect for the labours of those who had previously worked in the field—the names of Alexander Brown, J. S. Corbett, V. T. Harlow, A. P. Newton and J. A. Williamson come to mind as proximate predecessors, with Hakluyt and Purchas being the best known names from earlier centuries. However, while they corrected those who had gone before them in matters of detail they also distanced themselves from their more jingoistic and/or romantic conclusions. Where Quinn had done so by displaying an interest in, and concern for, the native populations and cultures (native American or Irish) that fell foul of the acquisitiveness of English adventurers, Andrews alluded repeatedly to the plunder and piracy that was pursued by the well-known Elizabethan sea adventurers such as Drake, Raleigh and Hawkins, and he demonstrated that some of London's leading merchants and several senior figures at court invested in, and profited from, extra-legal activities. When Andrews insisted that several of 'the most successful businessmen of the age' who, in 1600, constituted 'the nucleus of the East India Company', had previously been active promoters of Caribbean raiding and African slaving, he was also upholding his more general proposition that England's capitalist system was based on theft from European competitors no less than from native populations.[3] This contention was analogous to the more frequently invoked Marxist mantra formulated originally by Eric Williams which

---

[3] K. R. Andrews (ed.), *English Privateering Voyages to the West Indies, 1588–1595* (Cambridge, 1959), p. 32.

held that Britain's Industrial Revolution had been enabled by profits from the slave trade.[4]

If the propositions expounded by Andrews dovetailed with his ideological preferences, he recognised that they stood no hope of winning scholarly, much less popular, acceptance unless he could sustain them with fresh evidence. Here his earlier interest in languages came to his assistance and he delved into Spanish archival sources, particularly in Seville, as well as in the records of the High Court of Admiralty, housed at the then Public Record Office, to gain a balanced view of England's overseas endeavours. His guide to the Spanish material was the American historian Irene A. Wright who had been long immersed in a projected three-volume Hakluyt Society edition of Spanish accounts of English voyages to, and intrusions in, Spanish America during the sixteenth century. When the advance of years prevented her from proceeding beyond a second volume she presented Ken Andrews with the remaining notes she had extracted from the Spanish archives.[5] Andrews gladly accepted and augmented this material for his volume *English Privateering Voyages to the West Indies, 1588–1595*. Here he used the Spanish evidence to corroborate the information he had gleaned from English sources, but he valued it particularly for the insight it provided on the impact—'psychological and economic, naval and military'—that repeated English attacks had exerted upon settler Spanish communities scattered across the Caribbean.[6]

Andrews's prime source on the English side to England's privateering activities during those years came from the files of the High Court of Admiralty. One of his signal achievements in his very first volume was in reaching an understanding of, and then explaining, how that very complex court had operated and what strands of information could be garnered from the various complaints, testimonies, depositions, interrogations, and summations of day-to-day activities that are included within the archives of a court that had a vast range of responsibilities and involved a broad community of interests. The work of the court, as he made clear, ranged from licensing privateers to tracking and deciding upon the distribution of the loot they captured and to adjudicating upon disputes—

---

[4] E. Williams, *Capitalism and Slavery* (Chapel Hill, NC, 1944).
[5] I. A. Wright (ed.), *Documents Concerning English Voyages to the Spanish Main, 1569–1580* (London, 1932); I. A. Wright (ed.), *Further English Voyages to Spanish America, 1583–1594* (London, 1951); Wright's original interest had been in the Spanish Caribbean itself as shown in I. A. Wright (ed.), *Historia Documentada de San Cristobal de la Habana*, 2 vols. (Havana, 1930).
[6] Andrews, *English Privateering Voyages*, p. 2.

including international disputes—to which the activities of privateers and pirates inevitably gave rise.

This section of what is a very fine introduction to Andrews's first Hakluyt edition constitutes evidence of his concern to master whatever information proved necessary to understanding the mind and the world of all the different categories of people involved with Caribbean ventures. These people ranged from those who sponsored the ventures and those who designed, constructed and equipped the vessels, to those who manned the ships and charted and commanded successive expeditions. Andrews was at pains also to establish the licit and illicit profits that each group made from its involvement, and what benefit accrued to the government, and to the servants of the Admiralty Court, from both privateering activity and piratical pursuits.

As he set about his task, Andrews found a ready-made audience among the members of the Hakluyt Society and those interested in naval history. However, he became somewhat disenchanted to find that as Britain was entering upon the post-imperial phase of its development he was considered by most historians of his generation to be traversing obscure, and for them irrelevant, pathways of the Elizabethan era. It was reasonable for Andrews to conclude that he was being isolated from the historical mainstream because, with Geoffrey Elton as the rising star in Tudor studies, the focus of research activity in political history was shifting chronologically from the reign of Queen Elizabeth to that of King Henry VIII, and thematically from parliament to the royal court and the administrative instruments of government. However, Andrews had hoped that economic historians would have embraced his work, only to find that as these came to attach increasing store on quantification they showed scant respect for subjects for which precise economic or demographic data were either not available or had never existed. He voiced his frustration retrospectively in writing to a colleague in 1985: 'they [Economic Historians] certainly never regarded me as one of them—did I ever say anything about the cloth trade or the Merchant Adventurers? My relationship with them was never any better than my relationship with the naval historians, who generally failed equally to see the connections between overseas trade and maritime warfare. My work has been a long uphill battle to bridge this gap, bringing commercial and naval history into a fruitful partnership, but few have understood—Ralph Davis was one of the few.'[7]

---

[7] The quotation is from K. Andrews to Donald Woodward, 5 Sept. 1985, and supplied to me by Donald Woodward.

When he was confronted with the reality that the historical subjects to which he had devoted his life were even being dropped from the history and economic history undergraduate curricula of British universities, Ken Andrews saw the need to win readers for what he considered to be defining moments of Britain's historical past by educating them *ex nihilo*. Thus in successive publications he took to explaining the human and physical geography of the Spanish Caribbean and its climatic and seasonal variations; the intricacies of navigation during the early modern period; the design, construction and repair of sixteenth-century ships; and the financial instruments used to launch and profit from high-risk, but potentially high-gain, maritime ventures of the sixteenth century. Andrews saw the need for such explication even when writing for members of the Hakluyt Society who constituted a captive and well-informed audience. Then in his first monograph, *Elizabethan Privateering: English Privateering during the Spanish War, 1585–1603,* he located his chosen subject within a context that was familiar to readers of mainstream history, including professional historians.[8] Thus, when he set out to explain that privateering was piracy under another name, he described how a parsimonious Queen Elizabeth licensed English sailors, some of them former pirates, to attack Spanish ships because this was the only means, besides a formal declaration of war with its attendant cost to the state, by which English merchants could receive compensation for the losses they had suffered on those occasions when their cargoes had been seized by the Spanish authorities. He also made it clear that Elizabeth had a political purpose in mind when she licensed privateers to the extent that she hoped that this would prove an inexpensive way to persuade the Spanish government to desist from consolidating its military position in Flanders and thus threatening the security of England. Andrews also contended that however expedient such stratagems might have seemed to Elizabeth's government they were not generally favoured by London's principal merchants who previously had been profiting from peaceful trade with Spain and whose agents in Spain had been willing even to participate in Catholic worship whenever such compliance furthered their commercial ends. Such established merchants, he insisted, became reluctant privateers and risked their ships for such ventures only after open warfare between England and Spain made conventional trade impossible. Even then, he contended, they treated privateering as a supplement to, or a substitution for, orthodox trading activity.

---

[8] K. R. Andrews, *Elizabethan Privateering: English Privateering during the Spanish War, 1585–1603* (Cambridge, 1964).

Thus, Andrews explained, in a way that nobody had done previously, that there were various strands to Elizabethan privateering, and that London's leading merchants, who had profited considerably from privateering during the war years, resumed their traditional eastward-looking trade with Europe once peaceful conditions were restored. The marginal participants who had never drawn any distinction between trade and plunder had no 'normal' trade to return to after 1604, and Andrews explained how, in the absence of such, they persisted with unorthodox activity in the Caribbean and along the coastline of North America where conditions continued to be unruly and the power of Spain was less securely established. Here he anticipated the thesis that would be popularised and elaborated upon some years later by Robert Brenner.[9]

Whereas in *Elizabethan Privateering* Andrews was aiming to persuade professional historians of the relevance of his subject to their various interests, his *Drake's Voyages*, as was mentioned, was directed at a general audience and was more pedagogic and ideological in purpose in that it set out to inform and raise the political consciousness of a general public who had never had the opportunity to study history in a formal setting. In this volume, Andrews deployed to especially good effect his proven ability to detail and explain in simple language the complicated technicalities associated with forgotten crafts. Here also he set about demythologising the exploits of Drake and other Elizabethan mariners, and dispelled the romantic aura that had been cultivated by authors of previous centuries by exposing the brutal, ruthless, exploitative and temperamental sides to Drake's character. Not all was debunking, however, and Andrews cultivated a new respect for Drake's seamanship as this had been demonstrated both by his global circumnavigation of 1580, which Andrews ranked 'among the greatest feats of early European oceanic enterprise', and by Drake's ability to outwit and outmanoeuvre his Spanish opponents at close quarter and in confined space.[10] While he pointed, in several instances, to the lack of coherence in the various attacks that English adventurers launched against the Spanish presence in the Americas, and more particularly in the Caribbean, and to the inconsequence of individual assaults relative to Spain's military prowess, he showed how cumulatively these attacks undermined Spanish confidence in its ability to defend

[9] R. Brenner, *Merchants and Revolution; Commercial Change, Political Conflict and London's Overseas Traders, 1550–1643* (Princeton, NJ, 1993).
[10] K. R. Andrews, *Drake's Voyages: a Re-Assessment of their Place in Elizabethan Maritime Expansion* (London, 1970, Panther edn.), p. 98.

all its Atlantic (and even its global) empire. In this way he demonstrated how the success of Elizabethan adventurers laid the foundations for what would become a more significant English presence in the Caribbean in the seventeenth century.

However, as Andrews identified new reasons for lauding the achievements of Elizabeth's sea-dogs, he questioned the high-minded motives that had been attributed to them by the authors of previous generations who had cherished their memory either as the upholders of Protestantism and freedom against the tyranny of Catholic Spain, or as the progenitors of England's imperial power of the nineteenth century which its admirers had usually depicted as benevolent. To counter such presumption, Andrews reflected upon the economic crisis of the mid-sixteenth century and detailed how John Dudley, Duke of Northumberland, 'chiefly remembered as an unscrupulous plunderer of monasteries, guilds and chantries', had also patronised sea adventures and thus channelled into overseas endeavour the 'ambition, greed and ruthlessness' that he, and other members of the 'new nobility', had manifested when enriching themselves at the expense of the church. Their unscrupulousness, claimed Andrews, bore further fruit in Elizabeth's reign when 'the most active' of the 'great men in Court and Council ... formed a generation of gold-hungry men whose energy and greed was fortunately turned seawards into piracy, privateering, colonization, trade, exploration' and boosted 'the movement of maritime expansion'.[11]

Such emotive language which had characterised the prose of Kenneth Andrews from the outset of his career was absent from his next major publication; his Hakluyt documentary edition of 1972 which attempted a reconstruction of the *Last Voyage of Drake and Hawkins* that led to the death of both sea adventurers. In this, more than in his earlier publications, Andrews drew upon archival holdings in Spain and France acknowledging again that he had been guided in his search of the archives in Seville by Irene Wright, but now also by Engel Sluiter from the University of California at Berkeley.[12] However, he stated that he was now no longer interested in presenting 'another interpretation' of what transpired in the West Indian enterprise of 1595–6, and while he occasionally offered his 'own opinion' both on the personalities involved and on the course of events, he left it to his readers to 'draw their own conclusions' from the 'representative documents and associated information' that he was plac-

---

[11] Andrews, *Drake's Voyages*, pp. 20–2.
[12] K. R. Andrews (ed.), *The Last Voyage of Drake and Hawkins* (London, 1972), p. xi.

ing before them.[13] In doing so he was confident that the addition both of fresh evidence from Continental archives and of previously neglected papers concerning Sir Thomas Baskerville (who commanded the fleet after Drake's death), would lead his readers to the conclusion that the purpose of this expedition of 1595–6, that included 1,000 soldiers as well as 1,500 sailors, was to dislodge the Spanish from the Isthmus of Panama and to establish an English presence there. One of the justifications for this undertaking, which Andrews regarded as an act of folly, was to divert Spain from assembling yet another Armada; this time probably to invade Ireland rather than England. This invocation by Andrews of considerations from high politics to explain developments at sea, suggests that he was again bidding for admission to the academic mainstream, as does the attention he gave to court factionalism to explain the choice of those officers who held positions of authority in this expedition. That Andrews was seeking to make peace also with naval historians is suggested by his inclusion of an essay by Commander D. W. Waters on 'The art of navigation in the age of Drake' to round-off this Hakluyt edition.[14]

All of this laborious assembling, augmenting, editing and reflecting upon evidence appertaining to England's overseas ventures, particularly in the Caribbean, during the sixteenth and early seventeenth centuries was regarded positively by scholars but Ken Andrews was coming to realise that he was correcting rather than adding to what had been done by others and that he would never contribute further to fresh knowledge unless he could balance what he had come to know of English overseas ventures with details of Spanish achievements. The opportunity to do so came with the award of a Nuffield Fellowship which enabled Andrews to spend a full year in Seville freed from his onerous teaching and administrative responsibilities at Hull. His investigations in poorly catalogued collections continued to be guided by the previous investigations of Engel Sluiter and Irene Wright, the latter by now deceased. However, Andrews went much further than either of these scholars in the book that resulted from his fresh research, *The Spanish Caribbean: Trade and Plunder, 1530–1630*. There he created a vivid picture of a sector of Spain's Atlantic Empire that had come to be little regarded by historians of his generation but which, as he made clear, was vital to the interest of Spain throughout the early modern centuries.[15] He demonstrated how Spain's early involvement

[13] Ibid., p. 1.
[14] Ibid., pp. 259–65.
[15] K. R. Andrews, *The Spanish Caribbean: Trade and Plunder, 1530–1630* (New Haven, CT, 1978).

with the Caribbean following the Columbus voyages became a natural extension of its earlier exploitation of the people and resources of the Canary Islands and was characterised by the same indiscipline and 'colonizing attitude' that, as David Abulafia has recently established in greater detail, had led to the destruction of the indigenous population of the Canaries.[16] Andrews then showed how in practice the Greater Antilles proved more fertile and productive than the Canary Islands had ever been, and were soon producing a range of commodities that found a ready market in Europe—some, such as cotton, medicinal plants, salt and pearls, that were native to the Caribbean and others, notably sugar and hides, that had been introduced there by the Spaniards at a huge cost to the natural environment. He further explained that the development that provoked greatest interest in Spain was the discovery of gold on the island of Santo Domingo with a resulting brief gold rush that hastened the demise of a native population which was already faring badly from Spanish contact.

It becomes clear from Andrews's book why some Spaniards retained an interest in the Caribbean for its own sake even if it diminished in relative importance in the eyes of Spanish officials, and in the Spanish popular imagination, once Spaniards achieved even more spectacular successes in Central America and in Peru. Spanish achievements there, however, added a new strategic importance to the Caribbean, which Andrews describes as an 'American Mediterranean', because all the ships bearing precious metals from the New World to Spain had, of necessity, to pass that way. This also explains how, with the passage of time, smugglers, corsairs and privateers from other European nations were particularly attracted to the Spanish Caribbean with a view to lurking in places from which to attack the Spanish silver fleet on its return journey. The Spanish response was to give greater attention to administering and defending a part of its Atlantic Empire that had become a backwater, and their effort to recover their presence led ultimately to the conflict for the control of this area to which Ken Andrews would return in his next book.

This, his magisterial *Trade, Plunder and Settlement: Maritime Enterprise and the Genesis of the British Empire, 1480–1630*, which appeared in 1984, is the book for which the name of Kenneth Andrews is best known to economic historians, historians of colonial British America, historians of European expansion overseas and mainstream historians of early modern England.[17] Andrews had, by this stage, left the anger of youth and middle

[16] David Abulafia, *Atlantic Encounters in the Age of Columbus* (New Haven, CT, 2008).
[17] K. R. Andrews, *Trade, Plunder and Settlement: Maritime Enterprise and the Genesis of the British Empire, 1480–1630* (Cambridge, 1984).

age behind him, but this did not debar him from looking critically at England's imperial legacy, as he had done as early as 1939 when, as he put it himself, he had 'shocked his school-mates and masters by forecasting (without much argument or evidence) the downfall of the British Empire'. Now he insisted that his appraisal of that legacy was no longer 'motivated by any political or philosophical concern' because he had ceased almost twenty years before then to subscribe 'to any sort of Marxism ... and to any sort of political movement ten years before that'.[18] Thus in 1984 as Andrews traced England's engagement with the wider world from the close of the Middle Ages, through the crisis of the 1550s, to the even greater economic crisis of the 1620s, he contended that he was being guided to his conclusions by the empirical evidence he had been assembling during his working life rather than by any ideological fixation. One of these conclusions was that it was 'the crude pursuit of riches' added to the 'insatiable thrust for fame and honour' that motivated the cast of adventurers whose risks and hardships he chronicled and whose efforts led ultimately, but not inevitably, to the creation of a British overseas empire.[19] Few, he contended, were inspired by the other 'sentiments'—the desire to uplift or evangelise foreign peoples, or to create model settlements, or to achieve economic self-sufficiency for England—that were 'invoked to explain, justify or recommend projects'. These latter were important, he suggested, only because they helped to win support in England for 'the idea of a maritime empire' in the decades before this had gripped 'the imagination of the English people'.[20] While Andrews was satisfied that communal, and even governmental, support for this grander project was ultimately secured, he remained convinced that a successful outcome was never assured given the disadvantages under which English seafarers worked as compared with various Continental competitors in such matters as ship design and construction, the training of mariners, the mobilisation of finance, and the securing of consistent support from the state. This led Andrews to conclude that while 'a British empire overseas' was born at some point in the early 1600s what emerged from the womb was 'a sickly child and all but still born', as compared with the vibrant empires of other European powers (now the Dutch as much as the Iberians) that then flourished.[21] This reality, he was only too well aware, had done nothing to stem the glorification of these early achievements

[18] Andrews, *Trade, Plunder and Settlement*, pp. vii–viii.
[19] Ibid., p. 31.
[20] Ibid., pp. 31, 35.
[21] Ibid., p. 359.

that had contributed so much to the 'English nationalism' of his and previous generations. Therefore the final contribution of K. R. Andrews to correcting the distortions of his predecessors (and also those of some of his contemporaries) was in demonstrating that 'the involvement of England in the process of European overseas expansion was a natural consequence of her integral role in the commercial, political and cultural life of Europe'.[22]

Such a conclusion would have irritated the new right of Prime Minister Margaret Thatcher's generation no less than Andrews's previous Marxian explanations for the genesis of England's overseas empire had vexed academic supporters of previous Tory regimes. However, his ability to anchor his opinions in empirical evidence drawn from an extensive range of sources, his skill at situating his subject within contexts that were meaningful to political as well as economic historians, as well as his formal announcement that he had come in from the political cold, combined to explain why, in 1986, K. R. Andrews was elected a Fellow of the British Academy after he had been proposed by G. R. Elton, C. R. Boxer, D. C. Coleman, and Charles Wilson. Of these Elton was already the *doyen* of the political and constitutional history of the Tudor period; Boxer was the recognised expert on the history of Europe's overseas expansion; and Coleman and Wilson were authorities respectively on the economic and technological histories of the early modern centuries. Only such a combination could have done justice to the range of interests and competencies that K. R. Andrews had mastered during a long and productive career. In the citation he was credited with having 'effectively rewritten the history of Elizabethan expansion overseas, greatly enlarging and deepening what was thought to be a familiar story', in an extensive corpus of published work that bore 'the distinction not only of judicious powers of assessment but also of a lively and creative imagination'. Perhaps his most consequential achievement had been in convincing the then-recognised leaders of the different dimensions to early modern British history that the threads he had been weaving over a lifetime of scholarship had made a vital contribution to the better understanding of the subjects they had been explicating throughout their careers. On the other side it may have been their recognition of his achievements that provided Ken Andrews with the professional self-assurance that gave him the stimulus to engage in a final burst of archival investigation that brought his interests forward in time and culminated

[22] Andrews, *Trade, Plunder and Settlement*, pp. 363, 364.

in *Ships, Money and Politics: Seafaring and Naval Enterprise in the Reign of Charles I*, and which appeared when he was already 70 years of age.[23]

Belated peer recognition encouraged Ken Andrews forth from the cocoon within which he had sheltered for much of his life, partly because his first marriage, in 1949, to Hildegard Gurassa from Poland had brought him little happiness before it was finally dissolved in 1961. He was altogether more fortunate in his second marriage in 1969 to Ottilie Schobrová née Kalman, from Olomouc, whom he had met when he was a British Council Lecturer to what was then Czechoslovakia. As his wife, Otti, as she liked to be called, was a great home-maker and fine cook, and together they became generous hosts to a small group of close friends. Through Otti also, Ken, or Andy as he was known to his new family, acquired two stepsons and two step-grandchildren. He thrived on these new connections, and became particularly close to Barbara, Otti's grand-daughter, who lives in Vancouver, to whom he proved supportive, especially in her academic endeavours after she had sustained severe injuries in a road accident about twenty years ago. A great void came into Ken's life when Otti died suddenly in January 2000. However, the broader interests he had developed in walking, chess, swimming, and listening to jazz continued to enrich his life. These, together with his continuing interest in England's ventures overseas and his enthusiastic involvement with the local U3A, sustained him for twelve further years.

NICHOLAS CANNY
Fellow of the Academy

Note. Given that I only once met Ken Andrews and exchanged but a few letters with him I am especially indebted to Donald Woodward, his former colleague at Hull, for supplying details and reminiscences on a shy but a loyal and principled man. Ken's stepson, Professor Jan Schober, also provided some insights on the private man. Hamish Scott offered invaluable support, advice and information at all stages as I prepared this memoir.

[23] K. R. Andrews, *Ships, Money and Politics: Seafaring and Naval Enterprise in the Reign of Charles I* (Cambridge, 1991).

ANTHONY BLUNT

Courtesy of the Courtauld Institute of Art

Anthony Frederick Blunt
1907–1983

Introduction

IT IS MORE than thirty years since Blunt died, too long for the kind of appreciation normally accorded to the recently dead, yet perhaps not quite sufficient for him to have receded far enough into the depths of time past for the abnormal circumstances of his life to be reviewed without disturbing the calm detachment needed for straightforward historical research. He is still, though only just, within the living memory of those who could be said to have known him at all well, and the embers of feelings that once ran high in the aftermath of his exposure in 1979 may be rekindled by this belated reopening of the inquest. It is not meant to be an exculpation of his clandestine activities, though it may seem like that to some, since it attempts to correct the disproportion between the attention that has been given to the spying episode, and his academic life and career. It is still possible for this to be done, though there are few of us left who had insight into, or sympathy with, his thought world, and time is running out.

The reasons why art history has been consistently underrated or ignored in the literature about Blunt are that the authors have not been art historians themselves, and that the art historians of the Courtauld Institute who could have done something about it declined to do so. Even Miranda Carter, who in her admirable biography made a determined effort to ensure that her readers were aware that there was an art-historical side, seems to have done so in order to moderate the all-importance of the spying, instead of from a realisation that it was the core activity, and the

Biographical Memoirs of Fellows of the British Academy, XIII, 19–39. © The British Academy 2014.

spying peripheral.[1] A glance at the chronology should make that obvious. When he died in 1983 Blunt was nearly 76. His life divides into two nearly equal parts in 1947, when he took up the directorship of the Courtauld. The whole of the later part was preoccupied with art-historical matters. His involvement with Soviet intelligence lasted less than ten years of the first part, in fact the actual espionage was effectively confined to the five years that he spent in MI5 during the war, when art history was on hold. The rest of the first part was a preparation for the second.

Put like that, the spying was not 'another life', but an integral episode in his one and only art-historical life, and how to make sense of that is the besetting problem about Blunt. Figuratively it might be seen as a malignant cancer which, after a short period of activity, was in remission though not dead and, in the end, destroyed him. But a descriptive analogy, however graphic, is not an explanation. One does not take up spying in the way that one gets cancer. There were serious reasons for his decision to spy for Russia, and there is abundant evidence from both MI5 and Moscow that he did so with the zeal of a dedicated communist.

Relocating art history to the centre of attention does not make it any easier to understand how Blunt squared this particular circle, but it does get the perspective right in which the enigma should be seen. And, if nothing else, by bringing art history out of the shadow of the spying, it allows due acknowledgement to be made of what he achieved in the academic field, which is, or should be, the principal concern of the Academy.[2]

Up to the war

Blunt's parents were late Victorian middle class, not wealthy, but eminently respectable and well connected. His father was a clergyman; his mother was the daughter of a magistrate in the Indian civil service, and a distant relative of Princess Mary of Teck, who married the Duke of York, later King George V. Anthony was their third and youngest son, born on 26 September 1907. The family background was predominantly Church of England. His paternal grandfather had been the suffragan Bishop of Hull, and in an earlier age one at least of the brothers would have gone

---

[1] M. Carter, *Anthony Blunt, His Lives* (London, 2001).
[2] For a summary of the debate on his fellowship in 1980 see Peter Brown's contribution to the memoir of Sir Kenneth Dover—D. A. Russell and F. S. Halliwell, 'Kenneth James Dover 1920–2010', *Biographical Memoirs of Fellows of the British Academy*, XI (2012), pp 153–75.

into the Church. But the mind-set of the new century was moving away from religion and all three turned their backs on the clerical profession. The eldest, Wilfred, took up art and ended as art master at Eton; Christopher went into the city, but found time to make a name for himself as a distinguished numismatist.[3] Anthony's academic vocation was in no way exceptional.

There was one black sheep among his relatives: Wilfred Scawen Blunt (1840–1922). Not that he was in any way close, and his parents almost certainly made every effort to keep his face turned firmly to the wall. The one thing they could not do, however, was to inoculate their sons against the contagion of his notoriety—he was too well known, too much talked about. Scawen Blunt cultivated the image of an anti-establishment bohemian dilettante. This began with his conversion to Catholicism, and proceeded step by step down the road to perdition, which he delighted in parading before the public, to the outrage of his respectable relatives. He was not much interested in the visual arts, but his offences included open approval of dissident and avant-garde poets such as Yeats and Ezra Pound, who were far better known than painters. It is unlikely that young Anthony ever met him, but that did not matter. It needed only the inevitable curiosity of prurient schoolboys about his name to alert him to the existence of an alternative life style.

In 1911 his father became chaplain to the British Embassy in Paris, and the family went to live there for the next decade. It was during his boyhood years in France, mainly in Paris, that his life-long interest in French art and architecture began. When the war ended, Blunt was sent to a prep school in England, and in 1920 he won a scholarship to Marlborough College, as his brothers had done before him. He was at Marlborough for five years.

In 1973, when the Courtauld summer school which had planned to go to Cyprus was aborted on account of the Turkish invasion, an alternative programme had to be improvised at short notice, and Blunt agreed to give a lecture on his early life at school, university and up to the Second World War. It was repeated at the Institute in 1974, shortly before he retired, and that time it was recorded.[4] In retrospect it can be seen that the account was very carefully tailored. For obvious reasons one whole chapter was simply left out, along with details that would have been superfluous. But with these

---

[3] See I. Stewart, 'Christopher Evelyn Blunt 1904–1987', *Proceedings of the British Academy*, 76 (1991), pp. 347–81.

[4] Courtauld Institute Archive, no accession number.

reservations, there is no reason to doubt the essential accuracy of what he tells us about the formation and development of his ideas about art.

The greater part of the lecture was taken up with his time at Marlborough. In the history of the College, Blunt is briefly mentioned as one of a group of 'aesthetes', along with Louis MacNeice and John Betjeman, who, among other things, were responsible for a short-lived magazine called *The Heretick*.[5] In the lecture he fills in some of the details, and they sound a pretty stroppy lot, hell-bent on mischief-making at the expense of their bêtes-noires. But he also amplifies the connotation of 'aesthetes'. This was more than just a schoolboy affectation; it meant that they had discovered Bloomsbury. In the 1920s Bloomsbury was still the latest thing in fashionable intellectual circles, and that was clearly how it appeared to these precocious sixth formers. It allowed them to feel superior, and provided them with coherent sets of ideas that were shocking to their elders who did not know how to answer back. Bloomsbury was a kind of aesthetic ideology, which in its Cambridge brand made contact with the ethical philosophy of G. E. Moore. Not that the Marlborough aesthetes got that far. MacNeice and Betjeman were interested in its literary theories; for Blunt it was the artistic doctrine of 'significant form', preached by Roger Fry and Clive Bell.

What he understood by the 'significance' or 'purity' of form was not really made clear in the lecture, but whatever else it may have been, formal properties were the only ones that mattered in deciding whether a work of art was good or bad. They didn't take risks. The all important thing was to get the answers right; that put you among the angels, so in practice Blunt took his cue from Roger Fry, which meant that Cézanne was the peak of excellence, and the pre-Raphaelites were uniformly execrable. He candidly admits that they were extremely dogmatic, extremely intolerant and extremely naïve. At Marlborough they were cocooned in their certainties. Politics were never discussed, the rest of the world did not exist. And, rather surprisingly in view of his remarks about the school, 'we were very happy'.

These were the views they took with them when they went up to university in 1926, MacNeice and Betjeman to Oxford, Blunt to Cambridge. It might have been expected that with his command of French he would opt for modern languages, but in the event he got a mathematics scholarship to Trinity. This was passed over in silence in the lecture. Until the post-First World War years, Marlborough had a poor record in Oxbridge

[5] T. Hinde, *Paths of Progress* (London, 1992), p. 148.

scholarships.[6] The dramatic improvement was largely due to the head-master at the time who encouraged academic ambitions in potential high flyers, and Blunt was evidently considered to be one. His maths must have been good if Trinity was prepared to take him. It was the prestige subject at Cambridge, and the reputation it acquired through a succession of dis-tinguished mathematicians—Bertrand Russell, G. H. Hardy, J. Littlewood, S. Ramanujan, Ludwig Wittgenstein—made it the Mecca for those aiming for the top. Blunt was ambitious enough, but if he was hoping that maths was the route, he was in for a shock. He was very unhappy during his first year,[7] which suggests that he was out of his depth, and when at the end of it he took part one of the tripos and only got a second, he gave up. He switched at once to modern languages and with his customary ease got the first that had been anticipated.

Whether art history played any part in his decision to do languages is an interesting question. There is no compelling reason to think that it did, but there are indications that it might have done. Ostensibly his second language was Italian, which was almost as perfect as his French, and Italian art and architecture were as prominent as French in his subsequent art-historical career. But for the degree it was German. The explanation could be that German was the language of the principal art-historical publications, and that Blunt was already thinking of an academic future in that field.

In 1927 that would have been a very risky gamble without a private income, which Blunt did not have, unless he was aware of a possible devel-opment that was still at the exploratory stage, and almost certainly under wraps. At that time no British university had an art history department. There was a widespread feeling that it was not a fit subject, but part of the know-how of practical activities that lay outside the realm of thought and language. Its only *raison d'être* was as an asset in the operations of the art trade and, if it had to be taught, the proper place was an art school.

This attitude was poles apart from the dominant perception of art history in Mitteleuropa, where it had come to be held in high regard as one of the humanities, and an integral part of the concept of *Bildung*, i.e. shaping in the sense of cultivating the well-rounded personality of a civil-ised human being. In 1810, when he presided over the establishment of the new University of Berlin, Wilhelm von Humboldt took *Bildung* to be the fundamental purpose of a university education. Under this generous

[6] Ibid., p. 137.
[7] Carter, *Anthony Blunt*, p. 46.

remit, the visual arts of the past could take their place alongside literature, religion and philosophy in the accredited achievements of the human enterprise that are worth studying for their own sake. This gave art history its academic legitimacy.

There were a few academics in Britain who knew about this Continental alternative, and would have been delighted if it could displace the ingrained, insular prejudice; but they were too few to get anywhere themselves. The initiative had to come from outside the universities, and in 1927 there was a glimmer of hope. Lord Lee of Fareham began to seek support for his idea that an academic institute for the study of the history of art should be set up somewhere in the country. Lee was not thinking of the Continental model. He saw his institute as a way of improving the competence of the trade, perhaps because he had been badly stung by wrong attributions when he was collecting the pictures that he donated to Chequers. There was also the example of the dealer, Joseph Duveen, who fortified his attributions with the magisterial judgements of the distinguished American art historian, Bernard Berenson. It took Lee four years to bring his proposal to fruition, but in 1931, with the financial support of Samuel Courtauld, who put up most of the money for the endowment, and the good offices of Sir Robert Witt, the Courtauld Institute of Art in London University came into existence. After a brief stay at the Adelphi, it moved to 20 Portman Square, Courtauld's town house which he vacated when his wife died in 1932. It was to be the Institute's home for the next fifty years, and Blunt's for the twenty-eight years that he was director.

If he was aware of the Courtauld project as early as 1927, Blunt must have been told about it by someone in the know. My guess is that this was Andrew Gow, a classics don at Trinity. Gow had a formidable reputation, austere and caustic as a person, exact, meticulous and hypercritical in his scholarship. The clarity, though not the prolixity, of Gow's scholarship rubbed off on Blunt's own. Gow's other distinctive trait was his interest in the visual arts. In the course of his life he assembled a notable collection, mainly drawings, much of it with Blunt's advice. It was this that brought them together. One of the classics masters at Marlborough who had encouraged Blunt's exploration of the avant-garde art world may have contacted Gow to ensure that he had a sympathetic *patron* when he went up to Cambridge. If so, he succeeded. Blunt had an almost filial devotion to Gow that lasted a lifetime, and it was reciprocated. In 1965 Gow moved from his rooms in Trinity, and the Courtauld photographers were sent to photograph some drawings that had been left behind. Almost everything had gone, but on the mantelpiece was a faded postcard of a group of youthful freshmen, with Blunt among them, the most youthful of them all.

Gow was in touch with the London art market, and well-placed to pick up rumours of what Lord Lee was trying to do. He also had the weight needed to persuade the French department to allow Blunt to write his post-graduate thesis on a highly unorthodox art-historical subject: Poussin and his Italian literary sources. It was accepted in 1932, and Gow may have been instrumental in making sure that it found its way to W. G. Constable, the first director of the Courtauld, who was very impressed. From then on the way to the Courtauld was wide open.

There was no mention of any of this in the 1973 lecture. Gow was still alive then, and the absence of his name has been construed as implying that he had been involved in the spying business, though I doubt it.[8] If nothing else there would have been confirmation from Moscow, and no shred of it has ever surfaced. Gow's main role in Blunt's life was as a benign facilitator, though it is quite likely that he helped to focus his sights on the European perception of art history as one of the humanities. At first, however, Blunt may have found it difficult to distinguish that idea from the thought world into which he was about to be drawn.

According to Blunt, 1933 was the year in which Marxism hit Cambridge. This is where, with the benefit of hindsight, it can be seen that the narrative has been tailored. He gives the impression that his Marxism was quite innocent, like catching the common cold, something that happened to 'every intelligent undergraduate' in that year. There were just minimal references to the Marxists with whom he was acquainted at Trinity, notably Guy Burgess. Allegedly the sole importance of Marxism was its devastating impact on the aesthetics of Bloomsbury. Almost everything that had been taken for granted at Marlborough was now rejected out of hand, and superseded by an entirely new set of criteria for judging works of art. The aesthetic idyll was confronted by the harsh political realities of the outside world. Pure form gave way to socialist realism, and art acquired a mind-shaping function. It came reinforced by an ideological doctrine that really did put art into history, as that was understood by the party pundits. It was heady stuff for immature minds, barely out of adolescence, all the more so for being the first political movement to equip itself with a fully worked out philosophical underpinning, to which its critics had no answer.

---

[8] B. Sewell, *Outsider II* (London, 2012), p. 138.

In the lecture Blunt gives the impression that his reactions were immediate and total, like a religious conversion. In the event, however, it was
not quite like that. He never actually joined the party, and he never subscribed to the Marxist interpretation of art and art history. There were
equivocations which suggest that unlike the commitment of his colleagues
Burgess and Philby, which was total, his was always qualified. My guess is
that his sights were already too firmly fixed on the Courtauld to risk jeop-
ardising the prospect of a future there. As with many bright young men at
the time, his affectation of Marxist sympathies was viewed with indul-
gence by the Establishment, and put down to youthful idealism he would
grow out of. No man of his demeanour was ever less convincing as a
would-be communist.

However, he did try. At the end of 1932 Blunt became art critic of *The
Spectator*, and from then until the war there was a steady output of journalism, dogmatic and judgemental in tone, deliberately provocative, con-
troversial, even offensive in its avant-garde pugnacity—in other words a
repetition on a grander scale of his early efforts at Marlborough and the
complete antithesis of his later writing style. It was left-wing from the
start, and only became overtly Marxist after 1936. The critical moment
was his review of Picasso's Guernica in the Spanish Government's pavil-
ion at the Paris international exhibition in 1937, which he praised as an
expression of the horror of right-minded people at the barbarism of the
fascists in the civil war, but found wanting for doing nothing practical to
help the Republican cause.

The Spanish Civil War was a turning point for Blunt in many ways. It
marked the moment when the politics of the external world began to
intrude on the enhancement of his art-historical education, which had
been going on alongside the journalism throughout the thirties. Not that
it impeded progress. On the contrary, it added a measure of urgency,
which conspired to make it desirable that certain arrangements should be
clarified before the big war began and everything was shut down for an
indefinite duration.

Turning himself into a qualified art historian was a self-managed exercise for Blunt. It was centred on the Poussin thesis and the enlargement of
part of it into his first book, but it was mainly a matter of broadening the
horizons of his experience, both visual and intellectual. Gow introduced
him to Renaissance art, and Constable at the Courtauld put him in touch
with Walter Friedländer, who was the leading expert on Poussin. But by
far the most important factor was the arrival in England in 1933 of the
Warburg library from Hamburg, together with the community of scholars

attached to it. They were mostly Jewish and all formidably learned. In 1937 Blunt left Cambridge and came to London. He went straight to the Warburg, where the director Fritz Saxl created a sinecure for him, and the next two years were an intensive introduction to German art history. The Warburg library was a revelation to him. It must have been a humbling experience to discover the vast resources of historical material that were at the disposal of Warburg scholars which exposed his journalism as crass juvenilia, and made it only too clear that the art of the past was a closed book to him.

The Warburg was also an insulation against the extreme forms of Marxist art history. It was in London that Blunt made contact with Friedrich Antal, an émigré Hungarian who came to England in 1934. He was a hard-line communist, now remembered, if at all, for a remarkable study of early Renaissance painting in Florence, in which the dialectic was used to collate the avant-garde style of Masaccio with the emerging capitalist economy of the city.[9] They must have discussed this highly theoretical approach and, given Antal's overbearing personality, he would undoubtedly have tried to turn Blunt into another hard-liner. If so, he failed. In the introduction to his first book Blunt acknowledges Dr. F. Antal 'for instruction in a method which has, I fear, been applied in an only too slipshod manner ...'.[10] But if he got nowhere on the theory front, Antal may have put ideas of another sort into Blunt's mind.

Blunt's move to London in 1937 was almost certainly connected with events at the Courtauld. In that year W. G. Constable resigned as director. From the start there had been latent friction between him and the founding fathers over the basic policy of the Institute. Constable resented the sneer that the Courtauld was a young ladies' finishing school and wanted to develop the postgraduate side to improve its academic standing, perhaps even to make it entirely postgraduate. Lee, Courtauld and Witt, fearing that he would turn it into something as exclusive as the Warburg, were determined to keep the undergraduates and to attract students from the widest possible sections of society. Constable's resignation was probably not meant to be taken seriously, but it was accepted, and the question of who should succeed him became important. It seems to have been agreed that Blunt would eventually be the man for the job. He was already lecturing there, but in 1937 he was still considered to be too young—he was not

[9] F. Antal, *Florentine Painting and its Social Background: the Bourgeois Republic before Cosimo de' Medici's Advent to Power, XIV and XV Centuries* (London, 1947).
[10] A. Blunt, *Artistic Theory in Italy, 1450–1600* (Oxford, 1940), p. vi.

yet thirty. Finding a locum tenens was not easy, but in the end T. S. R. Boase from the Oxford History School, and totally unqualified as an art historian, was willing to do it for a short period, probably two years, until Blunt was ready. The likely date for him to take over was the autumn term of 1939; the war broke out on 3 September.

The spying issue

In the brouhaha that erupted after his exposure, someone asked Blunt why he had spied for the Russians, and his rather flippant reply was 'for the hell of it, I suppose'.[11] It was the sort of answer that was guaranteed to exasperate his inquisitors, but I think it was his evasive way of declining an impossible task: how to explain to an audience that lived in a different world, and knew no history, that what now seemed like blatant treachery could once have seemed an intelligent course of action. He revealed a little more at the press conference held five days after Mrs Thatcher's statement in the Commons, when he said that he 'bitterly regretted what he had done' and now 'realised that he had been totally wrong'. As an all-but confession of his iniquities, this had a hollow ring, and no one was taken in by it. Blunt was never remotely repentant in that sense. But that is not what he meant, and if the linking word had been 'because' instead of 'and' the meaning would have been clearer. What he regretted was getting it wrong. Getting it wrong inflicted a wound on his innermost being that would never heal, and it happened twice: first about Russia; and then about Poussin after the exhibition at the Louvre in 1960. For a man who spent his life trying to get at the truth of things, to have failed twice, once in each of the fields to which he had committed himself on the certainty that his insight could be trusted, must have been excruciating. Blunt was a proud man, quite unable to forgive his own failures.

How he got himself into the situation that ended with his disgrace can only be surmised. One assumption is fairly safe. When the first contacts were made, the likelihood that they would lead to the kind of spying that Blunt did was infinitesimal. The Marxism to which he succumbed in 1933 had much more to do with the Comintern than with Russia. The Comintern existed to promote Communist revolution in countries world-wide, not to make them into Russian satellites, and it was behind the widespread feeling on the political left in Britain before the war that a revolution was

[11] Carter, *Anthony Blunt*, p. 491.

inevitable and imminent. This was when Blunt first knew Antal. Antal had a political past. In 1919 there was a short-lived Communist *coup d'état* in Hungary, led by Béla Kun, a Lenin type of hardliner, in which all private art collections were promptly nationalised, catalogued and put on exhibition. Antal was in charge of this operation, and one might wonder whether Blunt ever saw himself as commissar of culture in a future Communist government, empowered to follow Antal's example; though it can never have been one of his more realistic expectations.

Blunt may have been under pressure from Burgess to commit himself before he left Cambridge, but it was the Spanish Civil War that brought things to a head. In 1962, I was in Versailles with him, getting illustrations for his book on Poussin, and in the first real conversation I ever had with him he asked me what my views were about the Civil War. I told him that I thought both sides were as bad as each other: 'Ah,' he said 'for us it was the moment of truth.' I did not know him well enough to take it any further, but in retrospect that is precisely what it was: the pivotal moment when indecision turns into purposeful activity. For intellectuals like Blunt the Spanish Civil War transformed the communist party from an agency for social change in domestic politics into the physical arm of resistance to the onward march of fascism on the international stage. The failure of the western democracies to lift a finger to help the legitimate government of the Spanish republic left the issue clearly defined as an ideological conflict. Spain was seen as the prologue of the greater war that was shortly to break out, and the obvious conclusion was that the only great power with the will and the means to take on the fascists was Soviet Russia. Two of his Cambridge friends, John Cornford and Julian Bell, were killed in Spain, and he may have been stung by the taunt: what were you doing about it? At any rate, in 1937, when he got to London, he was recruited by the NKVD, the Russian intelligence service, for clandestine work in the future, as yet unspecified. By what must have been a coincidence, no sooner was Blunt recruited than the NKVD's operation in this country was closed down and remained dormant for the next three years.[12] During this time the Comintern was converted into an instrument of Soviet foreign policy, and Blunt took the opportunity to acquaint himself with serious left-wing thinking about the international situation.

I do not know whether Blunt ever read a book by E. H. Carr called *The Twenty Years Crisis, 1919–1939*. It was written between 1937 and 1939, and published at the outbreak of war. For most of the twenty years

---

[12] Ibid., pp. 181–2, 198–200.

Carr was a civil servant in the Foreign Office, and he retired in order to write his book. Philby, who was in the Foreign Office when he was there, must have known him, and he made no secret of what it was about. Ostensibly, it purported to be an impartial examination of British foreign policy between the wars in the light of what he called the science of international politics; but in effect it was the damning exposure of a preference for pussy-footing with pious hopes instead of facing up to the realities of the situation created by the peace treaties. This was a clear sign that the effort to win the First World War had irretrievably drained the reserves of British power, and that the great power status that Britain had enjoyed since Waterloo was coming to an end. The fiction was maintained in the book, but the true state of affairs was shortly to be revealed to the world by Britain's ignominious expulsion from Europe at Dunkirk, and confirmed two years later by the disastrous surrender at Singapore, which sounded the death knell of the Empire.

If the spies had ever been called to account for their conduct, Carr's analysis provided a viable explanation for what they did. Britain was finished; there was only Russia. At the outbreak of war Blunt volunteered for the military police, and was in France with the army when the Germans struck. He got out through Boulogne, just in time, under no illusion that the situation was extremely precarious. It was then that he applied to MI5, and was accepted, presumably on the strength of his languages. He was already established there when the NKVD came back to life, and his spying career began. There was almost certainly a fortuitous element in this conjunction of circumstances, though he took full advantage of it. He probably did find spying exhilarating, and considered it his personal contribution to the war effort. The thanks he received from Russia for information that helped them to win the decisive tank battle of Kursk in 1943 must have given him particular satisfaction.[13] There is no doubt that he was in breach of the law, but it does not follow *ipso facto* that he was a traitor—which is not to say that he was never guilty.

Up to a certain point, perhaps after Kursk, when it at last became evident that the Russians were going to win their war, and the prospect of a communist Europe became a distinct possibility, Blunt might have hoped that he was going to be justified by events. But what the spies failed to foresee was that the Americans would come in and take over from the

---

[13] Carter, *Anthony Blunt*, p. 270; C. Andrew, *The Defence of the Realm: the Authorized History of MI5* (London, 2010), p. 280.

British in the west. This completely upset their calculations. Insofar as they thought at all about the Americans, they seemed to be safely locked up in their isolationism. The success of the Anglo-American invasion of 1944 ensured that when the war ended, at least the western half of Europe would be kept out of Russian hands, and the conditions were in place for the ideological war between left and right to be continued, albeit with the roles reversed and in non-violent form, for another forty-five years.

It had not been meant to end like this. When Blunt resigned from MI5 in 1945 the cold war was already in its early stages and he must have been apprehensive that the switch from Russia the ally to Russia the notional enemy would inevitably cause MI5 to take a close look at what he had been up to during the war. It was not long before he was under suspicion, and the unending rearguard action to keep exposure at bay began, at precisely the same time that he took up his appointment as director of the Courtauld Institute.

Blunt at the Courtauld Institute

Blunt became director of the Courtauld in October 1947. The Institute had been kept open for all but the first year of the war in a state of suspended animation, due largely to the efforts of Margaret Whinney, one of the old staff, a nucleus of which was still there when he took over from Boase. But almost at once he embarked on what was in effect a fresh start, the tone of which was set by his first two appointments.

In entirely different ways, these must have seemed peculiar to most people. The first was Johannes Wilde, ethnically German but a Hungarian national. He came from Vienna in 1939, and the one thing about him that would have been known to British immigration was that he had been Antal's assistant in Béla Kun's short-lived communist government in Hungary after the First World War. Whether he was ever a communist is doubtful, but the taint stuck and it helped to get him interned and deported to Canada in 1940. Thanks to influential friends in England he was allowed to return in 1941, and it was then that Blunt got to know him.

What mattered for Blunt was that Wilde spent eighteen years between 1920 and 1938 in the art-history world of Vienna. After the failure of Béla Kun's coup, it was expedient for Wilde to get out of Hungary, and a timely invitation from Max Dvorak at the University of Vienna enabled him to do so. Dvorak, who was impressed by his early work, had plans for Wilde at the university, but he died the following year and they came to nothing. Short though it was, the contact was long enough for a bond of like minds to form, and Wilde was as much a personal friend of Dvorak's as his intellectual heir. He spent the next eight years getting Dvorak's posthumous papers into print. The first set appeared in 1924 under the title *Kunstgeschichte als Geistesgeschichte*, which became the label for the point of view that Dvorak ended up trying to promote. [14]

Dvorak seems to have been one of the few really creative minds in the Vienna School, where well-established lines of thought came together, shedding fresh light on old subjects, and detecting the presence of unsuspected stylistic refinements such as 'mannerism' lurking in the borderland between the great conceptual entities. Wilde plunged into this exhilarating ferment of new ideas in his capacity as Dvorak's literary executor. But what set him apart from the rest of the younger art historians was the decision he made in 1923 to leave the university for the Kunsthistorischesmuseum, where during the next fifteen years he made a systematic study of individual paintings in the collection. In other words, for Wilde the works of art took precedence over the ideas that were exemplified in them. It was this forensic approach that convinced Blunt that Wilde should be the cornerstone of art history at the Courtauld.

Blunt's second appointment was totally out of character. This was Christopher Hohler, who succeeded Boase as the house medievalist. Like Boase, Hohler was a product of the Oxford History School, and Boase had known him as an undergraduate. During the war he was in military intelligence in the Middle East, and Boase met him out there in 1943. Four years later, when he left the Courtauld to return to Oxford, he remembered Hohler's intensely personal perception of the Middle Ages, and I suspect that he thought it would be no bad thing if an insular maverick were there to offset the Continental bias that he saw in Blunt's first appointment. It is said that when Boase put the offer to him, Hohler protested that he knew no art history, to which Boase replied: 'that's all right Christopher, you know everything else, you'll soon pick it up'; a fair indication of what the Oxford History School still thought about art history. At the time Hohler had no prospects of a job, and decided to give it a try. He stayed for over thirty years.

It is doubtful whether he ever did pick it up. He never thought of himself as an art historian, and was totally uninterested in artists, craftsmen

[14] M. Dvorak, *Kunstgeschichte als Geistesgeschichte*, Johannes Wilde (ed.) (Munich, 1924), p. 169, nos. 1, 4.

or style. In his later years he made no secret of his intention to protect the Middle Ages from art historians who knew nothing—which was not a bad description of what he was doing during the whole thirty years. Put like that, it sounds as though he was out of place at the Courtauld, but turned around it could be construed as an inverted plea for medieval art to be seen as an integral part of everyday life in the Middle Ages, which is not all that far from the Dvorak–Wilde position. In Hohler's hands 'everyday life' meant top people who could afford to surround themselves with status symbols in the form of art objects of every kind, from castles at one end of the scale to cutlery at the other.

How Blunt got on with Hohler, and vice-versa, is another puzzle. Hohler's politics must have been anathema to Blunt and in the house they had little to do with each other. I wonder whether Boase knew more about Blunt's wartime activities than has been made public. Behind his bland façade, he was very shrewd, and it would be like him to get a man from military intelligence into a position where an eye could kept on a suspect from MI5. But there is no proof.

Despite their differences, the triumvirate of Blunt, Wilde and Hohler set the tone of the place during the first fifteen years of Blunt's tenure. Brian Sewell, who was an exact contemporary of mine, summed it up extremely well in his autobiography:

> ... art history was the history of painting, sculpture, architecture and associated skills, from the ... Italian Renaissance ... to the present day; it was the history of those who worked in those fields; it was the history of patronage from the Church, the state and individuals; it was also the history of nations, dynasties, the middle classes and the poor, the history of political ambitions and the conflicts of religion—it was indeed the history of history itself. We recognised art's connections with literature and music, theology and heresy, philosophy and theory.[15]

Suitably amended, a medievalist would concur with every word. In effect, it was the blueprint for a *Bildung* education.

Something of this sort might be seen as the Institute's mission statement, but Blunt and Wilde had something else in mind as well. They were on the lookout for the high flyers who would go on to do research, and eventually join the teaching staff as new specialisms formed and the syllabus expanded. Courtauld students were under continuous assessment of a very discreet kind. The principal talent spotter was Wilde, though Blunt always had the last word. During the 1950s a succession of students of the

---

[15] Sewell, *Outsider II*, p. 141.

requisite calibre duly surfaced: John White, Michael Kitson, John Shearman, Alan Bowness, Andrew Martindale, Michael Hirst—all of whom were members of the teaching staff at some time; two of them, John White and John Shearman, were entirely home-grown, the rest were Oxbridge postgraduates. I think I must have been the only one of Hohler's students who eventually made it on to the teaching staff, though George Zarnecki and I were de facto members long before we were formally co-opted.

In those days there was no such thing as competition for places. Blunt and Lionel Robbins, who became chairman of the Management Committee in 1948 and remained there for the rest of Blunt's time, ran the Institute like a private fiefdom. You were simply invited. They knew what they wanted; it saved a lot of trouble. None of the new recruits was a replica of his tutor. They chose their own research topics, were never coerced, and left to develop at their own pace. By the 1960s they were ready to take charge of the subject. Wilde had retired in 1958, and his influence began to fade. Blunt's own position imperceptibly changed.

The enlargement of the teaching staff was one of a series of mutually connected expansions. The primary one was the steady increase in student numbers. In 1938 there had been forty-five; when Blunt retired there were 220. By the 1960s the pre-war syllabus no longer coincided with what students wanted. There was a tidal wave of interest in twentieth-century art, to cater for which entailed the complete restructuring of the entire course. The Renaissance lost its privileged status, and modern art was put on equal footing with the earlier periods. Blunt's Guernica lecture became an annual event, but he was happy to leave the rest of the subject matter to Alan Bowness.

Art history was a worldwide success story in the second half of the twentieth century, and the prestige of the Courtauld brought growing numbers of overseas students to the Institute. Many of them came to the annual summer schools, started in 1957, which were the direct result of Blunt's personal friendship with Barbara Robertson, a relative of Roger Fry, and the wife of Charles Robertson, the jam manufacturer. They continued until 1981. Starting in Bath, the school went to many countries in Europe and beyond. The student traffic went both ways. Courtauld graduates found jobs in the USA, Canada, Australia and New Zealand; members of staff took an active role in the increasing number of international conferences; and Blunt himself was honoured by the rare distinction of being invited to preside over the major exhibition of Poussin's paintings at the Louvre in 1960.

At home the glory days of the Courtauld probably peaked during the last decade of Blunt's regime. This came in the wake of the Robbins report of 1963, which led to the setting up of a series of new universities, most of which wanted departments of art history. Blunt was invariably consulted about the staffing, and the outcome was a scattering of Courtauld enclaves across the country. Older universities which had art history departments felt it incumbent to recruit Courtauld graduates, and most of those that had so far done without, like Cambridge, made good the deficiency. At first sight it looks very impressive, but it was an ephemeral ascendancy. The proliferation of Courtauld progeny soon put an end to Courtauld pre-eminence, and in the 1970s the flow of ready money began to dry up. Blunt's retirement in 1974 coincided closely with the end of an era.

The one thing, apart from the spying, that is generally known about Blunt is that he put art history on the academic map, and this alone would be sufficient for him to be remembered with respect. But whether, or how much of, the expansion was due to him is another matter. It was certainly not something that he set out to do in 1947, and once the ball was rolling it gathered momentum of its own accord. In effect he was the managing director of the only firm in the business that could have done the job and, that said, he handled the expansion with exemplary competence, in the best interests of the subject rather than the Courtauld. But I do not think that this was what he wanted to be remembered by.

When he returned to his academic life after the war, Blunt was obliged to devote a good deal of time and effort to the task of keeping a substantial part of his personal life very private indeed. Even what was nominally open to public scrutiny was bewilderingly enigmatic to those who had known him before the war. The contrast between his pre-war and post-war personas was a consummate performance of the dissimulation techniques and self-control that he perfected in his MI5 days. The confrontational journalist with Marxist sympathies simply evaporated—a wartime casualty. The fledgling Warburg scholar survived, but he had matured into a man of the world beyond the university, and was no longer just another academic don. The students at the Institute recognised this. Except in classes where he could let his guard down, they saw him as a somewhat remote, Olympian figure, hinting at connections which they took to be with the higher echelons of the social order. Quite correctly, Blunt surmised that if he was under suspicion of treason, there was no better place to be than in the Establishment itself. Services to the royal family at the end of the war opened the way to his appointment as Surveyor of the King's Pictures in 1945; a knighthood followed in 1956. After his exposure he claimed that he had never wanted these honours, which may be true. Nevertheless, he did want it to be widely known that he had them. For the same reason he took on all manner of public commitments to augment the image that functioned as protective clothing. But authentic academic honours came his way as well, offered and accepted as due recognition of his contribution to the world of learning. Foremost among these were his election as a Fellow of the British Academy in 1950 (followed by service on its Council and from 1965–6 as a Vice-President), and his appointment to the French Légion d'honneur in 1958. There was any number of honorary doctorates.

The nurture of his good name on the public stage was a necessity, but one that wasted far too much of his time. Blunt was only really happy when he was doing research. He was one of those true intellectuals for whom there is no experience to compare with the eureka moment, when an obsessive problem finally dissolves into a pattern of intelligible connections. This was the Warburg scholar in Blunt, or the adherent at one remove of Max Dvorak's school of thought, and he wanted above all to round off his career as an art historian with a tour de force in which the paintings of one of the world's great artists would be shown to be a complete vindication of this approach. This was, of course, Poussin.

Among his many publications are five books, four of which could, in varying degrees, be seen as preparation for the fifth. The first was the work that came out of his fellowship dissertation; the second was a monograph on Mansart, Blunt's counterpart to Poussin among the architects who were his contemporaries; the third was a catalogue of the French drawings in the royal collection at Windsor Castle, many of which were by Poussin.[16] Most of the work on these books was done before the war. The fourth book was *Art and Architecture in France, 1500–1700* for Pevsner's Pelican History of Art series, in which Mansart and Poussin were located among their artistic peers.[17]

The last of his Poussin studies was the magnum opus. It did not appear until 1967, seven years after the exhibition at the Louvre, by which time his critics were well prepared. Blunt never changed or concealed his perception of Poussin: 'To appreciate him as an artist, it is essential to understand the intellectual climate in which he worked, and the ideas—religious,

[16] Blunt, *Artistic Theory*; A. Blunt, *François Mansart and the Origins of French Classical Architecture* (London, 1941); A. Blunt, *The French Drawings in the Collection of His Majesty the King at Windsor Castle* (Oxford, 1945).
[17] A. Blunt, *Art and Architecture in France: 1500–1700* (London, 1953).

philosophical, or aesthetic—in which he believed, and which affected his method of work as well as his paintings.'[18] In other words pure *Kunstgeschichte als Geistesgeschichte*. As a display of Blunt's erudition, his Poussin book probably is the masterpiece that he always wanted to write, but if he expected the art world to fall about in agreement with his cerebral reading of Poussin and that 'it would soon be taken for granted everywhere',[19] he was on an ego trip. This naïve streak in Blunt was his Achilles' heel. Worse still was the criticism on stylistic grounds of his chronology of the paintings, which in the end he reluctantly had to admit was right. He took this very badly. His *amour propre* as an art historian was bruised, and it punctured the confidence with which he had identified himself with Poussin throughout his life. It hurt so much that for once his perfect manners failed him, and his behaviour in dealings with Denis Mahon was regrettably peevish.[20] He was never the same again.

I think it was no accident that Blunt's last major book was a study of the Italian architect, Borromini, 'one of the greatest—perhaps the greatest —genius of Baroque architecture. Furthermore he was a neurotic and unhappy man, constantly dogged by disaster.'[21] The book was about the genius rather than the darker side of Borromini's life, but it was based on the last series of lectures that Blunt gave at the Courtauld before he retired, and they were rather different. I heard those lectures. His usual dry, objective style was notably absent; instead we got a vivid sense of the empathy he felt for a man whose abstract forms so eloquently expressed the pain of personal misfortunes. For Blunt, that made him a perfect surrogate. As a farewell to the Courtauld it was distinctly low key, but that was not entirely out of character. He preferred to slip quietly away.

Blunt's private duel with MI5 went on throughout his directorship. He was under suspicion from the start, but there was no evidence that could be used in court, and it became a question of whether he would confess. After the defection of Burgess and Maclean in 1951 there was no longer any doubt, and after Philby's defection in 1963 there was no longer any point in holding out. MI5 got their confession in the following year in return for a promise of immunity. But that was not the end of the interrogation. MI5 was not interested in an exposure that would merely reveal their own incompetence, but they did want details and the names of anyone

[18] A. Blunt, *Nicholas Poussin* (London, 1967), p. ix.

[19] Ibid., p. x.

[20] For an account of the disagreements with Mahon, which ran for several years, see Carter, *Anthony Blunt*, pp. 421–35.

[21] A. Blunt, *Borromini* (London, 1979), p. 13.

else who was involved, and on that Blunt remained silent. The constant pressure inevitably wore him down. His health was affected, the consumption of alcohol escalated, but he might have got away with it had it not been for the American Freedom of Information Act, over which MI5 had no control. His name was mentioned by someone he had recruited at Cambridge in the 1930s.

The exposure, when it came in 1979, was the nemesis that had been threatening to overtake him for more than thirty years. He could be thankful that his life's work had not been contaminated, and perhaps that is why on this occasion his behaviour was immaculate. The calm stoicism with which he took the only course open to him, which was to ride out the storm without making any effort to defend himself, may not have won him many friends, but it did preserve his integrity, and infuriate the media. The issue may have lapsed, but no settled verdict has ever been reached. Personally, I suspect that historians in the future will be less censorious than his contemporary critics, and see his decision in 1940 to spy for Russia as his way of trying to keep the war against fascism going, at a time when most right wing opinion in the country was prepared to give up and get on with the Germans. He may have been naïve, but who is to say that his misreading of the situation was any worse than theirs?

His art-historical legacies are also equivocal. As I was in a different branch of the subject, I can only offer personal opinions on their lasting value. I have always felt that his best work was in architecture, revaluing underdogs like Mansart and Borromini, or resurrecting the virtually unknown Sicilian, Rosario Gagliardi. His reading of Poussin was far too closely bound up with his identification of himself with the artist to stand a chance of being accessible to a wider public. One would have to be another Blunt to see the connection between the paintings and the intellectual milieu. Denis Mahon was not that sort of man. An Anglo-Irish spokesman for the traditional English instinct to rate seeing above thinking, he probably won the argument on this side of the Channel. In France the issue may still be open. There was no French translation of the Poussin book in 1997, and the situation does not appear to have changed.

On the other hand, Blunt's search for evidence that sheds light on the meaning of works of art put him in touch with Michael Oakeshott's dictum that history is inference from evidence, and that has endured. Post-Blunt research students are second to none in trawling the archives for the last scrap of information that might have a bearing on their subject, and though historians have no use for style it is evidence, and cannot be excluded. They may misuse evidence, or wilfully ignore evidence that endangers their pet hypotheses, but those are occupational hazards to which all branches of history are exposed. Perhaps Blunt's most important achievement was that he did more than anyone else to break down the prejudice in British universities that art history is not really history, and to secure a rightful place for it among the humanities.

Anthony Blunt died on 26 March 1983.

PETER KIDSON
Courtauld Institute of Art

MARJORIE CHIBNALL

Marjorie McCallum Chibnall
1915–2012

MARJORIE MCCALLUM MORGAN was born on 27 September 1915 in the farmhouse at Preston, on the river Severn near Shrewsbury in Shropshire. She was baptised in the parish church of St Lucia, Upton Magna, although the farm was 'almost within sight of the church' of St Eata, in the next parish of Atcham, where Orderic Vitalis had been baptised in 1075.[1] In her 'Memoir', published in 2005, she says she 'was born into a family that had farmed for generations'.[2] Her father, John Christopher Morgan, born at Acton Burnell, Shropshire, in 1882, and her mother, Maggie Morgan, born in County Durham in 1885, were second cousins, sharing a great-grandfather, George Morgan (1788–1861), who in 1851 was farming at Tudhoe, County Durham. His two eldest sons, John Morgan (1818–99), who by 1851 was tenant of a substantial farm at Frodesley, near Acton Burnell, Shropshire, and George Morgan (1821–87), who farmed at White House in County Durham, were the paternal grandfathers of Marjorie's parents.

Marjorie's childhood was spent at Preston-on-Severn, and later she told a friend that her mother's farmhouse kitchen was 'always full of animals'. In her first book, *The English Lands of the Abbey of Bec* (London, 1946), a study of the medieval rural economy, she shows her familiarity

---

[1] M. Chibnall (ed.), *The Ecclesiastical History of Orderic Vitalis,* 6 vols. (Oxford, 1968–80), 1, p. v, and 2, p. vi.

[2] Except where otherwise noted, quotations in the text below are taken from this 'Memoir', which forms chapter 53 in Jane Chance (ed.), *Women Medievalists and the Academy* (Madison, WI, 2005), pp. 747–58. Together with a bibliography of her writings to 2000, it was the only document she lodged at the Academy for her obituarist. All her other papers were destroyed at her request.

Biographical Memoirs of Fellows of the British Academy, XIII, 43–62. © The British Academy 2014.

with the seasonal rhythms of the farming year and the practicalities of land management. It is dedicated to her mother and father. Her only sibling, her brother Thomas Christopher Morgan, who was her elder by a year, took over the tenancy of the farm on his marriage in 1941, and their father then moved to the Grange, a farm in Upton Magna. Later, Marjorie and her family spent holidays at the two farms. Her father died in 1959, aged 77, her mother in 1976, aged 91, and her brother in 2004 at the age of 89.

As a young girl, Marjorie knew that she wanted to be a writer: her first compositions were mostly poetry. Among the women of her family, only her maternal grandmother, Jessie McCallum, a Highlander from the Isle of Arran, had had a career other than child-rearing and housekeeping: she had been a primary-school teacher before her marriage. Marjorie assumed that in adulthood her own life would centre on home and family, and her writing would have to be squeezed between household duties. But her parents believed in education for women (later, as a county councillor, her father was to serve on the Education Committee of Shropshire County Council), and in 1923 she was sent to the local girls' grammar school, the Priory County School for Girls in nearby Shrewsbury. Her schooldays were happy. There were some good teachers, including a 'brilliant history mistress'. Marjorie went into the sixth form and took Higher School Certificate, though without any clear idea of what she would do thereafter. Rather to her surprise, she gained distinctions in English, French and History, and won a State Scholarship, thus relieving her parents, at a time of agricultural depression, of the expense of university fees: 'The doors of Oxford were open to me.'

Initially she havered between English and History, but by the time she submitted her application she had decided on History, with Somerville College as her first choice and Lady Margaret Hall (LMH) as her second.[3] At her successful interview at LMH, with the History Tutor and Vice-Principal, Evelyn Jamison (1877–1972), a 'most remarkable woman', Marjorie was encouraged and strengthened in her decision to read History. Miss Jamison, a distinguished medievalist with a particular interest in the Normans in southern Italy and Sicily, 'was probably the most brilliant and certainly the most beautiful academic woman in Oxford at the time'.

At this stage, however, Marjorie's historical interests lay in modern history. Awareness of the misery and poverty brought about by the First World War and the subsequent economic depression kindled in her, as in

[3] LMH Archives, Education Registration Forms vol. 10.

many of her contemporaries, a 'passionate idealism' and a desire to work for international peace and understanding. When presented with a choice of special subject, she opted for the most modern then available, Europe 1815–1914.

At the end of her first year, in the summer vacation of 1934, Marjorie went to Germany for six weeks, to learn the language and study German literature as part of her work on nineteenth-century European history. Her stay in Hessen was a life-changing experience: 'it was, I think, in Germany that I first began to see the past in the present'. Hitler had become chancellor in 1933 and it was while Marjorie was in Germany in the summer of 1934 that the President, Field Marshal Hindenburg, the last guardian of the old Germany, died on 2 August. Hitler immediately combined both offices, and as *Führer und Reichskanzler* was able to begin to implement the Nazi programme in full. Returning to Germany the following summer, Marjorie was shocked by the cruelty and anti-semitism that had been unleashed. She read *Mein Kampf* in the full original, very different from the bowdlerised translation available in England. She saw the distorting power of propaganda and longed to rectify its evil influence 'by teaching people the true history of the past and training their minds to be critical': 'My growing interest in the Middle Ages now appeared ... as a way of promoting peace and tolerance.'

In her second term at Oxford, she had enjoyed the 'electrifying experience' of being taught English medieval history by the inspirational V. H. Galbraith (1889–1976) of Balliol. He had impressed on her that 'history was "not anything you read in books; it's a habit of thought. In time you won't even be able to look at a chair without seeing its history"'. On her return to Oxford at the beginning of her third year, following her second German trip, Marjorie chose a medieval special subject, 'Church and State in the Time of Edward I', which was taught by the Regius Professor, F. M. Powicke (1879–1963). She was enthralled by the subject, for which Powicke used both theoretical sources, such as the treatise *De regimine christiano* by the theologian James of Viterbo, and practical administrative records, including the archiepiscopal register of John Pecham. Within a few weeks, Marjorie knew that she wanted to go on to medieval research. Miss Jamison 'was encouraging, with the proviso "of course you will need to get a First". Fortunately I was able to clear the necessary hurdle.'

Marjorie consulted Vivian Galbraith about research. He warned her of the sheer nastiness of life in the Middle Ages and of the difficulties of finding one's way through masses of documents, 'the long dark tunnel' of research, but he also gave her a glimpse of the intellectual rewards.

Maurice Powicke's advice was more low-key: the subject he suggested for her B.Litt. was a study of 'Christ Church, Canterbury, and the *sede vacante* jurisdiction of Canterbury during the thirteenth century'. Marjorie completed her thesis in one year. Although in many ways the discipline of working with ecclesiastical documents was to underpin much of her later work in the field of law and administration, she decided in 1937 that it was not the kind of topic on which she wanted to spend her life. For her research as an 'Advanced Student' she would move into another sphere.

Her supervisor for the B.Litt. had been W. A. Pantin (1902–73: Oriel), an ecclesiastical historian with a special interest in the Benedictines. He it was who drew her attention to a formulary in a Cotton manuscript (Domitian A xi) which concerned the relations between the Norman abbey of Le Bec-Hellouin and its English priories: thus she was to identify a fruitful subject for her next piece of research. Indeed, the relations between England and Normandy and the history of the Anglo-Norman realm in all its aspects were to dominate her work for the rest of her long life.

At an early stage, the search for manuscript material took her to France, where, supported by research scholarships, she spent the year 1937–8 in Paris, working in the Bibliothèque Nationale and attending lectures by Gabriel Le Bras (1891–1970) at the Sorbonne and by Étienne Gilson (1884–1978) at the Collège de France. She also worked in departmental archives and libraries in Normandy. At Caen, 'sitting in the glorious nave of the Abbey of Saint-Étienne, I began to feel certain that one day I would study the history of the men who were able to build such churches'.

On her return to England she started work on the great collections of charters and manorial records produced by Bec's English priories, which in the fifteenth century had passed, with their lands, into the possession of the royal foundations of King's College, Cambridge, Eton College, and St George's Chapel, Windsor. In Cambridge she met Helen Cam (1885–1968), Fellow of Girton College, who introduced her to two of the leading economic historians of the day, Eileen Power (1889–1940), Professor of Economic History at the London School of Economics (LSE), and her husband Michael Postan (1899–1981), Professor of Economic History in Cambridge. Marjorie became an enthusiastic member of their famous seminar at the Institute of Historical Research in London, encountering there for the first time the methodology of economic history and the influence of the *Annales* school. In 1939 the Oxford authorities agreed to register her study of 'The English priories and manors of the abbey of Bec-Hellouin' for the D.Phil. degree, without further residence in Oxford, to be supervised by Eileen Power.

The outbreak of the Second World War changed everything. Postan went to work as head of the Russian section of the Ministry of Economic Warfare, and Eileen Power went with part of the LSE to Cambridge. Marjorie, having volunteered for war service, and hoping to be called up, took Voluntary Aid Detachment (VAD) training, and was working in a short-term job as a night-nurse in the Royal Salop Infirmary, Shrewsbury, when she heard the devastating news of the sudden death of Eileen Power on 8 August 1940, at the age of 51.[4] She returned to Cambridge a little later, and Postan took over as her supervisor, but was not often available to see her: he had his war-work to do, and, unlike Eileen, he was not the type of supervisor to give regular and detailed guidance, but rather was 'immensely stimulating, pouring out his ideas' and leaving 'his students to use them as best they could'.

The book which developed out of the thesis, *The English Lands of the Abbey of Bec*, published by the Clarendon Press in 1946, is written in her characteristically clear, judicious and authoritative style. Its primary focus is administrative, tracing how the authorities at Bec regulated the lives and observances of the monks living in the abbey's English dependencies and controlled the exploitation of the English estates. Five years later a companion volume was published, *Select Documents of the English Lands of the Abbey of Bec*.[5] For Marjorie this was an invaluable introduction to the editorial art, and the book became a set text for Postan's Special Subject in the Historical Tripos, on English rural society in the thirteenth century.

A significant factor helping Marjorie to organise her research material and find her own lucid style of exposition was her experience of university teaching. In 1941 she was appointed temporary Assistant Lecturer in Southampton University College.[6] The city of Southampton had suffered heavy bombing, in which the hall of residence where Marjorie was to live, Highfield Hall, had suffered serious damage, and air-raids continued during her first year there. The Faculty of Arts was small, and Marjorie found herself teaching not simply medieval but 'almost everything in English, European and American history, as well as giving short courses to RAF cadets': 'It was a baptism of fire: I hope my pupils learned as much as I did.' She particularly enjoyed teaching the cadets, working backwards from the present day in order to trace the conditions that produced the

---

[4] Sixty years later, Marjorie wrote a profile of Power, in Chance, *Women Medievalists*, pp. 310–21.
[5] Camden Third Series, 73 (1951). Significant new material was identified much later, which Marjorie edited as 'Compotus rolls of the English lands of Bec (1272–89)', in *Camden Miscellany*, xxix, pp. 1–196, 409–16, Camden Fourth Series, 34 (1987).
[6] Southampton University Archives, MS 1/MBK 7/2.

Fascist and Communist regimes. In her spare time she was finishing her thesis, which was submitted and approved for the D.Phil. in 1942.

By 1943 student numbers at Southampton had fallen drastically, but just as Marjorie was about to volunteer for an educational commission in the Women's Royal Naval Service (WRNS), a vacancy for an Assistant occurred in the History department at the University of Aberdeen. With Powicke's encouragement, she applied and was appointed 'on the spot' at interview with Professor John Bennett Black (1883–1964), the Elizabethan historian. She began at Aberdeen in the autumn of 1943 and remained there until 1947, being promoted to the newly established post of Lecturer in Medieval History in 1945.[7] In 1946 she built on the 'conspicuous success' with which she had taught Medieval European History by instituting a new course in Medieval British History.[8] One of her students (later an ambassador) recalled how in her early days at Aberdeen Miss Morgan was 'very shy and very new ... and ready to blush, but when in the classroom a first-rate teacher'.[9] The historian of the Aberdeen History department comments that 'her students were expected to think for themselves as she discussed subjects with them, and, after adjusting to the intellectual shock, most did so, to their own considerable benefit. Of no other member of the department can it be said that some students wept on hearing of her decision to leave.'[10] Professor Black was to be a life-long friend, godfather to Marjorie's first child, Mary, in 1948, and dedicatee of her edition of John of Salisbury's *Historia Pontificalis* in 1956—'dominorum amicorumque karissimo'. He had hoped she would succeed him in the chair of History at Aberdeen. Indeed, Marjorie had begun to take on the role of a historian of Scotland, stressing her McCallum antecedents, and writing a paper on 'The organisation of the Scottish Church in the twelfth century', in which she showed a complete mastery of the early records of Scotland so far published.[11] She would have been happy to have stayed at Aberdeen.

'Fortuna, however, had other ideas for me.' In March 1947 Marjorie was approached by the Fellows of Girton College who were looking for a medievalist to share the teaching with Helen Cam for two years and then

---

[7] Aberdeen University Archives (AU), L Per Aa P23 Min Senatus Minutes, p. 436, 12 Oct. 1943, and p. 181, 11 Dec. 1945.

[8] Doreen J. Milne, *A Century of History: the Establishment and First Century of the Department of History in the University of Aberdeen* (Aberdeen, 1998), p. 46.

[9] AU, MS 3620/1/49, Interview with Sir John Adam Thomson (member of British Diplomatic service 1950–87, ambassador to the United Nations 1982–7).

[10] Milne, *Century of History*, p. 49.

[11] *Transactions of the Royal Historical Society*, 4th series, 29 (1947), 135–49.

succeed her,[12] and around the same time she became engaged to Albert Charles Chibnall (1894–1988), Professor of Biochemistry at Cambridge. Events moved swiftly. At Aberdeen the Senatus Minutes of 13 May 1947 record that Miss Morgan 'would be leaving to take up another appointment'.[13] At Upton Magna church on Wednesday 4 June, 'very quietly', Charles and Marjorie were married.[14] At Girton on Tuesday 10 June Dr Cam suggested to the appointments committee that Mrs Chibnall, whose possible appointment to a non-resident lectureship had been discussed earlier in the year, should be so appointed, although 'Mrs Chibnall is at present away from Cambridge'. On Thursday 12 June, however, she was back in Cambridge, attended for interview, and was duly appointed. Her letter of acceptance is dated 17 June.[15]

In the space of a few weeks, Marjorie's life had changed utterly. She moved into her husband's large house, Madingley Rise (now the Bullard Laboratory), just outside Cambridge, near the Observatory. Charles was a widower, twenty-one years her senior, with two daughters, Joan aged thirteen and Cicely aged eleven. Kate, his widowed and bed-ridden mother (born 1866), also lived in the house until her death in April 1948. Marjorie had met Charles, an accomplished amateur medievalist, through their mutual friend Vivian Galbraith, on whose recommendation he had consulted her on questions relating to the medieval open fields of his ancestral Buckinghamshire village, Sherington.[16] He had proposed marriage after only three meetings: much later she called this 'retrospective love at first sight'.[17] In 1950 their son was baptised John Vivian, after Galbraith. Charles has been described as being 'for a quarter of a century ... the central figure in British protein chemistry, itself, for the first time, at the centre of protein chemistry in the world'.[18] His tenure of the chair of Biochemistry came to an end on a triumphant note, when he presided over the First International Congress in Biochemistry in Cambridge in 1949. 'Madingley

[12] In the event, Helen Cam left after one year, on her appointment as the first Zemurray Radcliffe Professor of History at Harvard.
[13] AU, L Per Aa P23 Min Senatus Minutes, p. 476.
[14] *The Times*, 5 June 1947.
[15] Girton College Archives (GC), AR 2/5/6/1/10.
[16] His work was published later, *Sherington: the Fiefs and Fields of a Buckinghamshire Village* (Cambridge, 1965, reissued 2012). On his life and career, see R. L. M. Synge and E. F. Williams, 'Albert Charles Chibnall. 28 January 1894–10 January 1988', *Biographical Memoirs of the Fellows of the Royal Society*, 35 (1990), 56–96. After his death in 1988, Marjorie had a window restored in Sherington church in his memory.
[17] *The Times*, obituary, 12 July 2012
[18] Synge and Williams, p. 57.

Rise rose to the occasion: Marjorie and ACC lavished their hospitality ...
Most memorable, perhaps, was the farewell morning, with stirrup-cups of
champagne on the carriage sweep.'[19] After his retirement in 1949, Charles
continued to work in the 'Protein Hut' in Tennis Court Road, as well as
pursuing historical research in his spare time.

At Cambridge, Marjorie was an exceptional teacher—kind, generous,
courteous, but also rigorous in requiring students to examine and assess
the evidence for themselves. Since her death, many former pupils have sent
recollections in tribute: 'I remember her meticulous criticism of essays,
[demanding] precise justification for everything that one wrote ... "can
you say that? can you prove that? what is the evidence for that?"'; 'I revered
her and am remembering now how she gave me a sense that she believed
in me, even when I might not have deserved it'; 'Going into a supervision
with Mrs Chibnall was like entering a medieval world where she knew all
the characters personally. With her gentle high-pitched voice she always
tried to find the best in my work however inadequate it was.' One student,
later a professor of philosophy, writes: 'it wasn't until I began to work on
late medieval logic texts that I noticed that I was beginning to (try to) pay
meticulous attention to detail in the way she had always recommended in
classes on gobbets.' Students from her earliest years at Girton remember
the birth of her two children, Mary and John, born in 1948 and 1950
respectively, and how she conducted supervisions in the Stella Maris
Maternity Home.[20]

Marjorie shared Charles's delight in giving generous hospitality. There
were memorable 'Tripos Teas', which allowed exam-stressed undergraduates to relax at her home, either at Madingley Rise or later in Selwyn
Gardens, with strawberries and her own home-made cakes. There were
picnics on motoring tours of historic places in East Anglia: 'she took us
on that Ascension Day picnic in the middle of Prelims, to the East Anglia
wool churches ... I recall the food, all individually packed in cardboard
cake boxes.' There were At Homes in Girton, with drinks and canapés.
One strictly teetotal student wrote to her parents about one such party,
after the College Feast in 1955, at 'Mrs Chibnall's, where again it was a bit
embarrassing as there was no alternative to champagne.'[21]

Marjorie's career at Girton lasted from 1947 to 1965. She was elected
a Fellow in 1953, and on the resignation of her senior colleague, Jean

---

[19] Synge and Williams, p. 81.
[20] See the affectionate obituary in *The Daily Telegraph*, 3 July 2012.
[21] GCPP Bishop 2/1/1.

Lindsay (1910–96), in 1960 she became Director of Studies in History. She supervised Girton undergraduates, and some students from men's colleges, for papers in medieval English constitutional and economic history, medieval European history, the history of political thought, and medieval intellectual history. In the university, from time to time she took over Postan's Special Subject, on English rural society, and in the early 1960s she gave short courses of lectures for research students. Letters in the Girton Archives refer to her hopes of a University Lectureship—in 1947, 1949 and 1953–4. Other letters attest the high opinion of her scholarship and teaching among senior members of the History Faculty.[22] Her two books had been extremely well reviewed in academic journals.[23] But 'after two or three applications for university posts' had been turned down, she realised that 'I could carry on as a fellow and lecturer at Girton, but I would have no official standing in the history faculty.' 'It was very disagreeable' to recognise that in Cambridge, which had not allowed women to take their degrees until 1948, there was still considerable prejudice against women, particularly married women. So although at Aberdeen she had 'participated fully and equally in the work of university lecturers and was paid the same salary as a man', and although her three predecessors as Fellows and Directors of Studies in History at Girton had all held university lectureships, Marjorie gradually came 'to appreciate that, though socially men stood back and opened doors for women to pass through, professionally they slammed them in their faces'. 'I chose not to hammer on a closed door but to build on what I had: my fellowship and teaching at Girton and my experience of editing and translating medieval texts.'[24] She now embarked on an edition of one of the longest and most important of medieval texts, the *Ecclesiastical History* of Orderic Vitalis, and in 1965, feeling that she would never complete this work if she continued teaching, she resigned her fellowship to give herself full-time to her edition and translation of Orderic.[25]

---

[22] GCAR 2/5/6/1/10 (Personnel).

[23] e.g. David Knowles in *Economic History Review*, 16 (1946), pp. 147–9, David Douglas in *English Historical Review*, 62 (1947), pp. 117–18, and Norma Adams in *Speculum*, 27 (1952), pp. 540–2.

[24] The obituarist in *The Times*, 12 July 2012, evidently unaware of her 'Memoir' and ignorant of the ethos of the 1950s, resorts to misogynist clichés and thus belittles her dignified silence—'her refusal to ape the stridency of her more "political" contemporaries'.

[25] Marjorie's recollections of her career, especially her teaching at Southampton, Aberdeen and Cambridge, are recorded in an interview conducted by Kate Perry, then Girton archivist, on 27 May 1997 (GCOH/2/3/27/5). Marjorie abbreviated some of this material for her 'Memoir', written soon after 2000.

Preliminary to discussing Marjorie's major work, a word is needed about her early association with the series of Medieval Texts initiated by Nelson's and later taken on by the Clarendon Press. The idea of launching a series of Latin medieval texts with parallel translations came about towards the end of the Second World War through the friendship of H. P. Morrison (1875–1971), Managing Director of Nelson's publishing house in Edinburgh, and Vivian Galbraith, Professor of Medieval History at Edinburgh from 1937 to 1944. Having enlisted R. A. B. Mynors (1903–89), successively Professor of Latin at Cambridge (1944–53) and Oxford (1953–70), to monitor the Latin texts, Galbraith set about recruiting historians to provide translations and commentaries. He naturally called on Marjorie, his former pupil, and she was soon enlisted for John of Salisbury's *Historia Pontificalis*, which describes at first hand some of the decisive events of the years 1148–51, and is especially important for its narrative of the council of Rheims in 1148. This history, which she subtitled *Memoirs of the Papal Court*, occupied her research time in the early 1950s. The Nelson's series had been launched 'for the general reader and for undergraduates ... who are not experienced in medieval Latin',[26] but as time passed the aim shifted towards printing original critical editions, with historical annotation and introductions at a deeper level, intended for an academic readership. The *Historia Pontificalis*, published in 1956, together with the first volume of *The Letters of John of Salisbury*, edited by C. N. L. Brooke, which had appeared the previous year,[27] marked a milestone in the development of British medieval textual scholarship—and in John of Salisbury studies. Historical interpretation became an essential part of the editor's task. In the space of a mere thirty pages, Marjorie's masterly introduction to her edition set John in his historical context, explored the writing and sources of the *Historia*, and assessed its historical value.[28] Her elegant translation is worthy of one of the great Latin stylists of the Middle Ages.

Marjorie enjoyed the challenge of translation, the process of immersing oneself in a text, teasing out the meaning, and thus getting to know the writer: she wrote to a friend, 'Translation is the most exacting form of

---

[26] Preface to C. Johnson (ed.), *Dialogus de Scaccario* (Oxford, 1950).

[27] This edition was largely the work of Christopher Brooke, revising the text and translation initially provided by W. J. Millor and H. E. Butler.

[28] In 1984 she was to revise and expand her comments on 'John of Salisbury as historian', in M. Wilks (ed.), *The World of John of Salisbury* (Studies in Church History, Subsidia, 3), pp. 169–77, reprinted in M. Chibnall, *Piety, Power and History in Medieval England and Normandy* (Aldershot, 2000).

interpretation I have ever met.'[29] In July 1954 she had almost finished her work on John of Salisbury when she received the letter rejecting her final application for a university lectureship in Cambridge. She did not wish to apply for posts outside Cambridge: 'there was something I wanted to do more, which could be combined more easily with the supremely happy marriage that tied me to Cambridge.' The day she received 'the last discouraging letter', she wrote to Galbraith, offering to edit the *Ecclesiastical History* of Orderic Vitalis, 'which I had been hankering to do for some time'. He replied immediately and enthusiastically, 'It is the book of books that Morrison wants done or started before he dies.' A letter from Morrison himself followed four days later: 'You have a double portion of my blessing ... it was Orderic who founded the Medieval Texts series!' As a young man, Morrison had met Delisle in the Bibliothèque Nationale, and was thus a living link with the last edition, in which Delisle had collaborated fifty years earlier.

Orderic was born to an English mother in Atcham, Shropshire, in 1075, and at the age of ten was handed over by his father, a Frenchman (possibly a Norman), to become an oblate monk at the Norman monastery of Saint-Évroult, where he lived until his death in c.1142. He had a good education there, became a scribe and librarian of the monastery, and in c.1114 began his massive *Ecclesiastical History*, which eventually comprised thirteen books covering the period from the birth of Christ down to the year 1141. It was edited in five volumes in the middle of the nineteenth century by Auguste Le Prévost (1787–1859) and finished in collaboration with Léopold Delisle (1826–1910).[30] It was a rare book, of which there were only two copies in Cambridge libraries. Marjorie was a few years into the project before she obtained her own copy, delightedly cabling 'CUPIO' to a bookseller in Seattle. It was to take twenty-five years to complete her edition and translation. After 1965, with her resignation from Girton and the family's move to Millington Road (where she had an excellent new study), she was able to devote uninterrupted hours to the work and made rapid progress. During that time, she joked, it seemed as if she saw more of Orderic than of her husband. Charles was whole-heartedly supportive throughout and the edition was dedicated to him.

Marjorie decided to start publication at the point where Orderic himself had begun to write, with books III and IV, charting the rise of Normandy, the conquest of England, and the early history of the abbey of Saint-Évroult. The first volume of the *Ecclesiastical History* to appear, volume 2, was published late in 1968 by the Clarendon Press.[31] By this time Nelson's had been acquired by the newspaper proprietor Lord Thomson of Fleet (1894–1976), who promptly closed down the Edinburgh printing works and moved the publishing house to London. After an uncertain period in the mid-1960s, it became clear that the new owner had no interest in maintaining the Medieval Texts series. Marjorie was in despair, until Galbraith (by now Regius Professor in Oxford) and Christopher Brooke (who had joined the General Editors in 1959) were able to conclude negotiations with Oxford University Press, which accepted the series, henceforth Oxford Medieval Texts (OMT). Orderic's *Ecclesiastical History* 2 was one of OMT's earliest publications. The remaining volumes came out over the course of the next twelve years: 3 in 1972, 4 in 1973, 5 in 1975, 6 in 1978, and the final volume, 1, with its Introduction to the entire work, in 1980.[32] Mynors and Galbraith retired in 1974, and Brooke was then joined by Michael Winterbottom and Diana Greenway. Marjorie was the model contributor to the series. Her typescripts were impeccable: as the Public Orator said at her Honorary Litt.D. ceremony, 'she edited it so perfectly that her own text needed no editor'.[33]

Orderic's *Ecclesiastical History* is unusual among medieval chronicles for the purity of its text. All but two of the thirteen books survive in the author's holograph, preserved in two manuscripts in the Bibliothèque Nationale.[34] Reading the *History* in Orderic's own hand, observing his orthography, and noting his revisions and additions, gave Marjorie a special insight into his process of composition. In her edition she retained the holograph's punctuation, which she recognised as a guide to the reading aloud of the rhythmic and rhyming prose in which the whole work was composed.[35] As far as possible, her translation followed the sentence structure of the original and mirrored Orderic's often dramatic style. The *Index Verborum*, created by computer through advances in technology

---

[31] Some of the first copies to be issued bear the correct date 1968, but further copies, sent to the binder a little later, were dated 1969, which has passed erroneously into many bibliographies.

[32] Orderic's *Ecclesiastical History* is now available online.

[33] 'tam perfecte edidit ut editore ipsa nullo egere uideatur', 24 June 2002, reported in *Cambridge University Reporter*, 3 July 2002, online at <www.admin.cam.ac.uk/reporter/2001-02/weekly/5891/15.html>.

[34] For the two books (VII and VIII) not preserved in holograph, most of the text was available in copies deriving from the lost manuscript.

[35] This is discussed in a fruitful section of the Introduction, 'The Historian's Workshop', *Ecclesiastical History*, 1, pp. 100–10.

during the period Marjorie was working on the *History*, enabled her to chart Orderic's use of language, and in her translation to take account of its subtleties.

The historical commentary demanded much of the editor. Identifying Orderic's varied sources led Marjorie into a searching textual analysis in order to unpick the patchwork of material, both literary and documentary. She became fascinated by the interdependence of chronicles and charters in the eleventh century, publishing an article on the subject in 1976,[36] and illustrating Orderic's use of charters, especially *pancartes*, in the Introduction to volume 1.[37] But tracing Orderic's sources for books I and II, the life of Christ and the history of the early Church, was a task in which Marjorie took little pleasure. In 1960 she had tried, unsuccessfully, to persuade at least one former pupil to take it on. Although eventually she identified the texts which Orderic used, she never wholly embraced the first two books, and they finally appeared, in volume 1, drastically abbreviated, consisting for the most part of references to the sources from which Orderic had taken passages or made summaries, with marginal page references to Le Prévost's full edition. The French historiographer, Bernard Guenée (1927–2010), although very appreciative of the superb Introduction to volume 1, expressed 'une certaine tristesse' that after a quarter of a century's work, the new edition did not replace Le Prévost's text in its entirety.[38]

Marjorie was more at ease when dealing with the history of the Normans—in Normandy and England, and in southern Italy and the eastern Mediterranean. The *Ecclesiastical History* is of inestimable value for its information on the Normans in the eleventh and early twelfth centuries, and also for its insights into the mentality of contemporaries, especially the lay aristocracy. Marjorie's commentary goes to the heart of Orderic's testimony, interpreting his narrative in the context of the full range of available sources. But the constraints of an edition, even on the lavish scale afforded by OMT, did not allow her full rein to explore 'the world of Orderic' in its many aspects. A separate book on the subject had

---

[36] M. Chibnall, 'Charter and chronicle: the use of archive sources by Norman historians', in C. N. L. Brooke *et al.* (eds.), *Church and Government … Essays Presented to C. R. Cheney* (Cambridge, 1976), pp. 1–17 (reprinted in *Piety, Power and History*).

[37] *Ecclesiastical History*, 1, pp. 63–77.

[38] *Annales, 38 année* (1983), no. 1, pp. 184–5. For some interesting comments on the historiographical significance of books I and II, see Amanda Jane Hingst, *The Written World: Past and Place in the Work of Orderic Vitalis* (Notre Dame, IN, 2009), pp. 20–1, 81–4, and chap. 6, especially pp. 118–19.

been suggested to her by Morrison in the 1950s, and was on the 'back-burner' throughout, finally published by the Clarendon Press in 1984 as *The World of Orderic Vitalis*. There, in her own words in her 'Memoir', she was able to reflect on how Orderic's 'great book brings in every aspect of the life of the monks and knights whom he knew, from liturgy and monastic studies to warfare and castle building, from the lives of saints to epic songs'.

Orderic did not totally dominate Marjorie's research in the 1970s. Somehow she found time to write several articles. She contributed no fewer than twenty pithy entries on Shropshire religious houses to the *Victoria County History of Shropshire*, 2, published in 1973: for Marjorie, the Shropshire lass, these pieces probably provided light relief while coping with typescripts and proofs of Orderic. Her continued interest in the connections between Norman abbeys and their English dependencies produced more publications, most significantly her edition of *Charters and Custumals of the Abbey of Holy Trinity Caen*.[39] These documents, relating to the abbey's English lands, had been brought to her attention over forty years earlier by Eileen Power, to whose memory the volume is dedicated.

Marjorie was not a recluse during these productive years. A new chapter in her life opened in 1969, when she was invited to become a Research Fellow of Clare Hall, a college for graduates and visiting faculty (founded in 1966); in 1975 she became a full Fellow.[40] Clare Hall was to provide her with support and stimulating companionship for over thirty years. Marjorie was naturally collegial: she led lively discussions over daily lunch, attended evening meetings and dinners, and for a short time in the 1980s she acted as Praelector, conducting graduands with great dignity at degree ceremonies in the Senate House, where she was noted for her impeccable Latin pronunciation. Her interest in medieval law and legislation, which was reflected in much of her writing (as also in her enthusiastic membership of the Council of the Selden Society),[41] led to her being called upon to draft the college statutes, which were approved in 1984. The Festschrift to honour her seventieth birthday was presented at a splendid lunch in Clare

---

[39] *Records of Social and Economic History, new series*, 5 (London, 1982).

[40] For Marjorie at Clare Hall, see Eric Ashby, Richard Eden and Ekhard Salje, *Clare Hall: the Founding and History of a College of Advanced Study*, pdf at <www.clarehall.cam.ac.uk/history>.

[41] She joined the Selden Society's Council in 1979 and served as Vice-President from 1987 to 1990, attending whenever she could; if prevented for any reason she sent detailed comments on the agendas. On being dissuaded from resigning in 2005, at the age of ninety, she wrote to the secretary: 'I am glad now that you didn't allow me to resign, as a new hearing aid has greatly improved my ability to take part in discussion ... I enjoy my membership of the Council and would have missed it.'

Hall in 1985,[42] and to celebrate her eightieth birthday in 1995 her colleagues arranged for the vocal ensemble known as Gothic Voices to perform Anglo-Norman songs in the Hall.

Also during the 1970s, despite her demanding research programme, Marjorie was deeply involved in supporting girls' education, a cause close to her heart. An old members' record-form which she completed for Girton in 1976 reveals the extent of her work in this area. Under 'Previous voluntary work and service on committees' she entered: 'Governor of Cambridgeshire Girls' High School; Governor of Cambridge Grammar School for Girls; Executive Committee, Governing Body of the Girls' Schools Association'. Under 'Present' she entered: 'Chairman of Governors, Perse School for Girls; Chairman, Millington Road Nursery School Trust'.[43]

The Perse Girls' School had a special place among Marjorie's interests. Initially her contact was as a parent, for at the time of her marriage, in 1947, both Joan and Cicely were pupils, and later Mary also attended. In 1964 she became a governor, nominated by Girton College, and she served as Chairman of the Governors from 1972 until 1978. The period of her chairmanship was peculiarly difficult. In 1975 the government announced its decision to phase out direct-grant schools, and it was clear that there was no place for a small selective girls' school in Cambridge's maintained sector. If it was to survive, the Perse had to become wholly independent. Marjorie presided over this historic change, launching a major fund-raising initiative (the school had been without endowment), and conducting negotiations with the Charity Commission, the Perse Boys' School and other bodies. Her clarity of mind, precise exposition and foresight helped navigate the school through the transition and set it on the path towards a secure future.

The steady publication of successive volumes of the *Ecclesiastical History* encouraged a growing scholarly interest in Anglo-Norman studies, which was further promoted in 1978 by the establishment of the annual conference at Battle, close to the site of the battle of Hastings. The founding genius was R. Allen Brown (1921–91), Professor of History at King's College London, who invited Marjorie, as a leading scholar in the field, to give a paper at the inaugural conference. She delivered an address on 'Feudal society in Orderic Vitalis',[44] and thoroughly entered into the

---

[42] Diana Greenway, Christopher Holdsworth and Jane Sayers (eds.), *Tradition and Change: Essays in Honour of Marjorie Chibnall* (Cambridge, 1985).
[43] GCAR 2/5/6/1/10 (Personnel).
[44] *Proceedings of the Battle Conference on Anglo-Norman Studies*, 1 (1979), pp. 35–48, 199–202.

Battle spirit, becoming a mainstay of the conferences thereafter, sometimes giving papers, but more often simply being available for discussion
and the exchange of ideas. In 1987, when the conference, meeting at Caen,
visited Saint-Évroult, Marjorie proposed the toast to Orderic, before the
monument which commemorates him. The yearly meetings of the Battle
conference cohered round the presence of the charismatic Allen Brown,
who chaired every paper, and when he became terminally ill the conference might have collapsed. It was Marjorie who then took on the directorship: she was so much a focus of Anglo-Norman studies that she was the
one person who could take on the central role at a critical time. She directed
the conference, and edited the proceedings (*Anglo-Norman Studies*), from
1989 to 1993, convening the memorable meeting at Palermo in 1992. Her
last attendance at Battle was in 2006, when she was in her ninety-first year.
A photograph and a print of Battle Abbey accompanied her to her room
in the nursing home where she died.

One of the attractions of the Battle conferences was its international-
ism: scholars from the British Isles were joined by colleagues from Europe,
and from the southern and western hemispheres, especially from the USA.
Marjorie was fond of America and Americans. Charles had spent two
years working in New Haven in the 1920s, and she had accompanied him
on subsequent visits to the USA, enjoying the Huntington and other
libraries, and the chance to meet and discuss with medievalists. In 1996, in
her eighty-first year, she accepted an invitation to lecture at the annual
Colloquium in the University of the South at Sewanee, in Tennessee. She
relished the intellectual stimulation of the gathering and loved the campus,
with its 13,000-acre 'Domain' of forest, meadows and lakes.

Meanwhile, Marjorie maintained the French connection which had
begun in her time as a research student. Her bibliography includes at least
fourteen articles written in French for French publications, the first in
1955 and the last in 2000.[45] Throughout her life she maintained her interest in Bec, attending and reading papers at conferences on its most illustrious abbot, St Anselm: she gave a lecture in Canterbury cathedral in
1993 to mark the nine-hundredth anniversary of his elevation to the arch-
bishopric, and travelled to Rome in 1998 for the celebration of his *Cur
Deus Homo*—the last Anselm gathering she would attend. She cherished
also her association with the University of Caen and the colloquies on
Norman studies at Cerisy-la-Salle: her attendance at these meetings was

[45] A full bibliography of her publications up to 1985 is in Greenway *et al.*, *Tradition and Change*.

valued for 'son erudition ... son dynamism et son humour, mais aussi sa grande modestie, qui la rendait si accessible aux jeunes chercheurs'. [46]

As she showed in both teaching and informal discussion, Marjorie was committed to making her learning accessible. She responded speedily and helpfully, and without condescension, to queries from members of the public, as well as students, teachers and academics.[47] After the publication of the *Ecclesiastical History* and its companion piece, *The World of Orderic*, she began to write general books for the wider world. The first of these, *Anglo-Norman England 1066–1166* (Oxford, 1986), traced the development of government and feudal institutions in England after the Conquest: intended for students and teachers, it was clear and precise, an object-lesson in the pragmatic appraisal and use of historical evidence. Blackwells launched a series entitled 'A History of Medieval Britain', of which *Anglo-Norman England* became the first volume, and Marjorie the General Editor of the other nine. Several years later, in a second general book, *The Debate on the Norman Conquest* (Manchester, 1999), exploring the historiography of the Conquest, she dissected some of the concepts which she considered too large and vague, such as 'feudalism' and 'empire'. The third of her general books followed quickly, *The Normans* (Oxford, 2000), in which she enlarged her focus, both chronologically and geographically, and included a study of 'the Normans in the South', a tribute to her revered tutor at Oxford, Evelyn Jamison.

In January 1988, two weeks short of his ninety-fourth birthday, Charles Chibnall died peacefully after a brief illness. He had seemed indestructible, recovering from some serious illnesses in his final years, including chest infections, a broken leg, and a brain haemorrhage, but his heart had been severely weakened, rendering him house-bound for the last eight months of his life. After his death, Marjorie wrote to two friends: 'Charles was a wonderful husband, and since we did not find each other very early in life we were indeed fortunate to have forty years of supreme happiness.'[48] She did not feel able to write any history for a year, but instead immersed herself in the practicalities of clearing and selling the large house in Millington Road and moving to a delightful second-floor flat

---

[46] *Bulletin de l'Ouen*, 34 (July 2012), p. 1, a brief memorial note.
[47] A remarkable example is her reply to an enquiry from a campaigner against a proposed Bexhill bypass in 1995, about the sites of Duke William's camp and the battle of Hastings, in which she gives a masterly survey of all the historical evidence, <www.secretsofthenormaninvasion.com/corresp/chibnall.htm>.
[48] Letter to the author and Jane Sayers, Jan. 1988.

at the very edge of Cambridge, off Barton Road, with views of the countryside.

The first book published after Charles's death was her biography of *The Empress Matilda* (Oxford, 1991), a project she had been nurturing for some years, having given her Prothero Lecture in 1987 on 'Matilda and church reform'.[49] It is dedicated to Allen Brown's widow, Vivien, 'in memory of Allen who was as indomitable as the empress'. The book was the first in English to study Matilda's career as a whole, her German experience being given full weight. Arguably it is Marjorie's finest book. The writing bears the hallmarks of her mature style, especially her subtle analysis of sources, differentiating what was believed at the time, and what was thought later, from what probably happened. Matilda, the designated heir 'who happened to be a woman', is treated with sympathy and some admiration. Marjorie comments on contemporary criticisms of the Empress, that 'what might have passed in a man for dignity, resolution and firm control were condemned in her as arrogance, obstinacy and anger'.[50]

Soon after the publication of *Matilda*, Marjorie took on another text for OMT. *The Waltham Chronicle* recounts the foundation and early history of the secular college which was established by Earl Harold on the eve of the Norman Conquest. Its only complete printing was in a scarce edition of 1861 by William Stubbs. Leslie Watkiss (1928–2013), a retired schoolteacher of Classics, who lived in Waltham, had transcribed and translated the text, but a historian was needed to provide the introduction and notes. Marjorie enthusiastically agreed to collaborate on the volume, which appeared in 1994. In a BBC television programme just before publication she stood beside Harold's supposed tomb at Waltham and told the chronicle's moving story of how Harold's *handfast* wife, Edith Swanneck, who knew the 'secret marks' on his body, identified him among the heaps of the dead after the battle of Hastings.

The final volume which Marjorie edited for OMT was *The Gesta Guillelmi of William of Poitiers* (1998), bringing to completion an unfinished project of her friend, the late R. H. C. Davis (1918–91). This life of William the Conqueror was written by a chaplain in his household and is a fundamental contemporary source for the Norman Conquest. It was quoted at length and annotated by Orderic, so its text was very familiar to

---

[49] *Transactions of the Royal Historical Society*, 5th series, 38 (1988), 107–33; see also M. Chibnall, 'The Empress Matilda and Bec-Hellouin', *Anglo-Norman Studies*, 10 (1988), 35–48. Both these articles are reprinted in *Piety, Power and History*.

[50] Chibnall, *Matilda*, p. 97.

Marjorie. She revised Davis's draft translation and wrote the introduction and notes: characteristically, although hers was the major part, she insisted that Davis's name precede hers on the title-page.

Marjorie's exceptional scholarship was recognised in various awards and honours. In 1970 her old college, LMH, gave her honorary membership of the Senior Common Room for four years. Girton elected her to an Honorary Fellowship in 1988. In 1979 she received an Honorary D.Litt. at Birmingham University, and an Honorary Litt.D. at Cambridge was conferred in 2002. An OBE was awarded in 2004. But for Marjorie the most pleasing of honours were to be elected a Fellow of the British Academy in 1978, and a Corresponding Fellow of the Medieval Academy of America in 1983. She never took any membership or obligation lightly, so she threw herself into the British Academy's affairs with gusto, attending meetings and lectures, writing two biographical memoirs (of Eleanora Carus-Wilson and Dominica Legge),[51] and, after Council decided in February 1994 that the annual *Proceedings* needed an academic editor, Marjorie volunteered, and edited three volumes of Lectures and Memoirs, 87, 90, and 94 (1994–6).

With her fine golden hair, startlingly blue eyes and high fluting voice, Marjorie Chibnall was unforgettable, impressing all who met her with her brilliance, sincerity, and generosity of spirit. Her list of publications (eighteen books and more than eighty articles) extends over seventy-two years—the first article appeared in 1939 and the last in 2011. Her final public lecture, a sympathetic, somewhat motherly, account of 'William Rufus: the king and the man', was given in Winchester Cathedral on 12 October 2000. She said her goodbyes to the Battle conference in 2006. After a heart attack in 2008 she was lovingly cared for at home by her family until in 2011 she decided to move to Broomgrove Nursing Home in Sheffield. It was there that she died peacefully on 23 June 2012. A memorial service was held in Girton College Chapel on 1 March 2013.

DIANA E. GREENWAY
Fellow of the Academy

Note. I am indebted to members of Marjorie Chibnall's family—Joan, Cicely, Mary and John Chibnall, and her nephew Stuart Morgan—for help and encouragement in writing this memoir. I am also grateful for the assistance of many friends and archivists. Jane Sayers and Edmund King gave much support and advice throughout, and both kindly lent their collections of letters from Marjorie. Christopher Brooke (NMT/

[51] *Proceedings of the British Academy*, 68 (1982), 503–20, and 74 (1988), 389–403, respectively.

OMT), Gill Sutherland (Perse Girls' School), Victor Tunkel (Selden Society), and Ann Williams (Battle Conference on Anglo-Norman Studies) all sent invaluable memoranda. Material in archives was made available to me by Mary Sabiston (University of Aberdeen), Jacqueline Cox (University of Cambridge), Hannah Westall (Girton College Cambridge), Oliver Mahoney (Lady Margaret Hall Oxford), and Chris Woolgar and Sarah Maspero (University of Southampton). Former colleagues and pupils who sent reminiscences include: from Aberdeen Dr M. B. Gauld and from Cambridge E. J. Ashworth, Wendy Childs, Nicola Coldstream, Richard Eden, Christopher Holdsworth, Marie Lovatt, David Luscombe, Sandra Raban, Susan Ridyard, Julia Roskill, Pamela Taylor, Christabel Sworder, and Stephanie Waller. Quotations from Marjorie Chibnall's 'Memoir', in Jane Chance (ed.), *Women Medievalists and the Academy* (© Board of Regents of University of Wisconsin System, 2005), pp. 747–58, appear by kind permission of the University of Wisconsin Press.

STANLEY COHEN

Stanley Cohen
1942–2013

I. Introduction

I WAS ONE OF THE CO-AUTHORS of the biographical introduction to a Festschrift, *Crime, Social Control and Human Rights*, that was published in 2007 to mark Stan Cohen's retirement two years before from the Martin White Chair of Sociology at the London School of Economics.[1] This memoir is intended to complement and extend that biography and other chapters in the Festschrift rather than merely duplicate them, although it is inevitable that there will be some small acts of cannibalism. Whilst the introduction was largely literary in content and exegetical in method, this memoir will be more of an intellectual portrait or mosaic based on interviews and discussion with those who knew him well, and in writing it I shall try to trace a number of broad themes which gave contour to his life and his views of the world, sociology, politics and human rights. Unless there is a statement to the contrary, it should be assumed that any quotation is taken from those conversations. It should also be said that I have been mindful throughout that it is all too easy to impose an artificial coherence on what was a long, contradictory and complicated life, but a measure of simplification cannot be avoided.

[1] D. Downes, P. Rock, C. Chinkin and C. Gearty (eds.), *Crime, Social Control and Human Rights* (Cullompton, 2007).

II. A brief resumé

Stan Cohen was the eldest of three brothers born into a comfortable
Jewish family in Johannesburg, South Africa, on 23 February 1942, the
son of Ray and Sie Cohen,[2] themselves part of a larger family originating
in Lithuania but dispersed through emigration and flight from the oppressive regimes of Europe in the 1930s and 1940s. He attended Parktown
Boys' High School in Johannesburg, took a BA degree in social work at
the University of the Witwatersrand, worked briefly as a psychiatric social
worker in England between 1963 and 1964, and then studied for a Ph.D.
on *Hooligans, Vandals and the Community: a Study of Social Reaction to
Juvenile Delinquency*, in the fledgling field of criminology, under the supervision of Terence Morris and, for a while, David Downes, at the London
School of Economics (LSE). David Downes remembered that he was
'enormously vital, buoyant and creative, full of ideas but with a clear
sense of what he wanted to achieve ... it gave me a false idea of what it
was like to supervise Ph.D.s because he never had any doubt really as to
what he wanted to do. But he was open all the time to learning new things.'
The doctorate, awarded in 1969, was published in part three years later as
Folk Devils and Moral Panics,[3] and then again with new prefaces in 1987,
1999 and 2003.

A 'moral panic', Stan Cohen said, was 'A condition, episode, person
or group of persons [that] emerges to become defined as a threat to soci-
etal values and interests; its nature is presented in a stylized and stereo-
typical fashion by the mass media; the moral barricades are manned by
editors, bishops, politicians and other right-thinking people; socially-
accredited experts pronounce their diagnoses and solutions; ways of
coping are evolved or (more often) resorted to; the condition then disappears, submerges or deteriorates and becomes more visible.'[4] The notion
condensed ideas about the capacity of powerful groups to shape social
phenomena; the ineluctably political complexion of law and order; the
processual and interactive character of social problems; the ever-present
potential for irrational, ephemeral, distorting and punitive traits to colour
reactions to rule-breaking; and the frequent helplessness of deviants and
others effectively to counter what was done to them. It was not the first

---

[2] A fuller account of his boyhood is given by Adam Kuper in 'Growing up with Stan', in *Crime,
Social Control and Human Rights*, pp. 3–6.
[3] S. Cohen, *Folk Devils and Moral Panics* (London, 1972).
[4] Ibid., p. 9.

time anyone had written on and around that theme.[5] It was not the first time that Stan Cohen himself had published a piece on that topic. He and I had produced a chapter employing very similar ideas in a short history of the Teddy Boy that had appeared three years before,[6] but we had not used the term *moral panic*, a more colourful and elaborated concept that was to become celebrated in the academic literature,[7] and one of the very few sociological phrases to enter common currency (there were 2,750,000 'results' in response to a search on Google in the autumn of 2013). Moral panic was a powerful and seductive concept. It seemed to capture important truths about the condition of England in the 1970s and beyond, and it established Stan Cohen as a public intellectual at a very young age.

Stan Cohen married Ruth Kretzmer in 1963, and they had two daughters, one of whom, Judith, became a Reader in the Philosophy of Education at the Institute of Education, University of London, and the other, Jessica, living in the United States since 1997, was to become a translator from Hebrew into English of books by David Grossman, Yael Hedaya, Ronit Matalon, Amir Gutfreund and Tom Segev. Ruth Cohen, a delightful and highly principled woman, and a ceramic artist, died in 2003. He and Ruth were doting grandparents, taking great pride and pleasure in their grandchildren in London and America.

Stan Cohen's career took him from place to place and country to country. It was not always smooth. He was appointed lecturer in sociology at Enfield College (later Middlesex University) in 1965, but the patronage system of British criminology in the 1960s then blocked him from leaving to take a post at Bedford College, at the time part of the University of

[5] See, for instance, R. Fuller and R. Myers, 'The natural history of a social problem', *American Sociological Review*, 6 (1941), 320–9; E. Lemert; 'Is there a natural history of social problems?', *American Sociological Review*, 16 (1951), 217–23; and E. Sutherland, 'The diffusion of sexual psychopath laws', *American Journal of Sociology*, 56 (1950), 142–8.

[6] S. Cohen and P. Rock, 'The Teddy Boy', in V. Bogdanor and R. Skidelsky (eds.), *The Age of Affluence* (London, 1970), pp. 288–319.

[7] See, for example, the 35 references to books and articles on moral panics in the British Library catalogue <http://explore.bl.uk/primo_library/libweb/action/search.do?dscnt=0&vl(174399379UI0) =any&frbg=&scp.scps=scope%3A%28BLCONTENT%29&tab=local_tab&dstmp= 1382087986360&srt=rank&ct=search&mode=Basic&dum=true&tb=t&indx=1&vl(free Text0)=Folk+Devils+and+Moral+Panics&vid=BLVU1&fn=search>; the 214,000 'results' on Google Scholar <http://scholar.google.co.uk/ scholar?hl=en&q=moral+panic&btnG=&as_sdt= 1%2C5&as_sdtp=>; and the 1,413 citations on JSTOR <http://www.jstor.org.gate2.library.lse. ac.uk/action/doBasicSearch?Query=moral%2Bpanic&Search=Search&gw=jtx&prq= moral+panic&hp=25&acc=on&aori=a&wc=on&fc=off> (all searches conducted on 18 Oct. 2013). And see D. Garland, 'On the concept of moral panic', *Crime Media Culture*, 4 (2008), 9–30.

London, and it engendered some justified resentment against the professoriate of the London School of Economics. He did however eventually move in 1967 to become lecturer and then senior lecturer at the University of Durham; senior lecturer in 1972 and then Professor of Sociology in 1974 at the University of Essex; Professor at the Hebrew University, Jerusalem, in 1981; and then, on his return to England, Centennial Professor in 1994 and finally Martin White Professor of Sociology at the London School of Economics two years later, retiring in 2005.

If his first career was in criminology sociologically conceived, his second was in the linked field of human rights, epitomised by his *States of Denial: Knowing about Atrocities and Suffering*,[8] an exploration of how torture became socially and psychologically possible, which was awarded the 2002 British Academy Book Prize that had been instituted to 'celebrate books that significant [*sic*] contributed to scholarly understanding and, by being lucidly written, appeal to the general reader'.[9] It was a book described by Dame Gillian Beer, the Chair of the Judging Panel, as 'a powerful analysis of an extraordinarily important topic. How is it possible for witnesses—or participants—in atrocities to deny what has, incontrovertibly, occurred? Can one speak of a culture of denial? In exploring these questions Stanley Cohen has carved out a whole new field of enquiry relating sociology, psychology, philosophy, political theory and personal experience.'[10]

Amongst the other honours he received were the Sellin–Glueck Award ('given in order to call attention to criminological scholarship that considers problems of crime and justice as they are manifested outside the United States; internationally or comparatively'[11]) from the American Society of Criminology in 1985; his Fellowship of the British Academy in 1997; an honorary doctorate from the University of Essex in 2003; and the newly established Award for Outstanding Achievement from the British Society of Criminology ('intended to celebrate outstanding contributions made to the discipline by members of the BSC'[12]) in 2009. He died on 7 January 2013 after a long and harrowing illness bravely borne. The British Society of Criminology elected in that year to affix his name to the opening, plenary addresses that would be delivered thereafter at its annual conferences.

[8] S. Cohen, *States of Denial: Knowing about Atrocities and Suffering* (Cambridge, 2001).
[9] <http://www.britac.ac.uk/about/medals/book-prize.cfm>.
[10] <http://www.britac.ac.uk/news/news.cfm/newsid/115>.
[11] <http://www.asc41.com/awards/SellinGlueckAward.html>.
[12] <http://www.britsoccrim.org/prizes.htm>.

III. South Africa

Stan Cohen grew up in the South Africa of apartheid, and, although he was not politically active there, it did reinforce in him an abiding scepticism about the benevolence of the State, its ideology and its institutions. After all, his relatives had long known the cruelty of States (Robin Cohen headed part of an account of the family's history 'Beware the State', and had then moved on to allude to the 'Family's experience of the Russian, Nazi and Lithuanian States'[13]).

Stan Cohen once remarked to me that he was puzzled by the propensity of lawyers to look upon formal social control as benign. He took it to be malign. The social anthropologist, Adam Kuper, his oldest friend and a fellow South African, observed that 'that anti-authoritarian thing was very strong among us'. It instilled in Stan Cohen a restless, lively, questioning intelligence that would take nothing on trust, and certainly not the utterances of those in political power. He once talked of what he called the 'three voracious gods' that faced the sociologist, and, of those, one was 'an overriding obligation to pursue honest intellectual enquiry (however sceptical, irrelevant and unrealistic)'.[14] It led not only to systematic doubt but also to a rugged political and intellectual integrity, what Thomas Hammarburg called a 'stubborn search for honest answers',[15] that emboldened him publicly to confront atrocities in Israel, despite the calumny that could follow;[16] and to defend academic freedom against assault from even quite influential figures.[17]

If Stan Cohen had a political ideology at all, it was probably a liberal or humanist variant of the anarchism, not of Mikhail Bakunin or Sergey

---

[13] In the meeting held at the LSE on 10 Dec. 2013: 'From *Moral Panics* to *States of Denial*: a celebration of the life and work of Stan Cohen'.

[14] S. Cohen, 'Intellectual scepticism and political commitment', in P. Walton and J. Young (eds.), *The New Criminology Revisited* (London, 1998), p. 122.

[15] At the meeting, 'From *Moral Panics* to *States of Denial*'. Thomas Hammarburg was until recently the Council of Europe Commissioner for Human Rights.

[16] His erstwhile colleague at Hebrew University, Daphna Golan, talked at the LSE meeting of 10 Dec. 2013 about Stan Cohen's exceptional courage in talking about the occupation and torture in a university where 'lectures took place as usual as if there were no intifada'.

[17] See the reporting in *The Times Higher Education Supplement* of Stan Cohen's handling of the aftermath of Conor Gearty's critical article on Michael Ignatieff's *The Lesser Evil*, in the *Index on Censorship* ('Ignatieff ducks debate with critics in torture row', *The Times Higher Education Supplement*, 9 Sept. 2005). Ignatieff had attempted to ensure that the article would not be published but Stan Cohen, as guest editor, refused to comply. Conor Gearty commented that 'Stan behaved magnificently throughout—fending off telephone calls from the furious Ignatieff pleading friendship as a reason to help him handle "Mr Gearty"'.

Nechayev, but of William Godwin, that embraced a mistrust of the State, the millenarian[18] and big ideas. It was an allegiance that he had contracted very early in life. His brother Robin remembered that 'at our family dining table [in South Africa] we sometimes formally took positions on issues of the day—Stan anarchist, me socialist, Clive capitalist. This is relevant to ... Stan's close engagement with anarchism. And truth to tell the three positions—which were adolescent self-ascriptions—were not far from our final positions.'[19]

Stan Cohen particularly admired the British anarchist Colin Ward,[20] a family friend until his death, of whom it was said that he 'saw all distant goals as a form of tyranny and believed that anarchist principles could be discerned in everyday human relations and impulses'.[21] He was at one with Colin Ward in being particularly distrustful of the apocalyptic and the absolutist. It was no accident that what may have been Stan Cohen's very first publication[22] appeared (like those of some of his criminological contemporaries on the British Left[23]) in *Anarchy*, the journal which Ward edited between 1961 and 1970. And one of the later concomitants of that antipathy to the State and its institutions was his publication with Laurie Taylor in 1972 of a clandestine study of long-term prisoners' strategies of survival in Durham Prison[24] that was based on a remarkable empathy with the lot of the incarcerated (Paul Wiles called it 'one of the most sensitive accounts of prison life ever published'[25]) but which also led to protracted antagonism between the authors and the Home Office[26] and a wider and enduring souring of relations between criminologists and government.

[18] See S. Cohen, 'Criminology and the sociology of deviance in Britain', in P. Rock and M. McIntosh (eds.), *Deviance and Social Control* (London, 1974), p. 30.

[19] Email, 13 Nov. 2013.

[20] Colin Ward, 1924–2010, was the author of some 30 books and edited the journals *Freedom* and *Anarchy* between 1961 and 1970.

[21] K. Worpole, Colin Ward Obituary, *The Guardian*, 22 Feb. 2010 <http://www.theguardian.com/society/2010/feb/22/colin-ward-obituary>.

[22] The first was S. Cohen, 'Vandalism and the social structure', *Anarchy*, 64 (1966), 181–7.

[23] See D. Downes, 'What will happen to Jones and Robinson?', *Anarchy*, 53 (1965), 195–201; D. Downes, 'One boy's story', *Anarchy*, 64 (1966), 173–5; J. Young, 'The zookeepers of deviancy', *Anarchy*, 98 (1969), 101–8; L. Taylor, 'The criminologist and the criminal', *Anarchy*, 98 (1969), 114–21.

[24] S. Cohen and L. Taylor, *Psychological Survival: the Experience of Long-Term Imprisonment* (Harmondsworth, 1972).

[25] Review in *The British Journal of Sociology*, 24 (1973), p. 255.

[26] See S. Cohen and L. Taylor, *Prison Secrets*, Radical Alternatives to Prison and National Council for Civil Liberties (London, 1976).

Authority at large was ever problematic for him. He chafed when baulked by senior staff, officials and bureaucracies, in Israel, in London and elsewhere. He was not to be confined by rules. He was to be something of an innocent abroad in the highly regulated labyrinth of English higher education. One of his research students, Olga Jubany, recalled, quite spontaneously:

> He had no idea about the practicalities of the PhD, registrations or any other issue. In fact, I didn't even realise that I wasn't actually registered for a PhD (but formally for an MPhil) until almost a year on, when my colleagues told me so. He would not bother with any of the admin machinery (you would not expect him to do so anyway). If at the very beginning I ever asked him something about how I should submit the Aims and Methods paper,[27] or how the bursary system was for PhDs, or what was the research seminar timing; he would look at me like: 'you seriously expect me to know that? surely not!'. What's more, he would not follow up on what courses I registered for and would certainly not make me choose specific ones over others (except for the wonderful Criminology seminar, where he participated too and was really the best course of the whole PhD years).

If Stan Cohen was an anarchistically minded sceptic, he was also a sceptic about some of the forms adopted by anarchism itself, observing in one of those pieces in *Anarchy* that 'Anarchists, whose intellectual roots go deeper back than any other group fighting the horrors of today's society should be the first to see that a committed and passionate position is not incompatible with an orderly argument ... antagonism needs to be documented as much as acceptance.'[28] Jessica, his daughter, said 'he disliked the idea of hard-line ideological positions and movements. ... I think it just came from his suspicion of dogma and structure. He could never have been a member of a political party.' It was a scepticism that could even turn in on itself, serving reflexively, in Harvey Molotch's words, as a 'loyal nag that what he was thinking might be wrong'[29] and that those with whom he disagreed might be right. It even led him eventually to distance himself from criminology itself, the discipline that had suckled him, when he was living in Israel (although there are some, like David Downes, who believed that the title of his matricidal book, *Against Criminology*,[30] was ironically intended).

---

[27] The 'Aims and Methods Paper' was intended to serve as a test of the research student's competence to proceed to the second year of the Ph.D. course.

[28] S. Cohen, 'Notes on Detention Centres', *Anarchy*, 101 (no date), 210.

[29] At 'From *Moral Panics* to *States of Denial*'.

[30] S. Cohen, *Against Criminology* (New Brunswick, NJ, 1988).

Growing up in South Africa also instilled in Stan Cohen a desire to leave what he conceived to be a malevolent country for one more admirable, Israel. His adolescent world was permeated by Zionism. The Students Jewish Association at Parktown Boys' High School was steeped in it. The November 1961 issue of the school magazine, *The Parktonian*, recorded, for instance, how the Association's:

> ... first few meetings of the year were addressed by members of the Zionist Youth Movement, who spoke on different aspects of life on Communal Settlements. As usual films were shown at various times of the year. Their topics ranged from Communal Settlements to Jewish holidays.... Dr. H. Michel returned to the school and gave an awe-inspiring talk on 'The Tide of the New Immigration' concerning the emigration of Jews from Arab and Communist dominated countries.[31]

As an adolescent, Stan Cohen had travelled with his family to Israel, visiting relatives and the tourist sites, and he had spent brief periods of time with *Habonim* at the South African-affiliated Kibbutz Tsora and Kibbutz Yizrael in the winter of 1958–9. It was to Israel that he determined he would return. Adam Kuper remembered:

> He wasn't that radical in South Africa. Of course he was anti-apartheid ... and he had black friends and so on but he was not politically active in South Africa in the way that a number of us were. Because he belonged to this group which said, 'okay, you know, the situation is terrible, we're against it, we're going to go to Israel.' So for a number of his friends, not for me, but for a number of his friends who then went to Israel, the great issue was 'why didn't Stan ... get further qualifications and then he would join us'.

The lure of *aliyah* was strong, and it was thought to demand particular talents from those who chose to emigrate. Robin Cohen said: 'Stan was much more committed than either Clive or myself to a sort of Zionist dream. By dream I mean ... something that was ... idealistic and he had some idea that he needed some skills that he would be able to apply in that context. And I think he sort of stumbled into social work.' It was an unusual course to take. Stan Cohen acknowledged that he was something of a disappointment and *Luftmensch* in the eyes of his parents[32] (all three brothers had 'said "no" to my father's increasingly despairing pleas to take over his retail clothing business' said Robin Cohen). Social work was not the common aspiration of young Jewish men growing up in the South Africa of the 1950s and 1960s, but 'each of his cohort were supposed to

---

[31] R.D.W., 'Students Jewish Association', *The Parktonian*, LVII (1961), 18.
[32] A. Kuper, 'Growing up with Stan', p. 6.

have a specialism that would be particularly useful in Israel'.[33] Stan Cohen's daughter, Judith, reflected that he and Robin, who would also become a Professor of Sociology, 'were regarded as the mad ones. The younger brother [Clive] stayed in South Africa, went into finance and insurance and that was regarded as the sensible, reasonable thing to do. Whereas Stan and Robin were always … just a bit mystifying to our grandparents … as to how they could possibly have chosen that … and they never understood why he left South Africa.'

Leaving South Africa was Stan Cohen's first displacement. He had felt uncomfortable there and he departed, although he always retained an ambivalent affection for the country. Judith Cohen said 'he loved it. He always felt that that was his home and yet whenever he was there … every visit that we went on when we were little, there was horrible tension always in the background.' But, at the age of 21, Stan Cohen was to go first, not back to Israel, but to England. Robin Cohen said 'I think his idea was that he would get some practical experience as a psychiatric social worker. He would perhaps do an MA and then he would go to Israel. And then somehow the lure of LSE and the entrance to the things he was doing took him away from that.'

IV. England

By contrast with South Africa, London was a free and febrile place in the mid-1960s. David Downes recalled that 'he always said that he got an enormous amount just out of being here. Don't forget, South Africa was then such a closed society in almost every way … he came here and he could go to all the things that he and Ruth had seen in smuggled back copies of *The New Statesman*. You know, meetings about politics in Red Lion Square and so on. [He] just loved to go to all those things [and the] debate and discussion.' The sociological criminology practised with his fellow-students, Jock Young and others, at the London School of Economics, and indeed in the United Kingdom at large, was itself febrile at the time. I have described elsewhere[34] how the great university expansion that took place in the wake of the 1963 Robbins Report[35] created a

---

[33] Email 13 Nov. 2013.
[34] P. Rock, 'The present state of British criminology', *British Journal of Criminology*, 28 (1988), 188–99.
[35] *Higher Education: Report of the Committee appointed by the Prime Minister under the Chairmanship of Lord Robbins 1961–63* Cmnd 2154 (London, 1963).

substantial cohort of youthful scholars who formed an intellectually tumultuous and self-referential critical mass that set itself against what was seen as the orthodoxies, postures, politics and authority of a fusty older generation.

Stan Cohen was at the centre of it all. He had arrived in England just as that ferment began, and his thesis captured what was in effect the minor intellectual revolt that was in progress around him. The Young Turks of the so-called new criminologies[36] rejected what they conceived to be the atheoretical positivism and subservience to the State of criminology proper, and celebrated in its place a blend of the symbolic interactionism and phenomenology personified by the Americans, Howard S. Becker, Edwin Lemert and David Matza; a sociology from below that reported the world-views of those who had hitherto lacked credit and a voice;[37] and, a little later, the radical Europeans, Karl Marx, Nicos Poulantzas, Evgenii Pashukanis, Louis Althusser and others.

The arguments which Stan Cohen collated and examined in his Ph.D. *Hooligans, Vandals and the Community* presented a particularly prescient and articulate opening statement of a number of those 'recent developments in the sociology of deviance',[38] and they served as a platform on which he would build almost all his subsequent theorising, and, indeed, as something of a platform for much of British criminology itself.[39] He talked there about how what he called transactionalism was a loose approach rather than 'a fully fledged theory' (p. 10); an approach that was best 'understood as a reaction against traditional ways of looking at one's subject matter' (p. 11) and against the theoretical insulation of criminology. In his exegesis of the work of Howard Becker, Erving Goffman, Kai Erikson, Ronald Laing, Edwin Lemert, David Matza, George Herbert Mead and others, he sought to bring sociology back into criminology; reject what he believed to be the essentialising, static and dehumanising definitions current in the thought of those working in social control agencies and the orthodox criminology that was their handmaiden; acknowledge the diversity of deviants and deviant phenomena; and subscribe to an imagery of deviance that was centred on social and psychological process. Rule-breaking was said to be rooted in identities that were negotiated, step by

---

[36] See, for instance, I. Taylor, P. Walton and J. Young, *The New Criminology* (London, 1973).

[37] See H. Becker; 'Whose side are we on?', *Social Problems*, 14 (1967), 239–47.

[38] He was not then, or afterwards, much influenced by Marx and the Marxists.

[39] As our biographical entry in the Festschrift argued, Stan Cohen 'made his mark *before* the new criminologies forked, and he continued to exercise influence thereafter as an ancestral father figure over all the criminological lineages …', *Crime, Social Control and Human Rights*, p. xxiii.

step and reflexively, in an unequal conversation with others, often more powerful, in a sequence of transformations which Erving Goffman represented as a moral career. Critical to that processual model, Stan Cohen said, is 'the use of concepts such as meaning, mind and self [which] moves us far away from the tenets of positivism; ... alerts us not only to seeing the reactions of others ... but also to seeing the interaction process *from the point of view of the deviant*' (p. 29, emphasis in the original). There was in all this a part of him that toyed with the deviant and the risqué himself (and in the jointly written introduction to one work he celebrated taking drugs with students, watching pornography and organising street protests[40]) but one suspects that much of it was more vicarious than practised, however much it may have been eulogised by his collaborator, Laurie Taylor, who often reminisced in public about their daring exploits together.

In affirming his position, Stan Cohen could be quite perfunctory and scathing about the failings of those who differed from him. He opened a review of Irvin Waller's *Men Released from Prison* with the dismissal 'Standard criminological stuff';[41] called John Williams's *Narcotics and Drug Dependence* 'lunacy';[42] and noted how 'sad' it was that Richard Sparks had spent time 'on this sort of stuff [the mathematical modelling of penal systems]. Mathematical models might well have their place—but perhaps not in a book subtitled: "The Crisis in the English Penal System".'[43] In so doing, he made it clear how much he disliked positivism, grand theory, descriptions grounded in the workings of impersonal social systems,[44] and what David Matza called 'correctionalism',[45] the pursuit of criminology to punish or change the deviant. He disliked dogmatics, even the dogmatics of his friends and colleagues on the Left (although, as Adam Kuper observed, he was outwardly tolerant of a politics that was 'so much the orthodoxy in the circles he moved in'). He was certainly not persuaded that revolution would answer the problems of crime and criminology: it might conduce only to the substitution of one form of oppression by another, to a 'model of social control in which offenders wearing

[40] See S. Cohen and L. Taylor; *Escape Attempts: the Theory and Practice of Resistance in Everyday Life* (London, 1976), p. 2.
[41] S. Cohen, Review, *New Society* (30 May 1974), 526.
[42] S. Cohen, Review, *New Society* (5 Sept. 1974), 624.
[43] S. Cohen, Review of R. Sparks, *Local Prisons: the Crisis in the English Penal System*, *New Society* (23 Sept. 1971), 579
[44] Robin Cohen said 'He wasn't keen on ... structuralism as in Marx, or structuralism as in Levi-Strauss, as in Parsonian [theory], I mean none of that really resonated.'
[45] D. Matza, *Becoming Deviant* (Englewood Cliffs, NJ, 1969), pp. 15–24.

sandwich boards listing their crimes before a crowd which shouts "Down with the counter-revolutionaries!" are then led away to be publicly shot'.[46]

He was driven by extension to the biographical and the intimate in the micro-sociology of everyday life. That is why he followed Terence Morris and turned to the work of the so-called Chicagoans and their heirs with their focus on the sociology of everyday life (and that emphasis was to be reinforced by semesters spent at the University of California, Santa Barbara, in the company of scholars such as Harvey Molotch, himself a product of the University of Chicago). Robert Park, the founder of the Department of Sociology at the University of Chicago and one of the progenitors of the 'Chicago School', once remarked that William James had taught him that 'the real world was the experience of actual men and women and not abbreviated and shorthand descriptions of it that we call knowledge'.[47] Stan Cohen would have approved. He once told me that of all the books he would keep, it would be those that had been published by the University of Chicago Press. Adam Kuper remarked he had been 'terrifically influenced by that stuff ... the study of the pool halls. Those were very important to him.' In his review of that study, *Hustlers, Beats and Others*, Stan Cohen said that he 'was grateful to Ned Polsky [its author] for reminding us that sociology could be interesting and even entertaining'.[48]

The new sociology was to be institutionalised in the form of the National Deviancy Conference that met for the first time at the University of York in 1968. Stan Cohen was in the van (David Downes claimed that 'the anchor-men of the NDC were Stan Cohen and Laurie Taylor'[49]). He edited the very first collection of papers from the Conference, *Images of Deviance*, as a *de facto* group manifesto, and it was there that he announced, in an echo of his preamble to *Hooligans, Vandals and the Community*, that 'Our feelings towards official criminology ranged from distrust at its orientation towards administrative needs and impatience with its highly empirical, anti-theoretical bias, to simply a mild lack of interest in the sort of studies that were being conducted.'[50]

[46] S. Cohen, 'Guilt, justice and tolerance', in D. Downes and P. Rock (eds.), *Deviant Interpretations* (Oxford, 1979), p. 44.
[47] In P. Baker, 'The life histories of W. I. Thomas and Robert E. Park', *American Journal of Sociology*, 79 (1973), 255.
[48] S. Cohen, Review, *New Society* (3 June 1971), 969.
[49] D. Downes, 'The sociology of crime and social control in Britain, 1960–1987', *British Journal of Criminology*, 28 (1988), 46.
[50] S. Cohen, 'Introduction', in S. Cohen (ed.), *Images of Deviance* (Harmondsworth, 1971), p. 15.

But, if he was averse to positivism and all its works, to abstracted empiricism, to grand theory and to structuralism—to dogmas, ideologies and systems—his scepticism about orthodoxy encouraged him to be otherwise eclectic, not accepting any single theory *tout court*. He was an intellectual in love with ideas. His daughter, Jessica, said 'I think that he had difficulty relating closely to adults who were not academics or not intellectual. He ... wasn't comfortable, I think, with people who were not intellectual because they would not find a common language.' And his other daughter, Judith, agreed: 'that's right, that's how he related to people. That was the only way he related to people, to discuss ideas. You couldn't talk about just everyday stuff.'

Stan Cohen had a great liking for conversation, teaching and students, and his students were fond of him in their turn. In Israel and England, he was ever in their midst. Judith Cohen said 'he was always encouraging students to come and talk to him and ... he would spend hours talking to people ... but it was only if they had a shared intellectual language'. His was a teaching rooted in discussion, story-telling and anecdote. Olga Jubany recalled that 'His supervision relied almost entirely on our regular conversations that would focus on discussing the development and approach of the investigation. Later these would develop into personal chats ... but certainly never, ever, about any administrative or bureaucratic proceedings.'

Stan Cohen's thought was grounded in what he called transactionalism. He flirted with the ideas of Michel Foucault, Ronald Laing, ethnomethodology and anarchism. He was intrigued by the psychology of the self, being, as his brother Robin said, 'much more self-reflective, much more personally aware than ... either Clive or myself'. He had studied psychoanalysis, practised briefly as a psychiatric social worker, and received therapy in California. At the very opening of his intellectual career he had talked scathingly about the 'sort of philistine distrust ... which greeted the work of Durkheim and Freud.... How [some said] can the intrapsychic conflicts of middle-class Viennese Jews explain how the normal mind works?'[51] His answer was that they could do so pretty well. Indeed, just as Sigmund Freud's study was littered with small carvings of gods and idols from ancient Greece, Rome, Egypt and the Orient,[52] so Stan Cohen kept a plastic manikin of Freud on his desk at work. Malcolm Feeley, Claire Sanders Clements Dean's Professor of Law at the University

---

[51] Cohen, *Hooligans, Vandals and the Community*, p. 13.
[52] See <http://www.freud.org.uk/about/house/>.

of California, Berkeley, who used from time to time to occupy Stan
Cohen's office at the Hebrew University, recalled that 'the books of
psychoanalysis took up a big part of his library collection.... I do think
that underlying a lot of his work is some sort of implicit psychology....
Think of moral panics as something that creates anxieties in people....
States of Denial is implicit there.' Indeed, Stan Cohen was to talk often
and at length to Irene Bruna Seu, an academic and a psychoanalytical
psychotherapist, whilst he was writing the book.

Stan Cohen was, in short, something of a polymath and an eclectic.
One of his students, Megan Comfort, later a research sociologist working
in San Francisco,[53] remembered the diversity and breadth of his thought
as a teacher: 'it felt like he brought in a lot of different perspectives and
different theoretical ideas into our thinking through all of these different
issues'. He thought on a large, panoptic scale. His colleague at the LSE,
Claire Moon, put it that 'Typically, Cohen took an unsettling approach to
... problems [of the denial of human rights], what might be called a 360
degree approach ...,'[54] and by that she meant that he looked 'not just [at]
the state, but also the bystanders (the consumers of humanitarian campaigns and appeals), and the humanitarian entrepreneurs, the human
rights NGOs themselves. All of these were, he argued, complicit in denial
and "bystander passivity".'[55]

Perhaps Stan Cohen was above all *playful*. He enjoyed the life of the
mind. He had an abiding sense of humour, irony and the absurd (and the
transactionalism which he espoused had at times itself veered into a sociology of the absurd[56]). A reflexive sociologist who looked continually at
the interplay between biography and the social world, he loved anecdote
and narrative, teaching through stories, and funny stories above all (one
of his students, Sharon Shalev, said 'he was a wonderful gossip. There
were few things I enjoyed as much as sitting and just gossiping about
people with him.') His LSE colleague Conor Gearty said too that 'The
other memory I have is of course how funny he was. And that, to some

[53] Her full title was senior research sociologist with the Urban Health Program and an adjunct
assistant professor of medicine at the Center for AIDS Prevention Studies at the University of
California.
[54] C. Moon, '"Looking without seeing, listening without hearing": Cohen, denial and human
rights', *Crime, Media, Culture*, 9 (2013), p. 194.
[55] C. Moon, keynote lecture delivered to the Moral Panic, Society and Rights Conference in
Honour of Stan Cohen, University of Athens, Greece, 7 Dec. 2013.
[56] See, for instance, S. Lyman and M. Scott, *A Sociology of the Absurd* (New York, 1989);
P. Carlen, *Magistrates' Courts: an Ethnography in the Sociology of the Absurd*, Ph.D. dissertation,
University of London, 1974.

extent, comes through in the writing but the fun was rooted in such a strong sociological understanding of the self you know. I mean he was so aware that he was part of something. It was incredible.'

Stan Cohen had a great store of Jewish jokes, and he told them very well, often to poke fun at authority, the staid, the conventional and himself. Stan Cohen's colleague, Tim Newburn, said 'one of the things that's an overriding memory for me of Stan is [that he] had extraordinarily twinkly eyes which betrayed, I thought, a really important bit of his character which was, Stan was just a little bit naughty, I thought. And that naughtiness probably displayed itself in a variety of ways but I think that as a scholar, that naughtiness presented itself at least in part, as a desire in some small way, always to subvert.'

V. Israel

England in the 1960s and 1970s may have been intellectually exciting, Stan Cohen may have come into his own and prospered there professionally, but he was never quite at home. He liked individual Britons, and he and Ruth made close friendships, mostly through work, some of which endured for the rest of their lives. They did talk fondly about their life in Durham. Yet Judith, his daughter, reflected they had 'a sense of aloofness from "the Brits" as a nation'. He did not talk about 'us' but about 'the British' as if they were foreign to him. A political animal, he never became involved in British politics. ('I was', he said, 'acutely aware that [my] original commitments could never find a home in English politics. I couldn't read about what was happening in South Africa and Israel and then connect with the striking British trades unionists or university Trotskyists.'[57]) In the whole of England there was but one little area for which he had come strongly to care, Belsize Park, in North London. But the Cohens were living in Colchester in Essex in the 1970s, and that was another matter altogether. Robin Cohen said 'it was very grey and bleak and even within Wivenhoe or Colchester, wherever they were, they seemed to somehow pick out the greyest stucco and drabbest walls'.

Disengaged and rather rootless, Stan Cohen and his family quit England for Israel in 1981. Many were taken aback at their decision. David Downes said 'it took me completely by surprise ..., his going to Israel. I mean I hadn't been in on that, as it were. So it came as a bolt from

---

[57] L. Taylor, 'The other side of the street', *New Humanist*, 119 (2004), 4.

the blue ... that he found British society so boring. I mean that did surprise me 'cause I don't find British society boring. I find it really endlessly fascinating. But then, from his perspective, I could see how that could be. You know, there was no really powerful fundamental challenge going on to the powers that be.' It should be reported that Stan and Ruth Cohen also told Malcolm Feeley, their friend from Berkeley, that their emigration had been prompted by the anti-Semitism of the Left in England, although they seem to have said that to no one else, and certainly not to their daughters.

Other forces were in play. There was the residual influence of Zionism (Stan Cohen said afterwards that 'So strong was the brainwashing I'd received from the Zionist youth movement that I'd managed to avoid facing the full reality'[58]). Jessica Cohen claimed that there was a quest for the *frisson* of political commitment, what David Downes had called a 'really powerful fundamental challenge'. 'For obvious reasons', she said, they 'couldn't go back to South Africa ... before apartheid ended, so I think Israel was a place for them to feel involved in.' And her sister, Judith, concurred: 'They needed to be in a struggle ... there was the political thing, that they wanted to feel part of something, there was a connection ... at that point in Israel, there was a sense that there was a real political struggle that was going in a positive direction. There was Camp David and there was a sense that if you joined this swell of people who were you know, progressive and moving towards peace, then you could be part of this.' There were family links. Ruth's parents lived in Jerusalem. So did David, her brother, at that time the Bruce W. Wayne Professor of International Law at the Hebrew University. And thus it was that the family left.

It was not to be a wholly happy experience. Stan Cohen said it had been 'complete madness'.[59] Judith Cohen called it 'a complete fiasco'. Instead of a vibrant politics, they found, in the words of Jessica Cohen, that 'the South African friends they had who had moved to Israel ... most of them, the vast majority of them were just not involved in any kind of political activity. They were just living *bourgeois* lives.' Stan Cohen was not to be at home intellectually or socially in the Department of Sociology at the Hebrew University. He had been lauded in England but, Jessica Cohen continued, 'he felt under-appreciated in Israel, right from the

---

[58] L. Taylor, 'The other side of the street: an interview with Stan Cohen', in Downes *et al.*, *Crime, Social Control and Human Rights*, p. 20.
[59] Ibid., p. 20.

beginning, professionally'. He found Shmuel Noah Eisenstadt,[60] a power-
ful baronial figure in the department, a grand theorist in the tradition
of structural-functionalism, to be a difficult colleague. In turn, Shmuel
Eisenstadt and another colleague, Joseph Ben-David,[61] dismissed Stan
Cohen's work as not properly sociological, rejected his wish to remain in
the department,[62] and obliged him to move into the Institute of
Criminology where, again, he was to be ill at ease professionally. Malcolm
Feeley, who knew him in Israel and the United States, said 'Stan was just
head and shoulders above them ... [he] was not happy there and he got
increasingly unhappy ... he did not have a comfortable intellectual home.'
Adam Kuper put it even more pithily, 'he hated the Hebrew University,
hated the sociologists. He thought the university was not a very good university.' *Aliyah* had become something of an illusion. Robin Cohen said
'Israel he regarded as a pretty big mistake you know, he was living out that
interrupted adolescent dream ... he had friends, he had significant ...
achievements in the UK and in the United States. Israel was very much a
sort of backwards move.' He and Ruth began to question whether their
daughters could ever have a future in the country.

Some members of his immediate family did somewhat temper that
narrative of alienation and deracination. Jessica Cohen certainly did so—
her memories of life in Israel were more affectionate. But Stan Cohen had
undoubtedly become estranged from large portions of Israeli society,
sociology and criminology and, finding the 'Israeli military occupation of
the West Bank an ongoing source of pain',[63] he moved into the politics
and study of human rights, focusing especially on torture.[64] Adam Kuper
recalled too that 'he'd got a bit bored with sociology and criminology as
well ... in Israel, the most interesting people in any case were often

---

[60] Shmuel Eisenstadt (1923–2010) taught at the University from 1946 to 1990 and was head of the
Department of Sociology between 1949 and 1969. He was said to have 'developed comparative
knowledge of exceptional quality and originality concerning social change and modernization,
and concerning relations between culture, belief systems and political institutions. His work
combines sociological theory with historical and empirical research in the study of modernities
and civilizations' (citation for the Holberg Prize, 2006, <http://www.holbergprisen.no/en/shmuel-
n-eisenstadt/shmuel-noah-eisenstadt-1923-2010.html>).

[61] Joseph Ben-David (1920–86), the George Wise Professor of Sociology, a committed anti-
relativist, was a sociologist of science who had taught at the Hebrew University from 1950. See
R. Westrum; 'Obituary: Joseph Ben-David (1920–86): sociologist of science and of higher
education', *Social Studies of Science*, 16 (1986), 565–7.

[62] See N. Ben-Yehuda, 'Stan', *Crime, Media, Culture*, 9 (2013), 188.

[63] Ibid., p. 188.

[64] See B. Hudson; 'Professor Stanley Cohen: an appreciation', *Criminal Justice Matters*, 92 (2013),
<http://www.tandfonline.com/doi/full/10.1080/09627251.2013.805380#.Upd0wNJSiS8>.

involved in these human rights things'. So it was that he moved to work with others 'to expose the torture of Palestinian political figures. And Stan published not only key papers on it,[65] he was very involved with the pressure group which ... got the Supreme Court to see what could be done.'[66] Robin Cohen added, 'he had to find some space for himself which allowed him to live in this place that he clearly hated. And I think that's probably where the human rights stuff came from. Again, the biographical angle, the personal and the political connecting.' It was in the vigorous intellectual and political world centred on human rights in Israel that Ruth and Stan Cohen then came to find a new anchorage. Judith Cohen remembered:

> ... he did find himself—largely through political activity—connecting to a small group of intellectuals and activists on the Left, where he and Ruth were instrumental in founding and organizing groups and activities within the anti-occupation movement ... during their time in Israel, despite the problems, they were very involved politically—Ruth perhaps more than Stan—and the friendships they formed through this activity were hugely significant and provided them with a support network, a rich social life that, I think ... encouraged them to stay on even when things got difficult.

The Professor of International Law, Christine Chinkin, Stan Cohen's future colleague at the London School of Economics, met him first at a conference in Gaza organised by the Palestine Human Rights Association, and found in his work a complementarity with her own legal interest in genocide. But what Stan Cohen introduced analytically into what was then a largely legal and activist field was a sociological inflection unusual at the time. He began by transposing the psychoanalytic vocabulary of denial, sociological ideas about good people and dirty work,[67] and the criminological language of techniques of neutralisation[68] to a new empirical terrain:

> Human rights were colonised by law. There's no doubt about that at all.... I don't think other people have done the sort of sociological roots of human rights in the way he did, how issues emerge through a language and then through being identified in such a way that they can ... explor[e] that sociological root.

---

[65] See S. Cohen, *Denial and Acknowledgement: the Impact of Information about Human Rights Violations* (Jerusalem, 1995); and S. Cohen, 'Government responses to human rights reports: claims, denials and counterclaims', *Human Rights Quarterly*, 18 (1996), 517–43.

[66] He was referring to the consequences of the 1991 B'Tselem Report, co-authored by Stan Cohen, and discussed by Stan Cohen's brother-in-law, David Kretzmer, in 'The torture debate: Israel and beyond', in Downes *et al.*, *Crime, Social Control and Human Rights*, pp. 120–35.

[67] E. Hughes, 'Good people and dirty work', *Social Problems*, 10 (1962), 3–11.

[68] See G. Sykes and D. Matza, 'Techniques of neutralization: a theory of delinquency', *American Sociological Review*, 22 (1957), 664–70; and D. Matza, *Delinquency and Drift* (New York, 1964).

The States of Denial stuff.... Nobody else ... has really looked at this concept of what is the complicity of people with respect to human rights violations of those who are in some sense peripheral or on the margins or watching.

Another colleague in the same area, Claire Moon, would add that Stan Cohen then proceeded to apply a further idea integral to criminology, that of the politics of social control, to the comparative analysis of transitional justice, examining how societies policed the past by opening up and closing down access to discreditable and dangerous knowledge. The idea raised ancillary questions about how such knowledge should be acted on—about lustration and punishment—and about how (if at all) those who received that knowledge responded to what they were told[69] ('the assumption that drives a lot of human rights NGO work is, of course, if only people knew, they would act [but there are] defence mechanisms that prevent us from acting on information about suffering'[70] she said). And, moving even further down that spiral of actions and reactions, the idea invited an exploration of how states such as Israel responded to those selfsame responses by 'contest[ing] and rebuff[ing] claims by human rights organizations, such as those made by PCATI [the Public Committee Against Torture in Israel], Human Rights Watch or Amnesty International in their reports?'[71] Their official rejoinder, it seemed, was typically to redefine the victim, the perpetrator and the act in ways that softened the impact of knowledge about torture, restored a measure of legitimacy, distance and necessity to what was done and allayed the bystander's disquiet—accomplishing, in effect, the very antithesis of a moral panic. In short, Stan Cohen's criminology of human rights posed very big sociological questions of truth, acknowledgement, catharsis and reparation:

[T]he control by opening and the control by closing was a really interesting way of looking at it because he was pointing right early on to the political dimensions ... looking at the State institutions and at how people were made to speak, who was allowed to speak, who could speak, what kind of truths were being generated and so on.

In Israel, Stan Cohen had encountered what he considered to be an oppressive polity and his antipathy to Leviathan had grown. Robin Cohen

---

[69] S. Cohen; 'State crimes of previous regimes: knowledge, accountability, and the policing of the past', *Law and Social Inquiry*, 20 (1995), 7–50.

[70] See S. Cohen and B. Seu; 'Knowing enough not to feel too much: emotional thinking about human rights appeals', in M. Bradley and P. Petro (eds.), *Truth Claims* (Piscataway, NJ, 2002), pp. 187–228.

[71] C. Moon, keynote lecture delivered to the Moral Panic, Society and Rights Conference in Honour of Stan Cohen, University of Athens, Greece, 7 Dec. 2013.

said: 'I think part of what happened to him there was "it's every bit as bleak as I feared, the State is immutable, the populace is completely behind the State. This looks to me like I can't believe in any meaningful sense".' It is perhaps unremarkable then that one of the few intellectual positions he came to accept almost without cavil for a while was to be the work of Michel Foucault, because Foucault wrote allusively and polemically about the diffuse and overweening tyranny of the State. Foucault's *Discipline and Punish* was an especially graphic, almost poetic, account of the way in which the controls imposed by the State insidiously and systemically permeated every fibre of the body social.[72] Adam Kuper reflected that 'there was a stage where Foucault was really terrific' for him. Stan Cohen himself enthused in 1974 about 'the marvellously rich French school around Foucault [that] has built up an impressive theoretical edifice ...',[73] calling it 'wonderful' to Nachman Ben-Yehuda, his colleague at the Hebrew University. The consonance between the thoughts of the two men was especially pronounced in Stan Cohen's paper 'The punitive city',[74] published in 1979, and the influential book, *Visions of Social Control,* published in 1985 whilst he was in Israel, a book replete with references to Foucault, in which he explored how the apparent attenuation of State power perversely only extended State power through what he called boundary-blurring, 'net-widening' and 'mesh-thinning'. But they were references made at a later stage, and by then Stan Cohen had come to be somewhat dubious even about 'the marvellously rich French school',[75] wondering, Nachman Ben-Yehuda recalled, about its meagre empirical foundations.

VI. England Again

Belsize Park in North London was where Stan and Ruth Cohen had first stayed when he was a research student, and it was to become the *Heimat*

[72] M. Foucault, *Discipline and Punish* (English translation) (Harmondsworth, 1979).
[73] S. Cohen, Review of D. Rothman, *The Discovery of the Asylum, New Society* (7 Feb. 1974), 332.
[74] S. Cohen. 'The punitive city: notes on the dispersal of social control', *Social Crises*, 3 (1979), 341–63.
[75] He was to say that 'I am altogether unsympathetic to the intellectual climate in which his work flourishes and (being exactly the type of "humanist" he is always attacking) totally opposed to his structuralist denial of human agency. But to write today about punishment and classification without Foucault, is like talking about the unconscious without Freud': S. Cohen, *Visions of Social Control* (Cambridge, 1985), p. 10.

to which they returned on his appointment to the London School of Economics. His brother said 'he fixed on one place which was Belsize Park and he never really felt comfortable in any other space. By that I mean to say, did he feel comfortable in South Africa? No. In Israel? No. In the UK at large? No. In American space? No. It was just that little zone ... he needed a certain sense of buzz and activity, eating with friends, meeting interesting people.' The grand houses of Belsize Park are physically elegant and many of its inhabitants are intellectually animated and urbane. Judith Cohen described it as 'the hub of this ... political, cosmopolitan environment'. In that last decade or so of his life, working at the LSE and living in North London, he seemed to have become much more content with his lot. Jessica Cohen said 'I think by the time [the family had] sort of come to terms with all the turmoil of moving back and forth and just accepted that they were now in London.'

VII. The Marginal Man

Judith Cohen said 'in spite of all their moving around, [my parents] sustained close friendships, often for over fifty years, with individuals from all over world. Friends were hugely important in their lives and it was their close network of friends, both those that went back to the early days in South Africa or England, and more recent ones, that made them feel at home and rooted, especially here in London.' The family could never simply be described as homeless cosmopolitans. Yet there was, at the same time, a sense in which they were perennial outsiders. Jessica Cohen said they felt that they never completely belonged anywhere. Stan Cohen himself was frequently described by friends and colleagues as a wandering Jew, a marginal man, who had never quite settled. His friend and student, Sharon Shalev, called it 'the curse of the Jew ... we belong everywhere, we don't belong anywhere ... we look at the big ugly parts of the societies we live in and ... you belong but you don't really belong.' His brother reflected in like vein that Stan Cohen 'did have that habit of looking past you and that's what I'm calling displacement and you can put some other label to it which may be more slightly psychoanalytical, but it was a sense of unease with where he was'. And that was an engrained part of his background. At the LSE celebration on 10 December 2013, Robin Cohen further reflected that 'Identities are made on the move' and theirs had long been a family in motion.

Marginality has its consequences. It may inhibit a full taking of the role of the other, of empathy and *Verstehen*. Allied to the Young Turks' preoccupation with the deviant actor, it can bring about a descriptive neglect of the sensibilities of everyone else involved in volume crime—the victims, witnesses, bystanders, police, judges and others who are all too readily forgotten or reduced to stereotype—only when roles are reversed and the perpetrator is the state or corporate business do they merit attention. It can in its turn render almost all formal social control incomprehensible, futile or sinister. But marginality can also be propitious intellectually.[76] It leads to the attainment of an anthropological distance in which the familiar may become strange and problematic; and where, in Alfred Schutz's terminology, one can attain the *epoché* of the natural attitude.[77] The stranger can question what others accept.[78] He or she can be sensitive to what Robin Cohen called 'people out of place'. That was probably at the root of Stan Cohen's endemic scepticism and of his analytical strength. He was somewhat outside the taken for granted social and political world (Sharon Shalev said 'he was able, which very few of us are able to do, ... to look at what's happening in his own society and analyse it'). And he was also outside the very analytic frameworks, such as criminology, that examined it. His daughter, Judith, remembered 'I did discuss the kind of general idea of being on the outside of a discipline. And I remember once having a discussion in which he said he thought you were better placed to be critical of a discipline or an ideological position if you were on the outside. And that was a position that he'd adopted.'

Stan Cohen had as a consequence an extraordinary ability to interrogate apparently banal and commonplace problems anew, to say interesting things about them as if encountering them for the very first time. It was a trait commonly cited. Megan Comfort, a former student, captured it when she talked of how 'he suddenly ... turned everything on its head from what you had just been thinking ... you're ... thinking of this one lens and then, where you suddenly apply another lens into the picture, you realise that you have to rethink everything you had just been considering'. He had, she said, a flair for 'getting right in there and turning everything

---

[76] See E. Stonequist, 'The problem of the marginal man', *American Journal of Sociology*, 41 (1935), 1–12.

[77] A. Schutz, 'Common-sense and scientific interpretation of human action', in M. Natanson (ed.), *Alfred Schutz: Collected Papers*, Vol. 1 (The Hague, 1967), pp. 4–47.

[78] See G. Simmel; 'The stranger', in D. Levine (ed.), *Georg Simmel on Individuality and Social Forms* (Chicago, IL, 1971), pp. 143–9.

upside down and making you laugh and making you question'. Conor Gearty, Professor of Human Rights Law at the London School of Economics, captured it too:

> He had this incredible freshness. I mean to be able to pick up and run with ideas which were foreign to his area of academic life ... the problematising of it, the uncertainty about it, the awareness that the [ideas] which we supported were not obvious and needed to be understood and were multi-layered, was really quite new. And getting behind the term and understanding that it stands for something and could easily stand for something else in the hands and in the mouths of somebody else was important.

VIII. Conclusion

Originality, marginality, scepticism, moral purpose and a sense of the absurd encapsulate the defining contradictoriness of the man. He was a sociological relativist committed politically to the enlightenment project of universal human rights. He may have called himself 'a pessimist, a "miserabilist," even a depressive',[79] but his occasional gloominess about the world and a consciousness of its cruelty were leavened always by a besetting sense of the ludicrous. He was *homo ludens*. Even when he was very ill, *in extremis*, he joked to me that he felt he was, like Job, being punished by God for not believing in Him. He was the only person, his colleague, Claire Moon, remarked, 'who could shoehorn the odd genocide joke into a lecture'.[80] Laurie Taylor alluded in his obituary to 'his happy readiness to undermine anything too serious with a joke'.[81] And that sensibility occasionally surfaced in his writing. Frances Heidensohn reminded me about what she called 'some endearingly quirky pieces which show his sense of humour and maybe his anarchism', and she cited his 'Conference life: the rough guide'[82] and 'The last seminar',[83] 'a darker paper but also subversive', with its imagery of the university as a madhouse populated by the lost and the damned wandering around mouthing 'Commentaries on

---

[79] Response to Public Orator by Professor Stanley Cohen, University of Essex, 9 July 2003, p. 5.
[80] Moon, 'Looking without seeing, listening without hearing', p. 193.
[81] L. Taylor, Stanley Cohen obituary, *The Guardian*, 23 Jan. 2013.
[82] S. Cohen, 'Conference life: the rough guide', *Scottish Journal of Criminal Justice Studies*, 1 (1995), 33–59 (also published in *The American Sociologist*, 28(3) (1997), 69–84).
[83] S. Cohen, 'The last seminar', *The Sociological Review*, 27 (1979), 1–27.

commentaries. All sense of the world gone, washed away with the excreta of the Left Bank.'[84]

An intellectual, enamoured of ideas, he was nevertheless uninterested in history, the natural world and the physical sciences; he could not understand how campaigners could become involved in the preservation of animal species; and he did not go to the theatre (although he loved the opera). He was also far from being unremittingly bookish, having been fascinated by boxing and boxers, and especially Muhammad Ali, since boyhood; he gambled on the horses; and he adored watching old videos of the comedian and magician, Tommy Cooper, who died in 1984, and *Il Bacio di Tosca*, a 1986 film about the operatic denizens of the *Casa di Riposo per Musicisti*, a home founded in 1896 by Giuseppe Verdi for retired opera singers.

His quirkiness was a strength. Stan Cohen's prime achievement was not to be an ethnographer in the mould of Ned Polsky (he did none of that kind of work after *Folk Devils and Moral Panics* and *Psychological Survival*); nor a grand theorist, for he had emphatically eschewed that role; but as a theorist of what might be called the lower middle range,[85] injecting a number of illuminating, unusual, beautifully phrased and always enticing ideas into the analysis of the misuses of power in societies purporting to be benign. Tim Newburn put it well:

> my sense of Stan was that he was quite an unpredictable scholar, an imaginative, unpredictable scholar. So I would have said that there have been many people working as it were, in the field of criminology broadly defined, sociology, deviance and so forth, who have done great things. But I, having read one or two of their great things, I would sort of know what was coming next ... and that's not meant in any disparaging way ... I was never quite sure what he was going to do next and where he was going to come from other than a sort of overriding concern with justice in some broad form.

PAUL ROCK
Fellow of the Academy

Note. I am most grateful to Nachman Ben-Yehuda, Christine Chinkin, Jessica Cohen, Judith Cohen, Robin Cohen, David Downes, Malcolm Feely, Conor Gearty, Frances Heidensohn, Adam Kuper, Claire Moon, Tim Newburn and Sharon Shalev for their often detailed comments on an earlier draft of this memoir and to Joyce Lorinstein for transcribing the interviews.

---

[84] S. Cohen, 'The last seminar', *The Sociological Review*, 27 (1979), 12.
[85] See R. Merton, *Social Theory and Social Structure* (Glencoe, IL, 1957).

PATRICK COLLINSON

Patrick Collinson
1929–2011

PATRICK COLLINSON was the most compelling and influential historian of the religion and politics of Elizabethan and Stuart England of his generation, but he never intended to devote his life to studying the past. History was his second choice of vocation: his real passion was marine biology and he harboured an enduring fascination with the manifold mysteries of the natural world, in which he took intense delight. This was merely one of the many ironies and paradoxes that marked his life, just as they suffused and stimulated his scholarly writing. Although he was allocated the subject that made him famous by his Ph.D. supervisor, it proved a perfect fit and his research completely transformed it. Conspicuously left-wing in his politics and imbued with a radical social conscience, he nevertheless ended his career at the heart of the intellectual and social establishment: as Regius Professor of Modern History at the University of Cambridge and as a Fellow of Trinity College and the British Academy. His trajectory to the pinnacle of his profession was neither standard nor direct. Energetic, restless, and tossed and turned by circumstance, he held posts at the universities of Sudan, London, Sydney, Kent, and Sheffield, before receiving the invitation to succeed Geoffrey Elton at Cambridge. The longest he spent at any single institution was eight years. A man of large stature and sparkling brilliance, the several personal afflictions from which he suffered were less an obstacle to his achievements than a fillip.

The son of missionaries who met in Algeria, Patrick Collinson was born in Ipswich on 10 August 1929. His father Cecil was of Yorkshire and Quaker stock, the eleventh in a family of twelve. Apprenticed to a clothier after leaving school, he worked as a gentleman's outfitter in Suffolk before

his encounters with the fringes of the Islamic world during a cruise to the
Mediterranean inspired him to sell up his business and dedicate himself to
converting the Muslims of North Africa. A few months after the death of
his ailing wife, Hilda Quant, in 1927, leaving him a widower with four
young children, Cecil impulsively proposed to a young Scottish woman,
Belle Patrick, with whom he worked in Algeria. The pair were married in
Edinburgh in 1928. She was the daughter of a fish-buyer from Anstruther,
who committed suicide when she was nine after being diagnosed with a
brain tumour. Brought up in an atmosphere of intense religious fervour
and revivalist Baptist and Presbyterian piety, Belle was a highly intelligent
girl, who was obliged to turn down a bursary to St Andrews University
but later qualified as one of Scotland's first female solicitors. She never
practised law, however, exchanging it for the higher duty of spreading
the gospel and booking a passage to Africa immediately after passing
her final exams. Her vivid memoirs of the fisher folk of early twentieth-
century East Fife were eventually edited and published by the only child
of her marriage to Cecil Collinson, Patrick, in 2003. He himself recalled
his Scottish origins with pride and often evoked the image of his godly
grandmother reading her large print bible daily to her dying day and tri-
umphantly proclaiming that the air-raids by Mosquito planes on Berlin
were a sign of the second coming of Christ. He evidently found his elderly
father a rather remote figure, a stern Victorian patriarch who never went
out without a trilby hat and sometimes wore spats, but he was extraordinarily close to his mother, whom he described as 'the love of my life'.
She typed all his work and remained his constant adviser and guide until
her final illness and death in 1972.[1]

Patrick Collinson spent his early childhood in Ipswich and on a farm
at Great Blakenham, where he stayed while his parents were overseas, fish-
ing and roaming the fields. These and his idyllic holidays on the coast of
Scotland, bathing and investigating rock pools, nurtured his ambition to
become a naturalist. By his own account he was 'a strange little boy', distant in age from most of his older half-siblings and lacking many friends
outside the household of faith in which he was raised. But he was also a
child who 'longed to be famous'. The daily round of prayer meetings and
emotional mission gatherings which he regularly attended left an impression, and before he reached the age of 10 he wrote and published a small

[1] Patrick Collinson, *The History of a History Man: or the Twentieth Century Viewed from a Safe Distance* (Woodbridge, 2011), chaps. 1–2, quotation at p. 2. See also his preface to Belle Patrick, *Recollections of East Fife Fisher Folk* (Edinburgh, 2003), pp. vi–xvii.

evangelical magazine which was sent to missionaries in Egypt. It was anticipated that he would follow in the footsteps of his parents as an evangelist. In 1935, the family moved to north London, where his home was twice bombed during the Blitz. He found these wartime experiences alternately exciting and terrifying. He was later evacuated to the Cambridgeshire fens, where his parents ran a canteen for the armed forces. It was this eventuality that led to his enrolment in the King's School at Ely, which he called 'a place of unspeakable barbarity' and which he complained had left him poorly educated. One reason why he was initially bullied and marginalised was his disinterest in cricket and football; another may have been the large strawberry birthmark that covered half of his face, which was airbrushed out of photographs of him as an infant. Pat was so unselfconscious of this disfigurement that those who knew him very soon ceased to notice it too.[2]

Still intent upon studying Biology at University, he was steered towards History instead because of his weak ability in Mathematics. He failed to secure a scholarship at King's College, Cambridge, but won an exhibition to Pembroke, which he took up in 1949, after eighteen months of National Service in the RAF. He was trained as a radar mechanic, a trade for which he claims to have displayed no aptitude, and posted to a base in the Cotswolds and later a navigation school near Darlington. The redeeming feature of these years was his belated discovery of hills and mountains, which ignited a voracious appetite for climbing that lasted throughout his life. At Cambridge, mountaineering, together with rowing and the activities of the Christian Union, took priority over his academic studies, at least until he moved into Part II of the Tripos. A member of a class that included another future Regius, John Elliott, he took a Special Subject taught by Norman Sykes and graduated at the end of the year with a first, winning his college's Hadley Prize for History, some of the proceeds of which he spent on a copy of his soon-to-be supervisor Sir John Neale's *The Elizabethan House of Commons*.[3]

Inspired by his supervisions with Roger Anstey, Collinson toyed with the idea of doing research on colonial Africa, but his inadequate background in modern history pushed him towards the Tudor school at University College London (UCL), to which he went in 1952. His decision to pursue postgraduate study was taken despite the disapproval of his father and elder brother, who thought that one degree was quite sufficient. Neale was a formidable and somewhat dictatorial figure, who exercised his

[2] Collinson, *History of a History Man*, chaps. 3–4, quotations at pp. 1, 22, 38.
[3] Ibid., chaps. 6–7.

patronage in a ruthless fashion, and Collinson found him a less than satisfactory supervisor (indeed the adjectives he repeatedly used to describe
him were 'terrible' and 'dreadful'). He said that he did little to guide his
research beyond bestowing upon him the notes of a former student, Edna
Bibby, who had died before completing her MA thesis on the topic in
1929, though Collinson conceded that he always left his presence with a
spring in his step and fired up to pursue fresh discoveries. Neale's kindness
to him created a bond and he grew quite fond of him.[4] The years of
research in the Public Record Office, British Library, and local record
offices that followed were tremendously fruitful. Living virtually on top of
the UCL History Department, where he was allocated an office, he worked
until the early hours of each morning—a Stakhanovite regime that
reflected the intense work ethic instilled in him from an early age by the
admonitions of his father.[5] He found stimulus and company at the
Institute of Historical Research and benefited from the support of Joel
Hurstfield and S. T. Bindoff, although the first seminar paper he delivered,
in the presence of R. H. Tawney, allegedly sent that great man to sleep.

In October 1955 Collinson became Neale's research assistant and his
status as the favourite pupil of a historian who was heartily disliked in
some circles proved something of a handicap when it came to securing
more permanent employment. He was widely interviewed for assistant
lectureships, but nerves and naivety took over and he failed to secure one.
As something of a last resort, and against the advice of friends and mentors, he accepted a post at the University of Khartoum. His gigantic thesis,
which ran to nearly half a million words, and led to the introduction of a
formal word limit, was only completed and submitted when he returned
to England during the summer of 1957 on leave. He wrote later of the
peculiarity of 'sorting out the affairs of Puritan preachers in Elizabethan
Suffolk' surrounded by exotic and distracting sights like geckoes, praying
mantises, camel spiders, mongooses, and abdin storks. As ever, his eyes
were captivated by all forms of animal life.[6]

---

[4] Collinson, *History of a History Man*, chap. 8, esp. p. 78. See also his comments in Patrick
Collinson, 'The monarchical republic of Queen Elizabeth I', *Bulletin of the John Rylands
University Library of Manchester*, 69 (1987), 394–424, reprinted in Patrick Collinson, *Elizabethan
Essays* (London, 1994), pp. 31–2; and in his eightieth birthday speech at Trinity (5 Sept. 2009):
see <https://www.trin.cam.ac.uk/show.php?dowid=730> [last accessed, 15 April 2014]. See also
his essay on Neale: Patrick Collinson, 'Neale, Sir John Ernest (1890–1975)', *Oxford Dictionary of
National Biography*, <http://www.oxforddnb.com/view/article/31487> [last accessed 7 May 2014].
[5] Collinson, *History of a History Man*, pp. 77; see also below, n. 20.
[6] Ibid., chap. 8 and p. 89. The thesis was entitled 'The Puritan Classical Movement in the Reign
of Elizabeth I' (London, 1957).

It was in the Sudan, newly declared an independent republic, that Patrick Collinson lived for the following five years until 1961. He looked back with anger and regret at the 'cataclysmic mess' made by the British in a country which he came to love, but his experiences there, against the troubled backdrop of decolonisation and in the wake of the Suez crisis, were formative. They included his private tutorship of the son of the Muslim leader, Sayed Mohammed Osman el Mirghani, hair-raising adventures travelling in Egypt, Eritrea and the Holy Land, and expeditions to Erkowit in the Red Sea Hills, where he collected specimens of snake and lizard for the Khartoum Museum. Throughout this period, he was engaged in a lingering, long-distance, and ultimately unfulfilled relationship with Esther Moir, which remained etched on his memory. However, his disappointment in this affair of the heart was dispelled when he met and fell deeply in love with a nursing sister, Elizabeth (Liz) Selwyn, whom he married after a 'lightning courtship' in December 1960. Their honeymoon to Ethiopia coincided with an abortive rising against the Emperor Haile Selassie and they were passengers on a plane which had just delivered the body of a murdered provincial governor for burial.[7]

During the preceding years, Collinson had seriously considered ordination in the Church of England and secured a place at Ridley Hall, but uncertainty about his vocation and the prospect of a career teaching in a seminary led him to withdraw and instead to seek to return to academic life in Britain. He was appointed Assistant Lecturer in Ecclesiastical History at King's College London in 1961 and the next eight years saw him begin to flower as a published historian. Soon after his arrival, A. G. Dickens arrived from Hull to take up the chair of History at King's, and their time as colleagues boosted his confidence and extended his knowledge of the Reformation, which was the main subject of his teaching to theological students, among whom numbered a certain Desmond Tutu. Another source of encouragement and friendship was the pre-eminent historian of nonconformity, Geoffrey Nuttall. The first of his research students, Bill Sheils, recalls supervisions conducted in his partitioned-off office in the basement to the accompaniment of pile drivers and pneumatic drills.[8]

The book of Collinson's already legendary thesis (worn out by use in the intervening years) finally appeared in 1967 as *The Elizabethan Puritan Movement*. This was a landmark study of the ecclesiastical and political ramifications of puritanism, which reinterpreted it less as a subversive

---

[7] Collinson, *History of a History Man*, chaps. 9–12, quotation at pp. 123, 136.
[8] Ibid., chap. 13. On his thoughts of ordination, see pp. 112, 116, 128.

sectarian presence than as the expression of a reformist impulse within the Church of England determined to complete the imperfect religious settlement of 1559. If the book tracked the trials and tribulations of the Presbyterian militants who reacted to episcopal repression by calling for the abolition of the bishops, it situated this 'intransigent minority of puritan extremists' in the context of a broader and more moderate tendency, which by 1603 had become absorbed into the bloodstream of English Protestantism and constituted a kind of moral majority. The 'quiet and often unobserved revolution' effected by puritan divines and their lay supporters in England's parishes contrasted with the violent civil war which their successors were then widely credited with fomenting in the mid-seventeenth century. Collinson memorably defined puritans as 'the hotter sort of Protestants' and argued that what divided them from their conformist neighbours were 'differences of degree, of theological temperature ... rather than of fundamental principle'.[9] This not only laid the foundation for reassessing puritanism as a sociological rather than primarily doctrinal phenomenon, but also brought it back into the mainstream. It rescued it from the grip of Marxist and structuralist analyses that saw it as a vehicle for other secular and ideological concerns. In the process the book reconfigured the histories of both Anglicanism and the dissenting tradition. It embodied and foreshadowed the shift of perspective for which he called more explicitly in an important essay published in a Festschrift for Leland H. Carlson in 1975, which castigated the distorting tunnel vision exhibited by generations of denominationally committed scholars: a shift from documenting the latter's genealogy as a collection of sects towards exploring its horizontal and lateral connections.[10] Warm reviews of *The Elizabethan Puritan Movement* by Christopher Hill and Hugh Trevor-Roper took the sting out of A. L. Rowse's icy contempt for Collinson's 'somewhat rebarbative subject', though Rowse did not make the more sharply edged remark that 'we must all be grateful that he has finally got it off his chest' that Collinson later attributed to him .[11]

[9] Patrick Collinson, *The Elizabethan Puritan Movement* (Oxford, 1990; first pub. London, 1967), quotations at pp. 467, 433, 27, 26.
[10] Patrick Collinson, 'Towards a broader history of the early dissenting tradition', in Patrick Collinson, *Godly People: Essays on English Protestantism and Puritanism* (London, 1983), pp. 527–62, reprinted from C. Robert Cole and Michael E. Moody (eds.), *The Dissenting Tradition: Essays for Leland H. Carlson* (Athens, OH, 1975), pp. 3–38.
[11] Collinson, *History of a History Man*, p. 145, though he substitutes 'thoroughly' for 'somewhat'. A. L. Rowse, in *English Historical Review*, 83 (1968), 833–4, declared it an excellent study, but did say condescendingly that Collinson had been at work on the topic for many years 'and has at length mastered it; for which we can be grateful—one can hardly suppose there is much more usefully to be said'. How wrong that remark would prove!

In fact, the success of the book was such that at the age of 40 he received the offer of a chair at the University of Sydney, to fill the hole left by the departure of Jack McManners to Leicester. This followed another series of ill-fated interviews for senior posts at Durham, Exeter and Manchester, for which he applied anxious to augment his modest salary and provide for the four children (Helen, Andrew, Sarah and Stephen) who had arrived in quick succession between 1962 and 1968. The momentous decision to emigrate to the other side of the world was apparently taken after consultation not with Liz, but with his mother Belle, who accompanied the family to Australia and later died there. Remembering the episode on his eightieth birthday, Pat poked fun at himself as a 'Taliban husband'.[12] Neale, meanwhile, thought of it as the professional equivalent to convict transportation and the tone of his farewell was one of commiseration.[13]

The translation to Sydney proved both a liberating opportunity and a challenge. His gregarious personality and warm hospitality won him many friends among his colleagues and his witty lectures on Martin Luther and on the English Reformation inspired successive cohorts of able students. His non-managerial style was refreshing and he sowed the seeds for the rejuvenation of the curriculum. He relished the chance to put on innovative courses, including a Fourth Year Honours Seminar on 'Churches, Sects and Society', provoked by his engagement with the 'seductive' discipline of Sociology. It was typical of his impishness that he claimed that some signed up for the class because they had misheard the middle word of the title. This was the beginning of the interdisciplinary overtures which would become a hallmark of the rest of his career and which, his friends attest, transformed him as a historian. He built contacts with other scholars of the sixteenth and seventeenth centuries, including George Yule at Melbourne, and was instrumental in organising conferences that later crystallised into a more formal association of early modern European historians in Australia and New Zealand. He was honoured by his election to the Australian Academy of the Humanities in 1974.[14]

---

[12] Collinson, *History of a History Man*, pp. 147–8. Pat used the phrase 'Taliban husband' in his eightieth birthday speech.

[13] Personal communication from Bill Sheils.

[14] Collinson, *History of a History Man*, chap. 14, quotation at p. 154. His account of the Sydney years is supplemented by the recollections of Sybil M. Jack and Alison Wall in 'Patrick Collinson: an appreciation', which preface 'Protestants, property, puritans: *Godly People* revisited: a Festschrift in honour of Patrick Collinson on the occasion of his retirement', *Parergon*, NS 14 (1996), ix–xiii; and the obituaries by John Gascoigne and Sybil M. Jack in *Parergon*, 29 (2012), ix–xiv, and Ros Pesman and Richard Waterhouse in the *Annual Report of the Australian Academy of the Humanities* (2012), 25–6.

But at Sydney Patrick Collinson also found himself caught awkwardly between the demands of his position as a professor and head of department in what was still a very hierarchical institution and the aggressive and emotional demands for democratic reform swelling up from below. Some felt sympathetic to his efforts to reconcile these competing imperatives and praised the work he did to bring about change from within; others felt that the legalistic approach he adopted during this tumultuous phase in the university's history was out of character with his collegiality and with the inclusive and levelling principles to which he instinctively adhered.[15] He himself found the experience extremely arduous and trying and these struggles played their part in persuading him to return to England in 1976. Other factors that contributed to his leaving Australia were the difficulty of finding time for his own research and writing and the progressive spread of the 'fungus' of postmodernism.[16] But there were costs, including the sacrifice of the Collinsons' cottage retreat on a tidal creek feeding into the Hawkesbury River and Broken Bay at Patonga, where he fed his love of nature, found pleasure in bush-walking, and entertained fellow scholars and friends. Some of them described it as 'a historians' Mecca';[17] for Pat himself it was a kind of paradise on earth. Back in the financial stringency of Jim Callaghan's Britain, he dreamed of it every night for a year with a profound sense of desolation and loss.[18]

The post to which Collinson returned at the University of Kent at Canterbury proved to be no bed of roses against a backdrop of national and institutional austerity and the serious cut in salary which taking it had entailed. But he resisted an invitation to retrace his steps to Sydney and threw his energies into making the best of his situation. He took advantage of the flexible structures of the university, which encouraged mingling and experimental teaching with colleagues in other disciplines. Here he collaborated not only with other Tudor and Stuart historians including Peter Roberts, but also with literary scholars such as Michael Hattaway, with both of whom he taught an MA in Elizabethan and Jacobean Studies. These experiences invigorated him and widened his intellectual horizons. So did the cathedral archives, which he mined systematically and which supplied illuminating material for many subsequent

---

[15] For sympathetic accounts of this episode, see the items by Jack, Wall and Gascoigne cited above, n. 14. For a more critical appraisal, see Doug Munro's review of *History of a History Man*, in *Journal of Historical Biography*, 11 (2012), 123–31, esp. 128–9.
[16] Eightieth birthday speech.
[17] Jack and Wall, 'Patrick Collinson', p. ix.
[18] Collinson, *History of a History Man*, pp. 160, 163.

lectures and essays: as ever, he revelled in the disorderly detail of human lives which the depositions and defamation suits of the ecclesiastical courts revealed. Another legacy of this period was *A History of Canterbury Cathedral*, which he co-edited, and which eventually appeared in 1995.[19]

Patrick Collinson's eight years at Canterbury were also productive ones, and they saw the publication of the biography of the 'puritan' Archbishop Edmund Grindal upon which he had been working for much of the previous decade. It was a book in which he wore his sympathies for this prelate's brand of 'Calvinism with a human face' on his sleeve and in which he openly confessed to finding John Aylmer, Bishop of London, 'an unattractive figure'. The picture he painted of Grindal's primacy was of a highly creative phase of reform in which Protestantism successfully established an apostolate at the grass roots—an era which, echoing the Jacobean preacher Josias Nicholls, he thought of as 'a golden time, full of godly fruit'. Grindal's stubborn stance in the matter of prophesyings marked a descent into failure and paved the way for the ascendancy of clerics for whom Collinson harboured a lifelong distaste (Whitgift, Bancroft, and Laud). It was a failure of critical importance for the future of the Church of England and English civilisation, which became less monolithic and more diverse, and which fostered a 'fatal tendency to ideological fracture' and 'resentful dissidence' out of which sprang radical thought and political conflict. He could not disguise a note of personal lament at the miscarrying of the religious programme for which Grindal stood.[20]

These years also saw a series of new accolades, notably the invitation to deliver Oxford's Ford Lectures in Hilary Term 1979, which he believed to be 'the best thing that can happen to a historian of these islands' and which seemed to vindicate the risk his family had taken in the reverse migration from Australia. A relative stranger to Oxford, he found a warm welcome there, though the qualms he felt as he looked out upon the crowns and mitres capping the drain pipes of St John's College's Canterbury Quad were emblematic of his outlook. His discomfort sprang in part from his provocative pronouncement in the course of the lectures that 'Archbishop

---

[19] Collinson, *History of a History Man*, pp. 165–73. Patrick Collinson, Nigel Ramsay, and Margaret Sparks (eds.), *A History of Canterbury Cathedral* (Oxford, 1995), to which he contributed chapter 4—Patrick Collinson, 'The Protestant Cathedral, 1541–1660'.
[20] Patrick Collinson, *Archbishop Grindal 1519–1583: the Struggle for a Reformed Church* (London, 1979), quotations at pp. 11, 231, 283. In a letter to Brett Usher on 27 Oct. 1999, he wrote that he had read Usher's draft *ODNB* entry on Aylmer with 'a kind of horrified fascination. Can he have been as bad as this?': see B. Usher, 'John Aylmer (1520/21–1594), *Oxford Dictionary of National Biography*, <http://www.oxforddnb.com/ view/article/935> [last accessed 7 May 2014].

Laud', an illustrious alumnus of that college, was 'the greatest calamity
ever visited upon' the Church of England.[21] Developing themes that had
been implicit in his work from the very beginning, he dwelt upon the 'institutional equilibrium' of the Elizabethan and Jacobean Church of England
and its capacity to accommodate vigorous expression of religious volun-
tarism within 'its loose and sometimes anomalous structures'. Key to this
were the powerful alliances forged between magistrates and ministers, dedicated pastor bishops, and the entrenchment of a preaching ministry. In
exploring the struggles of the godly to restrain unruly elements of popular
religion he distanced himself from the tendency to see the impulses behind
the reformation of manners as a function of social antagonism and the
end-product of puritan evangelism as 'class war of a kind'. The lines of
fraction he discerned cut across the boundaries created by status and
wealth.[22] The story he told accorded well with wider revisionist tendencies
that were reassessing the inevitability of the mid-seventeenth-century revolution, especially the work of Nicholas Tyacke and Conrad Russell. Hints
can also be detected of the new and more pessimistic assessment of the
impact of the Protestant Reformation that was emerging from the research
of Christopher Haigh, among others.

Prepared for publication during a visiting fellowship at All Souls, *The
Religion of Protestants* was celebrated in the *London Review of Books*
(*LRB*) as 'a stirring event in the rediscovery of Early Modern England'
and praised by Christopher Hill in the *Times Literary Supplement* (*TLS*)
for its vast learning lightly worn, its deep humanity, and scrupulous fairness to scholars with whom it disagreed: 'What a Jacobean bishop he
would have made!', Hill exclaimed.[23] Collinson's election to the Fellowship
of the British Academy occurred in the same year. The first omnibus collection of his articles and essays on puritanism, *Godly People*, appeared in
1983. In the preface, he spoke of himself as 'an unsuccessful escapologist':
although he had laughed inwardly when Neale had told him in 1954 that
'I like to think of you spending the rest of your life on this subject' and
vowed to move on to other topics as quickly as possible, the prophesy had

---

[21] Collinson, *History of a History Man*, pp. 170–1. See also the preface to Patrick Collinson, *The
Religion of Protestants: the Church in English Society 1559–1625* (Oxford, 1982), pp. vii–viii. The
indictment of Laud is at p. 90. He was surprised to be asked to lecture on Laud at St John's in
May 1995 and reiterated this judgement on that occasion.
[22] Collinson, *Religion of Protestants*, pp. ix, 282, 240.
[23] Blair Worden, 'Rescuing the bishops', *London Review of Books*, 5/7 (21 April 1983), 15–16;
Christopher Hill, 'The godly community', *Times Literary Supplement*, 4172 (18 March 1983),
257.

come true and he was still striving to understand its implications for the politics, mentality and social relations of the Elizabethans and Jacobeans.[24]

Cambridge replicated the honour bestowed upon him by Oxford by asking him to present the Birkbeck Lectures in 1981. These took the form of an exploration of 'The roots of English nonconformity' and were a fruitful variation on the themes that preoccupied him through his career. In them, he memorably described dissent as a species of ecclesiastical acne and investigated its corrosive and divisive effects in English society, though mitigated and kept in check by an aversion to separatism. Sadly, these lectures were never published and the typescript of them now seems to be lost, a casualty of the scramble to clear his room in Trinity for a new occupant as he lay dying. There were several reasons why Patrick Collinson was unable to see them to the press in the immediately succeeding years, especially the testing period during which his son Andrew was being treated for a rare form of non-Hodgkin's lymphoma, from which few people had previously recovered. This seriously overshadowed the Birkbecks, the first of which he delivered on the same day as a sobering meeting with the oncologist.[25] Collinson had only just emerged from a tribulation of his own: a terrible accident in September 1980 getting off a train as darkness fell, as a result of which he lost most of his left foot. Cautioned by the railway police for alighting from a moving vehicle, he was sanguine about the episode and adapted quickly to his disability and the prosthesis which he was obliged to wear for the rest of his life. It did little to inhibit his strenuous physical activities, though he did admit that it wrecked the balance required for punting! A letter sent to Kenneth Fincham shortly after the accident reveals that he never indulged in self-pity, displayed courage during his convalescence, and looked forward to re-entering circulation as soon as possible after his hospital stay of seven weeks. Visits were sometimes hard to arrange because he was likely to be supervising postgraduates or holding a Special Subject class by his bedside.[26]

By 1983, things were turning sour institutionally too. The savage budget slashes of the Thatcher years began to take their toll within the University

[24] Collinson, *Godly People*, p. xi.
[25] Collinson, *History of a History Man*, pp. 171–2. On the Birkbecks, see also Collinson, *Godly People*, p. 18.
[26] Collinson, *History of a History Man*, pp. 171–2. Letter from Patrick Collinson to Kenneth Fincham dated 17 Sept. 1980. Memories of his convalescence after the accident can be found in Christopher Brooke's reflections prefacing the first of his Festschriften: Anthony Fletcher and Peter Roberts (eds.), *Religion, Culture and Society in Early Modern Britain: Essays in Honour of Patrick Collinson* (Cambridge, 1994), pp. xv–xx, at xix.

of Kent, where the Faculty of Humanities was obliged to shed a proportion of staff and where pressure upon people to take early retirement was
firmly exerted. It was in this climate of retrenchment that Collinson
applied for and was offered the Chair of Modern History at Sheffield. His
own Vice-Chancellor made no attempt to stop him from accepting and
said, on the contrary, that he would be doing a favour to his colleagues by
leaving. Although some of his friends felt that the manner of his departure from Kent was scandalous, Collinson never bore a public grudge to
that university, and in so far as he laid blame at anyone's door, it was the
Prime Minister's.[27]

The translation to Sheffield in 1984 was preceded by a year of leave,
half of which he spent as the recipient of an Andrew Mellon Fellowship
at the Huntington Library in San Marino, California. He was exhilarated
by his hikes in the San Gabriel mountains and by the discoveries he made
digging through the Ellesmere manuscripts and he wrote to a correspond-
ent at home that he was in 'Abraham's Bosom', sending 'a crumb from this
rich table'.[28] Through his exchanges with the occupant of the adjacent
office, John King, the fellowship further exposed him to recent trends in
literary scholarship, with which he engaged persuasively in subsequent
work. The research he did in this bibliographical haven and oasis of
botanical beauty in the midst of Los Angeles enabled him to sketch the
blueprints for his Stenton Lecture at Reading in 1985 and the Anstey
Memorial Lectures at Kent in 1986.

Signalling his turn towards evaluating the broader cultural impact of
Protestantism in England, the former set forth the stimulating thesis (since
revised and nuanced) that around 1580 the Reformation moved from an
iconoclastic to an iconophobic phase, setting aside its early flirtation with
the popular media of art, song and drama and moving into a sober middle
age marked by moral rigour and succoured by Ramist diagrammatic logic
and bibliocentricity.[29] This idea was developed further in chapter 4 of *The
Birthpangs of Protestant England*, which appeared in 1988, dedicated with
affection and respect to Geoff Dickens 'who both led and pointed the
way'. The thrust of the revised and augmented Anstey lectures was, however, at odds with Dickens's own convictions about the spontaneous, rapid

[27] Collinson, *History of a History Man*, pp. 172–3.
[28] Ibid., pp. 173–4, supplemented by a letter to Ken Fincham of 1 May 1984 and John King's
obituary in *Reformation*, 17 (2012), 3–6, at 3–4.
[29] Patrick Collinson, *From Iconoclasm to Iconophobia: the Cultural Impact of the Second English
Reformation*, The Stenton Lecture, 1985 (Reading, 1986).

and popular character of the English Reformation.[30] Its title nodded to the rival view that was then beginning to command consensus, that Protestantism was an unwelcome imposition by the Tudor state on the populace, which struggled painfully to put down firm roots over a more prolonged period; in brief, in the short term it was not a success but a failure. Collinson was prepared 'to assert, crudely and flatly, that the Reformation was something which happened in the reigns of Elizabeth and James I', and that everything before that was merely 'preparative' and 'embryonic'. It was 'only with the 1570s that the historically minded insomniac goes to sleep counting Catholics rather than Protestants'. The other chapters of *Birthpangs* were studies of its implications for urban piety and politics and subtle meditations on its side-effects: on the ambiguous role of the Reformation in the formation of national consciousness, in the history of the family and gender relations, and in the genesis of what, in keeping with Anthony Fletcher and John Morrill, he described as England's Wars of Religion. His focus, though, was not on the conflicts that broke out between King and Parliament in 1642 but on the squabbles over maypoles, Sunday sports, and church ales that erupted in its streets and the frictions created by puritans who shunned their unregenerate neighbours. He identified the antipathy between the godly and ungodly as 'the necessary mental condition' for the outbreak of fighting and in one of his most quoted lines he declared that puritanism was 'not a thing definable in itself but only one half of a stressful relationship'. The use of the term puritan in contemporary discourse was an index of 'dynamic and mutual antagonism'.[31] This presaged the even more nominalist position he adopted in a lecture on *The Puritan Character* at the Andrew Clark Library in Los Angeles, published in 1989, and in a series of suggestive essays on the role of the theatre and popular libel in the 'invention' of this phenomenon, though he later thought of the former as an 'extreme statement'.[32]

[30] For Collinson's relationship with Dickens, see Patrick Collinson, 'A. G. Dickens', *Historical Research*, 77 (2004), 14–23, esp. 18.

[31] Patrick Collinson, *The Birthpangs of Protestant England: Religious and Cultural Change in the Sixteenth and Seventeenth Centuries* (New York, 1988), quotations at pp. ix, 146, 143.

[32] Patrick Collinson, *The Puritan Character: Polemics and Polarities in Early Seventeenth-Century English Culture* (Los Angeles, CA, 1989); Patrick Collinson, 'Ben Johnson's *Bartholomew Fair*: the theatre constructs puritanism', in David L. Smith, Richard Strier and David Bevington (eds.), *The Theatrical City: Culture, Theatre and Politics in London, 1576–1649* (Cambridge, 1995), pp. 157–69; Patrick Collinson, 'Ecclesiastical vitriol: religious satire in the 1590s and the invention of Puritanism', in John Guy (ed.), *The Reign of Elizabeth I: Court and Culture in the Last Decade* (Cambridge, 1995), pp. 150–70. For his comments on *The Puritan Character*, see Patrick Collinson, *From Cranmer to Sancroft* (London, 2006), p. xiii. For earlier and later statements along these lines, see Patrick Collinson, 'A comment: concerning the name puritan', *Journal of*

The themes delineated in the final chapter of *Birthpangs* were further elaborated in a later study of the 'The cohabitation of the faithful with the unfaithful', which turned on the counterintuitive argument that the social segregation practised by puritans committed to remaining with the Church of England was more corrosive of harmonious neighbourly relations than the formal ecclesiastical separation of nonconformists. Meeting their psychological need for antagonism and suffering, their avoidance of 'familiar company keeping' with reprobates was a piece of 'adroit casuistry' that did its 'fair share in dividing and distracting communities and neighbourhoods which hoped to be at peace'. If the products of puritan apartheid were rarely 'actual violence', they were 'potentially explosive'.[33]

The emphasis in *Birthpangs* on the destabilising potential of puritan principles and piety represented Collinson's partial shift back towards the position that fervent Protestantism was a disruptive social force. Much of his work revolved around the problem of whether or not it was 'a solvent of parochial religion' and 'congregationalist in potential', as he argued (temporarily impressed by a suggestion made by Christopher Hill) in a paper delivered at a *Past and Present* Society conference in 1966, but retracted in the Ford Lectures in 1979.[34] This was indicative of a man who had sufficient humility to change his mind, but also of one who found it difficult to accept that puritanism was a recipe for sedition and famously declared it to be 'as factious and subversive as the Homily on Obedience'.[35] The same questions also simmered beneath the surface of his presidential lecture on 'The English conventicle' for the annual conference of the Ecclesiastical History Society on his chosen theme of 'Voluntary Religion' in 1986.[36]

Other lectures he delivered in this period proved to be even more influential, especially his John Rylands Library lecture on 'The monarchical republic of Queen Elizabeth I'.[37] The delicious oxymoron that lay at its heart was the notion that the late Tudor polity was simultaneously a kingdom ruled over by a hereditary sovereign and a self-governing entity which

Ecclesiastical History, 31 (1980), 483–8; and Patrick Collinson, 'Anti-puritanism', in John Coffey and Paul C. Lim (eds.), *The Cambridge Companion to Puritanism* (Cambridge, 2008), pp. 19–33.
[33] Patrick Collinson, 'The cohabitation of the faithful with the unfaithful', in Ole Peter Grell, Jonathan I. Israel and Nicholas Tyacke (eds.), *From Persecution to Toleration: the Glorious Revolution and Religion in England* (Oxford, 1991), pp. 51–76, quotations at 65, 63, 68, 74, 67.
[34] See Patrick Collinson, 'The godly: aspects of popular Protestantism', in Collinson, *Godly People*, pp. 1–17, and note on p. 18.
[35] Collinson, *Religion of Protestants*, p. 177.
[36] Patrick Collinson, 'The English conventicle', in William J. Sheils and Diana Wood (eds.), *Voluntary Religion*, Studies in Church History 23 (Oxford, 1986), pp. 223–59.
[37] Collinson, 'Monarchical republic'. See also Collinson, *History of a History Man*, pp. 189–90.

depended upon the cooperation of the crown's servants and within which there was space to wield power and indeed to resist. 'Citizens', he wrote elsewhere, 'were concealed within subjects',[38] and he meant this of both the privy councillors who advised Elizabeth and the humble people who took on responsibility at the grass roots. This striking conceit took its bearings from two archival finds: the document drawn up by the chief inhabitants of the village of Swallowfield in Berkshire in 1596 about how to govern their community and a memorandum written by Lord Burghley outlining where authority would lie in the event of an interregnum. The ideological roots of the hybrid species that was monarchical republicanism lay in humanism, but also in Protestant biblicism. It was in the texts of the Old Testament that the queen's advisers found the ammunition to coerce her into executing her cousin Mary Queen of Scots in 1586, a topic that he dilated further in his Raleigh lecture entitled 'The Elizabethan exclusion crisis and the Elizabethan polity', subsequently published in the *Proceedings of the British Academy.*[39] This intriguing set of ideas was the self-confessed 'hobby horse' of Collinson's later years and it has proved to be an acorn out of which has grown a mighty oak.[40] Reflecting Collinson's belated return to the terrain once occupied by his supervisor and by the towering figure of Geoffrey Elton—the realm of politics—they have set the agenda for understanding the early modern commonwealth of England for the last twenty-five years, giving rise to conference panels, round table discussions, and a volume of essays. To the latter Collinson contributed a reflective afterword, which predicted that the paradoxical notion of monarchical republicanism might not 'have an indefinite shelf life'.[41] The tide may now be beginning to turn in a fresh direction, but there can be no doubt that collectively these essays constituted a seminal intervention which injected fresh dynamism into a field of debate that had fallen into a state of relative stagnation. It is worth commenting on the ostensible tension

[38] See Patrick Collinson, *De Republica Anglorum: or, History with the Politics Put Back* (Cambridge, 1989), reprinted in Collinson, *Elizabethan Essays*, pp. 1–27, at 19.

[39] Patrick Collinson, 'The Elizabethan exclusion crisis and the Elizabethan polity', *Proceedings of the British Academy*, 84 (1994), 51–92. See also Patrick Collinson, 'The State as "monarchical commonwealth": Tudor England', *Journal of Historical Sociology*, 15 (2002), 89–95; Patrick Collinson, 'Servants and citizens: Robert Beale and other Elizabethans', *Historical Research*, 79 (2006), 488–511; Patrick Collinson, 'The politics of religion and the religion of politics in Elizabethan England', *Historical Research*, 82 (2009), 74–92.

[40] Collinson, *History of a History Man*, p. 197.

[41] See John F. McDiarmid (ed.), *The Monarchical Republic of Early Modern England: Essays in Response to Patrick Collinson* (Aldershot, 2007). Collinson's own comment is in the 'Afterword', pp. 245–60, at 258. For further discussion, see Stephen Alford, 'Patrick Collinson's Elizabethan commonwealth', *Reformation*, 17 (2012), 7–28.

between Collinson's emphasis on the latent subversion of his monarchical republicans and his insistence on the docility of puritans, though this may be more apparent than real.

Meanwhile, Collinson was enjoying his time at Sheffield, despite the renewed challenges of leading a department that had not hitherto worked well as a unit and of a university trying to find ways to reduce its spending. He helped to reform the curriculum, oversaw the merger of History with Economic History and Ancient History, secured posts that seemed in danger of being lost in the latest bureaucratic freeze, and continued to interact fruitfully with colleagues in English Literature. Always a team player willing to take his turn, his sense of humour, willingness to tell tales against himself, and unassuming and irenic style as Head were appreciated by many of his colleagues. Mark Greengrass and Anthony Fletcher speak of his arrival as 'a breath of fresh air'. They remember his gift for diplomacy and tact, the distinctive memos he typed at high speed on his battered Remington typewriter, and his prodigious appetite for work. His speeches at History Society dinners had students rolling in the aisles and he enthusiastically contributed his precious time to address local branches of the Historical Association. Tensions within the department remained, and there were those who felt that he exhibited a certain unwillingness to grasp nettles and who were rankled by his presence. Nevertheless, the impact he made in the course of just four years was out of proportion to the brief time he spent in Sheffield. He relished having the Peak District on his doorstep, which provided new opportunities for hill-walking and led to the purchase of a house with magnificent views of the Hope Valley at Hathersage, where he and Liz lived between 1989 and 2005.[42]

Collinson's relocation to Cambridge to take up the Regius Chair in Modern History in 1988 was a worthy index of the esteem in which he was held, but he was alive to the irony that the indirect author of his troubles in Kent, Mrs Thatcher, was now responsible for his elevation to one of the top jobs in the historical profession. He was genuinely surprised and greatly flattered by the invitation. *The Daily Telegraph* heralded his appointment with the headline 'Rise of Left-Winger' and he was certainly an unexpected choice under a Conservative government and a very different figure from his predecessor, Geoffrey Elton.[43] Before he took up his post, Elton put him in his place by ticking him off for cramming too much into a confer-

[42] On the Sheffield years, see Collinson, *History of a History Man*, pp. 174–8. I have been assisted by the reminiscences of Mark Greengrass, Anthony Fletcher, and Michael Bentley.
[43] Collinson, *History of a History Man*, pp. 177–9.

ence paper.[44] Once he arrived relations between them were cordial and he patiently tolerated Elton's reluctance to release the reins of power, which included continuing to attend the Tudor Seminar and behave as if he were presiding. Collinson was sufficiently indiscreet to tell one of his graduate students that Elton didn't have the 'organ' to understand religion and it is clear from his own rather unsympathetic British Academy memoir that they were men of sharply contrasting temperaments. There was a degree of mutual incomprehension. Elton's lack of interest in the open air and countryside and his failure to be impressed by the Blue Mountains in New South Wales, for instance, quite bewildered him.[45] And he did not hide his disagreement with the style and priorities of the scholarship practised by 'this pugnacious historian' in his polite but uncompromising review of his last book, *Return to Essentials,* which he regarded as an embarrassment.[46]

The faculty that Collinson inherited was full of frustrations. He was impatient and outspoken about the impracticalities of the Stirling prize-winning Seeley Building, admired by students of architecture from all over the world, but (still) incapable of coping with rain and extremes of cold and heat: 'for those who have to work in it, in all weathers', he wrote, 'it is not a friendly place'.[47] There were other irritations, including his thwarted attempts to bring about reform of what he saw as a conservative and antiquated Tripos. His Inaugural Lecture as Regius, 'De Republica Anglorum', was not only a powerful call for early modern British historians to explore 'the social depth of politics' and 'to find signs of political life at levels where it was not previously thought to exist', but also a critique of the artificial division between political and ecclesiastical and economic and social history enshrined in the existence of separate Tripos papers.[48] He wrote later of the need 'to put the Humpty Dumpty of the sixteenth century' back together and to reintegrate fields that had been unhelpfully demarcated.[49] He proved unable to overcome the resistance he

[44] Collinson, *From Cranmer to Sancroft*, p. xii.

[45] Patrick Collinson, 'Geoffrey Rudolph Elton 1921–1994', *Proceedings of the British Academy*, 94 (1996), 429–55, esp. 436, 454; Patrick Collinson, 'Elton, Sir Geoffrey Rudolph [*formerly* Gottfried Rudolph Otto Ehrenberg] (1921–1994)', *Oxford Dictionary of National Biography*, Oxford University Press, 2004 <http://www.oxforddnb.com/view/article/54946> [last accessed 17 Jan. 2014].

[46] As well as the items cited above, n. 43, see his review of *Return to Essentials*, *London Review of Books*, 14/11 (11 June 1992), 24–5; Collinson, *History of a History Man*, p. 185.

[47] Collinson, 'Geoffrey Rudolph Elton', p. 451; Collinson, *History of a History Man*, p. 183.

[48] Collinson, 'De Republica Anglorum', in *Elizabethan Essays*, p. 11.

[49] Patrick Collinson, *The Sixteenth Century 1485–1603* (Oxford, 2002), p. 9. See also Collinson, *History of a History Man*, p. 184.

faced from entrenched interests and as chairman of the faculty, a role which he took upon himself perhaps too early in his tenure, he felt like an outsider and was never wholly effective, despite the intellectual respect which his work commanded. He sometimes lacked political antennae and was not always watchful for the devious and ill-intentioned. Collinson found the faculty a little introverted and one colleague recalls a whiff of nostalgia for the congenial corridor and common room culture of Sheffield. But he learnt not to make the mistake of speaking of how things were done in other institutions and to bite his tongue when people complained that Cambridge had problems.[50]

Yet there were significant compensations. As ever, he took pleasure in his teaching and his Special Subject on 'Perceptions and Uses of the Past' produced a crop of devoted followers and some future historians, as well as the steady flow of essays on aspects of early modern historiography that marked his later years: studies of John Foxe, William Camden and John Stow, which asked refreshing and critical questions about the links between truth and fiction and interrogated the teleological myths that traditionally surrounded the subject.[51] Once again he established points of contact with literary scholars, notably Lisa Jardine, Anne Barton and Jeremy Maule. He warmly endorsed the M.Phil. in Renaissance Literature for its excellent combination of training in palaeography, textual criticism and contextual history and he was a strong supporter of the interdisciplinary Early Modernists seminar which then met in an offshoot of Jesus College, Little Trinity.[52] By contrast he did not make as much effort to forge links with the Faculty's Europeanists, including the distinguished historian of Reformation Germany, Bob Scribner.

The era in which he was Regius was a golden age for the study of sixteenth- and seventeenth-century Britain in Cambridge, and to the Wrightsonians, Spuffordians, Skinnerians, and the New Morrill Army

---

[50] Collinson, *History of a History Man*, p. 187.
[51] Ibid., pp. 184–5. A number of these essays—including Patrick Collinson, 'Truth, lies and fiction in sixteenth-century Protestant historiography', in Donald R. Kelley and David Harris Sacks (eds.), *The Historical Imagination in Early Modern Britain: History, Rhetoric and Fiction 1500–1800* (Cambridge, 1997), pp. 37–68; Patrick Collinson, 'One of us: William Camden and the making of history', *Transactions of the Royal Historical Society*, 6th ser. 8 (1998), 139–63; Patrick Collinson, 'John Stow and nostalgic antiquarianism', in Julia F. Merritt (ed.), *Imagining Early Modern London: Perceptions and Portrayals of the City from Stow to Strype, 1598–1720* (Cambridge, 2001), pp. 27–51; and Patrick Collinson, 'William Camden and the anti-myth of Elizabeth: setting the mould?', in Susan Doran and Thomas S. Freeman (eds.), *The Myth of Elizabeth* (Basingstoke, 2003), pp. 79–98—were reprinted in Patrick Collinson, *This England: Essays on the English Nation and Commonwealth in the Sixteenth Century* (Manchester, 2011).
[52] Collinson, *History of a History Man*, p. 186.

were added the Collinsonian elect. He gathered around him a large crop of research students from the United States, Canada, Switzerland and Australia as well as the UK, which he regarded as the 'jewels' in his crown and to whom, in a gesture that humbled them (and, as he jested, almost bankrupted him in gratis copies!), he dedicated his *Elizabethan Essays*.[53] He was a generous and supportive supervisor, though not always a very directive one, and he let those about whom he was confident out on a long rein. More generally, his willingness to go out of his way to offer encouragement to younger scholars, especially those to whom he had no obligations, is gratefully remembered. The letters commending articles which he sent to obscure young scholars without track records were immensely cheering to those who at the end of their Research Fellowships were wondering where they would end up next. One of those to whom he wrote encouragingly in the 1980s was Diarmaid MacCulloch. He could be brusque on the phone, which was not his favoured instrument of communication, but meetings with him were filled with amusing digressions and were occasions when the cup of his learning overflowed. He too had a gift for making his students leave his room with renewed hope and enthusiasm and the many typed notes he despatched through the internal university mail service were a source of much reassurance to those who received them. He struggled to come to terms with computer technology and he never mastered email.

As an examiner, Patrick Collinson could be a stern and hanging judge. He was impatient with incompetence and severe against those who displayed intellectual deficiencies or behaved ungraciously, though sometimes compassion coloured and tempered his judgement. His role at Cambridge made him a sought-after patron and he exercised this power extensively, sometimes weighing need in the balance alongside merit. He was a candid and sometimes capricious referee and was the subject of intense resentment by a few of those whose aspirations were disappointed. He could be obstinate in pursuing his preferences in faculty appointments and he ruffled some feathers in the process. The many obligations he accrued in this regard, as in others, explain why he ruefully described himself as a 'reading professor' during his term in Cambridge, forever marking up drafts of students' work and wading through mountains of meeting and committee papers. He often rose at 5 a.m. to catch up on his correspondence. External responsibilities also crowded in: the chairmanship of the British Academy John Foxe Committee, the Vice-Presidency of the Royal Historical Society between 1994 and 1998, the formation and first

[53] Ibid., p. 185; and Collinson, *Elizabethan Essays.*

Presidency of the Church of England Record Society in 1992, and membership of the History Panel of the Research Assessment Exercise. He emerged from his second bout of service on the latter 'deeply sceptical about its rationale and likely effects' and unconvinced of the applicability to the Humanities of 'a model of productivity which may make sense in a laboratory but which ultimately derives from industry and business'. He was doubtful whether 'rekindling a few spent volcanoes' and persuading 'some drones to become busy bees' was really worth the cost.[54]

All of this took its toll on his own work and it is notable that he had no sustained sabbatical leave and published no monographs during this period. He became, however, a consummate master of the occasional lecture and commissioned essay, many of which were later republished in his collected volumes *From Cranmer to Sancroft* and *This England*. In many ways pieces of article length, written under high pressure and fuelled by adrenalin, were the mode in which he flourished best and in which his most brilliant work found its natural home. He was also a splendid and prolific reviewer and his essays in the *TLS* and *LRB* are little masterpieces of insight and wit. He also found time to contribute several substantial chapters to the history of that puritan seminary, Emmanuel College.[55]

Above all, Patrick Collinson settled very comfortably into Trinity College, at which he accepted a professorial fellowship. Pembroke had expected its alumnus to return to its ranks, but was slow to make a direct overture, by which time it was too late. He felt awkward about this decision but this residue of guilt was perhaps finally appeased after his election as an Honorary Fellow of Pembroke a few months before his death. He came to love Trinity dearly, somewhat surprisingly given his political views, and he yearned for it when he retired to Derbyshire and moved from there to Devon, avidly reading the Council minutes and delivering a highly affectionate eightieth birthday speech in the Master's Lodge in September 2009.[56] Most of the fellows found him a delightful companion and he formed some firm and lasting friendships, though he had his detractors in college, who mistook his loquaciousness for pomposity and self-absorption and were baffled by his unwillingness to play the political games in which they engaged. He himself found 'the C. P. Snow-style feuds' to which Oxbridge colleges are prone of 'marginal interest' and was

---

[54] Collinson, *History of a History Man*, p. 187.
[55] A. S. Bendall, Christopher Brooke and Patrick Collinson, *A History of Emmanuel College, Cambridge* (Woodbridge, 2000).
[56] Collinson, *History of a History Man*, chap. 16, esp. p. 180; eightieth birthday speech.

not entirely adept at the wheeling and dealing required of electors in the annual Junior Research Fellowship competition.[57]

The years after he stepped down as Regius in 1996 saw no letting up of the frantic pace at which he had become accustomed to work. They were filled with multiple lectures, the Douglas Southall Freeman visiting professorship at the University of Virginia and a stint as an Honorary Professor at Warwick, not to mention honorary degrees at Oxford, Essex, Warwick, Trinity College Dublin, and Sheffield (adding to those he had already received at York and Canterbury), the receipt of three Festschriften, and the award of the Historical Association's Medlicott Medal in 1998.[58] Freedom from administration and teaching enabled him to undertake and complete new projects, including an edition of manuscripts relating to *Conferences and Combination Lectures* at Dedham and Bury St Edmunds, on which he collaborated with John Craig and Brett Usher and which appeared in 2003.[59] The archive of his letters collected by Dr Usher testifies to Collinson's meticulousness as a scholar, his discovery of the joys of collaboration, and his accomplishment at the art of juggling. They reveal the breakneck speed at which he wrote his little book on *The Reformation*, a short overview designed for the lay reader, which he freely admitted came out of his head and such books as he could find on his shelf. This revealed 'his love of Luther' but he felt less affinity with the 'choleric personality' of Calvin. Reviewers were kind, but although it fizzed with ideas and was translated into several languages, including Portuguese, this was not his best work. He was disappointed that it did not make more impact.[60] More profound were his earlier attempts to situate English Calvinism in its international context in a volume edited by Menna Prestwich and the introduction entitled 'The fog in the channel clears' he wrote for *The Reception of the Continental Reformation*, the offspring of a British Academy conference he organised with Polly Ha.[61]

[57] Collinson, *History of a History Man*, pp. 181, 196.

[58] The four Douglas Southall Freeman Lectures he gave at Virginia were published in the *Douglas Southall Freeman Historical Review* (Spring 1999). The Festschriften were Fletcher and Roberts, *Religion, Culture and Society*; Jack and Wall, 'Protestants, property, puritans: *Godly People* revisited', and Susan Wabuda and Caroline Litzenberger (eds.), *Belief and Practice in Reformation England: a Tribute to Patrick Collinson by his Students* (Aldershot, 1998).

[59] Patrick Collinson, John Craig and Brett Usher (eds.), *Conferences and Combination Lectures in the Elizabethan Church: Dedham and Bury St Edmunds 1582–1590* (Woodbridge, 2003).

[60] The late Brett Usher lent me a box file of correspondence relating to the edition cited above, n. 59. Patrick Collinson, *The Reformation* (London, 2003), quotations at pp. ix, 74.

[61] Patrick Collinson, 'England and international Calvinism 1558–1640', in Menna Prestwich (ed.), *International Calvinism, 1541–1715* (Oxford, 1985), pp. 197–223; Patrick Collinson, 'The fog in the channel clears: the rediscovery of the continental dimension to the British reformations',

During the early 2000s he was also preoccupied by his duties as an associate editor for the *Oxford Dictionary of National Biography*, to which he contributed twenty-seven articles, including a 36,000 word entry on Elizabeth I, which later appeared as a short book. The experience of writing the life of this long-reigning monarch ('an awful sweat') made him determined to 'have no more to do with the woman' ('no-one should be allowed to be queen for 45 years') and he returned the advance of £1,000 he had received from Blackwells for a full-scale biography.[62] What he really wanted to write, but which never transpired, was a book about the tragic story of his wife's parents' trial for the murder of a farm servant in early 1930s Kenya. Trailed in an *LRB* article called 'The cowbells of Kitali', it was to be called *Black and White Mischief* and to function as an emblem of colonialism in all its deleterious effects. Perhaps he thought of it as the fulfilment of his youthful wish to pursue research in African history.[63]

Patrick Collinson was not particularly troubled by giving up the power he had exercised as Regius, but in retirement he did sometimes succumb to feeling marginalised and he was sensitive to perceived slights and hurt by negative relationships. He felt cut off from Cambridge in the coastal town of Shaldon in Devon, to which he and Liz moved after she suffered from a stroke and a heart attack in 2005, in order to be closer to three of their four children. Always eager for gossip, in his declining years he relied upon John Morrill as his 'master spy'. Most of his final book, *Richard Bancroft and Elizabethan Anti-Puritanism*, was written after his diagnosis with terminal bladder cancer, with access only to a limited library and his yellowing Ph.D. notes. This was a case of turning full circle: it is *The Elizabethan Puritan Movement* viewed through the hostile lens of its chief antagonist. He regarded it as 'a kind of mental therapy' and his dogged determination to finish it before he died says everything about the stoicism and stamina that had always been part of his character.[64] Bancroft was the anti-hero of this study, which reiterated Collinson's long held-conviction that puritanism was the leavening lump, life-blood and 'vital chord' of the Church of England and a force too resilient for its most ardent and ingen-

in Polly Ha and Patrick Collinson (eds.), *The Reception of Continental Reformation in Britain*, *Proceedings of the British Academy*, 164 (Oxford, 2010), pp. xxvii–xxxvii.
[62] Patrick Collinson, 'Elizabeth I', in *ODNB*, reprinted as Patrick Collinson, *Elizabeth I* (Oxford, 2007). Letters to Brett Usher, 19 Oct. 2001, 29 Nov. 2001. Collinson, *From Cranmer to Sancroft*, p. x.
[63] Patrick Collinson, 'The cowbells of Kitali', *London Review of Books*, 25/11 (2003), 15–20. See Collinson, *History of a History Man*, p. 197; Collinson, *From Cranmer to Sancroft*, pp. x–xi.
[64] He died on 28 September 2011.

ious episcopal enemy to uproot.[65] Around the same time, on the poignant occasion on which he sat watching some of his students pack up his books for sale as a job lot, he came out with the pronouncement that Bancroft's predecessor at Canterbury, John Whitgift, was a complete 'bastard'.

The book on Bancroft was published posthumously, but Collinson's memoirs, *The History of a History Man: or, the Twentieth Century Viewed from a Safe Distance* appeared a few months before his death, though they had already been made available online via the Trinity College website.[66] He described the book as 'a picaresque chronicle of a wandering scholar in four continents' and it was less a set of reflections on his historical endeavours than a lively account of his mobile and adventurous life, with some highly confessional elements.[67] One reviewer rightly detected a degree of false modesty in his description of himself as 'a petit-maître' of the historical discipline,[68] and his presentation of his career as a chapter of accidents runs the risk of disguising his quiet ambition. He had no personal vanity and many commented upon his immense modesty and instinct for self-mockery, but he did take great pleasure in his achievements and in the honours showered upon him in later years. The presence of the autobiography (from which Collinson admitted some things had been 'deliberately omitted') is something of a hazard for his biographer.[69] It eclipses an inner complexity which his own discourse was designed to efface.

What does leap from its pages, as from his many letters and scholarly writings, is his distinctive voice, engaging personality, and lust for life in all its rich variety. His academic prose was colourful, allusive, and replete with extravagant metaphors. He had a mischievous, irreverent and sometimes macabre sense of humour. He enjoyed food and drink and was the life and soul of the parties he and Liz organised in Sydney, Canterbury, Sheffield and Cambridge for staff and students alike. He enjoyed singing lugubrious ditties, including one beginning 'Whenever you see a corpse go by', and had a repertoire of inspired shaggy dog stories which he told at his own expense.[70] Music was a passion, especially the Baroque masterpieces of Bach, and he kept and played a harpsichord and clavichord. He

---

[65] Patrick Collinson, *Richard Bancroft and Anti-Puritanism* (Cambridge, 2012). See the preface, p. ix, and p. 218.

[66] Collinson, *History of a History Man*.

[67] Eightieth birthday speech.

[68] Munro, review, 131; Collinson, *History of a History Man*, p. 52.

[69] Collinson, *History of a History Man*, p. 4.

[70] As remarked by Sheridan Gilley in a letter responding to Collinson's obituary, in *The Times* (15 Oct. 2011). This seems to have been a trait he shared with his father: see Collinson, *History of a History Man*, p. 19.

was also a remarkably talented cartoonist, who doodled pictures of the sixteenth-century people he studied and produced hilarious birthday cards for members of his family. Holidays were important to him, and he especially treasured annual trips to a cottage in Connemara in Ireland in the last decade and a half of his life. Everywhere he went he indulged his insatiable curiosity about nature and he had an intricate knowledge of the habits of birds, fish and mammals that would have impressed David Attenborough. But there was also a streak of danger. Mountaineering claimed the lives of several of his friends and he himself had more than a few narrow squeaks; he was thrilled by great heights; and he had a propensity for driving at recklessly high speeds. Above all, however, Liz and his children and grandchildren were at the very heart of his world, and they spilt into every conversation one had with him.

As has already been observed, Patrick Collinson was also a man who held pronounced political views rooted in his earnest Christian socialism. He was a member of the Campaign for Nuclear Disarmament, a peace campaigner and anti-war activist who marched in the streets and vocally opposed the invasion of Iraq in a letter to a leading newspaper, and a supporter of the call for gay rights. He was a dedicated Christian Aid man and spent much effort pioneering Traidcraft at Hathersage in Derbyshire. The priorities of American foreign policy gravely worried him and he spoke openly of 'the intellectual and moral failure' of the United States and its allies.[71] Although Tony Blair's drift from its historic principles dismayed him, he was a lifelong supporter of the Labour Party, who celebrated the fall of Thatcher at the beginning of a seminar in 1990. Shaldon proved to be a little too complacent and conservative (with a large and small c) for his liking. Nevertheless, this 'more than closet republican' found it possible to accept the honour of a CBE, diffusing the discomfort by receiving it at Trinity rather than at Buckingham Palace, where it was bestowed upon him by the Lord Lieutenant of Cambridgeshire, who had been his old captain of boats.[72] Nor can the manner in which his political outlook seeped into and shaped his historical writing be ignored: he saw the past partly through the prism of the burning issues that exercised him in the present and admitted that his portrayal of moderate puritanism was

---

[71] Collinson, *History of a History Man*, p. 196.
[72] Ibid., pp. 145, 191. He wrote that he accepted the honour as a mark of esteem for his office and the profession and that 'insofar as the queen was and is my head of state, I was happy, and proud, to receive it from her. It was how any of my sixteenth-century monarchical republicans would have responded.'

tinged with '*Guardian*-reading pinkness'.[73] Written in the shadow of the Cold War, *The Elizabethan Puritan Movement* draws a passing parallel between the drive against the godly and the anti-Communist initiatives of Senator McCarthy, while the original title of his last book, *The Archbishop and the War against Terror*, reveals that the international response to Islamic fundamentalism in the wake of 9/11 supplied him with a new set of spectacles. The first draft contained more than a few references to dodgy dossiers.[74]

Patrick Collinson often claimed that he had no real method as a historian, beyond assembling 'an omnium gatherum of materials culled from more or less everywhere'.[75] Fond of calling himself a 'butterfly collector' and 'hunter gatherer',[76] he relished the anecdotes and gems of evidence he collected from his forays into the archives and from the early printed texts he identified by his ritual yearly reading of Pollard and Redgrave's *Short Title Catalogue*. He believed that 'precious truths ... reside in particulars' and thought that there was 'no substitute for *ipsissima verba*'.[77] The empirical positivism of the London school of which he was a product left a profound mark on his scholarship, though his critique of the narrowness of Elton's vision of history reveals a recognition of the limits of Rankean thoroughness. He could not adhere to an 'epistemology which refuses to face the fact that no historian can tell the whole truth about all of the past, and that he therefore has to select, shape, and even in some sense invent his material'.[78] He generally kept historical theory at arm's length and his flirtations with it in Australia produced only 'a very superficial conversion'. He jettisoned it quickly on his return to England.[79]

But Collinson was by no means hostile to insights derived from other disciplines and to borrowing creatively from them. Marx's understanding of religion as a superstructure of political and economic forces was anathema to him and Durkheim's overly functional, but he admired the sociology of Max Weber, and found enduring value in his concept of 'elective

---

[73] See <http://theconventicle.blogspot.co.uk/2007/11/conventicle-q-with-prof-patrick.html> [last accessed 14 April 2014].

[74] Collinson, *Elizabethan Puritan Movement*, p. 397. The original typescript title-page is in my possession.

[75] Collinson, *History of a History Man*, p. 144. On his approach to the past, see also chap. 5 *passim*.

[76] Ibid., e.g. pp. 49, 51, 161.

[77] Collinson, *Religion of Protestants*, p. 39; Collinson, *History of a History Man*, p. 52.

[78] Collinson, 'Sir Geoffrey Rudolph Elton'; Collinson, 'Geoffrey Rudolph Elton', p. 441; Collinson, review of *Return to Essentials*.

[79] Collinson, *History of a History Man*, pp. 154, 161.

affinity'.[80] He thought that anthropological models of interpretation were underpinned by the unhelpful assumption that religion was a mistaken apprehension of fact, though he did engage playfully with Clifford Geertz's approach to culture and his classic analysis of the Balinese cockfight. In one essay he compared stalking puritanism to hunting the okapi in the Ituri rain forest (an apt analogy for a thwarted field naturalist) and directed practitioners of the technique of thick description to the evangelical fasts and mass communions conducted by the godly Protestants of sixteenth- and seventeenth-century England and Scotland.[81] For all his quarrels with Stephen Greenblatt and other New Historicist literary critics, he came to agree with them about the textual character of historical documentation.[82] Notwithstanding his diatribe against postmodernism as a fungus, his thinking did bear the imprint of the linguistic turn and of the sensitivity it cultivated to the nexus between language and reality. His conviction that puritanism was in large part a rhetorical construct owed something to this and he 'half agreed with Hayden White that the historian's task is not absolutely alien to the writer of fiction'.[83] Defying neat categorisation, his work never slavishly followed current trends. Instead it set them. While the elliptical and serpentine sentences in which his subtle thinking was encapsulated often puzzle students, for the initiated they yield fresh revelations each time they are read.

Finally, it is necessary to turn to the issue of Patrick Collinson's religious faith and its relationship with the work he did. His evangelical upbringing in a family of missionaries exerted considerable influence in his youth. He was baptised by total immersion at Bethesda Chapel in Ipswich in his late teens, but he never quite experienced the emotional conversion and re-awakening for which he strove during his adolescence.[84] By his early twenties he had migrated away from nonconformity towards

[80] See the discussion in Patrick Collinson, 'Religion, society and the historian', *Journal of Religious History*, 23 (1999), 149–67; Collinson, 'A. G. Dickens', pp. 22–3.
[81] Patrick Collinson, 'Elizabethan and Jacobean Puritanism as forms of popular religious culture', in Christopher Durson and Jacqueline Eales (eds.), *The Culture of English Puritanism, 1500–1700* (Basingstoke, 1996), pp. 32–57, at 34, 50. See also Collinson, *History of a History Man*, p. 49; and Patrick Collinson, 'The vertical and the horizontal in religious history: internal and external integration of the subject', in Alan Ford, James McGuire, and Kenneth Milne (eds.), *As by Law Established: the Church of Ireland Since the Reformation* (Dublin, 1995), pp. 15–32, at 22.
[82] Collinson, *From Cranmer to Sancroft*, p. x. For Collinson's interaction with scholars in this field, see Paulina Kewes, 'A mere historian: Patrick Collinson and the study of literature', forthcoming as part of a special issue on 'Patrick Collinson and his historical legacy', ed. Alexandra Walsham, to be submitted to *History*.
[83] Collinson, *History of a History Man*, p. 54.
[84] Collinson, *History of a History Man*, pp. 61, 28.

the Church of England, and he briefly thought of becoming ordained. The parish churches in which he successively worshipped spanned the spectrum of Anglicanism, from liberal to Anglo-Catholic, and unlike his father, who detested set forms of prayer, he had an affectionate respect for the liturgy. His time at King's School Ely seems to have instilled in him a fondness for the rhythms of Cranmer's *Book of Common Prayer*, but he was sheepish about having participated in a procession, accompanied by incense, in Shaldon.[85] By his own confession, he had 'a general difficulty with Catholicism', which, not coincidentally, was also something of a blind spot in his writing. And he distrusted clergy who claimed special knowledge or understanding, even of church history.

Yet it remains difficult to gauge the nature of his piety and to measure its precise impact on his scholarship. It is noticeable that he was interested less in theology and doctrine than in the people who applied and practised it in their everyday lives. Attentive to their frailties and foibles, he took pride in being 'a kind of resurrection man'. He frequently professed that he was 'methodologically atheist' and he bridled when Eamon Duffy described him as a Protestant historian.[86] But he also knew that he was a product of his environment, the prisoner of his own past, and a child of the movements that he studied. Despite his protestation that he would 'probably run a mile from those Puritans ... I study if I met them in the street', he was, in a sense, one of them.[87] He once wrote that the 'optimum position' was to be both an insider and an outsider, and his life, career and scholarship epitomise the benefits of this ambidexterity.[88] These varied experiences equipped Patrick Collinson with a unique ability to write 'history with a human face'.[89]

ALEXANDRA WALSHAM

Fellow of the Academy

---

[85] For his father's aversion to a formal liturgy, see ibid., p. 19. And note his review of *Common Worship: Services and Prayers for the Church of England* (2000); Patrick Collinson, 'Holy-rowly-powliness', in *London Review of Books*, 23/1 (4 Jan. 2001), 33–4.

[86] Collinson, *History of a History Man*, p. 52. For one use of the phrase 'methodological atheism', see Collinson, 'The vertical and the horizontal', p. 25; for his reaction to the label 'Protestant historian', see Collinson, *History of a History Man*, p. 53, reinforced by Eamon Duffy's own recollection of Collinson's response.

[87] Patrick Collinson, 'I believe ...', *Times Higher Education Supplement* (8 July 1996).

[88] Patrick Collinson, 'Part of the fun of being an English Protestant', review of Diarmaid MacCulloch, *Reformation: Europe's House Divided 1490–1700* (London, 2003), *London Review of Books*, 26/14 (22 July 2004), 22–3.

[89] Collinson, *History of a History Man*, p. 52.

Note.   In addition to the sources noted in the footnotes, I should like to acknowledge conversations and exchanges with Liz Collinson and with the following of Pat's friends, acquaintances, pupils and colleagues: Michael Bentley, John Craig, Eamon Duffy, John Elliott, Kenneth Fincham, Anthony Fletcher, Mark Greengrass, Boyd Hilton, Arnold Hunt, Paulina Kewes, Beat Kumin, Christine Linehan, John Lonsdale, Diarmaid MacCulloch, John Morrill, Kate Peters, Bill Sheils, and Susan Wabuda. I have also drawn on a box of the late Brett Usher's correspondence with Patrick Collinson and my own archive of letters. Additionally I have benefited from the papers delivered by Peter Lake, Kenneth Fincham, Peter Marshall, and Ethan Shagan at a symposium in Cambridge discussing his legacy, which it is hoped will appear as a special issue of the journal *History* in 2015.

BARRIE DOBSON

Richard Barrie Dobson
1931–2013

R. B. Dobson, known universally as Barrie, died in 2013, at the age of eighty-one. Over a long and distinguished career, he contributed distinctively and substantively to an understanding of the ecclesiastical, religious and social history of the English Middle Ages.

Born at Stockton-on-Tees on 3 November 1931, Barrie was the son of Richard Henry and Mary Victoria Dobson. The Dobsons had long been established at Brough and Middleton-in-Teesdale; Barrie's first name, Richard, had been given to the eldest son over successive generations. Barrie spent some of his early years in South America, where his father worked for the Great Western Railway of Brazil: some of the memorabilia of this great engineering adventure remained his proud possessions to the end of his life. In 1939 Barrie's mother brought him and his sister, Margaret, back to England to prepare for the birth of the youngest child, Marybelle; they first lived at Redcar, but after the outbreak of war evacuated themselves to Mickleton, a Teesdale village then in the North Riding of Yorkshire and later transferred to County Durham. His mother and sisters subsequently moved to Middleton, but Barrie remained with his aunt at Mickleton and made the daily journey from there to Barnard Castle School. Barrie's strong sense of personal and scholarly identity with Yorkshire and County Durham were developed through his early experience of the dramatic landscapes of Low Force and High Force in upper Teesdale. After school, Barrie went straight on to military service in the Army, including time in Malaya during the Emergency, where he was in the Education Corps teaching English.

In 1951, Barrie went up as a Scholar to Wadham College, Oxford, to read Modern History. While still on National Service, Barrie had written to the Warden to ask what he should bring with him. The response from Maurice Bowra, FBA, was just what was needed: 'Yourself and a toothbrush.'[1] Under Bowra, Wadham flourished as a diverse, cosmopolitan and intellectually vibrant community. Although Barrie was tutored for medieval papers by Lawrence Stone, his intellectual formation owed most to A. F. (Pat) Thompson, who had made his own academic journey from the Middle Ages to nineteenth- and twentieth-century labour history, and who became a life-long mentor and family friend. Among those of Barrie's group at Wadham who went on to professional careers teaching History at school and university were Alan Forey, Aubrey Newman and David Parry. His contemporaries remember Barrie's rapid emergence as an assured historian and the natural conviviality of a young man who delighted in walking, reading, music and the cinema—pleasures that remained with him throughout his life. The retired Wadham medievalist, R. V. (Reggie) Lennard, a distinguished expert on agrarian history, was a founder member of the Friends of the Lake District and organised reading parties there. It was on these occasions that Barrie first fell under the spell of Helvellyn and developed his lifelong passion for hill and fell walking. Much later, in 1989, Barrie became an Honorary Fellow of Wadham.

Barrie took a first in Modern History in 1954, and in 1957 was elected a Senior Demy at Magdalen College, where he later became Junior Lecturer. For his doctoral work he originally proposed a study of a bishop's register, but the Regius Professor, V. H. Galbraith, FBA, took a dim view of this and Barrie eventually fixed upon 'The Priory of Durham in the Time of Prior John Wessington, 1416–46'. His supervisor was W. A. (Billy) Pantin, FBA, whose own studies of the late medieval English Church remain classics of the genre today. Medieval history at Magdalen (and across Oxford) was dominated by the figure of K. B. McFarlane, an expert on the English nobility, and although Barrie never became an acolyte, he was clear that his own use of prosopographical method owed much to McFarlane's inspiration. The thesis was completed in 1963 and examined by Dom David Knowles, the mid-century doyen of monastic studies, who had become Regius Professor at Cambridge in 1954. Barrie's copy of Knowles's inaugural lecture, *The Historian and Character*,[2] contains a number of letters that track the evolution of a scholarly friendship. In 1972 Barrie sent

---

[1] Pers. comm., David Parry.
[2] Dom D. Knowles, *The Historian and Character: Inaugural Lecture* (Cambridge, 1955).

Knowles the first chapter of the reworked thesis, then in preparation for publication. 'Father David' wrote back to say that 'I began thinking it a chore, but read on with growing satisfaction and improvement of the mind … You have lived with it and thought about it, and you bring its characters to life.' He recommended the inclusion of good maps, since 'Those unlucky people who have never seen Durham will need them.' The book appeared two years later as *Durham Priory, 1400–1450*.[3] The experience of working intensively with the remarkable archive of the community of St Cuthbert established Barrie's abiding interest in the records of the northern English Church. With their searching analysis of the membership, the economic management and the intellectual life of Durham Priory in a period often cast as one of monastic decline, the thesis and the first book offered a different way of thinking and writing about the fifteenth century and helped set in train a major reassessment of the role of the religious orders in general, and the Benedictines in particular, during the last century of Catholic England.

Oxford gave Barrie intellectual purpose and friends; it also made him a family man. Early in 1958, Menna Prestwich introduced him to Narda Leon, a St Hilda's graduate who was completing a B.Litt. at the Institute of Colonial Studies and was about to take up a post in Paris. Barrie and Narda married a year later, by which time Barrie had moved to a lectureship at the University of St Andrews. While St Andrews was emphatically an ancient institution with an exceptionally strong sense of its special traditions (the insistence of Barrie's newly adopted department on the spelling of 'Mediaeval' in its title was a case in point), it was also undergoing a significant period of change. Under an inspiring and energetic Head of Department, Lionel Butler, Barrie had the chance to contribute fully to the new styles of teaching that were being introduced and to hone his skills in the lecture, the seminar and the tutorial. It was in St Andrews that Barrie and Narda's children, Mark and Michelle, were born, and the family entered with relish into their life in the bracing environment of the Kingdom of Fife.

In 1964 Barrie accepted the offer of a lectureship in the Department of History at the University of York. It was a big decision, and in many ways a very risky one: to leave an ancient and world-famous place of scholarship for one of the new group of 'plate-glass' institutions being developed in the wake of strong government determination to expand

[3] R. B. Dobson, *Durham Priory, 1400–1450*, Cambridge Studies in Medieval Life and Thought, 3rd series 6 (Cambridge, 1973).

higher education across the United Kingdom. Barrie joined the University
of York in only its second year of operations, with much of the physical
infrastructure and intellectual agenda still in development: he later
described the four-fold increase in the staffing establishment of the
Department of History over the first seven years of its existence as 'an
exhilarating, if at times exhausting, expansion'.[4] But it was clear to everyone that York offered a mix of tradition and innovation that appealed
strongly to Barrie's temperament. On the one hand, York was an ancient
city whose fabric and resources were themselves a constant inspiration to
the medievalist. The Minster, parish churches, walls and guildhalls conjured
up York's great days of wealth and political importance in the later Middle
Ages, and the exceptionally rich civic and ecclesiastical archives housed
within the city's bounds were a natural attraction to the documentary-
minded historian. Barrie quickly added studies of church life in York and
Selby to his on-going work on Durham.[5] On the other hand, the chance to
contribute to the formation of a distinctively modern academic community
was both an initial draw and a lasting stimulation.

The dual perspective was typified in the new working environment to
which Barrie was inducted. The Department of History started life in the
King's Manor, which had once been the abbot's lodging of the great
Benedictine abbey of St Mary's and, after the Reformation, was the headquarters of the Council of the North. History soon moved to its new
premises on the emerging Heslington campus, where the modernist vision
of the young architect Andrew Derbyshire was articulating in concrete
and glass the purist intellectual ideals of Barrie's own generation. If the
subsequent foundation of the Centre for Medieval Studies at the King's
Manor in 1968 offered Barrie the chance for a regular commute, as it were,
between the twentieth and the fifteenth century, there was never any sense

[4] R. B. Dobson, 'Claire Cross: a tribute', in D. Wood (ed.), *Life and Thought in the Northern
Church, c.1100–c.1700: Essays in Honour of Claire Cross*, Studies in Church History Subsidia, 12
(1999), pp. 1–9 at p. 5.
[5] R. B. Dobson, 'Richard Bell, Prior of Durham (1464–78) and Bishop of Carlisle (1478–95)',
Transactions of the Cumberland and Westmorland Antiquarian and Archaeological Society, NS 65
(1965), 182–221; R. B. Dobson, 'The last English monks on Scottish soil: the severance of
Coldingham Priory from the Monastery of Durham, 1461–78', *Scottish Historical Review*, 46
(1967), 1–25; R. B. Dobson, 'The foundation of perpetual chantries by the citizens of medieval
York', in J. G. Cuming (ed.), *The Province of York*, Studies in Church History, 4 (1967), pp. 22–38;
R. B. Dobson, 'The election of John Ousthorp as Abbot of Selby in 1436', *Yorkshire Archaeological
Journal*, 42 (1967), 31–40; R. B. Dobson, 'The first Norman Abbey in Northern England',
Ampleforth Journal, 74 (2) (Summer 1969), 161–76.

of withdrawal into the past, but instead an energetic embracing of the endless possibilities that History offers for its own reinvention.

Like other colleagues who joined the department at York in these early days, Barrie was motivated by the vision of the founding Vice-Chancellor, Eric James, and of the first Head of History, Gerald Aylmer, FBA. This, however, was to be no 'top-down' organisation. The historians, like their colleagues in other departments, worked in productive partnership to formulate an undergraduate curriculum that captured a shared vision of the discipline and its future. Long before such things were expressed in these ways at a national level, the resulting programme met all the benchmarks now considered essential to an excellent undergraduate training in History. Barrie played an important role in helping to ensure that the curriculum was at once utterly true to the intellectual ideals of History and sufficiently diverse and challenging as to test students' potential for the world of work that lay beyond. A major innovation was the compulsory course in Comparative History, where students studied a theme or phenomenon over time and space. The methods of assessment were especially bold, with open examinations the norm for most research-led courses. The challenges of delivering—and receiving—such a curriculum were significant. A natural collaborator, Barrie was a powerful advocate of team-teaching. He also strongly identified himself with the system of pastoral supervision that emerged as a hallmark of the department and the University, and gave significantly of his own (and his family's) time in supporting those students who found the going difficult. Among those who helped Barrie determine his direction of travel during these years was the charismatic Gwyn Williams, who joined the department in 1965; Williams's early training in the history of medieval London and his subsequent work on modern radicalism and revolt had a significant impact both on Barrie's teaching and on his emerging research interests. Over the following years, Barrie was to draw particular inspiration from close collaboration with the outstanding group of historians of medieval and early modern religion that gathered in York, including Peter Biller, FBA, Claire Cross, John Bossy, FBA, Richard Fletcher, Gordon (Bunny) Leff and David Smith.

The other major influence on Barrie's intellectual progress as a medievalist during his first decade at York was the emergence of interdisciplinary studies. In the mid-1960s Elizabeth Salter, founding professor of Medieval Literature in the university, began to formulate plans for a graduate Centre for Medieval Studies. Salter was a gifted literary historian with a very strong command of the artistic as well as the literary legacy of the Middle Ages. Barrie's special skills as negotiator were drawn on, first to ensure that the new centre should be a genuine collaboration between the Departments of English and History and, later, that its commitment to the visual should be supported by specialist appointments in the History of Art. The interdisciplinarity that is now regarded as a hallmark of York's intellectual culture across the Arts and Humanities owes itself in a very real and lasting way to Barrie Dobson's work in the pioneering Centre for Medieval Studies. With his great colleague and close friend, Derek Pearsall, Barrie co-directed the Centre from 1977 to 1988 and developed, within its taught graduate programme, the various specialist options that helped train a new generation of aspiring medievalists.

The quickly emerging international reputation of the Centre for Medieval Studies, coupled with Barrie's personal reputation as a stimulating and sympathetic supervisor, also brought many able young doctoral students to York. Among those whom Barrie guided in their doctoral work over his time at York and who subsequently went on to careers in universities and archives on both sides of the Atlantic were Lorraine Attreed, Margaret Bonney, Janet Burton, Patricia Cullum, Sarah Rees Jones, Heather Swanson, Brigette Vale and Juliet Vale, along with students of other universities who sought him out as an external supervisor, including Jeremy Goldberg (Cambridge) and Rosemary Hayes (Bristol). Barrie's supervisees remember his characterisation of their lot as that of the 'lone wolf', and the subtle (and not so subtle) ways in which he encouraged them out of their isolation into sociable lunches, visits to archives and historical sites, and the generous round of parties that he and Narda held at their home on Stockton Lane. One recalls being whisked away from a supervision to help Barrie load into his car a recently acquired interwar edition of the *Encyclopaedia Britannica*, only rapidly to realise (as Narda could have told her) that he had given no thought to how he was going to find shelf-space for it at work or home. The increase in his institutional and public responsibilities put pressure on Barrie's diary, but everyone emphasises the way that he made them feel important and gave validity and significance to their academic efforts. And he emphatically observed the adage that a supervisor is for life, busying himself in the writing of references and taking enjoyment and pride in the group's professional accomplishments and family lives.

The almost quarter-century of service that Barrie Dobson provided at the University of York saw both the maturing and the diversification of his own scholarly work. The medieval Church remained the abiding and dominant interest. Working intensively with the York archiepiscopal records held at the Borthwick Institute of Historical Research (now the

Borthwick Institute for Archives) and the records of the Dean and Chapter of York Minster, Barrie developed a detailed knowledge of the prosopographical, institutional and cultural history of the churches and religious houses of York in the late Middle Ages, and made fruitful comparisons between these and their counterparts in other major cathedral cities, especially Durham.[6] His 1977 contribution on this topic to *The History of York Minster* (itself a model for other scholarly cathedral histories to which Barrie contributed) was a particular highlight, as was his article on York's residentiary canons in 1979.[7] In 1982 he helped to host an important colloquium on the late medieval English Church at York, and edited its proceedings in a successful volume published in 1984.[8] He also continued his fascination with intellectual and educational developments during the later Middle Ages: his 1985 article on the university connections of the cathedral chapters of Durham and York heralded later contributions to the histories of both Oxford and Cambridge, and his 1995 article on the educational interests of Archbishop Rotherham of York stands as the definitive study of this great benefactor of learning.[9] The study of 'Richard III and the Church of York' published in a 1986 Festschrift for the eminent scholar of the Yorkist period, Charles Ross,

---

[6] R. B. Dobson, 'Cathedral chapters and cathedral cities: York, Durham and Carlisle in the Fifteenth Century', *Northern History*, 19 (1983), 15–44; R. B. Dobson, 'Mendicant ideal and practice in late medieval York', in P. V. Addyman and V. E. Black (eds.), *Archaeological Papers from York Presented to M. W. Barley* (York, 1984), pp. 109–22; R. B. Dobson and S. Donaghey, *Historical Sources for York Archaeology after AD 1100, Part 1: The History of Clementthorpe Nunnery*, The Archaeology of York 2 (1) (York, 1984); R. B. Dobson, 'The authority of the bishop in late medieval England: the case of Archbishop Alexander Neville of York, 1374–1388', *Miscellanea Historiae Ecclesiasticae*, 8 (1987), 181–91; R. B. Dobson, 'The political role of the Archbishops of York during the reign of Edward I', in P. R. Coss and S. D. Lloyd (eds.), *Thirteenth Century England III: Proceedings of the Newcastle upon Tyne Conference, 1989* (Woodbridge, 1991), pp. 47–64; R. B. Dobson, 'The Church of Durham and the Scottish Borders, 1378–1388', in A. Goodman and A. Tuck (eds.), *War and Border Societies in the Middle Ages* (London, 1992), pp. 124–54; R. B. Dobson, 'English Cluniac houses towards the end of their story', in G. Constable, G. Melville and J. Oberste (eds.), *Die Cluniazenser in ihrem politisch-sozialen Umfeld* (Münster, 1998), pp. 559–73.

[7] R. B. Dobson, 'The later Middle Ages, 1215–1500', in G. E. Aylmer and R. Cant (eds.), *A History of York Minster* (Oxford, 1977), pp. 44–109; R. B. Dobson, 'The residentiary canons of York in the fifteenth century', *Journal of Ecclesiastical History*, 30 (1979), 145–74.

[8] R. B. Dobson (ed.), *The Church, Politics and Patronage in the Fifteenth Century* (Gloucester, 1984).

[9] R. B. Dobson, 'Recent prosopographical research in late medieval English history: university graduates, Durham monks, and York canons', in N. Bulst and J.-P. Genet (eds.), *Medieval Lives and the Historian: Studies in Medieval Prosopography* (Kalamazoo, MI, 1985), pp. 181–200; R. B. Dobson, 'The educational patronage of Archbishop Thomas Rotherham of York', *Northern History*, 31 (1995), 65–85.

became widely cited a quarter-century later in the vigorous public debates that followed the exhumation of Richard's remains at Leicester.[10] Among the many honours that Barrie accrued over his career, the Presidency of the Ecclesiastical History Society (1990–1) was one that most surely captured his profound and enduring commitment to the history of the medieval Church.

Alongside the ecclesiastical was an equally abiding research interest in urban history. York's records again provided much of the stimulus for Barrie's early work in this field, the City Archive being located especially conveniently next door to the Centre for Medieval Studies' base at the King's Manor. In the 1970s, the history of late medieval towns was dominated by the 'growth or decline' debate, and there was much sparring over the methodology for testing the relative economic strength or weakness of any given community. Barrie's 1973 article in the *Economic History Review* championed a prosopographical approach by using admission to the freedom of the city of York as an index of urban prosperity.[11] But it was in his invited lecture to the Royal Historical Society on 'Urban decline in late medieval England', published in the Society's *Transactions* in 1977, that he fully demonstrated his more general powers of critical analysis. The discussion of the building of town walls captures brilliantly the aspirations, as well as the vulnerabilities, of English urban communities in the fourteenth and fifteenth centuries and helped move forward the debate over 'growth or decline' from one based (even supposed that we had them) on absolute numbers to one focusing on the aspirations, reputations and 'worship' of towns.[12] In 1980 Barrie published his acclaimed edition of the *York City Chamberlains' Account Rolls*, and later in life planned (but did not finish) a parallel volume for Cambridge.[13] In 1997 he contributed a significant essay to a publication marking the six-hundredth anniversary (in 1996) of the royal charter that elevated the city of York to the status of

[10] R. B. Dobson, 'Richard III and the Church of York', in R. A. Griffiths and J. W. Sherborne (eds.), *Kings and Nobles in the Later Middle Ages: a Tribute to Charles Ross* (Gloucester, 1986), pp. 130–54.
[11] R. B. Dobson, 'Admissions to the Freedom of the City of York in the later Middle Ages', *Economic History Review*, 2nd series 26 (1973), 1–22.
[12] R. B. Dobson, 'Urban decline in late medieval England', *Transactions of the Royal Historical Society*, 5th series 27 (1977), 1–22. See also R. B. Dobson, 'Yorkshire towns in the late fourteenth century', *Thoresby Society Miscellany XVIII*, Thoresby Society, 59 (1985), 1–21; R. B. Dobson, 'The City of York', in B. Ford (ed.), *The Cambridge Guide to the Arts in Britain, II: The Middle Ages* (Cambridge, 1988), pp. 200–13.
[13] R. B. Dobson, *York City Chamberlains' Account Rolls, 1396–1500*, Surtees Society, 192 (1980 for 1978–9).

an independent county and published an important essay on the historical context of the York Mystery Plays.[14] His wide-ranging contribution to the history of medieval towns, and his ability to work through the historiographical debates with both sensitivity and determination, made him the obvious author of the overview of the later Middle Ages in the relevant volume of the *Cambridge Urban History of Britain*, published in 2000.[15]

The legacy of the medieval Church and the medieval town, so evocatively summoned up on the streets and in the historic buildings of York, prompted in Barrie a further and, as it proved, abiding interest in the Jewish communities of England in the Middle Ages. His interest in the field had been awakened by a series of lectures given by Cecil Roth at Oxford, and by a reading of Roth's significantly revised 1964 edition of his *History of the Jews in England*.[16] In 1974 Barrie published, in the Borthwick Papers series, a masterly and compelling study of *The Jews of Medieval York and the Massacre of March 1190*.[17] The notoriety of the events at York in 1190 and the sensitivities that they continue to arouse both in the city and in a wider debate about the victimisation of religious minorities might have caused others to shy away from confronting the historical record and challenging received opinions. But Barrie managed to combine the proper disinterest of the professional historian with an innate (and, importantly, non-aligned) humanitarianism to tackle with honesty one of the most vexed moments in the history of York. The study has remained in print continuously for nearly forty years, and while its findings have inevitably been expanded, modified and sometimes challenged, it remains one of the great set pieces of modern Anglo-Jewish history.

Alongside the Borthwick Paper, Barrie also wrote a closer, academic study (eventually published in 1979) of the York Jewry in the century after 1190, thus establishing his position on the reasons for, and the consequences of, Edward I's general expulsion of the Jews from England in 1290.[18] He was

---

[14] R. B. Dobson, 'The crown, the charter and the city, 1396–1461', in S. Rees Jones (ed.), *The Government of Medieval York: Essays in Commemoration of the 1396 Charter*, Borthwick Studies in History, 3 (York, 1997), pp. 34–55; R. B. Dobson, 'Craft guilds and city: the historical origins of the York mystery plays reassessed', in A. E. Knight (ed.), *The Stage as a Mirror: Civic Theatre in Late Medieval Europe* (Woodbridge, 1997), pp. 91–105.

[15] R. B. Dobson, 'General survey, 1300–1540', in D. M. Palliser (ed.), *The Cambridge Urban History of Britain, I: 600–1540* (Cambridge, 2000), pp. 273–90.

[16] C. Roth, *A History of the Jews in England*, 3rd edn. (Oxford, 1964).

[17] R. B. Dobson, *The Jews of Medieval York and the Massacre of March 1190*, Borthwick Papers, 45 (York, 1974).

[18] R. B. Dobson, 'The decline and expulsion of the medieval Jews of York', *Transactions of the Jewish Historical Society of England*, 26 (1979), 34–52. See also R. B. Dobson, 'The medieval York Jewry reconsidered', *Jewish Culture & History*, 3 (2) (2000), 7–20.

also instrumental in the campaign to erect a memorial tablet to the Jews
at the site of the 1190 massacre, Clifford's Tower;[19] when the Chief Rabbi
arrived at York Railway Station in preparation for the resulting ceremony,
he immediately asked Barrie's opinion on the myth that Jews were formally forbidden from residing in the city. His work on the York Jews, and
his strong support for other medievalists working on English Jewry, led to
Barrie's election as President of the Jewish Historical Society of England
in 1990. His presidential address on 'The Jews of medieval Cambridge'
(consciously chosen to complement—and compliment—Roth's earlier
study of *The Jews of Medieval Oxford*) was delivered 'more or less seven
hundred years to the day since the last persecuted survivors of the once
substantial medieval English Jewry were crossing the channel into involun-
tary exile'.[20] Barrie's strong sense of occasion, and his deep determination
to mark and make sense of the events of 1190 and 1290, led him, as incom-
ing President of the Ecclesiastical History Society, to nominate 'Christianity
and Judaism' as the theme for the 1991 summer meeting of the Society. His
own address was on 'The Role of Jewish Women in Medieval England', a
topic that he also addressed in one of his two contributions to the Sewanee
Medieval Colloquium of 1991.[21]

The final area to which Barrie Dobson brought his particular talents
and perceptions as medieval historian was the study of outlaws and revo-
lutionaries. As with Jewish history, so with this topic, the choice was at
once personal and political. In 1970 Barrie published a landmark collection of translated texts on *The Peasants' Revolt of 1381*; much in demand
as a tool both for teaching and for research, the book was revised to mark
the anniversary of the Great Revolt and reissued in 1983, and remains in
print to this day.[22] Inspired by Gwyn Williams, Barrie worked his way
through a series of sometimes contradictory accounts of the events of the
summer of 1381 found in chronicles, official documents and imaginative
literature, organising them into a helpful sequence that at once allowed

[19] Borthwick Institute for Archives, University of York, SC Pamphlet Box 124/15.
[20] R. B. Dobson, 'The Jews of medieval Cambridge', *Jewish Historical Studies*, 32 (1993 for 1990–2),
1–24 (quotation at p. 1); C. Roth, *The Jews of Medieval Oxford*, Oxford Historical Society, NS 9
(1945).
[21] R. B. Dobson, 'The role of Jewish women in medieval England', in D. Wood (ed.), *Christianity
and Judaism, Studies in Church History*, 29 (1992), 145–68; R. B. Dobson, 'A minority ascendant:
the Benedictine conquest of the north of England, 1066–1100' and R. B. Dobson, 'A minority
within a minority: the Jewesses of thirteenth-century England', in S. J. Ridyard and R. G. Benson
(eds.), *Minorities and Barbarians in Medieval Life and Thought*, Sewanee Mediaeval Studies, 7
(Sewanee, TN, 1996), pp. 5–26, 27–48.
[22] R. B. Dobson, *The Peasants' Revolt of 1381*, 1st edn. (London, 1970); 2nd edn. (London, 1983).

the student to make sense of the material and yet adamantly resisted any notion that what emerged ought to be treated as a definitive account. Other than in his commentaries in this book, Barrie did not write extensively on 1381, though he was a significant participant in the public events around the commemoration of the Great Revolt in 1981 and contributed a particularly important study of the uprisings in York, Beverley and Scarborough to the volume of essays produced by the Past & Present Society to mark the occasion.[23] It is in his ruminations on the legacy of 1381 in *The Peasants' Revolt* that we can see most directly the human and political values that he shared with Wat Tyler, John Ball and their fellow rebels, and his deep understanding of the longer-term influence of the Great Revolt on the English intellectual and political tradition.

Similar instincts readily account for Barrie's fascination with the Robin Hood legend in medieval England. When Barrie was a research student, there had been a particularly highly charged debate in the pages of *Past & Present* over the figure of the medieval Robin Hood, and those who entered upon the subject a decade later did so not without some intellectual bravery and professional risk. In 1976 he and John Taylor, a medieval historian at the University of Leeds with whom Barrie had developed a long academic and personal friendship, published *Rymes of Robyn Hood*, in which they set out a critical edition of the earliest surviving outlaw ballads and an extended analysis of the historical contexts in which the original Robin Hood legends may have developed.[24] Taylor later described Barrie as 'the major partner in this enterprise', commenting that his co-editor was driven to the subject in part by his own instinctive search for 'the just society'.[25] The Robin Hood ballads have been re-edited several times since 1976 by literary scholars, but the historical notes in *Rymes* have become a classic source of reference. The title of the volume derived from the earliest known reference to the Robin Hood ballads in

[23] R. B. Dobson, 'Remembering the Peasants' Revolt, 1381–1981', in W. H. Liddell and R. G. E. Wood (eds.), *Essex and the Great Revolt of 1381* (Chelmsford, 1982), pp. 1–20; R. B. Dobson, 'The risings in York, Beverley and Scarborough, 1380–1381', in R. H. Hilton and T. H. Aston (eds.), *The English Rising of 1381* (Cambridge, 1984), pp. 112–42. See also R. B. Dobson, 'Beverley in conflict: Archbishop Alexander Neville and the Minster clergy, 1381–8', in C. Wilson (ed.), *Medieval Art and Architecture in the East Riding of Yorkshire*, British Archaeological Association Conference Transactions, 9 (1989), 149–64.
[24] R. B. Dobson and J. Taylor (eds.), *Rymes of Robyn Hood: an Introduction to the English Outlaw* (London, 1976). Their first joint publication on the subject was R. B. Dobson and J. Taylor, 'The medieval origins of the Robin Hood legend: a reassessment', *Northern History*, 7 (1972), 1–30.
[25] J. Taylor, 'Richard Barrie Dobson: an appreciation', in R. Horrox and S. Rees Jones (eds.), *Pragmatic Utopias: Ideals and Communities, 1200–1630* (Cambridge, 2001), pp. 1–10 at p. 4.

the B-text of William Langland's *Piers Plowman*, written around 1377; and it was Barrie's special interest in how the legends might in turn have influenced some of the ideology of the rebels of 1381 that led him to posit a relatively early genesis for texts otherwise known to survive only from the late fifteenth century. He was always inclined to locate Robin Hood in the Barnsdale setting of some of the early legends, and conjured evocative descriptions of the topography, society and culture of south Yorkshire in his support of a distinctively northern genesis for the outlaw hero. In the 1990s he and John Taylor were persuaded to prepare a new foreword for a revised edition of *Rymes*, published in 1997.[26] In the same year the Dobson–Taylor team contributed a review essay to *Northern History* in which they considered the extraordinary levels of scholarly and public interest that had developed over the twenty years since the publication of *Rymes* as a 'transformation of Robin Hood from medieval outlaw into heritage hero'.[27]

It was in his work on Robin Hood that Barrie established himself most obviously as a public intellectual, and some of the obituaries that appeared in the press in the weeks after his death concentrated on the undoubted contribution that he had made to that particular part of the English national heritage. For him, though, the lasting significance of the outlaw hero, as of the events and people of 1381, lay in his own profound commitment to an inclusive and thoughtful socialism. He was comfortable in the 'beer and sandwiches' culture of Labour Party activism and enjoyed lengthy sessions in the pub with friends such as Colin Richmond, where they would debate their commitment to progressive politics (and, in this particular conversation, the rights and wrongs of Philip Larkin's views on the history of jazz). Ultimately, his political vision owed most to Thomas More's *Utopia* (which he taught intermittently throughout his career), and his model of university life echoed his socialist principles in its complete commitment to freedom of opportunity and freedom of speech. In one of the Festschriften prepared for Barrie on his retirement, Rosemary Horrox

---

[26] Dobson and Taylor, *Rymes of Robin Hood*, rev. edn. (Stroud, 1997). In 1991 Dobson had written an appreciation of Taylor as well as a substantive essay on medieval historiography for the latter's Festschrift: R. B. Dobson, 'John Taylor: a tribute', and 'Contrasting chronicles: historical writing at York and Durham at the close of the Middle Ages', in I. N. Wood and G. A. Loud (eds.), *Church and Chronicle in the Middle Ages: Essays Presented to John Taylor* (London, 1991), pp. xi–xxiii, 201–18.

[27] R. B. Dobson and J. Taylor, ' "Merry men at work": the transformation of Robin Hood from medieval outlaw into heritage hero', *Northern History*, 33 (1997), 232–7. See also R. B. Dobson and J. Taylor, 'Robin Hood: the genesis of a popular hero', in T. Kahn (ed.), *Robin Hood in Popular Culture: Violence, Transgression and Justice* (Woodbridge, 2000), pp. 61–77.

commented on the debate among the contributors as to an appropriate theme and title for their collective enterprise. What emerged was a series of studies 'of pragmatic idealists, looking to achieve salvation or improvement within the structures of this world'.[28] Everyone who knew Barrie Dobson would readily recognise the type.

The national and international acclaim for the emerging body of work, coupled with his growing reputation for academic management, brought Barrie both honour and responsibility. In 1972 he was elected a Fellow of the Royal Historical Society and in 1979 a Fellow of the Society of Antiquaries. He held a British Academy-funded visiting fellowship at the Folger Library, Washington DC, in 1974, when he travelled to so many universities to give lectures that he was dubbed 'the Kissinger of the East Coast'.[29] He was also Visiting Professor at Swarthmore College, Pennsylvania, in 1987, when he and Narda again enjoyed the pleasures of extensive travel in the United States. In 1977 he was promoted to the title of Professor of Medieval History at York, and from 1984 to 1987 served as Deputy Vice-Chancellor of the University, working closely alongside another historian, the Vice-Chancellor Berrick Saul, and playing a key role in forging closer links between town and gown. His prominent contributions to the study of northern archives, cities and cathedrals also brought a range of offices, including the co-General Editorship of the Yorkshire Archaeological Record Society (1981–6) and the Presidency of the Surtees Society (1987–2002). His service to the wider historical profession led him to a term as Vice-President of the Royal Historical Society (1985–9) and to other roles including membership of the Victoria County History Advisory Committee and the Advisory Committee for the Public Records, and the chairmanship of the Friends of the Public Record Office. He was a prominent member of the York Archaeological Trust and was chair of the Trust during one of the busiest and most challenging periods of its development, between 1990 and 1996. His distinction as a scholar and his outstanding contribution to the profession were recognised in a high moment of his career with his election, in 1988, to the Fellowship of the British Academy.

The same year saw Barrie's appointment to the chair of Medieval History at the University of Cambridge. The move from York was a wrench, in several ways. Barrie had just taken over as Head of the Department of History, and his departure was a source of genuine sadness to his colleagues

[28] R. Horrox, 'Preface', in Horrox and Rees Jones, *Pragmatic Utopias*, pp. vii–viii, at p. viii.
[29] Pers. comm., Nigel Ramsay.

and friends in the North. The housing market also militated against a quick move, and it was only after some delay that Barrie and Narda were able to settle in their flat in Bateman Street, with its view (admittedly available only to those prepared to hang from the study window) of the spectacular roofscape stretching away to the chapel of King's College in the distance. After the relative informality of York's governance and the adaptability of its curriculum, the complexities of Cambridge and the Tripos system were a shock. So too with academic politics: a relatively cohesive group at York gave way to a strong tradition of individualism at Cambridge. Barrie's naturally conciliatory approach and quiet determination worked wonders, and he became a recognised force within the Faculty of History. He aimed to establish a firmer place for the history of the Church in Part I of the Tripos, and developed a new Special Subject on late medieval towns in Part II. He provided important leadership and direction for the taught M.Phil. in Medieval History, which had only recently been introduced. In all of this Barrie was guided and energised by two old friends: Christopher Brooke, FBA, who held the Dixie Chair of Ecclesiastic History, and Patrick Collinson, FBA, who arrived from Sheffield to the Regius Chair in Modern History in the year of Barrie's own appointment.[30]

Above all, the decade at Cambridge offered Barrie the opportunity to perform daily acts of assistance and kindness both to those in his charge and to those who, from across the globe, sought out his general advice and support. He was especially active in promoting the interests of the community of postdoctoral fellows and non-university teaching officers whose presence was so important to the success of the Cambridge History Faculty. The late 1980s and early 1990s saw few opportunities for the young generation of scholars to find positions in United Kingdom universities, and Barrie was indefatigable in his efforts to assist—not least by writing what must literally have been many hundreds of references. The counsel and encouragement offered to so many created its own virtuous circle, and medieval history continued to thrive across the university, with Barrie taking on the supervision of another generation of research students who went on to academic and writing careers, including John Aberth, Ruth Frost, Anthony Musson, Ben Nilson, Andrew Wines and Irene Zadnik. Barrie's decision to take a fellowship at Christ's College, driven initially by a natural affinity with a society founded at the end of the Middle Ages, also

---

[30] Barrie's contribution to the Brooke Festschrift was R. B. Dobson, 'Citizens and chantries in late medieval York', in D. Abulafia, M. J. Franklin and M. Rubin (eds.), *Church and City, 1000–1500: Essays in Honour of Christopher Brooke* (Cambridge, 1992), pp. 311–32.

proved socially and intellectually fruitful, and Barrie and Narda settled into a series of college friendships, above all a renewed acquaintance with the bursar, Graham Ballard (a contemporary of Narda's at Oxford and, like Barrie, a Wadham alumnus), and his wife Domini. Beyond Cambridge, Barrie was also much in demand as a speaker and session chair at important conferences organised by colleagues from North America, and increasingly from Japan, where Barrie did a lecture tour sponsored by the British Council in 1992. In 1994 he was able to develop a new set of international contacts when he took up a short Visiting Fellowship at Trinity College, Toronto.

Barrie's inaugural lecture at Cambridge, given in February 1990, had the title 'Preserving the Perishable: Contrasting Communities in Medieval England'.[31] It offered the opportunity to consider two lasting preoccupations in his work: the historian's responsibility as custodian of the historic fabric and the historic memory; and the nature and quality of community life in the Middle Ages. Margaret Thatcher's denial of the existence of society and the rampant individualism of the 1980s had raised interesting debates in academic circles about the cosier connotations of 'community' and provoked questions about the legitimacy and utility of the term in relation to the past. The medieval communities on which Barrie focused— monasteries, towns and universities—were formal collectives with their own corporate existence and their own strong sense of identity. None of this, of course, guaranteed that they were always necessarily functional and harmonious: as Barrie appreciated, major social or political disruptions such as the Peasants' Revolt or the depositions of medieval kings could often serve to expose and exacerbate latent stresses and blatant factionalism in a range of religious and secular institutions. This historical awareness, coupled with his acute perceptions of how collectivities flourish or fail, meant that the lecture had both deep historical insights and important contemporary resonances.

The lecture did more than inaugurate a period of office: it heralded a new phase of productivity in Barrie's scholarship. His Royal Historical Society lecture on 'English Monastic Cathedrals in the Fifteenth Century', published in 1991, drew together important work that had been in gestation over the previous decade on the prosopography of the religious orders

---

[31] R. B. Dobson, *Preserving the Perishable: Contrasting Communities in Medieval England. An Inaugural Lecture delivered in the University of Cambridge on 22 February 1990* (Cambridge, 1991).

in the later Middle Ages.[32] Meanwhile he had also further developed his longstanding interest in the monastic presence at the universities. 1992 saw the publication of his chapter on 'The religious orders, 1370–1540' in the official *History of the University of Oxford*, and this was followed up with a further detailed study of the members of Durham and Canterbury Colleges in 1997.[33] In 1995 came another magisterial study of monastic lives and personalities in his chapter towards the *History of Canterbury Cathedral*.[34] In 1999 Barrie published an illuminating study of 'The monastic orders in late medieval Cambridge' in the Festschrift for his esteemed York colleague, Gordon Leff.[35] The first of a number of volumes of Barrie's collected essays, *Church and Society in the Medieval North of England*, was published in 1996.[36] With further publications on urban history, medieval Jewry and Robin Hood, discussed above, the 1990s marked one of the most prolific periods in Barrie's writing career.

All of this was managed alongside an ever-expanding portfolio of duties and offices. A newly emergent feature of scholarly life in the Humanities during the 1990s was the large-scale project led by senior academics and staffed by specialist researchers. Barrie was in the vanguard of such developments. With the Cambridge historical geographer, Robin Glasscock, and a senior medievalist at the Public Record Office, David Crook, he set up the project known first as 'Lay Taxes in England and Wales' and later as 'Records of Government Taxation in England and Wales', which aimed to provide a definitive listing and complete place-name index of the extensive materials, covering the twelfth to the seventeenth centuries, in the Public Record Office series E 179. The existing search tools for the series were notoriously unreliable, and meant that a wide variety of users—local and family historians, historical geographers, social, economic and institutional historians—were often thwarted in their efforts to track down vitally important evidence relating to people,

[32] R. B. Dobson, 'English monastic cathedrals in the Fifteenth Century', *Transactions of the Royal Historical Society*, 6th series 1 (1991), 151–72.

[33] R. B. Dobson, 'The religious orders, 1370–1520', in J. Catto and R. Evans (eds.), *The History of the University of Oxford II: Late Medieval Oxford* (Oxford, 1992), pp. 539–79; R. B. Dobson, 'The Black Monks of Durham and Canterbury Colleges: comparisons and contrasts', in H. Wansbrough and A. Marett-Crosby (eds.), *Benedictines in Oxford* (London, 1997), pp. 61–78, 287–89.

[34] R. B. Dobson, 'The Monks of Canterbury in the later Middle Ages, 1220–1540', in P. Collinson, N. Ramsay and M. Sparks (eds.) *A History of Canterbury Cathedral* (Oxford, 1995), pp. 69–153.

[35] R. B. Dobson, 'The monastic orders in late medieval Cambridge', in P. Biller and R. B. Dobson (eds.), *The Medieval Church: Universities, Heresy, and the Religious Life. Essays in Honour of Gordon Leff*, Studies in Church History Subsidia, 11 (1999), 239–69.

[36] R. B. Dobson, *Church and Society in the Medieval North of England* (London, 1996).

places and taxes in medieval and early modern England. As the project developed it drew funding to Cambridge, London, York and Bangor from a wide variety of sources, including the Leverhulme Trust, the Economic and Social Research Council, the British Academy and the Arts & Humanities Research Board. Indeed, it took on an extraordinary life of its own that survived changes of name and function both among its funders and at its own archival headquarters, which transformed itself from the Public Record Office to The National Archives in 2003. The E 179 database is now a major online resource in the wider repertoire of search facilities offered by The National Archives, and the 'Records of Government Taxation' project has itself sponsored significant research in fiscal social and ecclesiastical history. Barrie remained active in the project throughout, and his 2000 article on aliens in York reflected his keen interest in the reconstruction of medieval lives from tax records.[37]

The energy and interest that Barrie gave to the E 179 project made him much in demand as adviser and chair for other major historical enterprises. He had long been involved with the British Academy's project, English Episcopal Acta, in which David Smith and Christopher Brooke were strongly associated, and he chaired the project from 1995 to 2007. The English Monastic Archives project, based at University College London, was similarly indebted to Barrie for his strong support over a decade of activity from its inception in 1999, as was Jeffrey Denton's major project housed at the University of Sheffield to edit the major assessment of clerical wealth in medieval England, the *Taxatio* of 1291. Barrie also became closely involved in the Harlaxton Medieval Symposium, an annual interdisciplinary conference founded by Pamela Tudor-Craig in 1983 and held at the British campus of the University of Evansville, outside Grantham. Barrie co-chaired the Symposium Committee with Andrew Martindale and after the latter's death in 1995 continued as chair until 2008. He worked closely with stalwarts of the symposium such as Janet Backhouse and Nigel Morgan and helped to bring in many new organisers and speakers from his extensive range of contacts in the UK and North America, including old friends such as Caroline Barron and Joel Rosenthal. He was especially attracted by the symposium's commitment to interdisciplinary studies, and contributed several important articles to the annual volumes of Harlaxton's proceedings: his 1999 essay on

---

[37] R. B. Dobson, 'Aliens in the city of York during the fifteenth century', in J. Mitchell and M. Moran (eds), *England and the Continent in the Middle Ages: Studies in Memory of Andrew Martindale*, Harlaxton Medieval Studies, 8 (Stamford, 2000), pp. 249–66.

monastic bishops and his 2003 study of 'Henry VI and the University of Cambridge', along with his article on aliens in York, nicely exemplify the continuing themes of Barrie's scholarship through the 1990s and on into the new millennium.[38]

In 1999 Barrie retired from Cambridge and he and Narda returned to live in York, taking up residence on St Olaves Road within a short walk of the city walls. The move brought them back into close contact with the University of York, which elected Barrie an Honorary Professor in the year of his return. Equally importantly, it enhanced family life. With Michelle and her husband Conrad close at hand in Leeds, Barrie was able to spend time with his young grandson, Theo; Mark, working in Bratislava, also bought a house in Leeds and was a regular visitor to his parents' new home. The retirement was marked with multiple appreciations of Barrie's extra-ordinary contribution. Sarah Rees Jones at York, and Barrie's Cambridge colleague, Rosemary Horrox, organised a memorable Festschrift under the title *Pragmatic Utopias: Ideals and Communities, 1200–1630*, which considered the lives and mental worlds of a wide variety of men and women from clergy and intellectuals, via Lollards and puritans, to indigents and criminals. The respect and affection that all the contributors shared was summed up in a notably warm appreciation from an old and trusted friend and collaborator, John Taylor.[39] Meanwhile, a number of other colleagues and former students drew together to publish *The Church in Medieval York: Records Edited in Honour of Professor Barrie Dobson*.[40] The 1999 Harlaxton Symposium chose to honour Barrie by adopting the theme of 'The Church and Learning in Later Medieval Society', and the resulting volume of essays, published in 2002, was formally dedicated to him.[41]

Barrie's retirement coincided with the honouring of a number of other esteemed former colleagues at York and other long-standing collaborators; Barrie co-edited the Festschrift for Gordon Leff, contributed the tribute to Claire Cross in the volume of *Studies in Church History* dedicated to her, and wrote a thoughtful comparison of the cults of St Cuthbert

[38] R. B. Dobson, 'English and Welsh monastic bishops: the final century, 1433–1533', in B. Thompson (ed.), *Monasteries and Society in Medieval Britain*, Harlaxton Medieval Studies, 6 (Stamford, 1999), pp. 348–67; R. B. Dobson, 'Henry VI and the University of Cambridge', in J. Stratford (ed.), *The Lancastrian Court*, Harlaxton Medieval Studies, 13 (Donington, 2003), pp. 53–67.

[39] Horrox and Rees Jones, *Pragmatic Utopias*.

[40] D. M. Smith (ed.), *The Church in Medieval York: Records Edited in Honour of Professor Barrie Dobson*, Borthwick Texts & Calendars, 24 (York, 1999).

[41] C. M. Barron and J. Stratford (eds.), *The Church and Learning in Later Medieval Society*, Harlaxton Medieval Studies, 12 (Donington, 2002).

and Thomas Becket for the essays in honour of John Bossy.[42] Slightly later he also published essays in the Harlaxton volume dedicated to Pamela Tudor-Craig and in the series of studies of medieval documents presented to Colin Richmond.[43] The irony of all this activity was not lost on this group of old friends: Claire Cross noted at a party in Barrie's honour how busy she had been kept writing not one but three essays for his Festschriften. Barrie's appreciation of the offerings made to him on his retirement was limited only by his own modesty in accepting them and by his own very clear determination—evident in the setting up of not one but two studies at the new house—to press on energetically with his own work. His conversations around this time suggested that his major ambition in retirement was to complete a book on cathedral chapters in England in the high and later Middle Ages. But while a number of the articles cited above were markers of this route, the final destination eluded him. Much in demand as fund-raiser, committee member and general public figure, Barrie continued to take genuine pleasure in helping others to achieve their personal and organisational goals. One journal that benefited greatly during this period from his general support was *Northern History*, which also published his study of 'The Northern Province in the later Middle Ages' in 2005.[44] In the same year he had the satisfaction of contributing the essay on the early years of his Cambridge college to the volume commissioned to mark the five-hundredth anniversary of the foundation of Christ's; his learned yet vivid evocation of the late medieval world of piety and learning provided a strong historical base to an intrinsically teleological project.[45] Barrie's last publication, a co-authored article on the religious houses of Kent, appeared in 2010, and in the same year Helen Birkett gathered together Barrie's earlier essays on medieval Jewry in a volume titled *The*

[42] Biller and Dobson, *The Medieval Church*; Dobson, 'Claire Cross: a tribute'; R. B. Dobson, 'Contrasting cults: St Cuthbert of Durham and St Thomas of Canterbury in the fifteenth century', in S. Ditchfield (ed.), *Christianity and Community in the West: Essays for John Bossy* (Aldershot, 2001), pp. 24–43.

[43] R. B. Dobson, '"The clergy are well lodged": the transformation of the cathedral precinct at late medieval Durham', in J. Backhouse (ed.), *The Medieval English Cathedral: Papers in Honour of Pamela Tudor-Craig*, Harlaxton Medieval Studies, 10 (Donington, 2003), pp. 2–40; R. B. Dobson, 'John Shirwood of York: a common clerk's will of 1473', in M. Aston and R. Horrox (eds.), *Much Heaving and Shoving: Late Medieval Gentry and their Concerns. Essays for Colin Richmond* (Chipping, 2005), pp. 109–20.

[44] R. B. Dobson, 'The Northern Province in the later Middle Ages', *Northern History*, 42 (2005), 49–60.

[45] R. B. Dobson, 'The foundation', in D. Reynolds (ed.), *Christ's: a Cambridge College over Five Centuries* (London, 2005), pp. 3–34.

Jewish Communities of Medieval England, with an appreciation by Joe Hillaby.[46]

A collaboration that bore particularly rich fruit after Barrie's return to York was that with the Director of the Borthwick Institute of Historical Research, David Smith. Barrie had been associated with the Company of Merchant Taylors of York since the 1980s, when he had been drawn in to assist with the ordering of the Company's archive and became a member. Two decades later, Barrie and David developed a plan for an academically robust and attractively presented account of the Merchant Taylors from the fourteenth to the twentieth century. Barrie recruited several former students and colleagues, including Heather Swanson, William Sheils and Edward Royle, wrote the chapter on the emergence of the company in the later Middle Ages, and organised much of the editing and production.[47] By the time of the launch in 2006, at a splendid event in the medieval surroundings of the Merchant Taylors' Hall, David Smith had retired, and in the meanwhile Barrie had collaborated with Christopher Brooke and with David's colleague at the Borthwick, Philippa Hoskin, to publish another notable volume of essays on English medieval ecclesiastical history.[48] In 2009 the Merchant Taylors' Hall was also the natural choice of venue for the generous party that Barrie and Narda organised to celebrate their golden wedding.

In December 2011 Barrie suffered a serious cardiac arrest that necessitated a long and difficult period of hospitalisation and rehabilitation. He was hugely relieved to return home but found some of the daily round difficult. He made sufficient recovery to enjoy a number of holidays, including a memorable trip to St Andrews with his son Mark. But some of the impairments were more lasting, and it was a particular source of frustration to all that he found it increasingly difficult to read. Family and friends rallied to assist: Barrie loved spending time with his grandson Theo, and close friends such as Mark Christodoulou and Beth Izak would share conversation and read aloud. Barrie became increasingly frail over the following winter and eventually died, at home, on Good Friday, 29 March

[46] R. B. Dobson and E. Edwards, 'The religious houses of Kent, 1220–1540', in S. Sweetinburgh (ed.), *Later Medieval Kent, 1220–1540*, Kent History Project, 9 (Woodbridge, 2010), pp. 79–110; R. B. Dobson, *The Jewish Communities of Medieval England: the Collected Essays of R. B. Dobson*, Borthwick Texts and Studies, 39 (York, 2010).
[47] R. B. Dobson (ed.), *The Merchant Tailors of York: a History of the Craft and Company from the Fourteenth to the Twentieth Century*, Borthwick Texts and Studies, 33 (York, 2006), including Dobson's 'The tailors of medieval York: from craft to company', pp. 23–51.
[48] P. M. Hoskin, C. N. L. Brooke and R. B. Dobson (eds.), *The Foundations of Medieval English Ecclesiastical History: Studies Presented to David Smith* (Woodbridge, 2005).

2013. The funeral was held at the St Saviourgate Unitarian Chapel in York on 16 April. Friends and colleagues, including David Parry, Peter Biller and Caroline Barron, spoke thoughtfully and affectionately of the different stages and aspects of Barrie's life; and Theo, rapidly emerging as an exceptionally talented young musician, performed a touching tribute to his grandfather.

If Barrie Dobson's public legacy lies in his enduring contribution to the study and understanding of medieval history, the abiding memory for all those who knew him rests inevitably in the integrity and warmth of his personality. Barrie had many pleasures in his life. When their families were young, he and John Taylor would take the boys off to watch Leeds United play at home; throughout his life, he enjoyed chess and took a serious interest in the game, playing avidly with John Bossy and other friends. The regular retreats to the Lake District for long, vigorous regimes of walking continued for many years; his other great outdoor pursuit was architecture, and his students and friends appreciated his special ability to 'bring stones to life' on tours of the great cathedrals and monasteries of the British Isles. The interest in film that Barrie had developed as a young man in Oxford and London also made him a leading campaigner for the development of an arts cinema in York. He was instrumental both in the foundation of a branch of the National Film Theatre in the city in 1968 and in seeking out civic support and participation in the venture. His passion for jazz led him, when in London, to Ronnie Scott's; and his penchant for a variety of literary forms from poetry to detective novels made him an avid book collector. His delight in words is evident in his academic writing and his private correspondence. He wrote and spoke in highly complex sentences: in the higher reaches of the university administration at York, he was affectionately known as 'Subordinate Clause Barrie'.[49] He had a wonderful story about being mistaken for Marlon Brando in the Harlem Apollo, which he recounted with a sharply self-deprecating wit. And his letters were full of mischievous asides. In 2008 he wrote to invite some friends from London to visit him and Narda: 'We could drive to all parts of Yorkshire from Holderness and Whitby to Haworth—which apparently worshippers of the Brontës now only visit at the cost of having their cars clamped.'[50] In his conversation, he was a master of the dry aside and the revealing anecdote, without ever resorting to the spiteful or the merely gossipy. Above all, he never dwelt on his own achievements or tribulations

[49] Pers. comm., David Foster.
[50] Pers. comm., Nigel Ramsay.

but always inquired about others: as everyone who knew him remarks, he was genuinely interested in the world around him and had the special gift of making one feel the most interesting and important person in the room. His fortunate and unusual combination of intellectual power and personal modesty made him an impeccable scholar, an inspiring teacher and a delightful friend.

W. MARK ORMROD
University of York

Note.   I am grateful to Graham Ballard, Peter Biller, FBA, Patricia Cullum, Cliff Davies, Ken Emond, David Foster, Ruth Frost, Jeremy Goldberg, Rosemary Hayes, Philippa Hoskin, Rosemary Horrox, Beth Izak, Anthony Musson, David Parry, Nigel Ramsay, David Reynolds, FBA, Sarah Rees Jones, Brigette Vale and the Dobson family, above all Narda Dobson, for sharing their memories of Barrie and providing much information on the facts and features of his career. Unless otherwise cited, sources and quotations are from Barrie Dobson's personal papers in the custody of his family. Barrie published variously as R. B., R. Barrie and Barrie Dobson; unless otherwise stated, all works cited here were under his sole authorship or editorship.

JOHN EHRMAN

John Patrick William Ehrman
1920–2011

JOHN EHRMAN was born in London on 17 March 1920, the only child of Albert and Rina (née Bendit) Ehrman. His paternal grandfather, whose forebears had been settled near the Rhine in Frankfurt, Württenburg and Alsace, migrated to England in the mid-nineteenth century and founded with an English partner a merchant firm specialising in the supply of industrial diamonds. It was the first such firm in England and became very successful. His only son, Albert, was called away from Charterhouse in 1906 to join the firm in High Holborn. Albert Ehrman was a cultivated man. Business trips to Amsterdam and Paris enabled him to learn Dutch and French, and he never forgot his school Latin. He married Rina in April 1919 and moved to the small town of Broxbourne, Hertfordshire. While 'recovering from a bout of influenza in Eastbourne' he saw in a bookstore by 'happy chance' a folio volume published in Venice in 1472; attracted by the beauty of the typography, he purchased it. A love of these early books combined with a developing enthusiasm for 'learning about the invention and spread of printing' led to an extensive and important collection of incunabula and other rare books which, for convenience of brevity, he named the Broxbourne Library.[1] With Rina and their son, John, he soon moved to London, residing at 38 Lowndes Street. But Albert Ehrman was fond of sailing and had taken instruction in navigation—as a boy at Charterhouse he had hoped to become a naval architect. In 1936 he built a house at Clobb Copse, Buckler's Hard on the Beaulieu

[1] A. Ehrman, 'Contemporary collectors II: The Broxbourne Library,' *The Book Collector* 3.3 (Autumn 1954), 190–1.

River in Hampshire and soon added a structure to house the Broxbourne Library. In due course he also found time to design a series of motor yachts for himself. Thus, while continuing to manage a successful business, he 'pursued his twin loves of boats and books'. Sixty years later, John Ehrman would write: 'I grew up, in London and on the banks of the Beaulieu River in Hampshire, against this dual background; when in London, a world of book collectors and curators, publishers and some of their authors and illustrators.'[2]

From an early age John Ehrman enjoyed reading history and was increasingly drawn to English history from the seventeenth to the nineteenth centuries. Entering Charterhouse in 1933 he became a 'History specialist' and had the good fortune to study under John Morgan and Robert Birley (later Sir Robert). There can be no doubt that he enjoyed his days at Charterhouse. In his last year he triumphed in the public schools sailing championship. His delight in wit and humour were scarcely suppressible. In 1983, Ian Wallace recalled that as a member of a small group of Sixth Form History Specialists he was 'forbidden to sit next to one of the outstanding historians of his generation, John Ehrman, because the resultant helpless laughter quickly infected' others. It was quite a group, gaining five entrance awards to Oxford and Cambridge. Two did not survive the war. Lawrence Stone became a historian of great distinction at Oxford and Princeton. Ian Bryce Wallace became an actor excelling in comic parts, a (bass-baritone) opera favourite, and the star of the BBC Radio 4 quiz show 'My Music'.[3] Those familiar with Wallace's unfailing good nature and robust sense of fun can readily understand why Ehrman was unable to stifle his laughter. In summer 1939 Ehrman and Wallace walked in the Cotswolds and travelled in America together.

Ehrman went up to Trinity College, Cambridge in autumn 1938. He had joined the Royal Navy Volunteer Reserve in the summer. He expected to be called up when war broke out in September 1939, but the government's policy for university students allowed him to finish a second year and take the examinations for Part I of the History Tripos, in which he earned a Starred First. He later observed: 'I thus had the advantage of two years under supervisors who included Philip Grierson, Charles Smyth, and above all, and influentially, George Kitson Clark.'[4]

[2] John Ehrman, British Academy memorandum lodged with the Academy in 1996.
[3] Ian Wallace's obituary of Michael Trollope in *The Carthusian*, Dec. 1983.
[4] Ehrman, British Academy memorandum.

Immediately after completing his examinations in June 1940 he was ordered to HMS *King Alfred* in Hove and from there to duty as an acting sub-lieutenant, reporting aboard HMS *Gloxinia* (K 22) on 8 August 1940, a fortnight before she was commissioned. The *Gloxinia* was a Flower-Class corvette. In 1939–40 the Royal Navy ordered hundreds of these small escort vessels to be built. Nicholas Monsarrat, author of *The Cruel Sea* (also from Trinity College, Cambridge but ten years older), was appointed to an almost identical corvette commissioned a fortnight later. As sailors remarked, 'A corvette would roll on wet grass.'[5] Thus the only offspring of Albert and Rina Ehrman was embarked in a small ship of war in dangerous seas. They were probably not able to see him off. From 1940 to 1942 they were in New York, where the firm had an office. Years before the war, apprehensive about international developments, Albert Ehrman had refused to sell industrial diamonds to Germany or Russia; his mission in 1940 was to ensure that the United Kingdom would be well supplied and that no diamonds would go to the Axis powers.[6] The Ehrmans also supported national defence by donating two 'presentation' Spitfires and two Fulmars, each plane reckoned by Lord Beaverbrook's scheme to cost £5,000.[7]

John Ehrman reported to his ship in Londonderry. Walking from the train station to the base he met with a nasty surprise, being pelted with rotten vegetables and probably worse because he had made the mistake of walking down 'a Catholic street'. The *Gloxinia* put to sea on 27 August and within a month was picking up survivors from two torpedoed vessels in its convoy.

After two and a half months of North Atlantic service the ship was assigned to the Mediterranean. She escorted supply ships from Gibraltar to Malta and assisted, in early 1941, the resupply of British forces defending Greece. Soon these forces had to be hurriedly evacuated, and small ships like *Gloxinia* were essential because minor Greek ports had to be used. These were hazardous missions. There was no air cover, so embarkations had to be done at night and as the ships sailed away in morning daylight they were bombed relentlessly by the German aircraft. Ehrman's ship missed the horrendous evacuation of Crete. She had been ordered to

---

[5] N. Monsarrat, *Monsarrat at Sea* (London, 1975), p. 26.
[6] N. Barker, 'Albert Ehrman, 6 February 1890–12 August 1969', *The Book Collector* (Winter, 1970), 458.
[7] H. Boot and R. Sturtivant, *Gifts of War: Spitfires and other Presentation Aircraft in Two World Wars* (Tonbridge, 2005), notes the Ehrman gifts (pp. 28, 227, 368, 384). Their gift of Fulmars, navy carrier-based aircraft, was almost unique.

Malta where the Grand Harbour was closed by mines; convoyed supplies
could not get in and a squadron of destroyers could not get out. *Gloxinia*
was specially equipped for magnetic mine-sweeping. Experimentally, on 9
May, depth charges were dropped by an assemblage of small vessels to
detonate the mines.

> The scheme was a triumphant success . . . It has to be recorded, however, that
> when the *Gloxinia*, towing her magnetic sweep, or 'fluffing her tail', as they
> called it, led the convoy into harbour the next day, nearly a dozen more mines
> went up as she steamed through the breakwater entrance.[8]

Shortly thereafter she was damaged by an acoustical mine and slated for
repair in Malta Dockyard. Since Malta was under continual aerial bom-
bardment in 1941 the work went slowly, and personnel understandably
complained of lack of sleep—evidently not John Ehrman, who was able
to sleep well all his life; this may have been the occasion when, off duty, he
slept through the moment when a bomb fell on his ship. He was promoted
to lieutenant in January 1942. During the early months of the year the
ship operated with the 'Inshore Squadron' that convoyed supplies from
Alexandria to beleaguered Tobruk, where she was also engaged in mine-
sweeping. On this service there was danger from both air and submarine
attack, but *Gloxinia* was unscathed. In June she was assigned to escorting
Levant convoys. Probably in April 1943 Ehrman left her under orders for
re-appointment.

After completing the specialised navigation course at Portsmouth he
became navigating and staff officer of an Atlantic Escort Group on board
HMS *Enchantress* (L 56). Mainly she supervised convoys which ran
between Freetown and Gibraltar, often stopping at Dakar and Casablanca.
It was a relatively safe and comfortable service, but at least once the group
was assigned to the dangerous Gibraltar–Londonderry route. Ehrman's
next appointment was ashore. In summer 1944 he became an instructor at
HMS *Dryad*, the Navigation School at Southwick House near Portsmouth.
Before long he was selected to join a team that was doing pioneering work
for the Action Information Organisation (AIO) in developing shipboard
operations rooms. The new system was essentially made necessary by
radar; a similar development, the Combat Information Center (CIC), was
occurring in the US Navy. In the months before Ehrman joined the team
a number of mock-ups had been created for various classes of ships, but

[8] A. B. Cunningham, *A Sailor's Odyssey: the Autobiography of Admiral of the Fleet Viscount Cunningham of Hyndhope* (New York, 1951), p. 361. Cunningham was Commander-in-Chief in the Mediterranean.

it was clearly a work in progress. Reflecting back upon it decades later, Ehrman wrote: 'I found the experience of considerable interest.'[9]

War, strategy and government

Ehrman was listed for early demobilisation at the request of Trinity College, Cambridge. The government knew that university teachers would be needed to meet the expected post-war influx of students. He arrived shortly after the start of the academic year in autumn 1945, eager to embark on historical research. But he needed a topic. The Regius Professor of Modern History, G. N. Clark, who had come from Oxford in 1943 and became a fellow of the college, suggested 'something maritime', and Ehrman, because he had served in the Mediterranean, thought of 'the survival of Venice's island colonies in the prolonged period of the city's decline'.[10] But the postwar situation of the Venetian archives seemed uncertain and Clark then suggested studying the navy during the early years of the Board of Admiralty when Samuel Pepys was no longer the leading administrator. The result was *The Navy in the War of William III: its State and Direction 1689–1697*, published by Cambridge University Press in 1953.

It is a long book, 622 pages of text. Ehrman conducted research and wrote at amazing speed, holding his pen with heavy gloves during the hard winter of early 1947. He was elected a fellow of the college later that year and began teaching undergraduates in the autumn. He might have taken time to reduce the long manuscript to conform to the university's word limit for Ph.D. theses but chose not to do so.

The book stands as an essential foundation for the history of modern British naval administration. In fact it is much more than this. It integrates the history of new administrative challenges with the navy's operational history—encompassing, for instance, the unprecedented achievement of wintering a battlefleet at Cadiz in 1694–5—while relating all this to the violent political upheavals that disturbed the navy's leadership after 1688. Furthermore—this may be its most significant contribution—it traces in substantive detail how the navy's rapid growth in size and expense during the 1690s prompted the development of all-important financial institutions upon which the power of Great Britain would thereafter depend.

[9] Ehrman, British Academy memorandum.
[10] Ibid.

Parliament's role in this was fundamental, and the modernised British navy, as its leading present-day historian has observed, was (unlike the army) an institution answerable to Parliament more than the monarch.[11] Ehrman's study probes the proceedings, contentious and chaotic, which shaped the crucial early years of administrative development. He notes that the Commissions of Public Accounts appointed by the House of Commons to scrutinise expenditures, though troublesome and sometimes behaving as misinformed nuisances, were charged with attempting to understand the navy's real needs. It helped that Parliament and public, despite misgivings about William III's strategic priorities, realised that the future of the realm as a protestant polity was at stake and that survival depended on a strong navy.

Yet Parliament's financial support, however strongly motivated, was chronically inadequate. Ehrman shows how credit crises compelled naval and Treasury administrators to acquiesce in financial methods that were suited to capital-market expectations, methods suggested by bankers and merchants. The pressures on government were immense. When, in 1694, the Navy Board's credit was completely exhausted all the merchants held back from tendering and delivering urgently needed naval stores. These naval contractors—mainly men of the City—were the only people who might provide a rescue.

Chief among the various proposals was a new institution, the Bank of England. Its foundation in May 1694 has been generally treated by historians as a milestone in the history of monetary and financial innovation and as a means of providing large wartime loans. Ehrman focuses on something else: how the Bank's issuance of paper notes transformed the navy's indebtedness. He gives prominence to the Bank's role in absorbing myriad tallies issued by the Navy Board. By this point in the war masses of tallies registering debts owed to merchants could only be cashed at a distant date, some being assigned to revenue funds so anaemic that eventual payment seemed hopeless. A great deal of potential wealth was thereby 'locked up in large bundles of wooden sticks . . . awaiting redemption'. The solution was 'the negotiable paper bill', but of course creditors had to be willing to trust it. 'With the emergence of the Bank of England . . . and the circulation of . . . powerful Bank of England notes, an answer was to be found.' In effect, the Bank united 'Parliamentary financial responsibility and departmental credit' (pp. 489–90). Later in the war an

[11] N. A. M. Rodger, *The Command of the Ocean: a Naval History of Britain, 1649–1815* (London, 2004), p. 579.

unavoidable but inefficient recoinage left the realm without hard money. The navy was unable to pay wages and the Bank again came to the rescue; in return it was given permanent privileges that insured its standing and future usefulness to the British state.

At least one-quarter of the book is concerned with naval materials, wages and financial problems. In discussing these Ehrman reveals his awareness that the interactions of Navy, Treasury and Parliament as they faced the dire challenges of the war of 1689–97 had an enormous long-term impact on the British state. Most reviewers in 1953–4 did not comment on this, though one did: 'William's reign witnessed a most remarkable development in government administration, but this vital change has been so neglected by historians that far more is known of the administration of Edward II than of William III.'[12] Arguably, the book's greatest achievement is to highlight a momentous stride in what has been described as 'the largest, longest, most complex and expensive project ever undertaken by the British state and society'.[13]

The manuscript was practically complete when Ehrman accepted an offer to write the final volumes on *Grand Strategy* for the official history of the Second World War. The offer was made by the general editor of the United Kingdom Military Series, Professor J. R. M. Butler, who became Regius Professor of Modern History at Cambridge in 1947; he had been a fellow of Trinity for many years and knew Ehrman well. Butler's selection of this relatively young scholar bespoke confidence in him as a careful historian who seemed likely to cope courteously yet firmly with criticisms made by high-ranking officers and distinguished statesmen. Most of these men were still living and would be allowed to comment on the finished draft. The work, supervised by the historical branch of the Cabinet Office, would be done in London. On 24 April 1948 Ehrman resigned his Trinity fellowship.

By this time he was engaged to be married to Susan Blake. It might be thought that he met her at a social gathering of persons involved in producing the Military Series because her father, Vice-Admiral Sir Geoffrey Blake, was a service adviser to the series, but in fact Ehrman met her during vacation time at Buckler's Hard. The Blakes and Ehrmans possessed adjacent mooring locations, and one day after she came in from crewing for her father John Ehrman offered to carry up the sails for stowage. A theatre invitation followed the next day and after five dates he proposed.

---

[12] J. H. Plumb in *The Spectator*, July 31, 1953, p. 138.
[13] Rodger, *Command of the Ocean*, p. lxv.

Learning that she wanted to accept, her father wrote to the renowned historian, Professor G. M. Trevelyan, Master of Trinity College, asking him about the young man. Trevelyan's reply was emphatically positive. The marriage took place on 1 July 1948. In 1954 the couple made their home at Sloane House in Chelsea. During the 1950s four sons were born: William, Hugh, Richard and Thomas.

The history of *Grand Strategy* in the last two years of the war required two volumes. Volume V begins in August 1943.[14] At this point Allied maritime and air superiority had been achieved, so the range of choices for land campaigns was broad. Ehrman believed that he should include options to which the strategic planners gave serious consideration before setting them aside; he warned readers that this might seem unnecessary and tedious in hindsight but argued that omitting them would present a distorted picture of the high-level deliberations. As a result, many pages of these two volumes deal with regions that the American strategists were inclined to call 'side-shows'.

The Americans' focus was on invading northwest Europe—Operation Overlord—and they feared that British interest in the Mediterranean might subvert and therefore postpone it. The question of whether Britain's leadership was properly supportive of Overlord has generated an enduring historical controversy. It had already begun when Ehrman addressed it in the early 1950s:

> It is important to be clear on this. Much was said at the time, and has since been written, on British, and particularly Churchillian, strategy in the Mediterranean during this period, which is misleading not only for the period but for the same problem in later periods. (*Grand Strategy*, V, p. 111)

He began by observing that British and American strategists fully agreed that Overlord's success depended on a diversion—on preventing the Germans from building up military strength in northwest Europe. The dispute was chiefly over how best to achieve this. The British thought the best way was to campaign in Italy. They had to admit that the offensive had stalled south of Rome but pointed out the main reason for this: the Germans had added divisions in Italy—which for the sake of Overlord was of course what was wanted. The Americans did not entirely agree. They pressed for a landing in the south of France, Operation Anvil. To this the British objected that pressure on the German lines in Italy would

---

[14] *History of the Second World War, United Kingdom Military Series*, ed. J. R. M. Butler. J. Ehrman, *Grand Strategy: Volume V, August 1943–September 1944* (London, 1956), Preface dated November 1955.

be diminished as forces would be withdrawn to prepare for Anvil and must remain inactive until the time of its launching.

Some American leaders feared that the British intended to substitute a push through the Balkans as an alternative to Overlord. Ehrman found that prior to the Normandy landings nothing beyond supplying arms to guerrilla forces was planned. Churchill sometimes talked as if he would prefer action in the Balkans and also wished to mount minor operations in the Aegean Sea with the hope of bringing Turkey out of neutrality, and all this made the Americans suspicious. Eighty days after the Normandy landings, however, Churchill seriously urged a thrust towards Vienna that would involve the northern Balkans. It was proposed with an eye on the postwar world (*Grand Strategy*, V, pp. 392–4). When British leaders gave it serious consideration Russian armies were in Romania and Stalin's forces were standing off and allowing the Warsaw uprising to be crushed.

The British made strenuous efforts to drop weapons and supplies into Warsaw to help the insurgents. Stalin refused to make convenient landing fields available. Ehrman reports that British leaders were deeply angry; the War Cabinet even considered stopping the Arctic convoys to Russia. At the end of his account Ehrman felt a need to write: 'The beginning of the last message from Warsaw deserves to be recorded. "This is the stark truth. We were worse treated than Hitler's satellites, worse than Italy, Rumania, Finland."' Ehrman's final observation: '[R]elations between Britain and Russia suffered a shock from which they never fully recovered' (*Grand Strategy*, V, pp. 369–76).

Throughout his discussion of strategic options Ehrman, as he states in his Preface, was intent on 'seeing each step against the background of resources, within whose iron limits the actors moved' (*Grand Strategy*, V, xiii–xv). The shortage of assault shipping, especially Landing Ships, Tanks (LSTs), is a recurring theme throughout the book. It has been suggested by some historians that the shortage of these in Europe was exaggerated by British military planners in order to postpone Overlord, but Ehrman's history shows that their planning was repeatedly constrained by its realities. It is interesting that Roosevelt's choice of Eisenhower, who paid close attention to logistics, to command Overlord was judged by Ehrman to be 'perhaps one of his best' appointments (*Grand Strategy*, V, p. 201).

Publication of this volume was delayed by Sir Winston Churchill. He had agreed that the official historians could look at his 'personal minutes and telegrams' but only on the understanding that any extracts or 'substantial use' made of these documents should be shown to him for approval

before publication. Having seen a critical account by Sir Stephen Roskill
of his decisions concerning naval strategy, he developed a loosely para-
noid view of the motives of the official historians, and while he was still
prime minister Ehrman's study of 1943–4 became 'the prime target'. But
he relented in August 1955 and allowed the relevant volumes to be
examined and approved by trusted persons.[15]

Among topics traced by the final volume are:[16] continuing disputes
over bombing strategy—railway versus oil targets—and RAF Bomber
Command's persistent favouring of area bombing. (These issues would be
fully explored in a later official history, *The Strategic Air Offensive Against
Germany, 1939–1945* by Charles Webster and Noble Frankland: London,
1961.) Also in the realm of strategy, Ehrman pays close attention to
Eisenhower's preference for attacking in the southern sectors where the
German army left its defences weak over Bernard Montgomery's steady
insistence on attacking in the northern sector where enemy concentrations
were strongest. He notes the importance of logistics in defining the limits
of penetration in the southern sector.

Matters affecting postwar positioning are prominent, such as the ultimate success of Britain's sustained interest in Greece and Churchill's
urgent desire to take Vienna before the Russians did. The conclusion
regarding Burma is interesting. Although the years of brutal fighting by
British and Commonwealth forces in the mountainous jungles were eventually crowned by a remarkable success as the Japanese were pushed out,
Ehrman ends by asking whether it was all worthwhile, since action in this
theatre could not contribute directly to Japan's surrender. He answers by
citing its diplomatic and military advantages, not least the tremendous
losses sustained by the Japanese army in the theatre (*Grand Strategy*, VI,
pp. 256–7).

Another prominent theme is the discussion of plans for British participation alongside the Americans in the effort to defeat Japan, most of the
plans rendered irrelevant when the war suddenly ended after atomic
bombs were dropped on Hiroshima and Nagasaki in August 1945. In
early 1951 Ehrman realised that this fact presented him with a problem:
how could he properly write a history of grand strategy in the final year of

---

[15] D. Reynolds, *In Command of History: Churchill Fighting and Writing the Second World War*
(New York, 2005), pp. 516–17.
[16] J. Ehrman, *Grand Strategy: Volume VI, October 1944–August 1945* (London, 1956), Preface
dated March 1956.

the war without discussing the decision to drop the atomic bomb which ended it?

He presented the problem to his general editor, J. R. M. Butler, who, on 21 March 1951, drafted a minute for the Cabinet Secretary responsible for the official histories, Norman Brook. Ehrman had volunteered to write about the decision to drop the bomb. He was directed to proceed and, evidently, was encouraged to explore the circumstances under which British scientists (many of them refugees from Europe) who had led the way in research on atomic energy turned their knowledge over to the Americans. But his main concern was the decision to drop it. There existed agreements between London and Washington, particularly one that Franklin Roosevelt signed at Quebec in August 1943, promising that the British government would be consulted before a decision to use the bomb was made: 'These agreements, though concluded during the war, were still very much of a live issue in international politics' and they were still kept secret, Brook minuted. (At this time speculation as to whether American bombers at East Anglian air bases were carrying atomic bombs was of intense public interest in Britain.) It was decided that Ehrman's book would be restricted to internal government use only.[17]

Since his primary concern was to be able to write a chapter on the decision in his official history, the difficult question of clearance remained, and on 8 January 1953 he wrote to Professor Butler, laying out the problem. 'To say nothing of the decision that ended the war would be an undoubted gap in the official history of the war. Nor do I think, on reflection, that the Western Allies need be unduly ashamed of their reasons, which (in my opinion) can bear scrutiny.' There were, however, 'three possible objections'. First, 'a published account must include all or nothing'. The factors justifying the decision were complex and omissions would 'lead to distortion . . . It would therefore, I think be extremely difficult and unwise, as well as dishonest, to write a partial account; and I could not consent to do so.' A second objection was that the wartime agreements between the British and the Americans were still secret. Third, since the British were only partially involved, the account 'cannot hope to be based on all the available evidence. This is an undoubted drawback, particularly in a delicate and controversial subject.'[18] These were powerful

---

[17] J. Ehrman, *The Atomic Bomb: an Account of British Policy in the Second World War*. The Preface is dated July 1953. The book remained classified as Top Secret until the early 1990s.
[18] These documents and others involving Ehrman's proposals are to be found in TNA CAB 140/61.

objections, and how the chapter managed to be approved for publication in Volume VI cannot be traced here, but it may be said that whole pages of the Top Secret book appear in it.

As his work on *Grand Strategy* was coming to an end Ehrman was honoured to be asked to give the Lees Knowles Lectures in Military History at Trinity College, Cambridge. The four lectures, delivered in 1957, were published.[19] He began by observing that strategic planning for armed defence of Britain and its empire had been virtually absent during the half-century before 1890, and ended by observing: thus, 'one of the three classic activities of government, after a long period of disuse' was brought 'into the framework' in a way that preserved the traditional attributes and authority of Britain's system of cabinet government (p. 132). His attention to persons was limited to 'a small group of men'—Arthur Balfour, Robert Haldane, David Lloyd George, Winston Churchill, George Sydenham Clarke and Maurice Hankey ('above all Hankey')— who moved the process forward and a few others who obstructed it. But the focus is on structure, not men, nor even political situations or intractable issues.

The book's concern with structure exposes the way in which the presence of the Committee of Imperial Defence (CID) obscured the need for the Cabinet to deal with the fundamental requirements of national and imperial security. As Ehrman points out, the CID 'had developed as an alternative to, rather than as a regular instrument of, the Cabinet in strategic affairs', yet only the Cabinet could make the basic decisions. It failed to do so. Foreign policy wound up being excluded from discussion by Sir Edward Grey and the Foreign Office—most Cabinet members, preoccupied by domestic policy, were willing to allow this—and the CID, although 'set up to consider problems of strategy in general . . . [became] increasingly involved in the detailed preparations for a specific campaign', namely the sending of regiments to support France on the Continent. One sees why, when war broke out, the CID and its sub-committees were scarcely consulted; instead, the Cabinet resorted to a 'formless search for professional advice' (pp. 52, 54, 57). Lurking in the background is the fact that Britain's unique situation—global yet European—presented choices so profoundly divergent that no system of committees, not even the Cabinet, could have reached a consensus without enormous strain.

Aware that Ehrman had been one of the official historians, Robert Blake regretted that the book's scope did not extend to 1945: 'the reader

---

[19] J. Ehrman, *Cabinet Government and War, 1890–1940* (Cambridge, 1958).

longs to know what he would have said about Sir Winston Churchill's war-time administration'.[20] Perhaps this gave Ehrman the idea for a paper he read to the Royal Historical Society on 8 October 1960, 'Lloyd George and Churchill as War Ministers'.[21] This beautifully written paper looks at the two statesmen with sensitivity, deep knowledge and wise perception. 'Both,' Ehrman writes, 'had that rare and indefinable quality, of catching the imagination of their times' (p. 102) and both had a remarkable capacity to 'inspire, and at least sustain, the morale of the nation' (p. 105). But, Ehrman then observed,

> inspiration by itself is not enough . . .; [it] will fail after quite a short time if it is not based on competence, . . . [so a leading war minister] needs knowledge and experience, as well as imaginative flair . . . Both Lloyd George and Churchill, it is well known, possessed the imaginative flair. It is not so often appreciated to what extent they also possessed the knowledge and experience . . . Both in fact were very good administrators for war. (pp. 106–7)

When concluding this paper Ehrman remarked that it is often asked 'which of these two wartime Prime Ministers was the greater'. His response was (for him) predictable and interesting: 'It is not a question I should like to answer', and he added, 'Nor is it, I suspect, the sort of question that historians think should be asked, at least of them.' Instead, he offered a reflection: '[I]t is fortunate, for the survival of the country itself and of its traditional institutions in this century, that the normal political world should have thrown up such a figure on each occasion, to work within its framework and to preserve by his unusual methods a tried and familiar form of government' (p. 115). He avoided saying which wartime Prime Minister was the greater while giving his audience the means to decide. Yet one may detect a preference for Churchill:

> He was far more generous in big issues, more loyal to his associates, possessed of much greater humanity, than one who was, as Keynes divined, ultimately remorseless and rootless . . . The central sanity of his character—supported and strengthened, I think, by his historical sense, a quality entirely lacking in Lloyd George—became increasingly apparent as time went by. So did the central irresponsibility of Lloyd George. (pp. 104–5)

Two months after presenting this paper John Ehrman was struck down by poliomyelitis and the doctors were fighting for his life. An early breathing apparatus had to be utilised. (The four boys had received the vaccine but he had not.) While immobilised he recorded books for the

[20] *The Spectator*, 18 April 1958.
[21] *Transactions of the Royal Historical Society* 5th series, 11 (1961), 101–15.

blind. Upon recovery he no longer had the use of one leg.[22] But he was determined to remain as active as possible. Outings in rough terrain were eagerly anticipated, and he and Susan soon purchased an old house on a hillside in Corfu and restored it; it became a favourite spring and late-summer retreat for the remainder of their lives together.

The Younger Pitt

When the author asked Susan Ehrman why her late husband chose to study the younger Pitt her reply was swift and succinct: 'He always wanted to do Pitt.' He undoubtedly pondered it from time to time during the years 1948–57 when he was engaged in historical tasks chosen for him by others. The question remains: why Pitt? In reality he never publicly provided an answer except to say in the Preface of the first volume that 'various developments in our knowledge of his times enabled us to look again' at how Pitt 'met the conditions and turned them to advantage'.[23] This was more like a justification of his choice than an enticement.

A reviewer of the final volume mused 'Writer and subject are so comfortable with one another that the reader imagines them shaking hands on their first meeting in Elysium.'[24] Yet personal affinity had its limits—quiet and steady bearing, genuine competence, and gentlemanly conduct, to be sure, though Pitt too often did not treat people he met with appropriate courtesy whereas John Ehrman always did. Regarding personal life, Ehrman was lucky enough to marry the woman he loved and, as their eldest son said at the funeral, 'For 63 years they found the key to happiness, working as a pair, always full of joy in each other's company.' In contrast, the Younger Pitt appears to have been for reasons unknown—and quite unlike his father—terrified by the thought of acquiring a female partner.

Ehrman's principal motive lay in the public sphere. When he returned to Cambridge in 1945 he had thoughts of 'trying to do something on Harley and the politics of Queen Anne's reign', but G. N. Clark dissuaded

---

[22] I recall being shocked to see him on forearm crutches in the early 1960s. He had been my Cambridge Ph.D. supervisor to whom I had been referred by George Kitson Clark, who had taught him before the war. My draft chapters were discussed in an upstairs room at the Garrick Club after a nice lunch.

[23] J. Ehrman, *The Younger Pitt: the Years of Acclaim* (London and New York, 1969), p. xii.

[24] *The Economist*, 20 July 1996.

him on the ground that it would be 'full of dangers for a neophyte'.[25] It is likely that at Charterhouse and Cambridge he had learned that Harley was a politician who also cared greatly about policy. Pitt's durable and conscientious commitment to responsible governing undoubtedly attracted Ehrman: the predominant concern of all three volumes is to ascertain the challenges that Pitt assiduously laboured to meet.

Possibly this enquiry may be carried further, into the sphere of personal political values. In a letter to me in January 1976 Ehrman remarked, probably in response to some comment I had made about the deplorable state of politics in both Britain and America at that time: 'I disagree with Dr. Johnson about the effect of public affairs on private satisfactions.'[26] He may have been referring to the couplet wherein Johnson observed how little of what 'human hearts endure, . . . laws or kings can cause or cure' or had in mind the assertion that 'living under one form of government rather than another' is 'of no moment to the happiness of an individual', perhaps both. In any case, he knew that William Pitt the Younger avowed the English constitution as forged in the Revolution Settlement of 1689 to be his guide. That Ehrman himself placed a high value on the English constitution is evident in the closing paragraph of his paper on Lloyd George and Churchill where he made it a point to observe that, despite the dire challenges of the world wars, both men preserved the constitution's essentials.[27]

The first volume was published in 1969. A number of reviewers did not comprehend Ehrman's purpose. Some thought the book too long; others complained that Pitt was insufficiently visible.[28] These complaints were often joined to a questioning of why a biography should include detailed discussions of every issue confronting government. Was Ehrman actually writing a 'life and times' instead of a political biography, as he claimed?

---

[25] Ehrman, British Academy memorandum.

[26] To the author, 6 Jan. 1976.

[27] See above, p. 157.

[28] A peculiarly unfriendly review in *The Times* (Saturday Review), 18 Oct. 1969 came from J. H. Plumb, who had praised Ehrman's book on William III's navy. After gushing appreciation of Fox, Pitt's merits are dismissed and it is stated that 'Pitt always gets the benefit, and more than the benefit of every doubt' from Ehrman (a point on which other reviewers disagreed). The review ends with a judgement that Ehrman had 'attempted a task beyond his powers'. Plumb felt that his own acceptance as an accomplished historian was too slow (see D. Cannadine, 'John Harold Plumb 1911–2001', *Proceedings of the British Academy*, 124, *Biographical Memoirs of Fellows*, III (2004), 269–309) and may have considered Ehrman's acceptance unfairly rapid. I am grateful to Professor David Cannadine, who wrote that memoir, for suggesting where I might find this review.

Colonial issues and worldwide trade along with diplomacy and European
trade occupy 189 pages.

Ehrman wished to show what could and could not be done in these
spheres. To show how Pitt manoeuvred between the constraints and
opportunities, and to understand the choices he made, a comprehensive
view of the circumstances seemed necessary. Although Pitt is absent in the
chapter on India (Henry Dundas handled the government's dealings with
the East India Company), in other spheres he was much involved, not
only in decision-making but also execution.

Perhaps his most comprehensive effort concerned trade. In December
1786 a London newspaper observed that Pitt was engaged in 'no less than
a general arrangement of the commerce of the greatest commercial power
that ever existed, with almost all the great commercial powers of the
world' (*The Years of Acclaim*, p. 502). It appears that in an early stage of
his research Ehrman had grasped the dimensions of this vast undertaking—'a succession of unexpected findings'—and wisely decided to
publish the details of the commercial-treaty negotiations in a separate
book.[29] Only one negotiation, the important one with France, produced a
treaty, but the total effort strongly suggests the influence of Adam Smith,
both in respect to free trade and to the desirability of trading with
Continental Europe. As will be seen, this effort did not signify that Pitt
valued European trade more than transoceanic.

As to the latter, he very much wanted to restore liberal access to the
valuable market that was now the United States. Still, he believed there
was a factor more important than trade (as Smith allowed). Ehrman states
that he 'never sacrificed "navigation" to the principle of free trade'. When,
in an August 1785 interview, John Adams 'argued the ill effects of continued protection' Pitt replied that the Navigation Act 'would not answer its
end, if we should dispense with it towards you' and added that Americans
could not blame Englishmen 'for being attached to their ships and seamen
which are so essential to them' (*The Years of Acclaim*, pp. 335, 341).

Ehrman leaves no doubt that Pitt's motivation for ending British
participation in the slave trade was grounded in humanity and morality: 'I
hope', he said in a famous speech of spring 1792, 'we shall hear no more
of the moral impossibility of civilising the Africans.' Still, the 'whole
oration' illustrated Pitt's customary approach—'the reconciliation of an

[29] J. Ehrman, *The British Government and Commercial Negotiations with Europe, 1783–1793*
(Cambridge, 1962), quotation on p. vi.

ideal . . . with arguments . . . designed to satisfy the objections of practical men' (*The Years of Acclaim*, 401–2).

In the field of foreign affairs during the 1780s Pitt cared little about Europe: 'He wanted to avoid continental entanglements, his interests lay elsewhere.' As one British envoy remarked, he had 'concluded a permanent Alliance with that most formidable of all Powers, the Power of Surplus' (*The Years of Acclaim*, p. 516). Nevertheless, as Ehrman skilfully narrates, in his cautious but firm handling of the challenge posed by Amsterdam radicals aligned with France in 1787 Pitt restrained some overly eager envoys while alertly assessing and taking advantage of emerging developments (*The Years of Acclaim*, pp. 520–38).

A reader of the three volumes should not fail to notice that 'handling of finance' was 'perhaps his favourite occupation, the work in which he felt most at home. He knew that most people were bored by the subject', but a 'financial issue could always rouse him, when apparently greater issues might not' (*The Years of Acclaim*, p. 280). Most historians, it may be said, are bored by the subject, and in most histories dealing with Pitt's era it appears only when the much admired British financial system collapsed in 1797.[30] In this first volume Ehrman makes us see the importance of Pitt's dedication and skill in the aftermath of the American Revolutionary War. The annual charge of interest on the National Debt was £9m; the permanent taxes which could be used to pay this charge amounted to about £10m. It was, as Ehrman remarks, a 'nightmare'—'an annual charge which was largely responsible for an annual deficit which in turn was increasing the debt on which an annual charge must be paid' (*The Years of Acclaim*, p. 280). In addition there was a pressing need to deal with unfunded Navy bills and other wartime bills which amounted to over £14m. If annuities were to be employed in providing long-term funding of these, more permanent taxes would be required, and a new permanent tax was something that no ministry wanted to ask of Parliament. Pitt tried a Shop Tax—it was loudly unpopular and had to be withdrawn—but his 'main object was to increase the yield from *existing* taxes'. His attention turned to smuggling, a big business which was estimated to divert an amount equal to one-sixth of the customs revenue. The duties on tea were very high. Pitt proposed steep cuts in the existing rates—to one-quarter or less. What is fascinating, as Ehrman reports, is how shrewdly the change had to be carried out: to cover the two-year

[30] A noteworthy exception is J. S. Watson, *The Reign of George III, 1760–1815* (Oxford, 1960), pp. 283–93.

delay before the East India Company could get additional supplies to England and prevent the smuggling fraternity from making most of it, large quantities had to be bought secretly in Amsterdam; this needed government approval and Pitt was in the thick of it. A good deal has been made of Pitt's Sinking Fund. It was designed to inspire confidence in the National Debt and thus enable interest payments to be reduced. But the hidden force behind his almost magical financial success was what would today be called economic growth, and it appears that Pitt was aware of this. Ehrman found among notes and reports of a speech evidence of Pitt's concern for the volume more than the balance of trade, noting how the 'accumulation of capital [which] arises from continual application of a part at least, of the profit obtained each year, [serves] to increase the total amount of capital to be employed in a similar manner' (*The Years of Acclaim*, pp. 274–5).

Pitt's friend William Wilberforce once said that [Pitt] suffered from 'the necessity of . . . speaking upon subjects of a low and vulgarising quality, such as the excise on tobacco, wine, &c. &c.' Ehrman remarks: 'These impressions could be dangerous, when a clerk-like care for figures was not much admired. But in the right hands, as Pitt well knew, it was a source of the greatest strength' (*The Years of Acclaim*, p. 280). Great Britain was fortunate in having at this critical time a head of the Treasury who seemed to enjoy probing the sums and intricacies. It seems likely that he inherited this trait from his mother Hester Grenville, beloved by all her brothers and demonstrably furnished with Grenville competence—like her brother George but with more common sense—in business matters.

In a trenchant review A. J. P. Taylor commented: 'Time and again the younger Pitt disappears. The policy of the British government in Pitt's period takes his place, and this policy had many dreary aspects.'[31] One place where Pitt disappears is certainly regrettable. Chapter VI, 'The Struggle for Power', deals with Pitt's ascendancy from the level of a young Chancellor of the Exchequer with a famous name and budding reputation as a debater to the height of leading minister, a position he would retain for the next seventeen years. Yet Ehrman's account of Pitt's role in this process is obscured. Charles James Fox in coalition with Lord North headed the government in 1782. George III detested Fox and wanted to be rid of him. Fox's East India Bill could easily be criticised—unfairly, Ehrman too sympathetically suggests—as transferring the company's patronage to his ministry. During the resulting uproar Pitt took a

---

[31] *The New York Review of Books*, 9 April 1970.

calculated risk when he finally accepted the king's proposal that he should lead a new administration. After Fox and North were dismissed and Pitt installed, it was expected that, lacking a majority, the new ministry would initially suffer defeats. Pitt's task, as Ehrman points out, was to demonstrate to MPs 'waiting to be convinced' that his ministry could survive (*The Years of Acclaim*, pp. 128–9).

The task involved trying to defend George III's use of Crown prerogative at this juncture while somehow finding a way to persuade members that he was not merely a compliant instrument of royal power. Ehrman recognises that Pitt's vital asset was the persuasiveness of his speeches in debate, yet the reader must traverse fourteen pages discussing political manoeuvres in which Pitt was rarely involved before reading: 'a new dimension had been added by Pitt's own performance. Starting from a posture of great weakness in a series of gruelling debates, he had held his own, virtually singlehanded, against a formidable array, and had slowly forced Fox himself, at the height of his vigour, to recognise an ultimately hopeless position' (*The Years of Acclaim*, p. 142). Pitt carried the burden of debating almost alone, night after night. Yet the book fails to highlight any of these speeches—a departure from Ehrman's customary method, which is to enable readers to form impressions and conclusions from factual and circumstantial details rather than by simply being told. Nor is anything said about whether they had an impact 'out of doors', a phenomenon that had played a key role in his father's rise to greatness. This is all the more puzzling because the ensuing general election awarded Pitt's administration a resounding victory.

Taylor's other complaint, about policy, asks Pitt, and indeed eighteenth-century England, to be something they were not. Ehrman quotes the economic historian, T. S. Ashton, where he remarked that 'the characteristic instrument of social purpose was not the individual, or the State, but the club', and Ehrman suggests concrete examples: 'from the Jockey Club and the Dilettanti to the Freemasons and Lloyds, from the Society for the Reformation of Manners and the Chamber of Manufacturers to the literary and dining clubs in the taverns. This zest for voluntary associations swelled the demands for official retrenchment' (*The Years of Acclaim*, p. 168). Indeed, aside from the basic need to guarantee security from internal violence and invasion from abroad, retrenchment and reform were Pitt's missions in the 1780s. He sought to render government effective in an age when toleration of cluttered ancient procedures was diminishing. It had 'dreary aspects', to be sure, but its achievements were much approved at the time.

When the consequences of the French Revolution interrupted this mission, Pitt found the reality hard to bear. With great reluctance and fervent hope that the interruption would not last long, he turned his attention to the problems of security; it proved to be a dismaying challenge in both its external and internal expressions. The subtitle of the second volume captures Pitt's disappointment.[32]

The external challenge was unprecedented. Pitt's administration would be overwhelmed by persistent failures in a European war that he had wished to avoid. He gave the French Revolutionary government ample warning that the Low Countries should not be disturbed, but after France declared war against Britain in January 1793 she immediately issued threats against the Netherlands. On Henry Dundas's recommendation it was decided to capture Dunkirk. Surprise, an essential factor in a siege, was lost because the general commanding a nearby Austrian army chose to besiege a French stronghold many miles inland, and in early August *The Times* reported that Dunkirk would be the next objective. British troops arrived in time, but the siege equipment did not. Although British arms lacked recent experience in conducting a European siege, Dunkirk's fortifications were not formidable and the Ordnance department's planners overestimated the requirements, so everything came late. Nor was the assisting naval force given its orders soon enough. Despite these delays Dunkirk might have capitulated if the Austrian troops, after their successful siege, had marched towards the coast to rebuff a French army that was, at long last, coming to the rescue. The outnumbered British force had to retreat. Britain had rarely performed well in the beginning of a war, yet everyone knew that France was in chaos and her armed forces in disarray. Success should have been easy, and an important opportunity was lost.

Since a successful siege depends on well-coordinated preparations it is clear that much of the responsibility for the failure lay in London. Ehrman's account makes this obvious.[33] Pitt himself was occasionally involved in relaying orders and did so inconsistently. Moreover, and this was of great importance, neither he nor his close associates understood the rhythm of campaigns. During the Seven Years War his father had been intent on allowing plenty of time for transports to be gathered, loaded and provided with naval escorts; he anticipated that adverse winds and

[32] J. Ehrman, *The Younger Pitt: the Reluctant Transition* (London, 1983).
[33] He was able to draw on Michael Duffy's thorough and penetrating article, '"A Particular Service": the British government and the Dunkirk expedition of 1793', *English Historical Review*, 91 (1976), 529–54. Duffy gives powerful reasons why Dunkirk was a well-chosen objective.

administrative lapses might produce ruinous delays. The son was far too optimistic. Admittedly, France's political turmoil would throw up new opportunities quite suddenly, so there was little time for adequate preparations. But Pitt's optimism, shared by his colleague William Wyndham, Lord Grenville, was itself a problem. Everything was expected to go right and on time, and under eighteenth-century conditions of warfare, especially where shipping was required (as of course it was in Britain's case), this was far from likely.

Ehrman leaves us with no doubt that Pitt remained dedicated to supporting a comprehensive coalition against the French government's military effort to extend revolutionary principles in Europe. But trying to get coalition forces to focus on the French enemy was a century-old problem. In the case of the Netherlands it was aggravated by the fact that while Prussia, by a recent treaty, was formally responsible for helping to defend the Low Countries, the army on the spot was Austrian, committed to defending its Netherlands provinces. Pitt wished to rely on a cooperative effort by both powers to resist French Revolutionary aggression, but their mistrust of each other was deep and long-standing, and intensified by Prussia's current eagerness to carve out a portion of Poland. Difficulties of this kind foreshadowed the ongoing military and diplomatic disappointments that would characterise Britain's war effort, and Pitt's optimism, stimulated by his hope of a short war, would have pervasive ill-effects.

To readers of this second volume Ehrman conveys not only a realisation of the ill-consequences of Pitt's optimism but also a glimpse of its advantages. Despite repeated military disappointments Pitt did not despair, and because his hopefulness was genuine he was able to impart it to parliament and public. Yet there was one respect in which Pitt's optimism was quite guarded, namely the capacity of the nation and its people to accept the expense of a long war. If he mistakenly assumed that France's finances under revolutionary government would bring her down, he was intensely aware that British finances might not be publicly supported in a long European war. Ehrman makes clear that when this prospect loomed in 1796 Pitt seriously looked toward making peace, but French Revolutionary politics blocked the effort. Ironically, the strategy of pursuing West Indian conquests, which resulted in the slaughter of so many soldiers by disease, proved fundamental to enabling Britain to hold out in the long struggle that lay ahead.

Regarding internal security Ehrman's chapters are thorough and carefully balanced, though more inclined than most writings on the subject to see that the administration's viewpoint is presented. Perhaps the most interesting discussion concerns Pitt's abandonment of the Dissenters; they had good reason to anticipate that he would repeal the Test and Corporation Acts that rendered them politically second-class citizens, and, as Ehrman points out, the later 1780s were a promising moment for Pitt to act. Yet he did nothing and the moment was lost. This was, Ehrman comments (a rare case where he offers a judgement), 'Pitt's greatest default in the pre-war period'. Observing what seemed to be Pitt's rationale for inaction, he writes, 'When precisely, it might be asked, would Pitt's conditions be fulfilled? His function was not simply to reflect opinion: there are occasions when a Minister should lead and persevere.' He adds that Pitt 'could have reaped a reward in the course of the next few years. For when he embarked on repressive measures . . . he would have achieved a more willing consensus if he had first tried for a moderate reform' (*The Reluctant Transition*, pp. 85, 87).[34] As for 'dimensions of unrest', the two chapters dealing with domestic insecurity are, as one expert reviewer commented, 'among the best in the book'.[35] Reflecting the extreme anxiety provoked by the unfolding French Revolution among the propertied classes, Pitt and his colleagues overestimated the danger that French Revolutionary ideas might lead to an overthrow of British constitutional monarchy. When the government, particularly alarmed by the resonance of Thomas Paine's *Rights of Man*, moved in May 1792 to suppress all radical publications it thereby announced an irretrievable hostility to political change. In a later chapter, 'Dearth and Discontent', one sees the dangerous mixing of severe food shortages with all this, creating a crisis to which Pitt responded too slowly. At one point, in October 1795, an immense crowd in St James's Park shouted 'No Pitt, No War, Bread, Bread, Peace, Peace' as his carriage passed through.

Six years after completing the final volume Ehrman wrote:

> I embarked the other day on a rereading of The Younger Pitt—a curious thing to do, but really quite interesting thanks to the passage of time. I find I had forgotten more parts of it than I had expected, and [was] amused to discover how one's perspective can alter with the passage of years. I think less of Vol. III than I did, but more of I, and still obstinately hold II in quite high regard.[36]

---

[34] Betty Kemp, in the *English Historical Review*, 100 (1985), 630 sees Pitt's conduct here as stemming from narrowly conceived political advantage rather than misjudgement. Her review is relentlessly hostile to both Pitt and Ehrman; so was her review of the first volume in the same journal, 86 (1971), 804–7.

[35] George Rudé in *International History Review*, 7 (1985), 309.

[36] To Dr Anthony Smith, 28 Aug. 2002, Cambridge University Library [hereafter CUL] Additional Manuscript 9975.

The title of volume III is *The Younger Pitt: the Consuming Struggle.*[37] At 854 pages of text it is the longest of the three volumes. In August 1994 when he was almost finished he wrote: 'I don't know about this final volume—maybe a curate's egg. Anyway I enjoyed myself on the way.' He did not enjoy all of it. In late December 1995 came a one-line note: 'Having a rough time seeing my book through the press.'[38] The words 'consuming struggle' might well be thought to apply to the biographer as well as his subject, but Ehrman survived.

He might have wondered whether his discussion of Pitt's conduct prior to the king's outspoken rejection of Catholic Emancipation could be one of the bad ingredients of the 'egg'. The failure to pass a law for moderating Catholic political disabilities as a necessary companion to the Act of Union (which eliminated the separate Irish parliament in 1801) was one of the great legislative lapses in British history. To be sure, the blame rightly falls on George III, who stubbornly adhered to the belief that easing Catholic civil disabilities violated his Coronation Oath to uphold the Church of England. But it appears that Pitt made no concerted effort to leave an opening for overcoming the king's veto in future—quite the contrary: when George III announced his intention somewhat publicly, Pitt resigned, and in due course promised never to raise the question again. Ehrman notes that Pitt was ill at the time and also had reason to fear that if he pressed the king too hard, the result would be royal insanity, and everyone expected that the Prince of Wales would seek to change the entire administration. But evidence is presented that Pitt had readily given up on Catholic relief when pressing for the Act of Union. It does not serve to clarify the minister's conduct that the discussion of how the act was passed is separated from the story of royal refusal and Pitt's resignation by 300 pages.

That said, this volume is an impressive achievement. From 1797 onwards dreadful events came thick and fast. The French Revolutionary government's refusal to make peace, the naval mutinies, a run on the Bank of England, two frightening invasion threats, the 1798 rising in Ireland, the collapse of European coalitions, the most serious harvest failure in a century—even these do not exhaust the list. One observes Pitt, now aware that the war against France must be considered interminable, making the politically brave decision in late 1797 to increase taxation and introduce an income tax. It meant an 'invasion of liberty, the prying by the Crown

---

[37] London and Stanford, CA, 1996.
[38] Letters to the author, 10 Aug. 1994, Dec. 1995.

into the personal affairs of the subject', and would establish in Pitt's own words an 'inquisition which would be generally invidious', things to be suffered only in a war for national survival. The tax was graduated, carefully avoided direct demands on the poor, and worked (*The Consuming Struggle*, pp. 263–5). In dealing with the great dearth occasioned by the worst harvests (1799–1800) in over a century Ehrman manages to get the details as well as the larger picture right. His clear exposition shows how much more quickly and wisely Pitt dealt with this crisis than the one in 1794–6, both by supporting relief efforts and obtaining food supplies from abroad. Not much could be done except to encourage concrete, visible measures by which the government and ruling classes could demonstrate their concern and provide some amelioration. Pitt recognised it as a very serious matter, involving issues of humanity and trust in government, but also, as Ehrman remarks, 'the forbidding conjuncture of riots and the rising tide of petitions for peace' (*The Consuming Struggle*, p. 314).

What remained unsuccessful was strategic and logistical preparation. One sees, especially in the launching of an expedition to Holland (*The Consuming Struggle*, pp. 246–8), that Pitt and his colleagues never did learn how to plan and execute a major campaign. The larger problem remained: Pitt's continuing desire, strongly reinforced by Lord Grenville, to keep up diplomatic and military pressure in Europe regardless of persistently adverse circumstances. By the year 1800 Dundas was openly— and constructively—critical of the repeated wasteful efforts in Europe which seemed to accomplish nothing but frustration and humiliation. Ehrman's rich texture allows us to move beyond the prevalent yet simplistic criticism that Pitt failed to pursue a consistent policy. The dispute between Grenville and Dundas was grounded in a profoundly genuine question: were there not times when a land war in Europe against Napoleon was utterly fruitless (which Grenville did not wish to acknowledge) while the Royal Navy, equally invincible, might be employed in furthering Britain's worldwide resources of strength during this long war and afterwards? Given this situation and because eventually in this interminable war, as Pitt understood, France would have to be resisted in Europe, Ehrman offers a narrative wherein Pitt is to be commended for trying to keep the two men near at hand, notwithstanding the strategic ambivalence. This does not excuse the profusion of orders and counter-orders that George III himself rightly complained about. In respect to this Ehrman steadily reveals Pitt as a poor war minister, though he does not come right out and say it.

One comes away with a conclusion which Ehrman appears to have intended: that in respect to Great Britain's waging of a long war involving countless adversities and disappointments Pitt had got four big things right. First, he had made certain that the navy would be strong, a matter to which he devoted personal attention during the period of peace in the 1780s. One might recall that within the scope of this final volume (1797–1806) discouragement occasioned by failed coalitions was countered by boosts to morale stimulated by four striking naval victories. Second, he understood that the struggle, however long it was to last, would require economic prosperity, without which revenues, public borrowing and public political support for continuing the war would be lacking. In this connection it should be noted that although the claim that Pitt upheld 'the Establishment' was certainly true in many respects, few persons at the time would have placed in that domain the merchants and manufacturers to whom Pitt gave so much access of his time and consideration in his policies. Third, if his strategic plans undertook too much and relied too often on hopes for a short conclusion, he nevertheless allowed Dundas's plans for Caribbean conquests to go forward in strength. As has often been pointed out, the loss of soldiers to tropical diseases in these campaigns was horrendous, but Ehrman's careful narrative of the European aspects of the war reminds us of the counter-balancing stream of costly reversals there. The fourth big thing is suggested by Ehrman when he writes of 'a development of far-reaching importance . . . what one may genuinely call a more professional, dispassionate appreciation to the problems of government'. Pitt encouraged his assistants to develop this appreciation. He thereby gave 'a modernising tone to the practice of government' (*The Consuming Struggle*, pp. 844–5). Ehrman left it to others to show how these efficient modes of administration improved Britain's ability to wage war—understandably, since the effects became most noticeable during the years following Pitt's death.

Last years

After an exhausting time 'buried—drowned, take your choice—in proofs: horrible things' Ehrman delivered the corrected proofs to Constable on 2 January 1996. Before the end of February he responded to the British Academy requirement to provide a memorandum concerning his early life. He added two afterthoughts. One was his regret that he had tended to hurry when noting references in his book on William III's navy and had not found time to check them before publication. The other was a bit startling: 'I would like to say that I am more satisfied with my efforts to assist libraries and archives than with my performance in all as an historian.' This was written during the time familiar to authors when exhaustion and doubt dominate anticipation of reviews. It was also written before a conference was organised in his honour at the Institute of Historical Research. On that occasion he was prepared to speak a word of thanks, 'But when they stood up, and seemed unwilling to sit down quietly, the only way to end proceedings was—to end proceedings. A pity really, but very generous of them.' He added: 'I have certainly been uncommonly fortunate in both the number and the tone of reviews.'[39]

The reviews, many by prominent historians, were indeed numerous and positive. The volume was carefully examined and looked upon as a strong finish. Thorough exploration combined with fondness for laying out tableaux of interacting elements—Pitt regarded George III as a formidable and unsettling element—again resulted in 'acute insight and measured judgement'.[40] Like Pitt, Ehrman believed in information. Historians working in all aspects of the period turn first to these volumes to discover what the government did and did not do, and why, and this will be the case for a long time. One reason is, as Ian Gilmour observed, 'Everything is seen in the conditions of the day; hindsight is largely absent.' Yet Pitt 'is not submerged beneath the history. The theatre is crowded, the action is continuous . . ., but Pitt is . . . just as he always remained centre-stage throughout his political life.' Many reviewers took the occasion to appraise the whole three-volume accomplishment. Homage was repeatedly paid. Gilmour's closing words capture the spirit:

> Pitt's life lasted only 46 years. John Ehrman has spent almost as long researching the three majestic volumes of his biography. Vast stamina has been needed as well as an unrivalled understanding of Pitt, great literary skill, historical sympathy and limitless erudition—a combination of qualities which has produced the major political biography of the last half-century.[41]

---

[39] Letter to Anthony Smith, 2 July 1996, CUL MS 9975. The conference was held on 4 May 1996. The April 1998 number of *History* was devoted to publishing the papers.
[40] Michael Duffy, 'The Premier killed by government', *The Times Higher Education Supplement*, 29 Nov. 1996.
[41] Ian Gilmour, 'Centre-Stage', *London Review of Books*, 1 Aug. 1996.

The Economist's reviewer wrote: 'He can take complete pride in everything he has done.'[42] Clearly, he had ample reason to reconsider his February pronouncement.

Yet it is certain that he wanted posterity to know that he judged his efforts to assist libraries and archives to be of great importance. These were not activities carried on in retirement. It was an 'aspect of my life, . . . [which] occupied a substantial part of it from the late 1940s, and one which increased markedly from the start of the 1970s until the end of 1994'. His own words in 1996 should be recorded:

> My time as Hon. Secretary and later Treasurer of the Friends of the National Libraries; on the Reviewing Committee on the Export of Works of Art, where I chaired a new subcommittee on archives and helped introduce the reserved purchase fund for documents, administered by the V and A Museum; on the H. M. C.; as the first chairman of the National Mss Conservation Trust, seem to me to have perhaps made a useful contribution in aggregate.[43]

He was a commissioner of the Historical Manuscripts Commission for a remarkable twenty-one years (1973 to 1994) during which he was always a regular and faithful attender at meetings and in touch with matters between meetings, ready to discuss everything from the allocation of manuscripts accepted for the nation in lieu of tax to the unending struggle for obtaining government funding.[44] Ehrman was the first chairman of the National Manuscripts Conservation Trust. Lord Egremont, current chairman, states that the organisation 'would not exist without him. I always enjoyed—and learnt from—our meetings, not least because he spoke the most exquisite English. What a fine and generous man and not at all a pushover! John could recognise anything or anyone bogus with unerring accuracy.'[45]

Ehrman's list is not complete. He was chairman of the British Library Advisory Committee, 1979–84. He served as a trustee of the National Portrait Gallery. Richard Ormond, young Assistant Keeper at the time, remembers him as quiet in meetings but helpful at negotiating a contested issue and prepared to offer words to summarise a consensus.[46] This talent plus Ehrman's experience with the document purchase fund may have enabled him quietly to negotiate a way for the National Maritime Museum

[42] *The Economist*, 20 July 1996.
[43] Ehrman, British Academy memorandum. In 1954 he published a brief history of 'The Friends of the National Libraries (*The Book Collector*, 3, 1 [Spring 1954], 55–60).
[44] Message to the author from Christopher Kitching, 21 Jan. 2013.
[45] Message to the author from Lord Egremont, 1 Feb. 2013.
[46] Author's interview with Richard Ormond, 4 Nov. 2012.

to purchase the papers of Admiral David Beatty. The list also omits Ehrman's long service on the Council of the Navy Records Society, twice in the office of Vice-President (1968–70, 1974–6). Undoubtedly he served other organisations. The voluntary and philanthropic services taken together were by themselves enough to warrant honours, which he refused. He was a Fellow of the Royal Historical Society, a Fellow of the Society of Antiquaries, and was elected a Fellow of the British Academy in 1970.

He also undertook a weighty personal obligation arising from inheritance—the responsible disposal of his father's valuable book collection. In 1977 he presented incunabula and sixteenth-century printed books to the British Library. An extensive collection of bookbindings and book-trade lists and catalogues went to the Bodleian Library. To the Cambridge University Library he gave the books exhibiting early type specimens. Other libraries were also recipients of books and materials from his father's Broxbourne Library. Most of the rest was sold at Sotheby's in 1977 and 1978.[47] Giles Mandelbrote remembers him in connection with his father's collection: 'He was always immensely encouraging and supportive of my interest . . . [in the Broxbourne Library]. At the same time, beneath his kindness there was also steely determination and toughness: I remember . . . the postcards which used to arrive, urging me to get on with it.'[48] The author remembers those postcards too—kind and supportive but usually occasioned by a (timely) urge to prompt; he was an ideal Ph.D. supervisor.

In the late 1970s he and Susan were preparing to move to the country. She discovered some abandoned structures called the Mead Barns in the village of Taynton near Burford in Oxfordshire and devised a plan for restoring the buildings. A large and congenial library was created to accommodate her husband's books and there was an adjacent study. They moved in 1980; Sloane House was sold: 'Pitt has had to be put aside for some weeks, in this mammoth distraction of moving house. But I hope to start sniffing in Bodley next week, and back to harness thereafter.'[49] When the second Pitt volume was finished, he decided he must take on a research assistant to help with the third. It was no longer easy to get to the Public Record Office (now The National Archives). Dr Anthony Smith, an Oxford D.Phil. in medieval studies, accepted the position, which he retained from 1983 to 1986.

[47] Electronic British Library Journal, Department of Printed Books, 1980.
[48] Message from Giles Mandelbrote to the author, 12 Feb. 2013.
[49] Letter to the author, 26 Nov. 1980.

After completing the third volume Ehrman thought that his historical labours were over, but soon came an invitation from the 'New DNB', now the *Oxford Dictionary of National Biography*, to write the long article on the younger Pitt. He could not have done it without Dr Smith who readily answered Ehrman's call for help and wrote nearly all of it, making use of the three volumes. As Smith has commented, 'Certainly he felt the constraints of the summary approach were not best suited to his manner of working and his temper of mind' and he was 'glad for me to wield the editor's pen.'[50] The task took its toll—on both of them, but especially Ehrman who had an attack of pneumonia in early 1998; 'no vim or vigour—had to rely on S[usan] to pull me up'. The following November he wrote: 'I know that 79, as I shall be in the coming spring, is no great shakes these days. But I suppose that the legacy of the polio, which centred on my lungs all those years ago, tells increasingly nonetheless—I was warned it might—and I would be glad to see this undertaking completed'. A typically gentle prompting; but he added: 'It was extremely kind of you to have agreed to take on this demanding task, and I hope you are not cursing the day. I will do what I can to ease the load.'[51] Proofs were not in hand until early 2003. The result is an expert condensation of the many challenges and undertakings of Pitt's administration. Worth particular attention are: Pitt's proceedings antecedent to the war of 1793; all aspects of the difficulties posed by Ireland; the decisions Pitt made during the severe subsistence crisis of 1799–1801; the forming of the Second Coalition; circumstances of Pitt's resignation in February 1801; and a skilful account of his conduct and ruminations during his three years out of office.[52]

Ehrman could not do as much as he would have liked to 'ease the load'. He had always loved to walk, but in March 2000 he reported: 'my legs just don't want to take the trouble anymore'. He had managed to give a talk to the Pitt Club in London—'quite a business working it all out'— but 'it seems to have passed off all right and nobody threw anything at me'. But in late April 2001 he 'was carted into hospital in the middle of the night', a recurrence of pneumonia-bronchitis. His recovery was slow

---

[50] Message from Dr Smith to the author, 27 Dec. 2012.
[51] CUL MS. 9975, 2 March 1998, 9 Nov. 1998.
[52] J. Ehrman and A. Smith, 'Pitt, William (1759–1806)', *Oxford Dictionary of National Biography*, 2004 <http://www.oxforddnb.com/view/article/22338> [accessed 30 May 2014]. Ehrman was anxious to make sure that Michael Duffy's recent biography, which he greatly admired, would be included in the list of sources. It was: M. Duffy, *The Younger Pitt* (Harlow, 2000).

and, as he put it, he 'staggered on'.[53] Reflecting back on the whole experience, Smith wrote: 'John was quite simply the most kindly, decent and admirable scholar I have ever met and I count it as a great privilege that I was enabled to know him.'[54]

In June 2010 he wrote to me: 'I have not written you for quite a long time because I could not. I lost the power to write legibly—a maddening experience . . . But, equally oddly it is starting to recede . . . I am now 90, and if I continue to live for a bit longer and you happen to visit this country . . . I would of course love to see you. So here is a line of encouragement.'[55] Unfortunately he died on 15 June 2011, of pneumonia, six weeks before my planned visit. He is buried in the churchyard of St John the Evangelist, Taynton.

DANIEL BAUGH
Cornell University

Note. I could not have written the memoir without help from the Ehrman family. Mrs Susan Ehrman welcomed me to her home in Taynton, answered my questions and shared some delightful recollections. Richard Ehrman facilitated my visit and obtained answers to my numerous questions thereafter; Sir William Ehrman provided a copy of his funeral address at the church and offered leads for learning about his father's post-war years at Trinity, Cambridge. Hugh Ehrman supplemented my collection of book reviews. Some of John Ehrman's papers are deposited in the Cambridge University Library.

Mrs Catherine Smith, Charterhouse Archivist, sent me information as wonderful as it was unexpected. I wish to express my gratitude for the help given me by the staffs of the Swem Library of the College of William and Mary and the Williamsburg Regional Libraries.

To Captain Roger Richardson-Bunbury, RN, a friend for decades, I record my heartfelt thanks for his willingness to go to the archives to discover details concerning Ehrman's naval service. I also wish to thank Joe Logan, Secretary of the Navigating and Direction Officers' Association, Commander Peter Selfe, Captain K. C. D. Watson, and Rear-Admiral J. R. Hill for their responses regarding the pioneering AIO work done at HMS *Dryad*. For information about Ehrman when a fellow at Trinity, Cambridge I am grateful to Sir John Bradfield and Sir Philip Goodhart.

In connection with his efforts to assist libraries and archives I received valued help from Lord Egremont, Nicolas Barker, Richard Ormond, Giles Mandelbrote, and Dr Christopher Kitching. Michael Duffy has helped me assess Ehrman's historical

[53] CUL MS. 9975, 27 March 2000, 3 May 2001.
[54] Message from Dr Smith to the author, 15 Dec. 2012.
[55] Letter to the author, 22 June 2010. Oddly, the post-affliction handwriting appeared more legible to me than the former.

achievement, and Dr Anthony Smith generously shared with me his thoughts about John Ehrman and suggested significant improvements to the memoir while also saving me from errors. Professor Roger Knight gave me his notes of an interview with John Ehrman on 31 March 2008 at Taynton; his wife Jane helped to facilitate my research. Their enduring hospitality, helpfulness, and unwavering kindness I can never repay.

RICHARD ELLMANN

Richard Ellmann
1918–1987

RICHARD ELLMANN was fortunate to begin his career just as modernism was becoming an admissible academic topic. It was his genius to give it critical mass in his work on the three Irish titans, Yeats, Joyce and Wilde. It was genius too, as well as good fortune, that led him to approach them in that order, three monosyllables that will be his epitaph. The first step in this progress began in September 1945 when, assigned from the US Navy back to the Office of Strategic Services and posted to London, he was able to find his way to Dublin and visit the poet's widow, George Yeats. She was already the watchful guardian of Yeats's posthumous reputation, as aware as T. S. Eliot that he was 'one of those few poets whose history is the history of their own time, who are part of the consciousness of an age which cannot be understood without them'. But previous visitors had been few. Yeats had died at Roquebrune in January 1939, and his fame dwindled, his books out of print during the war. So that meeting, three years before Yeats's body returned to be reinterred 'under Ben Bulben', was as full of significance for Mrs Yeats as for Dick Ellmann, American and just half her age. On the face of it, the situation was ripe with possibilities for mutual misunderstanding, but, as he recalled in the preface to the second edition (1979) of *Yeats: the Man and the Masks*, they hit it off at once.

Such a dénouement, determining his future, could hardly have been imagined as he grew up in Highland Park, Detroit, where he was born on 15 March 1918. He did well at school, well enough to go on to Yale, where he graduated 'with exceptional distinction' in English in 1939. He went on to complete an MA thesis on 'The social philosophy of Thomas Carlyle'

(1941). But this overlaid an earlier and deeper passion. His Yale colleague Ellsworth Mason, lifelong friend and collaborator, whose job at the University Library it was to put out for public use duplicate catalogues from the acquisitions department, observed that he 'was already heavily into Yeats, and when I noticed him looking at the catalogues I volunteered to call his attention to all Yeats items in the catalogues I handled. From an ample allowance he was able to buy most of what I found, and had bought more than two-thirds of Yeats in first editions at prices from US¢3.50 to US$8.00 before he left Yale for war service in 1942.'[1]

This was another stroke of luck; even a year later he might not have found catalogues or books as easily or frequently. His MA thesis complete, Mason recalls that Ellmann took the same route as other Yale graduate students. Armed with a recommendation from Frederick Pottle, Director of Graduate Studies in English, he called on another Yale man, Wilmarth Sheldon Lewis, who had abandoned the pursuit of Horace Walpole to become head of a section of the Coordinator of Information, a new government agency that was to become the Office of Strategic Services. There he became a unit head in March 1942, but in August he was invited to become an instructor at Harvard, where he spent the next year. It was then that he read Joseph Hone's *W. B. Yeats*, just published (London, 1942), thoroughly, and his verdict, 'competent and safe', already shows that he surmised how much more there was to be found out. A year later he was drafted into the US Navy. He found relief from the boredom of a unit in Virginia that dealt with constructing airfields and other buildings by writing poetry, some published in the *Kenyon Review* (he did not take up Dodd, Mead's offer to publish a book of them). He was later moved to Washington, but at the end of the year a better chance came his way, when he was transferred back to the Office of Strategic Services and posted to Paris, on the staff of the Commander of US Naval Forces, France.

Paris was the first European city that Ellmann lived in long enough to attempt the difficult task of extracting from its outward appearance, the townscape, and from the speech of the people he met, its essence, to be rendered in the original or in translation. He could absorb an amazing amount of heterogeneous facts and impressions, as quickly as a dry sponge soaks up water, and as quickly put both in order. In 1945 this was an instinctive trait, born of a desire to order new material, factual or

---

[1] E. Mason, 'Ellmann's road to Xanadu', in S. Dick, D. Kiberd, D. McMillan and J. Ronsley (eds.), *Omnium Gatherum: Essays for Richard Ellmann* (Gerrards Cross, 1989), p. 6.

imaginative, in a logical or at least useful order. One outlet was writing verse, and more of his poetry appeared in the Yale *Furioso* and the *Kenyon Review*. In the long term, however, meeting Henri Michaux proved more important. Cosmopolitan, orientalist, artist as well as poet, Michaux's references were both difficult and challenging. The sense of a mind barely in control of characters struggling to impose order on a fluid universe, with only the writer's own ironic humour to relieve the struggle, made new demands on his intellect and linguistic skill. Two dozen poems in translation, published separately in the *Partisan*, *Kenyon* and *Sewanee Reviews* and elsewhere between 1946 and 1953, culminated in *L'Espace Dedans: the Space Within* (New York, 1951), translated and with an introduction by Ellmann. Absorbing the impressions of his year in Paris in 1945 and translating Michaux's abstract and 'difficult' prose and verse were an apprenticeship for other practical and semantic challenges that lay ahead.

While in Paris he met his Yale colleague Norman Pearson, now head of the Office of Strategic Services in London, who summoned him there. London was a new city to explore, English English a new language to learn, but it was from this point of departure, by this circuitous route, that Ellmann arrived in Dublin in September 1945.

> At 46 Palmerston Road, Rathmines, the first sight of Mrs Yeats's study, which had been her husband's, was astonishing. There in the bookcases was his working library, often heavily annotated, and in cabinets and file cases were all his manuscripts, arranged with care by his widow. She was very good at hunting up at once some early draft of a poem or play or prose work, or a letter Yeats had received or written. When complimented, she said she was just a hen picking up scraps. Among the scraps were all Yeats's letters to Lady Gregory, done up in innumerable small bundles according to year, with ribbons to hold them together. I asked her about Yeats's first meeting with Joyce, and she showed me an unpublished preface to *Ideas of Good and Evil* (1903) in which Yeats described that singular occasion. I evinced a perhaps unexpected interest in the magical order to which Yeats belonged, the Golden Dawn; she opened a chest and took out his implements and regalia and rituals. Agape at such profusion, I could only say that I would like to return after the War, and she replied, 'I hope you will.' So it came about that I spent the year 1946–7 in Dublin, working with these books and papers.[2]

Ellmann already knew, or sensed, what was needed if such an encounter was to be fruitful: knowledge, intimate and sympathetic, of every least detail that could be found out in advance, about life, then limited to Hone's biography, and works, now being reprinted, and the background, literary

[2] R. Ellmann, *Yeats: the Man and the Masks*, 2nd edn. (Oxford, 1979), pp. xi–xii.

and political, behind both. He knew Yeats in print as well as anyone could; already aware of the textual complexities (Yeats had passively or by accident authorised different printed editions in his last decade), he had now to come to terms with a wealth of manuscript beyond computation. Beyond that, he had also to relate a sociology of Ireland learned from print to the reality around him, picking his way through the minefields of a family with three Yeatses (as seen by widow, son and daughter), with Maud Gonne MacBride still alive, Gogarty self-exiled in New York, other friends old and new at odds over every aspect of his complex character, with lowering suspicion from the clergy, and the embers of politics, quiescent during the war, blown red by Seán MacBride and the newly founded Clann na Poblachta. Just as with George Yeats, Ellmann won all hearts by his unforced charm, his wit, always an asset in Dublin at any time, and his integrity, proof against seduction or battery.

This familiarity, so early acquired, saw him through all the far-ranging enquiries that followed. He knew well what they would be: 'He had fallen into a gold mine and was fully confident that he would emerge from it with most of the important nuggets already shaped into imperishable form.'[3] The work to which he had set his hand did not cease when he returned to Washington that autumn. Ellsworth Mason was already back at Yale, whence he sent extracts of Yeats's letters from John Quinn's sale catalogue, but on 5 May Ellmann was able to report: 'This is the eve of my demobilization. I go to Bainbridge[4] tomorrow and prepare to re-enter the world of the living.' Next month he was back in Dublin, ensconced at the United Arts Club.

There is a vivid picture of that second and longer visit in John Kelleher's 'With Dick in Dublin',[5] revealing the ease with which he picked up the threads, not only of last year's visit, but of still vital memories of Yeats. They met his younger brother, the painter Jack Yeats, met Maud Gonne, or rather Madame MacBride. She did most of the talking, reciting familiar facts. Kelleher wondered if Dick had got anything useful out of the interview: 'It wasn't until much later that I realized that in these interviews he could perceive clearly many things, small significant traits of personality for instance, that I, with my all-too-ready judgments, might miss completely.' They met H. O. White at Trinity College, who opened more doors in Dublin than anyone else and said 'Yeats is still everywhere in this

---

[3] Dick *et al.*, *Omnium Gatherum*, p. 10.
[4] The Naval Training Center in Maryland.
[5] Dick *et al.*, *Omnium Gatherum*, pp. 13–22.

town.' Kelleher bought a bicycle and explored the south, returning to urge Dick to join him on the last leg of his trip. They climbed Ben Bulben, and met those who remembered Yeats. As they headed north to Donegal, Ellmann came to dislike the bicycle. He took the train back to Dublin from Londonderry, leaving his companion with a lasting impression of what he intended:

> I really came to understand what Dick was doing. His way was to come armed with more, and generally more detailed and reliable, knowledge than he could expect the person interviewed to have, yet never to bring this forward, scarcely ever to interrupt. He let them talk; he showed himself grateful for what they told him; now and then with a quiet question he would elicit some particular point, and in leaving would express his thanks again. He left them smiling and thinking what a nice young man!

> Though I then wondered that he thought the trouble worth it, for in view of what he already knew the ore he could extract from these interviews would scarcely assay at one-percent, when, a year later, I was reading his book in type-script I saw how much this constant concern for small facts, minor interrelations, contributed to the consistency and authenticity of the portrait.[6]

This method, thus sympathetically and shrewdly described, underlies Ellmann's three great books, *Yeats: the Man and the Masks* (New York, 1948), *James Joyce* (New York, 1959) and *Oscar Wilde* (London, 1987). That is not to diminish his mastery of the biographer's regular resources, the reading of documents, letters, diaries, directories, timetables, the ever critical balance between fact, in print and script, against the spoken evidence of witnesses, and beyond both the words and images in creative writing. The eye and ear for detail was like a dynamo, always gently humming, applied to a pupil's essay or response to a seminar question as well as his own critical writing. It was one of the reasons why he was much admired and loved as a teacher; those who read what he wrote knew they were in safe hands.

The winter and spring of 1946–7 found Ellmann in Dublin, shuttling between the United Arts Club and Buswell's Hotel, suffering from flu, and writing two theses at once, 'William Butler Yeats: the fountain years' for a Litt.B. from Trinity College, Dublin, where H. O. White was a constant friend and guide to Yeats's early years, and 'Triton among the streams: a study of the life and writings of William Butler Yeats' for his Yale Ph.D. (all but lost in transit by Pan American in April). This combination was no light task, but it was punctuated by another visit to the Continent, and

[6] Ibid., p. 19.

the beginnings of work on Joyce, shared with Ellsworth Mason, for whom he bought a map of Dublin and *Thom's Official Directory of Dublin* for 1904. By August he was home at Highland Park, and September found him at Harvard, picking up the threads of his pre-war stint as an Instructor. His Yale thesis was duly rewarded with a doctorate, awarded the John Addison Porter prize for the best dissertation of the year in 1947; it was the first given by Yale for work on a twentieth-century writer. Swiftly adapted for publication, it was accepted by Macmillan and came out in 1948. Its reception made it clear that Ellmann's was a rising talent; it also recognised his work as a milestone in the understanding of Yeats's poetry. Articles followed in the *Kenyon Review, Western Review* and *Partisan Review.* Harvard promoted him to be Briggs-Copeland Assistant Professor of English Composition, with five years' tenure.

Before his first year was out, an event of lasting significance to his future took place: he met Mary Donahue and they were married on 12 August 1949. Women, apart from Mrs Yeats, had not been conspicuous in Ellmann's life hitherto. Mary Donahue was already conspicuous. Famous as a feminist critic, the future author of *Thinking about Women* (London, 1968) in which she ruthlessly examined male stereotypes of women from Jane Austen to Norman Mailer, she brought a sharp edge, a touch of acid, to what was always an equal partnership. What united them was wit, Dick's like the summer lightning that plays about the clouds, Mary's a bolt that struck straight to earth. They did not, in the event, stay long in Cambridge, Ellmann diverging from his teaching duties to begin a critical study of Yeats's poetry. As his tenure at Harvard was only temporary, in 1952 he accepted appointment as Professor of English at Northwestern University, three years after the university's first computer was installed in a spare room in the observatory. The Ellmann family moved to Evanston, Illinois, a dozen miles north of Chicago, which was to be their home for the next sixteen years.

In 1954 Ellmann's study of Yeats's poetry was published as *The Identity of Yeats* (London), to further applause, and he became a regular reviewer, every literary editor's first choice, of any and every book on Yeats that appeared, with occasional diversions to James Gould Cozzens, Conrad, Hemingway, Wallace Stevens, Tom Stoppard and Auden. Beckett too was never far away, but increasingly Joyce came to dominate Ellmann's work and life. When he reached Evanston, one of the first of the new colleagues that he met was Walter B. Scott, who introduced him to the parodies in 'The oxen of the sun'. Another was James F. Spoerri, whose Joyce collection, seen before it was sold to Kansas University next year, convinced him that a biography could be written. He corresponded with Joyce's bibliographers, John Slocum and Herbert Cahoon, and picked up the first threads lain down by Harry Levin. A first essay on Joyce and Yeats appeared in the *Kenyon Review* in 1950, reprinted as 'The hawklike man' in *Eminent Domain* (New York, 1967). Six more such studies, all important, appeared in the next three years, one of them, 'The grasshopper and the ant', reflecting on Joyce and his brother Stanislas. He edited the latter's *My Brother's Keeper: James Joyce's Early Years*, long in gestation but published posthumously only in 1958 (London); with his old friend Ellsworth Mason, he also edited *The Critical Writings of James Joyce* (New York, 1959).

But these were casual ports of call on the long journey from *A Portrait of the Artist as a Young Man* to *Finnegans Wake*. With the encouragement of Frank O'Connor and Carroll G. Bowen, he set to work, going to Europe in 1953, 1954 and 1956, visiting every place in which Joyce's wandering life had been spent and revisiting Dublin to walk the streets that are the setting, the greatest of all walking-on parts, of *Ulysses*. The copious pages of acknowledgements read like a travelogue: Joyce's surviving friends and acquaintances, collectors of his works, libraries and archives— he visited them all, making friends wherever he went, who saw him depart with sadness. Harriet Shaw Weaver, Joyce's muse, publisher and now literary executor was, he wrote, 'constantly generous to me; otherwise I could not have proceeded with the book'. She let him read her letters, published and unpublished and, although in her eighties, read the eventual manuscript. That ran to some 350,000 words, a prodigious achievement, the more so as there is not a wasted word in it from start to finish. There are 265,000 words in *Ulysses*, and if ever an author deserved to have half as many words again written about him as he himself wrote, it was Joyce. Time after time, the minute details of daily life weave in and out of Joyce's imaginings, and through them into his writings. The record wanders on, as shapeless and as shaped as the epigraphs to each chapter that Ellmann chose from *Finnegans Wake*: 'The verisimilitude in *Ulysses* is so compelling that Joyce has been derided as more mimic than creator, which charge, being untrue, is the greatest praise of all.'[7]

A biographer cannot get behind the skin of his subject without becoming, to some extent, part of the subject. If the subject is also in part the creation of his or her own fiction, that image has to be fitted into the mould of the day-to-day reality of the occurrences making up the life. These

---

[7] R. Ellmann, *James Joyce* (New York, 1959), p. 363.

parallels and paradoxes returned to Ellmann when he gave his inaugural
lecture on 'Literary Biography' at Oxford in 1971. Now, in 1959, the critics
were overcome less by the concept of nature imitating art than by the sheer
volume of all the new information about Joyce, and with it the inwardness
of his fiction. Long as it was, Ellmann's biography was not long enough for
those to whom Joyce's life and writings were an unending mystery. The
symbolisms that lay everywhere were now accumulated in a labour that
was not itself laborious because it was patently a labour of love. It was
clear to the critics that the talent seen growing in *Yeats: the Man and the
Masks* had now matured in a gigantic masterpiece that set in focus the
largest and most intractable monument of modernist writing. 'That great
biography of yours has it all', wrote Mason, 'we can throw the other books
away.'[8] A reputation in his own field was exchanged for a larger one on an
international scale. His pupils, a small army on their own, found they had
to share their devotion with hundreds of admirers stretching beyond academic bounds. He rewarded them with more writing and an influence freely
lent to forward the careers of his students. 'The power you wield!' exclaimed
Mason, 'God save us you never take over the Mafia!'[9]

He did not, even if his reputation in Dublin fell not far short of it. He
continued to pursue Yeats and Joyce, and in 1966 that other figure, never
far away among all his Irish explorations, finally entered the scene. The
impetus came from Charles Ryskamp, professor of English at Princeton,
whose idea it was, with E. D. N. Johnson and Alfred Bush, to put on an
exhibition 'Wilde and the Nineties', drawing on the university collections
and that of Mary Hyde (later Viscountess Eccles), near by at Four Oaks
Farm, New Jersey. It was Ryskamp's inspiration, too, to ask Ellmann to
contribute an essay to the catalogue. 'The critic as artist as Wilde' was the
result, launching Ellmann fairly on his third great biographical voyage.
This was followed shortly after by *Eminent Domain: Yeats among Wilde,
Joyce, Pound, Eliot and Auden* (New York, 1967), five essays whose titles—
'Oscar and Oisin', 'The Hawklike Man', 'Ez and Old Billyum', 'Possum's
Conversion' and 'Gazebos and Gashouses'—revealed an easy familiarity
with all the complex relationships of his heroes.

In 1965 he and his Yale classmate Charles Feidelson published *The
Modern Tradition* (New York), an anthology of key modernist texts that
became a manifesto for a branch of study, remote twenty-five years earlier,
that had become a new orthodoxy. Ellmann was now at the summit. He

[8] 28 Dec. 1974.
[9] 6 Oct. 1978.

had enjoyed two Guggenheim Fellowships in 1950 and 1957; another came in 1970. Other universities pressed their claims on him, but he remained faithful to Northwestern, which promoted him to a personal chair in 1964, the Franklin Bliss Snyder Professorship of English, named after the university's president in 1939–49. He was a Fellow of the School of Letters in Indiana University in 1956 and 1960, Senior Fellow 1966–72, and Frederick Ives Carpenter Visiting Professor at the neighbouring University of Chicago in 1959, 1967 and 1975–7. He was chairman of the Modern Language Association session on contemporary literature in 1955, member of the Executive Council 1961–5 and the Editorial Committee 1968–73, and American Scholar 1968–74. He became a member of the American Academy, and won the National Book Award in 1960. He was Fellow of the Royal Society of Literature and elected a Fellow of the British Academy in 1979. He had honorary degrees from the National University of Ireland, Boston College, Emory, Northwestern, McGill, Gothenburg and Rochester universities.

All this had happened or was in the wings when Ellmann left Northwestern in 1968 to take up the chair of English at Yale. He was to return to the scene of his first academic triumphs, and seemed set to end his career there. But despite the solidity of the reputation thus consecrated, despite the honours, awards and responsibilities that went with it, there was a gipsy streak in Ellmann that resisted proprieties and certainty. Among the many who had courted him before were his English admirers, and even after leaving Northwestern, for good, it seemed, he had not been dismissive of such approaches: 'established at Yale, he could predict exactly which meetings he would be attending on any given day in the foreseeable future; Oxford offered no such predictability'.[10] In 1969 he was invited to apply for the Goldsmiths' chair of English at Oxford. His mind was now increasingly bent on Wilde, and the chance to be within easy striking distance of the places where Wilde had spent so much of his life, besides the archival and library resources, was too tempting to be resisted. All seemed set for another, more adventurous change of direction when in December Mary Ellmann had a cerebral haemorrhage; an operation on the aneurysm failed, and she found herself condemned to a wheel-chair existence. Ellmann quickly adapted to this change at the centre of family life. Mary was adamant that the planned move should go ahead, and Dick was duly elected to the chair, and the fellowship of New College that went with it.

[10] John Kelly, 'Ellmann, Richard David (1918–1987)', *Oxford Dictionary of National Biography*, <http://www.oxforddnb.com/view/article/39805> (accessed 24 March 2014).

They made their home at 39 St Giles', where they kept open house to graduate students, new friends and old, visiting from America. Nothing at Yale, Harvard or Northwestern had quite prepared the cosmopolitan Ellmanns for Oxford, but they took to it with an infectious gaiety, his wit striking sparks off the local wits, her now slow speech adding trenchancy to hers. He gave his inaugural lecture on 'Literary Biography' on 4 May 1971. Lecturing came easily to him, but he preferred the give and take of the seminar, to ask questions, to suggest not dictate answers. No text was impenetrable to inquiry: 'Let's take the poet's part', he would urge,[11] certain that the clue could be found.

More books followed: his extraordinary return journey, *Ulysses on the Liffey* (New York, 1972), 'a Great Pyramid filled with beautifully worked out puzzles and penetrations', reconstructing the text from its Dublin roots (he was always the most scientific of symbolic critics), and *Golden Codgers* (London, 1973), a series of 'biographical speculations', including 'Literary Biography' and 'The Critic as Artist as Wilde', and other essays on George Eliot, Wilde's *Salome*, André Gide and T. S. Eliot. *The Consciousness of Joyce* (London, 1977) pursued a constant theme in both *Ulysses* and *Finnegans Wake*. A second edition of *Yeats the Man and the Masks* came out in 1979 (Oxford), with a new preface recounting how Mrs Yeats had introduced him to the manuscripts and her memories, and how that had led to meeting Maud Gonne, the first flame of Yeats's life.[12]

But all the time the life of Wilde was hammering away in Ellmann's mind, waiting to be let out. He had edited his critical writings, collected a series of critical essays on Wilde (*The Artist as Critic: Critical Writings of Oscar Wilde*, and *Oscar Wilde: A Collection of Critical Essays*: both in London, 1969). He had lectured on Wilde in love and at Oxford. He had edited *The Picture of Dorian Gray* (New York, 1982). But these were side-shows. In attempting the life of Wilde he had one great asset that was also a huge disadvantage. Allan Wade, actor, collector and bibliographer of Yeats, had over many years collected, and in 1954 finally published, *The Letters of W. B. Yeats* (London). This had come too late for *Yeats: the Man and the Masks*, but Ellmann had known Wade and references to 'unp. Ltr' acknowledge his help. Wade had also been pursuing the letters of Oscar Wilde as industriously, but had not finished his work when he

---

[11] Dick *et al.*, *Omnium Gatherum*, p. xiv.
[12] He made one uncharacteristic error. He described the copy of *A Selection of the Love Poetry of W. B. Yeats* (Dublin, 1913) that Yeats had given to her as with 'the only pages that she had troubled to cut were the ones that contained poems written to her'. It was those that were uncut.

died in 1955. He left the task to his publisher, Rupert Hart-Davis, who had brought out *The Letters of W. B. Yeats*. Already the author of *Hugh Walpole: a Biography* (London, 1952), Hart-Davis had a fair idea of the task ahead, but no one could have foreseen how long it would take, how much time to satisfy the standards of accuracy in transcription and annotation that Hart-Davis set himself and his many helpers. *The Letters of Oscar Wilde* came out in 1962 (London), to universal applause, almost every one of the reviewers announcing that despite all the many previous biographies it would obviate the need for any other. All this mass of material was already there for Ellmann; it also stood in his way.

Finally, he set to work, threading his way through the still smouldering embers of the controversies of Wilde's life and those who had tried to explain them with his usual grace and tact. As with Joyce, he left no detail unexplored, a harder task than with Joyce: all the events were that much longer ago, and overlain, then and later, with contradictions and argument. Many had been cleared up by Hart-Davis's *Letters*, but inevitably there were others unmentioned in Wilde's correspondence. Some of these aspects of the 'hidden Wilde', so to speak, such as the belief that syphilis contracted at Oxford, present but latent until his final illness, explained much of his sexual ambiguity, were risky, but Ellmann was not averse to risks and surprised his peers by the ease with which he accepted correction if it came. He made many new friends as well as new discoveries during the research and writing which increasingly occupied his time. Rupert Hart-Davis was foremost among them, reading what he wrote as he wrote it. Merlin Holland, Wilde's grandson, provided family photographs and memories. Mary Hyde, later Lady Eccles, gave him full access to her collection. The William Andrews Clark Library at Los Angeles, with the largest institutional collection in the world, was as generous.

Besides the various chips from the Wilde workbench, he continued to write on all the subjects that had engaged him. A great deal of work went into a second edition of *James Joyce*, substantially revised with the help of Catherine Carver (Oxford, 1982); used to the editorial supplications of Saul Bellow and John Updike, she worked on Ellmann's prose with the same affection and acumen. Mary Reynolds provided other suggestions and 'a new and much more elaborate index', a great improvement. The new edition came out in 1982, and won the James Tait Black and Duff Cooper Prizes the following year. He gave the British Academy's Sara Tryphena Phillips Lecture on 'Henry James among the aesthetes' on 19 May 1983, and lectured twice at the Library of Congress, 'W. B. Yeats's second puberty', about Yeats's experiment with the Steinach operation, on 2 April

1984, and 'Samuel Beckett, Nayman of Nayland', his first formal approach to the fourth Irish pillar of modernism, on 16 April 1985. His most recent occasional pieces were gathered together in *Four Dubliners: Wilde, Yeats, Joyce and Beckett* (London, 1986). His last new writing to be published in his lifetime was his 'Preface' to Hans Walter Gebler's monumental *Ulysses: the Corrected Text* (New York, 1986).

In 1982 Ellmann had become Woodruff Professor of English at Emory University, Georgia, held in conjunction with his Oxford chair, from which he retired in 1984. New College made him an Honorary Fellow, and Wolfson College, Oxford, elected him Extraordinary Fellow, also in 1984. A new future uninhibited even by the teaching that he enjoyed seemed to lie open before him. All too soon, however, came the first signs that his physique was not what it had been. A big man, well built, he had coped with Mary's disability without strain. In the autumn of 1985 he fell twice while jogging; that winter his voice was unaccountably hoarse; travelling to Canada in June 1986 for his honorary degree from McGill he found difficulty standing or sitting upright, and his speech was now slurred. When he got home he went to London for a specialist opinion. He came back to find Mary with company. 'How did it go?' she asked. He paused, then said, 'He didn't tell me anything I didn't know.' 'Did you expect to live for ever?' she replied. It was motor neurone disease, they learned. She had to watch the frame fall in on itself, muscles, hands, then voice failing, a progress that acupuncture or Chinese medicine could not delay. Ultimately, a simple keyboard with roll-printer became his sole means of communication; even so, his words showed that the mind within was undiminished. He died on 13 May 1987.

The pace of writing Wilde, never slow, had since become a race against time, in which he was abetted by Mary and both his daughters, Lucy and Maud. Owen Dudley Edwards, Wilde scholar since 1954, came to wait on him hand and foot and eye. Catherine Carver again edited the text thoroughly, making criticisms from which, he was still able to write, 'I have greatly profited.' She also read the proofs, and was relieved to find marks in his set that showed that he had been able to finish them up to the last page. Mary Reynolds provided another admirable index. *Oscar Wilde* came out posthumously in September 1987 (London).

The reviews were as much elegies to Ellmann as praise for his last work. 'A master of the biographer's art', wrote John Gross in the *New York Review of Books*, 'Ellmann has the first, indispensable virtue of telling his story well—not just the big story but the lesser stories that lie coiled inside it.' All the other critics were in accord, and *Time Out* added

'Ellmann's life is likely to remain as revered and read as the same author's lives of two other Anglo-Irish prodigies: Yeats and Joyce.'

Time is not likely to alter that verdict. Any biographer facing the task that he took on three times, how to relate the realities of life to the creations of the mind, will do well to read his words. Those who do will come to realise that he had another gift, perhaps the greatest: to be able to enter into the mind of each of his subjects, instinctively to become them, even to write about them as they would have written.

> Had Yeats died instead of marrying in 1917, he would have been remembered as a remarkable minor poet who achieved a diction more powerful than that of his contemporaries but who, except in a handful of poems, did not have much to say with it ... His prose would have continued to come forth in the same beautiful, bottomless style as in *Per Amica Silentia Lunae*, published just before his marriage, built up out of evasion so skillfull that the reader is never sure whether he is being presented with a doctrine or with a poem in prose.[13]

> Joyce is Gabriel Conroy when 'The time has come for him to set out on his journey westward': 'The bubble of his self-possession is pricked; he no longer possesses himself, and not to possess oneself is in a way a kind of death. It is a self-abandonment not unlike Furey's, and through Gabriel's mind runs the imagery of Calvary. He imagines the snow at Oughterard, lying "thickly drifted on the crooked crosses, on the spears of the little gate, on the barren thorns." He thinks of Michael Furey who, Gretta has said, died for her, and envies him his sacrifice for another kind of love than Christ's. To some extent Gabriel too is dying for her, in giving up what he has most valued in himself, all that holds him apart from the simpler people at the party. He feels close to Gretta through sympathy if not through love; now they are both past youth, beauty and passion; he feels close also to her dead lover, another lamb burnt on her altar, though she too is burnt now; he feels no resentment, only pity. In his own sacrifice he is conscious of a melancholy unity between the living and the dead.[14]

> *Patience* was turned against the satirist: 'So Wilde found ways to act and speak in full knowledge that they could and would be mocked. To be derided so was part of his plan. Notoriety is fame's wicked twin: Wilde was prepared to court the one in the hope that the other would avour him too.' Nor did Wilde spare his old teacher: 'Wilde might have treated Mahaffy nostalgically, but the erect pen has no conscience'.[15]

Richard Ellmann has been long dead now, and others knew him better than the present writer. Besides the Ellmann who will live on in the three biographies and his many lesser writings, there is the more elusive but as

---

[13] Ellmann, *Yeats: the Man and the Masks* (1948 edn.), p. 220.
[14] Ellmann, *James Joyce*, pp. 258–9.
[15] Ellmann, *Oscar Wilde* (London, 1987), pp. 131 and 271.

vital figure preserved in the memories of friends and students, among them those who contributed to *Omnium Gatherum: Essays for Richard Ellmann*, edited by Susan Dick, Declan Kiberd, Dougald McMillan and Joseph Ronsley, begun before his death and published in 1989. There Jane Lidderdale recalled 'one of his traits … his artistry in opening a lecture: a challenging and often witty first sentence, accompanied by a little turn of the head, a signal to his listeners that he was glad to be addressing them'. Owen Dudley Edwards remembers what made him an honorary citizen of Dublin. Among the questions after a lecture he gave in Dublin was one that made him laugh: 'now Mr Garvin knows perfectly well that he knows far more than I do about this point and I'm not going to be foolish enough to answer his question'. He knew that John Garvin knew more about Joyce than anyone else in Dublin. He also knew that he was a civil servant in local government, as such a mere amateur to most academics. It was characteristically graceful as well as wise to give credit where credit was due.

Ellmann knew the value of facts; establishing the truth, the whole truth and nothing but the truth was to him a sacred duty. He also knew that there was a further kind of truth, unsupported by facts, the legend that grows up round the great that can never be wholly detached from reality. It was not right to treat it as just a failure in the record, a defect for which allowance had to be made, but rather as part of a greater reality, no less real because less true. Charity, sifting grain from chaff, made moral sense of both. Charity was what he saw as common in the lives of Yeats and Joyce and Wilde, different though they were. It was what drew him to them. Charity he had himself in abundance, extended not only to his heroes, with all their strengths and weaknesses, but to everyone who came his way, students, colleagues, anyone he met. He was a lovable and much loved man.

NICOLAS BARKER
Fellow of the Academy

CHRISTOPHER EVANS

Christopher Francis Evans
1909–2012

THREE YOUNG MEN—two Anglican, one Methodist—studying Theology at Cambridge at various times in the 1930s were destined, though they did not know it, to become the three most influential British New Testament scholars of their generation. All were to become Fellows of the British Academy. The first was Charles Francis Digby Moule (always known as 'Charlie'), who read classics at Emmanuel College, but then studied Theology at Ridley Hall in preparation for ordination; he became Lady Margaret's Professor of Divinity in 1951. Youngest of the three was Charles Kingsley Barrett (known by his friends as 'Kingsley'), who studied mathematics at Pembroke before switching to Theology and preparing for the Methodist ministry at Wesley House; he spent almost all his teaching career in Durham, where he became Professor of New Testament.[1] In between them, and overlapping with Charlie Moule, was Christopher Francis Evans, who was for a short time Lightfoot Professor at Durham before moving to the University of London, as Professor of New Testament at King's College.

'Overlapping with', and perhaps overshadowed by, Charlie Moule, who had gone up to Cambridge a year before him. In later life Christopher would relate how, as an undergraduate, he had ventured to enter for various university prizes, but would inevitably recognise Charlie's slight figure at another desk in the examination room, whereupon his heart would

---

[1] Both have been the subject of memoirs in this series: W. Horbury, 'Charles Francis Digby Moule, 1908–2007', *Proceedings of the British Academy*, 161, *Biographical Memoirs of Fellows*, VIII, 281–301; J. D. G. Dunn, 'Charles Kingsley Barrett, 1917–2011', *Biographical Memoirs of Fellows of the British Academy*, XII, 3–21.

Biographical Memoirs of Fellows of the British Academy, XIII, 195–214. © The British Academy 2014.

sink, and he would conclude that he had no hope of success—though he did, in fact, win the Jeremie Hellenistic Prize in 1932. Throughout his life Christopher found it incredible that he should be taken seriously as a scholar, and no doubt this experience of believing that there were better scholars in the room contributed to his diffidence. So, too, did the fact that like many other students of his generation, he went straight from university and curacy into teaching, without undertaking 'research' for a Ph.D. Even as a professor, he would be diffident about supervising Ph.D. students. After all, he had never taken a Ph.D. himself, so how could he tell them what to do? And how had he come to be elected to a chair, and to have honours heaped upon him? Typical of his modesty was the note he wrote on the cover of the copy of the inaugural lecture delivered in Durham which he gave to the author of this memoir, who happened to lodge in a bed sitting-room in his house: 'To the real theologian who lives above the study.'[2] The note was, of course, as generous as it was absurd: the reason that he regarded me as a *real* theologian was because I was engaged in full-time 'research'. How, he wondered, could *he* dare to pontificate on scholarly matters, when the Germans were so thorough in all their studies, and when he was increasingly surrounded by young British scholars who all needed to undertake postgraduate research if they were to become university teachers? Yet precisely because he did *not* 'pontificate', but continued to question all assumptions, it was *he* who was in truth 'the real theologian'.

I

Christopher was born in Small Heath, Birmingham, the second son of Frank Evans, a businessman, and his wife Beatrice, on 7 November 1909. He attended the famous King Edward's School, Birmingham, which numbered Cambridge New Testament Professors J. B. Lightfoot and B. F. Westcott among its alumni, and where Charles Dugmore—who later became a fellow professor (in Ecclesiastical History) at King's College—Robert Leaney—who, like Christopher, wrote a commentary on Luke[3]—and the future Conservative MP, Enoch Powell, were among his contemporaries. He was a member of the 1st Rugby XV, where he played

---

[2] C. F. Evans, *Queen or Cinderella*, inaugural lecture delivered 23 Feb. 1960 (University of Durham: 1960); republished in C. F. Evans, *Explorations in Theology 2* (London, 1977), pp. 84–100.
[3] A. R. C. Leaney, *The Gospel According to St Luke* (London, 1958).

scrum-half, so setting something of a family tradition, since his son Jonathan also played scrum-half for school and club, and his grandson played scrum-half and captained Manchester University. The tradition is now carried on by his great-grandson Luke, playing scrum-half for his preparatory school. Christopher's love for the game continued in later life, and when in Oxford he was a regular attender of games at the University's grounds at Iffley Road.

As a boy, Christopher came under the influence of Alec Vidler, who was curate at St Aidan's church, Small Heath. In 1929 he went up to Cambridge, having been awarded an exhibition to read classics at Corpus Christi College, with the intention of switching to theology after a year, and it was this initial training in classics that would colour his approach in later years. Cambridge could boast many first-class New Testament scholars at that time: J. M. Creed was Ely Professor, and F. C. Burkitt was Norris-Hulse. Other New Testament teachers included P. Gardner-Smith and W. L. Knox. But by far the greatest influence on Christopher was exercised by Sir Edwin Clement Hoskyns, who was lecturing on the Theology and Ethics of the New Testament (and who was going to have a similar influence on C. K. Barrett, who attended the same series of lectures a few years later). Hoskyns combined fearless examination of the text with deep personal devotion, and made his pupils familiar with the rigorous critical work being done in Germany, which was felt by more timid scholars to be an attack on the Christian faith itself. Hoskyns was also the translator of the immensely influential commentary on Romans by Karl Barth,[4] and appreciated Barth's engagement with scripture. He introduced his pupils to the idea of 'biblical theology', which was to become prominent in biblical studies in the mid-twentieth century. Christopher had 'the great good fortune', as he described it, to be a pupil of Hoskyns,[5] and in a public lecture delivered on 22 October 1981, in which he reflected on the work of Hoskyns, he tried to describe the effect that this pre-eminently great teacher had on him: 'any attempt to do so would be inadequate which did not account for the fact that at the end of a supervision one might have to be careful in walking down the stairs because one was feeling rather drunk'.[6] Christopher's own students might well feel later that this was a good description of their experiences of his own teaching![7]

[4] E. C. Hoskyns, *The Epistle to the Romans* by Karl Barth, trans. from the 6th edn. (London, 1933).
[5] Evans, *Explorations*, p. vii.
[6] C. F. Evans, 'Crucifixion–Resurrection: some reflections on Sir Edwyn Hoskyns as theologian', *Epworth Review*, 10.1 (1983), pp. 70–6, and 10.2 (1983), pp. 79–86, at p. 84.
[7] Commenting on Christopher's Inaugural Lecture (see above, n. 2), Gordon Wakefield described him as 'a genuine successor to Hoskyns'. See E. C. Hoskyns and F. N. Davey (eds.), with a

In the introduction to a collection of essays published in 1977, Christopher picks out three things, in particular, that he learned from Hoskyns.[8] The first of these was 'the importance of the critical method in the study of the New Testament'. Hoskyns's pupils, he remarks, 'had their noses rubbed in [the critical method], and were not allowed to talk theology apart from it'. Hoskyns's confidence in the method 'as serving to uncover where the principal theological issues were, breathed through the book *The Riddle of the New Testament* which he wrote in conjunction with his ... pupil F. N. Davey'—a book which exercised an enormous influence not only on his Cambridge pupils, but on future generations of students far beyond Cambridge.[9] For Christopher, the historical-critical method was always the essential starting point for any investigation, as he demonstrated in the section entitled 'The New Testament in the making' which he contributed to the volume of *The Cambridge History of the Bible* co-edited by himself.[10]

The second insight he learnt from Hoskyns was, he writes, his 'concern with Christology'—not as 'a subject in itself and on its own', but as 'an aspect of theology and of the doctrine of God'. This concern, he suggests, was in part a reaction to the prevailing 'liberalism' of the time, 'according to which the words and message of Jesus were of primary, and the person of the one who uttered these words of secondary, importance'. For Christopher also, however much he subjected the words of Jesus to scrutiny, it was the person of Jesus himself who was primary. It was a theme that he himself explored in a lecture entitled 'Christology and Theology', where he discusses the way in which the Old Testament is appealed to by our New Testament writers. Such appeals are aimed, he writes, 'at establishing the continuity and identity of Jesus with the agelong purposes of God'.[11] In Acts 13, for example, the Old Testament is used 'to show Jesus as not being a figure in his own right, but as one who is in the closest connection with the purposes of God'.[12] And writing of the central role of

---

biographical introduction by G. S. Wakefield, *Crucifixion–Resurrection: the Pattern of the Theology and Ethics of the New Testament* (London, 1981), p. 79.

[8] Evans, *Explorations*, pp. vii–ix.

[9] Sir Edwyn Hoskyns and N. Davey, *The Riddle of the New Testament* (London, 1931). Christopher notes that the book was translated into eighteen languages.

[10] P. R. Ackroyd and C. F. Evans (eds.), *The Cambridge History of the Bible Volume 1* (Cambridge, 1970), pp. 232–84. I owe this observation to the Revd Dr R. Parsons, one of his students.

[11] C. F. Evans, 'Christology and Theology', the Albrecht Stumpff Memorial Lecture delivered at Queen's College Birmingham in May 1959, and published in Evans, *Explorations*, pp. 101–20, at p. 106.

[12] Evans, *Explorations*, p. 107.

Christology for Paul, he commented: 'It would ... be quite inadequate to Paul's thought to say that as a Christian he had added to a previous satisfactory belief in God a belief in Jesus as the Messiah; rather had belief in Jesus as Messiah brought to light for the first time what belief in God really was, and had made it operative.'[13]

The third insight he attributed to Hoskyns was that although theology was 'very properly pursued as an academic discipline in the universities, [it] was in the last resort a function of the church, and sooner or later the theologian must show himself responsible to the man and woman in the pew, and if possible to the man and woman in the street'. It was this fundamental answerability of the theologian to the church that was to characterise Christopher's own approach as a teacher.

In 1932 Christopher graduated with first-class honours and began preparation for ordination at Lincoln Theological College, where he was taught by a team which included Michael Ramsey, future Archbishop of Canterbury. Many years later, he related how he and a friend had consulted Sir Edwyn Hoskyns regarding the choice of a theological college. 'In your case, Evans,' Hoskyns had said, 'I think you would be well advised to consider going to Lincoln. They teach some theology there, and there is a young man named Ramsey who has recently joined the staff: I think you might learn a good deal from him.' As for his friend, he continued, he had 'advised [him] to go to Cuddeston [sic]. After all Cuddeston [sic] is for gentlemen, isn't it?'[14] Hoskyns's recommendation of Lincoln proved good advice, and from Ramsey Christopher learned, among other things, about the writings of two very different theologians—F. D. Maurice and P. T. Forsyth—whose work had hitherto been unknown to him.

On Hoskyns's advice, he also spent several months in Tübingen, where he heard some of Germany's leading New Testament scholars, and was shocked by the activities of the National Socialist Party. A research stipend enabled him to spend some time at Hawarden, where he worked on St Luke's Gospel: already, it seems, he was concentrating on the Gospel which was to be the subject of his last and greatest book. He was ordained deacon in 1934, priest in 1935, and from 1934 to 1938 served as a curate at St Barnabas, Southampton. Among those who met and were influenced by this lively young clergyman were Tom Baker (later Principal of Wells Theological College, and subsequently Dean of Worcester) and Dennis

[13] Ibid., pp. 112 f.
[14] C. F. Evans, *Humanity, Holiness—and Humour*, The Michael Ramsey Memorial Lecture (Durham, 1995), p. 1.

Nineham (future Regius Professor of Divinity at Cambridge, then Warden of Keble, Oxford, and finally Professor of Theology at Bristol).

In 1938 he returned to Lincoln Theological College as Tutor, and remained there for most of the Second World War, with bombers heading for Germany passing regularly overhead. The Principal at that time was Eric Abbott, later Dean of King's College London (1945–55) before becoming Dean of Westminster, and Eric Mascall (who joined King's as Professor in 1962, in the same year that Christopher himself arrived there) was also on the staff: together, they made a formidable team. During this time he met his future wife, Elna Mary Pasco, whom he married in 1941. He was the first member of staff to be married, and he was required to live out of College, which necessitated a long cycle home at night after compline. Their son, Jonathan, was born in 1943.

After six years of teaching at Lincoln Christopher moved—but not far, since he now took up a post as Chaplain and Lecturer in Theology at the Training College for Teachers in Lincoln. The post was not equal to his capabilities as a scholar, but provided him with the opportunity to enhance his teaching skills and to use his pastoral gifts.

His knowledge of German was put to good use shortly after the war, when he took part in a visit of British churchmen to Germany and was embarrassed to find himself lecturing to some of Germany's prominent theologians. A few years later, in 1951, he was invited to lecture as 'Gastprofessor' at a summer school in Hamburg, where he formed a lasting friendship with his host, Dr Eduard Lohse, who was to become Professor of New Testament at Kiel and then Göttingen, and was later elected Presiding Bishop of the United Evangelical Lutheran Church in Germany.

In 1948, Christopher's scholarly gifts were recognised when he was elected Chaplain, Fellow, and Lecturer in Theology at Corpus Christi College, Oxford.[15] Here, instead of teaching all the subjects in the Theology Honours School, as had traditionally been done, he formed a 'teaching circus' with J. R. Porter (later Professor at Exeter University), who was teaching Old Testament at Oriel College, and Dennis Nineham, by now Chaplain at Queen's College, followed by David Jenkins (later Bishop of Durham), who both taught early church doctrine. Undergraduates would spend one or two terms writing weekly essays for one of the three before moving on to the next. One former student describes how Christopher opened her eyes to 'the excitement and value of critical approaches to the Bible', and notes how much she appreciated the personal interest that he

[15] He became an Emeritus Fellow of the College in 1977.

took in his pupils.[16] Another, who studied in Oxford in the mid-1950s, recalls the brilliance of his lectures on Luke;[17] he was, it seems, continuing to work on that Gospel. At the same time, however, he was working on St John, editing the commentary left unfinished by R. H. Lightfoot, former Dean Ireland's Professor in Oxford.[18] He also joined with Dennis Nineham in delivering a joint series of lectures on the Synoptic Gospels, fascinating the undergraduates with their different approaches and with the unanswered questions they raised. Among his pupils were John Bowden, who was to become a firm friend and—as editor of the SCM Press—the publisher of his books, and Frederick Borsch, who was later to become Dean and President of the Church Divinity School of the Pacific, and who remarked that Christopher had taught him 'the value in gospel research, not only of asking questions but of asking questions about the questions'.[19]

But Christopher never forgot that he was also a churchman. In addition to his pastoral work in his college, he served as Proctor in Convocation for the University of Oxford from 1955 to 1958. For some years he was a member of the Church of England Doctrine Commission.[20] He was much in demand as a spiritual director and retreat conductor. Like his mentor, Hoskyns, his roots lay in Anglo-Catholic piety.

In January 1959 he moved to Durham as Lightfoot Professor of Divinity and Canon of the Cathedral. He was teaching early church history, which was not his specialism. It is not surprising then, that he was attracted by the invitation to accept one of the new chairs in Theology being created in the University of London, and based in King's College. Having only just arrived in Durham, however, he felt that he could not move in 1961, as requested. As it happened I was still resident in his house, working as a Research Fellow in the University, and so, happily for me, the idea was born that I would fill the gap until Christopher could decently move to London the following year. It is to him, therefore, that I owe the opportunity to begin my teaching career, since at the end of the year I was given a post at King's in my own right, and so began a fruitful period of

---

[16] Note from the Revd Jean Mayland in *The Church Times*, 14 Sept. 2012.
[17] Miss Margaret Flemington, in personal conversation with the author.
[18] R. H. Lightfoot, *St John's Gospel: a Commentary*, ed. C. F. Evans (London, 1956).
[19] F. H. Borsch, 'Jesus, the wandering preacher?', in M. Hooker and C. Hickling (eds.), *What About the New Testament? Essays in Honour of Christopher Evans* (London, 1975), pp. 45–63, at p. 61.
[20] The Commission's report was published as *Christian Believing: the Nature of the Christian Faith and its Expression in Holy Scripture and Creeds* (London, 1976). Christopher contributed an appendix entitled 'The unity and pluriformity of the New Testament' (pp. 43–51).

working with Christopher in teaching New Testament in King's. At first
Dennis Nineham did some of the teaching, but then we were joined by
Colin Hickling, followed by Sophie Laws, and finally, when I left King's in
1970, the team was completed by Graham Stanton, who eventually succeeded to the chair when Christopher retired. Christopher was always hugely
supportive of his younger colleagues, one of whom expresses it well when
she recalls his 'humanity, informality and kindness', and remembers with
gratitude the concern he had for us all.[21]

Christopher's arrival at King's brought a breath of fresh air to the
department there. His predecessor, who retired in 1961, had sadly failed to
inspire his pupils. One former student writes of the 'magic' of Christopher's
teaching, and describes 'the total transformation' that the new regime
'brought to a moribund New Testament department', saying that he will
'never forget the sheer excitement of Professor Evans's lectures on John . . .
Even then, we knew how very fortunate we were, as later years of teaching
and ministry have confirmed.'[22] They were amazed by the wealth of meaning that he discovered in the text. Dazed undergraduates would emerge
from his lectures on the Fourth Gospel, wondering how anyone could take
a whole term to deal with the Johannine Prologue, and whether he would
ever get to the end of the book; but they came back for more! As Graham
Stanton later expressed it, Christopher 'was a master teacher who had the
knack of encouraging students to think about the text for themselves'.[23]

Christopher and I continued the collaborative form of teaching which
he had adopted in Oxford, deliberately adopting different approaches.
The resulting weekly Seminars for New Testament specialists 'remain an
inspiration' to this day for at least one former member of the group.[24]
Christopher's contributions to the seminar were characterised by excitement and determination. Sitting on the edge of his seat, he would expound
one or other of the New Testament passages we had chosen for in-depth
study, introducing the students to critical analysis of the text. One week *he*
would lead the discussion, the next it would be my turn—and though he
was ever ready to ask questions, he was not necessarily prepared to accept
the answers I offered him. 'Rubbish!' he would splutter when he disagreed
with my analysis. The students loved to watch us locked in dispute, and *we*
certainly enjoyed our shared explorations. Our sessions were not, how-

[21] Lady Laws, in a private letter to the author.
[22] Letter from the Revd Canon Anthony Phillips in *The Church Times*, 14 Sept. 2012.
[23] Endorsement on the back cover of the 2008 edition of C. F. Evans, *St Luke* (London).
[24] The Revd Canon Robin Gill in *The Church Times*, 24 Aug. 2012.

ever, designed as entertainment, but rather to serve as demonstrations of the problems involved in any serious engagement with the text. There was always more than one way of approaching the problems, always more than one possible solution answer to any question. One member of the group was Desmond Tutu, who came from a very different background in Africa 'where there were right answers which you regurgitated as a student'. He was astonished to be invited to think for himself, and was utterly bowled over by this new experience, which he found both 'exhilarating' and 'liberating'. He writes: 'I cannot erase from my memory the image of [Christopher] puffing away at his pipe whilst listening attentively to the spewings forth of us students.'[25]

Christopher was rarely seen without his pipe in those days. Another student remembers him with great fondness, and describes how he would walk around his room excitedly while discussing an essay, spilling sparks from his pipe and almost setting fire to the carpet.[26] His experience was typical, for Christopher was not only a brilliant lecturer but also a patient supervisor. He would spend hours with the students specialising in New Testament studies, and they speak gratefully of his conscientiousness and care. He was, indeed, primarily a teacher rather than a writer, and as a result progress on his Commentary on Luke was slow, though occasional articles appeared as a result of his work.[27] He took a sabbatical in Australia with the purpose of 'completing' it, but it was another twenty years before it finally appeared.

In some university departments, concerned as they were to prove that theology was a proper 'academic' study, and where any kind of belief was regarded as unscholarly, Christopher would have been lost. In the King's of the 1960s and 1970s, where more than 90 per cent of the students were preparing for ordination, he was in his element, and in his teaching he demonstrated the relevance of academic study to personal faith—though it was left to his hearers to make the vital connection. As Leslie Houlden expressed it in his review of *Saint Luke*,[28] when it was finally published, 'This commentary ... will not yield good sermons at the press of a button,

---

[25] The Most Revd Desmond Tutu, in a private letter to the author.
[26] The Revd Dr David Cornick, in personal conversation with the author.
[27] See, for example, C. F. Evans, 'Uncomfortable words—V', *Expository Times*, 81 (1969–70), 228–31 (a study of Luke 16:31); C. F. Evans, 'Tertullian's references to Sentius Saturninus and the Lukan census', *Journal of Theological Studies*, NS 24 (1973), 24–39.
[28] C. F. Evans, *Saint Luke* (TPI Commentary, London, 1990; 2nd edn. with preface by Robert Morgan and Michael Wolter, 2008).

but ... it may prevent bad ones' from being written.[29] Christopher himself was acknowledged to be an outstanding preacher.

Christopher's own situation, as scholar and priest, enabled him to sympathise with his research students, who were almost all training for ordination. One of them comments:

> That connection between study and ministry, while having the potential to bring many good fruits, carries with it some serious risks, not least that rhetorical or pious sleights of hand might crowd out the rigour of intellectual questioning ... what is needed is a gentle empathy with the student's ministerial motivation combined with a persistent, though not strident, return to the hard questions— again and again. If I know that, it is because it is what I received from Christopher. Part of the gentle empathy is an awareness that there are things which cannot be known, whose uncertainty will always be part of the theological agenda, but that there are also things which, at least to those who have faith, can be affirmed.

Referring to the many statements in Christopher's own work which lie 'on the boundary between certainty and uncertainty, faith and doubt, affirmation and intellectual inquiry', this former student continues: 'to be supervised by CFE was to be invited to join him there'.[30]

College students were not the only people to benefit from Christopher's teaching skills. Already in 1948, he had published a small booklet to help study-groups grappling with the Bible.[31] A series of Lenten addresses on the Lord's Prayer delivered in Durham in 1962 was reproduced in printed form, and became a best seller.[32] While at King's, he took part in two series of televised lectures, the first on the Gospels, the second on St Paul.[33] Television lectures in the 1960s were totally unlike those of today, where presenters wander through some exotic landscape, or stand (momentarily) in a building with a tenuous connection with the subject of the lecture. In those days the lecturer was filmed standing behind a lectern, addressing a hall full of students, and the only movement of the camera throughout the allotted thirty minutes was from lecturer to audience and back. It was

---

[29] L. Houlden, Review of *Saint Luke*, *Theology*, 93 (1990), 317.

[30] The Rt Revd Dr Peter Selby, in a tribute given at a Choral Evensong celebrating the life of Christopher Evans held at King's College London 15 Jan. 2013.

[31] C. F. Evans, *The Bible* (London, 1948).

[32] C. F. Evans, *The Lord's Prayer* (London, 1963).

[33] The second of these, 'His Writing', a television lecture given in 1966, was published in C. F. Evans, M. Hooker and J. C. O'Neill, *The Apostle Paul* (London, 1966), pp. 7–20. Christopher wrote almost nothing on Paul, the main exception being a lecture on 'Romans 12.1–2: the true worship', given at the 5th Ecumenical Pauline Colloquium held in Rome in 1974, and published in Lorenzo De Lorenzi (ed.), *Dimensions de la Vie Chrétienne (Rm 12–13)* (Rome, Série Monographique de "Benedictina" 4, 1979), pp. 7–33.

necessary to engage one's audience—and Christopher did so—as he evidently did once again in some lectures on St Mark's Gospel delivered in 1968 in the University of Kent.[34]

Christopher was a regular contributor to the series of weekly lectures in Theology provided at King's College London for 'non-theological' students, studying for the Associateship of King's College (AKC). Not surprisingly, he was asked to give similar lectures elsewhere, and some of these have been preserved in a volume of essays which appeared in the SCM series entitled *Explorations in Theology*. Four lectures on 'The Passion of Christ' printed here were given at Bryn Mawr College, Philadelphia, in March 1975,[35] and three on 'The Christian' were delivered in the Queen's University of Belfast in 1972.[36]

One of the issues that engaged him throughout his teaching career was what he termed 'The Use of Scripture'—the title he gave to a group of papers republished in *Explorations*.[37] All of them reflect the understanding of the role of the theologian which he attributed to Hoskyns, that 'sooner or later the theologian must show himself responsible to the man and woman in the pew, and if possible to the man and woman in the street'.[38] The first, 'Hermeneutics',[39] arose out of his experiences as a member of a group set up by the World Council of Churches to consider the relevance and meaning of the Bible today, of which he wrote: 'The writer's membership of the British group was not only for him a great privilege and pleasure but also one of the most creative experiences of his life.'[40] The second essay is the inaugural lecture he gave in Durham in 1960, which considered the limitations of the historical method in the pursuit of theology. The Christian gospel, he wrote, must be investigated by historical means, since it 'is contained in an event which is genuinely historical ... On the other hand however, it escapes a purely historical description, and the historical method does not suffice to penetrate to its

[34] C. F. Evans, *The Beginning of the Gospel ...: Four Lectures on St Mark's Gospel* (London, 1968).
[35] Evans, *Explorations*, pp. 3–66.
[36] Ibid., pp. 141–82.
[37] Ibid., pp. 69–137.
[38] Ibid., p. ix.
[39] A paper read to The London Society for the Study of Religion in 1974. First published in *Epworth Review*, 2.1 (1975), 81–93.
[40] Evans, *Review*, 2.1, p. 84; Evans, *Explorations*, pp. 72 f. On the experiences of this group, see also E. Flesseman-Van Leer, 'Dear Christopher', in M. Hooker and C. Hickling (eds.), *What About the New Testament? Essays in Honour of Christopher Evans* (London, 1975), pp. 234–42.

heart.'[41] Two lectures—one on 'Christology and Theology',[42] the other on 'Parable and Dogma',[43] in which he explored some of the ways in which later theological debates and pronouncements had distorted the significance of the earliest material—complete this section of the book.

King's recognised Christopher's contribution to teaching and to the Faculty by electing him to a Fellowship of the College in 1970. Recognition came, too, from the University of Southampton, which awarded him an honorary D.Litt. in 1977. On his retirement, in 1977, he moved, with his wife Elna, to Cuddesdon, Oxford, a couple of hundred yards from the theological college there, a recent amalgamation of Ripon and Cuddesdon Colleges. He began a happy association with the College, where he taught some students, while continuing his work on a Commentary on Luke which he had begun many years before. Elna died in 1980, and he took many years to come to terms with her loss. After teaching for a month at Bishop's College, Calcutta in 1982, he returned to Durham as Visiting Fellow at Trevelyan College in 1982–3, but it was two terms spent in Glasgow in 1986 and 1987 as the Alexander Robertson Lecturer that restored him to his old form—though he nearly lost his life there when he was taken seriously ill while addressing a group of students; he was saved by the quick thinking of some medical students who were present.[44] In Glasgow he lectured on St John's Gospel and conducted seminars on St Luke's Gospel, on which he was still at work. Students found him an 'absolutely inspirational teacher who amazed them because he was still puzzling over things that puzzled them. He did not always understand their Scottish accents, but they loved him dearly!'[45] The University of Glasgow awarded him an honorary DD in 1987.

Back in Cuddesdon, he continued to work on St Luke, and the resulting commentary was finally published in 1990.[46] His election as Fellow of the British Academy in the following year brought him much pleasure. He continued his close connection with the theological college—a relationship which proved to be of mutual advantage. He learned to cook, attending evening classes in Oxford, and would cook his own Christmas cakes and serve dishes such as Beef Wellington and Pavlova at dinner parties.

[41] Evans, *Queen or Cinderella*, p. 21; Evans, *Explorations*, p. 99.
[42] See above, n. 11.
[43] The Ethel M. Wood lecture: C. F. Evans, *Parable and Dogma* (London, 1977), delivered in the University of London in 1976, and reprinted in Evans, *Explorations*, pp. 121–37.
[44] The Revd Dr Anthony Bash, in a private letter to the author.
[45] Professor John Barclay, in a private letter to the author.
[46] Evans, *Saint Luke*.

All his visitors were familiar with the terrifying Cona machine powered by methylated spirit which looked as if it would be at home in a chemistry laboratory, in which he brewed coffee.

During these years Christopher's eyesight deteriorated to the point that he could no longer read, except with the aid of a special magnifying machine. He disposed of his theological books—but retained his precious run of Wisden! In 2008, increasing infirmity led him to move to the Foundation of the Lady Katharine Leveson at Temple Balsall, in the West Midlands, where he was well cared for, while contributing richly to the life of the community. He retained his razor-sharp inquiring mind to the last. A former research student describes how, when arranging a day and time when they could meet for a meal, Christopher said that he would write down the date with 'ISAAC' next to it, explaining that 'ISAAC' meant 'If Still Alive And Compos'.[47] No one else had any fear that he would *not* be 'compos'! His eyesight gone, he preached his last sermon—lasting twenty minutes!—without notes on Advent Sunday in 2011. After a final short illness, he died on 30 July 2012, aged 102.

There was of course far more to Christopher than the scholar and churchman. One of the things that endeared him to others was that he *enjoyed* life—and his enjoyment was infectious. He enjoyed good food and wine and conversation, and loved going to good restaurants and to the theatre. He took pleasure in throwing parties for his students, who remember them still with great pleasure, and he lit up any gathering by his presence. It is true that there were bleak years for him after Elna's death, and at the end of his life he found the limitations of old age frustrating, but he never lost his immense capacity for friendship; he enjoyed meeting people and found them interesting. He would greet one with an impish grin and a twinkle in his eye. A large number of family members and friends gathered to celebrate his hundredth birthday—another occasion on which Christopher spoke at length without notes. One of the last photographs taken of him shows him with his friend Leslie Houlden at Temple Balsall, each with a glass in hand. For many of his friends, their abiding memory of him is of a shared meal. One describes how he and two other friends were taken out to lunch by Christopher when the latter was 100; he writes: 'Christopher was the life and soul of the party, mixing gossip from the 1920s with a sharp command of contemporary ecclesiastical gossip, and cracking many a joke about both.'[48] He loved watching cricket, and had a

[47] The Rt Revd Peter Selby, see above, n. 30.
[48] The Revd Professor Diarmaid McCulloch, Kt, in a private letter to the author.

secret passion for all-in wrestling, but the hobby he listed in *Who's Who* was fly-fishing, a sport which demanded great patience both from him and from Elna. At the end of his life, he took great pleasure in the achievements of his two grandsons—Martin, a naval chaplain, and David—and in his three great-grandchildren—Isabelle, Luke, and Alexandra, who was just 100 years younger than himself.

II

It was not until Christopher was working in Oxford that his first serious published work appeared—a fact which may well have contributed to his diffidence in regarding himself as a 'true scholar'. The first piece to appear, in 1954, was an essay in the prestigious *Journal of Theological Studies* entitled 'I will go before you into Galilee'.[49] In this he argued that Mark 14:28 was to be understood as a promise by Jesus that, following his resurrection, he would lead his disciples back into Galilee, and that this symbolised the beginning of the Gentile mission. Tentatively, Christopher invited his readers to choose between this interpretation and one that was popular at the time, which understood the words as a reference to Jesus's return at the Parousia. At the end of the article he touches on the problem of the abrupt ending of Mark's Gospel, and comments that it is not alone, since 'The end of any Christian book is a problem, for eloquent perorations are reserved either for those who believe optimistically that they have the answers, or for those who believe cynically that there are no answers to have; perorations are debarred to those for whom God's act is the last word.' It was an appropriate declaration for a scholar who, in his future work, never made perorations, and who always worked with the conviction that the text on which he was commenting was 'God's act'.

In the following year, he contributed an article to a volume written in honour of an Oxford New Testament scholar, R. H. Lightfoot, formerly Dean Ireland's Professor of Exegesis at Oxford.[50] In this, Christopher turned to Luke's Gospel, and looked at the enigma of the long central section (9:51–18:14), a passage which has no parallel in Mark's Gospel (almost certainly used as a framework by Luke), and which purports to tell the story of Jesus's journey from the Mount of Transfiguration to

---

[49] *Journal of Theological Studies*, NS 5 (1954), 3–18.
[50] C. F. Evans, 'The central section of St. Luke's Gospel', in D. E. Nineham (ed.), *Studies in the Gospels: Essays in Memory of R. H. Lightfoot* (Oxford, 1955), pp. 37–53.

Jerusalem. This passage had long proved a problem, since it seemed to possess no clear structure, but rather appeared to be an amorphous collection of diverse material with little reference to either time or place. Christopher found clues to the passage in the opening verses, where the language reflects expressions used in the Septuagint, the Greek translation of the Old Testament. As elsewhere in the Gospel, we may suppose that Luke is pointing us towards the Jewish scriptures. Especially significant was the word 'assumption' in 9:51, a word used in apocryphal literature to refer to Moses's ascension to heaven. Christopher argued that Luke's purpose here was to present Jesus as 'the prophet like Moses' promised in Deuteronomy 18:18, and spelt out a series of parallels between Luke 10:1–18:14 and Deuteronomy. For good measure, he pointed to parallels —or rather contrasts—between Luke 9:52–62 and stories in 1–2 Kings about Elijah, and suggested that both Moses and Elijah, the two figures who feature in the story of the Transfiguration, are important to Luke as witnesses to Jesus.

This scintillating thesis had a mixed reception. For some commentators it was clearly too *avant garde*, and they simply ignored it. Some accepted it with enthusiasm,[51] while others argued vigorously against it, protesting that the parallels were not convincing, and that there were other passages in Deuteronomy that offered better parallels, though not in the sequence presented in that book.[52] The evidence, it was argued, suggests only that Deuteronomy may have been drawn upon from time to time. It is true that his critics were right in arguing that some of the suggested links were far less persuasive than others, but there are sufficient parallels to support the belief that there must be some truth in Christopher's suggestion. He himself seems to have lost his initial enthusiasm for the thesis as he originally presented it, however, since he refers to it only tentatively in his Commentary on Luke, published nearly forty years later.[53] Although he again sets out the links between Deuteronomy and Luke, he makes far less of their significance and of the importance of Moses and Elijah. Nevertheless, in the scholarly world of today, where critics are far less concerned with depicting Luke as an 'historian' whose primary interest

---

[51] See, for example, J. Drury, *Tradition and Design in Luke's Gospel* (London, 1976), pp. 67 f., 138–64. See also D. Moessner, *Lord of the Banquet: the Literary and Theological Significance of the Lukan Travel Narrative* (Minneapolis, MN, 1989).

[52] For example, C. L. Blomberg, 'Midrash, Chiasmus, and the outline of Luke's central section', in R. T. France and D. Wenham (eds.), *Gospel Perspectives: Studies in Midrash and Historiography*, III (Sheffield, 1983), pp. 217–61.

[53] Evans, *Saint Luke*, pp. 34–6, 435.

was accuracy, and regard him rather as someone who wished to bring out the theological implications of his story, the theory offers what may well be the best explanation of Luke's intention in composing this section of his Gospel.

The following year saw the publication of another article in the *Journal of Theological Studies*,[54] in which Christopher once again raised questions about a commonly held interpretation. This time he focused on the view, initially propounded by C. H. Dodd[55] and by the 1950s widely regarded as an established conclusion, that the speeches in the first part of Acts, together with certain 'pre-Pauline fragments' in Paul's letters, reflected the early *kerygma*—that is, the preaching—of the early Jerusalem church. Although it was recognised that Luke stood in the tradition of ancient historiography, and could therefore be expected to compose speeches which he considered appropriate to his characters and to the occasion, Dodd had argued that the faithfulness with which he used his sources in composing his first volume (Luke's Gospel) suggested that he would adopt the same method used in the Gospel in writing Acts. These passages were therefore regarded as supremely important in tracing the development of Christian belief. Moreover, these speeches—which were said to 'sound primitive'—contained aramaisms, suggesting that they preserved very early material, while those attributed to Paul appeared to echo Pauline language.

Christopher argued that a comparison of Luke's method in writing Acts with the one he adopted in composing his Gospel is invalid, since Luke would have felt himself far freer in composing his second volume than in his first, where he was dealing with words attributed to Jesus himself, not the words of apostles. Moreover, the material in the Gospel—compilations of sayings—is very different from the speeches in Acts; to describe Luke as composing speeches in the tradition of Greek history tradition is insufficient, however, since this tradition 'was open to a wide variety in practice'.[56] Luke was a 'biblical' writer who was strongly influenced by the Septuagint. Moreover, he was a dramatic historian, 'gripped by the conception of Christianity as a great event projecting itself into history', who aimed 'to interpret it not to his fellow Christians, and not ... to the Jews, but to the subjects of the Empire itself'.[57] The speeches,

[54] C. F. Evans, 'The Kerygma', *Journal of Theological Studies*, NS 7 (1956), 25–41.
[55] C. H. Dodd, *The Apostolic Preaching and its Developments* (London, 1936).
[56] Evans, 'The Kerygma', p. 29.
[57] Ibid., p. 30.

Christopher argued, were composed to demonstrate the theme of the book, which is clearly stated in 1:8: 'Ye shall be my witnesses both in Jerusalem, and in all Judaea and Samaria, and unto the uttermost part of the earth.' He shows how this theme is set out and developed in all these speeches, and how it explains why Acts ends as it does, with Paul in Rome, preaching the Gospel without hindrance in spite of Jewish opposition. It is because the speeches were composed to fit this overarching theme that they sometimes seem inappropriate for the occasions on which they are said to have been delivered. Luke's purpose, to show how the apostles bore witness to the Gospel 'to the uttermost parts of the world', also explains his strange repetitions—in the early speeches in Jerusalem, in the accounts of the conversion of Cornelius (Acts 10–11), and in the threefold recounting of Paul's conversion, with their growing emphasis on Paul's commission to take the gospel to the Gentiles (Acts 9, 22 and 26). He concludes by suggesting that the very elements in the speeches which seem to us to be 'primitive' may in fact be characteristic of the preaching of Luke's own day.

This essay built on the work of Martin Dibelius, already renowned as a form critic of the Gospels, whose study of the speeches in Acts had recently been published,[58] and who was concerned with the literary forms of the material, rather than with positing fragmentary 'sources' which might or might not embody historical tradition. Christopher was not content, however, to label them all as 'speeches', but argued that each had a particular purpose. It is no accident that his approach to Acts coincided with the development of 'redaction criticism' of the Gospels; the evangelists were now being regarded as authors with a purpose rather than gatherers-up of fragments. Like Christopher's study of the central section of Luke's Gospel, this essay on Acts portrayed Luke as a man with a mind of his own and a clear purpose. He returned to the theme of the speeches in an essay contributed to a Festschrift published in 1970, once again building on the work of Dibelius.[59]

The relationship between form and content is once again the theme of his last major public lecture, published some twenty years later, though on this occasion his subject was the relationship of form and content in the

[58] M. Dibelius, 'Die Reden der Apostelgeschichte und die antike Geshichtsschreibung', *Sitzungsberichte der Heidelberger Akademie der Wissenschaften, philosophisch-historische Klasse* (Heidelberg, 1949); republished in *Aufsätze zur Apostelgeschichte* (Göttingen, 1951), and subsequently translated in M. Dibelius, *Studies in the Acts of the Apostles*, ed. H. Greeven (London, 1956), pp. 138–91.
[59] C. F. Evans, '"Speeches" in Acts', in A. Descamps and R. P. André de Halleux (eds.), *Mélanges Béda Rigaux* (Gembloux, 1970), pp. 287–302.

Epistle to the Hebrews.[60] Most of Christopher's published work was based
on lectures given on various occasions. The same is true of his most substantial study of one theme (apart from the Luke commentary), a volume
exploring the idea of Resurrection.[61] The original three lectures have,
however, been expanded into 180 somewhat dense pages, which led one
reviewer to remark that 'some of [the book] is heavy going'.[62] Its value lies
in what the same reviewer describes as 'its scrupulously careful and scholarly analysis of what the New Testament says about resurrection, and its
refusal to let the reader get away with facile interpretation'.[63] Christopher
begins by showing the scant evidence for the idea of resurrection at the
time of Jesus, goes on to a detailed examination of the New Testament
tradition regarding Jesus's resurrection, and concludes with a discussion
of the meaning of resurrection and its relation to exaltation, which he
considers to be the more inclusive idea. A few years later he returned to
the theme in an essay entitled 'Resurrection in the New Testament and
now', which undertook the even more difficult task of relating the biblical
doctrine to the modern world.[64]

His greatest achievement, however, was undoubtedly his Commentary
on Luke, which was eventually published in 1990, when he was 80. It had
originally been commissioned to replace a somewhat thin volume in the
series of Penguin commentaries. Christopher's volume, of some 933 pages,
certainly cannot be described as 'thin'! Unlike many modern commentaries, which become clogged up with references to secondary literature,
however, this one succeeds in distilling the insights gained from a lifetime
of studying the views of others. Not surprisingly, given Christopher's
training, the commentary 'continues the English tradition of classicists
becoming theologians rather than Judaica providing the essential background for New Testament scholars ... but among New Testament writers
Luke is the one most naturally read with a classicist's spectacles'.[65]
Intended for clergy and students, it offers reliable comments, and is notable for its sound judgement. Above all, it offers us the author's own

---

[60] C. F. Evans, *The Theology of Rhetoric: the Epistle to the Hebrews* (London, 1988).
[61] C. F. Evans, *Resurrection and the New Testament* (Studies in Biblical Theology, 2:12, London, 1970).
[62] C. F. D. Moule, review in *Theology*, 73 (1970), 457–9, at p. 459.
[63] Ibid., p. 457.
[64] C. F. Evans, *Is Holy Scripture Christian? And Other Questions* (London, 1971), pp. 64–77. An earlier attempt to relate biblical faith to the modern world was made in an essay entitled 'The faith of the New Testament', in D. M. MacKinnon (ed.), *Christian Faith and Communist Faith* (London, 1953), pp. 117–45.
[65] R. Morgan and M. Wolter, preface to the 2008 edn. of Evans, *St Luke*, pp. xvi–xvii.

understanding of Luke, his background, and his Gospel. The reviewers were united in their praise; one described it as 'a welcome combination of vigour and freedom from dogmatism', and welcomed the fact that it 'ducks none of the problems'.[66] When the book was republished in 2008, another wrote:

> C. F. Evans' Commentary on Luke is extraordinarily rich, reflecting a life-time's close engagement with the Gospel. The Commentary opens up not only the world of Jesus but also that of the author of the text as he sought to inter-pret the traditions about Jesus to his own setting. Pastors, interested lay people and students will find challenging questions that direct them afresh to the text, while more experienced students and scholars will find more new insights and suggestions than in many a much-longer Commentary.[67]

Throughout his life, Christopher continually posed similar 'challenging questions'. In a lecture provocatively entitled 'Is "Holy Scripture" Christian?', he raised the fundamental question as to whether the notion of a 'holy book' was compatible with Christianity.[68] It was no accident that a phrase he often used was 'the curse of the canon'. Here, he reminds us that the final choice of books for inclusion in the canon had been made on the belief that they were 'apostolic'—a belief which he described as 'fantastic'—and argues that 'it was of the essence of the Christian gospel in its earliest period that it abolished the category of the holy except as applied to God himself (and perhaps to the community which was in living touch with him)'.[69] The lecture was included in a book with the same title,[70] in which he posed other questions that some may have found disturbing: 'Should the New Testament be taught to Children?' raised the eyebrows of some readers. 'Is "the Jesus of History" Important?' sounded dangerously Bultmannian to others. As for 'Is the New Testament Church a Model?', that challenged the prevailing orthodoxy of the day by declaring that 'one of the results of critical analysis of ... the New Testament [is] that it puts a question mark against the assumption that there is *a* or *the* New Testament view of anything'.[71] For Christopher, the task of the New Testament scholar was to 'put a question mark' against *all* assumptions—and to subject any answers offered in response to those question marks to further scrutiny.

---

[66] L. Houlden, review in *Theology*, 93 (1990), 317.
[67] Judith Lieu, endorsement on the back cover of the 2008 edn. of Evans, *St Luke*.
[68] Published in Evans, *Is Holy Scripture Christian?*, pp. 21–36.
[69] Ibid., p. 34.
[70] Evans, *Is Holy Scripture Christian?*
[71] Evans, *Is Holy Scripture Christian?*, p. 79.

It was for this reason that the editors of a volume of essays presented to him on his sixty-fifth birthday chose a question—*What about the New Testament?*—as the title for that book.[72] To those who knew him, its appropriateness was obvious. What *about* the New Testament? What are we to do with this strange collection of documents? What makes them special? In what *ways* are they special? How do we probe the questions the New Testament raises regarding history and literature, theology and authority? It was no accident that all the essays in that volume raised questions—many reflected in the titles the authors gave to their pieces. As his friends, we knew that we could honour him best by asking questions, however radical they might seem, rather than by producing a set of polished answers. When the time came to present the book to him, one of his oldest friends, Dennis Nineham explained, in his after-dinner speech, that his friends had decided to recognise his birthday by presenting him with a book. Christopher commented afterwards that he had sat listening to these words, wondering which book we had decided to buy for him! It did not occur to him that we might have written the book ourselves. He could not believe that he deserved such an accolade.

Throughout his long life, Christopher Evans neither sought nor expected praise or honour, though he cherished them when they came his way, for he possessed the great gift of serendipity, enjoying to the full what fortune brought him. Above all, he embodied the characteristics he attributed to his hero, Michael Ramsey—humanity, holiness, and humour.[73]

MORNA D. HOOKER
University of Cambridge

Note. I am grateful to the Revd Jonathan and Mrs Susan Evans and to the Revd Robert Morgan for assistance in composing this *Memoir*.

---

[72] Hooker and Hickling, *What about the New Testament?*
[73] Evans, *Humanity, Holiness—and Humour.*

PHILIP FORD

Philip John Ford
1949–2013

PHILIP FORD was a leading scholar of French and Neo-Latin Renaissance literature, especially poetry. He participated throughout his career in the movement that has seen the vast body of literary works written in classicising Latin from the fifteenth century onwards come to be taken seriously as an object of study. When Philip's research career started, Neo-Latin studies were just beginning to acquire the status of a discipline. He became arguably the most energetic, ambitious, and persuasive promoter of that discipline to emerge from his generation onto an international stage. At a time when the relation of Neo-Latin studies to classics, modern languages, and English was still in the process of being worked out, his last book, on language-choice in sixteenth-century poetry, was a pioneering model of how to integrate the study of Neo-Latin and vernacular (French) writing in a reflective, dynamic, and non-hierarchical way. His expertise in humanist imitation of antiquity stretched to Greek as well as Roman literature: he transformed our understanding of the Renaissance reception of Homer in and beyond France. Among the many writers whom we understand better thanks to him, two colossi preoccupied him most: Ronsard, the greatest French poet of the sixteenth and indeed perhaps of any century; and the Scottish humanist George Buchanan, who lived for many years in France.

Philip's scholarly achievements were not compartmentalised from the rest of his life. They were symbiotic with a vast range of activities undertaken with unusual gusto. These ranged from teaching, mentoring, organising, leading, and language-learning to cooking, music, and above all family life. The intensity of Philip's engagement with all of these was

Biographical Memoirs of Fellows of the British Academy, XIII, 217–248. © The British Academy 2014.

made possible by a certain regulating of time and space. Home was largely separate from work; having risen early, he would cycle from one to the other. Work was centred for decades on an attic office spectacularly strewn with piles of papers and books whose order was apparent to him alone (and above which hung two oars from student days). While Graduate Admissions Tutor in his Cambridge college, each day he would make himself spend fifteen minutes in the Tutorial Office before lunch and another fifteen after. Such regulating was not for him an end in itself; it is what enabled him to give his utmost across the board. At a deeper level than that of routines and of distinctions between spheres, it is striking that the people who knew him in different spheres speak of the same qualities: curiosity, kindness, amiability, humour, integrity, modesty, dependability, judgement, determination, energy, pragmatism, enthusiasm. Whatever the sphere, he 'was always entirely Philip', and 'remained very Philip'.[1] The overriding impression is of a unified purposefulness centred on discovering, nurturing, developing, serving—and enjoying.

He died from cancer on 8 April 2013, aged 64, having known only for a few weeks that he was gravely ill. His death produced shock and grief throughout those different spheres and in many countries, not just because it was premature and sudden and because he was widely admired and relied upon, but because he inspired deep affection and gratitude. This memoir, while put together by someone who knew him mainly in just one sphere (as departmental colleague), incorporates much that has been supplied by those who knew him in others.

I

While Philip's adult life was in many respects far removed from that of his upbringing, it seems also to have been continuous with it in deep-seated ways.

He was born into a working-class London family on 28 March 1949 to a mother from the East End and a Catholic Liverpudlian father. Philip's mother Leah was descended from Sephardic Jews, originally Portuguese-speaking, who had arrived from the Netherlands in the seventeenth century. Up until the late nineteenth century, the men on her father's side had been rag merchants, general dealers, pen cutters and eventually commercial travellers. The first male in the family to marry outside the Sephardic

---

[1] Conversations with Simon Franklin and John O'Brien respectively (both Dec. 2013).

community seems to have been Philip's great-grandfather Moses, who married an Ashkenazi Jew, Leah Joel. Although Philip's mother's family continued to think of itself as Sephardic rather than Ashkenazi, she herself used some Yiddish words.

The younger of Moses and Leah's two children was someone who had a strong early influence on Philip: his grandfather, Abraham, who possessed, and helped instil in younger family members, a powerful sense of self-belief. A Communist, he tried (but failed) to organise London cab drivers into a cooperative. Abraham's own marriage marked a stage in the loosening of the family's ties to Judaism as a religion. He married a non-conformist Christian, Esther Annie Cooper, in a Registry Office. (The males of this Cooper line had been London bakers at least as far back as the mid-eighteenth century.) But culturally the family remained proudly Jewish. Abraham stood with the Jewish community when Oswald Mosley's Fascists marched on the East End in 1936; but, equally, he may have done this because of his strong socialist principles. And Philip's mother Leah, who was Esther and Abraham's first child, went to shul as a child. Philip saw Judaism as an important influence on his life, without seeing himself as Jewish. He referred to his mother's extended family as the 'Jewish relatives'.[2]

Philip was not alone in inheriting this energy, drive, initiative, and self-belief from Abraham and others. When growing up, Philip thought of Paul as his uncle, whereas in fact he was Philip's half-brother. Paul had been brought up as Abraham and Esther's son after Philip's mother Leah had him when unmarried, years before meeting Philip's father. It was only about two years before Paul's death that Philip learned all this. Paul co-founded an amateur theatre company and remained in retirement an exceptional swimmer at Masters level. Another of Abraham and Esther's children, Alf, a world champion at Masters level, had founded the Sans Egal swimming club in Ilford. The young Philip swam there too, and won many medals.

In comparison, the family background of Philip's father, Peter Ford, loomed less large in Philip's early life. Having lost an eye in Africa during the Second World War (as a result of a Jehovah's Witness bomb), Peter became a guard in a prisoner-of-war camp in Scotland. After the war he became a London postman with a Fleet Street beat. He was partial to a bet on the horses. Peter's Catholicism became strong at the end of his life, but the outcome of Philip's Jewish–Catholic parentage was that Philip

---

[2] 'parents juifs', entry for 20 July in Philip's 1968 diary.

himself did not have a religious upbringing. While Philip seems to have
ended up being close to an atheist, as a student he had often attended
chapel and talks on religion; and his own wedding, funeral, and son's baptism were held in the chapel of Clare College, Cambridge.

Philip's parents belonged to a working-class generation that wanted
something different and better for its post-war children. However, he
apparently decided when he was about twelve that, for this to happen, he
would have to devise a suitable regime rather than expecting his parents
to.[3] They were proud of and occasionally baffled by his eventual life-path.
His mother, a vivid and ebullient personality, was distressed when he left
home for university.[4] His parents' marriage was not always harmonious,
and during his childhood and youth he was especially close to his mother,
albeit in a way that involved a degree of shouting. Although the young
Philip was less focused on his father (and chided himself later in life for
having sometimes been dismissive of him), people who met Peter emphasise qualities of courtesy and kindness that were perhaps, one cannot help
suspecting, part of his own subterranean legacy to his son.

Philip attended a primary school in Dagenham. He was later grateful
to it for giving him a good start. He recalled that the backgrounds of
many of the children were so deprived that the school assumed that their
chances in life would depend to a high degree on whatever the school
could offer them. Philip then got into a grammar school in Ilford, the
County High School for Boys. He threw himself into activities and leadership roles that were to become, or to morph into, lifelong ones. He was
a Prefect. He became General Secretary of the Classics Society. He swam
for the school and captained his House swimming team. He played tim-
pani in the school orchestra, played piano (eventually to Grade 8), went to
concerts (such as Bach's St John's Passion with Peter Pears and the English
Chamber Orchestra at the Proms on 26 July 1967).[5] These were not disparate activities. They were partly connected by pleasure in discipline, endur-
ance, rhythm, sound. Not particularly coordinated or balanced in his
movements—as a La Clusaz ski trip later confirmed—Philip eventually
gravitated towards another rhythmically pounding kind of sport: rowing.
As a student at King's College, Cambridge he rowed both bow-side (leading the pace-setting) and stroke-side (a sign of exceptional adaptability).
Although he could still be seen later in life at US conferences going for a
6.30 a.m. swim, it was rowing that became more prominent. Not only did

---

[3] Philip told this to his wife, Lenore Muskett. It was mentioned by the Revd Gregory Seach in his
address at Philip's funeral in Clare College, Cambridge on 24 April 2013.
[4] Extra entry for 27 Aug., inserted between August and September, in Philip's 1968 diary.
[5] Programmes for this concert and others are among Philip's personal papers.

he eventually row for several years in the Fellows' Eight of Clare College, Cambridge but the mid- and late 1980s saw him doing three 7.15 a.m. fitness sessions per week with fellow crew member Simon Franklin. The balance and dexterity required by water polo, however, proved more elusive, at least if one can judge by the regular defeats suffered by the King's team he set up when a graduate, eager as ever to initiate and try out new things. That drumming, swimming, and rowing should come naturally to him would make sense to observers of his trademark gait—fast, vigorous, bouncing, angular, purposeful, accelerating when he spotted ahead someone whom he wished to greet in a conference corridor. It is perhaps not fanciful to see Philip's fascination for, and unusual sensitivity to, the metres of Latin verse (as handled by Buchanan and others) as grounded in this gift for rhythmic physicality.

To return to grammar school days: while Philip was in the Lower Sixth Form, the headmaster wrote to suggest that he tried for Oxbridge. As was standard in such contexts, the letter was addressed not to both parents, nor to the person who had taken charge of Philip's education (Philip), but to the person who, in this case, possibly had the least say in the matter, Philip's father. The long-serving H. S. Kenward was experienced at explaining to the parents of first-generation university applicants the middle-class rites, such as the gap year, which surrounded higher education. He suggested that Philip take the entrance examination after staying on for a term beyond A-levels (as was common): 'Dear Mr Ford, . . . The six months after leaving and before going to a University can be spent in employment and the candidate goes up with some money in his pocket and also more mature: the Universities approve of this.'[6]

Philip won an Exhibition to read French and Latin at King's College, Cambridge, to which he made the unusual addition of Modern Greek later in the course. The choice of college was perhaps determined both by King's College's particularly positive attitude towards applications from state schools and by Harry Kenward, who had studied at King's himself (1921).[7] King's may have given financial support to Philip,[8] as it did subsequently to fund the first year of his doctorate.[9]

[6] Letter of 27 Jan. 1966 by H. S. Kenward to Peter Ford, in Philip's personal papers.
[7] See the obituary for John Andrew Wilkins in *King's College, Cambridge: Annual Report 2011*, pp. 229–31 at 229. Wilkins, later a renowned VAT expert, was another working-class child who went to King's College from the Ilford County High School with Kenward's encouragement.
[8] Philip was exchanging letters with the college's Financial Tutor in the weeks before arriving: entries for 20 and 22 Aug. in 1968 diary, in Philip's personal papers.
[9] Philip mentioned this in the acknowledgements preceding his Ph.D. thesis, 'The Poetical Works of George Buchanan Before His Final Return to Scotland' (University of Cambridge, 1977).

With characteristic regularity, Philip kept diaries in his youth. Remarkably, he often wrote them in French (and occasionally ancient Greek), both to stretch himself and also to maximise privacy. The 1968 diary chronicles his gap year (during which he and his parents moved from Ilford to Bournemouth) and his first months at King's. It shows him driving himself onwards, castigating himself for the odd lie-in, urging himself to lose weight (having been a chubby child). It shows him interested in world politics (in that momentous year) in a way that continued throughout his life: well informed, keen on mutual understanding, tolerance, non-violence, and compromise, disliking any ideology that wanted victory over others.[10] He liked the Liberals best, hearing Jeremy Thorpe and David Steel in his first term, and joining the Cambridge University Liberal Club Society in 1970.

University was a sudden transition from what had been a fairly fixed if intensively social framework of schoolfriends (such as Edward Garner) and extended working-class family to a world where 'Number of people you meet is incredible.'[11] Many, mostly from middle-class backgrounds, were famously involved at King's in student activism, but Philip was not. Some of the life-long friendships he forged at King's as undergraduate and postgraduate were with other working class and/or grammar-school boys, such as Jerry Wilde (a medical student; Philip and he became godfathers to each other's children) and Allan Doig (architectural historian and now chaplain of Lady Margaret Hall, Oxford). Allan Doig, who arrived from Vancouver in 1973, remembers Philip as never intimidated by or preoccupied with the class hierarchies that pervaded Cambridge life but as intent on ignoring them, on encouraging others to do so, and on mixing with people from all backgrounds. Philip became in his third year Gastronomic Secretary of the King's Boat Club, licking his fingers to test the food he had prepared, with his all-consuming focus on the task at hand. He was an extraordinary cook. Planning and/or preparing meals was for him a fundamental means of forging community, from those student days, in which he was known for brilliant improvisation with whatever scraps happened to be in the shared fridge, to a later time in which at Clare College he would host dinners for the institutions he founded and co-founded—Cambridge French Colloquia and the Cambridge Society

---

[10] For example, entries for 22 Feb., 6 April, 24 May, 5 and 6 June, 21 Aug., in 1968 diary, in Philip's personal papers.
[11] Ibid., entry for 4 Oct. 1968.

for Neo-Latin Studies—or would carefully select wines that connected to the conference or seminar topic, or indeed to the speaker's nationality.

II

Philip's intellectual itinerary took its turn towards both Neo-Latin and French Renaissance studies through the influence of Robert Bolgar. He and the amiable Patrick Wilkinson were Philip's undergraduate Latin supervisors at King's.

But before embarking on a Ph.D., Philip devoted a year to acquiring another language, Italian. He spent 1971–2 in Milan, tutoring the twin sons of a *contessa* (Giulia Maria Mozzoni Crespi, whose family owned the *Corriere de la Sera*) and teaching English at the Centro linguistico e audiovisivi. (He liked hearing Italians remark subsequently on his Milanese accent.) Wandering through the Galleria Vittorio Emanuele II one autumn Saturday afternoon he stopped to listen to a fire-brigade brass band playing Verdi overtures and encountered someone who had stopped for the same reason—Michael Tilby, the future Balzac authority, whom Philip knew a little from Cambridge. So began another life-long friendship. Philip bought a Fiat 600 and the two spent weekends motoring around Northern Italy in this sixties icon.

In his late teens Philip would repair the family's temperamental car and worry about his parents driving it, his father being visually impaired and his mother having apparently once inadvertently run Philip over. But cars also became for Philip a means of curiosity and freedom. His relationship to them was as revealing as that of one of his favourite authors, Montaigne, to horses. It was hands-on; loyal; determined; optimistic to a point that could verge on comedy. Jerry Wilde recalls a Morris Minor van lovingly serviced by Philip himself before the pair took it around Europe in the summer of 1970. After the vehicle had spluttered at some 5 miles per hour to the summit of a mountain pass leading from France to Italy, onlookers in the panoramic car park burst into applause, to Philip's intense indignation. Jerry remembers similar indignation two years later when Philip's relief that there was little import duty to pay on the Fiat 600 was tainted by the insulting level of the Dover customs' valuation (£25).

When Philip returned to King's College, Cambridge in 1972 he began a Ph.D. on Buchanan under the supervision of the pioneering Neo-Latinist

I. D. (Ian) McFarlane,[12] several of whose supervisees became leading practitioners of French Renaissance and Neo-Latin studies (Terence Cave, Dorothy Gabe Coleman, Ann Moss, John O'Brien).

Philip's thesis, completed in 1976 and approved in 1977, was entitled 'The Poetical Works of George Buchanan Before His Final Return to Scotland'. It is in two parts. Part I is a selective intellectual biography of Buchanan that focuses on educational, social, and religious dimensions. It tracks the humanist from his birth in Scotland in 1506, through his years of alternating from 1520 between France (mainly), Scotland, England, Portugal, and Italy—famously teaching at the colleges of Guyenne, Coimbra, and Boncourt—up to 1561 when he embraced Protestantism and returned to Scotland, where he died in 1582. Part II of the thesis is a study of Buchanan's (Latin) poetry, focusing on a wide range of genres (satires, elegies, and others) while mainly excluding some (tragedies, epigrams, psalm paraphrases, and the cosmological poem *De sphaera*). The thesis is highly original, though one would not know it from the modesty of the framing and self-presentation—which came to characterise all Philip's work. The thesis corrects numerous errors in previous biographical accounts and was the first serious and substantial study of Buchanan's poetry.

Part II in particular fed, in further-researched form, into Philip's first book, *George Buchanan, Prince of Poets: With an Edition (Text, Translation, Commentary) of the 'Miscellaneorum liber'* (Aberdeen, 1982). The book aimed to provide readers with the tools to read and evaluate Buchanan's poetry using criteria that were germane to it, notably the principles and practice of Neo-Latin versification, as enshrined for example in the bestselling *Ars versificatoria* (1511) by Johannes Despauterius. This aesthetic historicising was crucial to Philip's rehabilitation of Buchanan and others against the anachronistic charges (for example of false quantities) that classicists previously levelled at Neo-Latin poetry. Aesthetic evaluation of this kind is not currently widely practised in literary scholarship on the French Renaissance. Yet it was an enduring preoccupation of Philip's. He further pursued it in various publications, such as a 2009 article in which he argues that, unlike the authors of Renaissance verse manuals, Buchanan had an instinctive feel for sound and rhythm, for the variation in metrical practice between different ancient genres, and that, bending metre without seeming to fight it, he used 'rules' as opportunities for self-expression. Few if any critics would be equipped to show, as Philip

---

[12] See T. Cave, 'Ian Dalrymple McFarlane, 1915–2002', *Proceedings of the British Academy*, 124, *Biographical Memoirs of Fellows*, III, (2004), 182–203.

does in that article, how Buchanan handled common metres in a way that was sensitive to meaning and tone.[13]

The title *George Buchanan, Prince of Poets* alludes to the widespread presentation of Buchanan (in the phrase 'poetarum nostri saeculi facile princeps') as 'easily the leading poet of the age'. This first occurred in Henri and Robert Estienne's 1565 or 1566 edition of Buchanan's hugely successful psalm paraphrases. As well as introducing Neo-Latin versification, Philip's book succinctly discussed Buchanan's poetry and drama before 1547, his relation to Horace and Catullus, and the poetry of his final years. Since the aim of getting Buchanan read once more was hampered by the absence of a modern critical edition of his works, Philip included in the volume a critical edition, with translation, of Buchanan's *Miscellaneorum liber*, which he chose because it included poems written at different times of the Scot's life and in different genres and metres. This edition was prepared in collaboration with the classicist W. S. Watt.[14]

The enormous project of a complete critical edition of Buchanan's poetical works, including his tragedies, remained a preoccupation of Philip's.[15] Years later he came to an understanding with the Swiss publisher Droz that they would publish such an edition, with Philip as its general editor. He recruited a team, and the one volume to have appeared to date is Roger Green's edition of the psalm paraphrases.[16] After Philip's death, overall responsibility was taken over by Ingrid De Smet, but the project remains at an early stage.

By the time that Philip gave a paper in 2006 in the church hall of the village of Killearn, where Buchanan was born, at a session of one of the two quincentenary conferences held in Scotland that year,[17] he had made

---

[13] P. Ford, '*Poeta sui saeculi facile princeps*: George Buchanan's poetic achievement', in P. Ford and R. P. H. Green (eds.), *George Buchanan, Poet and Dramatist* (Swansea, 2009), 3–17. Further examples include P. Ford, 'Leonora and Neaera: a consideration of George Buchanan's erotic poetry', *Bibliothèque d'Humanisme et Renaissance*, 40 (1978), 513–24 (Philip's first academic publication); P. Ford, 'George Buchanan's court poetry and the Pléiade', *French Studies*, 34 (1980), 137–52.
[14] See R. G. M. Nisbet, 'William Smith Watt 1913–2002', *Proceedings of the British Academy*, 124, *Biographical Memoirs of Fellows*, III, (2004), 358–72.
[15] Ian McFarlane and Jozef IJsewijn had earlier envisaged an edition of just Buchanan's secular poetry (the *Poemata*): see R. Green, 'The poetry of George Buchanan 1973–2013', Annual Lecture of the Society of Neo-Latin Studies, 8 Nov. 2013, p. 9 <http://www2.warwick.ac.uk/fac/arts/ren/snls/events/pastevents/annuallecture2013> (last accessed 18 February 2014).
[16] George Buchanan, *Poetic Paraphrase of the Psalms of David*, ed. and trans. R. P. H. Green (Geneva, 2011).
[17] The conference, co-organised with Roger Green, was mainly held in Glasgow. Philip's paper was published as '*Poeta sui saeculi facile princeps*: George Buchanan's poetic achievement' (see above, n. 13).

a huge contribution to putting Buchanan at the heart of European Renaissance and also Scottish studies. The other early modernist to do so was Philip's supervisor, Ian McFarlane, whose monumental biography, *Buchanan*, appeared in 1981. McFarlane explained the division of labour: he did not focus much on the Latin poetry, because Philip had studied it (at that point only in his thesis), though the latter 'has very kindly allowed me to include some findings of his research'.[18] It may have been at least in part because of McFarlane's 1981 book that Philip pruned some of the biographical material of his 1977 thesis from his own 1982 book. If the overlap of interests was at all uncomfortable, Philip seems never to have shown it. He remained inspired by what Ann Moss calls 'McFarlane's ground-plan for a full recovery of the rich and little excavated treasure house of Neo-Latin poetry, with particular regard for that written in France'.[19] In what turned out to be his own final months, Philip wrote, with characteristically self-deprecating generosity:

> This book is dedicated to my Ph.D. supervisor, Ian McFarlane, who died ten years ago this year on 17 August 2002. In writing certain chapters, I kept finding that Ian had got there before me, publishing many years ago documents whose importance I thought I had discovered myself, opening paths of research whose originality was not always fully recognised at a time when Neo-Latin studies were still thought of as an eccentric side-show, and always bringing to bear a deep literary sensitivity to French Renaissance writing. In addition to this, he was a profoundly humane and generous scholar and teacher, from whose close attention and gentle mentorship I benefited enormously in my own develop-ment as a scholar.[20]

Philip is probably alluding in particular here to a book manuscript by McFarlane, *Neo-Latin Poetry in Sixteenth-Century France*. It was com-pleted some three decades before McFarlane's death but never published, possibly because the author felt there would be insufficient interest among readers at the time. In 2009 Philip joined, as co-leader, a project initiated by Ingrid De Smet to edit the typescript for publication. He negotiated a contract with a publisher; the editorial work continues.

The gentleness that Philip remembered in McFarlane's mentoring lurked beneath an austere surface. Handwritten notes that, like much else,

---

[18] I. D. McFarlane, *Buchanan* (London, 1981), p. xi. For an assessment of contributions of Ford and McFarlane to Buchanan studies as symbiotic and yet distinctive, see Green, 'The poetry of George Buchanan'.

[19] Ann Moss, pers. comm. (Jan. 2014).

[20] P. Ford, *The Judgment of Palaemon: the Contest between Neo-Latin and Vernacular Poetry in Renaissance France* (Leiden, 2013), p. xii.

Philip never threw away, began 'Dear Ford, . . .', in contrast with the 'Dear Philip, . . .' that his undergraduate supervisor Patrick Wilkinson had written from the start. Lavishing supportive praise was not McFarlane's style. Student friends remember Philip being on tenterhooks when heading to Oxford for supervisions, sure that McFarlane approved of what he was doing, less sure of the extent to which McFarlane approved of *him*. A moment recalled by one of the world's leading Neo-Latinists, Ann Moss, who was to become a firm friend of Philip's, suggests that he need not have worried:

> I first met Philip in 1973 at the second congress of the International Association for Neo-Latin Studies [in Amsterdam], in circumstances that deserve at least a Latin epigram. We were both research students of Ian McFarlane, the father of Neo-Latin studies in this country, though Philip was much younger. We were all on a boat on one of the canals. McFarlane drew us together, introduced us, and made a gesture that could only be interpreted as 'Bless you, my children'.[21]

Philip continued this genealogical conception of the discipline's growth: at the 2012 Münster Congress of the International Association for Neo-Latin Studies, at which two panels were dedicated to McFarlane's memory, Philip delighted in calling his own supervisees—of whom some were present—McFarlane's 'grandchildren', as one of them (Ingrid De Smet) recalls.

III

However, after Philip had submitted his Ph.D. thesis in the summer of 1976, the institutional marginalisation of Neo-Latin studies meant that Buchanan, for all he had written and done in France, did not seem to have been a particularly canny choice for someone wishing, as Philip did, to forge a career in a university French department, especially in a period when undergraduate teaching needs drove appointments more than in some subsequent decades. Philip's future looked uncertain and bleak. He spent 1976–7 teaching English as a lector at the Centre Pédagogique Régional in Bordeaux. His friend Michael Tilby encouraged him to develop research interests that would translate more readily into French undergraduate teaching. Philip gravitated towards what was then an undergraduate staple: seventeenth-century French theatre. Under the supervision of Bernard Tocanne of the Université de Bordeaux III he gained a *maîtrise ès lettres modernes* by completing a project on the

---

[21] Ann Moss, pers. comm. (Jan. 2014).

tragedy *Panthée* (first published in 1624) by the prolific Alexandre Hardy. The project later turned into Philip's critical edition of that play, published in 1984.[22]

Panthée, its plot drawn mainly from Xenophon, actually kept Philip firmly in the Renaissance. He presented Hardy, born in 1570, as operating within a humanist tradition that influenced his conception of tragedy (strongly influenced by Seneca) and poetry (open to neologism and dialectal variety, equivocal about Malherbe's attempts to standardise and pare down the rich French language cultivated by Renaissance authors). Indeed, although Philip later became an expert teacher of seventeenth-century literature, he seems to have retained a temperamental aversion, if not to the period, then to a certain dimension and image of it—'classicism' in the sense of restraint, uniformity of register, separation of genres, adherence to dramatic unities, and so on—that was more prevalent in the teaching experienced by him and his contemporaries than it is nowadays.[23] Or, as he put it in only the second week of his very first undergraduate term: 'Incredibly boring lecture on Corneille.'[24] Days later, Boileau, who served as the fulcrum of this neo-classicising vision of seventeenth-century French culture, and so was set as Philip's first undergraduate essay, reduced him to an uncharacteristic struggle for focus: 'Did some reading, but found it difficult to get down to Boileau essay' (27 October); 'Tried to do Boileau essay this afternoon but listened to "Rite of Spring" on radio' (29 October).[25] For this timpanist and swimmer, the stifling prescriptiveness of the *Art poétique* was no match for Stravinsky's atavistic rhythms. But the struggle was still continuing eight years later, during Philip's first weeks in Bordeaux: 'I do not <u>like</u> Boileau. Can I therefore live with him, or should I change to something more sympathetic, such as Malherbe, for example?'[26]

If that 'something more sympathetic' for which Philip was searching was in the first instance Hardy, in the longer term it was the great poet Pierre de Ronsard—a sixteenth-century Stravinsky, as one might loosely

---

[22] Alexandre Hardy, *Panthée*, ed. P. Ford, Textes Littéraires series 53 (Exeter, 1984).

[23] See also P. Ford, 'Montaigne in England', *Montaigne Studies: an Interdisciplinary Forum*, 24.1–2 (2012), P. Ford (ed.), *Montaigne in England*, 3–6 at 6. When Philip did venture deep into the seventeenth century, it was for a Latin didactic poem that was markedly heterodox and free-thinking: P. Ford, 'Claude Quillet's *Callipaedia* (1655): eugenics treatise or pregnancy manual?', in Y. Haskell and P. Hardie (eds.), *Poets and Teachers: Latin Didactic Poetry and the Didactic Authority of the Latin Poet from the Renaissance to the Present* (Bari, 1999), pp. 125–39.

[24] Entry for 14 Oct., 1968 diary, in personal papers.

[25] Ibid.

[26] Entry for 10 Oct. [1976] in notebook, in personal papers; underlining in the original.

call him, with his quest to explore extremes of bodily and mental experience and sensation through rhythm, sound, variety, formal experimentation, myth, and arresting imagery. Philip already knew Ronsard from his undergraduate work. Indeed, his undergraduate essay on Ronsard's *Amours* opened with a mission statement to which we have already seen him hold for Buchanan, and which would govern years of work on Ronsard: 'When criticising poetry of an age when criteria differ a great deal from those of today, it is easy to condemn the poetry unfairly. Perhaps the fairest approach is to decide what were the poet's aims and see whether he was successful in them.'[27] Just as Philip did not espouse the modern critical theories, from structuralism onwards, that travelled from Paris to many parts of UK French studies from the 1970s onwards, so he seems not to have espoused the decontextualising New Criticism of I. A. Richards and others. Close reading and aesthetics, yes; decontextualisation, no. He remained consistent in pursuing his kind of historicising— not as an antiquarian end in itself, but partly as a means of detecting and evaluating the aesthetic power of poetry. This approach might have seemed more old-fashioned to some in the 1970s than it did twenty years later, by when there had been a reinjection of history into Renaissance literary studies (thanks especially to New Historicism) and by when book history—of which Philip was a longstanding practitioner (culminating in his work on Homer and Montaigne)—had become central to Renaissance studies.[28]

   The opportunity to start serious work on Ronsard came in the form of a Research Bye-Fellowship at Girton College Cambridge (1977–8), where he was part of the college's first intake of male Research Fellows. Although no stipend was involved, this was a lifeline. Hoping in Bordeaux that the appointment would be confirmed, Philip reflected that 'if not, things will

---

[27] Undated essay in personal papers.

[28] Two critical movements that largely post-dated his doctoral supervisor's generation but did go on to inform some of Philip's work, though not in a way that involved overt engagement with theory, were feminism and postcolonial studies. He published pieces on women writers (Camille Morel, Marguerite de Navarre), on the question of women's education, and on the demonisation of Catherine de Médicis, as well as co-editing volumes on women's writing and on masculinities. The impact of feminist approaches is also evident in his emphasis on the role of fantasy in the representation of women in male erotic poetry: see P. Ford, 'Jean Salmon Macrin's *Epithalamiorum liber* and the Joys of Conjugal Love', in P. Ford and I. De Smet (eds.), *Eros et Priapus: érotisme et obscénité dans la littérature néo-latine* (Geneva, 1997), pp. 65–84 at 83. For examples of the impact of postcolonial studies on Philip's work, see P. Ford, 'Anti-colonialism in the poetry of George Buchanan', in R. Schnur (ed.), *Acta Convenus Neo-Latini Abulensis: Proceedings of the Tenth International Congress of Neo-Latin Studies, Ávila 4–9 August 1997* (Tempe, AZ, 2000), 237–46; Ford, *The Judgment of Palaemon*, esp. p. 7.

indeed look extremely grim'.[29] He was welcomed by two distinguished
French early modernists at Girton, Odette de Mourgues, and his future
serial collaborator Gillian Jondorf, as well as by another down the
Huntingdon Road at what was then New Hall, Dorothy Gabe Coleman.
The latter two in particular shared Philip's deep interest in the classical
underpinnings of Renaissance literature. They both helped him with
Ronsard. After several articles, his work on the poet eventually culminated
in a 1997 monograph, *Ronsard's 'Hymnes': a Literary and Iconographical
Study* (Tempe, AZ). He wrote in its preface that 'Dorothy Gabe Coleman,
who died in 1993, was a source of considerable inspiration to me in her
close reading of texts and her numerous demonstrations of the importance
of textual allusion for a full understanding of Renaissance writers.'[30]

   Ronsard's 'Hymnes' is an important and distinctive contribution to the
vast field of Ronsard studies. Its distinctiveness lies in the seriousness with
which it takes Ronsard's engagement with painting on the one hand, and
with Neo-Platonism on the other. The first of those dimensions had
already been announced by the title of an article Philip published in 1986,
'Ronsard the painter',[31] a rejoinder to that of an influential collection
edited by Terence Cave, *Ronsard the Poet* (London, 1973). The 1986 article examined a 1550 ode—an ecphrastic description of a painting—in
which the underlying reality of the actual painting being described is left
underspecified, at least at first reading. The article provides a brilliant
reconstruction of the underlying scene being described by Ronsard's
poem. The reconstruction rests on the poem itself and on ancient sources
(Virgil, Homer, Heraclitus). This kind of approach was taken further in
the 1997 monograph. It focuses on the remarkable hymns that Ronsard
published in 1555–6 and 1563 on a range of philosophical, natural, and
mythological subjects, such as gold, Bacchus, demons, death, justice, or
the seasons, imitating classical models such as Hesiod, Lucretius, the
Homeric hymns and Neo-Latin ones such as Marullus. Ronsard's hymns
are rich and difficult, allusive and elusive, full of apparently allegorical
narratives and motifs whose precise meaning is not immediately clear.

[29] Entry for 24 April [1977] in notebook, in personal papers. On Philip's time at Girton, see the
obituary by Gillian Jondorf listed in the present piece's concluding 'Note'.
[30] P. Ford, Ronsard's 'Hymnes', p. viii. See also P. Ford, 'The androgyne myth in Montaigne's "De
l'amitié"', in P. Ford and G. Jondorf (eds.), *The Art of Reading: Essays in Memory of Dorothy
Gabe Coleman* (Cambridge, 1998), pp. 65–74 at 66.
[31] P. Ford, 'Ronsard the painter: a reading of *Des peintures contenues dedans un tableau*', *French
Studies*, 40 (1986), 32–44.

Ronsard's 'Hymnes' forges a powerful critical framework for under-standing Ronsard's aims in this poetry. It argues that Ronsard's practice of ecphrasis often shades off into hypotyposis, the presentation in vivid visual terms of a real or imaginary scene that does not have a primary existence as a painting or sculpture, as it does in ecphrasis. So, although Ronsard probably knew the Château de Fontainebleau paintings commis-sioned by François Ier from Primaticcio and others—research trips took Philip there—many of the hymns are persuasively interpreted by Philip as *quasi*-ecphrastic, even in their structure: for example, some scenes in the hymns function as framing devices and vignettes, like the decorative elements in mannerist painting. This cohesive yet semi-secret overall architecture of the poems is connected in this interpretation to the feeling of harmony that Ronsard wishes ultimately to create in the reader, in keeping with Neo-Platonism. Going further than those who argue that for the Ronsard of this period Neo-Platonism was a vehicle for imagination and aesthetics, a poetic toolkit, Philip argues that Ronsard and others at the French court actively subscribed to a Neo-Platonising form of Christianity. Much of the book involves erudite, syncretist decoding of the poetry's allegorical elements within the terms developed notably by the fifth-century CE Neo-Platonist philosopher Proclus, whose views were disseminated especially by Conrad Gesner's partial 1542 edition.

So Philip's work on Ronsard is in the tradition of Edgar Wind's *Pagan Mysteries in the Renaissance* (London, 1958).[32] It acknowledges, but diverges from, the critical-theory-inspired reading of works by Ronsard and others—as being not so much cohesive as torn between centripetal and centrifugal forces—that had recently been provided by Terence Cave:[33] 'Ronsard's style is copious, certainly, but that *copia* has a purpose.'[34] Yet Philip's contribution to the hermeneutic debate is nuanced: he acknowledges not only that much textual detail continues to resist interpretation,[35] but also that there is now, and was in Ronsard's time, a degree of disconnect between the different elements that constitute actual reader experiences of the poetry:

[32] 'Like them [sc. Botticelli, Primaticcio, Titian], Ronsard was representing pagan mysteries in his works, often in largely visual terms.' P. Ford, 'Neoplatonic Fictions in the Hymnes of Ronsard', in N. Kenny (ed.), *Philosophical Fictions and the French Renaissance* (London, 1991), pp. 45–55 at 55.
[33] T. Cave, *The Cornucopian Text: Problems of Writing in the French Renaissance* (Oxford, 1979).
[34] Ford, 'Neoplatonic Fictions', p. 55.
[35] Ibid. See also T. Cave, 'Epilogue' in the same volume, pp. 127–32 at 128.

The discovery of a unifying significance in a work of art may be an intellectually satisfying experience, but it is just one of a number of pleasures offered by Ronsard's poetry. ... As with the frescoes of the Galerie François Ier [at Fontainebleau], the sensuous beauty, wit, and harmony of Ronsard's work would have been appreciated by many more readers than those who would have grasped the intricacies of its thematic structure and allegorical significance.[36]

IV

Turning to Ronsard, however momentous in professional terms, was dwarfed in its significance for Philip's life by another encounter that occurred around the same time. In 1978, while holidaying with his college friend Allan Doig in the latter's home city of Vancouver, Philip met a humorous, eloquent, straight-talking, bibliophilic,[37] history-graduate cousin of Allan's, who was also visiting, in her case from California. Philip met Lenore Muskett again in 1979 and 1981. Allan remembers Philip putting down the receiver in Cambridge after a transatlantic telephone call and announcing that he and Lenore were to marry, which they did in 1982. This very happy marriage was the rock on which the rest of Philip's life was built.

In 1987 Lenore gave birth to their son, Thomas, or Tom. It was not a straightforward birth. Tom was extremely premature, and the lives of both mother and baby were in danger. This crisis, and its fortunate outcome, had a profound and lasting effect on Philip. He was overwhelmed with joy. Lenore recalls a change that occurred in this man whose all-round capability had developed, partly through childhood circumstances, into a high degree of self-sufficiency: fatherhood now focused him on someone who was part of him in a sense and yet other to him. And, although he spent much time with Tom, Philip was very good at respecting that otherness. On the one hand, Philip, who became a parent governor at Tom's comprehensive (The Netherhall School in Cambridge), was interested in whatever his son was doing and proud of his achievements: colleagues remember Philip's glow when Tom got a First in Latin American Studies at the University of Liverpool and later a M.Sc. in Global

---

[36] P. Ford, 'Ronsard's erotic diptych: *Le Ravissement de Cephale* and *La Defloration de Lede*', *French Studies*, 47 (1993), 385–403 at 402.

[37] Having been the acquisitions librarian at Binghamton (State University of New York) when she left the USA to marry Philip, Lenore Muskett later spent several years managing the 'Books for Amnesty' shop in Cambridge.

Governance and Ethics at University College London. On the other hand, Philip was not an overbearing father. Indeed, Philip's Ph.D. students describe a judicious and supportive but light-touch and freedom-granting approach that seems to have been an extension of that domestic parenting style. In Philip's everyday conversations with his close colleagues, Lenore and Tom were constant reference points: 'None of this would be worthwhile without them', as he wrote in the preface to his last book. One of his colleagues remembers encountering father and son at lunchtime in the centre of Cambridge on a mission to buy Tom an interview suit. And the present writer is not alone in recalling with amusement how meetings in Philip's college study would occasionally be halted by telephoned requests for advice regarding homework and similar. Philip's mock-exasperated response, 'What do you want *now*?', might have been disconcerting were it not for the beam of utter delight on his face; he seemed to love being interrupted by his son.

To return to 1978: the partial reorientation towards French vernacular writing through Hardy and Ronsard bore fruit with Philip's appointment to a lectureship in French at the University of Aberdeen, where he stayed for three and a half years (1978–81). He embraced his new Scottish existence in his usual positive and open way. It shaped *George Buchanan, Prince of Poets*. The volume appeared with the Aberdeen University Press and Philip's collaborator W. S. Watt was the university's Regius Professor of Humanity. Philip joined a strong group of early modernists in the French Department, working alongside Alison Saunders, the authority on emblems,[38] and Henry Phillips, the seventeenth-century theatre and church specialist (who was to leave Aberdeen at the same time as Philip and for the same destination). Philip did not appear to harbour the least nostalgia for England. Indeed, an absence of tub-thumping nationalism was the flipside of his cosmopolitanism: his wife Lenore reports that he deemed the French way of life to be superior to the English in virtually every respect, with the exception of the institution of Oxbridge, which he thought preferable to the way in which the elite sectors of higher education in France are structured. One activity into which he threw himself in Aberdeen was the same as that pursued over many years by his half-brother Paul: theatre. Philip's new friends included Carolyn and Bill Kirton, and Philip acted in plays directed by Bill—as Monsieur Smith in Ionesco's *La Cantatrice chauve* in the department's annual French play,

---

[38] Years later, Philip co-edited her Festschrift: A. Adams and P. Ford (eds.), assisted by S. Rawles, *Le Livre demeure: Studies in Book History in Honour of Alison Saunders* (Geneva, 2011).

234 *Neil Kenny*

and as the lead in a children's play written by Bill for a local drama group: 'Philip seemed to get pleasure from everything.'[39] A hardy non-complainer, he also seemed oblivious to the freezing temperatures to which his garret flat descended in winter, as his friend Jerry Wilde found to his discomfort when visiting.

In 1981, Philip left Aberdeen. He returned to Cambridge, this time for good. He was appointed University Assistant Lecturer (till 1986) and then University Lecturer (1986–99) in French, before becoming Reader in French and Neo-Latin Literature (1999–2004), and Professor of the same (2004–13). In 1982 he was elected Fellow of Clare College, Cambridge, the start of a 31-year-long attachment during which he would develop warm friendships with longstanding modern languages colleagues (Simon Franklin, Alison Sinclair, Tess Knighton) and more recent ones (Rodrigo Cacho, Helena Sanson). Alison Sinclair was on the college body that selected him: 'When asked in 1982 by the Fellowship Committee at Clare about his reasons for returning to Cambridge, his reply was characteristically brief, good-humoured, revealing, and remarkably simple. Cambridge was 500 miles closer to France.'[40]

V

Within the Department of French at the University of Cambridge Philip was a quiet—in the sense of non-attention-seeking—new member, while starting to initiate and develop what became an extraordinary twin-tracked tradition of research events, one focused on French Renaissance studies, the other on Neo-Latin studies. For each, he exploited to the hilt the infrastructure and resources available to him at Clare College.

He initiated a 1985 colloquium and publication that was initially cash-strapped but turned out to be the first in a series of ten Cambridge French Colloquia, held 1985–2008 and published 1986–2012. His co-organiser for the first, 'Ronsard in Cambridge', and several more was his good friend Gillian Jondorf; the pair co-edited the first six volumes, before other co-editors replaced Jill alongside Philip. Some of the volumes were devoted to major authors (two are on Montaigne), but most provided a new look either at an established issue within Renaissance studies (human-

[39] Bill Kirton, pers. comm. (Dec. 2013).
[40] S. Franklin and A. Sinclair, 'Philip Ford: Fellow of Clare 1982–2013', forthcoming in the *Clare Association Annual* (Cambridge), quoted with kind permission.

ism and letters in the age of François Ier), an under-studied one (intellectual life in Lyon; poetry and music), or an emergent one (women's writing; self and other; masculinities). These events became the backbone that enabled the community of UK-based *seiziémistes* to identify and debate new research developments in the company of leading specialists from France and North America, who were also invited. Philip was invariably the initiator, the driving force, the chief fundraiser and organiser, and the 'immensely kind, genial, welcoming and ever-smiling host'.[41] The present writer recalls seeing him bound onto the rostrum to deliver the opening address while pouring with sweat from dashing around resolving last-minute logistical issues. Philip also took sole care of the marketing and sale of the volumes.

Having something like the Cambridge French Colloquia up and running might have sufficed for most academics of the enterprising kind, but not for Philip. Ann Moss witnessed his role in forging Neo-Latin research communities and traditions:

> In 1991, Philip initiated a series of Cambridge Neo-Latin symposia that were to meet in Clare College every two years out of three, and which he organised with the prodigious efficiency also in evidence in his parallel series of French colloquia. They were open to a growing band of postgraduate students, young research fellows, and a devoted following of national and international scholars. The symposia were variously themed and many of their sessions resulted in published collections of papers. These meetings were enormously important for the encouragement and companionship they gave to young researchers in this emerging field and contributed very effectively to its rising professional status.[42]

Themes of the consequent volumes that Philip also co-edited include erotic writing, pastoral, drama. Out of these symposia emerged in 1992 the Cambridge Society for Neo-Latin Studies, co-founded by Philip, Ingrid De Smet (his first Ph.D. student), Philip Hardie, Hugo Tucker, and Zweder von Martels. The new society oversaw both the symposia and also 'the Cambridge Neo-Latin research seminars, instituted around the same time under Philip's guidance, and meeting at Clare on usually two evenings a term'.[43] Fellow stalwarts of this Cambridge Neo-Latin scene came to include over the years, in addition to those just mentioned, Yasmin Haskell, David Money, Andrew Taylor, and Paul White.

---

[41] Ann Moss (describing Neo-Latin conferences), pers. comm. (Jan. 2014).
[42] Ibid.
[43] Ibid.

Philip did not however only embed Neo-Latin at a research level in the university. He also pulled off the unprecedented feat of embedding it at undergraduate level.

> Post-medieval Latin, with the creditable exception of the Low Countries, has rarely had a place of its own in the university syllabus. In the United Kingdom, it was until very recently spurned by classicists, and only existed as a just about tolerated research interest of a few eccentric scholars employed in recognised departments such as History, English, and, very often, as in Philip's case, Modern Languages. McFarlane started the Neo-Latin renaissance at Cambridge, but it was Philip who brought it to birth. It was Philip's ability to get things done that has ensured it a place within the Modern Languages Tripos, with two papers on offer and available to undergraduates from other faculties.[44]

He did not stop at the Cambridge level, for, in Ann Moss's words:

> Philip was concerned that there should be a national Society for Neo-Latin Studies. Thanks to his prompting and his early oversight, this has now come into being [in 2005].[45] In addition to organizing conferences, it has deliberately decided to champion new initiatives involving public outreach by the way of its website with its links to Neo-Latin collections and research tools.[46] Its most innovative, and particularly useful, activity is an evolving on-line anthology of short poems or extracts from Latin writing produced between the fifteenth and the eighteenth centuries. Members contribute items subscribing to a template that comprises brief introduction, text, English translation, and notes that elucidate the more unusual linguistic features and point up some analogies in other authors. The anthology is targeted at undergraduates, postgraduates and others who need to practise or improve their Latin reading skills, and it is being used as a textbook for elementary Latin courses in several places. As Philip hoped, the community is committed to user-friendly strategies for the survival and growth of Latin language learning, without which research in the early modern field can be seriously deficient.[47]

Nor did Philip stop at this national level:

> Over-arching all these ventures is the International Association for Neo-Latin Studies. It is surprisingly large. Its triennial congresses, held at different locations in Europe and North America since 1971, are big enough to necessitate several parallel sessions, and if it does not quite have the razzmatazz of the MLA, it scores on its congenial and collegiate atmosphere. This is at least one advantage of the fact that Neo-Latin is a haven for refugee enthusiasts, not a

---

[44] Moss, pers. comm. (Jan 2014). The two papers are 'Introduction to Neo-Latin Literature 1350–1700' (available to second- and final-year undergraduates; first taught in 2001–2) and 'A Special Subject in Neo-Latin Literature: Selected Authors' (available to final-year undergraduates).
[45] Having worked behind the scenes for the society, Philip joined its executive committee in 2011.
[46] <http://www2.warwick.ac.uk/fac/arts/ren/snls/> (last accessed 14 April 2014).
[47] Moss, pers. comm. (Jan. 2014). Ann Moss was the society's founding President.

battleground for competition between professional rivals. Philip was a committed member of the Association from its second congress, at which we first met, and later, as was his wont, gladly shouldered administrative responsibility.[48]

As the Association's Second Vice-President, he was chief organiser of its triennial congress (held at Cambridge in 2000) before serving for nine years as First Vice-President (2003–6), President (2006–9), and Past President (2009–12).[49]

Within French studies too, he took on both national and international roles.[50] The twin tracks of French Renaissance and Neo-Latin studies came together in two further international leadership roles, one as Vice-President (2006–9) of the main learned society within France itself that promotes the study of sixteenth-century literature and culture (the Société Française d'Étude du Seizième Siècle),[51] the other as President (2007–13) of the umbrella organisation of Renaissance societies and institutes across the world, including for example in Japan and Israel (the Fédération Internationale des Sociétés et des Instituts pour l'Étude de la Renaissance: FISIER). Philip was forever heading off to catch a Eurostar.

VI

In the midst of all this enabling and editing of other people's work, Philip's own research thrived. He did like a challenge: following the giants Buchanan and Ronsard came a larger one, Homer. The three were in fact intimately connected, not only because Philip often worked on them concurrently and because Buchanan and Ronsard partly moved in the same circles and had aesthetic common ground,[52] but also more specifically because of a poet and teacher whom Buchanan and Ronsard both knew[53] and who had a famous impact on the course of French poetry by immersing Ronsard and his fellow Pléiade poets in ancient Greek literature: Jean Dorat.

---

[48] Ibid. Philip himself wrote an overview of the discipline's institutional and other progress: P. Ford, 'Twenty-five years of Neo-Latin studies', *Neulateinisches Jahrbuch: Journal of Neo-Latin Language and Literature*, 2 (2000), 293–301.
[49] Ingrid De Smet, pers. comm. (April 2014).
[50] In 2011 he joined the Executive Committee of the UK Association of University Professors and Heads of French.
[51] He was also a member of the Executive Committee 1997–2009.
[52] See Ford, 'George Buchanan's Court Poetry and the Pléiade'.
[53] See McFarlane, *Buchanan*, p. 163.

The great scholar of humanism Paul Oskar Kristeller (d. 1999) had brought to the attention of the Neo-Latinist Geneviève Demerson a manuscript held in the Biblioteca Ambrosiana in Milan. Demerson encouraged Philip to undertake a critical edition of the intriguing student notes (dated by Philip to 1569–71) which were among the manuscript's contents.[54]

> Philip was very proficient in Greek, and this enabled him produce in 2000 a publication that is particularly valued by specialists in Renaissance commentary. It is a carefully transcribed, translated, and annotated edition of the Latin notes of an anonymous student attending lectures on the *Odyssey* delivered by the influential French scholar, Jean Dorat. Entitled *Mythologicum*, the student's manuscript conserves Dorat's oral notes on Books X–XII and on part of one of the Homeric hymns. They constitute above all an interpretative account of Homer's narrative, exemplifying Dorat's attachment to that search for meaning beyond the surface of the text that beguiled so many of Dorat's predecessors and contemporaries. The manuscript reveals him applying the whole range of exegetical tools they used to extract 'deep' meaning: etymologies, word-play, anagram, numerology, moral and physical allegorisation, Biblical parallels.[55]

In comparison with many contemporary mythographers Dorat emphasises the moral and physical meanings less than the philosophical and religious truths conveyed by Homer, whom he sees as a prophet or *vates*. Philip shows how this kind of interpretation was made possible by the humanist dissemination in the first half of the sixteenth century (by Gesner and others) of ancient and Byzantine commentaries on Homer's epics (Heraclitus the Rhetor, Porphyry, Eustathius of Thessalonika, Proclus).[56] Echoing his own interpretation of Ronsard's hymns, Philip argues that Dorat's engagement with the long tradition of Homeric exegesis is also innovative in its attempt to produce a unified interpretation of a given myth, and even of the *Odyssey* as a whole, rather than the discrete and unrelated interpretations of its details that characterise standard medieval and even humanist practice: 'Dorat suggested that the whole of the *Odyssey* had a single, coherent explanation: the passage of the human soul from life through death to the afterlife.'[57]

---

[54] Jean Dorat, *Mythologicum ou Interprétation allégorique de l'"Odyssée" X–XII et de l'"Hymne à Aphrodite'*, ed. and trans. P. Ford (Geneva, 2000).

[55] Ann Moss, pers. comm. (Jan. 2014).

[56] For a succinct but full list of these commentaries, see P. Ford, 'Classical myth and its interpretation in sixteenth-century France', in G. Sandys (ed.), *The Classical Heritage in France* (Leiden, Boston, MA, and Cologne, 2002), pp. 331–49 at 334–5.

[57] P. Ford, 'Homer in the French Renaissance', *Renaissance Quarterly*, 59 (2006), 1–28 at 16.

This important edition was just one plank in a vaster project, that of assessing the Renaissance reception of Homer, and in particular of the *Iliad* and *Odyssey*. Philip was able to undertake it thanks to a British Academy Research Readership, which freed him from university teaching and administration for two years (2003–5). The outcome was his magisterial *De Troie à Ithaque: réception des épopées homériques à la Renaissance* (Geneva, 2007). Although its stated focus is the one that so fascinated Philip—did people interpret the epics allegorically?—it ranges beyond even that large question.

The first half (chapters 1–3) surveys the European printing history of editions of the *Iliad* and *Odyssey* from the 1470s to the end of the sixteenth century. The scale of the enterprise is indicated by the valuable research tool that Philip appended to his volume, a 56-page bibliography of editions of Homer (excluding vernacular translations and the pseudo-Homeric *Batrachomyomachia*). This first half of *De Troie à Ithaque* examined Greek editions, Latin translations, and commentaries. Faced with a welter of potential material, Philip took the astute decision to track the changing patterns of interpretation by focusing especially on treatments of two controversial passages, the love-making of Zeus and Hera on Mount Ida (*Iliad* XIV. 341–56) and the Cave of the Nymphs (*Odyssey* XIII. 92–112). The survey's unprecedented breadth and depth enabled Philip to produce an original chronological framework that distinguished between the initial humanist reception of Homer's epics (up to 1540), a golden age of intensified and broader interest in them (1541–70), and a twilight (1571–1600). The volume's second half (chapters 4–6) then examines, against the backdrop of that chronology, the reception of the epics in France in particular, first by the great humanist Guillaume Budé and his generation (Jean Lemaire de Belges, François Rabelais, and others), then by Dorat and his generation (for example Denis Lambin), and finally by those such as Ronsard and Montaigne who wrote in the wake of the influential favouring of Virgil over Homer by Julius Caesar Scaliger in his posthumously published *Poetics* (*Poetices libri septem*, 1561). As some of these names indicate, this second, France-specific half of *De Troie à Ithaque* extends the analysis beyond editions, translations, and commentaries to include also imitations of Homer in vernacular prose fiction and poetry, as indeed in the art of Fontainebleau.

De Troie à Ithaque reshapes our understanding of the Renaissance reception of Homer's epics; it reveals in detail a degree of humanist and broader engagement far beyond what had been uncovered for example by the only previous monograph treatment of the subject in relation to

France (a decent slim 1962 volume by Noémi Hepp,[58] which Philip presents in characteristically generous terms). Although Philip had long enjoyed an international reputation as an excellent Renaissance scholar, this project established him as a star of the discipline. He summarised some of the findings when invited to give in 2005 the prestigious Josephine Waters Bennett Lecture at the largest gathering anywhere of Renaissance specialists, the annual meeting of the Renaissance Society of America.[59] In 2009 he was elected Fellow of the British Academy. He had already been honoured by the French Government, which appointed him to the Ordre des Palmes Académiques (first as Chevalier in 2001, then as Officier in 2004), as well as by the Académie Royale de Belgique, which elected him Associate Fellow in 2004.

VII

Philip's attention then turned from Homer to yet another giant: Michel de Montaigne.

The immediate catalyst for this was an external circumstance, but the author of the *Essais* had been looming on Philip's research horizon especially since 1998, when he published a persuasive case for a homo-erotic element in what Montaigne wrote about his much mourned friend Étienne de La Boétie.[60] Philip had moreover explored Montaigne's connections both to his erstwhile teacher Buchanan and also to Homer.[61] That Montaigne spoke to Philip as a human being as well as fascinating him as a scholar was evident from Philip's choosing as a reading at his funeral a passage—on grateful acceptance of the embodied human condition—from the chapter 'De l'expérience'. By gravitating towards Montaigne in what turned out to be the last years of his life, he was in fact following the same path as that taken by two early modern departmental predecessors

---

[58] N. Hepp, 'Homère en France au XVIe siècle', *Atti della Accademia delle Scienze di Torino, II. Classe di Scienze Morali, Storiche e Filologiche*, 96 (1961–2), 389–509.

[59] Published as Ford, 'Homer in the French Renaissance'.

[60] Ford, 'The androgyne myth'. He had not contributed an essay to his 1989 co-edited volume on Montaigne.

[61] P. Ford, 'George Buchanan et Montaigne', in John O'Brien and Philippe Desan (ed.), *La 'familia' de Montaigne, Montaigne Studies: an Interdisciplinary Forum*, 13.1–2 (2001), 45–63; P. Ford, 'Montaigne's Homer: poet or myth?', *Montaigne Studies: an Interdisciplinary Forum*, 17 (2005), 7–16.

for whom he had such admiration and affection: Odette de Mourgues and Dorothy Coleman.[62]

The external circumstance was the death in 2000 of the financier Gilbert de Botton. He had tried to acquire as many as possible of the copies known to have been in Montaigne's library: he reached nine (possibly ten). Where he could not buy Montaigne's actual copy, he bought another copy of the edition known to have been used by Montaigne. He also collected editions of Montaigne's works, from the earliest to the most recent. For a while after de Botton's death, it was uncertain where this remarkable collection would go. Jill Whitelock was at the time Head of Rare Books at Cambridge University Library, where she is now Head of Special Collections:

> Philip was instrumental in securing the magnificent Montaigne Library of Gilbert de Botton for the University Library in 2007.... When the books arrived in Cambridge he publicised the acquisition with energy and enthusiasm, as advisor to the 2008 exhibition *'My booke and my selfe': Michel de Montaigne 1533–1592*, as author of the accompanying monograph *The Montaigne Library of Gilbert de Botton at Cambridge University Library* (Cambridge, Cambridge University Library, 2008), and as organiser of another international conference, for the French Department's Cambridge French Colloquia in September 2008, devoted to the 'Librairie de Montaigne'.[63]

> One fruitful outcome of the conference was the collaboration between the Library and the Université François-Rabelais, Tours to digitise books from the Montaigne Library—including Montaigne's annotated copy of Lucretius' *De rerum natura* (1563), the jewel of de Botton's collection—for the freely available web resource on Renaissance humanism, 'Les Bibliothèques virtuelles humanistes'.

> Philip also gave many talks on the collection and hosted numerous private viewings of the Montaigne Library, including a visit on 6 May 2009 by Maurice Gourdault-Montagne, Ambassador of France to the United Kingdom. He was always generous in sharing his expertise not only with visitors, but also with

---

[62] Montaigne was 'the author whom Odette [de Mourgues] most admired' according to Peter Bayley's obituary for her in *French Studies*, 43.1 (1989), 118–19 at 119. Although she lectured regularly on Montaigne, the only publication she devoted to him was her very last, elicited by Philip among others: O. de Mourgues, 'Passé, présent, futur dans les Essais', in P. Ford and G. Jondorf (eds.), *Montaigne in Cambridge: Proceedings of the Cambridge Montaigne Colloquium 7–9 April 1988* (Cambridge, 1989), 1–6. Dorothy Coleman's increasing turn to Montaigne towards the end of her career culminated in her last book—D. Coleman, *Montaigne's 'Essais'* (London, 1987)—and a posthumous collection of her articles—D. Coleman, *Montaigne, quelques anciens et l'écriture des 'Essais'* (Paris, 1995).

[63] P. Ford and N. Kenny (eds.), *La Librairie de Montaigne: Proceedings of the Tenth Cambridge French Colloquium 2–4 September 2008* (Cambridge, 2012). The volume includes an essay by Philip on 'La Bibliothèque grecque de Montaigne' (pp. 25–38).

> Library staff, whom he continued to support in recommending acquisitions to
> enhance the collection.
>   Philip had a close relationship with Cambridge University Library over
> many years ... He served as the Chairman of the Library Syndicate from 2010.[64]

He was 'a supportive and engaged Syndicate Chairman' characterised by
'kindness, humour, and above all, . . . integrity'.[65]

VIII

Philip produced one more monograph. It arose from the life-long love of
poetry that he shared with Montaigne. It was also grounded in Philip's
other great cultural passion: multilingualism. Rooted in years of research
and reflection, *The Judgment of Palaemon: the Contest between Neo-Latin
and Vernacular Poetry in Renaissance France* (Leiden, 2013) was written
fairly quickly once he got the opportunity with a research sabbatical year
(2011–12).

The book charts for the first time, and on one level in precise statistical
terms, the evolving language-choice of poets: should they write in Neo-
Latin or in standard French (which was itself in fact just 'Francien', the
dialect of most of North-Western France)? Philip's doctoral student
Harry Stevenson assisted him in establishing the evidential and statistical
basis. By showing that non-Francien speakers were at times more likely
than Francien-speakers to choose to write poetry in Latin, *The Judgment
of Palaemon* concludes that composing in Latin was felt by many to be
more natural. French was more alien than Latin to many poets in France
(Dorat among them). It is difficult to assess the likely influence of a book
that has only appeared recently, but in the present writer's view this pow-
erfully developed insight is likely to have a long-lasting impact—both
unsettling and invigorating—on French Renaissance studies, not least
because of the profound expertise with which Philip then develops it on
his favoured terrain of textual analysis. Chapters are devoted to Joachim
Du Bellay; Neo-Catullan poetry (Janus Secundus, Marullus, Baïf, Belleau,
Labé); Martial and Marot (and the latter's Neo-Latin imitators); multilingual funerary collections or *tumuli*, Latin translations of Ronsard; and
finally the Morel salon in Paris, movingly presented—in a spirit overtly

---

[64] Jill Whitelock, with input from Anne Jarvis (University Librarian, Cambridge University
Library), pers. comm. (Dec. 2013).
[65] Ibid.

inspired by Philip's undergraduate supervisor Robert Bolgar—as an eirenic, Erasmian, Latin- and poetry-based language community, holding out against the forces that brought civil war to France.

The Judgment of Palaemon is Philip's 'great gift to Neo-Latin studies';[66] not because it privileges Latin over the vernacular, but because it uncovers in such compelling detail a two-way dynamic relationship—of influence, imitation, translation, emulation—between the two:

> . . . indeed, with hindsight we can take it as a summation of all his work in the Neo-Latin field, brought here into close collusion with the French-language poetry of the Renaissance that was the subject of Philip's parallel research trajectory. There is much learning here, lightly worn. There is evidence drawn from manuscript sources, as well as printed books. There is a continuation of Philip's analytical expertise in detailed matters of language choice, metrics, and stylistic manoeuvres, now tellingly applied to a comparison of poems translated and imitated from Latin originals into French and, mainly, from French originals into Latin, with further comparative excursions into Greek, classical Latin, and Italian Neo-Latin writers. . . . Numerical tables account for all French poets of the period, their language of choice, and their geographical distribution, . . . Most impressive of all is the consummate ease with which Philip is able to move about the whole of Latin poetry, ancient and modern, picking up specific vocabulary, turns of phrase, and images with which his Neo-Latins constructed their *ancienne poésie renouvelée*. The captivated reader senses that she is entering the very mind of the Renaissance humanists. McFarlane would have been very proud, . . .[67]

A few days before he died, Philip was gratified to hold a copy of the printed volume in his hands.

IX

Philip wrote on many other topics and writers in the ninety or so articles he published in addition to co-editing no fewer than nineteen collective volumes or special issues (five of which appeared in 2011 and 2012 alone). A twentieth was almost finished at his death: the vast, two-volume *Brill's Encyclopaedia of the Neo-Latin World* (Leiden and Boston, MA, 2014). Its other two editors are Jan Bloemendal and Charles Fantazzi: '[Philip] was the one who was the architect of the structure of the *Encyclopaedia*, the chief editor.'[68]

[66] Ann Moss, pers. comm. (Jan. 2014).
[67] Ibid.
[68] Jan Bloemendal, pers. comm. (Dec. 2013).

Staggering though Philip's research achievements and activities were, they were only vaguely or barely known by many colleagues and under-graduate students in Cambridge who knew him well but in *other* respects. There were perhaps three reasons for this discrepancy: those other, non-research respects *also* appeared to be all-consuming, and so were easily assumed to be; no single individual had the energy or knowledge to follow Philip across all his spheres of activity; he did not broadcast his achievements.

He saw his teaching of undergraduates and postgraduates as part of his central mission. He supervised doctoral students working on a wide range of Neo-Latin and other topics, mainly early modern (including Ingrid De Smet, Margaret Duncumb, Paul White, Emilia Wilton-Godbertforde, Harry Stevenson, Adam Kay, David Porter, and Jaspreet Singh Boparai) but also medieval (Venetia Bridges). When sending him messages shortly before his death, his current and former undergraduates singled out his kindness and inspiring passion for the subject as a teacher, the reassuring smiles with which he greeted them at their admissions inter-views, and the gentle and discreet rigour of his prompts to them: 'The moment in my interview when you raised your eyebrows at me and asked me whether I was really sure that "it was all Madame Bovary's fault" is engraved in my memory! I promise I will do exactly as you told me and put that "bit more effort" into final year.'[69] He did not do his fair share of undergraduate admissions interviews: he did more than it, being the spe-cialist in the most applied-for language (French) at what was in most years the most-applied for Cambridge college in modern languages (Clare). Quietly mindful of his own origins, he was passionate about widening participation in higher education long before most of his colleagues. Yet he was a traditionalist in the sense that he was more cautious than some about giving applicants the benefit of the doubt if their grammar was weak.

As in his research worlds, he both continued such ground-level involve-ment—in his Cambridge college, department, and faculty, for example as Director of Studies at Clare for twenty-five years from 1982—while also assuming ever-higher leadership roles. He was Admissions Tutor at Clare (1985–93), also chairing for the last three of those years the university-wide forum for admissions tutors (the Cambridge Admissions Forum). He was Chair of the Faculty of Modern and Medieval Languages (1996–9),

[69] Reproduced by kind permission of Anna Wagner. These messages were collected and conveyed to Philip by his friend and colleague Rodrigo Cacho.

having been its Academic Secretary. He progressed to roles at school and university level: from 2006 to 2010 he was Deputy Chair of the Council of the School of Arts and Humanities (forming a duo with his old Clare friend the Russianist Simon Franklin when the latter became Chair in 2009), a member of the university's General Board, and of the General Board's Education Committee. Philip implemented at these higher levels the holistic approach to graduate welfare that he practised himself as a supervisor and mentor: having been Graduate Admissions Tutor at Clare (1995–9), as Deputy Chair of the School he enthusiastically led the implementation, within the university's arts and humanities, of the new regime of support for postgraduate skills training and career development that had been ushered in by the 2002 Roberts Report. This culminated in the establishment of the School of Arts and Humanities Graduate School (1 January 2010).

Philip's style in such roles was not to adopt an Olympian blue-skies-thinking position or to ignore some issues in order to devote all his attention to others, but to be pragmatically engaged across the board in issues large and small. Whoever emailed him about anything would get a prompt and courteous answer, from first-year undergraduate to Vice-Chancellor. He thrived in the committee-led decision-making environment of the University of Cambridge because he was honest, had no secret agendas or self-promoting aims, and so could be entrusted take the out-of-committee decisions upon which such a system relies for the wheels to keep turning. He was an astute, realistic appraiser of personalities and political possibilities. His fundamental gentleness could be laced with toughness or even obduracy when he felt it was needed: not one to be plagued by self-doubt, he could dig his heels in. One colleague and devoted friend describes his can-do approach as verging occasionally on the 'maddeningly optimistic', while also pointing out that he would look to build bridges after a heated argument. He was not a bearer of grudges. He was a facilitator who got people with different outlooks to work together constructively, and so was easy to take for granted because so dependable and not attention-seeking. He was not prone to gossip, nor to a sense of superiority in relation to the majority of academics whose energy, commitment, and gifts were dwarfed by his. The only person whose organisational skills the present writer heard him criticise was himself, when fatigue or the sheer volume of his activities led to oversights or delays, as inevitably happened on occasion. Some things certainly irritated him: unwillingness to take one's routine turn at a task; allowing personal issues such as resentments to interfere with one's professionalism; and intellectual showiness if he thought its aim was to conceal an absence of knowledge.

Although he was profoundly public-spirited, believed strongly in the institutions for which he worked, and pushed himself very hard, he seems to have done so more because he wanted to than because he felt he ought to. He hugely enjoyed most of his work. Researching, learning, and teaching were for him different facets of one and the same enterprise; and the pull that Renaissance humanism exerted on him was due in part to the primacy it gave to education. For him, learning was not just something to get others to do. His own language-learning was extraordinary. Acquiring a new language was a joy. In addition to French, Italian, Latin, and ancient and modern Greek, he had a very good grasp of Dutch (acquired to help him work on Erasmus and interact with Dutch and Flemish scholars), German, and Spanish (influenced by his son Tom—the pair also took a night class in Russian together at Tom's school); Philip also had a very basic knowledge of Hebrew;[70] he could at least order a meal in Hungarian; and he had a go at Swedish (Lenore remembers the air filling with surprising sounds as he practised his pronunciation at home). Students and teachers in his own faculty found him turning up in their classes when he took a Diploma in Italian (1994) and a Certificate in Dutch (2000), gaining a Distinction in each. Applicants for an undergraduate place in French and Italian found him putting them through their paces in both languages. Members of the International Society for Neo-Latin Studies had in him a President who could address them in a range of languages at their famously polyglot congresses. Language was the prime medium—with cuisine coming a close second—through which, with relish, he discovered and experienced difference. He loved spending every summer in Burgundy where he and Lenore owned a house, not because it was an escape from all the calls on him, but because he could immerse himself in the ways and the everyday exchanges of French village life. Not batting an eyelid, indeed rather enjoying it, when colleagues at the Arizona Center for Medieval and Renaissance Studies would address him as 'Phil' came as naturally to him as modulating forms of address in the languages he spoke.[71] Yet, whatever the situation, he would somehow remain visibly and utterly himself, helped by a lack of modulation in one department, that of his dress,

[70] It was put to telling use in P. Ford, 'Le Rôle de la poésie hébraïque dans l'enseignement de Charles Utenhove', in I. Zinguer, A. Melamed and Z. Shalev (eds.), *Hebraic Aspects of the Renaissance: Sources and Encounters* (Leiden and Boston, MA, 2011), pp. 182–90.
[71] His undergraduates affectionately nicknamed him 'Pipford' and 'PFord'.

as his wife Lenore recalls once pointing out to him, to his surprise, as he strode happily alongside her on a Californian beach—in jacket, trousers, sandals, and socks. Always neat and smart, he spent no time whatsoever, according to Lenore, trying to picture how he looked visually to others.

This physical artlessness actually made him an expressive, unique physical presence. Most striking of all was his laugh: an explosive guffaw, frequent and generous, in the sense that Philip had the gift of making one feel that one's lame quips really were funny—many a conference and seminar speaker must have felt grateful.

> But there was another characteristic sound. Around the coffee-table in the [Clare College] SCR, with people looking with more or less interest at the papers . . ., Philip would look up, say, 'Right', or 'So', or occasionally 'Now', by way of introducing a discussion about things that collectively we might need to do—or to think about doing. You knew when you heard one of these monosyllables from Philip that he was preparing to get us in gear, reminding us of tasks to be done, and always with some view of what the obligations (or the way forward) might be.[72]

On tricky issues, Philip's whole body would become a vehicle for thought as he stood, head back, hands on hips, rocking from foot to foot while deliberating, then leaning wholly forward when a decision was reached.[73]

I see this unstudied expressiveness in the photograph that precedes the present memoir. If Philip looks pleased, that is because he was. The picture was taken by Lenore, in the dining room of their home, for the British Academy website when he was elected Fellow: 'Philip was incredibly proud of being elected to the BA, but he would never have told anyone about it. . . . For him, his achievements were personal goals, a sort of life plan that unfolded. If anyone asked what he did for a living, he would just say that he taught French, and he left it at that.'[74] This was not false modesty; it was an absence of the ego and arrogance that sometimes accompany academic distinction. Philip's pride at his achievements was of a straightforward, limited, skin-deep, not profoundly self-regarding kind. He was fundamentally orientated towards others, and most deeply of all towards two people, one of whom, in her reflections on what made him tick, omits to mention her own incalculable role: 'Philip was proud of his academic achievements, but he was prouder still of his son. In later life, it

---

[72] Alison Sinclair, pers. comm. (Dec. 2013).
[73] I am grateful to Allan Doig for this formulation.
[74] Lenore Muskett, pers. comm. (Dec. 2013).

was Tom rather than his academic life that offered the greatest pleasure and gave the deepest meaning to his life, and I think this rather surprised him.'[75]

NEIL KENNY
Fellow of the Academy

Note. Since so much of the above relies on what has been communicated to me by others, their contributions have not as a rule been individually acknowledged, except in cases of direct quotation. I am deeply grateful to Lenore Muskett and Thomas Muskett-Ford for talking and writing to me about Philip, and for allowing me to see and quote from his personal papers. Ann Moss kindly contributed a written assessment of his contribution to Neo-Latin studies, from which I quote at length; she thanks Jim Binns and Roger Green for supplying information. My warm thanks go to many people who supplied me with documents, insights, and memories, including Philip's nephew Mark, Jan Bloemendal, Venetia Bridges, Rachel Deadman, Allan Doig, Rodrigo Cacho, Ingrid De Smet, Erna Eagar, Stephen Fennell, Simon Franklin, Roger Green, Liz Guild, Yasmin Haskell, David Holton, Ann Jarvis, Bill and Carolyn Kirton, Jim Laidlaw, Marc Laureys, Michael Moriarty, John O'Brien, Alison Sinclair, Astrid Steiner-Weber, Harry Stevenson, Elsa Strietman, Andrew Taylor, Michael Tilby, Paul White, Jill Whitelock, Jerry Wilde, and Emma Wilson. Obituaries of Philip Ford, on some of which I have drawn for particular points, have been written by Ingrid De Smet in *RHR: Renaissance, Humanisme, Réforme*, 76 (2013), 8–10, and in the *Neulateinisches Jahrbuch*, 15 (2013), 5–9; Gillian Jondorf in *The Year 2012–2013: The Annual Review of Girton College* (Cambridge, 2013), pp. 109–10; Neil Kenny in *French Studies*, 67.4 (2013), 593–5; Michael Moriarty in *The Independent*, 15 May 2013; John O'Brien in *The Times*, 20 June 2013, and in the *Bulletin de Liaison: Société Française d'Étude du Seizième Siècle*, 77 (May 2013), 27–8. A forthcoming issue of the *Clare Association Annual* (Cambridge) will include three pieces devoted to Philip Ford, two of them jointly authored by Simon Franklin and Alison Sinclair (an obituary; an address read out at the funeral) and the other a trilingual elegy (Greek, English, Latin) by Stephen Fennell. A memorial volume of essays is in progress: *Sodalitas litteratorum: la sodalité dans la littérature néo-latine et française de la Renaissance et de l'époque moderne (1500–1675) / 'Sodality' in Early Modern French and Neo-Latin Literature (1500–1675). Études à la mémoire de Philip Ford / Studies in Memory of Philip Ford (1949–2013)*, ed. Ingrid De Smet and Paul White.

[75] Muskett, pers. comm. (Dec. 2013).

JOHN HAJNAL

John Hajnal
1924–2008

Introduction

JOHN HAJNAL was born on 26 November 1924 in Darmstadt, a town close to Frankfurt, which was then in the German State of Hesse. His full name was John Hajnal-Kónyi, reflecting the family's Hungarian background. The family was also Jewish, and with increasing discrimination and persecution during the Nazi regime it decided to leave Germany. John was sent to a Quaker school in The Netherlands in 1936. A notable linguist, he became fluent in Dutch and later in life would sometimes lapse into Dutch. He described this as the happiest time of his life (Seneta, 2010). His parents left Germany for England and John rejoined them in 1937. He then attended University College School in Hampstead, London, and entered Balliol College, Oxford, at age 16. John was highly academically talented and was also multilingual. Initially he studied classics, but switched to politics, philosophy and economics in his second year and gained a First Class Honours degree in 1943.

Although without an academic background in statistics or mathematics, he had a strong interest and flair for these subjects and was a member of the staff of Britain's Royal Commission on Population in the period 1944–8. During that time, he contributed to the work of the Commission but also started to develop his wider interests in demography, which led to a number of publications in the premier journal in the discipline, *Population Studies*, and elsewhere, including the *American Sociological Review* and *Population Index*, in the late 1940s and early 1950s. At the same time, two demographers who were to play important roles at the

Biographical Memoirs of Fellows of the British Academy, XIII, 251–269. © The British Academy 2014.

London School of Economics (LSE), David Glass and Eugene Grebenik, were also working with the Commission.

Although relatively young, his contribution to the work of the Commission was well recognised and he was recruited to work on demography at the UN in New York (where he met his future wife Nina) by Frank Notestein, who was the first director of the UN Population Division. He stayed at the UN from 1948 to 1951, but then moved to Princeton University when Frank Notestein, who had been on leave from his post as Director of Office of Population Research (OPR) at Princeton University, returned. Frank Notestein was one of the fathers of demographic transition theory and he attracted a number of distinguished scholars—the calibre of staff that he recruited included Irene Taeuber, Frank Lorimer, Dudley Kirk, Kingsley Davis, Robert Potter, and Charles Westoff, indicating the standing of John Hajnal at that time. He spent the time there not only working with Notestein but he also, importantly for his future development, spent considerable time in developing his mathematics skills (William Feller was at Princeton during John Hajnal's 1951–3 period there). The family then returned to England, where John took up a post in the Department of Social and Preventive Medicine at Manchester University in 1953. John Hajnal was influenced and encouraged by the probabilists Maurice Bartlett and Walter Ledermann during his time at Manchester.

The family moved to London in 1957, when John obtained a lectureship at the London School of Economics. John was recruited by LSE principally as a demographer, but over time his interests increasingly turned to theoretical statistics. He was promoted to Reader in 1966 and to Professor of Statistics in 1975. He became an elected member of the International Statistical Institute (ISI) in 1961 and a Fellow of the British Academy in 1966. He retired from the LSE in 1986, although he continued contact with the institution both socially and intellectually; he was still publishing papers with members of the Statistics Department in 1999.

Since he had both substantive interests and strong statistical technical skills, he was able to attract research students with interests that overlap these two areas. The most notable was probably Bill Hamilton who became a major figure in evolutionary theory, producing a number of key findings including the kinship coefficient of altruism. Bill Hamilton transferred from Cambridge to be supervised by John Hajnal and Cedric Smith of University College London (UCL), apparently because Ronald Fisher was regarded there as a 'mere' statistician. However, Hamilton did not feel entirely at home in his new environment and after a year transferred to UCL. Norman Carrier appears to have been the member of staff who left the greatest impression from his time at LSE (Hamilton, 1995, pp. 3–4).

John Hajnal's teaching at LSE concentrated on theoretical statistics, especially in actuarial mathematics, although his most influential research work is in demography. He was a member of the Statistics Department and there was very little overlap with the postgraduate M.Sc. Demography courses that were mainly taught by a group of specialist demographers— David Glass, Norman Carrier and Chris Langford.

In his time at LSE, a number of developments took place in demography. Under the leadership of David Glass, who was then the foremost scholar in the discipline in the country, funding had been obtained from the Ford Foundation to set up an M.Sc. in Demography from 1965–6 (Langford, 1988). LSE also housed the Population Investigation Committee (PIC), members of which, especially David Glass, had been responsible for undertaking much of the work of the Royal Commission on Population. The PIC continued its activities, including organising a number of large-scale studies such as the 1946 Birth Cohort Study (NSHD: Wadsworth, 2010) and later studies such as ones on birth control and fertility in Great Britain (e.g. Langford, 1976). The PIC also publishes the journal *Population Studies*. However, John Hajnal played little role in these activities; he was never a member of the editorial board of the journal although he was a frequent contributor to book reviews not only in *Population Studies* but in other journals as well.

Although he served as member of the PIC for a number of years, he does not seem to have been active in the Committee or in the establishment of a number of major initiatives at the time. David Glass was setting up a large-scale demography training programme and running the PIC. Bill Brass at the London School of Hygiene and Tropical Medicine was devising new methods for measuring fertility and mortality in countries with poor data collection systems and also building up an active research centre. Tony Wrigley and Peter Laslett at Cambridge were founding the Cambridge Group for the History of Population and Social Structure (HPSS) as well as writing books for the wider informed public, such as *The World We Have Lost* (Laslett, 1965), which appeared in the same year as John Hajnal's most famous paper on European marriage patterns (Hajnal, 1965), and *Population and History* (Wrigley, 1969). Although he did not play a prominent role in major scientific congresses and learned societies, Hajnal built up a series of links with scholars with overlapping interests in a number of institutions. He made frequent visits to Cambridge to discuss work with members of HPSS, including Peter Laslett with whom he had a close relationship even though they had very different personalities, and other scholars with overlapping interests such as Jack Goody and Alan MacFarlane. His periods of study leave included Visiting Fellow at Trinity College, Cambridge, OPR at Princeton (where he wrote his 1982 paper) and Rockefeller University, New York, where he collaborated with Joel Cohen. We now summarise his various contributions to scholarship.

Demographic Modelling

Population projections in practice and in theory

John Hajnal had started work at the Royal Commission on Population in 1944. The Commission had been proposed in 1936 when there was substantial concern about population decline—a book by Enid Charles, the wife of Lancelot Hogben, one-time professor of Social Biology at LSE, *The Twilight of Parenthood* (Charles, 1934) had suggested that the British population might fall substantially. If the recent trend in Sweden occurred there too, the population of England and Wales would fall by 90 per cent to about four million over the next century (Charles, 1938). The establishment of the Commission was interrupted by the Second World War and it did not formally gain approval by Royal Warrant until 1944. John Hajnal was well placed with his quantitative skills to contribute to its work. In his time there, together with Bryan Hopkin, a life-long friend who was Assistant Secretary to the Commission and later became Chief Economic Adviser to the Treasury and Head of the Government Economic Service, he undertook the first large-scale and systematic set of population projections for Britain. In the past methods for doing so had been based on procedures for which the justification was unclear. However, in the 1930s models using matrix algebra were developed by scholars like Whelpton and Leslie. These provide a coherent way for incorporating assumptions about the components of population change and showing the implications of these in both the short and the long term. The work involved in making projections was time-consuming given the limited technology available at the time for undertaking the substantial number of calculations required. Nevertheless, John Hajnal produced a set of sixteen alternative projections which formed the basis for much of the debate about trends in the post-war period (Royal Commission on Population, 1950).

These population projections used different combinations of assumptions for fertility, nuptiality and migration (mortality, which was a topic that John Hajnal showed little interest in, received less attention).

Fertility was assumed to depend on marital status, age and time married. This model, with a particular emphasis on marriage as a key variable, was therefore more complex than ones often used today (a similar approach incorporating marriage explicitly was adopted in British official population projections in the 1960s, but was abandoned when the projections were found to be of poor quality). The alternative assumptions covered what were regarded as a range of plausible scenarios. There was no preferred (or 'central') projection identified. The projections were produced for a 100-year horizon starting from a base population of 48.2 million in 1947. For 2007, the GB projected population values ranged from 39.8 to 57.0 million. The actual 2007 official estimate turned out to be 59.2 million. Thus the projections that were made underestimated population growth in the rest of the century for reasons relating to each of the determinants of population change—fertility, migration and mortality:

1. the reversal of the long-term decline in fertility of earlier decades and the emergence of the so-called post-war 'baby boom' was unexpected;
2. there was a change in international migration whereby Britain ceased to be a net exporter of people mainly to the Commonwealth and became a net importer of people from parts of the same area; and
3. mortality improved more than anticipated, leading to greater than expected numbers of older people.

However, the importance of this work was in developing a coherent framework for discussion about future scenarios rather than its accuracy (all projections will turn out to be wrong), a point John Hajnal was to elaborate in his later 1955 paper.

Hajnal's work showed that some of the more alarmist projections of the pre-war period, such as by Enid Charles, were based on implausible, over-simplified models and that it was highly unlikely that there would be rapid population decline. In fact, population started to increase during the 1950s as fertility increased from the mid-1930s low point of 1.72 in 1933 to a maximum value of the total fertility rate (TFR) of 2.93 children per woman in England and Wales in 1964—although, as discussed later in the section on population models, John Hajnal would have been sceptical of this most conventional and widely used measure as a reliable indicator of the 'level of fertility'. However, the fact that there was a substantial rise in fertility in many developed countries in the post-war period was not in dispute. The issue of over-population had not yet become a topic of interest and indeed many saw population growth as a positive trend in contrast to the conditions of the pre-war depression years. Public and policy interest waned, only to reappear a decade later when the implications of rapidly growing populations in both developed and developing countries became a topic of major concern, but by that stage John Hajnal had moved on to other interests.

Population projections in theory

John Hajnal had been directly involved in the production of the first major set of 'modern' population projections in Britain. The methods used directly modelled the demographic processes by which populations change—births, deaths and migration—so permitting use of specialised insight and experience of the individual components and allowing the relative importance of these factors to be assessed. However, that work also made John Hajnal sceptical about over-extending the limits of forecasting. He presented a paper entitled 'The prospect for population forecasts' at the 1954 World Population Conference in Rome, which was published in the proceedings of the conference and an expanded version in 1955 in the *Journal of the American Statistical Association* (*JASA*). Hajnal's main arguments were: '(1) that population projections in the future as in the past will often be fairly wide of the mark—as often as simple guesses would be; (2) that, nevertheless, the frequent preparation of projections will continue; (3) that a projection can be useful as a piece of analysis even if its accuracy is low; (4) that simple, unpretentious short term projections should be used to meet most practical needs for population forecasts; (5) that greater flexibility and variety in techniques for projecting births need to be developed'. He finished by stating 'If there is a general lesson to be drawn from all this, it is, I think, first that as little forecasting as possible should be done, and second that, if a forecast . . . is undertaken, it should involve less computation and more cogitation than has generally been applied. Forecasts should flow from the analysis of the past. Anyone who has not bothered with analysis should not forecast. The labor spent in doing elaborate projections on a variety of assumptions by a ready-made technique would often be much better employed in a study of the past. Out of such study may occasionally come important insights about unexpected possibilities in the future' (Hajnal, 1955, p. 321).

Unlike his earlier empirical work, this was a reflection on his own and others' work in the area. The statement about the relative importance of cogitation and computation resonated with Louis Henry with whom John Hajnal corresponded following publication of the paper. Henry wrote to Hajnal on 29 December 1955 that since understanding of demographic phenomena 'could result only from the study of the past, I believe, as you do, that one should spend more time on that study than on computing complicated projections or forecasts. Yet I am not sure that these long and apparently unprofitable studies are always well regarded; the quest for profitability remains very strong and I fear that the desire for immediate apparent usefulness may often cause people to prefer a deluge of supposedly precise calculations to a slow elaboration of methods capable of improving actual effectiveness—but only later' (Rosental, 2003, pp. 103–4). These conclusions were later endorsed by Paul Demeny (2004) in his commentary on the courageous production of population projections for the next three centuries by the UN. However, while this measured approach has been endorsed by such perceptive analysts, the recent UN projections have been based on Bayesian statistical methods using more specialised and complex methods than hitherto (Raftery *et al.*, 2012).

Demographic methods

The relationship between period and cohort indicators of demographic variables has become a topic of particular importance in recent decades with very low levels of period fertility experienced in many countries, and TFR values of below 1.3 children per woman common in the 1990s (Billari and Kohler, 2004). If 100 women have only about 60 surviving daughters on average, then in the long term and in the absence of in-migration the population would fall by about 40 per cent each generation. Period measures such as TFR have been historically volatile and they might not be the best indicator of long-term patterns. John Hajnal was the first demographer to investigate this issue in detail, introducing ideas of postponement and anticipation of fertility which can affect such period indices. In his 1947 *Population Studies* article he analysed the sharp fluctuations in period rates that had occurred in developed countries in the 1930s and early 1940s drawing especially on the patterns in Germany in the 1930s. Couples had the ability to alter the timing of their births and so 'a change in the rate at which people are having children in a given year [could] no longer be taken as an indication of a change in the number of children they [would] bear altogether in the course of their reproductive lives'

(Hajnal, 1947, p. 143). He concluded that 'demographic analysis in future must study changes in the number of children born over the whole of their married lives to successive cohorts of marriages and relate yearly fertility rates to the number already born to the marriages in question' (Hajnal, 1947, p. 153)—he noted that this would also hold for birth cohorts, but that availability of data in practice restricted analysis to married couples. He was clear that the issue was conceptual rather than one that more sophisticated measures could address: 'It is, however, clear that no more complicated calculation will take the place of the net reproduction rate, which, according to the view now common, is the index of the prospects of population growth. For, if the argument of this paper is sound, it follows that the question "To what extent is the population replacing itself according to the rates of this year?" is a futile question' (Hajnal, 1947, p. 162). With regret, it must be noted that 'replacement rates' based in period measures are still widely cited by both national and international statistical agencies.

This is not to say that the Royal Commission work of John Hajnal and colleagues was greeted with universal acclaim. In a discussion meeting of the Institute of Actuaries in 1950, Bernard Benjamin, later professor of Actuarial Studies at City University, London, opened his remarks by stating that 'it was easy to criticize destructively a report based upon so many shades of opinion, a report whose compilers had been handicapped by having to draw less upon fact than upon speculation' (Benjamin *et al.*, 1950, p. 38), but even he was positive about the work of John Hajnal:

> For example, temporary postponement of births during an unemployment crisis might not seriously affect ultimate family size but it would upset 'reproduction rates'. Hajnal (*Population Studies*, 1947, 1, 150) quoted the experience of Germany after the Nazis came to power 'that the rates of those (marriages contracted before the dictatorship) who had postponed births to make up rose more than the fertility rates of those who had not' showing that 'family size changes fairly slowly'. Hajnal, dealing in the same article with the stability of family size, put an important point.
> To establish that changes in fertility rates are not necessarily an indication of changes in family size it is not necessary to have any very extravagant idea as to the extent to which the number of children is planned and foreseen. It is not necessary to assume that all married couples begin their married life with a fixed idea (afterwards invariable) as to the number of children they want, that they are all completely successful in having this number of children, no less and no more, and in 'postponing' and 'anticipating' childbearing exactly when they wish.   (Benjamin *et al.*, 1950, pp. 41–2)

The 1947 paper introduced a range of ideas that form the basis for much later work, including the relationship of period and cohort measures, the need for standardisation for previous marriage and childbearing (by use of marital status and parity-specific indices), the distinction between fixed and moving targets, and the complications that would be likely to arise as couples gained more control over their fertility which would need new approaches moving beyond the 'natural fertility' model where couples were assumed not to alter their behaviour in the light of previous fertility experience. This work has been taken forward by perceptive scholars such as Ryder (1964), Bongaarts and Feeney (2008) and Ní Bhrolcháin (1992).

Standardisation

In addition to his work on projections, John Hajnal was particularly concerned with formal modelling of fertility and, in particular, marriage processes. He did work concerned with the two-sex problem (Hajnal, 1948). Models involving one group are relatively straightforward but once the cooperating and competing interests of two or more groups have to be taken into account, the technical problems become formidable and in some cases intractable without specific and sometimes arbitrary assumptions. However, the practical application of such models has been limited, in part because the detailed data required for both men and women were rarely available.

On the other hand, he developed a new simple measure of nuptiality that is still widely used in demography. He formulated the key idea of a singulate mean age at marriage (SMAM: Hajnal, 1953a). The idea behind this was straightforward in retrospect. The average number of years spent before marriage (i.e. in the single state) by a group of people who eventually marry is simply equal to the mean age at first marriage of that group. In practice calculations are usually based on women between the ages where the great majority of first marriages take place, typically 15 to 50. Therefore it is possible to derive estimates of the mean age at marriage in societies where there may be information about the cross-sectional marriage status of the population by age from diverse sources such censuses or tax rolls, even if no explicit information is collected about age at marriage itself (although some assumptions are required). As with much of his other work, John Hajnal used data from a range of countries to show how the indicator can elucidate marriage patterns in his article on the marriage boom in *Population Index* (Hajnal, 1953b). In this paper he shows that crude marriage rates and proportions single are inadequate for making useful cross-national comparisons, and SMAMs were used extensively in discussing the results. SMAM remains a key global demographic indicator: the *World Fertility Report 2009* contains data on the singulate mean age at marriage for 190 countries or areas with the total population of 100,000 or more inhabitants in 2009 for three reference dates where available (United Nations, 2011). It has also been widely used with historic census data to elucidate research questions, for example by Woods and Hinde (1985) and Wrigley (1994).

The series of Royal Commission reports and associated academic papers were landmarks in both the development of new methods and in setting out clearly the context and options for future population growth. However, John Hajnal followed his own advice in his 1955 *JASA* paper and looked for insight from the past, where he was to achieve his greatest prominence.

Historical Demography

John Hajnal's most influential work was the chapter 'European marriage patterns in perspective' in the 1965 volume *Population in History* (Hajnal, 1965). He identified a clear discontinuity in marriage patterns in Europe in the period before 1900 (the latest date included) between those living on either side of an imaginary line connecting St Petersburg (Leningrad at the time of publication) and Trieste. With his innate modesty John Hajnal would be unlikely to characterise it as such, but it is now generally referred to as the 'Hajnal line'. It remains a key organising concept in social and demographic history as evidenced by a recent book *Marriage and the Family in Eurasia: Perspectives on the Hajnal Hypothesis* (Engelen and Wolf, 2005) and a special edition of the *Journal of Comparative Family Studies* (Brădăţan, 2012).

John Hajnal was familiar with living arrangements in much of Europe, especially Central Eastern Europe, given his Hungarian background. There had been earlier work on family forms in historic Europe, especially the work of Frédéric Le Play (1855). This had led to discussion about the so-called stem family system in Europe and the extent to which it varied across the Continent. However, detailed analysis of European patterns was lacking and it was not until 1965 that John Hajnal produced the seminal paper bringing together information on the distribution of marriage patterns across the Continent drawing on a wide variety of statistical and non-statistical sources. He argued that there was a clear distinction between Eastern and Western Europe (although he uses the term

'European' to refer to what is now usually called the Western or sometimes Northwest European marriage pattern). The Western marriage
pattern was characterised by relatively late age at marriage, an average age
of first marriage for women about 23 and 26 for men with spouses
relatively close in age; high fractions, 10–20 per cent, remained unmarried;
and marriage involved the establishment of an independent household by
the young married couple. Eastern Europe was characterised by higher
proportions marrying and at earlier ages, with large residential groups,
typically involving multiple generations, and higher fertility being offset
by higher mortality. Although non-European evidence was sparse, Hajnal
reviewed the available studies on marriage patterns in other societies and
concluded that the West European marriage system appeared to be unique.
As a result, only about half of all women aged 15 to 50 years of age were
currently married in the West compared with about 70 per cent in the
East.

The Western European pattern of late and non-universal marriage
was crucial for population growth since it restricted fertility, given that the
great majority of births in most countries occurred in wedlock (although
very shortly after in many cases). Late marriage therefore had a very
substantial impact on overall fertility levels.

Subsequent research has identified some exceptions to this simple
pattern and shown that variations exist within each area, but the central
conclusion that there are substantially different patterns in these two
broadly distinct regions in Europe is not challenged. The relevance of the
findings and research agenda remain undiminished in the light of subsequent research (for example, van Zanden and de Moor, 2010).
Consequently, the debate moved on to the interpretation of these findings.
While the data presented referred mainly to the sixteenth to late nineteenth centuries, the question of provenance remained unclear. Was the
pattern of long standing or one that had arisen more recently? Was the
pattern common to all groups in society, or did it vary by social status?
Were gender relations substantially different in Western and Eastern
Europe? A second set of questions related to the wider implications of
these findings. Was it coincidence that early industrialisation occurred in
these Northwestern European countries, or did their apparently unique
marriage patterns play a role? These issues were identified as topics for
further research in the paper and they have been vigorously debated since.

While not the only source of information on historical social structure, this work provides a framework both for more localised studies and
for debating wider socio-economic trends. John Hajnal's work on the

European Marriage Pattern was influential with social scientists in other disciplines such as Jack Goody and Alan MacFarlane (Goody, 1983; MacFarlane, 1976). In a sequel article, 'Two kinds of preindustrial household formation system',[1] in *Population and Development Review* (*PDR*: Hajnal, 1982), he narrowed the Western component to Scandinavia, Britain, Iceland and parts of France and Germany where the data were both more complete and more consistent with the formal rules for household formation he set out, but the disciplinary perspective broadened. His interest in the life-cycle of servants and its link with marriage age was especially important from a social structural as well as demographic perspective. He also broadened the comparator areas to include India and China, in particular using 1951 Indian Census data extensively. While the 1965 paper had considered household formation, marriage has been the main focus, although in those periods they were intimately related of course. The 1965 paper had concentrated mainly on presentation of findings, but it was underpinned by a Malthusian framework, whereby the gatekeeper to marriage was the ability of the young couple to establish an independent livelihood which might require, for example, inheritance or gaining control of a family farm. However, marriage was not the only factor involved in household formation and he set out two kinds of household formation systems that differed along three main axes with stylised rules of normal household formation behaviour. These were referred to as the Northwest European simple household and joint household systems respectively. Their characteristics were as follows:

Northwest European simple household system	Joint household systems
Late marriage for both sexes	Earlier marriage for men and rather early marriage for women
After marriage a couple are in charge of their household (the husband is head of household).	A young married couple often start life together in a household of which an older couple or a formerly married older person continues to be head. Usually the young wife joins her husband in the household of which he is a member.
Before marriage young people often circulate between households as servants.	Households with several married couples may split to form two or more households, each containing one or more couples.

Source: based on Hajnal (1982), p. 452.

[1] This paper is often cited under the title 'Household formation patterns in historical perspective'.

He showed that these rules could explain the main differences in household size and structure between these major regions, while also emphasising that Northwest Europe was distinct not only from Eastern Europe but
also other parts of the world for which information was available.

Only one area, his 1965 tentative conclusion that the Western European
marriage pattern emerged relatively late, possibly around the sixteenth
century, has been seriously challenged (Smith, 1983), although even here
in his 1982 article he had already downplayed this earlier suggestion. He
argued there that these rules were unlikely to have emerged in the sixteenth century and that fragmentary evidence suggested that the rules
were in operation for many centuries earlier.

Statistical Methods

His 1960 paper in the *Journal of the Royal Statistical Society* (*JRSS*) on
the probability of incestuous marriages owing to artificial insemination
(i.e. a couple could unknowingly have a common father who was an
artificial insemination donor) marked a shift in emphasis from the core
demographic topics John Hajnal had been concerned with previously
(Hajnal, 1960). The paper was a probabilistic analysis using approaches
from statistical genetics. This shift was also evident in his later paper in
Proceedings of the Royal Society B (Hajnal *et al.*, 1963) which extended
earlier work on consanguinity to the case of overlapping generations by
making random mating between a man and a woman depend on the
interval between their dates of birth. A theoretical model is developed
which is compared with observed values. The paper was one in a volume
based on a discussion meeting at the Royal Society concerned with the
interface of demography and biology, and included contributions from
the major scholars in demography at the time, including Louis Henry,
David Glass, Ronald Freedman, Bill Brass and Frank Notestein. By this
time, Hajnal was also well regarded as a mainstream probabilist since he
had been invited to join the editorial board of the *Journal of Applied
Probability* in 1964. His work in later years was concerned in particular
with inhomogeneous Markov chains, where he made a number of substantial contributions summarised in Seneta (2013). He published relatively little of a purely mathematical nature: only about eight papers in
total, almost all as sole author.

Public Policy

John Hajnal did not play a substantial part in public affairs, but he was particularly concerned with education. He obtained a fellowship from the Nuffield Foundation in 1968 to write a book on reforms of the sixth form and university undergraduate curricula. He believed passionately that the UK's 'A-level' system which restricted the long-term choice of students from around age 14 to a narrow set of options was wrong and that they should have a broader education and only specialise later. It may be that he was conscious that he would have preferred to take a subject like mathematics at university rather than classics. In the event, he was able to draw on his extensive knowledge on the organisation of schools and universities in a number of countries. He argued that the English system in contrast to those in Scotland, USA and Continental Europe led to students who fail to have both literate and numeric skills. The result was a short book *The Student Trap*, published by Penguin (Hajnal, 1971).

Postscript

John Hajnal was fortunate to enter demography at a time when new methods such as those for population projection were only recently developed and there was considerable scope for imaginative use in applications. He was possibly less fortunate in that much of his work was based on a topic of high importance and interest at the time, namely that of marriage. Marriage is not only important in itself as a demographic variable, but the strong association between fertility and marriage meant that it was the key variable for attempting to understand changing patterns of fertility. The great majority of childbearing in England had taken place within marriage and marriage was frequently followed very shortly by birth so marriage retained a direct role in determining population change. Most of the contemporary information that was used for analysis was derived from vital registration data and censuses, which only collected information about married women's experience. Indeed little demographic information had been collected since the 1911 Census of England and Wales and even basic information such as age of mother had only started to be collected in vital registration since 1938. Therefore scholars of this time had to use these published data, but within two decades much more information started to become available from other sources, particularly social surveys for contemporary populations and record linkage studies of historical populations. The focus of analysis tended to move towards statistical modelling of survey data rather than the analysis of census and vital registration tabulations. The focus of policy and substantive interest, unsurprisingly, turned toward the measurement and implications of rapid population growth in Third World countries.

John Hajnal's demographic work largely concentrated on marriage. He was to make major contributions to elucidating the role of marriage for historical populations, especially in cross-national context. Work by Hajnal and others emphasised the key role of marriage as a gatekeeper of fertility in the past. The ability to marry was a major restriction on population growth. Late marriage age and high fractions never marrying reduced the number of births a woman expected to have over her lifetime.

However, for a number of reasons the role of marriage became less prominent in contemporary demographic research. Economic restrictions became much less relevant as couples were able to marry when they felt appropriate rather than being subject to external constraints such as having to wait to inherit a family landholding. Childbearing outside marriage became much more common, now accounting for close to 50 per cent of births in England and Wales. While John Hajnal had produced a number of important studies on contemporary marriage published in major journals such as the *American Sociological Review* (Hajnal, 1954*a*, 1954*b*), these have attracted relatively little attention in the last half-century or so, reflecting the changing emphasis in the discipline. In contrast, his 1965 paper on the Hajnal line has been cited 1,741 times (Google scholar as at August 2013); it has been suggested that this is possibly the most highly cited publication in historical demography. His second most cited paper is the 1982 *Population and Development Review* paper, which has over 600 citations.

John Hajnal was not a person who was inclined to push himself into prominence. He did not establish a research group, nor was he highly visible in international statistical or demographic conventions. Some of his best work was contained in the publications of the Royal Commission on Population and thus failed to receive the attention that might have been expected in more mainstream academic outlets. For example, postponement of fertility was later to form a topic of strong interest in the context of the major declines of fertility in countries in the later part of the twentieth century. The roots of technical analyses in this area are usually traced back to influential work by Bongaarts and Feeney (1998). Hajnal's early work was closely related to cohort rather than period approaches to the analysis of fertility, but in this area most work is traced back to the important work of Norman Ryder (1964). It is perhaps not surprising that Hajnal's work on postponement failed to become a major topic of interest in the middle of the twentieth century. At that time, childbearing was getting younger rather than older and so concerns with the implications of changes in timing of births, if any, centred not on postponement but rather the reverse. John Hajnal himself did not follow up much of his early work for the Royal Commission and therefore this work, referred to as 'superb' by Hobcraft (1996, p. 486), tends to be overlooked. There is only a single citation in the major book covering technical demography—*Applied Mathematical Demography* (Keyfitz and Caswell, 2005)—and that to his 1955 paper in the *Journal of the American Statistical Association* on population forecasting. A similar comment can be made about his work on population projections. He was the foremost expert in the area in Britain in the late 1940s, and he wrote the influential and insightful 1955 *JASA* essay reflecting on his experiences. He was capable of lively writing; his comment in that paper that population projections would benefit from a little more cogitation and a little less computation is one that is now widely acknowledged. However, this also was his swan song in this particular area and his interests moved on elsewhere as noted above.

The reputation of his work on historical demography rests substantially on only two papers, one published in 1965 and the other in 1982. In the intervening period, he produced little work in this area even though it had become a major focus of interest. In 1972, a substantial work edited by Peter Laslett with Richard Wall (1972), *Household and Family in Past Time*, included studies from eminent scholars. Many of these had been stimulated by the work of Hajnal, and included in-depth studies on household structures on both sides of the Hajnal line. John Hajnal himself did not appear in the volume, even though attempts were made to encourage him to contribute to such volumes. The reason why he was not involved remains unclear.

John Hajnal was able to make substantial contributions to a number of distinct academic fields. His output was not large but has been enormously influential. The Hajnal line work created interest across a range of disciplines and in a number of areas: after more than half a century it is still widely used as a framework for discussing household structure and change within Europe. Questions that arose included the extent to which the pattern that he identified mainly for the sixteenth to early twentieth centuries, had been a long-standing pattern or had arisen due to social and economic changes such as feudalism. It also provided a potential framework for explaining the diverging development patterns in Eastern and Western Europe. It raised the question of how far the Western (or Northwestern) European marriage pattern was a factor in the emergence of industrial development in that part of the globe.

John Hajnal had a keen interest in ideas but he was not as visible in administrative and scientific organisations as might have been expected for someone of his standing. He did not organise scientific meetings or edit books. He 'went his own way', as his gravestone says. However, he was unfailingly courteous and his work continues to have a major influence on historical demography. He died on 30 November 2008.

MICHAEL MURPHY
Fellow of the Academy

Note. As the author had only limited interaction with John Hajnal, this memoir relies heavily on contributions from Chris Langford, Richard Smith, Eugene Seneta, Tony Wrigley and members of the Statistics Department at LSE, whose help is gratefully acknowledged. See also the obituaries by Eugene Seneta in the *ISI Newsletter* (Seneta, 2010) and one in the *Jewish Chronicle* of 5 February 2009 <http://www.thejc.com/social/obituaries/obituary-john-hajnal>.

References

Benjamin, B. *et al.* (1950). 'Report of the Royal Commission on Population: abstract of the discussion', *Journal of the Institute of Actuaries*, 76: 38–59.

Billari, F. C. and Kohler, H. P. (2004). 'Patterns of low and lowest-low fertility in Europe', *Population Studies*, 58: 161–76.

Bongaarts, J. and Feeney, G (1998). 'On the quantum and tempo of fertility', *Population and Development Review*, 24: 271–91.

Bongaarts, J. and Feeney, G. (2008). 'Afterthoughts on the mortality tempo effect', in E. Barbi, J. Bongaarts and J. W. Vaupel (eds.), *How Long Do We Live?: Demographic Models and Reflections on Tempo Effects* (Dordrecht), pp. 263–9.

Brădăţan, C. (2012). 'Guest editor comments to Special Issue: Whatever Happened to Hajnal's Line? "East European" Family Patterns, Historical Context and New Developments', *Journal of Comparative Family Studies*, 43: preceding p. 335.

Charles, E. (1934). *The Twilight of Parenthood: a Biological Study of the Decline of Population Growth* (London).

Charles, E. (1938). 'The effect of present trends in fertility and mortality upon the future population of Great Britain and upon its age composition', in L. Hogben (ed.), *Political Arithmetic: a Symposium of Population Studies* (London), pp. 73–105.

Demeny, P. (2004). 'Population futures for the next three hundred years: soft landing or surprises to come?' *Population and Development Review*, 30: 507–17.

Engelen, T. and Wolf, A. P. (eds.) (2005). *Marriage and the Family in Eurasia: Perspectives on the Hajnal Hypothesis* (Amsterdam).

Goody, J. (1983). *The Development of the Family and Marriage in Europe* (Cambridge).

Hajnal, J. (1947). 'The analysis of birth statistics in the light of the recent international recovery of the birth-rate', *Population Studies*, 1: 137–64.

Hajnal, J. (1948). 'Some comments on Mr Karmel's paper, "The relation between male and female reproduction rates"', *Population Studies*, 2: 352–60.

Hajnal, J. (1953*a*). 'Age at marriage and proportions marrying', *Population Studies*, 7: 111–36.

Hajnal, J. (1953*b*). 'The marriage boom', *Population Index*, 9: 80–101.

Hajnal, J. (1954*a*). 'Analysis of changes in the marriage pattern by economic groups', *American Sociological Review*, 19: 295–302.

Hajnal, J. (1954*b*). 'Differential changes in marriage patterns', *American Sociological Review*, 19: 148–54.

Hajnal, J. (1955). 'The prospects of population forecasts', *Journal of the American Statistical Association*, 50: 309–22.

Hajnal, J. (1960). 'Artificial insemination and the frequency of incestuous marriages', *Journal of the Royal Statistical Society. Series A*, 123: 182–94.

Hajnal, J. (1965). 'European marriage patterns in perspective', in D. V. Glass and D. E. C. Eversley (eds.), *Population in History: Essays in Historical Demography* (London), pp. 101–43.

Hajnal, J. (1971). *The Student Trap: a Critique of University and Sixth-form Curricula* (Harmondsworth).

Hajnal, J. (1982). 'Two kinds of preindustrial household formation system', *Population and Development Review*, 8: 449–94.

Hajnal, J., Fraccaro, M., Sutter, J. and Smith, C. A. B. (1963). 'Concepts of random mating and the frequency of consanguineous marriages (with discussion)', *Proceedings of the Royal Society. Series B Biological Sciences*, 159: 125–77.

Hamilton W. D. (1995). *Narrow Roads of Gene Land: the Collected Papers of W. D. Hamilton. Vol.1, Evolution of Social Behaviour* (New York).

Hobcraft, J. (1996). 'Fertility in England and Wales: a fifty-year perspective', *Population Studies*, 50: 485–524.

Keyfitz, N. and Caswell, H. (2005). *Applied Mathematical Demography* (third edition) (Dordrecht).

Langford, C. M. (1976). *Birth Control Practice and Marital Fertility in Great Britain: a Report on a Survey Carried Out in 1967–68* (London).

Langford, C. M. (1988). *The Population Investigation Committee: a Concise History to Mark its Fiftieth Anniversary* (London).

Laslett, P. (1965). *The World We Have Lost* (London).

Laslett, P. and Wall, R. (1972). *Household and Family in Past Time* (Cambridge).

Le Play, F. (1855). *Les Ouvriers européens*, 1st edition, 1 volume in folio, 1855; 2nd edition, 6 volumes (1877–9) (Tours).

MacFarlane, A. (1976). *The Origins of English Individualism: the Family, Property and Marriage in Europe* (Oxford).

Ní Bhrolcháin, M. (1992). 'Period paramount? A critique of the cohort approach to fertility', *Population and Development Review*, 18: 599–629.

Raftery, A. E., Li, N., Ševčíková, H., Gerland, P. and Heilig, G. K. (2012). 'Bayesian probabilistic population projections for all countries', *Proceedings of the National Academy of Sciences*, 109: 13915–21.

Rosental, P.-A. (2003). 'The novelty of an old genre: Louis Henry and the founding of historical demography', *Population-E*, 58: 97–130.

Royal Commission on Population (1950). *Reports and Selected Papers of the Statistics Committee Volume II, pp. 213–301. Population Projections for Great Britain 1947–2047. Report by the Assistant Secretary* (London).

Ryder, N. B. (1964). 'The process of demographic translation', *Demography*, 1: 74–82.

Seneta, E. (2010). 'In Memoriam John Hajnal', *ISI Newsletter—Volume 34, Number 1 (100) 2010*, p. 10, available at <http://isi.cbs.nl/NLet/ISINewsletter2010-1.pdf> [accessed 16 April, 2014].

Seneta, E. (2013). 'Inhomogeneous markov chains and ergodicity coefficients: John Hajnal (1924–2008)', *Communications in Statistics—Theory and Methods*. Published online: 31 May 2013 DOI: 10.1080/03610926.2012.754468 [accessed 16 April 2014]

Smith, R. M. (1983). 'Hypothèses sur la nuptialité en Angleterre aux XIIIe–XIVe siècles', *Annales, Économies, Sociétés, Civilisations*, I: 22–73.

United Nations, Department of Economic and Social Affairs, Population Division (2011). *World Fertility Report 2009* (New York).

van Zanden, J. L. and de Moor, T. (2010). 'Girl power: the European marriage pattern and labour markets in the North Sea region in the late medieval and early modern period', *Economic History Review*, 63: 1–33.

Wadsworth, M. (2010). 'The origins and innovatory nature of the 1946 British national birth cohort study', *Longitudinal and Life Course Studies*, 1: 121–36.

Woods, R. I. and Hinde, P. R. A. (1985). 'Nuptiality and age at marriage in nineteenth century England', *Journal of Family History*, 10: 119–44.

Wrigley, E. A. (1969). *Population and History* (London).

Wrigley, E. A. (1994). 'The effect of migration on the estimation of marriage age in family reconstitution studies', *Population Studies*, 48: 81–97.

EMRYS JONES   *Photograph: Deborah Elliot*

Emrys Lloyd Jones
1931–2012

EMRYS JONES was the most original scholar–critic of his generation in the field of Shakespeare and sixteenth-century literature. He was born on 30 March 1931 in Hoxton. His parents, Peter and Elizabeth (née Evans), had moved to London from Wales in the 1920s, and ran a corner shop and dairy at 155 Pitfield Street. Emrys used jokingly to refer to himself as a cockney, and as Pitfield Steet is not much more than a mile from St Mary-le-Bow, as the crow flies, he almost certainly had a right to that title. At the outbreak of the Second World War he was sent, for safety, to Wales, where he boarded with relatives of his mother at 59 High Street, Glynneath.

He attended Neath Grammar School, where he was in the same form as Peter Lewis, later a Professor of Medieval History at Oxford, David Nicholas, later Sir David, head of Independent Television News, and Roger Howells, who became a senior administrator with the Royal Shakespeare Company and was a close friend. As this suggests, the school was distinguished academically. Notable on the staff were the English master Elis Jenkins and the Latin master W. J. Stratton. There was a strong musical tradition, with an orchestra led by John Hopkin Jones. Emrys sang in the choir, but his main interest was drama. The school magazine records him directing and acting in several plays, and Howells recalls their intensive rehearsals of the tent scene from *Julius Caesar* for a school competition, with Emrys playing Cassius to Howells's Brutus.

In June 1949 Emrys entered for, and won, a Violet Vaughan Morgan Scholarship. This was a privately endowed scholarship, worth £80 a year for three years, and eligible for supplementation by the Ministry of Education. A scholarship had been advertised the previous year, but not awarded, so Emrys was the first ever Violet Vaughan Morgan Scholar. In his year there were twenty-one competitors and the chief examiner was Lord David Cecil. The scholarship did not guarantee admission to an Oxford college, and in his acceptance letter Emrys asked if he might do his national service before coming up as this would give him more time to arrange college admission. In the event he applied to and was accepted by Magdalen.

Having passed his army medical examination, 22343242 Gunner Jones, E. L., Royal Artillery, spent his two years of national service performing clerical duties at the HQ of 6 Ack Ack Brigade at Orsett Camp near Grays in Essex. He later said that he was grateful to the army for teaching him to type.

Howells did his national service in the Royal Engineers, but they kept in touch and would meet on weekend leaves and, later, at Oxford where Howells read law at Pembroke. They went to the theatre and concerts together—Howells recalls a Colin Davis concert in Oxford in 1952, and Berlioz's *The Trojans*, a rare staging of the complete work, at Covent Garden in 1957. He vividly remembers their seeing Ugo Betti's *Summertime* at the Apollo in Shaftesbury Avenue in 1955. It was Dirk Bogarde's last stage appearance, and when they came out the smog was so thick that men were walking in front of the buses with blazing torches. Emrys, who had a precise knowledge of London's streets and buildings, led the way and Howells followed with a hand on his shoulder until they reached Hoxton where the welcoming Jones parents insisted on him spending the night.

At Magdalen Emrys's tutor was C. S. Lewis. In those days the Oxford English syllabus terminated at 1832, so there was no opportunity to study Victorian or modern literature, and Emrys's own scholarly interests were to be largely in the Renaissance and the seventeenth and eighteenth centuries. Surprisingly, perhaps, he did not act at Oxford. But he was a naturally reserved and reticent man and may not have found Oxford's undergraduate thespian community quite to his taste. He took Schools in 1954 and did outstandingly well, gaining, by all accounts, the top first.

When C. S. Lewis was elected to the Chair of Medieval and Renaissance Literature at Cambridge, Emrys, seemingly on the strength of his Schools papers, was appointed his successor as Fellow and Tutor in English at Magdalen, taking up the post in Michaelmas Term 1955. His reputation as a brilliant tutor and lecturer quickly spread, and undergraduates at other colleges clamoured to be taught by him. His lectures, drawing on his experience as an actor, were vividly histrionic, and not only when he was lecturing about plays. A lecture on Thomas More's *History of King*

Richard III is remembered as virtually a dramatic performance. His tutorials were similarly enlivened. During a discussion of Johnson's poem 'On the Death of Dr Robert Levet' he surprised the two students present by remarking, 'It's really a hymn, isn't it?' and proceeded to sing it. He shared his passion for opera with his students, playing records for them of an evening. His breathless commentary on *Tristan und Isolde* has lodged in several of their minds. His favourite operatic composer, though, was Bellini.

Another passion was architecture. He had a close knowledge of London's churches, both in the city and further afield. Martin Dodsworth remembers being rushed off from outside the British Museum to admire Hawksmoor's St George's, Bloomsbury—'You *must* see it!' One of my own memories of Emrys is meeting him one day as I came out of the Bodleian Library and, instead of passing with a nod and a smile as he normally would, he stopped me and, taking in with a sweep of his arm the whole vista—the Radcliffe Camera, St Mary's, All Souls—he exclaimed 'Isn't it *wonderful*!' It was as if a sudden impulse had broken through his usual reserve. He lived in college until his marriage to Barbara Everett in 1965, and Dodsworth recalls the lovely rooms he had in Magdalen's eighteenth-century New Building, overlooking the Deer Park.

He was increasingly in demand as a supervisor of postgraduates, and in 1977 he was appointed a University Reader in English. Though he was unfailingly kind and helpful, the depth and range of his learning could make his supervisions demanding. Colin Burrow, now a Senior Research Fellow at All Souls, recalls arriving in Oxford from Cambridge to write a thesis on Spenser, and being placed in Emrys's care.

> He meticulously corrected small errors in the first piece of incoherent work I gave him (over sherry—blue glasses I remember) and since it didn't have a point worth talking about he said, 'You should read Ariosto'. Which I did. When I gave him a piece on Ariosto he then said, 'You should read Tasso'. When I gave him a piece on Tasso he said, 'You should read Chapman's Homer'. It wasn't until my third year that he confessed he didn't like Spenser, and I realised why I had been steered towards the *Faerie Queene* by such a circuitous route.

His first book was an edition of the *Poems* of Henry Howard, Earl of Surrey, in the Clarendon Medieval and Tudor Series (Oxford, 1964) and it combines two factors that were to become hallmarks of his work—precise learning and imaginative innovation. Previously Surrey had been chiefly known as a Petrarchan sonneteer. Emrys, however, switches the focus to the translations from Virgil's *Aeneid,* which most commentators had neglected. For him they are primary—the arena where Surrey learned his distinctive verbal skills. Anticipating some of the arguments that he was to marshal in the first part of his book *The Origins of Shakespeare*, he sees Surrey as a neo-classical poet, a forerunner of Milton, Dryden and Pope, and a product of the 'prime age of northern humanism'. He was, he contends, a beneficiary of the educational ideals of Erasmus and Colet, and of a new way of teaching Latin, promoted by them and by Lorenzo Valla in his *Elegance of the Latin Language*, that concentrated not on abstract rules but on the example of the best ancient authors.

He considers Surrey the first English poet to respond to this new teaching, and he sees the movement of his verse as 'neo-Latin', echoing the 'rich orchestration of Virgil and Horace'. Surrey, he suggests, invented blank verse in order to allow himself to compose unrhymed verse after the Virgilian pattern, and his working rule was fidelity to the syntactical and rhetorical forms of Virgil, as far as it was possible to imitate them in an uninflected language. Influenced by Virgil's 'magnificent inventiveness in syntactical forms' he tried, in many cases, to follow Virgil's word order, and the structural unit in his verse as in Virgil is the phrase or clause not the line. Compared to the Virgil translations, Surrey's Petrarchan sonnets are dismissed as 'insipid and excessively smooth', though interesting as 'performances in elocution'. Besides, Surrey turned to Petrarch, as Emrys sees it, only because Petrarch was the original instigator of the neo-classical movement, modelling his vernacular poems in diction and clausal structure on the Roman poets. The Introduction to the edition offers several analyses of lines from Surrey that capture 'the interwoven density of Latin', and which make one regret that Emrys never wrote on Milton.

Other characteristic features of the Surrey edition are its honesty and modesty. Though he writes more searchingly about Surrey than anyone had previously done, he admits that 'a severe criticism' will find Surrey's achievement 'small in scale and flawed'.

His first full-length book, *Scenic Form in Shakespeare* (Oxford, 1971), is remarkable for its authority, its sensitivity and the precision of its knowledge, but above all—like the Surrey edition—for its originality. Unlike most books about Shakespeare it is not concerned with interpretation, nor with biography, historical context or the other common topics. It looks at Shakespeare's plays in a new way, focusing on the scene as the crucial unit of drama and on Shakespeare as an artist in scenic form. Plays, it claims, 'are made of scenes before they are made of words', and the structural shaping of the individual scene is so fundamentally important that it shows up even when a play is performed in an unfamiliar language or in an operatic version (as in the banquet scene in Verdi's *Macbeth*).

It is, the book argues, primarily because of Shakespeare's mastery of scenic structure that his plays have held the stage so well. For the inventor of scenes needs an exceptional degree of insight into the psychology of an audience. In his hands the audience must become a 'charmed crowd' who look, listen and wait for something to happen. The dramatist must anticipate, monitor and control their reactions, creating expectancy and nurturing an informed interest in what will happen next. In this respect, it is suggested, plays are comparable to musical works as experienced in a concert hall or opera house: 'When we see them performed what we enjoy is, in part, the process of "going through" the work, taking pleasure in its texture and structure in a way which critical accounts which limit themselves to interpretation can hardly do justice to.' An instance of this is the way we laugh at jokes in plays even when, as with the gravedigger's jokes in *Hamlet*, they are stale and feeble. 'When the joke comes it feels new; it is in fact made new by being part of a new performance.'

The dramatist's management of time, and his ability to control how the audience experiences time, are crucial to scenic form. To illustrate this, the letter scene in *Twelfth Night* (II. v) is analysed from a temporal aspect, bringing out the 'nature of its movement': 'In performance a certain tempo is established akin to that maintained in an orchestra by the conductor's beat.' This, though, is only one of a rich profusion of intricate and illuminating scenic analyses offered in the book. Even scenes mainly concerned with conveying information to the audience are 'choreographed', it is shown, so that 'the effect is of watching a game or a group dance'—a claim supported by an analysis of the four speakers in *2 Henry IV*, I. iii, who are discussed as if they were players in a musical quartet.

An important element in the book's argument is frequent reference to Shakespeare's sources so as to show how scenic art converts its raw materials into exuberant dramatic form. These source studies repeatedly reveal a deep and precise knowledge of the other dramatists of Shakespeare's time and earlier. It is suggested, for example, that the structural source for *Julius Caesar*, I. ii, might have been the first scene of Greene's *James the Fourth*—a play in which Shakespeare may have acted. Scenic form does not necessarily relate to the subject matter of the scene, and the book's alertness to it reveals patterns of resemblance between scenes that might at first sight seem markedly disparate—the forum scene in *Julius Caesar*, for example, where Antony works on the credulous plebeians, and the temptation scene where Iago works on Othello.

The examination of Shakespeare's time-management distinguishes between scenes that make us want to speed time up and others that make

us want to slow it down. The balcony scene in *Romeo and Juliet*, for
example, or the scene in *The Merchant of Venice* where Bassanio chooses
between the caskets, show Shakespeare exploiting 'the elementary fact
that time passes' so as to make us wish to linger in 'the precincts of a particular situation'. Recognition scenes (for example, Lear awakening to
Cordelia) are comparable, though different, in that they resemble drawn-
out rituals, for which the ultimate prototype in Western drama is, it is
suggested, the recognition scene in Euripides' *Iphigenia in Tauris.*'The
essential beauty of these scenes lies in their deployment of time', in that
the ritual depends on breaking time up into small steps or segments and
on the use of repetition. Again, scenes that seem very different in tenor are
found to be similar in scenic form—Hal and Falstaff's tavern scene in *1
Henry IV*, ii. iv, for example, and the scene at the start of *King Lear* Act ii
where Goneril disputes about the number of knights Lear is to retain.

The book's sophisticated understanding of time-management allows
it to expose the fallacies inherent in the critical approach that busies itself
with detecting 'double-time schemes' in plays such as *The Merchant of
Venice, Macbeth, Othello* and *Julius Caesar*. To expect the time references
within a play to adhere to a coherent chronology—as in a detective
novel—is, it is argued, pedantic and mistaken. An understanding of
Shakespeare's art requires that we should think of time 'in terms of a
more illusionist and mimetic system, in which the prime concern is not
duration but continuity, and above all continuity between scenes'. Viewed
in this way the treatment of time in the plays displays a 'brilliant expedi-
ency'. Shakespeare introduces references to 'tonight' or 'tomorrow' and
suchlike when it suits him dramatically, and with no thought for any strict
overall chronology.

Being concerned with scene-to-scene continuity, the book questions
the customary division of the plays into acts and scenes. This division
(begun in the First Folio, but not found in the Quartos) has, it is argued,
obscured the plays' real structure, which will normally be found to consist
of two unequal movements, corresponding roughly to the first three and
the last two acts in modern editions. The 'natural interval' between the
two needs to be observed as scrupulously in performance as the pause
between movements in symphonic works. Each of the two parts has its
own 'imaginative unity', and characterisation may be 'radically modified'
in the transition from the first part to the second (the character of Richard
in *Richard III* is a case in point). In *Hamlet* the natural break comes
unexpectedly late—after what is in modern editions iv. iv—and there is
'structural rhyming' between the two parts, in that each ends with the

appearance of Fortinbras. Examples are cited to show Shakespeare using the two part structure at all stages of his career.

That career emerges from the book as itself a continuity, in that it reveals Shakespeare repeatedly borrowing from himself. The fineness of critical perception brought to this task is remarkable. Shakespeare is shown, for instance, remembering the affray scene in *Romeo and Juliet* when he wrote the affray scene in *Othello*, and Tyrell's description of the murder of the princes in the Tower in *Richard III*, IV. iii. 1–22 is remembered in Othello's soliloquy when he murders Desdemona. Many examples are marshalled to show that the structural sources of the mature tragedies can be detected in the early history plays, which emerge as of crucial importance for Shakespeare's development, providing him with a source of 'scenic form and contrivance' until the end of his career.

The book brilliantly combines two aptitudes which might be thought mutually inhospitable—an acute sensitivity to the immediacy of the theatrical experience and, collaborating with that, an incisive scholarly intelligence that seeks and finds parallels to the plays in unexpected places. The appeal to what one actually feels in the theatre is used, for example, to reject F. R. Leavis's criticism of Othello's character. What Leavis fails to take into account is that in the theatre 'we are *with* Othello'. Like Hamlet, he is the focus for 'the readily available erotic feelings of the audience'. Othello as a character 'acquires full reality only in the presence of a theatre audience'.

Working with—or against—this theatrical immersion is the detached scholar–critic, who observes how much affinity *Othello* has with comedy. It takes its main action from *Much Ado* (the Don John–Claudio plot) and in its earlier part it adapts incidents from *Merry Wives*. Another comedy it draws on is Jonson's *Every Man in his Humour* (the first version with the Italian setting). The comic provenance of this material explains why so much of *Othello* 'seems to take place in a comic setting, with its shrewd sanity and worldliness and its commonplace sense of actuality'. *Othello*'s comic affinities explain, too, why the play seems 'so much more a theatrical contrivance than a dramatic poem' compared to other tragedies.

Much of Emrys Jones's finest criticism seems to reflect, as here, a dialogue with himself—or, perhaps it is more correct to say, with his wife, the scholar and critic Barbara Everett. She is the book's dedicatee, and he acknowledges his great debt to her for 'encouragement and support, criticism and innumerable discussions'. As it happens a chance to see and hear the two of them talking about Shakespeare, and to compare their personal styles, has been preserved. In Al Pacino's 1996 film *Looking for*

Richard, which is available on DVD, they speak briefly about *Richard III*. Interestingly, Emrys comments vehemently about social class: 'Shakespeare saw Richard of Gloucester and Buckingham as gangsters, they were thugs, high-class, upper-class thugs.' Is this the boy from the Hoxton corner-shop remembering the snobbery which, some say, he encountered in 1950s Oxford?

The Origins of Shakespeare (Oxford, 1977) is as strikingly and persistently original as the first Shakespeare book and even more remarkable in scope. It, too, pays tribute at the outset to Barbara Everett's collaboration, and is dedicated to her. In its first section it demonstrates, with convincing precision, Shakespeare's dependence on the classical knowledge that was disseminated through the Elizabethan grammar schools and radically influenced by Erasmus. In its second section it sheds new and vivid light on Shakespeare's debt to the passion story as mediated through the traditional structure of the medieval mystery plays. Its third section shows how closely the *Henry VI* plays, *Richard III* and *King John* are involved in the political life of their time.

What we need, it insists at the outset, is 'a more historically adequate idea' of Shakespeare the man and of the age that produced him. A work to which it pays tribute, in supplying that need, is T. W. Baldwin's painstaking detection of Shakespeare's multiple debts to the sixteenth-century grammar school syllabus in *William Shakspere's Small Latine & Lesse Greeke* (Urbana, IL,1944). Building on Baldwin's foundations, the claim that *The Origins of Shakespeare* makes is that the grammar schools and the dissemination of print culture brought about an 'educational revolution' in the sixteenth century, creating levels of literacy not matched in any previous era. Far from being directed at unlettered groundlings, Shakespeare's plays were 'the most intellectually demanding entertainment ever put before a large audience in the history of England'.

Taking issue with his former tutor, C. S. Lewis, who saw humanism as the 'new ignorance', Jones celebrates the depth, richness and variety of the knowledge of men and ideas that spread from Colet's St Paul's through the Tudor grammar schools, Shakespeare's at Stratford among them. Shakespeare, he claims, 'unavoidably breathed the neo-classical atmosphere' and 'responded more deeply than anyone to the Erasmian paradoxes of the wisdom of folly and the folly of wisdom'. To exemplify this he shows how the plays exploit, and assume knowledge of, Erasmus's *Adagia*—a standard grammar school text—and argues that the society Shakespeare wrote for, which could pick up such allusions, was 'by modern standards pedantically bookish'.

It is a frequently noted feature of Shakespearean drama that it does not allow us to identify with a single point of view. Romantic critics ascribed this to Shakespeare's 'myriad mindedness' , but it is actually the direct result, *The Origins of Shakespeare* argues, of academic rhetorical training in the writing of *controversiae* which was standard in grammar schools, and which also influenced Shakespeare's choice of subject for his plays. Instances can be found of grammar school students being asked 'Was Brutus right or wrong to murder Caesar?' or required to compare Henry VI and Richard III. *Imitatio*—the imitation of a classical source in a new context—was another universal grammar-school practice and accounts, Jones claims, for the uncanny and curious resemblance between the Hostess's description of the death of Falstaff and the account of Socrates' death in Plato's *Phaedo* (an aperçu that he brilliantly extends by proposing affinities of a general kind between Falstaff and Socrates). Noting the 'freedom and casualness and audacity' with which the classical text is put to work in this instance, he observes that 'it is often as if at some deep level of his mind Shakespeare thought and felt in quotations'. In illustration, Hamlet's 'O, what a rogue and peasant slave am I' speech is shown to derive from passages in Quintilian and Seneca's *Thyestes*; and Desdemona's 'lie' at her death (saying she has killed herself to deflect blame from Othello) is shown to be traceable to a heroically faithful wife in Horace, *Odes*. III. xi.

The most challenging of the book's claims in this section is the proposal that Shakespeare knew of Greek tragedy, notably Euripides, probably from Latin translations. It is argued that Euripides' *Hecuba* was Shakespeare's chief dramatic model for *Titus Andronicus*—'Titus is in essence nothing else than a male Hecuba'—and that the quarrel scene between Brutus and Cassius in Julius Caesar IV. iii (the scene that Emrys had rehearsed at school with Roger Howells) is based on the quarrel between Agamemnon and Menelaus in Euripides' *Iphigenia in Aulis*.

These new perceptions are matched by equally spectacular findings when the book turns to the subject of Shakespeare and the mystery cycles. The last performance of the Coventry cycle, it is noted, was in 1579, so Shakespeare might have seen it as a boy. However it is not part of the book's argument that Shakespeare necessarily knew any of the four surviving cycles. Much Catholic drama was destroyed in the Reformation and texts have disappeared. The aim, rather, is to show that Shakespeare knew something sufficiently like the extant cycles for us to posit a deep indebtedness. Shakespeare, it is claimed, carried the passion and death of Christ and the manner of their presentation in the mystery cycles 'perhaps half consciously, at the back of his mind' as a dramatic paradigm. To give a specific instance, the mystery cycles' baiting scenes, in which the enemies of Jesus, the high priests Caiaphas and Annas, revile and persecute the redeemer, are the model, it is argued, for the fall and death of Duke Humphrey of Gloucester in *2 Henry VI*. The nobles who conspire against Gloucester are a secular version of the high priests, while Henry VI as head of state is, like Pilate in the mystery cycles, sympathetic to the hero-victim. That is not to say that Gloucester is a 'Christ-figure'. The book is not interested in making that sort of vague claim. It is concerned only with resemblances in structure. The insulting diatribes of Christ's mockers in the mystery cycles are, it is shown, also reflected in the murder of York by Margaret and Clifford in *2 Henry VI* (the comparison with Christ is in this case made explicit in Shakespeare's source, Holinshed)

Interestingly, the book finds, Christ's passion as the paradigm of tragic drama suggests itself to Shakespeare in relation only to some of the histories and tragedies. Others—*Titus Andronicus, Hamlet, Romeo and Juliet*—owe nothing to the scenes of group violence in the mystery cycles. But plays that derive their crucial power from that source include *King Lear* (the baiting of Lear by Goneril, Regan and Cornwall) and *Coriolanus* (the humiliation and threats Coriolanus is subjected to in Act III). In catching glimpses of the passion story in Shakespeare's texts, the book's critical procedures are at their most brilliantly sensitive. We are shown that Coriolanus appearing disguised after his banishment mirrors the play in the mystery cycles where Christ appears to his disciples on the road to Emmaus, and that the scene where the three women of Coriolanus's family appeal to him to spare Rome resembles in theatrical effect the scene in the mystery cycles where the three Marys visit Christ's tomb. In *Timon of Athens*, the scenes (II. ii and III. iv) where Timon is arraigned by bankrupt and predatory creditors, together with Timon's angry responses ('Cut my heart', 'Tear me'), also make the passion analogy apparent. Again, there is no attempt in this critical analysis to make Timon into a 'Christ-figure' as Wilson Knight strives to do. Timon's relation to Christ is, it is argued, as much a matter of contrast as of similarity. Nevertheless the claim is unequivocally made that without the gospel narratives and the passion plays *Timon* would not have come into being.

The book's perception of links between the passion narrative and the plays can be breathtaking—both completely new and totally convincing. This is nowhere more true than in the sections on *Othello* and *Macbeth*. Behind *Othello*, I. ii (the 'Keep up your bright swords' scene) we are made startlingly to see a biblical prototype—the arrest of Jesus in the Garden of

Gethsemane, with Jesus telling Peter to sheathe his sword. Both are scenes of torch-lit tumult, with the central figure remaining majestically calm, and the fact that the resemblance is more visual than verbal makes us wonder, again, whether the young Shakespeare might have seen, and remembered, the mystery play being acted. Behind the banquet scene in *Macbeth* we are made aware of two episodes from the mystery plays, the Massacre of the Innocents and the Death of Herod, and within this nexus we are shown how Macbeth meeting the three sisters parallels Herod meeting the three kings. Though Herod is the chief prototype of Macbeth in the mystery plays, we are also shown that there are links between Macbeth and Judas. Macbeth's 'If it were done when 'tis done, then 'twere well | It were done quickly'—spoken while Duncan is eating his last supper—picks up Jesus's words to Judas at the last supper (John, xiii. 27) 'That thou doest, do quickly.'

The book's third section stresses the topical relevance of Shakespeare's early histories, relating them to current political concerns (notably the fear of civil war and the danger of having two rulers in one realm) in the period between the Babington Plot of 1586 and the execution of Mary Queen of Scots in 1587. Jones sees Richard III as essentially a 'dynastic drama'. The ghost scene and dreams at the end make the establishment of the Tudor dynasty part of a divinely controlled universe. Richmond's dream relates to a famous vision of the true cross that came to Constantine before battle, and Queen Elizabeth is shadowed in the person of Richmond, her grandfather, whose queen's name she shared. Richmond is the play's Constantine and Queen Elizabeth a 'second Constantine', empress and head of the church.

For a student of Jones's work this third section is of particular interest in that it makes two suggestions that are not (so far as I know) matched elsewhere in his writing on Shakespeare. He thinks that *3 Henry VI* may be part of the official propaganda campaign which continued after Mary's death, and thus shows Shakespeare and his company cooperating with a government initiative. In his comments on *1 Henry VI* he makes the equally unusual suggestion that Shakespeare's feelings about his subject matter can be detected from the way he writes. Shakespeare, he contends, was 'far too reasonable to give the full weight of his sympathy to simple fame-hungry Talbot. The play accordingly suffers from a lack of authorial conviction in many of Talbot's scenes: the writing often rings hollow. More than anything else, perhaps, it is this felt insincerity that has prevented *1 Henry VI* from surviving the century in which it was written.' Extending this claim, Jones points to other areas of Shakespeare's work where he senses a lack of engagement on the dramatist's part. When Shakespeare was writing with 'deep creative involvement', he argues, a 'clash of viewpoints' is felt. But this is lacking in, for example, *3 Henry VI* and *Two Gentlemen of Verona* and after Mercutio's death in *Romeo and Juliet*, when the play 'runs aground into dramatic shallows'.

A challenging initiative in the book's third section is the case that Jones makes out for Shakespeare's *King John*. While admitting the play's weaknesses, he believes that it has been 'absurdly underrated'. Its chief concern, he argues, is the acquisition of moral experience, and in pitting innocence against worldliness it resembles morality plays like *Mundus et Infans* and *Respublica*. The Bastard Faulconbridge is a 'sensitive moral agent' who brings the play 'within hailing distance of *Hamlet*'. He relates to morality play figures such as Conscience, Honesty and Faithful Service, and is in effect a 'folk-hero' who 'speaks for the unknown multitude who make up the people of England'. The reign of King John, as presented in the play, shows 'the abject plight of England during the Dark Ages, when the Pope made the King do what he wanted', and consequently it throws into relief Elizabeth's role as England's Constantine, asserting her imperial authority against the meddling priests of Rome.

Jones's edition of *Antony and Cleopatra* in the New Penguin Shakespeare series came out in the same year as his *Origins of Shakespeare* and is, like it, provocative and challenging. Whereas *Antony and Cleopatra* is often thought of as a work of cosmic scope with larger-than-life characters, it is, Jones contends, 'essentially a small-theatre work'. He suggests that Shakespeare wrote it primarily as a Blackfriars play, intending it, that is, for an indoor theatre with a small intimately placed audience. It works, he points out, through short scenes and small groups of characters. Unlike Shakespeare's other Roman plays it has no crowd scenes, and its verbal effects are often of minute delicacy.

In part Jones's Introduction is an illustration of his scenic form theory in operation. He takes readers through the play's first scene, showing how Shakespeare manipulates our expectations and our responses, and keeps us guessing about the two main characters—their sincerity, their pasts, their futures. Shakespeare's source, Plutarch's *Life of Antony*, is, he points out, essentially interested in character—a man's habits and way of living 'What sort of a man is he?' is the question it asks, and *Antony and Cleopatra* reflects these aspects of Plutarch in a way central to its structure and meaning, accounting for some of its puzzling features. Antony is always either on stage or being talked about when off. He is 'the observed of all observers' much more than Hamlet, or for that matter Othello, Lear or

Macbeth. In this respect the play is closer to Shakespeare's two other Plutarchan tragedies of the same period, *Coriolanus* and *Timon*, and like them is permeated with anecdote, gossip and reminiscence.

The drifting movement of *Antony and Cleopatra*—its virtual lack of plot—is also ascribable, Jones argues, to Plutarch's influence, and its comic scenes reflect Plutarch's concern with the realism of comedy rather than with epic or tragedy, directing attention to the 'tangle of good and bad, honourable and dishonourable' in the actions of the characters. Nothing in Plutarch's *Life* suggests dramatic form—it consists of a multiplicity of small incidents—and Shakespeare, Jones suggests, decided to accept and exploit this lack of structure in order to represent life in all its haphazardness, wastefulness, untidiness and inconclusiveness. The view of human activity reflected is one of 'discontinuity and multiplicity, volatility and impulsiveness', and this encourages in the audience (in the first half of the play) a critical and ironical frame of mind. We see that Antony has surrendered to passion—he is dominated by will and impulse—and that he struggles in a formless, watery void (epitomised in his fatal choice to fight by sea).

Plutarch thought of Antony as a great man ruined by sexual passion, and Jones raises the question of whether the play endorses this traditional, moralistic view. As he sees it, for many modern readers Antony's love is justified by its transcendence, whereas Caesar's circumspect worldliness is mean and hollow—and by remaining ambiguous and open on this question the play encourages differences in response. Antony's behaviour is condemned by a wide range of characters in the play, but no one speaks up for the lovers except the lovers themselves. So the play allows readers to give Antony and Cleopatra's love their blessing, but does not require them to do so. On the other hand, Antony's earth-scorning, transcendent love ('Let Rome in Tiber melt') might, Jones suggests, be expected to strike a note in a Christian audience, reflecting a Christian contempt for the world, and so might the lovers' vision of themselves in the afterlife together. 'We are surely invited to respond sympathetically', Jones thinks, to their vision of reunion after death. So he concludes that the play—as always in Shakespeare—'refuses to identify reality with any one viewpoint'.

He sees the style of *Antony and Cleopatra* as 'lyrical'. But whereas the lyrical style of *Romeo and Juliet* is sometimes clearly modelled on Petrarch, the stylistic qualities of *Antony and Cleopatra* are, he believes, those of Horace's *Odes*. The themes of empire, love and wine are Horatian and, he notes, Horace wrote a famous ode on the defeat and death of Cleopatra (I. 37). This is a suggestion that leaves us longing for a fuller elaboration, and adds to one's regret that, after his 1977 book, Jones unaccountably did not again write at book-length about Shakespeare.

Or for that matter about anything else. It seems at first sight surprising that in the twenty years between *The Origins of Shakespeare* and his retirement in 1998 no further book appeared, even though his election in 1982 to a Fellowship of the British Academy and in 1984 to the Goldsmith's Chair at Oxford, which necessitated a move to New College, can have left him in no doubt about the esteem in which his published work was held. The answer to this apparent conundrum is to be found, I think, in the scope of his erudition and his personal modesty. If we look at the short things he produced—reviews, lectures—we realise that anyone else would have made them into book-length studies. This is particularly true of his two British Academy lectures, 'Pope and Dulness', the Chatterton Lecture on Poetry, given on 13 November 1968, and 'The First West End Comedy', the British Academy Shakespeare Lecture for 1982.

The first of these (*Proceedings of the British Academy*, 54 (1969), 231–63) starts with the suggestion that to see Pope, in the *Dunciad*, as a defender of cultural values is too narrow, and ignores the extent to which he was dramatising his own divided cultural feelings in the poem. The *Dunciad*, the lecture suggests, allowed him to escape from the distrust of the imagination and the dogmatic rationalism of Augustan culture, and gratify his desire to write about 'the low, the little, the trivial, the squalid and the indecent'. A topos like the garret life-style of a Grub Street poet, which Jones finds recurrent in seventeenth-century literature, cultivated images of the sordid and gross that were, he argues, both repulsive and exciting to Pope. The games and the diving match in the second book of the *Dunciad* allowed him to regress into the world of childhood, where ordure and physicality are free from shame or inhibition. This world of pre-literate infancy is adjacent to the world of Bedlam and madness and perhaps, Jones suggests, to the Freudian unconscious. It represents the challenge of the unconscious mind to the over-confidently conscious.

As the argument develops it becomes more and more apparent that there is a book here—an investigation not just of Pope but of Augustan culture. It would show how the forms Jones touches on—the mock-heroic, and the mock-encomium or adoxography, a classical form revived in the Renaissance and applied to gross or indecent subjects—provided writers with an outlet from rationalism, and allowed them simultaneously to repudiate the anarchic and respond to its vitality and excitement. But it was a book that remained unwritten.

The Shakespeare lecture, 'The First West End Comedy' (*Proceedings of the British Academy*, 68 (1983), 215–58), starts with a topical reference to Noel Coward's *Present Laughter* currently, Jones tells his audience, enjoying a revival at the Vaudeville, just up the road. That play starts with a famous actor rising late in the morning and being fussed around by friends and attendants—a scene that might be called, generically, Jones suggests, 'the levee of a man of fashion'. He then proceeds to find similar scenes in various eighteenth- and seventeenth-century plays until he reaches Jonson's *Epicoene*, first performed in 1609, which the title of his lecture refers to. But it does not stop there. He traces the genre further back, via Jonson's *Poetaster* and Donne's first satire, to Persius's third satire which opens with the poet still in bed. Then, in what is really a separate lecture, he traces the growth of London's 'West End', noting how the fashionable addresses in the late sixteenth century were the Savoy and the Strand, and how Inigo Jones created the first West End square with his piazza in Covent Garden and the first West End church with St Paul's. A book about theatre history and urban history and their connection with fashion seems the obvious follow-up to a lecture like this. But it, too, never got written

Another answer, though, to why no book appeared after 1977 is that one did—an enormous one—but it was an anthology. Concluding *The Origins of Shakespeare*, Jones observed that 'despite all that has been done we still need an adequate literary history of the sixteenth century, bold in outline and not overloaded with detail—a map of the region that will bring out the shape of the terrain and help explorers to master it'. His *New Oxford Book of Sixteenth-Century Verse,* published in 1991, answers this need, at any rate in relation to verse-writing. What is remarkable about it, apart from the astonishing wealth of knowledge, is its uncompromising modernity and its rejection of almost everything that its predecessor, Sir Edmund Chambers's 1932 *Oxford Book of Sixteenth Century Verse*, stood for. In his introduction Jones makes it clear—though with tact and courtesy—that he differs radically from Chambers both in his understanding of what constitutes poetry and in his estimate of what a just and adequate representation of sixteenth-century verse would look like. Chambers's anthology, though 'admirable' on its own terms, belongs irretrievably, in Jones's account, to a world that has gone. Behind Chambers's *Oxford Book,* he argues, stood Palgrave's *Golden Treasury* which 'lyricized' the expectations of generations of English readers of poetry. It had inclined them to identify poetry with short personal poems, and Chambers, following this prescription, had conceived of Elizabethan poetry largely in terms of 'dainty' pastorals and pretty love songs, giving inordinate coverage to the lesser late Elizabethans and failing to find space for a whole range of other writing. His partiality for the pretty and genteel, and his avoidance of the grotesque and ugly, confirmed a 'trivializing' image of the whole period. He represented Skelton, for example, by two extracts from *Philip Sparrow* and three short lyrics addressed to highborn ladies from *The Garland of Laurel* while excluding Skelton's satirical and didactic writing.

Another limitation of Chambers's book was that, equating poetry with ease and naturalness, it fought shy of anything difficult. Modernism has changed our perspective in this respect, and Jones takes advantage of this change of taste to include, for example, excerpts from Skelton's *Speak Parrot*, one of the most resplendently witty and versatile of sixteenth-century poems, as well as one of the most difficult. He recognises, too, that the huge expansion and experimental audacity of the English language in this period has left its texts full of words that are unfamiliar to most modern readers, and consequently he steels himself, 'even at the risk', as he puts it, 'of disfiguring an otherwise handsome page', to including footnote glosses far more extensively and helpfully than previous Oxford Book editors judged needful.

His selection also gives a new sense of the bewildering range of verse-production in the century, 'probably the most disorientating age of transition ever' in his estimate, with its change from feudalism to early capitalism and from Catholicism to the Protestant Reformation. In its poetry, he argues, forms and styles differ so radically that it is not possible to think of it as a single period. In the 1590s, poets are writing satires in heroic couplets that anticipate Dryden and Pope. But at the start of the century we are still in the middle ages, with an unknown Cheshire poet celebrating the English victory at Flodden in 1513 in the alliterative metre of which the greatest achievement had been *Sir Gawain and the Green Knight* in the fourteenth century.

For Jones, sixteenth-century verse is in another respect a broader category than Chambers's selection allows because he recognises how much of it was written for practical purposes by people with no literary ambitions. He includes, for example, extracts from Thomas Tusser's *One Hundred Points of Good Husbandry*, a work intended to teach the reader how to be a good farmer or housewife, and from William Warner's *Albion's England*, an enormous hotchpotch of history, romance, folklore and travelogue which, though it may seem crude to us, had wide contemporary appeal.

The new *Oxford Book* finds room, too, for the unnamed and unknown. There are sixty-three anonymous entries—more than for any named writer except Shakespeare. Alongside the great and famous are obscure people who are remembered for only one poem. Here is Chidiock Tichborne, a young Catholic gentleman executed for his part in the Babington Plot, whose 'My prime of youth is but a frost of cares' is said to have been written just before his death. Here is Francis Tregian, an imprisoned recusant, writing a poem to his wife, using the carbon from his candle wick as ink and a pin as pen. There are poems by women as well as men, and children as well as adults. The destitute and down-and-outs, though they have regrettably left no written account of themselves, being illiterate, are recorded in Robert Copland's little-known poem *The High Way to the Spital House*—a dialogue with a hospital porter about the vagabonds, tramps and beggars who come his way. Atheists and unbelievers have also for the most part been written out of the century's poetic record, but Jones discovers a broadside ballad by Thomas Gilbart, about the execution of an otherwise unknown heretic called John Lewes who, when he came to the place where he was to be burned to death, refused to kneel or repent and replied only, 'Thou liest', when a pious bystander told him he would go to hell. Generally speaking Jones's scholarly objectivity and self-effacement prevent any indication of his religious or political views, but he allows himself the comment that Lewes's words 'strike a refreshing and heartening note' in a period when repeated expression of orthodox religious belief can become 'somewhat oppressive'.

For that matter, a personal preference for the democratic and the anarchic might be deduced from the overall aim of his anthology which, he says, is to 'evoke however faintly a sense of the resistant, unassimilable disorderliness of the period's actual life, as opposed to what usually gets into the historian's tidied narrative'. His strong sense of himself as a Londoner is reflected in his rejection of the tendency, among previous commentators, to emphasise the poetry of the court as opposed to the town. Counteracting this, he gives special attention to 'poet-observers of society' like Sir John Harington and Sir John Davies, 'social poets of a new and forward-looking kind', and also to the foremost of the London poets, John Donne. Chambers's prettified notion of Elizabethan lyric poetry had excluded Donne from his *Oxford Book*, classifying him as a seventeenth-century poet. Jones, however, emphasises that the verse satires of the 1590s, which Donne pioneered, were an exclusively Elizabethan phenomenon, and he also includes some of Donne's *Songs and Sonnets* that can be shown to belong to the 1590s. (In an excusable moment of partiality he finds space for 'The Anniversary' among these, though from its references to 'kings' and 'favourites' it is clearly Jacobean.)

A constant characteristic of his critical approach is his awareness of both the classical and the contemporary European context of English writing. This shows itself in his *Oxford Book* in his emphasis on the crucial part played in the Elizabethan literary renaissance by the Pleiade poets, notably Ronsard and du Bellay, who, he claims, revitalised French poetry by rediscovering the natural world. A major difference, he suggests, between early Tudor and late Elizabethan poets is that Wyatt and Surrey were pre-Pleiade, whereas Sidney and Spenser took full advantage of the Pleiade's example, with the result that whereas early Tudor poetry is relatively poor in natural imagery, the post-Pleiade Elizabethans make themselves free of a freshly apprehended world of living things.

The same outward-looking perspective makes him aware of the important part translation played in the poetry of the period. The common prejudice against verse translation makes no sense, he insists, in the sixteenth century, when much of what counts as original poetry (the sonnets of Wyatt and Surrey, for example) is actually translation, and many translations are also original poetry. Accordingly his *Oxford Book* gives prominence to excerpts from Wyatt's Petrarch, Horace, Seneca and *Penitential Psalms*, Surrey's Virgil, Golding's *Metamorphoses*, Marlowe's *Amores* and Lucan, Harington's Ariosto, Chapman's Homer and Fairfax's Tasso—all important in their own right as English poems.

Emrys Jones's achievement, not just in this remarkable anthology but in all his work, rested on painstakingly acquired knowledge. He was a scholar first, a critic second. It seems right to point out, too, that his grammar school education was vital because it introduced him to Latin and the Latin classics, and revealed to him the foundations of European culture which are hidden from the Latin-less. In that respect Neath Grammar School has as much reason to be proud of him as has Oxford University.

Emrys enjoyed a long and happy retirement, pursuing his love of theatre and opera. He died of stomach cancer in Oxford's John Radcliffe Hospital on 20 June 2012, and is survived by his widow, Barbara Everett, and their daughter Hester who is a lecturer in English at the University of Bristol.

JOHN CAREY
Fellow of the Academy

Note. A number of people have helped me to gather material for this Memoir, and I should particularly like to thank Dr Colin Burrow, Robin Darwall-Smith, Professor Martin Dodsworth, Professor Katherine Duncan-Jones, Professor Paul Edmondson, Roger Howells and Professor Henry Woudhuysen.

MARTYN JOPE

Edward Martyn Jope
1915–1996

MARTYN JOPE, a chemist by early inclination and training and a productive biochemical researcher at the start of his career, was also a self-taught archaeologist who early on established himself as a formative figure in the emerging discipline of medieval archaeology. He was able to change career paths, establish a new department of archaeology in the Queen's University of Belfast, set up the Northern Ireland Archaeological Survey and achieve distinction both as a medievalist and as a recorder and interpreter of Early Celtic Art. His background as a scientist allowed him ultimately, too, to become an important bridge between archaeology, especially as represented within the British Academy, and the world of science.

The Jopes were of Cornish extraction, the name being traceable back to the early fourteenth century when a Jope was Portreeve of Liskeard. Martyn's grandfather was a Methodist minister in Devon and Cornwall and his father, Edward Mallett Jope, was born in Devon, though by 1915 he and his Lincolnshire-born wife Frances Margaret were living in Carshalton, Surrey where their only child Martyn was born on 28 December 1915. (Edward Jope was a civil servant, ending his career as a Principal in the Unemployment Assistance Board.) They moved to nearby Wallington and Martyn attended Whitgift Grammar School in Croydon before going as a boarder to his father's much-loved old school, Kingswood in Bath, where he was Head of House and a member of the rugby XV. He took to Kingswood with as much enthusiasm as his father had, revelling in the setting and getting to know the North Somerset and Gloucestershire countryside within cycling distance of the school. His long association with the west country and intimate knowledge of its archaeology began in

Biographical Memoirs of Fellows of the British Academy, XIII, 295–311. © The British Academy 2014.

part from this and in part from family holidays to Padstow, where his grandfather had long been minister.

Even at Whitgift Martyn showed an interest in chemistry to which he turned with some zest, blowing himself up in his home lab, he used to recall, by mixing potassium chlorate and red phosphorus in a marble mortar. He had a successful and enjoyable time at Kingswood, excelling in Physics and Chemistry but at the same time acquiring distinctive skills and powers of observation as an artist and draughtsman that were to serve him well in archaeology.

In 1935 he went up to Oxford with Oriel's Senior Chemistry Scholarship, having explained at interview that he would really like to devote his life to 'pursuing the molecular mechanisms which must operate underlying all biological processes', which in a certain sense he eventually did. He looked back to his first term as providing him with the basic philosophical concept that guided his thinking throughout his life. The University Lecturer in Chemistry, Neville Vincent Sidgwick, systematically went through the main elements in their periodic order demonstrating how their chemical behaviour was directly related to the electronic structure of the atom nucleus, showing more clearly than Martyn and his undergraduate contemporaries had ever hitherto grasped the fundamental principle of the properties of matter. By the end of his undergraduate career Organic Chemistry had relentlessly beckoned him towards the biological sciences and his first professional scientific work was to be on the biology of blood.

Meanwhile, however, Martyn's already substantial knowledge of archaeology and architectural history had propelled him into another and parallel interest at Oxford and he became an active member, Secretary, then President of the Oxford University Archaeological Society. The society's resources were urgently called upon late in 1936 and early in 1937 when a vast area of ancient tenements north of Broad Street was demolished and a huge mechanical excavation ensued to accommodate the New Bodleian Library. Building recording was done under the leadership of W. A. Pantin and recovery of below-ground archaeology was coordinated by R. L. S. Bruce-Mitford. Martyn gave weeks of assistance in excavation, recording and artefact recovery—a baptism of fire in what a later generation would describe as rescue archaeology. It not only brought him into a close working relationship with two scholars who were to remain friends and powerful influences on his life for years but also gave him an insight into the disciplines of field archaeology and the potential of archaeology to supply missing elements of medieval history, not least the early history and topography of towns and the organisation of economic life as evidenced by artefacts, notably pottery. The rapid analysis of the discoveries and their prompt publication by Pantin and Bruce-Mitford was another object lesson.

Fresh from his experiences at the New Bodleian site, but already deeply acquainted with the archaeology, historic buildings and archaeologists of the west country, Martyn and his friend Ian Threlfall in 1938 and 1939 excavated a thirteenth-century long house and associated structures at Beere near North Tawton in Devon. This was one of the first medieval peasant houses in the country to have been investigated by modern archaeological techniques. The prolific ceramic finds led him to regional studies of west country medieval pottery which benefited from his similar studies in the Oxford region. It eventually led him to forge new techniques of study and especially to develop distribution maps as a tool to define what he saw as elements of regional cultures in medieval England. Martyn's eventual report on the Beere excavation lies at the head of several subsequent generations of work by others to investigate rural settlement and the nature of medieval peasant life in Britain.[1]

With his Oxford reputation as an archaeologist outpacing his work as a chemist he was persuaded in 1938 to accept appointment to the staff of the Royal Commission on the Ancient and Historical Monuments of Wales. Working from London he briefly became involved in field investigations in Caernarvonshire and gained insight into the working methods of the commission, valuable when he himself became a commissioner many years later. By 1940, however, he had returned to biochemistry, working on Nuffield and Medical Research Council projects, mainly at the London Hospital, though he continued to live in Oxford. In 1941 he married Margaret Halliday, a Scottish research biochemist working at the Dyson Perrins Laboratory in Oxford, and they began a life-long and mutually supportive professional and personal partnership. Initially there was joint work on haemoglobins, jointly published. Increasingly, too, Margaret participated in the archaeological projects Martyn carried out throughout the 1940s in parallel with his biochemical research. By the end of the decade there were significant achievements in both fields.

The New Bodleian excavations had confronted Martyn with copious amounts of medieval pottery, then little understood or valued, and only dateable within broad terms. By dint of studying and publishing numerous

[1] E. M. Jope and R. I. Threlfall, 'Excavation of a medieval settlement at Beere, North Tawton, Devon', *Medieval Archaeology*, 2 (1958), 112–40.

groups of excavated pottery from these and other excavations in Oxford and the Oxford region, he was able to determine the range of ceramic fabrics and forms found in the region throughout the medieval period. By the use of distribution maps, showing both the locations where different types had been found and—importantly—the negative evidence, where in excavated pottery groups they had not been found, he was able to define the geographical range of each category. The problem of dating the various ceramics was tackled partly by recording which types or fabrics were consistently found associated together and partly by identifying archaeological sites that were themselves inherently dateable by documentary or other evidence. Two excavations on earthwork castles which were thought to have a limited period of occupation in the mid-twelfth century—Ascot Doilly and Swerford—produced groups which helped to define the ceramics of that time. An ingenious and opportunistic small excavation below Oxford Castle Mound, erected in 1071, revealed ceramics below the mound which must therefore have dated to before 1071—Oxford's Late Saxon pottery.[2] Another approach was to find the kiln sites which produced the various wares. Martyn's excavation of the Brill kilns revealed the source of one series commonly found in the Oxford region. In a decade Martyn had in effect defined and demonstrated the disciplines upon which the study of medieval pottery could be based, established and dated the ceramic sequences for the Oxford region—and also for parts of Devon and of Gloucestershire—and laid foundations for the discipline to develop nationally later in the twentieth century.

Pottery, though of great interest to Martyn, was a means to an end—the application of the techniques of prehistoric and Roman archaeology to the study of medieval life. His many excavations in and around the city of Oxford for the first time provided archaeological evidence for the extent and character and growth of the Saxon and medieval town—one of the first systematic attempts at medieval urban archaeology.[3] The report on his work at the Clarendon Hotel site in the centre of the city stands at the head of much later work on urban archaeology throughout Britain.[4] The nature of the earliest castles in England was another subject that he felt could be elucidated by field study and excavation. His work at the small

---

[2] E. M. Jope, 'Late Saxon pits under Oxford Castle mound: excavations in 1952', *Oxoniensia*, 17–18 (1952–3), 77–111.
[3] E. M. Jope, 'Saxon Oxford and its region', in D. B. Harden (ed.), *Dark Age Britain: Essays Presented to E. T. Leeds* (London, 1956), pp. 234–58.
[4] E. M. Jope 'The Clarendon Hotel, Oxford', *Oxoniensia*, 23 (1958), 1–83.

castle sites at Swerford, Hinton Waldrist, Ascot Doilly,[5] and Deddington demonstrated it. The long-running rescue excavation at Deddington ultimately led to the site being taken into Guardianship by the then Ministry of Works. This frenzy of archaeological work on so many fronts produced a regular flow of publications many of which, seven decades later, are still used or thought of as standards.

Martyn's biochemical work, on haemoglobins in human blood, produced a similar flow of seminal papers in the *British Medical Journal*, *Journal of Physiology*, *Cancer*, *Biochemical Journal*, *Proceedings of the Royal Society of Medicine*, *Spectrochimica Acta*, *Nature* and elsewhere. An example was his study of the toxic action of sulphonamides and TNT on workers in Royal Ordnance factories which led to highly significant findings on the dynamics of red cell destruction. The abnormal pigment sulphemoglobin was found to persist in circulating or drawn blood after cessation of contact with such causative agents as sulphonamides or TNT. It appeared therefore that the red cell has no mechanism in it for the transformation of sulphemoglobin; however the sulphemoglobin disappeared from the blood of seven TNT workers in linear fashion in about 116 days after withdrawal from contact with TNT. This related to the destruction of the red cells which contained the pigment. The implication was drawn that red cells have a fixed life within small limits.[6] Other research gave similar results for both the slope of the decay curve and the life span of red cells, for the first time demonstrating the dynamics of red cell destruction.

By 1948 Martyn and Margaret were developing research proposals, apparently favourably received by the Medical Research Council and other bodies, in what was leading to Molecular Biology and Molecular Cytology and his career path seemed clear. At this juncture, however, he received an approach from Christopher Hawkes, a long-time acquaintance and by now Professor of European Archaeology at Oxford, to see whether he might be interested in taking up a post at the Queen's University of Belfast to set up a new Department of Archaeology. The university was looking for an archaeologist who could develop the science side of the discipline and was inclined towards a medievalist who could complement the ethnographic work of E. Estyn Evans in the Geography Department at Queen's and continue the pioneering work of Oliver Davies in the

[5] E. M. Jope and R. I. Threlfall, 'The twelfth-century castle at Ascott Doilly, Oxfordshire', *The Antiquaries Journal*, 39 (1959), 219–73.
[6] E. M. Jope, 'Disappearance of Sulphemoglobin from the blood of TNT workers in relation to the dynamics of red cell destruction', *British Journal of Industrial Medicine*, 3.3 (1946), 136–42.

medieval to seventeenth century field in Ulster. Martyn, after much heart searching, applied, was offered the post and he and Margaret changed career.

The newly created post at Queen's was a joint university and Northern Ireland Government appointment. This presented opportunities for collaboration between the State, with responsibilities for conservation and presentation of the Ancient and Historical Monuments of Ulster, and the university, with its role in researching and understanding the meaning of the province's prehistoric and historic monuments. Martyn's work therefore rapidly fell into two parts—or more precisely into three, for he and Margaret maintained their home at Oxford, returning there religiously every university vacation for the whole of their thirty-two years at Belfast, thus maintaining English research interests and contacts.

In Northern Ireland the Ministry of Finance was responsible for ancient monuments and he worked there with a senior, Claude Blake Whelan, himself a progressive amateur Stone Age archaeologist, under an enlightened Minister of Finance, Major John Sinclair. Within a year the Archaeological Survey of Northern Ireland had been set up, two inspectors—Dudley Waterman and A. E. P. (Pat) Collins, old acquaintances— had been hand-picked and head-hunted by Martyn and work on the Archaeological Survey of County Down had begun along lines that he had encountered in his work for the Welsh Royal Commission but without the irksome constraints that had contributed to his leaving it. After a massive campaign of investigation, excavation and fieldwork the volume appeared under Martyn's editorship in 1966, the first of its kind for any Irish county, and relatively quickly for a work of this sort.[7] The survey continued into other counties but the next volume, on County Armagh, did not appear until 2009, forty-three years later and decades after Martyn's involvement had come to an end.

There were equal opportunities in the Queen's University. The new department was to be one of very few in the United Kingdom which at that time offered undergraduate teaching in archaeology and Martyn was determined that it should find a place in both the Science Faculty and in the Humanities. The former, which he achieved through the good offices of the Professors of Biochemistry and Physical Chemistry, both old friends from Oxford, ensured that the new department was funded in the order of a science department, and set a new pattern for archaeology in British universities. Estyn Evans had envisaged the new archaeology initia-

---

[7] E. M. Jope (ed.), *An Archaeological Survey of County Down* (Belfast, 1966).

tive as being within his Department of Geography but Martyn, with the support of the Vice-Chancellor, Sir David Lindsey Keir, and his science departments allies, ensured its independence—long a source of tension with the geographers. Appointed as a Lecturer, Martyn became a Reader in 1954 and Professor in 1963 during which time he built the department into a small but effective team—largely left to run its own affairs as Martyn would have expected of the kind of staff he sought—that offered an introduction to archaeology to large numbers of first and second year students, and latterly a full Honours course for more committed archaeologists. Its graduates went on between them to occupy many of the significant posts in archaeology in the Province and elsewhere in Ireland and Britain for a generation. Jope had a genius for identifying potential in those he appointed as research assistants and colleagues, many going on to make important contributions in their various fields. His research assistant Brian Davidson, for example, went to the English Department of the Environment, later English Heritage, where for many years he led medieval research initiatives and developed the castle studies he began under Jope's stimulus in Belfast. Peter Addyman as a medievalist and Arthur ApSimon as a prehistorian were to become founding staff at the new Department of Archaeology in Southampton in 1972. Tom McNeill remained in Belfast to set Irish castle studies on a new course while several of Jope's archaeological science appointees achieved pre-eminence in their various fields—some openly recognising their debt to the stimulus of their contact with Martyn, the interest he took in their work and his subtle influence upon its direction. Others though, because Jope was a very difficult person to work for, were less ready to do so. He was a jealous guardian of his time, often difficult to contact, the despair of university administrators—and never in Belfast after the end of term. His and Margaret's moves back and forth between Belfast and Oxford became legendary, their camper van, packed to the roof with books, files and personal effects, with cats peering out through a forest of ferns and potted plants, a regular thing of wonder in the Belfast or Heysham docks. Frustrating though these absences were for his Belfast staff, the regular returns to Oxford enabled him to continue his archaeological researches in Southern England, maintain contact with English colleagues and use research resources simply not available in Belfast.

Martyn and Margaret came to Belfast with a vision to develop what eventually became known as palaeoecology as a discipline complementary to more conventional archaeology. To this end he obtained a Nuffield Foundation grant which enabled a Nuffield Quaternary Research Unit to be set up with a team of four, botanists Alan Smith, subsequently Professor of Botany at Cardiff University, and Michael Morrison, soils specialist V. B. Proudfoot, subsequently Professor of Geography at St Andrews, and Margaret Jope, who by now had made herself a national expert on faunal remains in archaeology, especially birds. This small cross-departmental team addressed itself amongst other things to the potential provided by the peats and tree remains in Irish bogs for the study of climate history. Radiocarbon dating, then a relatively new technique, provided a means to date the enormously long sequences of pollen data, though far greater precision was required than 14C dating could then provide. Martyn and his team made the case for the establishment of a radiocarbon laboratory in Queen's that would address itself to precision dating—ultimately achieved through the dating of the long tree ring sequences obtained from trees from Irish bogs and elsewhere. Grants were obtained and a small but serviceable laboratory was set up—incongruously in garages behind the Department of Archaeology, the university then being very pressed for space and the available funds being limited. Under Gordon Pearson, formerly a senior technician at Windscale, exhaustive preparation and evaluation of every possible source of error or uncertainty took place and standards of precision were obtained equal to those of the best 14C laboratories in the world. For a time Belfast and Minze Stuiver's Seattle laboratory stood as the world leaders in precision dating and Martyn developed close international friendships with Hans Suess and others working on the calibration of radiocarbon dates. Work stemming from these initiatives by Jonathon Pilcher, and subsequently developed by Professor Mike Baillie, led to Belfast's pre-eminence in the field of high precision dendrochronology.

Martyn, on his arrival in Belfast in 1949, pointed out to his appointment committee that he knew 'absolutely nothing about prehistory' and similarly he had no experience whatsoever of Ireland or of Irish archaeology. With the zeal he had displayed in the previous decade in developing medieval archaeology in the Oxford region he set about putting this right. He and Margaret, in exhausting weekend sallies in their transit van, rapidly acquainted themselves with the geography and the archaeological resources of the six counties, a particular emphasis being on County Down where the Archaeological Survey began its work and where he undertook a number of field investigations on behalf of the Survey. Opportunities presented themselves at every turn and the volumes of the *Ulster Journal of Archaeology*, whose editorship he took over, were for twenty years full of Jope papers which between them helped to propel

Ulster archaeology up to twentieth-century standards and sometimes placed it at the forefront of new developments. Most were studies of particular artefacts or specific sites, always starting with meticulous and perceptive descriptions of the evidence often illuminated by his sensitive and perceptive drawings and figures, but then broadening into more general statements of the implications of whatever was being studied. He and Margaret even managed to find the time to carry out significant excavations, beautifully done and elegantly recorded, for example at the Ballymacash rath near Lisburn, where they wanted to provide a control study to validate the excavation recently done on the nearby Lissue rath by the German expatriate archaeologist Gerhard Bersu.[8] Martyn seemed as at home when dealing with the Neolithic axe factory on Tievebulliagh Mountain in County Antrim and its porcellanite polished stone axes, which his distribution map showed were traded throughout the British Isles, as he was with the buildings in the North of Ireland designed by John Nash four millennia later—and everything in between.

It was not quite true, as he had claimed at interview, that he knew nothing about prehistory on arrival in Ireland. In fact for several years he had been helping another expatriate German scholar, Paul Jacobsthal, to assemble illustrations for a projected volume on Early Celtic Art in the British Isles in the course of which, and in discussions and museum visits with Jacobsthal, he had acquired a wide knowledge and expertise in the study of Iron Age objects. Towards the end of his life Jacobsthal invited Martyn to become joint author of the projected work. Many of Martyn's Ulster papers, therefore, were devoted to studies of Iron Age objects from the province, including weaponry, decorated artefacts and in particular bridle bits and horse gear germane to another of his academic preoccupations, the use of draught animals and the technology of transport in the past.

His long-standing interest in the medieval castle led him to initiate investigations at Carrickfergus, the main stronghold of the twelfth-century Norman conqueror of Ulster, John de Courcy, and, working with Dudley Waterman, research was also put in train at other castles of conquest. He even investigated what he considered a misunderstood native copy of a castle, Harry Avery's Castle outside the Norman province in the wilds of County Tyrone. Another particular interest, and well before its time as a general field of study, was his work on the settlements of the Plantation of Ulster by the London companies in the sixteenth and seventeenth centuries

---

[8] E. M. Jope and R. J. Ivens, 'The Rath at Ballymacash, County Antrim', *Proceedings of the Royal Irish Academy*, 98C (1998), 101–23.

with their dwellings and fortified bawns—post-medieval archaeology well before the term became current and the activity a respectable academic discipline. A paper, 'Moyry, Charlemont, Castleraw and Richhill: from fortification to architecture in the north of Ireland' brought archaeological study up to the modern period, demonstrating incidentally Martyn's equal facility in the analysis, recording and interpretation of standing buildings.[9]

Martyn's Oxford region work brought him early recognition with election as a Fellow of the Society of Antiquaries in 1946. Election to the British Academy came in 1965, rather to his surprise for his work in the field of scholarship representing 'European Pre and Proto-history' rather than as a medievalist. The same year saw him President of Section H of the British Association for the Advancement of Science when his presidential address at the Cambridge meeting addressed 'Man's use of natural resources'.[10] His impact upon the archaeology of Ulster brought similar recognition in 1971 when he became a Member of the Royal Irish Academy. The year 1963, twenty-five years on, had found him back with the Royal Commission on Ancient and Historical Monuments of Wales but this time as a Royal Commissioner sitting with old friends such as Sir Cyril Fox, Sir Goronwy Edwards, Arnold Taylor and Idris Foster and later W. F. Grimes and D. Ellis Evans, Professor of Celtic at Oxford. His discussions there he found hugely stimulating in the context of his own work on Early Celtic art. In the end he served on the commission for twenty-five years, during which time the Welsh Commission changed its focus towards the study of houses, small and large, their detailed structural analysis and their historical, social and economic contexts. This gained his warm approval as the study of vernacular architecture was another of his interests, having learned the disciplines from W. A. Pantin at Oxford, and himself having produced important papers, for example the study of Cornish houses in the Festschrift *Studies in Building History*, which he edited in honour of Bryan H. St. J. O'Neil, or the paper he produced with his old friend C. A. Ralegh Radford on the great hall of the twelfth-century Bishop's Palace at Hereford.[11]

Martyn's election to the British Academy in 1965 brought to the Academy an archaeologist with a scientific background. He soon became

[9] *Ulster Journal of Archaeology*, 23 (1960), 97–123.

[10] E. M. Jope, 'Man's use of natural resources', *Advancement of Science*, 22 (1965–6), 1–9.

[11] E. M. Jope (ed.), *Studies in Building History, in Recognition of the Work of B. H. St. J. O'Neil* (London, 1961); E. M. Jope with C. A. R. Radford and J. W. Tonkin 'The great hall of the twelfth century Bishop's Palace at Hereford', *Medieval Archaeology*, 17 (1973), 78–86.

a bridge between the Academy and the Royal Society, conceiving and helping to arrange joint meetings of which the first was 'The Impact of the Natural Sciences on Archaeology' in 1969. This addressed the way in which dating techniques based in the natural sciences were providing a new chronological framework for prehistoric archaeology—very much the kind of work his Belfast Palaeoecology Laboratory was by then doing. One of the sequels to this meeting was a report produced by Martyn and Derek Allen, at that time the Secretary of the Academy, which made the case for the deployment of research funding for archaeological science. The case was in due course accepted by the Science Research Council, releasing funds on a scale well in advance of those for conventional archaeological research and making possible projects which placed British work at the forefront of archaeological science. A Science-based Archaeology Committee of the Science Research Council soon came into being. The move coincided with the burgeoning of archaeological field-work occasioned by the Rescue Archaeology movement and an urgent national need for improved methods of archaeological prospecting, investigation and analysis. This in turn led to a need to expand the numbers of those trained to carry them out.

Martyn's work on the development of archaeological science brought him stimulating contact with those at the forefront in a number of fields. Amongst these was Gordon Brown, Professor of Physics at the University of Bradford. Brown had already made significant progress in developing archaeological science, using spare capacity in his Physics Department to apply nuclear methods of analysis to the study of archaeological ceramics and lithics, a subject close to Martyn's interests. Stanley Warren there was applying X-ray fluorescence analysis to the study of ancient glass and other materials. Similarly his colleague Arnold Aspinall had established a reputation in the development of geophysical prospecting. Postgraduate and undergraduate courses were already being taught. Martyn's own scientific background and by now immense archaeological experience and insight meant that he was soon persuaded to help with the development of archaeological science at Bradford and the nurturing of the young archaeological scientists for which both he and Brown saw the need. He was Visiting Professor from 1974–81, being awarded an Honorary D.Sc. by the university in 1980. Subsequent to his retirement from Belfast he became Professor Emeritus at Bradford.

Throughout his career and because of his capacity for lateral, percep-tive and innovative thinking Martyn was frequently invited to take part in collaborative projects. His early interest in the use of mapping medieval data led to an invitation from H. C. Darby to co-author the Oxfordshire chapter for the *Domesday Geography of South-east England* (Cambridge, 1962). His interest in medieval carts and transport brought an invitation from Charles Singer to contribute to the Singer, Holmyard and Hall eight-volume *History of Technology* (London, 1954–84)—eventually expanding, as other contributors failed to produce, to include essays on horse harness and vehicles; agricultural implements; and post-classical ceramics. This led him to see the history of technology as a real sub-discipline in the history of science and of archaeology. He incorporated it in his Belfast courses and supported staff in his department such as Henry Hodges, subsequently with an international reputation as lecturer in archaeological technology at the Institute of Archaeology in the University of London, in its development. His papers always saw the technological implications of whatever he was studying. A further stimulus to his thoughts on the subject also came from his contacts with Joseph Needham, another erstwhile biochemist now engaged on a magisterial and con-troversial interpretation of Chinese culture history in which technology was a binding theme. He was delighted when in 1996 the Academy established a broadly based 'History of the Sciences Subject Committee' as a forum for the encouragement of interdisciplinary interchange and activities, the history of technology specifically taking its place within that setting. He saw the committee as a 'much needed intercommunicating link between the several (and indeed rather separated) Academy Sections'.

It was the invitation to help Paul Jacobsthal to complete his projected survey of Early Celtic Art in the British Isles, however, that changed the emphasis of Martyn's academic work. In a sense it kept him occupied, as circumstances allowed, right to the end of his life—the two-volume book eventually being published forty-three years after Jacobsthal's death and four years after Martyn's. By the time it appeared in 2000 it had become very much Martyn's own study, and Oxford University Press insisted that his name alone appeared as author. It remains the main academic achievement of his lifetime and his most substantial published work.

His involvement began very simply. Jacobsthal, having in 1944 published his well-received *Early Celtic Art* dealing with Continental material, had moved on to survey the British and was looking for help in assembling the high-quality illustrations his research methods demanded. Martyn was recommended to him as someone with archaeological know-how who, in time of war, had access to a photographic laboratory. Soon the cooperation became more profound as Martyn's expertise in the subject grew and when, after his move to Belfast, he was himself faced with the publication of important decorated Iron Age objects. As Jacobsthal grew infirm he invited Martyn to become joint author and on his death in 1957 left him with the task of completing the project. Quite how much Jacobsthal had achieved by this time is a matter of debate. His draft text was never found by the Jopes though it is clear that the eventual publication was very much as Jacobsthal had planned it, and recent finds of elements of the text in the Ashmolean Museum archives show that much of that survived through into the published work.

Jope, particularly concerned with the chronology of the British material, published a number of preparatory studies including his 'The beginnings of La Tène ornamental style in the British Isles' and his important 'Daggers of the early Iron Age in Britain' which posited a developmental sequence with chronological implications.[12] These papers established his eminence in Iron Age studies. He had been impressed by the work of Peter Shorer in the conservation laboratory at the British Museum in preparing electrotypes of important Early Iron Age bronzes which made it possible to see the detail of the decoration more easily— without the distraction of colour differences and corrosion effects—and of course the replicas could be more readily handled. Soon he had established a small conservation laboratory in his department at Belfast and appointed a young but brilliant conservator, Stephen Rees Jones, subsequently head of the technology department at the Courtauld Institute of Art, who had the skills to take the necessary latex moulds and the trust of the British Museum conservation staff to be allowed access to selected objects. Jope soon had a growing collection of electrotypes in Belfast that he could handle readily and study and describe at his leisure—and an encyclopaedic knowledge of the then-available British material. What he did not have, however, was a similarly extensive personal acquaintance with Continental material on which so much of the interpretation of insular art depended. At this period he hardly ever travelled abroad. When he had done so, in his early days, he had yet to develop an interest in Early Iron Age studies. This, in the eyes of colleagues both in Britain and abroad, had to constitute a weakness in his analyses.

The slow accumulation of data for *Early Celtic Art in the British Isles* (ECABI: Oxford, 2000) continued throughout Martyn's later career,

---

[12] E. M. Jope, 'The beginnings of the La Tène ornamental style in the British Isles', in S. S. Frère (ed.), *Problems of the Iron Age in Southern Britain* (London, 1960), pp. 69–83; E. M. Jope, 'Daggers of the early Iron Age in Britain', *Proceedings of the Prehistoric Society*, 27 (1961), 307–43.

taking its place alongside his myriad other interests and projects, but consolidating his national reputation in the subject. It provided him with material for the Munro Lecture which he gave in Edinburgh in 1953, and the O'Donnell lecture in Oxford in 1968 on masterworks of Early Celtic art in Britain. In the Rhys lecture to the British Academy in 1987 he explored how 'the practice and enjoyment of the visual arts have enriched the lives of Celtic peoples through some two and a half thousand years'—ending up with a feisty analysis of a work by Augustus John.[13] Early Celtic art also took him to Rome with Stuart Piggott and Christopher Hawkes as part of the British Academy team for the British Academy/Accademia Nazionale dei Lincei exchange lectures at the Palazzo Corsini. His paper on four British parade shields, showing the predominantly Italic background of the 'Gaulish' shield in Britain, caused as much interest for the shields themselves as for the interpretation he put on them. For Martyn it was also a chance to experience the British School at Rome where, like so many of its guests, he found the living conditions surprisingly Spartan but the atmosphere magical.

His work on the shields provided material for other papers in the 1970s and it seemed the publication of ECABI, as it became known, was imminent. Martyn certainly thought so, for he predicted it, wrongly, in his *Who's Who* entries, first as 'in press' in 1971, then in 1974 it was '1974'; for years his *Who's Who* entry had it as '1977'—misleading later obituarists—and so on. Some scholars doubted its existence and it became a joke, not least amongst his long-suffering staff in Belfast who lived with Martyn's ECABI preoccupations for more than two decades. But it did exist, in page proofs whose preface is dated 1972, and why it was not then published is a mystery.

For more than a decade ECABI was untouched but for the collection of photographs of newly discovered artefacts. It was amazing that every time a new artefact appeared there was an appropriate space on one of Jope's plates. The situation changed about 1983 when two colleagues were shown the proofs, helped to check some of the references and encouraged him towards publication. In order to update the text he decided to add an Annotated List of the illustrations—a form of catalogue that could include recent information without unduly affecting the existing text. Progress, however, was still painfully slow, in part because he allowed himself to be distracted by other Iron Age projects including the 1987

---

[13] This was published as E. M. Jope, 'Celtic art: expressiveness and communication through 2500 years', *Proceedings of the British Academy*, 73 (1987), pp. 97–124.

Rhys lecture for the British Academy, in part because of a late-flowering burst of international travel to conferences and to see colleagues in connection with Margaret's own research on the amino acids of fossil brachiopods and their implications for phylogeny. The text was finally completed and handed over to the inordinately patient Oxford University Press a few months before Jope died in 1996. It still needed a bibliography, provided by the last of a long-suffering succession of Martyn's research assistants, R. J. Ivens, and was nursed through the press, with minimal textual revision or updating, by Ian Stead. It includes much of the 1972 text word-for-word, thus 'the newly found gold from Ipswich' discovered in 1968 and 1970. Additions include a chronological chart, maps and accompanying text and an appendix on the dating of the Battersea shield. The latter had been a crucial problem for Jope (and others) and he was overjoyed to have an 'answer' provided by scientific investigation in part carried out by one of his own students. The additions, and Annotated List, are useful but it would have been a better book if it had been published in 1972 so that a whole generation of scholars could have benefited from it.[14]

Jope became involved in British Iron Age studies at a time when they were dominated by his friend Christopher Hawkes, whom he greatly admired. But he quietly ignored Hawkes's ABC approach, devised more for pottery than metalwork, preferring the Continental Hallstatt C and D and La Tène I–III. He had little experience, however, of Continental antiquities other than through Jacobsthall's *Early Celtic Art* (ECA) and his main foray in that direction (the Waldalgesheim master, in the 1971 Hawkes Festschrift) was not successful.[15] Jope, though, had more than enough to occupy himself with British antiquities and championed artefact studies at a time when they were being neglected by most British students.

In ECABI his descriptions are accurate and imaginative, using carefully chosen words and a technical vocabulary explained in a glossary. The book is full of fresh insights, has a wealth of hitherto unpublished information and a fine selection of photographs. He not only appreciated and described Celtic art but became increasingly confident that he could interpret it. In the Rhys lecture, for instance, he sees on the Colchester mirror a representation of the 'Tree of Life: harvest in autumn, seeding

[14] E. M. Jope *Early Celtic Art in the British Isles* (2 vols., Oxford, 2000).
[15] E. M. Jope, 'The Waldalgesheim master', in J. Boardman, M. A. Brown and T. G. E. Powell (eds.), *The European Community in Later Prehistory. Studies in Honour of C. F. C. Hawkes* (London, 1971), pp. 167–86.

time and renewal in spring . . . The interpretation can hardly be denied.' Some of his descriptions are so vivid and original that the student is obliged to see through Jope's eyes—the Great Chesterford Mirror, for instance with its 'unsteady lurch and a leering face, with wicked eyes . . . and spidery arms like tentacles wandering crazily'. These idiosyncracies enliven his texts, but perhaps they should not be taken too seriously. The Rhys lecture is somewhat eccentric, but ECABI is an invaluable standard work that will not be superseded for a very long time.

On Martyn's retirement from his Belfast chair in 1981 he and Margaret returned permanently to their Oxford home in Chalfont Road and to a number of years of vigorous and fruitful participation in the business of their respective research fields. He remained on the Science-based Archaeology Committee, having helped to organise various joint symposia of the Royal Society and the British Academy on 'The Early History of Agriculture' in 1975 and 'The Emergence of Man' in 1980, and to edit the subsequent publications;[16] the latter included his paper 'The emergence of man: information from protein systems'. This in part reflected Margaret's latest research—but also harked back to his biochemical background and his undergraduate wish to pursue the molecular mechanisms behind all biological processes. His paper 'Ancient bone and plant proteins: the molecular state of preservation' in Hare, Hoering and King's *Biogeochemistry of Amino Acids* (New York, 1980) shows in what direction his interests had now turned. In parallel he actively maintained his participation in the development of archaeological science at Bradford. Membership of the Ancient Monuments Board of English Heritage brought him to more conventional archaeological issues but also gave him the opportunity to champion the role of archaeological science within the national monuments service.

'Retirement' was a period of considerable satisfaction to Martyn and Margaret, allowing them to refresh Oxford contacts which they had never entirely given up, attend academic meetings with a frequency that had rarely been possible during the Belfast years and travel to meetings and academic contacts abroad which they had hardly ever done while at Belfast. There was more time for music, which they had both enjoyed and in their earlier days enthusiastically practised, Martyn playing the viola. Once again, as they had done several times in their lives, they began renewing their collection of recordings to take advantage of finer sound

---

[16] Sir J. Hutchinson, G. Clarke, E. M. Jope and R. Riley (eds.), *The Early History of Agriculture* (Oxford 1977); J. Z. Young, E. M. Jope and K. P. Oakley (eds.), *The Emergence of Man: a Joint Symposium of the Royal Society and the British Academy* (London, 1981).

reproduction provided by new technology. They still cherished their collection of early water colours, one of which, a view of the Victoria and Albert Museum, they presented to the British Academy. Hitherto they had rarely taken holidays. The story is told of a day's idleness in the Glenluce sandhills, which Margaret had insisted they take on one of their regular end-of-term journeys from Belfast to Oxford. Typically Martyn's eagle eye spotted artefacts and using the picnic cutlery he rapidly excavated a medieval coin hoard: 'The day has not been completely wasted then' was his comment. Nor did he waste his retirement. Papers continued to come out throughout the 1990s, into Jope's ninth decade, on Celtic art, on radiocarbon in the archaeological and biological sciences, on molecular preservation in archaeological and geological contexts, and, with the help of his research assistant Richard Ivens, on fieldwork and research projects of long ago—excavations he had carried out at the rath at Ballymacash near Lisburn in County Antrim in 1953 and 1954 some forty years before—the report appeared posthumously—or at Deddington Castle, a project started with 17-mile bike rides from Oxford by the Jopes half a century ago and eventually taken up by Ivens. It is a credit to Martyn that he was able, unlike so many archaeologists of his generation, to publish or make provision for the publication of virtually all his research backlog. More remarkably, in a vast lifetime product there is scarcely a single paper that does not have some new insight, or perception, or original thought or invaluable record—and on a range and scope of subjects that few if any of his contemporaries could match.[17]

Martyn died at Oxford on 14 November 1996 aged 80. His wife, co-researcher and fiercely loyal and devoted partner Margaret died in 2004. They had no children.

PETER ADDYMAN
Formerly Director, York Archaeological Trust

Note. Much of this memoir is based on biographical notes left by Martyn Jope at his death. I am also much indebted to Dr Ian Stead and Professor Roy Hodson for advice on his work on Iron Age matters and in particular for their notes on his publication of *Early Celtic Art in the British Isles*. Professor Bruce Proudfoot provided valuable insights into Jope's early years in Belfast and on his work as a biochemist.

[17] No full list of his writings has been published; a recently compiled list is available at Peter Addyman (2014) Memoir of Martyn Jope (Bibliography) [data-set]. York: Archaeology Data Service [distributor] (doi:10.5284/1027060).

IAN LITTLE

Ian Malcolm David Little
1918–2012

IAN LITTLE, who died on 13 July 2012, at the age of 93, was one of Britain's foremost economists and, for a time, the world's most influential development economist. Ian had a mind of unusual penetration, subtlety and creative power. The quantity and quality of his scholarly output was impressive, and he wrote or edited around twenty books and about a hundred papers, some of which were path-breaking. He also made an impact beyond the groves of academe. His seminal writings undermined the orthodox post-war view that protectionism, and *dirigiste* central planning, were the road to prosperity for developing countries. He became, thereby, one of the intellectual leaders of the shift in most of these countries towards liberal trade policies, which made a major contribution to lifting millions of people out of poverty in the last quarter of the twentieth century. Astonishingly, he was not knighted.

This memoir is divided into several sections. The first is an account of his life, career and personality. Later sections discuss his writings in the main areas which bear his imprint: theoretical welfare economics; applied welfare economics (project evaluation); trade and development; and the Indian economy. The last section appraises his work as investment bursar of Nuffield College. As there is no published complete bibliography of Ian Little's writings, this is appended to the memoir: full details of all items referred to in the text can be found there.

Life, career, personality

The sketch of Ian's life below is an inferior substitute for his own account in *Little by Little* (hereafter *LbL*), a remarkable autobiography that combines detached frankness with dry humour.[1] Another useful source for details of his life and views is *Collection and Recollections* (hereafter *CaR*), which reprints some of his articles (selected by him), interspersed with his later reflections.[2]

Ian was born on 18 December 1918 into a large, upper middle class, family. He writes in *LbL* that his lineage both on his father's and his mother's side was devoid of intellectual distinction. A harsh judgement but, even if true, distinction as such was not lacking. His grandfather was a general in the British army, his father a brigadier general, and they both commanded the 9th Lancers. On his mother's side, he was descended from Thomas Brassey, the great Victorian entrepreneur, who built railways all over the world. The family was well-off: according to *LbL*, Ian's childhood home had

> 23 bedrooms . . . and an appropriate number of reception rooms, servants' rooms and offices and so forth. It stood in about four acres of garden. There were six cottages, housing four gardeners, the butler, the head groom . . . There were ten or more horses . . . two motor cars . . . Within the house, there were eight or nine servants making about 20 in all. This was all apart from the mixed farm of about 180 acres with another three cottages for the bailiff and other farm workers . . .

But family relationships were distant; 'it is Nanny who was the real parent'.

After early instruction at the hands of a governess and a prep school, Ian went to Eton. He did quite well in examinations but was not regarded as a high-flier, partly because of his inability to learn by heart. He describes himself in *LbL* as painfully shy and fearful of sexual advances by older boys: he took up carpentry to avoid being in his house during the evening hours. He left school as soon as he was admitted to Oxford, because he was terrified of making the customary end-of-year speech to a gathering of parents. Travel during his gap year gave him 'some self-confidence which was woefully lacking'. All in all, while it would be an exaggeration to say that he suffered his Etonian education, he certainly did not much enjoy it.

Ian went up to New College, Oxford, to read Philosophy, Politics and Economics (PPE) in 1938. For some time, he was by his own account a

---

[1] I. M. D. Little, *Little by Little* (Privately Printed, 2004).
[2] I. M. D. Little, *Collection and Recollections* (Oxford, 1999).

hunting, drinking, gambling man, lacking any focus or direction. Things improved after the first two terms, when his intellectual interests were stimulated by philosophy tutorials with Isaiah (later Sir Isaiah) Berlin, and his friendship with Monty Woodhouse (later Lord Terrington). Even so, he writes in *LbL*, 'if it had not been for the war, I would not have got a first, perhaps not even a second'. Called up soon after war was declared, he served for nearly the full six years in the Airborne Forces Experimental Establishment of the Royal Air Force. At first he flew autogyros, which were used to calibrate the ring of radar stations that warned of approaching enemy planes. Later, he was a test-pilot and flew some hair-raisingly dangerous contraptions such as the 'rotachute', an innovative rotary-wing device designed by Raoul Hafner to be a super-parachute for dropping airborne soldiers, and the 'rotabuggy', also designed by Hafner, that was intended to convert a jeep into a flying machine by attaching a two-bladed rotor.[3] Much skill and courage was required in these obligatory adventures; he had several crashes and nearly met his death in one of them. Though he made light of the dangers (he compares himself in *LbL* to 'a sort of James Bond trying out Q's inventions'), the Air Force Cross that he was awarded towards the end of the war was clearly well deserved.

In 1945, he was demobilised with the rank of 'squadron leader' and returned to undergraduate studies at New College. The war had changed him profoundly. Before, he had been an amiable playboy, uninterested in scholarship. Now, he threw himself into academic study and resolved to become an academic. He took papers in philosophy (tutors: Isaiah Berlin and Herbert Hart) and economics (tutor: Philip Andrews) and got an outstanding First in PPE in the summer of 1947, and then a scholarship to Nuffield College to do graduate work in economics. He chose economics over philosophy because it offered wider possibilities and, as he says in *LbL*, 'it seemed to me that philosophers were cleverer than economists and so the competition would be less severe'.

His graduate supervisor was the eminent J. R. (later Sir John) Hicks, but they got on very badly. Ian was critical of his supervisor's work and Hicks was so affronted that he tried, thankfully without success, to get Ian's scholarship discontinued.[4] Shortly thereafter, Ian was elected to a prize fellowship (a fellowship by examination) at All Souls College,

---

[3] During the intervals between these test-flights, Ian trained as a pilot of the Sikorsky helicopter that had just arrived in England.
[4] On Hicks, see J. Creedy, 'John Richard Hicks 1904–1989', *Biographical Memoirs of Fellows of the British Academy*, XII (2013), 215–31.

Oxford. Isaiah Berlin is said to have remarked that Ian 'was the most ignorant person to get a fellowship at All Souls'. Presumably he meant that his breadth of knowledge fell far short of a typical young fellow's, but he made up for that in superior analytical power. At All Souls, Ian finished in two years his doctoral thesis, *A Critique of Welfare Economics* (hereafter *A Critique*). Though it was largely self-directed, he acknowledged helpful conversations with William Baumol, Jan Graaff and Lionel McKenzie. The thesis was examined by Arthur (later Sir Arthur) Lewis and David Worswick. It was however rejected for publication by Macmillan.[5] This was a bad business decision: it was published instead by Oxford University Press (OUP) in 1950, became a classic, sold 70,000 copies, and established his world reputation as an economic theorist. *A Critique* was motivated by a deep conviction that welfare economics had become a pretentious subject, insulated from good sense. What does it mean to say that one economic outcome is better for society than another? This is among the most basic, foundational questions in welfare economics. Ian demonstrated in *A Critique* that an ethical judgement about the distribution of income is intrinsic to any legitimate answer to this question, and that the search for some objective, value-free criterion of economic improvement is doomed to failure. While that is the justly famous central point of the book, we can see, retrospectively, that it made another advance. It clearly foreshadowed the theory of the second best, the idea that if one of the Pareto conditions is violated, satisfaction of one or all of the others would not, in general, constitute an improvement in efficiency. This proposition is stressed time and again in the middle chapters of *A Critique*, though a formal proof had to wait for the famous article by Richard Lipsey and Kelvin Lancaster in the *Review of Economic Studies*.[6] Ian himself followed up *A Critique* in 1951 with a short paper in the *Economic Journal*, refuting the alleged superiority of direct over indirect taxes. This was a rigorous exercise in the economics of the second best, of which there is not, so far as we know, another such early example, except Jacob Viner's work on customs unions, which appeared at about the same time.

---

[5] In *LbL* Ian speculates that the referee was A. C. Pigou. The passage is worth quoting: 'The anonymous referee's report said that I seemed incapable of grasping the elementary distinction between the size of a cake and the way it is sliced. As it was a central and closely argued message of the thesis that no such distinction can be drawn, because one does not know the size of the cake until one knows how it is sliced, this was a frustrating comment. I do not know for certain who the referee was, but I think it was A. C. Pigou . . .' (*LbL*, p. 81).

[6] R. G. Lipsey and K. Lancaster, 'The general theory of second best', *The Review of Economic Studies*, 24 (1956–7), 11–32.

In 1950, Ian succeeded Anthony Crosland as Fellow and Tutor in Economics at Trinity College, Oxford. He was there for two years, during which he wrote two well-known papers: a review article (for which he retained a special fondness) in the *Journal of Political Economy* (1952) of Kenneth Arrow's *Social Choice and Individual Values*, and the paper on 'Direct versus indirect taxes' mentioned above. He was elected an Official Fellow of Nuffield College, Oxford in 1952, and it remained his base thereafter, despite several spells away. After a year at Nuffield in which he wrote a policy-orientated book, *The Price of Fuel*, he was seconded in 1953 to Whitehall for two years as Deputy Director of the Economic Section of the UK Treasury, under Sir Robert Hall. This spell of government duty stimulated an abiding interest in problems of economic management and policy. He continued writing books and articles after his return to Nuffield. During 1955–8, he directed and published (jointly with Richard Evely) a study of concentration in British industry, and wrote articles on capital theory, as well as (jointly with Robert Neild and C. R. Ross) a long memorandum of evidence for the Radcliffe Committee on monetary policy. In addition, he collaborated with Paul Rosenstein-Rodan on a study of nuclear energy in Italy. Looking back, he later described himself in this phase as lacking in focus. He was clearly still searching for an area of specialisation.

To this end, the Rosenstein-Rodan connection proved to be critical: he invited Ian to join the MIT India Project. The Project Team that went to India in 1958 consisted of Ian, George Rosen and Trevor Swan. Ian and Swan established a close relationship with Pitambar Pant, the head of the Perspective Planning Division of the Planning Commission, and became intimately involved with producing India's Third Five Year Plan. The nine months in India were a turning point in Ian's career: thereafter, he became primarily a development economist.[7] For Ian, the road to Delhi was to be the road to Damascus. At that preliminary stage, however, his work did not depart much from contemporary orthodoxy, and was supportive of central planning. The India trip also got him interested in the economics of foreign aid. After a three-month tour of Africa in 1963, funded by the Overseas Development Institute (ODI), he wrote two books on the subject (*Aid to Africa*, and *International Aid*, the latter co-authored with Juliet

[7] 'The nine months that I spent in India was a turning point in my career. I became a development economist. I felt that there were problems that an open-minded economist could help to solve; and the terrible poverty would greatly increase the value of any material improvement one could help to bring about. But this was not the main influence. I think this was simply that I liked India and Indians' (*LbL*, p. 107).

Clifford) in the next two years. These were sympathetic to the objective of aid but expressed severe doubts about the absorptive capacity of African developing countries at that time.

The breakthrough in Ian's work on development came after his second trip to India in 1965, again on behalf of the MIT India project. This time, relations with the Planning Commission turned out to be less cordial. So Ian made his services available to the Bell Mission of the World Bank, which was visiting the country. As part of this consultancy, Ian was asked to do an economic appraisal of a heavy electrical plant in Bhopal. This project was a clear instance of plan-driven import substitution. If the Indian five-year plan model was soundly based, this project should have scored high marks. Ian came to the opposite conclusion. While doing the project evaluation, he realised that the investment made sense only if inputs and outputs were valued at domestic market prices. Valued at world prices, which are the true measures of opportunity cost in an open economy, the project was a waste of money. This was the seed from which sprouted his cardinal insight that economic progress in many developing countries had gone off the rails, as a result of neglecting the use of foreign trade.[8] This idea was to provide the focus of his work for the next ten years, during which he wrote two path-breaking books.

Both books were initiated during a two-year stint as Vice-President of the OECD Development Centre in Paris from 1966–8. Both were written with others but Ian was the driving force. The first, *Industry and Trade in some Developing Countries* (1970), was co-authored with Maurice Scott and Tibor Scitovsky. Using theory, as well as empirical evidence from six background country studies, it argued that trade controls, and inward-

[8] 'My work on Bhopal was a major factor in changing my ideas about planning development. I concluded that this very large project was seriously flawed in conception, implementation, and current operations, and that it promised a very low rate of financial and social return. The project evaluation work of other members of the Bell mission suggested that Bhopal was no exception. If planning threw up many projects that seemed to have a very low rate of return, belief in planning—anyway, planning as it was actually done was undermined. A related lesson was that one of the reasons for the low calculated rate of return was that the advantages of international trade were being neglected. This insight, blindingly obvious as it now appears, was then quite a revelation, for the ethos of development economics at the time prohibited any attention to the advantages of trade' (*LbL*, p. 129). Note that Ian's change of view about economic planning constituted an abandonment of the earlier influence of Rosenstein-Rodan whose big-push theory of economic development argued for rapid industrialisation on all fronts in economies with surplus labour in agriculture, to take advantage of network effects. While undoubtedly well intended, the big-push theory is toxic to rigorous and effective economic planning. It makes it acutely difficult to consider economic performance piecemeal, as any apparent local failings may be offset by network effects, which are easy to invoke but impossible to measure.

looking policies more generally, impose large economic costs and reduce employment and growth. It advocated radical trade liberalisation, but not laissez faire: it was explicitly in favour of using taxes and subsidies to off-set domestic market failures. It also showed that some developing countries, notably South Korea and Taiwan, were already breaking out of economic stagnation on the basis of export-oriented policies. The book had a huge impact on development thinking and policy and its message has stood the test of time. There is now a wide consensus that an open trade policy is a necessary, though not a sufficient, condition of economic transformation. Ian's other outstanding book on development, also initiated at the OECD, was *Manual of Industrial Project Analysis II, Social Cost Benefit Analysis* (1969), published later in revised form as *Project Appraisal and Planning for Developing Countries* (1974). It was written in collaboration with James (later Sir James) Mirrlees and proposed an original and constructive scheme of social cost–benefit analysis for project evaluation, sensitive to foreign trade opportunities as well as distributional considerations. It had a major influence on the practice of project selection in the World Bank and elsewhere. (Notably, Ian himself succeeded in persuading the Indian Planning Commission to set up a Project Appraisal Division.)

For many years, Ian's work as a development economist did not give him entry to the UK development economics community. The circle of UK development economists was then a closed shop dominated by a 'structuralist' view that held underdeveloped countries to be a separate family, to which orthodox (and especially neoclassical) methods had no application. The role of prices in economic development was underplayed because they were seen as chiefly to do with distribution, in which regard they could easily be offset by taxation and price regulation. That prices have crucial effects through the incentives that they create for action, however obvious that may now seem, was not then regarded as important.[9] If Ian's decision to become a development economist gave him no entry to the national community, it proved to be worth even less when it came to recognition in Oxford where, in the 1950s and 1960s, there were two regnant camps: Professor Hicks and his followers, and the development economics establishment led by Thomas (later Lord) Balogh. The former

---

[9] This last description applies better to British thinking on development than to development theory world-wide. Albert Hirschman in particular based his theory of unbalanced growth on the idea that what the state does creates incentives and outcomes in the private unplanned sector of the economy.

kept him at a distance, the latter met his ideas with active hostility. Nuffield College was the sanctuary in which Ian flourished. Along with Max Corden, James Mirrlees and Maurice Scott he made it a centre of excellence to which many of Oxford's brightest graduate students in economics gravitated.[10] Looking back on Ian Little's life it is difficult not to feel some sadness and embarrassment for British economics. He rarely received the credit due to him, and even when granted it was often reluctantly delivered. *A Critique of Welfare Economics* was not generally recognised as the masterpiece it undoubtedly represents, and Sir John Hicks's churlish rejection of Ian's work was a disgrace. But it is in the field of development economics that the embarrassment is greatest, and it is in Oxford that it reaches its peak. Ian Little was a giant of development economics, and the Oxford colleagues who rejected him and tried to lock him out were shown to be completely misguided. To assume that good ideas always win in the end is too optimistic. However, in the case of trade and development Ian, notwithstanding his early rejection, has proved to be on the winning side.

In 1970, Ian was elected to the Professorship of the Economics of Underdeveloped Countries at Oxford, and in 1973 to a Fellowship of the British Academy. He resigned the Oxford chair after four and a half years, in part because he was uncomfortable in the lecture theatre and hated public speaking. He then moved to Washington for two years as Special Adviser in the Development Economics Division of the World Bank. While there, he initiated a research project on small-scale manufacturing enterprises. (After he left, it made slow progress. He returned to the Bank for a few months in 1984 to write the overview.) He retired to Provence in 1978 but came back to live in Oxford after the death of his first wife.

Two of Ian's non-academic positions are noteworthy: board membership of the British Airports Authority (BAA) from 1968–73, and investment bursarship of Nuffield College off and on (including a short stint after retirement).[11] As member of the BAA board, he had a major influence in scuppering the mooted Third London Airport at Maplin. He argued that the Roskill Commission had greatly over-estimated the bene-

---

[10] 'As already indicated, I was now in my own mind a development economist but this was not recognised in Oxford. With only two exceptions no postgraduate student of the subject, or from a developing country, was assigned to me by the university before I became 'professor of the economics of underdeveloped countries' a decade later and acquired some say in the matter . . . However, Nuffield College always appointed a college supervisor for its students in addition to the university supervisor, and in this way I did acquire a few students, the most famous of whom was Manmohan Singh, Finance Minister of India from 1991 to 1996' (*LbL*, p. 114).

[11] He was also a member of the UN Committee for Development Planning from 1972–5.

fits of a new airport by failing to consider the use of peak-load pricing at existing airports. The case for Maplin was at first accepted by the Heath government. But Ian advised Tony Crosland, in opposition in 1971, that at most one new runway was needed in the London area in the twentieth century. He describes the ensuing course of events as follows: 'Sometime early in 1974 I had a telephone call from Tony Crosland, then again a Minister . . . asking what he should do about Maplin. I said "ditch it". He did. . . . If I had any decisive influence on this issue I reckon I earned my somewhat niggardly salary many times over' (*LbL*, pp. 145–6). Ian was co-investment bursar at Nuffield College with Donald MacDougall from 1958–62 and Uwe Kitzinger from 1962–5, and investment bursar from 1968–70 and 1990–2.

In retirement, Ian remained active and intellectually vigorous and wrote several major books and articles. The first was *Economic Development: Theory, Policy and International Relations* (1982), a brilliant, insightful survey of the field of development economics. In 1984 he was invited by Anne Krueger, then Vice-President of the World Bank, to design a large multi-country research project on the macroeconomic policies of developing countries. Seventeen countries were studied. Ian's involvement was considerable. He co-wrote the synthesis volume *Boom, Crisis and Adjustment* (1993) with Richard Cooper, Max Corden and Sarath Rajapatirana.[12] In addition, he co-wrote one of the country studies, *India—Macroeconomics and Political Economy, 1964–1991* (1994), with Vijay Joshi. This was shortly followed by another book co-authored with Vijay Joshi, *India's Economic Reforms, 1991–2001* (1996). In his eighties, he edited two books, and wrote two others: *Ethics, Economics and Politics*, a concise introduction to the interrelationship of the three component subjects of PPE; and *Little by Little*, the personal memoir mentioned above. He was appointed CBE in 1997.

At Nuffield College, Ian inspired many pupils and colleagues. One of his great satisfactions was that his doctoral student and friend, Manmohan Singh, became Finance Minister and then Prime Minister of India, and instigated many of the reforms that he had advocated. Ian's conversational style was quiet and reflective, not flashy; its hallmarks were the discerning throwaway remark, the *mot juste*, and the brief but incisive comment that goes to the heart of the matter. Despite the economy of

[12] Developing-country macroeconomics is an area in which Ian could fairly be claimed to have had a major influence. We have left out any discussion of his contribution to this field to keep the length of this memoir within reasonable bounds. For Ian's thoughts on the subject and on the World Bank project see *LbL*, pp. 172–3 and *CaR*, pp. 90–2 and 250–69.

words, his presence was magnetic; and its impact is captured by Francis Seton when he writes: '. . . [his] views, however modestly expressed, would command immediate acceptance for their lucidity and independence. He had no need to seek effects, to hedge about, manipulate the waverers, or lobby the influential . . . nothing seemed more alien to him than showmanship, conformity, plodding exertion, or nail-biting discomfiture.'[13] It is no surprise that this style did not endear him to the great and the good, and it may account for the fact that, like his illustrious ancestor Thomas Brassey, he received few of the honours in this country that one might have expected to come his way.

Ian's personality was complex. He was outwardly diffident but had an inner core of iron self-confidence. He was deeply serious and high-minded, but he was not a puritan; he loved the food, wine, and sun of Provence. He was rather reserved but gave wonderful parties. He had no ear for music but a very good eye for the visual arts. He was well-born but un-snobbish, hated ostentation and pomposity, and believed in taxing wealth more harshly than any of the political parties do today.[14] He was in some ways a correct English gentleman but there was also a wild streak in him, manifested by his love of fast cars and by the houses he designed and lived in, with their lethal spiral staircases. It was difficult to know what was going on behind his steely blue eyes, so people sometimes found him reticent or unapproachable, or even slightly frightening. But he was a warm and affectionate friend; and in the company of friends he would melt, and talk about people and events with ironic amusement. And these apparently contradictory elements did not in any way add up to a fractured or inconsistent personality. They were held together by his personal integrity, his humane and liberal outlook, and his zest of life.

Ian married twice. Both his marriages brought him fulfilment, though different in kind. He met Doreen Hennesey, known to friends as Dobs, while he was in the Royal Air Force. They married in 1946. They were a stylish couple and gave sensational parties that came to be known in Oxford as the 'parties for dancing economists'. The marriage was not peaceful during its middle years because Dobs was battling alcoholism and depression, but its last fifteen years were serene. Dobs died in 1984. Life as a widower did not suit Ian and, as he often remarked, he was very lucky to meet and marry Lydia Segrave in 1991. With her, Ian became young again. They had two decades of a rewarding and contented life,

---

[13] See Francis Seton, 'Ian Little—a salute *Inter Vivos*', in M. FG. Scott and D. Lal (eds.), *Public Policy and Economic Development: Essays in Honour of Ian Little* (Oxford, 1990), pp. 1–9.
[14] See J. Flemming and I. Little, *Why We Need a Wealth Tax* (London 1974).

travelling the world, visiting art museums, doing the *Times* crossword, seeing friends, and working. Lydia sculpted and Ian continued to write. He was very proud of Lydia's talent as a sculptor. She survives him, together with his two stepchildren, and a son and daughter by his first marriage.

Theoretical welfare economics

A Critique of Welfare Economics was the major contribution from Ian Little in his early career as an economist. It can also take its place beyond doubt as one as the most important publications on economics from the decades of the early post-war years. It is striking then to note that it reads less as pure economics than do many comparable works of the time. The author is certainly an economist, thoroughly grounded in the history and theory of the economics of welfare. Yet more than any other writer in the field, with the possible exception of Kenneth Arrow, he is also a philosopher. We recognise this from his insistence that welfare economics is about ethics, and that this aspect of the subject cannot be disguised or evaded.

To appreciate this work it must be seen in the context of its time. These were the years of the New Welfare Economics. This was founded in the rejection of the old welfare economics of Mill, Bentham, and Marshall, which depended upon measurable utility. To these writers it made sense to discuss whether it is a good idea to take £10 from a rich man to give the proceeds to a poor man, even if leakage created by this transfer reduced the poor man's gain to £3. A comparison of the marginal utility of money of the two parties provides a precise numerical answer. This kind of reasoning was a victim of the revolution in philosophical thinking that was logical positivism, and the ideas of the Vienna School. Taken to extremes, as it sometimes was, this new philosophy reached such bizarre conclusions as the refusal by the Oxford philosopher A. J. Ayer to admit to being an atheist, on the ground that the proposition 'There is no God' is untestable, and hence without meaning.

If arguments are valid only if they discuss exclusively the observable and the measurable, there is no room for cardinal utility. The tendency of an economics that adopted a positivist outlook was to eschew discussion of the distribution of welfare gains and losses, and to focus on efficiency, and the possibility of changes that could make everyone better off. One escape from the constraint of positivism was to confine attention to Pareto improvements of this kind. If a change could give the rich man £10 *and* the poor man £3, then surely it could be recommended, regardless of the measurement of utility. Here the problem is that changes that are Pareto improvements are quite unusual. Normally there are losers, even with the most attractive interventions.

It is in response to this difficulty that John Hicks and Nicholas Kaldor came up with the concept that came to be called the Kaldor–Hicks criterion (the K–H test). According to this test, a change can be recommended if the gainers are able to compensate (bribe) the losers and still be better off. That looks appealing, but what exactly does it mean? Are we asked to accept that a change that passes the K–H test, plus the required compensation, is to be recommended? That is no more than a particular case of the Pareto test, and is similarly limited in scope. Instead of such a narrow application, the K–H test did not require that the compensation be paid.

Then Tibor Scitovsky showed that the reversal of a K–H improvement could also pass the K–H test. With inefficient states, well inside the production possibility frontier, there is plenty of surplus to pay compensation, so Scitovsky's finding is not unexpected. It is to this confusing tangle of ideas that Ian Little brought his sharp and precise intellect. In place of the K–H test, he proposes a two-item check list for a change to count as a welfare improvement. First, it would produce a not-unfavourable redistribution of income; and secondly, the losers from the change could not bribe the gainers to vote against it. These two tests together define *the Little Criterion*. The second test takes care of Scitovsky's point.

The first three chapters of *A Critique* develop carefully and thoroughly the theory of welfare comparisons based on the choices made by individuals in market-situations. It is shown how consistent choices can generate indifference curves (or behaviour curves) that provide a behavioural definition of 'better off' for an individual consumer. The many difficulties that this approach encounters are noted at every step. Ian eventually relies on the possibility that the theory might work better for an average individual, than for a particular genuine individual. One of the striking features of *A Critique* is its focus on the central field of a basic welfare economics. Its author refuses to be diverted towards extensions, such as dynamics, or the cardinal utility measures of von Neumann and Frank Ramsey. He is aware of this material, but chooses not to go down those side-roads. As the reader will learn from this volume, there is plenty to be done with the most elementary welfare economics; and the author does just that.

The balance between rigorous scepticism, and a determination to achieve what can be achieved, is perfectly captured in the short paragraph that closes chapter III of the volume:

> But we must certainly not pretend that our analysis is anything but rough and ready. As we have already implied, it is particularly inapplicable in respect of choices between jobs, and different hours and kinds of work. Nevertheless, enough has, I think, been said to show that it would be foolish to dismiss the whole of welfare economics solely on the ground that the analysis of 'individual' behaviour, on which it rests, is hopelessly at variance with the facts.

Chapters IV and V of *A Critique* move on from the behaviour of individuals and the evaluation of individual welfare to the difficult fields of the distribution of welfare, interpersonal comparisons, and value judgements. This is economics, yes; but truly it is high-standard philosophy. Central to Ian Little's case is a head-on assault on the clear fact-value distinction of David Hume and G. E. Moore. These writers insisted that 'is' propositions cannot yield 'ought' propositions. The same distinction was the basis of Lionel Robbins's claim that when economists argue that the abolition of the Corn Laws was a good thing, this is not Science. If the effect of Corn-Law-abolition was to harm landlords, and benefit workers, the evaluation of that change depends upon the value judgement that the landlord losses count for less than the worker gains. The K–H test is designed to jump over that difficulty without confronting it. Ian Little allows himself no such easy ride. He shows in detail how slippery is distinction between fact and value.

Central to Little's argument is the observation that terms such as 'happy' or 'better off' do not refer to the entirely subjective and personal, as it might be maintained does 'tastes good'. Even this last term cannot be completely subjective. A man who says that raw sewage tastes good is not truthful. Also some terminology that appears to be no more than a value judgement reflects commonly understood criteria for its application. So while the description 'a good man' may be less precise than 'a tall man', it is not available for anyone to use as he likes. To say that a mass murderer is a good man is simply to reveal linguistic incompetence. Now the sentence 'John would be happier if he gave up drinking' can be considered a positivist statement. One who insists on a rigid fact-value distinction cannot claim that this last sentence does not entail a value-loaded recommendation that John gives up drinking. Clearly the positivist statement does imply a recommendation in favour of abstinence in John's case. A crucial conclusion of Ian Little's detailed analysis heads a list at the end of chapter IV: 'Interpersonal comparisons of satisfaction are empirical judgements about the real world, and are not, in any normal context, value judgements.'

Chapter VII is a short chapter devoted to the social welfare function, such as is proposed by Bergson and Samuelson. In the Preface to the 2002 reissue of *A Critique*, Little states that he has not taken note of Kenneth Arrow's book on social choice,[15] because he does not think 'that this subject has much relevance to classical welfare economics'. This view is strange, because Arrow arrived at his impossibility theorem after he had attempted unsuccessfully to arrive at a formal justification of the social welfare function. His analysis shows that given his other axioms, one individual must be decisive concerning a pairwise choice, which violates his no-dictatorship axiom. This is quite similar to the conclusion reached by Little, who characterises the social welfare function as the objective of 'a Superman', i.e. a dictator.

Chapters VIII and IX examine the optimal conditions of production and exchange: equal marginal rates of substitution for different individuals or producers. Yet the important point delivered by these chapters is that the satisfaction of one of these conditions is not sufficient for an optimum, however defined, if other marginal conditions are not satisfied. For example, direct taxation is not necessarily superior to indirect taxation when direct taxation destroys the equality between the rates of transformation and substitution of leisure and goods. This type of argument is now always called the theory of the second best. Ian Little is perhaps its originator, although few would realise that. As Ian himself puts it: 'Unfortunately for me, I did not name the theory!' (*CaR*, p. 8).

Marginal conditions do not work when there are indivisibilities. A bridge across a river is either built or not built; one cannot have a little less bridge. Ever since Alfred Marshall, this problem has been treated by applying the theory of consumer surplus to focus on the difference in total utility that the bridge delivers. This approach was obviously undermined when cardinal utility was abandoned. John Hicks applied much energy to rehabilitating the concept without cardinal utility, while Little took a different route, preferring direct ordinal assessments of lumpy changes. So Hicks and Little differed sharply on two separate questions: the K–H test, and consumer surplus.

The remaining chapters of *A Critique* (XI to XIV) examine output and price policy for public enterprises; the valuation of national income;

[15] K. J. Arrow, *Social Choice and Individual Values* (New Haven, CT, 1951, 2nd edn. 1963).

welfare theory and international trade; and welfare theory and politics. Chapter XV concludes. There are numerous sharp insights in these discussions, and also some intriguing surprises. Take, as an example of cutting analysis, the question of marginal-cost pricing for public enterprises. It is evident that the theory of the second-best will take issue with a simplistic argument in favour of marginal-cost pricing. This is because with average costs far higher than marginal costs, as is typically the case with public enterprises, such as the railways, strict marginal-cost pricing leaves a large revenue gap to be filled. There is no non-distorting way of raising that revenue, so the case in favour of marginal-cost pricing collapses. Little goes further by showing marginal cost to be a slippery concept. In the short run marginal cost oscillates wildly, as when the marginal cost of a rail journey varies according to how crowded are the carriages. In the extremely long run marginal cost is much the same as average cost.

Given his espousal of the second-best, one might expect Ian Little to reject the case for free trade. His actual position is more subtle and interesting. In the Preface to the 2002 edition he writes:

> The basic fallacy is that the free trade dogma neglects the distribution of income. Fifty years later I can find no fault with this. However I fear that the cursory reader might think that I believe that free trade generally worsens the distribution of wealth both between and also within countries. On the contrary, I believe that for most developing countries, especially the poorest, trade benefits the poor: this is because exports are relatively labour intensive, and raising the demand for labour reduces poverty.[16]

A good way of assessing the weight of the contribution that is provided in *A Critique* is to ask what a contemporary undergraduate studying welfare economics would lose if told to read nothing but that one volume. The answer must be that this imagined student would not be badly disadvantaged. Of course there are numerous other references that would benefit that individual. Ideally he or she should certainly study some social choice theory, which does have relevance for classical welfare economics. Also the welfare economics of risk and uncertainty, and inter-generational welfare, should not be neglected. And analysis using welfare weights, rejected by Hicks and only adopted later by Little, is hugely valuable. Yet a must-have tool-kit of welfare economics, with the correct emphasis on the distribution of welfare, is all to be found in the pages of *A Critique*.

---

[16] Preface to the 2002 edition of *The Critique*, p. xii.

Project evaluation

Many economists if asked to nominate Ian Little's major contribution to development economics would select his work on project evaluation. Given that, it is notable that Ian's entry to that field was almost accidental. It was not that he sought out the question of how to evaluate projects. Rather the issue landed on his desk while he was with the OECD in Paris:

> The other main product of my two years at the Development Centre was the OECD *Manual of Industrial Project Analysis.* This was jointly authored by myself and Jim Mirrlees. This was not the outcome of research that I had started. The Development Centre had already commissioned a French consultancy firm to produce such a manual, soon after it heard that the UN was doing so. A draft arrived which I thought terrible. I criticized it fundamentally, and revisions were promised. I considered the revised draft which eventually arrived to be still unacceptable. A small conference was called, most participants of which sided with me. But I had to threaten resignation to get the ball rolling. Baron [the then President of the OECD Development Centre] was convinced that my opposition simply stemmed from an Anglo-Saxon attitude.   (*LbL*, p. 132)

Here the discussion of the contribution made to project evaluation theory by Little and Mirrlees (henceforth L&M) will concentrate on their 1974 publication (henceforth *Project Appraisal*) rather than the original 1969 manual.[17] Two reasons support this choice. First, the 1974 book develops and presents their ideas more thoroughly and richly than the original. Secondly, the later publication responds in detail to the UNIDO *Guidelines* volume published between the two in 1972.[18] A comparison of the L&M approach and that of UNIDO is made difficult because the two volumes have distinct orientations. To put it simply, UNIDO is far more theoretical whereas L&M originated as a manual and remains such in the developed 1974 exposition. A manual is literally something to be held in the hand, like a guide book for workers in the field. For this reason the L&M exposition is intensely practical and offers detailed guidance concerning short-cuts and approximations.

Fundamentally, L&M and UNIDO follow similar paths in that they adjust market based returns by using shadow prices that are designed to

---

[17] The two publications are: I. M. D. Little and J. A. Mirrlees, *Manual of Industrial Project Analysis, II, Social Cost–Benefit Analysis* (Paris, 1969), and I. M. D. Little and J. A. Mirrlees, *Project Appraisal and Planning for Developing Countries* (London, 1974).
[18] P. S. Dasgupta, S. A. Marglin and A. K. Sen, *Guidelines for Project Evaluation* (New York, 1972).

better reflect social valuations. A difference between the two methods that received great attention is in itself of limited significance: the two systems use different numeraires (accounting units). The choice of a numeraire cannot of itself make a great difference. However once a numeraire has been selected, conversion factors are required; that is, formulae to convert other values, such as wage rates, into values expressed in the numeraire. Then the details of conversion can make a substantial difference. The L&M numeraire is 'uncommitted social income measured at border prices', which contrasts with UNIDO's 'aggregate consumption measured at domestic market prices'. To cut short what could become a lengthy discussion, it suffices to say that the L&M method is simpler and more reliable in practice. This is because it avoids the complex issue of deciding how far domestic market prices correctly reflect their contribution to consumption. In a highly distorted economy this is a complex exercise. L&M, on the other hand, avoid this tangled maze, either because if the good is traded one goes directly to the border price or, if it is not traded, its value can be measured at its marginal cost of production, broken down into its direct and indirect traded-good content (valued at border prices) and labour costs.

The focus of any project evaluation exercise is on the particular project and the numerical values associated with it. For that reason the impression is too easily arrived at that the theory is entirely microeconomic, concerned only with the project itself. This would be a mistake, and it is a great merit of the L&M method that it shows in a clear light how the evaluation of the individual project must be embedded in a global perspective that reflects the entire economy. The point can be illustrated via the consideration of a crucial value in any social return calculation, the shadow price of labour. The L&M formula for the shadow wage (SWR) is derived from:[19]

$$SWR = m + (c' - c) + \left(1 - \frac{1}{s}\right)(c - m)$$

where
c' = value of consumption at market prices including items that do not directly contribute to welfare such as transport costs;

---

[19] Little and Mirrlees, *Project Appraisal*, p. 271. The formula shown in the text is not quite correct given the definitions of the variables at the top of the same page. This problem has been taken care of here by the provision of different definitions of the variables to make the formula correct.

c = welfare producing consumption;

m = marginal productivity of the wage earner; and

s = the value of uncommitted government income in terms of consumption.

The first term in the above equation is the marginal product of labour; the second term adds the costs of delivering consumption, such as transport costs; the third term shows increase in consumption of the marginal worker minus that part of it which is reckoned to be a benefit. The final total SWR is in domestic local-currency value. That must be converted to the numeraire (foreign exchange) by the application of the shadow exchange rate. This last number is an economy-wide value with which all project evaluators will be provided.

The derivation of the shadow wage rate illustrates beautifully some of the basic principles that underlie the L&M analysis. Wages display two contrary aspects. On the one hand they are a welfare benefit; they provide workers and their families with consumption, and the higher they are the more consumption they provide. On the other hand they are a cost to the national budget, because each rupee of wage paid out might otherwise be applied to beneficial government expenditure. In a simple case let $(c'-c)$ be zero, so no additional resources are devoted to the provision of consumption. Also, let m equal zero, because for example labour employed on the project comes from agriculture where the marginal worker adds nothing to output. Furthermore assume that workers consume all their wages, there being no saving. These are not realistic assumptions, but they help to show the principles of shadow wage rate calculation in a clear light. Then the formula for the shadow wage rate reduces to:

$$SWR = \left(1 - \frac{1}{s}\right) w$$

where w is the market wage rate that the project will have to pay. Note that the shadow wage rate is below the market wage rate. This implies that public sector projects evaluated positively by the L&M method will be more labour intensive than would be a similar project chosen to maximise profit in the private sector.

Another important value for the accurate assessment of projects is the accounting rate of interest (the *ARI*), the number that measures how future numeraire values are weighted relative to current numeraire values. This rate of interest may vary over time, but the discussion concentrates reasonably on the case where it is nearly constant. The role of the *ARI* is to act as a gate-keeper for the projects being assessed. It must not accept too many, when taxes would have to rise sharply, and present consumption would be depressed excessively. Equally it must not accept too few, when welfare-increasing possibilities would be wasted. The questions at issue here are easier to answer in a classroom on a blackboard than in reality. The two fundamental effects that need to be taken into account are the rate at which per capita consumption will rise, and the root discounting of the future that reflects the impatience of the planner (or the population). Growth of per capita consumption argues for weighting future consumption more lightly. Impatience adds an additional effect in the same direction. These two effects together generate an *ARI* that should be equated to the rate of return on the marginal project—the one that only just gets accepted. L&M discuss an interesting, although special, case in which the return on private investments provides a useful estimate of the *ARI*.

The OECD Manual was hugely influential. It generated important empirical studies that applied its methods in the field.[20] It also played a crucial role in promoting formal rule-based project evaluation methodology in the World Bank. For many years in that institution project evaluation and Little/Mirrlees became synonymous. These successes were in sharp contrast to the largely hostile reception of the OECD Manual in Britain, and notably in Oxford. As Ian Little writes:

> The OECD Manual was strongly attacked by the development establishment, especially the Oxford branch. The essential principle it promoted was that, in considering the costs and benefits of domestic production of something, both export possibilities and the alternative of satisfying domestic demand by importing should be carefully considered. The implied insistence on trying to use international trade optimally was anathema to those who had been taught that free trade was a colonial tyranny designed to ensure that developing countries would for ever produce only primary commodities . . . Since those days relatively open trading policies have become more widely practised in developing countries, and few would now deny the benefit of such policies. But I myself continue to be reviled as The Great Satan in some development schools. (*LbL*, p. 138)

---

[20] See, inter alia, I. M. D. Little, T. Scitovsky and M. FG. Scott, *Industry and Trade in Some Developing Countries* (London, 1970); M. FG. Scott, J. MacArthur and D. M. G. Newbery, *Project Appraisal in Practice: the Little/Mirrlees Method Applied in Kenya* (London, 1974); and N. H. Stern, *An Appraisal of Tea Production on Small-Holdings in Kenya* (Paris, 1972).

The critiques of L&M pursued many arguments, these of variable merit. The February 1972 edition of the *Bulletin of the Oxford Institute for Economics and Statistics* was devoted entirely to a symposium concerned with the OECD Manual. Several of these papers, including one by Vijay Joshi, took a favourable view of L&M, and the paper by Nicholas Stern on an application to tea farming in Kenya provided a valuable example of the L&M method in practice. Partha Dasgupta's paper compared the OECD and UNIDO manuals. In contrast, the long paper by Frances Stewart and Paul Streeten is not unlike a prolonged artillery assault on L&M.[21] Elsewhere, a paper by Amartya Sen explored the issue of irrational (or at least immovable) government policies,[22] a point also stressed by Stewart and Streeten.

Leading issues raised by the Oxford critics of L&M are the following: irrational governments; economic linkages; and non-traded goods. It was claimed that L&M assume that the government of the country to which project evaluation is applied is as rational and detached as the authors themselves. Another assertion is that L&M ignore the multiple linkages—forward, backward, and sideways—that are characteristic of under-developed countries. The final claim from the prosecution is that L&M give insufficient weight to non-traded goods and fail to price them correctly.

In the final paper in the *Bulletin of the Oxford Institute* issue Little and Mirrlees provide a vigorous and robust reply to their critics. They agree that recommendations may be conditional on a rational government response but note that the implication of an irrational response is often contained in the recommendation. Thus if the project evaluator recommends the adoption of a scheme to manufacture motor vehicles domestically, provided that the engines are imported, this implies, and that could be made explicit, that the scheme should not be adopted if the government insists on all production being domestic. On linkages, L&M confirm their scepticism concerning their universality and measurability, yet point out that if a linkage is evident and important it becomes part of the project, to be assessed with other components of the same. They underline their flexibility concerning the shadow pricing of non-traded goods, such as electricity supply in many countries. Non-traded goods can often be

[21] F. Stewart and P. Streeten, 'Little–Mirrlees methods and project appraisal', *Bulletin of the Oxford Institute of Economics and Statistics*, 34 (1972), 75–91. All the other papers (except Sen's) mentioned in this and the succeeding paragraph are to be found in the same issue of the journal.
[22] A. K. Sen, 'Control areas and accounting prices: an approach to economic evaluation', *Economic Journal*, 82 (1972: Special Issue), 502–30.

priced by their opportunity costs in terms of traded goods. If that is not possible the values in domestic prices can be translated to border values using the conversion factor that already figures in their analysis. Notable in the L&M response is how, rather than mounting new arguments, these authors usually point their critics to what is already there in the Manual.

The 1970s were the years when project evaluation based on cost–benefit analysis was at its high-point, both in developed and developing countries. Since then its status has declined, although it is still used (or abused).[23] A leading problem that emerged when institutions such as the World Bank tried to impose the method is that project evaluation proved to be strongly liable to manipulation. As L&M show clearly in their writing, estimates and guesses have important parts to play. That opens the door to biased estimates designed to achieve a particular result— usually the acceptance of a dubious project. A senior Indian civil servant once told one of the authors of this memoir that, given the book of rules, he and his colleagues could arrange for almost any favoured project to get over the finishing line. In fact the bias affecting project evaluation is two-sided. Governments receiving aid favour certain projects and will twist the assessment process to favour those schemes. And lenders have their own biases. They are not paid for turning down projects; their job is to lend money. So a rigorous tough approach to project proposals does not suit donors any more than recipients. Ian Little was sharply aware of the problems created when political forces encroach on project evaluation. He writes: 'The main difficulty facing cost–benefit analysis is that large public, or publicly subsidized, investments are a source of prestige, patronage, and kick-backs for those in power, and their relatives and cronies. They do not want their projects submitted to hard-nosed appraisal by economists' (*LbL*, p. 142).

Aside from the problems of manipulation discussed above, there is another major reason why cost–benefit analysis on L&M lines has declined in importance. A leading motivation for the L&M approach, and the same could be said of the UNIDO method, is to surmount the misleading price signals prevalent in highly distorted economies, especially those subject to strong and unbalanced trade protection. All this has become far less important as developing countries have become more open, their markets

---

[23] A current case in point is the claimed benefits of the proposed hugely expensive high-speed rail link in the UK between London and Birmingham, and points north. The benefits concerned are hard to measure and highly impressionistic. The costs are massive, and sometimes neglected. This is an exercise more in political persuasion than in genuine evaluation.

less interfered with, and their tariffs and controls diminished, often to levels below those of rich industrial countries. A great deal of credit for this belongs to Ian Little and to economists who thought on similar lines. So perhaps Little the trade and protection specialist was the executioner of Little the project evaluation innovator. If that is the case he would probably not have minded that outcome.

Trade and development

So influential have been the ideas of Ian Little, and parallel thinkers, on the role of trade in economic development that it is difficult now to recover the intellectual climate of early post-war economic thinking on this topic. To put it simply, an orthodoxy of that time held that trade was ineffective, unnecessary, and a dangerous break on development. This view was underpinned by the belief that the way to economic advancement took the form of industrialisation, and that this required the protection of infant industries from foreign competition. One finds this kind of thinking in many newly independent countries, but it is well illustrated with India because that country produced one of the most articulate expressions of anti-trade thought.[24] Two ideas powered this philosophy. First, it was felt that colonialism had hampered Indian industrialisation for selfish reasons, a claim that was not without foundation, and that policy should now reverse that tendency. Secondly, self-sufficiency was seen to be an ideal, supposedly because it offered more security than the perils of dependence on trade.

For India the Soviet Union provided a model of successful economic development for a large country based on forced industrialisation and little international trade with the capitalist west. There was an appreciation of undoubted Soviet successes, including the defeat of Nazi Germany, rapid growth, and impressive development of some sectors. The Soviet Union had by a long way the world's largest shoe industry. There was less understanding of the severe deficiencies of the Soviet economy. Agriculture was a disaster sector, the victim of forced confiscation of output, collectivisation, and discriminatory pricing. The delivery of consumer goods was extremely poor. Even those millions of shoes were in wrong sizes and styles. Crucially the basic mechanism of the planning system was

---

[24] The Prebisch–Singer theory that held that the terms of trade would inevitably move against primary-product exports was another argument for industrial self-sufficiency.

misguided. Output was crudely measured with quantity counting for much more than quality. Producers operated with soft budgets, encouraging them to waste such inputs as they could obtain. For such a lavishly forested nation to produce a timber shortage was an astounding achievement. The closed nature of the economy implied that economic planning was directed to producing to targets without the question of whether national comparative advantage favoured those outputs ever being considered.

Indians, like everyone else, were in a poor position to view the true nature of the Soviet economy, hidden as it was behind propaganda and misleading statistics. Had they been able to enjoy a clearer view they could have drawn useful lessons concerning economic management and economic planning. Among these lessons would have been the danger of grandiose projects undertaken without proper assessment of costs and benefits. Another lesson would have been the cost of neglecting export opportunities. Had forestry not been starved of inputs, the Soviet Union could have exported timber to its benefit, rather than failing to meet even domestic needs. Finally, the five-year plan model, under which growth targets for various sectors were laid down in advance, led to the misallocation of scarce inputs, and the underweighting of consumer needs.

Whatever the problems of economic planning, it was required in some form by newly independent countries. Hardly anyone thought that simply introducing laissez faire would produce the results required. The question was what form should planning take, and particularly in what direction it should point economic development. Should it favour heavy industry over light? What place should it give to international trade, to imports and to exports? Ian Little was a product of his time, and he started out firmly in favour of economic planning. Over time, experience and sharp observation modified his views. Autobiographies too often take the form of a prolonged monologue on the lines of 'I was always right, and everyone else was wrong.' This is foreign to Ian's character. He freely admits to alterations in his position:

> I am widely regarded as having shifted from uncritical belief in *dirigiste* planning to excessive trust in the price mechanism. Apart from the adjectives, this is broadly true. All economists are conversant with the faults of the price mechanism, some would suppress it altogether. Many liberals, including myself, wanted to tinker with it, and to rely on government to implement the tinkering. We were slow to realize that the most prevalent reason for market failure was government itself. Governments were driven by false economic ideology—heavy industry, protection, and import substitution—and also became increasingly

> self-serving and corrupt. My own change in emphasis is obvious. . . . It was driven by experience and research. However, although the change is insidious from 1960 to 1990, my India visit of 1965 was a watershed. It led directly to my research programme at the OECD, and hence to increasing emphasis on free trade and the reduction of domestic controls. (*CaR*, p. 81)

Ian's evolving views on trade and development were laid out extensively and provided with solid empirical support in the fine volume that he co-authored with Tibor Scitovsky and Maurice Scott, henceforth *Industry and Trade*. This volume draws together the conclusions of several OECD studies of individual countries—Brazil, India, Mexico, Pakistan, the Philippines, and Pakistan. The essence of the approach adopted in this volume is the following. Beginning students of economics learn that the advantages of international trade lie in the exploitation of comparative advantage: a country should do what it does relatively best, and rely on imports for what it does badly. It then seems clear that numerous qualifications destroy this simple conclusion. Among these are terms of trade that vary with the volume of exchange, externalities and infant-industry considerations, issues of income distribution, and more. In *Industry and Trade* we find a forensic analysis of the multiple effects of protection and economic planning biased towards heavy manufacturing, and hence inevitably biased against agriculture and light manufacturing. Most importantly, this policy obliterates the possibility of taking advantage of opportunities for exports, that is, exactly those exports that have proved to be the foundation of economic growth in the successful East Asian countries, such as South Korea and Taiwan.

Industry and Trade is a volume that cannot be fairly summarised in a short essay. It examines the issues involved in great depth and breadth. However picking out some of its leading points gives a good sense of its contributions. Chapters 2 and 5 discuss the magnitude of protection, and distinguish between the 'nominal' rate of protection (how much protection raises domestic prices), and effective protection (how far protection permits the value added in production to exceed what it would be in its absence). Effective protection is often far higher than its nominal cousin, and sometimes, when outputs are more heavily protected than inputs, even allows activities with negative value added at world prices to survive.

Chapter 6 looks at the pernicious consequences of reliance on controls, a characteristic of a planned, and over-planned, economy. Widespread controls on investment and other activities are costly and they blunt private initiatives. Entrepreneurs gain more from playing the planning system than from innovation and productivity improvements.

Industrialisation has aggravated income inequalities. The extra profits made in industry are not a net gain to the community. Protection of large-scale industry implies the anti-protection of light industry and agriculture, sectors in which incomes are low. Chapter 2 notes that a major source of saving and investment is the profits of heavy industry inflated by protection. These profits are invested to a great extent in the same industries that generated them, thus adding force to the bias against light manufacturing and agriculture. Protection biased in favour of heavy industry is bad for employment and the full utilisation of capital. Finally, and crucially, protection of heavy industry leads to the neglect of comparative advantage. This echoes points made above concerning biases in the Soviet system.

The Indian economy

Ian Little's connection with India extended for more than fifty years and was the inspiration for a good deal of his work after he wrote *A Critique*. We have already covered his first visit in 1958, while he was favourably disposed to Indian planning, and his second visit in 1965, when he became disillusioned with it. A major reason for the disillusionment was that he became convinced of the falsity of 'elasticity pessimism', which was one of its central tenets. This change of view, in conjunction with his field experience in project analysis, strongly influenced his thinking on methods of project selection for developing countries. The first fruits of this can be seen in 'Public sector project selection in relation to Indian development', an article that was published in an obscure book in 1969.[25] Many of his distinctive ideas, in particular the use of world prices as shadow prices for tradable goods, later refined in collaboration with James Mirrlees, can be found in this seminal piece. More generally, his second thoughts on India's development strategy, along with early evidence of the success of export-oriented growth in the 'Gang of Four', prompted him to mount the large OECD project on trade and industrialisation policies in developing countries. Six countries were selected for close examination; one of these was India. The volume on India, written by Jagdish Bhagwati and

[25] The article was written in 1965. One of the authors of this memoir attended the seminar in Nuffield College at which it was presented and remembers the mixture of admiration and outrage with which it was greeted. The article was published in A. V. Bhuleshkar (ed.), *Indian Economic Thought and Development* (Bombay, 1969); it has since been reprinted in *CaR*.

Padma Desai, became a classic in its own right.[26] Following the OECD project, and until his retirement, Ian did not work directly on India but maintained his strong links with the country.

After he retired, Ian wrote extensively about the Indian economy. This came about as a result of the project on macroeconomic policy in developing countries that he initiated at the World Bank in the mid-1980s. Ian wrote the India volume with Vijay Joshi as his co-author, and it was published by OUP in 1994 under the title *India—Macroeconomics and Political Economy, 1964–1991*. This was the first systematic assessment of Indian macroeconomic policies from the death of Pandit Nehru until the inauguration of the liberalising reforms of 1991. The book was divided into three parts. Part One was an introduction to India's history, institutions and markets. Part Two examined four major macroeconomic crises that the country experienced during this period—in 1965–7, 1973–5, 1979–81, and 1990–1. To put it very crudely, the first three crises were mainly the result of exogenous events, in particular droughts and oil price increases. The fourth was different. It resulted from the pursuit of unsustainable fiscal policies during the 1980s. The authors analysed in depth the causes and resolution of the crises, with particular attention to the shortcomings of stabilisation policy. Part Three was concerned with longer-term trends in policy. Separate chapters were devoted to fiscal, monetary, and trade and payments policies, and to the connection between macroeconomic policy and long-run growth. A distinctive contribution of the book was that it demonstrated a link between microeconomics and macroeconomics in the Indian context. Before this book, the fashionable view about Indian economic policy was that it was unsound microeconomically but sound macroeconomically, and that these phenomena were positively related—in other words, the controls that led to microeconomic inefficiency helped to attain macroeconomic stability. In contrast, one of the central conclusions of the book was that India's control system was not only microeconomically inefficient but macroeconomically perverse. In *CaR*, Ian writes about this book, 'It was the first and only macroeconomic history of India since the death of Nehru and will, I hope, prove to be the definitive study of the period.'

By the time that book was published, India had embarked on an ambitious reform programme designed to move the economy towards greater openness and market orientation. Vijay Joshi and Ian Little got a grant from the Overseas Development Administration to carry out an appraisal

---

[26] J. Bhagwati and P. Desai, *India: Planning for Industrialization* (London, 1970).

of this programme. The book that resulted—*India's Economic Reforms, 1991–2001* (1996)—was the first systematic assessment of India's reforms. It went into seven impressions and made a significant impact. There were five chapters, apart from an introductory and a concluding chapter. Chapter 2 on stabilisation policy showed that government deficits and debt were on an unsustainable track, and that fiscal consolidation was imperative. On balance-of-payments policy, it was supportive of India's decision to opt for a managed exchange rate, buttressed by targeted capital controls, and by occasional sterilisation of reserve accumulation, in order to prevent excessive exchange rate appreciation caused by exuberant capital inflows. This policy proved its worth during the build-up to the East Asian crisis of 1997. Chapters 3, 4 and 5 undertook a critique of structural reform. The authors took the view that while India had made a good beginning, the reforms were partial and incomplete. On trade and indirect taxation, they argued that India should move to a uniform value-added tax harmonised between the Centre and the States, with few exemptions, supplemented by a uniform tariff no higher than 10 per cent for industry as well as, more controversially, for agriculture.[27] They drew attention to the super-abundance of government subsidies, explicit and implicit. Fertilisers, fuel, electricity, irrigation water, and many other goods and services that are not public goods were sold well below their costs of production. The beneficiaries were preponderantly the better-off sections of society. Winding up these subsidies would improve resource allocation and yield more than enough fiscal savings to compensate the poor. On industrial policy, the book argued for privatising state-owned enterprises producing tradable goods. In these sectors, international competition would annul the main argument for nationalisation—viz. the possibility of monopolistic exploitation. Public sector enterprises producing non-tradables should be broken up into competitive and naturally monopolistic elements. The former should be privatised; the latter could be privatised or left in state ownership but in either case independent regulation was essential. The economy's poor infrastructure, which was mainly in state ownership, was identified as a critical constraint on growth. The book also argued strongly that liberalising output markets was not

---

[27] The authors recognised that there is a theoretical case for non-uniformity but preferred a uniform rate for various pragmatic reasons. On agricultural trade liberalisation, they argued that it would raise prices and profits for farmers producing the principal crops. This would enable the elimination of various ill-judged subsidies to agriculture. The rise in output prices would hurt the poor but they could and should be compensated by direct transfers, which would require reform of the public distribution system. These changes would not be easy but the net benefits would be large.

enough. Factor markets needed reform. Company laws, labour laws and urban land law had combined to make the economy highly inflexible and to impede labour-demanding, inclusive growth. Chapter 6 considered the social sectors. It argued that well-designed public employment schemes were superior to food subsidies (distributed via the highly inefficient public distribution system) as instruments of poverty alleviation.

Since the book was written, India's reform programme has made significant progress. But many shortcomings remain, including a bias against employment, and continuing presence of counter-productive subsidies. These failings were clearly identified and analysed in the 1996 book.

Ian as investment bursar

Ian Little's experience of portfolio investment began with his appointment as one of the two investment bursars at Nuffield College in 1958. At that date Nuffield College ceased to be a department of the university and became responsible for the management of its own funds. He served with Donald (later Sir Donald) MacDougall, and subsequently with Uwe Kitzinger. The college's broker was Vickers da Costa, and its Chairman Ralph Vickers advised the bursars directly, this advice being delivered via a daily telephone call that reported on the state of the market. The performance of the college's investments in the first four years, with Ian partly in charge, was outstanding. This owed much to Ralph Vickers's unusual investment skills. He studied company reports with forensic care, an approach that served Keynes well when he was a successful investor, as it did later for Warren Buffett.

Ralph Vickers was an extraordinary individual. His warmth and huge generosity gave him friendships with left-leaning academics despite his own right-wing politics and his support for apartheid South Africa. He was an active and daring investor. He was not afraid to select the unorthodox and to bet on relatively short-run movements. Riding price bubbles is notoriously dangerous, and it is a measure of Ralph Vickers's judgement and intuition that it protected him and his clients from the worst perils of high-risk investment. A striking example of this comes from a time long after Ian Little had ceased to be an investment bursar. Ralph Vickers put the college into Asil Nadir's *Polly Peck* conglomerate, to show a considerable profit, and got out of that stock in good time before the company was exposed as a sham and went bust. The daily telephone conversations with Ralph Vickers were hugely enjoyable, but resulted inevitably in too much trading (churning as it is now called), a bad investment strategy, though profitable to a broker on commission for trades.

One of the investment trusts that served the college well was the Vickers da Costa Insecs (Investing in Success) fund. This fund was based largely on the principle of investing in firms that had shown a high rate of growth of earnings per share in the past. This strategy was surprisingly successful for some time. The success is surprising because the policy is based on two assumptions. First, it is assumed that earnings are positively serially correlated. Secondly, the strategy only succeeds if stock prices do not reflect that correlation, as what would now be called the efficient markets hypothesis would require. The serial correlation of earnings is such a natural and intuitive idea that it takes an unusual intellect to question it. That intellect was Ian Little's. As he writes: 'However I was unhappy that there was no statistical proof that past growth was a good predictor of future growth. I feared that our success might be based on an illusion, which could not last' (*LbL*, p. 113).

The result of these ruminations was a short paper with what Ian describes as 'the eye-catching title of "Higgledy-Piggledy Growth"' published in November 1962, and subsequently a small book co-authored with A. C. Rayner, published in 1966, *Higgledy-Piggledy Growth Again.* These studies destroyed the notion that there are growth stocks whose future earnings performance can be predicted from the past. This discovery was embarrassing because Ian Little was an Insecs director (a position from which he resigned shortly thereafter), and because his findings could be seen as ungrateful in view of the great benefits that had accrued to Nuffield from its investment in Insecs. As Ian writes: 'Donald MacDougall also thought I was "rather letting the side down". I did not see it that way, as I did not believe success could continue for long if based on error. Perhaps I also thought that an academic scholar should put the dissemination of truth before profits' (*LbL*, p. 113). As it happens, opinion in the City was catching up with Ian's thinking. The fashion for growth stocks was soon in decline, and the analysis of company prospects became far more sophisticated. Ian's friendship with Ralph Vickers survived this history, and he became a Director of the General Funds Trust, the other big beast in the Vickers da Costa stable.

CHRISTOPHER BLISS
Fellow of the Academy
VIJAY JOSHI
Emeritus Fellow, Merton College, Oxford

Bibliography of works by I. M. D. Little

Books

A Critique of Welfare Economics (Oxford, 1950, 2nd edn., 1957).
The Price of Fuel (Oxford, 1953).
(with P. N. Rosenstein-Rodan) *Nuclear Power and Italy's Energy Position* (Washington, DC, 1957).
(with R. Evely) *Concentration in British Industry: an Empirical Study of the Structure of Industrial Production 1935–51* (Cambridge, 1960).
Aid to Africa: an Appraisal of U.K. Policy for Aid to Africa South of the Sahara (London 1964).
(with J. M. Clifford) *International Aid: a Discussion of the Flow of Public Resources from Rich to Poor Countries with Particular Reference to British Policy* (London, 1965, repr. Chicago, IL, 1967).
(with A. C. Rayner) *Higgledy Piggledy Growth Again: an Investigation of the Predictability of Company Earnings and Dividends in the UK, 1951–61* (Oxford, 1966, repr. New York, 1971).
(edited with H. B. Chenery, F. Baade, J. Kaufmann, L. H. Klaassen, and J. Tinbergen) *Towards a Strategy for Development Co-operation, with Special Reference to Asia* (Rotterdam, 1967; Little contributed a chapter on 'Aid: Project, programme, and procurement tying').
(with J. A. Mirrlees) *Manual of Industrial Project Analysis in Developing Countries, II, Social Cost–Benefit Analysis* (Paris, 1969, also French trans.).
(with T. Scitovsky and M. FG. Scott) *Industry and Trade in Some Developing Countries: a Comparative Study* (Oxford, 1970, also French and Spanish translations).
(with D. G. Tipping) *A Social Cost–Benefit Analysis of the Kulai Oil Palm Estate West Malaysia* (Paris, 1972).
(with J. A. Mirrlees) *Estudio Social Del Costo–Beneficio en la Industria de Paises en Desarrolla: Manual de Evaluacion de Proyectos* (trans. from *Manual of Industrial Project Analysis, II*, Mexico City, 1973).
(with J. A. Mirrlees) *Project Appraisal and Planning for Developing Countries* (London, 1974).
(with J. S. Flemming) *Why We Need a Wealth Tax* (London, 1974).
(with W. M. Corden and M. FG. Scott) *Import Controls versus Devaluation and Britain's Economic Prospects* (London, 1975).
(edited with M. FG. Scott) *Using Shadow Prices* (London, 1976).
Una Critica dell' Economica del benessene (Milan, 1976, trans. Guido Tesarum and with a new introduction by the author).
(with M. FG. Scott and W. M. Corden) *The Case against General Import Restrictions* (London, 1980).
Economic Development: Theory, Policy and International Relations (New York, 1982).
(with D. Mazumdar and J. M. Page Jr.) *Small Manufacturing Enterprises: a Comparative Study of India and Other Economies* (Oxford, 1987).
(with R. N. Cooper, W. M. Corden, and S. Rajapatirana) *Boom, Crisis and Adjustment* (New York, 1993).

Macroeconomic Analysis and Developing Countries: 1970–1990 (San Francisco, CA, 1993).

(with V. Joshi) *India: Macroeconomics and Political Economy 1964–1991* (Washington, DC, and Delhi, 1994).

(with V. Joshi) *India's Economic Reforms 1991–2001* (Oxford and Delhi, 1996).

Picking Winners: The East Asian Experience (London, 1996).

Collection and Recollections: Economic Papers and their Provenance (Oxford, 1999).

(edited with I. J. Ahluwalia) *India's Economic Reforms and Development: Essays for Manmohan Singh* (Delhi, 1998, 2nd edn., 2012).

Ethics, Economics and Politics: Principles of Public Policy (Oxford, 2002).

A Critique of Welfare Economics: a Retrospective Reissue (Oxford, 2002).

Going to War and Global Morality (London, 2004).

Little by Little (Privately Printed, 2004).

Contributions to books

'Fiscal policy', in G. D. N. Worswick and P. H. Ady (eds.), *The British Economy 1945–50* (Oxford, 1952).

'Direct versus indirect taxes', in R. A. Musgrave and C. S. Shoup (eds.), *Readings in the Economics of Taxation* (London, 1959).

(with R. R. Neild and C. R. Ross) 'The scope and limitations of monetary policy', in *Principal Memoranda of Evidence Submitted to the Committee on the Workings of the Monetary System*, iii (London, 1960).

'Fiscal policy', in G. D. N. Worswick and P. H. Ady (eds.), *The British Economy in the 1950s* (Oxford, 1962).

'Comment on 'Evaluation of "Social income": capital formation and wealth' by P. Samuelson', in D. C. Hague (ed.), *The Theory of Capital* (London, 1963).

'Tax policy and the Third Plan' and 'The real cost of labour and the choice between consumption and investment', in P. Rosenstein-Rodan (ed.), *Pricing and Fiscal Policies* (London, 1964).

'Executive, co-ordinating, supervisory and evaluation machinery', in R. Robinson (ed.), *Overcoming Obstacles to Development: Impressions and Papers of the Fourth Cambridge Conference on Development Problems* (Cambridge, undated).

'Direct versus indirect taxes', in K. J. Arrow and T. Scitovsky (eds.), *Readings in Welfare Economics* (Homewood, IL, 1969).

'Public sector project selection in relation to Indian development', in A. V. Bhuleshkar (ed.), *Indian Economic Thought and Development* (Bombay, 1969).

'Regional international companies as an approach to economic integration', in P. Robson (ed.), *International Economic Integration* (Harmondsworth, 1971).

(with J. A. Mirrlees) 'Further reflections on the OECD Manual of Project Analysis in Developing Countries', in J. Bhagwati and R. S. Eckaus (eds.), *Development and Planning: Essays in Honour of Paul Rosenstein-Rodan* (London, 1972).

'On measuring the value of private direct overseas investment', in G. Ranis (ed.), *The Gap Between Rich and Poor Nations* (London, 1972).

'Social choice and individual values', in E. S. Phelps (ed.), *Economic Justice* (Baltimore, MD, 1973).

'A critical examination of India's Third Five-Year Plan', in C. D. Wadhva (ed.), *Some Problems of India's Economic Policy* (New Delhi, 1973).

'The economy of poor countries and their population stabilization: an introduction', in H. B. Parry (ed.), *Population and its Problems: a Plain Man's Guide* (Oxford, 1974).

(with K. M. McLeod) 'The new pricing policy of the British Airports Authority', in G. P. Howard (ed.), *Airport Economic Planning* (Cambridge, MA, 1974).

'The use and abuse of capital in developing countries', in Y. Ramati (ed.), *Economic Growth in Developing Countries—Materials and Human Resources: Proceedings of the Seventh Rehovot Conference* (New York, 1975).

'Bretton Woods', 'Development economics', 'Necessary and sufficient conditions', 'Take-off point', 'Underdevelopment', and 'Welfare, welfare economics', in A. Bullock and O. Stallybrass (eds.), *The Fontana Dictionary of Modern Thought* (London, 1977).

'Welfare criteria, distribution and cost–benefit analysis', in M. J. Boskin (ed.), *Economics and Human Welfare: Essays in Honor of Tibor Scitovsky* (New York, 1979).

'An economic reconnaissance', in W. Galenson (ed.), *Economic Growth and Structural Change in Taiwan* (Ithaca, NY, 1979).

'The developing countries and the international order', in R. C. Amacher, G. Harbeler, and T. D. Willett (eds.), *Challenges to a Liberal International Economic Order* (Washington, DC, 1979).

'Distributive justice and the new international order', in P. Oppenheimer (ed.), *Issues in International Economics* (London, 1980).

'Comment on Richard S. Eckaus, "Strategies of development and the international division of work"', in *Conference Internacionale Sobre Economia Portuguesa* (Lisboa, 1980).

'Social democracy and the international economy', in D. Lipsey and D. Leonard (eds.), *The Socialist Agenda: Crosland's Legacy* (London, 1981).

'The experience and causes of rapid labour-intensive development in Korea, Taiwan Province, Hong Kong and Singapore and the possibilities of emulation', in F. Lee (ed.), *Export-led Industrialization and Development* (Geneva, 1981).

'Comment on S. Kuznets's "Driving forces of economic growth: what can we learn from history?"', in G. Giersch (ed.), *Towards an Explanation of Economic Growth: Symposium 1980* (Kiel, 1981).

'Indian industrialization before 1945', in M. Gersovitz *et al.* (eds.), *The Theory and Experience of Economic Development: Essays in Honour of Sir Arthur Lewis* (London, 1982).

'Import controls and exports in developing countries', in R. K. Ghosh (ed.), *International Trade and Third World Development* (Westport, CT, 1984).

'Discussion', in A. P. Thirlwall (ed.), *Keynes and Economic Development* (Macmillan, London, 1987).

'A Comment on Professor Toye's Paper', in L. Emmerij (ed.), *Development Policies and the Crisis of the 1980s* (Paris, 1987).

'Crosland, Anthony', in J. Eatwell, M. Milgate and P. Newman (eds.), *The New Palgrave: a Dictionary of Economics* (Macmillan, 1987).

'Comments on Wolfram Fischer, "Swings between protection and free trade in history"', in H. Giersch (ed.), *Free Trade in the World Economy: Towards an Opening of Markets* (Tubingen, 1987).
'Resource use efficiency and the small scale enterprise', in K. B. Suri (ed.), *Small Scale Enterprises in Industrial Development: the Indian Experience* (New Delhi, 1988).
'Comment on Professor Findlay's Paper', in G. Ranis and T. P. Schultz (eds.), *The State of Development Economics: Progress and Prospects* (Oxford, 1988).
'The macroeconomic effects of foreign aid: issues and evidence—a comment', in C. J. Jepma (ed.), *North-South Co-operation in Retrospect and Prospect* (London, 1988).
(with V. Joshi) 'Indian macroeconomic policies', in G. Calvo, R. Findlay, P. Kouri and J. Braga de Macedo (eds.), *Debt, Stabilization and Development: Essays in Memory of Carlos Diaz-Alejandro* (Oxford, 1989).
'Ethics and international economic relations', in B. Barry and R. E. Goodin (eds.), *Free Movement* (Hemel Hempstead, 1992).
(with V. Joshi) 'Future trade and exchange rate policy for India', in R. Cassen and V. Joshi (eds.), *India: the Future of Economic Reform* (Delhi, 1995).
(with V. Joshi) 'Macroeconomic management in India 1964–94', in V. N. Balasubramanyam and D. Greenaway (eds.), *Trade and Development: Essays in Honour of Jagdish Bhagwati* (London, and New York, 1996).
'Protection and the industrialization of developing countries', in I. M. D. Little, *Collection and Recollections* (Oxford, 1999).

Articles

'A reformulation of the theory of consumer behaviour', *Oxford Economic Papers*, NS 1 (1949), 90–9.
'The valuation of social income', *Economica*, 16 (1949), 11–26.
'The foundations of welfare economics', *Oxford Economic Papers*, NS 1 (1949), 227–46.
'A note on the interpretation of index numbers', *Economica*, 16 (1949), 369–70.
'Welfare and tariffs', *Review of Economic Studies*, 16 (1949), 65–70.
'The economist and the state', *Review of Economic Studies*, 17 (1949–50), 75–6.
'Economic behaviour and welfare', *Mind*, 58 (1949), 195–209.
'The theory of consumer behaviour: a comment', *Oxford Economic Papers*, NS 2 (1950), 132–5.
'Direct versus indirect taxes', *Economic Journal*, 61 (1951), 577–84.
'Electricity tariffs: a comment', *Economic Journal*, 61 (1951), 875–82.
'Social choice and individual values', *Journal of Political Economy*, 60 (1952), 422–32.
'L'Avantage collectif', *Economie Appliquée*, 5 (1952), 455–68.
'Classical growth', *Oxford Economic Papers*, NS 9 (1957), 152–7.
'The economist in Whitehall', *Lloyd's Bank Review*, NS 44 (1957), 29–40.
'Die Rolle des Nationalokonomen in Whitehall', *Konjunkturpolitik* (Berlin, 1957).
'The aims of monetary policy', *Bulletin of the Oxford Institute of Economics and Statistics*, 9 (1957), 29–40.
'The role of the economist in Whitehall', *Administration*, 6 (Summer 1958).
'Atomic Bombay', *Economic Weekly*, Bombay, 10, 29 November 1958.

(with R. Evely) 'Some aspects of the structure of British industry, 1935–1951', *Transactions of the Manchester Statistical Society*, Session 1957–8.

'The strategy of Indian development', *National Institute Economic Review*, 9 (1960), 20–9.

'The Third Five-Year Plan and the strategy of Indian development', *Economic and Political Weekly*, 12 (1960).

'The real cost of labour and the choice between consumption and investment', *Quarterly Journal of Economics*, 75 (1961), 1–15.

'A critical examination of India's Third Five-Year Plan', *Oxford Economic Papers*, NS 14 (1962), 1–24.

'Welfare criteria: an exchange of notes', *Economic Journal*, 72 (1962), 229–31 and 233–4.

'Higgledy piggledy growth', *Bulletin of the Oxford Institute of Economics and Statistics*, 24 (1962), 387–412.

'Two comments', *Economic Journal*, 73 (1963), 778–9.

'Welfare economics, ethics and essentialism: a comment', *Economica*, 32 (1965), 223–5.

'Regional international companies as an approach to economic integration', *Journal of Common Market Studies*, 5 (1966), 181–6.

'Direkte Gegen Indirekte Steurn', *Finanztheorie* (Cologne, 1969).

'Symposium on project appraisal in lesser developed countries', *Journal of Agricultural Economics*, 22 (1971).

'Trade and public finance', *Indian Economic Review*, NS 6 (1971), 119–32.

(with K. M. McLeod) 'The new pricing policy of the British Airports Authority', *Journal of Transport Economics and Policy*, 6 (1972), 101–15.

(with J. Mirrlees) 'A reply to some criticisms of the OECD Manual', *Bulletin of the Oxford Institute of Economics and Statistics*, 34 (1972), 153–68.

(with Robert Mabro) 'Coping with Arab billions', *Financial Times*, 22 December 1973.

'Economic relations with the third world: old myths and new prospects', *Scottish Journal of Political Economy*, 22 (1975), 223–35.

'Perspectives for the second half of the Second UN Development Decade', *Journal of Development Planning*, 9 (1976).

'Import controls and exports in developing countries', *Finance and Development*, 15 (September 1978), 20–2.

'Robert Cooter and Peter Rappaport's "Were the ordinalists wrong about welfare economics?"; a comment', *Journal of Economic Literature*, 23 (1985), 1186–8.

'Small manufacturing enterprises in developing countries', *World Bank Economic Review*, 1 (1987), 203–35.

(with V. Joshi), 'Indian macroeconomic policies', *Economic and Political Weekly*, 22 (28 February 1987), 371–8.

'Small manufacturing enterprises and employment in developing countries', *Asian Development Review*, 6 (1988).

(with V. Joshi) 'Les politiques macro-economiques Indiennes', *Revue Tiers Monde*, 30 (1989), 797–821.

(with J. Mirrlees) 'Project appraisal and planning twenty years on', *Proceedings of the World Bank Annual Conference on Development Economics* (1991).

'Trade and industrialization revisited', *Pakistan Development Review*, 33 (1994), 359–89.

'India's economic reforms 1991–96', *Journal of Asian Economics*, 7 (1996), 161–77.

'Comment on "Review-debt adjustment and recovery"', *World Economy*, 19 (1996), 595–8.

Reviews

A la recherche d'une discipline economique by M. Allais, *Economic Journal*, 60 (1950), 558–60.

Income and Wealth, series I, ed. F. Lundberg, *Journal of Political Economy*, 60 (1952), 172–3.

Welfare and Competition by T. Scitovsky, *Econometrica*, 20 (1952), 703–4.

Welfare Economics and the Theory of the State by W. J. Baumol, *Economica*, 20 (1953), 78–80.

Principles of Private and Public Planning by W. Keilhau, *Economic Journal*, 63 (1953), 133–5.

The History of Economic Analysis by J. A. Schumpeter, *Economic History Review*, 8 (1955), 91–8.

An Expenditure Tax by N. Kaldor, *Economic Journal*, 66 (1956), 116–20.

The Role of the Economist as Official Adviser by W. A. Johr and H. W. Singer, *Economic Journal*, 66 (1956), 34–136.

Theoretical Welfare Economics by J. de V. Graaff, *Economica*, 24 (1957), 262–4.

Some Economic Aspects of the Bhakra Nangal Project by K. N. Raj, *Economic Journal*, 71 (1961), 413–15.

Indian Economic Policy and Development by P. T. Bauer, *Economic Journal*, 71 (1961), 835–8.

Equilibrium and Growth in the World Economy by R. Nurkse, *Economic Journal*, 72 (1962), 688–9.

The Development of the Indian Economy by W. B. Reddaway, *Economic Journal*, 72 (1962), 722–3.

The Management of the British Economy by J. C. R. Dow, *Economic Journal*, 74 (1964), 983–5.

Project Selection for National Plans by A. Papandreou and U. Zohar, *Journal of Economic Literature*, 12 (1974), 1336–7.

Economic Growth and Social Equity in Developing Countries by J. Adelman and C. T. Morris; and *Redistribution with Growth* by H. Chenery *et al.*, *Journal of Development Economics*, 3 (1976), 99–116.

Pioneers in Development, ed. G. M. Meier and D. Seers; and *The Hobbled Giant: Essays on the World Bank* by S. Please, *Finance and Development*, 22 (1985), 47–8.

The Role of the State in Economic Change, ed. H.-J. Chang and R. Rowthorn, *Journal of Development Economics*, 53 (1997), 471–4.

ALAN MILWARD

Alan Steele Milward
1935–2010

ALAN MILWARD was a profoundly original British historian who was elected by the Modern History Section to the Fellowship of the British Academy in 1987. Although he is commonly regarded as an economic historian, he worked across many fields including economic theory and policy, economic and political history, and contemporary economic and political studies; he was indeed a modern political economist of a very rigorous kind. He published between 1964 and 2007 in three major fields of European history. These were: first, the operations of Fascist and war economies; secondly, the economic development of European economies from the mid-nineteenth century; and, thirdly, the political and economic construction of the European Union. Alan's work was based on detailed primary research—he knew and used a very wide range of available archives, and his work had deep empirical foundations. This was supported by linguistic skills (he spoke French, German, Italian and Norwegian) which gave him access to archives across Europe, so the geographic scope of his work was unusually wide.

On the basis of this original-source research, his work frequently challenged conventional wisdom (often in rather brusque terms), and introduced fundamentally new perspectives. For example, his analyses of European development suggested that these economies were highly diverse in structure, and shaped by very diverse national decision-making. This approach undercut general economic narratives of both left and right. The European array of nation states was also highly vulnerable to the Fascist challenge: in fact few survived the onslaught. In the aftermath of the Second World War, he argued that the much-vaunted Marshall

Biographical Memoirs of Fellows of the British Academy, XIII, 353–362. © The British Academy 2014.

Plan was of relatively small significance in European reconstruction; this generated a continuing controversy. Then came perhaps his most powerful 'contrarian' argument: he showed that policy-makers negotiated the creation of the European Communities not as a path to unification but as a framework for realising national economic interests. Rejecting both past and present myths about the EU he argued that, far from being a federal project to transcend the nation state, it was (and is) a complex instrument aimed at maintaining the viability of nation states in Europe. Of course he recognised the profound long-term implications of integration. But his approach calls into question the 'founding myths' of European unity associated with the names of Jean Monnet and Robert Schuman, while convincingly demolishing one of the long-standing clichés of anti-EU rhetoric in the UK, namely that the EU is a unifying federal project.

Although Alan had a serious and subtle understanding of economic theory, particularly with respect to international trade and payments, he did not, as some economic historians do, work by applying theory to empirical data. Rather, he attempted to let empirical research inform conceptual understanding, and this led to innovations in his work. One key innovation was an insistence on the importance of diversity among economies, and hence an understanding of European development resting on heterogeneity rather than a uniform adaptation to the spread of capitalism and markets. A second innovation was that he rejected the distinction between states and markets that is frequently found in economics, in favour of an approach that saw states, and hence policy decision-makers, as central to establishing and operating market systems; this was a powerful and continuing theme in his work. He was capable of drawing together insights from his three major areas of work into original perspectives that are acutely relevant to a historical understanding of modern Europe (examples of this will be offered below).

Alan was born on 19 January 1935 and raised in Longton, in Stoke-on-Trent, an only child. His family's circumstances were rather poor, but his parents were articulate and intelligent people, and he remained close to them. At the beginning of the Second World War his father joined the armed services, but was subsequently moved back into civilian life as a post-office clerk; he later became a postmaster in Lichfield. He clearly had important influences on his son, not least that he was a keen cricket player, in which Alan followed him. Alan played cricket at his grammar school, enjoyed cross-country running, read rather widely and listened to classical music (but not opera, for which he had an abiding dislike mainly on class grounds). In due course, he developed a well-informed appreciation of literature, the theatre, painting and architecture, became keen on bird watching as an escape from academia, and deeply enjoyed wild country in places as far apart as Tanzania (where he went camping), Spitsbergen, the Scottish Highlands and north Norfolk (where much later in life he bought a cottage). At that time too, in his small garden in London, he made an unexpected collection of fruit trees and delicate Mediterranean plants. He also made a notable collection of nineteenth-century German postage stamps. After he left school, Alan took with him a continuing dislike of Stoke-on-Trent. Although not estranged, he remained distant from most of his relatives in and around Stoke, while he continued to be close to his parents and to one school friend, Alan Pedley. He followed the fortunes of the town's two football teams, Stoke City and Port Vale, for the rest of his life and retained his early interest in the novels of Arnold Bennett. His love of cricket also stayed with him all his life, and included playing for the university teams in Manchester, the London School of Economics (LSE), and for some years in a team in the little-known cricket league of Italy.

Alan went to University College London (UCL) with a scholarship, and was happy there as an undergraduate (1953–6), taking a First in Medieval and Modern History. Although Alan did not play an active role in party politics, his best friend from his university days at UCL, the economist Russell Butler, stood for Labour against Edward Heath in the 1966 general election, halving the Conservative majority. When Margaret Thatcher came to power, Alan joined the Labour Party.

Alan's trips abroad began early. In 1955, when he was twenty, he went on an adventurous bicycle trip in Finland using a university travel grant. He cycled into the north of Norway, forming an attachment to that country which never disappeared, and he began to learn the language. This had an impact on his cultural life: he enjoyed theatre, especially Ibsen, and very much liked the work of Edvard Munch.

Alan started his graduate studies at the LSE in 1956, yet had some problems finding a supervisor for his proposed Ph.D., on the armaments industry in the German economy during the Second World War. Contemporary history was regarded as a contradiction in terms, but he found a productive working relationship with Professor William Medlicott (a diplomatic historian), and submitted his Ph.D. in Economic History in 1960. After a short-lived junior position teaching Indian Archaeology at the School of Oriental and African Studies, he became assistant lecturer and then lecturer in Economic History at Edinburgh in 1960. This was a formative period in both his intellectual and personal life, when he made warm and lifelong friendships with his colleagues Michael Flinn and Christopher Smout, and began to work closely with Berrick Saul on the trajectory of European economic development. In Edinburgh he also met his first wife Claudine Lemaître from whom he gained his fluency in French.

From 1965 he became lecturer and then senior lecturer at the University of East Anglia's School of Social Studies. In 1969 he was invited to the USA as an associate professor of Economics at Stanford but returned to Britain three years later, becoming Professor of European Studies at the University of Manchester Institute of Science and Technology, in the Department of European Studies which he created. Alan was responsible for appointing to that department the young political scientist, Helen Wallace, and the economic historian, Richard Griffiths. He was also close to Ian Kershaw and John Breuilly in the History Department at Manchester at the time. It was also in Manchester that Alan met Frances Lynch, who was later to become his second wife.

He spent two periods, from 1983 to 1986 and then from 1996 to 2003, as professor of the History of European Integration at the European University Institute (EUI) in Florence where he developed major research programmes. In between the two periods in Florence, from 1986 to 1996, he was Professor of Economic History at the LSE.

In 1993 he was appointed official historian at the Cabinet Office, with the task of writing the history of Britain's decision-making and negotiations with the European Communities and later the EU. This resulted in the first volume of the Official History, *The UK and the European Community: the Rise and Fall of a National Strategy, 1945–1963* (2002), which offered a comprehensive historical perspective on British postwar policy thinking about the UK's place in the emerging world economy. The second volume was written by Sir Stephen Wall, who is also writing the third volume.

Alan published extensively and creatively: nine books as sole author, two major volumes with S. B. Saul on European economic development, two co-authored books and three edited volumes, plus twenty-one journal articles, sixty book chapters, and more than two hundred book reviews across all of his areas of interest.[1]

His first theme was the organisation of war economies, looking at war organisation and its impact in the UK, and at the economic impact of

---

[1] A full list of his publications is available in F. Guirao, F. Lynch and S. M. R. Perez (eds.), *Alan S. Milward and a Century of European Change* (London, 2012). A collection of all Milward's book reviews will be published by Routledge in 2015, edited by F. Guirao and F. Lynch.

Nazism both in Germany and in two important occupied economies. This work resulted in *The German Economy at War* (London, 1965), *The New Order and the French Economy* (London, 1970), *The Economic Effects of the Two World Wars on Britain* (London, 1970), and *The Fascist Economy in Norway* (Oxford, 1972). These were followed by an important work of synthesis, *War, Economy and Society 1939–1945* (Harmondsworth, 1977). With his usual realism he insisted that war was not at all an exceptional condition, that it was not becoming more costly over time, and that economic planning for war was a normal element of economic policy in peacetime. His general argument was that it is impossible to separate strategic concepts from the underlying economic organisation that supported them. So he maintained, for example, that the strategy of *blitzkrieg* was consonant with an economy that could produce high-quality but rather standardised weapons in quantities that could over-whelm opponents in short, intense conflict. But this kind of economic organisation, which was chronically short of raw materials and oil and with relatively high levels of civilian consumption (higher than in Britain), was deeply unsuited for the protracted war that emerged after the failure of the initial attack on the USSR, and after the declaration of war on the USA. This interpretation of the Nazi war economy, which was contested initially by Richard Overy, continues to be debated by younger historians in the field. At the same time, Alan took the political dimensions of the war very seriously, showing that many aspects of Axis strategy depended on underlying Fascist views about the inseparability of society and war, and in particular the idea that war was essential to German and Italian renewal and to overcoming the false gods of liberalism and democracy: '... the basis of existence in Hitler's view was a struggle of the strong for mastery and war was thus an inescapable, necessary aspect of the human condition'.[2] This ideology and its racialist associations did not conflict with purely economic calculation. The Fascist economies could not use trading networks or colonial resources, and were at their core autarkic. However, it was autarky combined with aggression, and so the attacks on Norway, the Ukraine, and the attempt to seize the Caucasus, for instance, were driven by purely economic objectives linked to critical resources. Despite serious conflicts within the German state, in managing the conquests Fascist ideas merged with long-standing German economic ideologies about the viability of 'large economic spaces' to create an autonomous zone subservient to the New Order. Alan saw this as a serious

---

[2] Alan S. Milward, *War, Economy and Society 1939–45* (Harmondsworth, 1977), p. 6.

'inward-looking' strategic alternative to the global trading strategies of the UK and the USA.

His work on the economic development of Europe was carried out in collaboration with S. B. Saul, and resulted in major works: *The Economic Development of Continental Europe 1780–1870* (London, 1973) and *The Development of the Economies of Continental Europe 1850–1914* (London, 1977). Each of these is a most important book, of wide scope. The first is organised in part thematically, with studies of agricultural organisation, land management, demographics (including migration), and technological change, and in part geographically, with detailed discussion of these processes in France, Germany, Belgium, Switzerland and Scandinavia. The thematic part of this work covers the Netherlands, Poland, Russia, and Romania. The second volume, covering the consolidation and acceleration of industrialisation that occurred after the mid-nineteenth century, is more geographical, covering Germany, France, the Low Countries, Spain, Italy, Austria-Hungary, Russia, and South-Eastern Europe. Central to Milward and Saul's approach is the issue of diversity:

> It is indeed the basic tenet of our work that processes of development vary more widely in accordance with national historical backgrounds than with anything else. Countries with different structures, in different geographical circumstances, with different timing of change, were bound to have different patterns of development. It is for this reason above all that we have paid scant regard to the thesis of the so-called globalité, or unity, of European development. The fact that natural resources such as coal fields and forests spanned political frontiers gave an international dimension to the growth experience, but the differences were far more important than the similarities. Indeed, it might well be argued that eighteenth-century society was more pan-European than it was in the nineteenth.[3]

The emphasis on diversity and heterogeneity in Europe contrasts with frequent assumptions among economic historians that economic development consists of countries pursuing essentially similar paths of institutional change, investment and industry creation. This idea of capitalism unfolding in an essentially similar dynamic everywhere really goes back to Marx ('the more developed country only shows to the less developed its own future') but it can also be found in many anti-Marxist writers such as Walt Rostow, and in many institutional historians. Milward and Saul rejected this, on the basis of an approach to development that was far

[3] Alan S. Milward and S. B. Saul, *The Economic Development of Continental Europe 1780–1870* (London, 1973), pp. 36–7.

more than merely economic. Their argument was that across European regions and countries, economic development required promotion and support by ruling elites and direct intervention by states. However, elites and states faced widely different political contexts as they sought to support economic change, and this gave rise to very different patterns of investment and forms of economic and political organisation. The result was divergent paths to development, not unity; at its worst, the outcome was a form of fragmentation that made European countries fragile in the face of the determined assault that came from Fascism in the twentieth century.

These themes of difference persist in Milward's powerful analyses of the history of the European Union. His analysis is complex but there are two major themes: first, the factors shaping the creation of the European Communities and the deepening of economic integration within it; and, secondly, British decision-making on Europe and the UK's role in the global economy. There are two broad pieces of theory about the growth of the EU. One is the economics of customs unions, which suggest that when countries remove tariffs between themselves then there is an incentive for neighbouring countries to join, and for the union to grow bigger thereby. The other is from political science, suggesting that common policy functions lead to integration, as a method of simplifying policy systems across countries. Beyond this there is what Alan considered a lazy cliché, though it is still widely held in some British political circles: that the EU was the result of an aggrandising federal strategy promoted by such figures as Schuman and Monnet, and reflecting a Franco-German accord aimed at domination by erasing national states. Alan pointed out that all these rather abstract approaches failed to account for the dynamics of the EU, and instead he conducted a detailed examination of the strategies and negotiations that had led to expansion. The causal factors changed over time, but his overarching argument was that the negotiators who created the European Communities (first around coal and steel, then Euratom, then the economic community) had specifically national economic and political objectives in mind. On the one hand they sought to rebuild allegiance to nation states, and to establish their economic viability in a world of increasing trade and interdependence. On the other hand, they sought to solve the great political challenge of the post-war settlement, namely the role of Germany in European politics, as the transition was made from occupied zones to West Germany as a national state. He argued trenchantly that no concessions of sovereignty were ever made in the European Communities unless they committed Germany more fully to the European structure. What emerged out of this was a framework for ensuring the viability and compatibility of nation states in a Europe that had long been riven by economic fragmentation and war. The 'Eurosceptic' nightmare of an encroaching federal project was in Alan's view a serious misrepresentation of the record.

But if Alan Milward was uncomfortable reading for Eurosceptics he was no easier for Europhiles. In *The UK and the European Community: the Rise and Fall of a National Strategy, 1945–1963* (London, 2002), he took on the idea (also still common) that the UK had made a major mistake in not linking firmly to the European Community initiatives of the 1950s, from the Schuman plan onwards. Milward was initially sympathetic to this criticism, but his views evolved. In a major effort to identify and think through the context of UK decision-making he came to feel that, taken together, the combination of the Commonwealth, sterling as a reserve currency, global trading links, nuclear and other military assets, and the alliance with the USA, were at the very least a reasonable foundation for the decision to remain outside the emerging EC initiatives. The British policy then was in effect that the creation of wider free trade areas, particularly with the United States, was preferable to the creation of a large internal market in Europe. But if this was justifiable (he argued that the independent British strategy was 'neither vain nor ill-conceived') in the post-war period it soon enough became clear that many of these UK advantages were insubstantial. It was then that British policy changed. But it changed on the basis of a calculation of national interests, just as it had done among the European Community partners themselves.

Alan Milward was, as Charles S. Maier described him, 'an inspired contrarian'. He could be a difficult man—he did not suffer fools gladly and was intolerant of 'wooden tops' who accepted the clichés of the day. Alan fought his corner strongly and tenaciously. He worked incessantly, wrote book reviews on holiday, and switched off only on the most remote beaches. He supervised twenty-seven doctoral theses during the period 1981–2006—and earned the affectionate nickname 'Milvy' with EUI students.

Alan was a member of several journal editorial boards including *Journal of Common Market Studies, Journal of European Integration History, Explorations in Economic History, The International History Review*, and later of *Contemporary European History* and *Zeitschrift für Staats- und Europawissenschaften*: he was a founding member of the *Review of European Economic History* and for six years he was adviser to Macmillan for their series 'Themes in Comparative History'. He was

President for five years of the University Association of Contemporary European Studies (UACES), having been its Publications Secretary and in that capacity responsible for the series 'Studies in the European Community'. He was a member of the Scientific Board of the Institut d'Études Européennes, University of Louvain-la-Neuve and the British representative since its creation on the Groupe de Liaison des Professeurs d'Histoire Comtemporaine auprès de la Communauté Européenne, along with Professor D. C. Watt of the LSE.

Alan taught for many years at the College of Europe in Bruges. Much sought after, he also held visiting posts in Paris, Siegen, Illinois, Bruges, Oslo, Trondheim, Århus, and Vienna. He served in the Economic History as well as the Modern History Section of the British Academy and joined the Academy's Overseas Policy Committee (1989–94), he was elected Fellow of the Norwegian Society of Sciences and Letters in 1994, and won a distinguished Italian history prize in Florence. He was also given an award for life-long achievement from UACES.

Alan was immensely creative in following through the implications of what he found in the archives that he explored so thoroughly, and he inspired a devoted following of younger scholars who have carried his originality and insights forward. One result of this is a major book on his life's work, *Alan S. Milward and a Century of European Change* (London, 2011), edited by Fernando Guirao, Frances Lynch and Sigfrido M. Ramirez Perez, with contributions from many colleagues and students. Alan was willing to think, without illusions, about the implications of his historical work, also for modern life in Europe. One example of this was his prescient views on the Euro, which he argued was the result of acts of political choice rather than adaptation to a globalising world, and would result in chaotic adaptation processes that would benefit only the wealthy economies. Alan argued in 1998 that the stabilisation conditions for the Euro would make it impossible to achieve acceptable levels of employment and growth.[4]

Likewise, his reflections on the origins and course of Nazism may be very relevant to our current situation. His thoughts here are worth quoting at length:

> Speculation about the German character or the supposed peculiarities of German political thought and tradition is escapism. It is to us and our societies that the lesson of history points. And if we are to arm ourselves with moral outrage it should be directed against the first steps of all those who turn the

[4] Alan Milward, 'Bad news for the downtrodden', *Times Literary Supplement*, 4982, 25 Sept. 1998, pp. 4–5.

power of government and the law from its true purpose of protecting all citizens to the purpose of protecting the government: domestic spies of all kinds, unknown and unknowable security services subject to no control but that of their masters, ministers and judges contemptuous of the people they govern. It may be noted that the law of Britain, as approved by the present Attorney-General, would appear to forbid under severe penalty any British civil servant from doing what we are asked to criticise Nazi civil servants for not doing. This does not mean that anti-Semitism is irrelevant to the story . . . Anti-Semitism was one factor, among many, that helped the Nazi movement into political prominence. It helped the Nazi Party and Hitler, once in power together, to fix in the mind of much of the population that there was something called 'the Jewish question'. And every question needs an answer. The Nazi movement itself had several and could not agree on them. After summer 1941 Hitler had only one, most dreadful of all, the one which, in Himmler's words, was 'never to be written', and it was Hitler who made sure that it was this one which was chosen. The machinery with which he put it into practice did not especially depend on the many peculiarities of the Nazi movement or the Nazi state. It could exist—it does exist—in several developed, civilised countries and will probably come to exist in many more in the future.[5]

The kind of thinking that Alan exemplified will continue to be necessary. We have been left with uniquely important scholarly work, which was brought to an end far too soon. Alan was deeply humane, passionate and he was a loyal friend. He was also good company. He was a proud parent, a loving husband to Frances Lynch, and he had a large network of international friendships. In so many ways generous, he is much missed and will continue to be so. He died on 28 September 2010.

KRISTINE BRULAND
University of Oslo

Note.   I wish to acknowledge my deep debt to Frances Lynch, who gave me a lot of her time and deeper insights into Alan's life. I was kindly provided with important contributions also from Christopher Smout. I thank them both.

[5] Alan Milward, 'It can happen here', *London Review of Books*, 7 (No 8, 2 May 1985), 3–6.

ROBIN NISBET

Robin George Murdoch Nisbet
1925–2013

ROBIN NISBET (known professionally as R. G. M. Nisbet), who was born in Glasgow on 21 May 1925, was one of the most distinguished and influential Latin scholars of his time. He studied at the University of Glasgow before going to Balliol College, Oxford, in 1947, for a second BA. On graduation in 1951, he moved at once as a Junior Research Fellow to Corpus Christi College (CCC), Oxford, where he became a Tutorial Fellow in 1952, and then moved across to the Corpus Christi Chair of Latin in 1970. He retired in 1992 and was (unusually) elected to an Honorary Fellowship at Corpus; other distinctions included an Honorary Fellowship at Balliol (1989), a Fellowship of the British Academy (1967) and its Kenyon Medal (1997).

Nisbet himself composed an autobiographical memoir, a paper delivered to the Oxford Philological Society at Corpus on 20 May 2005, the day before his eightieth birthday, entitled 'A Retrospect' (cited hereafter as *AR*). Its terse and witty texture, elegantly written with significant and often ironic asides on various issues, gives a good impression of its author's style of public discourse.[1] Its account of his family background is worth quotation:

> I had the good fortune to be born into a classical family, where in 1936 the death of Housman was mentioned at the breakfast-table, the first time I heard the name. My father, Robert Nisbet,[2] was a lecturer in Glasgow University in the

---

[1] The full text of the unpublished paper can be found in the Nisbet papers, Archives, Corpus Christi College, Oxford. All footnotes to Nisbet's text are mine.
[2] R. G. Nisbet (1872–1955); for his career (MA, Glasgow 1898; Exhibitioner and MA, Christ Church, Oxford, some time in London and Germany, lecturer at Glasgow from 1903) see J. Henderson, *'Oxford Reds': Classic Commentaries on Latin Classics* (London, 2006), pp. 114–15, and the brief anonymous obituary in *The Glasgow Herald*, 10 March 1955, p. 9, which stresses his modesty and interest in teaching and his membership of the University's Senate.

Department of Humanity, as Latin was still called in the Scottish universities; his commentary on Cicero's *De Domo*, published in 1939, is sometimes attributed to me in the bibliographies, though I was only fourteen at the time.[3] His own father had been a village schoolmaster in Lanarkshire, and the respect for education in rural Scotland should not be underestimated. If you go back a couple of centuries, John Nisbet of Hardhill was a militant Covenanter, for which he was hanged in 1685; this is the world depicted in Scott's *Old Mortality*, where he shows his Shakespearian gift for understanding people he didn't agree with. If you go back to the sixteenth century, Murdoch Nisbet, from whom I derive my third initial, was a Lollard who translated the New Testament into Lowland Scots, and hid from his persecutors in a secret vault under his house. You may wonder whether this learned man translated the New Testament from the Greek Vulgate, so I must confess that he translated it from English.

My mother, Agnes Husband, had read Latin and French with great distinction at Glasgow University;[4] as the teaching of Greek declines in schools, Oxford ought to remember that Latin can combine well with a Romance language. My mother was not learned in Latin syntax the way my father was, but she had an instinctive feeling for literature and an eye for what was interesting. There was said to have been a notable ancestor in her mother's family, who may have been responsible for larger ambitions if not a genetic inheritance. In the late eighteenth century George Broun, Lord Coalston, was a prominent judge in Edinburgh, whose daughter Christian married Lord Dalhousie, and is described in Scott's *Journal* as an intelligent, amiable and lively woman. I am supposed to be descended from another daughter, Euphemia Broun, who ran away with the factotum of a neighbouring landowner, and as a consequence was cut off with a silver spoon. I cannot vouch for the truth of the tale, but my sister[5] still has Euphemia's spoon. (*AR*, p. 1)

Nisbet had a highly successful career both at school (the independent day-school Glasgow Academy), where he records an awakening interest in Cicero and his prose-rhythm, and first learning about Catullus on wartime fire-watch (*AR*, p. 2); both were authors who would feature in his future work. At Glasgow University he came first in Humanity [Latin] and Greek (Honours) and Modern History (ordinary) in finals (1947), and won the most prestigious classical awards.[6] In mid-course he spent two years of war service working as a clerk in a Glasgow machine-tool factory (1943–5), having been rejected for the army on account of his poor eyesight. At Glasgow, apart from his father, who retired in 1942, his main influence

---

[3] R. G. Nisbet, *Cicero: De Domo* (Oxford, 1939); the confusion easily arose from Nisbet *fils'* similar initials and similar commentary on a Cicero speech for the same publisher twenty years later (see below, n. 18).

[4] First Class Joint Honours, 1917.

[5] Robin's twin sister Nanette, his only sibling, who became a consultant geriatrician and now lives in retirement at Pittenween in Fife.

[6] The Jeffrey Medal, the Ramsay Memorial Medal and the Cowan Medal.

was C. J. Fordyce, whom he regarded in later life as an excellent technical Latinist but as a formidable and forbidding character.[7] In 1947 he won the prestigious Snell Exhibition to Balliol College, Oxford, the previous holders of which include Adam Smith (1740) as well as Fordyce himself (1920) and W. S. Watt (1933), soon to be Nisbet's Balliol tutor.[8] This he regarded as the key point in his life (*AR*, p. 2). At Balliol, in the *de facto* absence of graduate degrees at that time,[9] he read for a second undergraduate degree in Classics.

This placed him in a golden cohort. The 1947 generation of classical undergraduates at Balliol was especially distinguished, and included the philosophers John Lucas, a future neighbour at Merton and always a good friend, and the future Sir Bernard Williams, a colleague at Corpus in the 1990s,[10] as well as Dick (Baron) Taverne QC, later a Labour cabinet minister. In a higher year and just finishing his classical degree there was Donald Russell, who became Nisbet's closest friend and Oxford colleague, to whom he was introduced by his Latin tutor W. S. Watt, who had been a student of Nisbet's father at Glasgow.[11] At Balliol Bill Watt, with whom he kept up and whose obituary he later wrote,[12] was a key influence on Nisbet, stimulating his interest in textual criticism; he was also taught Greek by the future Sir Kenneth Dover, later to be his President at Corpus (1975–86),[13] philosophy (which he found over-theoretical) by R. M. Hare, who also became a Corpus colleague as White's Professor of Moral Philosophy (1966–83), and ancient history, which he much liked as a subject, by the legendary Russell Meiggs.[14] All four of his tutors became

[7] Personal conversations with the author. The gentler Roland (R. G.) Austin (1901–74), who had been his father's close colleague in Glasgow 1923–37 and later became Professor of Latin in Cardiff (1937–55) and Liverpool (1955–68), was also a family friend and an influence (personal conversations); he too produced an influential Oxford commentary on a speech of Cicero (*Cicero: Pro Caelio*, Oxford, 1933; new edns. 1952, 1960) which may have been a model for the *In Pisonem*.
[8] For a full list see <http://archives.balliol.ox.ac.uk/History/snell.asp> [accessed 23 Dec. 2013].
[9] See his own account in R. G. M. Nisbet and D. A. Russell, 'The study of classical literature at Oxford, 1936–1988', in C. A. Stray (ed.), *Oxford Classics; Teaching and Learning 1800–2000* (London, 2007), pp. 219–38.
[10] As White's Professor of Moral Philosophy (1990–6); for his career see S. Blackburn, 'Bernard Arthur Owen Williams, 1929–2003', *Proceedings of the British Academy*, 150, *Biographical Memoirs of Fellows*, VI (2008), 335–48.
[11] Confirmed by Donald Russell (personal information).
[12] R. G. M. Nisbet, 'William Smith Watt, 1902–1989', *Proceedings of the British Academy*, 124, *Biographical Memoirs of Fellows*, III (2004), 355–72.
[13] Dover comments on this generation of Balliol undergraduates in his autobiography *Marginal Comment* (London, 1994), p. 68, that 'there was not much I could explain to them which they did not already understand'.
[14] For their careers see Kenneth Dover, 'Russell Meiggs, 1902–1989', *Proceedings of the British Academy*, 80 (1991), 361–70; A. W. Price, 'Richard Mervyn Hare, 1919–2002', *Proceedings of the*

Fellows of the British Academy. He attended E. R. Dodds's class on translation, in which students offered their own versions of Greek poetry (*AR*,
p. 2) , and of course Eduard Fraenkel's seminars on literary texts, which
left a lasting impression: he was in no doubt of the value of the German-
style seminar, which Fraenkel was the first to introduce in Oxford, but
deprecated the great man's perceived need for dominance: '. . . he came
with his mind firmly made up on every problem, and didn't encourage the
suggestion of alternatives. It was even more dangerous to produce a
crumb of information that he himself didn't possess' (*AR*, p. 3).[15] Nisbet
duly got Firsts in both parts of the classics course (Mods and Greats) and
won all the major classical prizes.[16]

He was elected a Junior Research Fellow at Corpus in 1951, apparently owing to the influence of Fraenkel, who in the manner of the time
simply informed him that the offer was available without any prior application or interview; he was later dined at Corpus and duly elected (*AR*, p.
3). Fraenkel wanted him to work on the fragmentary early Roman historians (*AR*, p. 3), but Nisbet, characteristically independent, chose to follow
his father in working on Cicero and after a term of looking for a subject[17]
spent most of the 1950s on his commentary on Cicero's *In Pisonem*, a
masterpiece of Roman invective oratory against a political enemy, which
was published in 1961.[18] Though Fraenkel helped him in various ways
with the project, and they would meet weekly for scholarly talk, Nisbet
learnt after an early experience that it was best not to show him work in
progress, since he would suggest that it needed laying aside for a couple of
years (*AR*, pp. 3–4).[19] On the *In Pisonem* Nisbet made significant contributions to both text and interpretation, making effective use of Campana's

---

British Academy, 124, *Biographical Memoirs of Fellows*, III (2004), 117–37; D. A. Russell and
F. S. Halliwell, 'Kenneth James Dover, 1920–2010', *Biographical Memoirs of Fellows of the
British Academy*, XI (2012), 153–75.
[15] For a more detailed and nuanced account of Fraenkel's seminars cf. Stephanie West, 'Eduard
Fraenkel recalled', in Stray, *Oxford Classics*, pp. 203–18.
[16] Chancellor's Latin Prose Prize 1948, Craven Scholarship 1948, Hertford Prize 1949, Dean
Ireland's Scholarship 1949.
[17] His fixing on the topic is noted in a letter of his to President Hardie of Corpus of 30 Dec. 1951
(Nisbet papers, Archives, Corpus Christi College, Oxford; in those days one could be elected to a
research fellowship without a clear plan of research), and the preface to the book is dated
September 1960.
[18] R. G. M. Nisbet, *Cicero: In Pisonem* (Oxford, 1961). It was extensively and positively reviewed;
for a free-wheeling modern account see Henderson, *'Oxford Reds'*, pp. 128–51.
[19] Fraenkel had made the same suggestion to C. J. Fordyce about a sample of a potential
commentary on Seneca's *Controversiae* in the 1930s (Fraenkel papers, Archives, Corpus Christi
College, Oxford); the commentary never emerged.

recent rediscovery of Poggio's copy of the speech, the important readings of which had before then to be reconstructed from later evidence; his penchant for textual emendation shows only a little here, perhaps thinking of Fraenkel's future critical scrutiny, with just two tentative suggestions in the *apparatus criticus*,[20] along with suggestions by his tutor Bill Watt and friend Gordon Williams.[21] This commentary's introduction contains what is still the best miniature guide to the principles of Ciceronian metrical prose-rhythm,[22] which was always a topic of key interest to him, and which he there and elsewhere stressed as a useful criterion for deciding between textual variants.[23]

Alongside these technical achievements, the commentary is keen to stress that this is a work of literature, something similarly evident in an essay of 1965 which drew attention to Cicero's supreme artistry in his speeches while making some characteristically robust and lapidary observations about his sincerity and ethics:

> Cicero was the greatest prose stylist who has ever lived, with the single exception of Plato. He had supreme intellectual gifts, especially for a public man . . . yet most of his speeches fail to satisfy. Though both eloquent and serious, he was seldom both at once. He championed unworthy causes for short-term results in front of audiences that he despised. He turned on spurious emotion so often that it is difficult to know when he is being sincere. He used his outstanding talents to frustrate rather than to promote action. Except at the beginning and end of his career, the moral authority of a Demosthenes or a Lincoln or a Churchill eluded him.[24]

In the first half of the 1960s he also published similarly lively and important essays on Horace's *Odes* and Persius's *Satires* which showed that classical texts deserved close stylistic and thematic scrutiny as well as traditional textual criticism and biographical or historical analysis;[25] this

---

[20] Both plausible (a rearrangement of the word-order at 32, and *confero* for *conferam* at 38).
[21] Suggestions by Williams at 17 (adding a word), 43 (deleting three words) and 47 (adding a word), and Watt at fr.ix (*subdolo* for *subito*), 47 (adding a word), and 94 (rewriting a crux).
[22] I still copy pp. xvii–xviii for my students half a century on.
[23] See *In Pisonem*, pp. xix–xx, and R. G. M. Nisbet, 'Cola and clausulae in Cicero's speeches', in E. M. Craik (ed.), *Owls to Athens: Essays on Classical Subjects Presented to Sir Kenneth Dover* (Oxford, 1990), pp. 349–49; R. G. M. Nisbet, 'Cola and Clausulae in Apuleius, *Metamorphoses* 1.1', in A. Kahane and A. Laird (eds.), *A Companion to the Prologue of Apuleius' Metamorphoses* (Oxford, 2001), pp. 16–26.
[24] R. G. M. Nisbet, 'The speeches', in T. A. Dorey (ed.), *Cicero* (London, 1965), pp. 47–79 at 77–8.
[25] R. G. M. Nisbet, '*Romanae fidicen lyrae*: the odes of Horace', in J. P. Sullivan (ed.), *Critical Essays in Roman Literature: Elegy and Lyric* (London, 1962), pp. 181–21; R. G. M. Nisbet, 'Persius', in J. P. Sullivan, *Critical Essays in Roman Literature: Satire* (London, 1963), pp. 39–71.

position was not always widely held at the time.[26] Though he later felt that
the Horace paper was 'one-sided and over-rhetorical' (*AR*, p. 5) and (as
with the Cicero paper) did not choose to reprint it thirty years later in his
collected papers (see below), it too combined high praise and literary
appreciation with blunt and well-crafted comment on the poet's perceived
shortcomings:

> The Odes could only have been written by a poet of unusual energy and intelli-
> gence. Horace created a style which was both original and inimitable. He covered
> a far wider range than most lyric poets. He transferred the metres and the
> themes of Greek poetry to an alien setting, and somehow gave them a genuinely
> Roman quality. Yet his limitations must be acknowledged. His high standards
> of technical perfection brought a loss of spontaneity: only those who write fast
> can express all the shades and subtleties of thought. He lacked style and grace
> of the Catullan sort (his social origins may be relevant here); he had no appreci-
> ation of certain sorts of beauty; he was unusually self-conscious, for a poet,
> about expressing emotion. When he turned to public subjects he could not
> speak as an autonomous agent; and freedom to conform is not enough for
> anyone who is any good ... The Odes are most successful when they reveal
> something of the poet's own humanity and scepticism.[27]

With his willingness both to conduct detailed stylistic readings and make
forthright aesthetic judgements, he played a key part in the emergence of
literary criticism in Latin studies in the UK in the 1960s, alongside such
figures as E. J. (Ted) Kenney, W. J. N. (Niall) Rudd, J. P. Sullivan,[28] P. G.
(Peter) Walsh[29] and David West,[30] all friends or associates of his. The significance of his work in this period was already recognised by election to
the British Academy in 1967.

Horace was no casual choice for his essay of 1962, for that was the
year in which Nisbet conceived (in a moment of inspiration on the sands
of St Andrews: *AR*, p. 5) the idea of a commentary on the whole of

---

[26] For the dearth of literary criticism in classical studies in the 1950s and early 1960s see Niall
Rudd, 'Introduction', in Niall Rudd (ed.), *Essays on Classical Literature Selected from Arion*
(Cambridge, 1972), pp. vii–xvii.

[27] Nisbet, *'Romanae fidicen lyrae'*, p. 217. 'Humanity and scepticism' suggests key qualities of
Nisbet himself.

[28] For John Sullivan, who was an Oxford colleague from 1954 to 1961 but then left for the USA,
see Gareth Schmeling, 'Sullivan, John Patrick (1930–1993)', *Oxford Dictionary of National
Biography*, <http://www.oxforddnb. com/view/article/53361> [accessed 23 Dec. 2013].

[29] For an obituary of Peter Walsh see <http://www.royalsoced.org.uk/cms/files/fellows/obits_
alpha/walsh_pg.pdf> [accessed 23 Dec. 2013].

[30] For an obituary of David West see <http://www.telegraph.co.uk/news/obituaries/10130699/
Professor-David-West.html> [accessed 23 Dec. 2013].

Horace's *Odes*.[31] The original commentary team was to have consisted of four Oxford colleagues (himself, Margaret Hubbard of St Anne's College, A. F. 'Freddie' Wells of University College, and Gordon Williams of Balliol College), all what were then known as 'Mods dons', heavily occupied undergraduate teachers giving instruction in Latin and Greek languages and literature, at that time limited to the first part ('Mods', Honour Moderations) of the Oxford 'Greats' (Literae Humaniores = Classics) course (see further below). Hubbard and Williams were contemporaries and friends of Nisbet, and both are already thanked by him in the preface to the *In Pisonem*; Wells (b.1911) was somewhat older and had worked on the *Thesaurus Linguae Latinae* in the 1930s. The team was rapidly reduced to two: Wells suffered from severe ill-health in the early 1960s, effectively retired in 1963 and died in 1966,[32] while Williams moved to the Chair of Humanity at St Andrews in 1963 and took no further part in the Oxford project. In the preface to the first volume of commentary, Wells is briefly but warmly memorialised as an earlier 'partner in our enterprise' (p. vi), but Williams is not mentioned, presumably because he had in the end contributed little, and seems to have incorporated his work on Horace into the many Horatian analyses of his *Tradition and Originality in Roman Poetry*, in the preface of which Nisbet's help is acknowledged (p. viii), and into the small-scale edition of *Odes* 3 which he published in 1969.[33]

All the original four-person team were connected with Fraenkel, whose *Horace*, itself replete with many close analyses of the *Odes*, had come out in 1957, when its author was a few years into retirement from the Corpus Chair of Latin but still very much an active scholar and teacher; by that time Nisbet had been his colleague at Corpus for six years, Williams his Oxford colleague for three,[34] while Wells (like Nisbet) was warmly acknowledged in the preface of *Horace* for helping shape the

[31] This section draws on the research in S. J. Harrison, 'Two-author commentaries on Horace: three case studies', in C. A. Stray and C. S. Kraus (eds.), *Classical Commentary: Explorations in a Scholarly Genre* (forthcoming), and is informed by several conversations with Robin Nisbet in 2012.
[32] For obituaries see that by Nisbet himself in *The Oxford Magazine* (1966), p. 10, and an unsigned piece in the *University College Record*, 5.1 (1966), 6–11.
[33] G. W. Williams, *Tradition and Originality in Roman Poetry* (Oxford, 1968), and G. W. Williams, *Horace: Odes Book III* (Oxford, 1969). For Williams's later career, ending as Thacher Professor of Latin at Yale, see the obituary and memorial addresses at <http://www.yale.edu/classics/news_williams.html> [accessed 23 Dec. 2013].
[34] Their friendship since 1954 is highlighted by Williams in the preface to *Tradition and Originality*, p. viii. Williams's letters to Fraenkel from the 1960s are available in the Fraenkel papers in the Archives, Corpus Christi College, Oxford, and show clearly that Fraenkel supported Williams for the Corpus Chair in 1969.

volume's English, and Fraenkel had been a keen supporter of Hubbard's appointment at St Anne's in 1957.[35] The eventual two-person team of Nisbet and Hubbard clearly had something of an ambivalent relationship with Fraenkel, whom (as seen above) Nisbet at least regarded as too domineering over younger colleagues, and the last paragraph of the preface to Book 1 is a masterpiece of tact worth citing in full:

> One debt remains to be acknowledged. Like many of our generation we owe to Eduard Fraenkel our whole approach to ancient literature, and in particular to Horace. He has always taken a sympathetic interest in our work, and lent us his books freely: if we have shown him nothing of what we have written, it is because we wish to remain as independent as we can. He will often find us guilty of plagiarism, sometimes of recalcitrance. We must trust to his magnanimity to forgive us for both.

The commentary indeed takes much from Fraenkel's work (its historicist concerns, its focus on literary patterning and models, and on literary history) but also differs from it in some key respects (an interest in candid literary evaluation and, in the later reception of the poems, a more nuanced approach to the poet's use of the first person, and a grittier and less idealistic approach to the poetry's political context). Its most distinctive feature, its assembling of extensive parallels from Greek and Latin literature, in some ways drew on Fraenkel's work (always aware of the Greek substrate to Horace's poetry), but went much further.[36] The preface to Book I confronts this issue directly:

> We have cited a large number of parallel passages, many of which we believe to be new. It is easy to misunderstand this procedure: classical scholars must seem a strange breed of pedants who refuse to admit that life is short unless they can find ten parallels to prove it. In fact we are trying to show how a very literary poet takes over themes conventional in various genres and adapts them to his new idiom. We also believe that many problems, both large and small, can be illuminated by the collection of evidence, and that without such evidence the most ingenious theorising is often misdirected. We hope that our stores may be found serviceable by commentators on other works of ancient literature.

The last sentence here is prophetic: there is virtually no commentary written on Latin poetry since 1970 that does not use the material of the first volume of Nisbet and Hubbard, and the detailed exegesis of the book's poems after that date inevitably starts from its parallels and judge-

---

[35] See M. G. Leigh, 'Margaret Hubbard', *The Ship* (2011–12), pp. 76–7 (available at <http://www.st-annes.ox.ac.uk/fileadmin/documents/Publications/TheShip_2012.pdf.pdf> [accessed 23 Dec. 2013]).

[36] For an interesting review discussion of this feature of the commentary by a former partner in the enterprise see G. W. Williams, *Horace* (Oxford, 1972), pp. 2–3.

ments, though it has been criticised by some for its underestimation of some aspects of Horatian poetics, e.g. imagery and literary structure.[37] The fact that the material is often austerely presented in compressed form, simply citing the parallel without further elucidating its function, has paradoxically added to the longevity of the commentary, leaving the reader to apply his or her interpretation to the suggested resemblance or connection.

One further element from the preface deserves notice. Nisbet and Hubbard deny that they are doing literary criticism: 'We do not rule out the possibility of serious literary criticism on a Latin poet, but we had neither the confidence nor the time to take on the job ourselves' (p. v). Though this is meant to draw a contrast between their work and that of more overtly literary critics of the time such as Kenneth Quinn,[38] it seems both to be in contradiction with their statement on the same page that 'we have occasionally suggested that some odes may be better than others' and to underestimate the value for literary-critical purposes of the interpretations which the commentary provides, though it is true to say that it does not provide the structural analyses and linear readings of the *Odes* to be found (for example) in Quinn's later commentary of 1980.[39] Here Nisbet and Hubbard are surely over-influenced by Housman's celebrated but over-austere view that scholarship and literary criticism are separate gifts rarely combined in the same person.[40]

Both volumes of Nisbet and Hubbard were fully joint enterprises, with both partners reading and commenting on the whole set of drafts. One partner would begin the work on a particular poem by producing a first draft for comment, discussion and redrafting: according to Nisbet, he wrote the first draft on slightly more poems in Book 1 than Hubbard and on a considerable majority of poems in Book 2. Nisbet himself felt that the collaboration worked more effectively for the first volume, when the enterprise was fresh for both partners, and neither had other major distractions: after 1970 Nisbet had the considerable administrative burden carried by the Corpus Chair of Latin at Oxford (see below), while Hubbard

[37] Their famous statement that 'his metaphors are sparse and trite' (I: xxii) has been justly criticised (see e.g. Quinn's review, see below, n. 38): for a richer view see e.g. D. West, *Reading Horace* (Edinburgh, 1967).

[38] For example, K. Quinn, *Latin Explorations* (London, 1963). For Quinn's initial mixed reaction to Nisbet and Hubbard see K. Quinn, 'The new Nisbet–Hubbard Horace', *Arion*, 9 (1970), 264–73.

[39] K. Quinn, *Horace: the Odes* (London, 1980).

[40] A. E. Housman, *The Name and Nature of Poetry* (Cambridge, 1939), p. 1.

was already engaged on the work which would lead to her important book on Propertius.[41]

As with many collaborative enterprises, it is hard for readers to ascribe particular parts of Nisbet and Hubbard to one or the other, even if there is some record of original allocations of poems between them for initial drafts.[42] This was neatly encapsulated by L. P. Wilkinson's improvised verses on Book 1:[43]

> This is a book of Hubbard and Nisbet:
> Some of it's her bit and some of it's his bit.
> I leave it to you to decide who did what,
> But all of it's sense and none of it's not.

Occasional guesses were usually wrong: some supposed that the commentary on the Archytas ode (1.28) with its copious philosophical material was principally Hubbard, others that 1.12 with its especially rich set of literary models was Nisbet, but both were incorrect according to Nisbet himself. The parallels from English poetry (an interestingly innovative feature of the commentary) came from both authors, though Nisbet regarded Hubbard as more expert there. Nisbet at least could change his mind over time: the commentary's somewhat austere denial that the wintry Mount Soracte in *Odes* 1.9 symbolised old age was withdrawn in one of his later articles.[44] A generation on, these two commentaries remain remarkable achievements and must be consulted by all serious readers of Horace's *Odes*.

Alongside this considerable research activity, Nisbet was a dedicated classical tutor at Corpus in the period 1952–70. Then, as now, classics was a key subject at Corpus. In 1952 the college had only eleven fellows, three of whom were classicists: Fraenkel and the ancient historian Frank Lepper in addition to Robin himself. On Fraenkel's retirement in 1953 Sir Roger Mynors,[45] with whom Nisbet had a warm relationship and whose commentary on Virgil's *Georgics* he saw through to publication after his

---

[41] M. Hubbard, *Propertius* (London, 1974).

[42] Nisbet's reading text of the *Odes* (Wickham's *editio maior*, now in the possession of Richard Tarrant) contains a list of the initial planned division of first drafts for Book 1 under the original four-person team, each containing roughly the same number of lines (Nisbet: 2, 9, 11, 18, 20, 22, 25, 28, 32, 37; Hubbard: 4, 7, 16, 17, 21, 31, 34, 35, 38; Wells: 1, 3, 5, 8, 14, 15, 23, 24, 26; Williams 6, 10, 12, 13, 19, 27, 29, 30, 33, 36) and for Book 2 (Hubbard: 1–3, 5, 8–9, 13, 15, 18–19; Nisbet: 4, 6–7, 10, 11, 12, 14, 16–17, 20). These were clearly not maintained in practice for Book 1, given that two of the team had dropped out by 1963, and may not have been for Book 2 (see above).

[43] Known to me from a postcard, perhaps in Wilkinson's own hand (Nisbet papers, Archives, Corpus Christi College, Oxford).

[44] R. G. M. Nisbet, *Collected Papers on Latin Literature* (Oxford, 1995), pp. 414–15.

[45] For his career see M. Winterbottom, 'Roger Aubrey Baskerville Mynors, 1903–1989', *Proceedings of the British Academy*, 81 (1991), 371–401.

death,[46] came back from Cambridge to the Corpus Chair, which meant at Corpus evenings in the 1950s and 1960s one could find oneself with Fraenkel, Mynors and Nisbet together, an impressive concentration of Latinists. A further collection of classical colleagues appeared over the next two decades: (Sir) Hugh Lloyd-Jones in 1954 (moving to the Regius Chair of Greek in 1960), the philosopher J. O. Urmson in 1959, the Hellenist Gerald Toomer in 1960 (moving to Brown in 1965), the philosopher Christopher Taylor in 1963, the Hellenist Ewen Bowie in 1965, the Roman historian John Matthews in 1969 (moving to Queen's in 1976, later to Yale) and John Bramble as Nisbet's own successor as Latin tutor in 1970.

In these years he was jointly responsible for Corpus's emergence as an undergraduate classical powerhouse, and the college's performances in Mods and Greats improved greatly. He taught a large number of distinguished schoolteachers and academics as undergraduates: amongst the academics one could mention Gerald Toomer, Nigel Wilson, Peter Brown and Oliver Taplin, all of whom became Oxford tutorial fellows, and other distinguished scholars such as John Briscoe, William Harris, John Moles, Andrew Wallace-Hadrill and Harry Hine in classics, not to mention Jonathan Dancy in philosophy. He also taught others of high achievement in other fields, for example Sir Martin Wolf, the leading financial journalist, William (Baron) Waldegrave, Corpus's first cabinet minister since the 1930s, and many outstanding civil servants and lawyers.

Both before and after his election to the Corpus Chair (see below), Nisbet played a central role in the administration of classics at Oxford, chairing the Classics Faculty Board and Sub-Faculty of Languages and Literature and acting as Director of Graduate Studies: he would often aver that there were two types of academics on committees, those who 'greased the wheels', and those who 'gummed them up' (he regarded himself as a wheel-greaser). In particular (along with Donald Russell and others) in the 1960s he was a leader in the most important reform of his academic generation, establishing the study of classical literature at Oxford as an equal part of Greats with Philosophy and Ancient History from 1970, a crucial step for the Sub-Faculty of Languages and Literature and for the study of classical literature generally.[47]

---

[46] R. A. B. Mynors, *Virgil: Georgics* (Oxford, 1990).
[47] For these reforms see further Nisbet and Russell, 'The study of classical literature at Oxford, 1936–1988', pp. 219–38.

In 1969, with the first volume of the Horace commentary in press and some of its contents known to the electors, Nisbet was elected to the Corpus Chair of Latin Language and Literature. His referees were an interesting selection: his former Corpus colleague Hugh Lloyd-Jones, Regius Professor of Greek, and the Hellenist Rudolf Kassel of Köln, who had visited Oxford and declined the Regius Chair of Greek in 1960, with Roger Mynors (the then holder of the Corpus Chair) as the only Latinist. Fraenkel, supporting Gordon Williams, was not available for Nisbet, though he wrote to congratulate him afterwards.[48] Mynors's reference does not survive, but the other two are preserved:[49] both mention having read parts of the forthcoming commentary, and both provide perceptive views of their subject. Lloyd-Jones, acutely analysing a character very different from his own more mercurial nature,[50] stated that 'his quiet, unruffled personality makes him able to get on terms with almost anyone, yet he has strong opinions, and is ready to defend them. He is highly congenial to his colleagues, easy of access and ready to discuss scholarly topics at all times.' Kassel's reference naturally stressed the excellence of the Greek parallels in the draft commentary, but its most effective aspect was a lengthy quotation from an anonymous former undergraduate student of Nisbet's:

> I think I can say without any hesitation that he is the best teacher I have had, and that he has opened my eyes to a great deal in classical literature which I am sure I would otherwise have failed to notice. He is also extremely conscientious, and takes an interest in the people he comes across . . . his teaching technique is well suited to research supervision, as it consists rather in asking awkward questions about work which a man has done than in filling a pupil with knowledge. He always encouraged us to have ideas of our own, even though his own ideas were so persuasive that we didn't much want to disagree with them.

Anyone taught by Nisbet at any level will recognise the accuracy of this account.

The year of Nisbet's election to the Corpus chair also marked a key change in his personal life. In his first years at Corpus he had lived the then life of a bachelor don and dedicated tutor in college, but in 1969 he married Anne Wood, with whom he had worked closely as College Secretary in his progress through the various college offices; he was Senior Tutor (1967–70) and twice Vice-President (1960–2, 1972–3), and Corpus

---

[48] The letter (dated 12.5.69) is in the Nisbet papers, Archives, Corpus Christi College, Oxford.
[49] In the files of the Presidential office at Corpus Christi College, Oxford.
[50] See N. G. Wilson, 'Peter Hugh Jefferd Lloyd-Jones, 1922–2009', *Proceedings of the British Academy*, 172, *Biographical Memoirs of Fellows*, X (2011), 215–29.

and its affairs and interests were always close to his heart. The pair moved to Cumnor, close to Oxford, where they enjoyed a long and happy marriage, a garden and cats, and for some years they also had a summer retreat at Barton-on-Sea in Hampshire.

As Corpus Professor (and indeed before) he had a stream of distin-guished graduate students who have gone on to occupy major positions in universities all over the world, and to do sterling work in schools and colleges. Amongst scholars, these included Richard Tarrant and Kathleen Coleman at Harvard, Denis Feeney at Princeton, Jonathan Powell at Royal Holloway, Michael Dewar in Toronto, the late Adrian Hollis and Don Fowler in Oxford, John Henderson at Cambridge and Charles Martindale at Bristol. There was also a stream of bright young colleagues in the P. S. Allen Junior Research Fellowship—his former students John Briscoe, Richard Tarrant and Harry Hine, and also Philip Hardie and Arnd Kerkhecker, all of whom enjoyed his support and help and went on to distinguished careers.

As a graduate supervisor he was a conscientious, rapid and acute reader of his students' work, often well into their professional careers, which he supported generously. His graduate seminars were fundamen-tally formative for his students, taking a Latin text, whether well-known or not, and subjecting it to the widest range of scrutiny, textual, literary and cultural; his stance, consciously differing from Fraenkel's need for domination, was essentially that of a midwife, to encourage, point students towards key bibliography and ideas, and very occasionally correct. For many, these seminars exemplified true and tolerant scholarship in action.

He did not travel overseas, academically or otherwise; in later years, he used to say to younger colleagues that they did his travelling for him. Wherever they went, his name achieved instant recognition, and if it was anywhere in the Anglophone academic world, they would inevitably find a colleague who owed something to Nisbet's help or teaching. And though he did not himself bring overseas scholars to Oxford, he was always kind and welcoming when they appeared, and keen to know what was going on elsewhere in the classical world. He did occasionally make it as far as Liverpool and Leeds, where he much enjoyed the colloquia organised by Francis Cairns and the chance to talk to old friends such as David West and Tony Woodman, and to London, where he served as Vice-President of the Roman Society and on the editorial committee of its journal.

Having spent most of the 1960s and 1970s on Horace, from the mid-1970s he began to produce a wide range of essays on Latin authors. Perhaps most famous amongst these were his co-authorship of the first edition of the Gallus papyrus from Egypt in 1979, resurrecting the missing link in Latin literature, Cornelius Gallus, the poet who stood at the head of the rich tradition of Latin elegy later developed by Tibullus, Propertius and Ovid. His brilliant paper of 1978 on the text and interpretation of Catullus both opened up and cleared up a number of issues in one of the most central and often-read Latin poets, and his splendid account of Virgil's Fourth Eclogue showed that the long-known similarities between Virgil's poem and the prophecies of Isaiah were likely to have been due to the Hellenised Jewish culture of Alexandria; he also produced important work on the style of the *Eclogues*, on the historical background of Horace's *Epodes*, on Seneca's tragedies, on Statius, and on Juvenal, as well as several pieces on scholarly methodology. In the end there were more than twenty essays over fewer than twenty years, later published in his *Collected Papers on Latin Literature* (1995), a volume which all intending professional Latinists should read.[51]

In 1992 he retired, and was feted by a splendid international collection of scholars at a conference on Horace at Corpus, later published as a Festschrift entitled *Homage to Horace*.[52] Characteristically careful and methodical, he moved his extensive classical library to Cumnor by the simple expedient of taking two shopping bags of books home each day on the bus for nine months. He was a man of some austerity: he did not drink, drive or type, and computers and the internet came too late for him, despite attempts by colleagues at his conversion. As often happens, having been a reformer in his early career he became more conservative later on, and did not always approve of the emergence of literary theory

---

[51] Nisbet, *Collected Papers*. I add here for completeness' sake the articles and chapters published after 1995 by Nisbet and therefore not included in the full bibliography (pp. 435–8) in that volume. Apart from the 2001 piece on prose-rhythm in Apuleius (see above, n. 23), the 2004 obituary of W. S. Watt (see above, n. 12), and the 2007 historical piece with Donald Russell on classics in Oxford (see above, n. 9), these were: R. G. M. Nisbet, 'The word-order of Horace's Odes', in J. N. Adams and R. G. Mayer (eds.), *Aspects of the Language of Latin Poetry* (Oxford, 1999), pp. 135–54; R. G. M. Nisbet, 'Epilegomena on the text of Juvenal', *Acta Antiqua Hungarica*, 39 (1999), 225–30; R. G. M. Nisbet, 'Sera vindemia: marginal notes on the text of Horace and Juvenal', in J. F. Miller, C. Damon and K. S. Myers, *Vertis in usum: Studies in Honor of Edward Courtney* (Munich, 2002), pp. 56–66; R. G. M. Nisbet, 'A wine-jar for Messalla: Carmina 3.21', in T. Woodman and D. Feeney (eds.), *Traditions and Contexts in the Poetry of Horace* (Cambridge, 2002), pp. 80–92; R. G. M. Nisbet, 'Horace: life and chronology', in S. J. Harrison (ed.), *The Cambridge Companion to Horace* (Cambridge, 2007), pp. 7–21; and R. G. M. Nisbet, 'Housman's Juvenal' [a revision of his 1989 article of the same title], in D. Butterfield and C. A. Stray (eds.), *A. E. Housman: Classical Scholar* (London, 2010), pp. 45–63. Some further conjectures on Juvenal await publication in the Italian journal *Segno e testo*.

[52] S. J. Harrison (ed.), *Homage to Horace: a Bimillenary Celebration* (Oxford, 1995).

in Latin studies, driven in the 1990s in this country by two of his most brilliant graduate students, John Henderson in Cambridge and the late Don Fowler in Oxford. Likewise with the new area of classical reception in recent years: he could see that Milton and Tennyson drew interestingly on their classical knowledge, and respected and praised the work of Charles Martindale (another former graduate student) on translation, but was sceptical about reception studies (now a key part of classics) as a field of endeavour.

Horace was not forgotten in retirement. After the publication of Book 2 in 1978, Hubbard had turned to other work, but Nisbet had continued drafting a commentary on Book 3, following the original intention of the project to cover the whole of the four books of *Odes*. By the mid-1980s Nisbet was clear that he would not go on to *Odes* 4 (which he found less inspiring than the early books), and others took on that book, on which we have now two major commentaries.[53] When he retired, friends and colleagues urged Nisbet to complete *Odes* 3, but he was initially unsure whether he would be able to do so.

Help came from an old friend.[54] In the mid-1990s, Niall Rudd, who had retired from his chair of Latin in Bristol in 1989 and was already the author of a widely used smaller-scale commentary on Horace *Epistles* 2 and the *Ars Poetica*,[55] approached E. J. Kenney as the main Latin editor of the 'Cambridge Greek and Latin Classics' series ('green and yellow' format), asking whether the series wanted a commentary on Horace *Odes* 4. Kenney replied that the series had already commissioned such a volume (from Richard Thomas), but would Rudd be interested in *Odes* 3 instead? At this point Rudd recalled that Nisbet was working on a larger-scale project on that same book and contacted him to see if he was interested in a collaboration. Nisbet replied that he had a good deal of handwritten material and would welcome collaboration to finish the project; Rudd (a user of computers) then agreed to type up that material, and add occasional elements of his own where he felt it was appropriate. The two partners agreed that whatever emerged would be a third volume for Oxford, in a longer and more detailed format, rather than for the leaner Cambridge series.

---

[53] P. Fedeli and I. Ciccarelli, *Q. Horatii Flacci: Carmina Liber IV* (Florence, 2008), R. F. Thomas, *Horace: Odes Book IV and Carmen Saeculare* (Cambridge, 2011).

[54] In what follows I am most grateful to Niall Rudd for help and discussion as well as to the late Robin Nisbet for several conversations. Quotations are from a letter from Niall Rudd to the author, dated 14.5.2013.

[55] N. Rudd, Horace: *Epistles II and Ars Poetica* (Cambridge, 1989).

Rudd had already begun work on his admirable Loeb edition of Horace's *Odes* and *Epodes* (published in 2004),[56] so he had thought through most of the major interpretational problems of the third book, and he sent Nisbet an outline of the main issues in each poem and of his own views, while Nisbet sent Rudd his draft commentaries on the same poems. Rudd's own words take up the story: 'as the packets of material arrived, it became clear that our approaches were very much the same, though I was happy to stand aside when he plunged into the more thorny thickets of *Wissenschaft*. It also became clear that in a few cases, where he thought I was wrong but not insane, he was willing that I should have my say.' Nisbet estimated that 20 per cent of the final draft came from Rudd, whom he viewed as more conservative than himself and more liable to be content with the traditional text and interpretation; the differences between the two partners are (unusually) enshrined in the commentary, where their divergent views are regularly reported under their initials. Discussions took place at regular Sunday meetings at Nisbet's home in Cumnor, where they would spend most of the day on the commentary. The commentary was duly completed and published in May 2004, almost exactly on Nisbet's seventy-ninth birthday.

In retirement Nisbet had been regularly and willingly enlisted in his wife Anne's active charitable life in Cumnor, for example delivering 'meals on wheels'. Her death in 2004 a few weeks after the publication of *Odes* 3 was a sad blow, and Nisbet's serious ill-health which followed a few years later eventually confined him to his home, leaving him unable to visit his beloved Corpus as he had done weekly since retirement; he found some consolation in listening to Classic FM and in even more extensive reading in modern history. He was sustained in Cumnor by a team of excellent carers and by the devotion of his friends Esme and Tony Wyatt. He kept in touch with other friends and colleagues largely by telephone, always keen to know and discuss the latest news, whether political or academic. He died on 14 May 2013, a week before his 88th birthday.

Nisbet's career as a scholar was influenced by three major figures in particular, as well as by his father and undergraduate teachers. His life-long profound interest in history led him to Syme, whose emphasis on the explanatory power of prosopography he followed, not least in his interest in the relevance of the *Odes* of Horace to the careers of their addressees, whose realistic and ironic approach to politics he found highly congenial,

---

[56] N. Rudd, *Horace: Odes and Epodes* (Cambridge, MA, 2004).

and whose lapidary style he greatly admired and sometimes imitated.[57] His interactions with Fraenkel from his undergraduate days were a crucial part of his development as a scholar:[58] Fraenkel's range of learning was a source of wonder to him, and his refusal to compartmentalise classical studies into Latin and Greek and his application of a vast spectrum of texts and information to the study of poetry was a key influence on Nisbet's commentary technique. Bill Watt's encouragement of Nisbet's interest in textual criticism led him to Housman, whose capacity to identify problems in a Latin text and solve them via the application of clear reason and encyclopedic knowledge was a constant inspiration and the subject of his last paper;[59] textual criticism of both prose and poetry was a keynote of Nisbet's career from first to last.

Though Housman and Fraenkel were scholarly models, Nisbet could see and avoid their darker sides. As already noted, while he was personally much influenced by and grateful to Fraenkel, he was clear (as already suggested) that the great man's capacity to discourage the research of others was his Achilles' heel: 'in spite of his immense contribution to Oxford classics, research did not prosper under him; to quote the fable in Horace, the tracks led into his den but none came out' (*AR*, p. 4).[60] Nisbet was the opposite: his capacity to encourage research at every level was one of his key contributions to the subject, as the numerous successful theses and books of his many pupils and protégés make more than clear. In the case of Housman, he found the latter's needless aggression unprofitable and unworthy: 'to professional rivals he was persistently offensive . . . and the effect on rising scholars was inhibiting'.[61] Again, in published work, he himself pursued the converse course, for example in a review of Shackleton Bailey's text of Horace: 'A review concentrates on points of doubt or disagreement, but it cannot do justice to the many occasions where Professor Shackleton Bailey has made one reader reconsider. It is a privilege and delight to debate with him about these interesting problems.'[62] In private, he could be mischievously amusing about other scholars: in response to the publication of a (in his view) learned but misguided volume on a

[57] See the Syme-style summaries of the careers of Cicero and Horace (see above, nn. 24 and 27).
[58] A letter survives from Fraenkel to the undergraduate Nisbet, dated 2.1.1949, congratulating him on the award of the Craven Scholarship and inviting him to his Plautus seminar (Nisbet papers, Archives, Corpus Christi College, Oxford).
[59] See above, n. 51.
[60] The reference is to *Epistles* 1.1.73–5 (the clever fox refuses to enter the lion's den).
[61] Nisbet, 'Housman's Juvenal', p. 61.
[62] Nisbet, *Collected Papers*, p. 201.

classical author X, he once quipped in his inimitable Scots accent: 'You'll learn a lot from it, but not about X' (but note how even here there is some praise). In general, kindness and thoughtfulness was a key feature of his life as well as of his scholarship, as his friends, colleagues and students can bear manifold witness.

S. J. HARRISON
Corpus Christi College, Oxford

Note. In preparing this memoir I have had generous assistance from Professors Donald Russell and Niall Rudd, from Julian Reid, the Archivist of Corpus Christi College, Oxford, from the Presidential office at Corpus, and from Dr Robin Darwall-Smith at University College, Oxford (himself a former Nisbet graduate student). Most useful of all was the extensive material prepared with typical method and forethought by Robin Nisbet himself for his future memoirist, which is now in the Archives of Corpus Christi College. I take this opportunity to salute him, my teacher, colleague and friend for over thirty years, and to hope that this small tribute is some return for his support and example over all that time. *Ave atque vale*.

JACK POLE

Jack Richon Pole
1922–2010

A DISTINGUISHED HISTORIAN of colonial British America and the United States, Jack Richon Pole was elected a Fellow of the British Academy in 1985 and an Honorary Foreign Member of the American Historical Association in 2002. He was born in London on 14 March 1922, to Joe and Phoebe Pole. His father, who had immigrated as a youth from Kiev, was head of publicity in London for the Hollywood film company United Artists. His mother taught French in a secondary school, was an active suffragette, and later served as a Labour member of Finchley council. In the words of Jack's close friend Godfrey Hodgson, they 'were classic Hampstead intellectuals of the period' who 'moved in a world of academics, psychoanalysts and socialists', Jack's father being acquainted with 'all the stars of Hollywood's Golden Age'.[1] They sent Jack at age 3 or 4 to the highly experimental Maltinghouse school in Cambridge, where his godmother, Susan Isaacs, a prominent child psychologist and educationalist, taught, and later to the progressive King Alfred School in Hampstead. The Second World War, during which he served as an anti-aircraft officer at Scapa Flow in Orkney and in the Horn of Africa in the campaign against the Italians, contributed to a long interruption in his formal education. After he was demobilised in 1947, he went up to The Queen's College, Oxford, where he obtained a first in modern history in 1949.

How and when Jack first developed an interest in United States history is a subject we never discussed, but in 1949, in a highly unusual move for a British historian of his generation, he won a Proctor Visiting

[1] *The Guardian*, 4 March 2010.

Biographical Memoirs of Fellows of the British Academy, XIII, 385–402. © The British Academy 2014.

Fellowship at Princeton University and sufficiently impressed his teachers that he was asked to stay on to complete his Ph.D., which he received in 1953. Perhaps his mother's involvement in the suffrage movement affected his choice of a dissertation topic, 'The Reform of Suffrage and Representation in New Jersey: 1774–1844'. This work won the New Jersey Prize, and over the next few years Jack published its main findings in three substantial journal articles.[2] Having taught for a year as an instructor in history at Princeton, Jack returned to Britain in 1953 to take up the lectureship in American history at University College London, where, for the next decade, he taught all areas of American history and rose to the rank of Senior Lecturer. In 1960–1 he was a Visiting Professor at the University of California, Berkeley. In 1963, he moved to Cambridge as University Reader in American History and Government and Fellow of Churchill College, posts he held for the next sixteen years. From 1975 to 1978, Jack also was Vice-Master of Churchill College. In 1979, he moved to Oxford to become Rhodes Professor of American History and Institutions and Fellow of St Catherine's College, positions he held until his retirement in 1989.

From the beginning of his professional career, Jack's goal was to do the quality of work that would win the respect of historians in the United States. As he put it in the introduction to a collection of his early essays published in 1979, his objective was 'to ask difficult questions, and then to find ways of answering them' by 'reading the published and archival records of American history' and producing 'books which any student of American history would be required to read in order to get an adequate grasp of the literature of the subject'.[3] As he went on to point out, such work from British hands had begun to appear only in the 1960s, when a few members of his generation, including W. R. Brock[4] and Marcus Cunliffe,[5] produced substantial and deeply researched volumes that, as the American historical community rapidly began to appreciate, contributed to change the landscape of or to rethink critical issues in United States history.

---

[2] J. R. Pole, 'The suffrage in New Jersey, 1770–1807', *Proceedings of the New Jersey Historical Association*, 71 (1953), 39–68; J. R. Pole, 'Suffrage reform and the American Revolution in New Jersey', *Proceedings of the New Jersey Historical Association*, 74 (1956), 173–94; J. R. Pole, 'Jeffersonian democracy and the Federalist dilemma in New Jersey, 1798–1812', *Proceedings of the New Jersey Historical Association*, 74 (1956), 260–92.
[3] J. R. Pole, *Paths to the American Past* (New York, 1979), pp. xviii–xix.
[4] W. R. Brock, *An American Crisis: Congress and Reconstruction* (London, 1963).
[5] Marcus Cunliffe, *Soldiers and Civilians: the Martial Spirit in America 1775–1865* (Boston, MA, 1968).

But no member of that pioneering generation of historians of the United States in Britain turned out to be a more prolific scholar than Jack. A review of his publications reveals that, as of 2000, he had published two major monographs (one of which subsequently came out under a new title in a considerably expanded form), four smaller interpretive books, a collection of essays, a textbook, five booklets, three collections of edited documents, one anthology, three edited or co-edited books, one co-edited encyclopaedia (subsequently expanded and republished under a different title), twenty-eight journal articles, and seventeen chapters in books.[6] At least 90 per cent of these publications were in the fields of colonial British American and United States history. And he was far from done, publishing over the last five years of his life what is widely regarded as the best edition of *The Federalist*[7] and yet a third monograph which appeared shortly after his death.[8]

In creating this extraordinary corpus of work, Jack had a lot of external support. He won two Rockefeller Research Awards, one in 1952 and the other in 1960, and numerous fellowships or research grants: from the Commonwealth Fund (UK) for American Studies in 1956, the American Philosophical Society in 1957, the American Council of Learned Societies in 1968, the Center for Advanced Study in Behavioral Sciences at Stanford in 1969–70, the Woodrow Wilson International Center for Scholars in Washington, DC, in 1978–9, and, from the British Academy in 1988, a Leverhulme Visiting Research Fellowship. Following his retirement, he held the Goleib Fellowship at New York University Law School in 1990, a Senior Research Fellowship at the Institute of Commonwealth Studies and a Visiting Fellowship at the Institute for the Bill of Rights at the Marshall-Wythe Law School at the College of William and Mary in 1990–1, and a Leverhulme Trust Emeritus Fellowship from 1988 to 1994. These prestigious awards and fellowships, which enabled him to pursue his passion for archival work in United States repositories, testify to the high esteem in which Jack was held by his peers on both sides of the Atlantic.

During his decade in London, Jack published several valuable monographic articles in local or regional American historical journals relating to the larger project he was formulating and for which he was collecting

---

[6] For a list of Jack's publications in English to 2005, see Rebecca Starr (ed.), *Articulating America: Fashioning a National Political Culture in Early America: Essays in Honor of J. R. Pole* (Lanham, MD, 2000), pp. 259–66.

[7] J. R. Pole (ed.), *The Federalist* (Indianapolis, IN, 2005).

[8] J. R. Pole, *Contract & Consent: Representation and the Jury in Anglo-American Legal History* (Charlottesville, VA, 2010).

materials.[9] But he did not make a major splash in American history circles
until 1962, with the publication in the *American Historical Review* of his
influential article, 'Historians and the problem of early American democracy'. In the 1950s the historians Robert E. and B. Katherine Brown had
published impressive empirical studies showing that the franchise in two
of Britain's oldest and most populous colonies, Virginia and Massachusetts,
was far wider than earlier historians had suspected. Their findings
challenged the longstanding but previously only lightly investigated
assumption that the wealthy colonials who dominated elective offices did
so by limiting the franchise and employing other means of social control
to keep political participation low. This work pointedly raised the question
of why, as Jack put it, 'the great mass of the common people might
actually have given their consent to concepts of government' that, 'by
systematically' excluding them 'from the more responsible positions of
political power', restricted 'their own participation in ways completely
at variance with the principles of modern democracy'. Jack's answer to
this question was that colonial British and Revolutionary America, like
eighteenth-century Britain, was 'a deferential society', a term 'coined by
Walter Bagehot in his account of Victorian England', that operated within
a fundamentally elitist and integrated structure of ideas that assumed that
government should be entrusted to men of merit; that merit was often
associated with wealth and high social position; that such men were
obliged to use their superior talents for the benefit of the public; and that
deference to them was the implicit duty of the rest of society. Most historians, myself included, took up this suggestion with alacrity, and *deference*
rapidly acquired a prominent place in the conceptual lexicon of American
historians.[10]

   If this influential intervention clearly displayed Jack's early mastery of
the issues in early modern American historiography and his capacity for
systematic thinking about large historical problems, his first book,
published four years later, established his credentials as an original and
perceptive contributor to his field. *Political Representation in England and*

---

[9] J. R. Pole, 'Election statistics in Pennsylvania 1790–1840', *Pennsylvania Magazine of History
and Biography*, 82 (1958), 217–22; J. R. Pole, 'Representation and authority in Virginia from the
Revolution to reform', *Journal of Southern History*, 24 (1958), 16–50; J. R. Pole, 'Suffrage and
representation in Maryland from 1776 to 1810: a statistical note and some reflections', *Journal of
Southern History*, 24 (1958), 218–25; J. R. Pole, 'Election Statistics in North Carolina, to 1861',
Journal of Southern History, 24 (1958), 225–8; J. R. Pole, 'Constitutional reform and election
statistics in Maryland, 1790–1812', *Maryland Historical Magazine*, 55 (1960), 275–92.
[10] J. R. Pole, 'Historians and the problem of early American democracy', *American Historical
Review*, 67 (1962), 626–46.

the Origins of the American Republic (London, 1966) was an unusually bold undertaking for a younger scholar. It took up a major problem, the concept and practice of political representation, and covered a wide scope of time and space: the Anglo and American worlds from the late seventeenth century to the Reform Bill of 1832. It was explicitly comparative in two ways, comparing Britain with the American colonies and the new United States and three American colonial/state polities with one another. Deeply, if not exhaustively, researched, it was also enormous, its more than six hundred pages instantly invoking terms such as *magisterial* and *weighty* to describe it.

The wide scope of subject matter and density of data proved a major organisational problem that Jack did not fully resolve. He divided the volume into five parts, the core of which consisted of three parts, each broken into from six to fifteen chapters, many of them with four or five subsections. The first of these, Part Two, occupied a quarter of the text and consisted of close and largely self-contained case studies of three of the most important American colonies—Massachusetts, Pennsylvania, and Virginia, representing three different areas of Britain's North American empire. Part Three, the second and longest of the core parts, constituted two-fifths of the text and covered developments in the same three polities as they transformed themselves into republican states beginning in 1776 and also in the hastily contrived American national government constructed after 1774 to handle the general matters required to fight a war against Britain and pursue foreign alliances. In considerably less detail, Part Four, taking up just over a fifth of the text, considered the British case from the late seventeenth century to 1832. These three substantial core parts were book-ended by a short introduction summarising the thoughts of James Harrington, Algernon Sydney, and John Locke on the nature of representation, and a comparative summary in which Jack impressively laid out his principal conclusions and considered the import of his findings.

This organisation was not well-suited for guiding the reader through his text to his principal conclusions. The compartmentalisation of the volume into discrete studies of so many separate polities and the fact that its rich materials were not from the beginning of the volume tightly subordinated to a well-worked out general argument made it seem less like an integrated account of the subject than seven independent studies, loosely tied together by an argument fully enunciated only in the summary. The result, as R. R. Palmer lamented in an otherwise highly favourable review, was that Jack had been 'so generous with his information, so absorbed by all aspects of his subject, and so scrupulous in perceiving nuances, that the clarity of his main argument' tended 'to be obscured'.[11] Only in the closing summary did Jack make it entirely clear that the grand theme he had been developing was the transition from a system of representation based on corporate entities such as towns or counties to one based on the numbers of enfranchised people or, as he termed it, political individualism. The same was true of his contention that, despite the differences he treated in such detail in the body of the volume, in the rate and character of this transition from place to place and from time to time and the different constitutional systems that ultimately resulted, he regarded the process in Britain and America as leading in the same direction and deriving out of an alliance between political reformers and powerful new interest groups concerned to protect new forms of property and to use the principle of numbers to undermine older arrangements.

Jack's organisation was considerably more effective in illustrating how peculiar circumstances affected the development and understanding of representation in different polities as they changed over time. It enabled him to capture in richly textured detail the complex interplay among ideas, ordinary politics and social context in each of the seven polities he treated and, in the case of his American data, was particularly valuable in working out the distinctive features of the internal histories of each of the colonies he treated during the colonial and early national eras. It also helped him fully to explore the process by which those colonies moved toward the achievement of legislative supremacy in colonial governance and the many ways that that development contributed to the establishment of 'capable self-government' and thereby served as an important precondition for independent governance. Equally important, his comparative approach enabled Jack to produce an account of his subject that was far less parochial than much of the contemporary historical literature being produced by American scholars at that time and suggested the possibility of a transatlantic approach that would have for its theme the understanding of how British peoples would adapt British culture and institutions in new physical and social situations. If Jack's discursive and sprawling organisation suggested that, at this stage of his career, he was better at dealing with precise data sets on specific problems than with

---

[11] R. R. Palmer, Review of *Political Representation in England and the Origins of the American Republic*, *Journal of American Studies*, 1 (1967), 131.

working out efficient frameworks for presenting extensive data, his text was, as Gordon Wood noted in his review, 'incredibly rich'.[12]

Even more ambitious, Jack's second major book, *The Pursuit of Equality in American History* (Berkeley, CA, 1978), was the first systematic analysis of the changing fortunes of the idea of equality during the first two centuries of the American republic and in its temporal range represented a departure from most of his earlier work. Although he had published three short booklets on Abraham Lincoln[13] and an edition of documents on *Slavery, Secession and Civil War* (London, 1975), his publications during the dozen years after the appearance of *Political Representation*, 1966 to 1978, showed a heavy concentration on the colonial, revolutionary, and early republican eras,[14] and the same would be true of his later publications. Sweeping in scope, tightly argued, and penetrating in its analysis of detail, the *Pursuit of Equality* had none of the organisational problems of his first book.

Starting with the observation that the world to which the American states announced that 'all men are created equal' in the Declaration of Independence in 1776 was dominated by ideas of order and hierarchy that were essentially hostile to all ideas of equality, Jack noted that natives and outsiders alike had always perceived the free population of the British North American colonies as more equal than perhaps any other contemporary society. Among that population, ideas of subordination seemed to be visibly weaker, opportunities to acquire property and independence demonstrably more abundant, the distribution of wealth considerably less unequal, and differences in wealth and social position, while sometimes inherited rather than earned, at least not built, as in Europe, upon laws of

---

[12] G. S. Wood, Review of *Political Representation in England and the Origins of the American Republic, Journal of Modern History*, 41 (1969), 238.

[13] J. R. Pole, *Abraham Lincoln and the Working Classes of Britain* (London, 1959); J. R. Pole, *Abraham Lincoln* (Oxford, 1964); and J. R. Pole, *Abraham Lincoln and the American Commitment* (Cambridge, 1966).

[14] The principal ones being J. R. Pole, *The Seventeenth Century: the Sources of Legislative Power* (Charlottesville, VA, 1969), a trenchant exploration of the development and foundations of legislative authority in Virginia and Massachusetts; J. R. Pole, *The Revolution in America: Documents of the Internal Development of America in the Revolutionary Era, 1754–1788* (London, 1970), a useful and extensive documentary collection; J. R. Pole, *Foundations of American Independence: 1763–1815* (Indianapolis, IN, 1972), an unusually well-designed textbook; J. R. Pole, *The Decision for American Independence* (Philadelphia, PA, 1975), a short documentary collection designed for American university students; and J. R. Pole, *The Idea of Union* (Alexandria, VA, 1977), a short but cogent account of the process by which the formerly disconnected colonies that came together to form the United States developed a sense of commonality during the era of the American Revolution.

privilege. At the same time, however, he also pointed out that by 1776 colonial societies were already deeply etched by great—and growing—economic and social inequalities within the free population, while the social chasm between that population and the rapidly rising number of black slaves was enormous. Moreover, he also found that relatively few free Americans saw much wrong with these inequalities and that the conception of equality in Revolutionary America did not extend much beyond equality of political and legal rights (for those entitled to such rights) in the English common-law tradition, equality of conscience in religion (primarily for Protestants), and, to a considerably lesser extent, equality of esteem (among free men).

As Jack made clear, the idea of equality was yet far from being a universal theory in America any more than in Europe. Nevertheless, he found that the egalitarian implications of the Revolution were sufficient to insure that the quest for equality would 'thenceforth . . . remain one of the most vital and magnetic forces in American life'. His principal contribution in this study was to trace with clarity and insight the shifting orientation of that quest from one generation to the next, from the gradual emergence between the Revolution and the era of Andrew Jackson of the relatively new notion of equality of opportunity; the growing commitment to the principle of equal protection under the law after the Civil War; the rapid subversion of that principle as it applied to Blacks over the next quarter century; the failure of women, like Blacks, to achieve genuine parity after the attainment of suffrage after the First World War; and the development after the Second World War among large segments of the population of a profound commitment to equality as a social goal to be achieved through various combinations of exhortations, legislation, and constitutional law.

Like *Political Representation*, however, *Pursuit of Equality* was not only a study in the history of ideas but also an exploration of the 'relationship of those ideas to social structure and political policies', and one of the most intriguing aspects of the book was Jack's analysis of the glaring discrepancy between America's unwavering public commitment to equality after 1776, and the relatively weak public concern to translate that commitment into policy. Jack cited a variety of reasons to explain why the American pursuit of equality was not more systematic and intense before the 1950s, but he kept coming back to one powerful underlying theme: the continuing predominance of the idea of incentive over the idea of equality in American culture. To an important degree, he suggested, the most important American contribution to the transformation of received views about social organisation during the eighteenth century was the conception—vivified by much actual example—of the social order as fluid rather than fixed, and based upon personal achievement through the exercise of individual talent and industry rather than upon ascribed rank or inherited and legally sanctioned social position. Inevitably, he showed, the high premiums Americans continued to put upon the virtually unfettered pursuit of individual goals produced ever-widening economic and social inequalities and acted as a powerful brake upon the emergence of a stronger and more comprehensive drive for equality.

In his later historical work, Jack never got very far away from the themes he explored in his two major books. In *The Gift of Government: from the English Restoration to American Independence* (Athens, GA, 1983), he returned to and treated more expansively problems that he had broached in *Political Representation*, usefully pushing them backward in time to the middle of the seventeenth century. In the early 1990s, he published a substantially enlarged and refined second edition of the *Pursuit of Equality*[15] and often endeavoured, without success, to interest publishers in issuing a revised version of *Political Representation*. And throughout the 1980s and 1990s, he published many valuable short essays on subjects relating to his earlier research, always with new materials, fresh insights, and his customary penetration.[16]

By the time he retired in 1989, however, Jack had already begun research on yet another large and difficult subject—the changing role of the law in Anglo-America from the seventeenth through the early nineteenth century. Noting the neglect of law by historians and its pursuit by lawyers as a specialised and largely self-contained subject, Jack believed that the legal process was so fundamental to the historical development of Britain and its American colonies that it was too important to be left entirely to legal scholars and that historians should give it a central place and endeavour thoroughly to integrate it into the fabric of the history of those places. Specifically, as he pursued this goal through research in

[15] J. R. Pole, *The Pursuit of Equality in American History*, 2nd edn. (Berkeley, CA, 1993).
[16] J. R. Pole, 'The politics of the word "state" and its relation to American sovereignty', *Parliaments, Estates and Representation*, 81.1 (1988), 1–10; J. R. Pole, 'Vocabolario Politico: notes on the word "state" in the Anglo-American tradition', *Il Pensiero Politico*, 21 (1988), 93–8; J. R. Pole, 'The ancient world in the new republic: the founders' use of history', in R. Kroes and E. Van De Bilt (eds.), *The U. S. Constitution After 200 Years* (Amsterdam, 1988), pp. 1–19; J. R. Pole, 'What is still vital in the political thought of the founders?', in R. C. Simmons (ed.), *The American Constitution: the First Two Hundred Years* (Manchester, 1989), pp. 203–24; and J. R. Pole, 'The individualist foundations of American constitutionalism', in H. Belz, R. Hoffman, and P. J. Albert (eds.), *To Form a More Perfect Union: the Critical Ideas of the Constitution* (Charlottesville, VA, 1992), pp. 73–106.

numerous libraries and archives in the eastern United States, he set out to study how various colonies adapted English common law to their peculiar situations, how it formed a central building block in their political and cultural constructions, and how it continued to inform the legal systems of American states long after they had become independent and leagued republics.

By the early 1990s, Jack thought he had become literate enough in American legal documents to accept an invitation to venture some of his tentative findings for a forum in the *William and Mary Quarterly,* the leading journal in his field. This forum consisted of Jack's thoughtful and surprisingly well-informed essay followed by three comments by legal history specialists. In his essay, Jack argued that colonial courts and juries were significant agents in colonial governance, that they founded their actions on common-law principles, that jury modification of those principles established local custom as community norms and therefore took on the character of local common law, and that this system throughout the states persisted well into the nineteenth century and was significantly less affected by the adoption of republican government than historians, taking at face value the words of contemporaries, had suggested. As trained legal experts, his commentators were rather critical, one of them remarking on his 'unfamiliarity with the law', pointing out a few errors in Jack's understanding of specific legal cases and legal terms, and complaining that his evidence derived from little more than 'an unsystematic rummaging through the papers of assorted lawyers and judges'. To the extent that this last charge was valid, however, Jack's citations showed that he had done a vast amount of rummaging, and his critics by and large did not so much challenge his central arguments as endeavour to qualify them.[17]

Although Jack continued to do research on this subject for another decade, the onset of the disease that debilitated him in his final years prevented him from ever fully pulling his materials together. His last book, *Contract & Consent: Representation and the Jury in Anglo-American Legal History* (Charlottesville, VA, 2010), was no more than a fragment of the large study he had initially envisioned and consisted of a series of loosely related essays on a wide range of topics subsumed under the title of the volume. Like all Jack's work, however, it represented a series of thoughtful

[17] J. R. Pole, 'Reflections on the law and the American Revolution', *William and Mary Quarterly*, 3rd ser., 50 (1993), 123–59; B. H. Mann, 'The evolutionary common law: a comment on J. R. Pole's 'Reflections', *William and Mary Quarterly*, 3rd ser., 50 (1993), 169–75; J. R. Pole, 'Further reflections on law and the American Revolution: a comment on the comments', *William and Mary Quarterly*, 3rd ser., 50 (1993), 594–9.

and informed ruminations that often challenged or qualified received wisdom and endeavoured to explore the relationship among ideas, institutions, and the political and social milieus in which they operated. Together, these essays made a strong case for the importance of courts, juries, and the common law as agencies of political representation and promulgators of law in America and for the continuities in legal culture from the colonial to the national era of American history. Certainly, it represented a strong step in his effort to bring the study of law into a central position in the analysis of the American past.

As the new century began, Jack was also hard at work producing a new edition of *The Federalist*, a substantial series of essays written by Alexander Hamilton, John Jay, and James Madison to explain the details and make the case for the ratification of the American national Constitution of 1787. Scholars had long used these essays as the single best index to the intentions of those who wrote the Constitution, and several modern editions of them had been published during the last four decades of the twentieth century. When Jack entered upon this project, his friends wondered why another edition was necessary and why he wanted to do it. The answer to those questions was immediately revealed upon publication of his edition in 2005. No previous edition had included such extensive annotations in which Jack used his extraordinary erudition to identify all historical references, quotations, and unidentified literary allusions, to clarify key concepts, and to explain contemporary uses of linguistic terms and uses. This feature of the book made it the richest edition of *The Federalist*, an impressive work of scholarship, and yet another significant contribution to the historical literature on the formation of the United States.[18]

Over the decades since Jack had introduced it to the United States American historical community, the concept of deference had been applied so widely and uncritically as to become little more than a caricature of Jack's early formulation, and several studies had shown that deference was more of an elite prescriptive aspiration than a description of an operational political and social system. In 1998, the *Journal of American History* published a round table discussion on 'Deference or defiance in eighteenth-century America?', in which five historians considered the continued utility of the concept.[19] Of these, Michael Zuckerman impressively

---

[18] Pole, *The Federalist*.
[19] J. R. Pole, 'Deference or defiance in eighteenth-century America?: a round table', *Journal of American History*, 85 (1998), 13–92.

pulled together a considerable amount of evidence to argue that the concept had little explanatory value for colonial American studies, in the process suggesting that Jack bore responsibility for later historians' abuse of the concept,[20] to which Jack, pleased at the critical attention his early effort continued to elicit nearly four decades after its initial publication, effectively took exception in a subsequent letter to the journal.[21]

A compulsive and careful writer, Jack by no means limited himself to the specialised historical work discussed in this memoir. During his career, he published thoughtful essays on American politics;[22] appreciative accounts of the achievements of several leading American historians, with all of whom he had had a close association;[23] various commentaries on contemporary intellectual and social issues;[24] and a few essays on cricket, one of his main passions.[25]

Beginning in the early 1980s, Jack's collaborations with me led to yet more publications. We first met in the early summer of 1961 when, having recently read one of my early articles and then visiting his in-laws in Pittsburgh, he drove over to meet with me in Cleveland, where I was then teaching at Western Reserve University. In his later years, Jack liked to muse that our decades-long friendship grew out of the fact that we both had the same given name, which forced us into endless explanations that Jack was not merely a nickname for John. As we quickly discovered, however, we also shared a deep interest in the history of governance in

[20] M. Zuckerman, 'Tocqueville, Turner, and turds: four stories of manners in early America', *Journal of American History*, 85 (1998), 13–42.

[21] J. R. Pole, 'A target respectfully returns the arrow', *Journal of American History*, 86 (1999), 1449–50.

[22] J. R. Pole, 'Forward from McCarthyism: the radical right and the conservative norm', *Political Quarterly*, 33 (1962), 196–207; J. R. Pole, 'The language of American politics', in L. Michaels and C. Ricks (eds.), *The State of Language* (Berkeley, CA, 1980), pp. 421–31.

[23] J. R. Pole, 'Daniel J. Boorstin', in M. Cunliffe and R. Winks (eds.), *Pastmasters* (New York, 1969), pp. 63–78; J. R. Pole, 'On C. Vann Woodward', *Journal of American Studies*, 32 (1988), 503–8; and J. R. Pole, 'Richard Hofstadter: the historian as critic', in R. A. Rutland (ed.), *Clio's Best: Leading Historians of the United States* (Columbia, MO, 2000), pp. 68–83.

[24] J. R. Pole, 'Misusage and abusage,' *Times Higher Educational Supplement*, 9 July 1989; J. R. Pole and F. N. L. Robinson, 'Mortuary science: a proposal', *Oxford Magazine*, 67 (1991); J. R. Pole, 'A bad case of agoraphobia: is there a market place of ideas', *Times Literary Supplement*, 4 Feb. 1994; J. R. Pole, 'Colour casting', *Oxford Magazine*, 80 (1992); J. R. Pole, 'A letter from Gamma Airlines', *Oxford Magazine*, 145 (1997); J. R. Pole, 'Freedom of speech: from privilege to right', in R. Cohen-Almagor (ed.), *Challenges to Democracy: Essays in Honour and Memory of Sir Isaiah Berlin* (Aldershot, 2000), pp. 11–54; and J. R. Pole, 'Letter from the Kingdom of Poland, Research Funding Council (1498) to Dr. Mickaus Kopemick', *Times Higher Educational Supplement*, 2 June 2000.

[25] J. R. Pole, 'Test cricket commentaries', *The Listener*, 17–24 Dec. 1981; J. R. Pole, 'Ramadhin and Valentine', *London Review of Books*, 13 Oct. 1988.

colonial British America and in the relationship among inherited ideas, social conditions, and institutional development. We shared as well a powerful conviction that the colonial world could only be fully understood as an extension of the transatlantic British world. And we were also profoundly secular and avid social networkers.

Whatever the explanation, the friendship grew as Jack generously helped my first doctoral student win a Fulbright Scholarship to University College London, and then guided him while he was in London. When in the early 1960s I undertook to edit a seven-volume text on American history, I enlisted Jack to write the volume covering the Revolution and the early national era, and, as a historical advisor to the Bicentennial Commission of the Thirteen Original American States, I helped them recruit Jack to write his book on the idea of union, which was intended as the first of thirteen volumes on the major themes that emerged out of the American Revolution. (Also, in the mid-1960s, St Martin's Press asked me to be a reader for Jack's first book, and in my anonymous report I qualified my great enthusiasm for its contents with a strong recommendation that it be thoroughly reorganised before publication. When the book appeared, however, the organisation was unchanged, and I never knew whether the press did not send it to him or whether he rejected my suggestions for reorganisation. This subject never came up for discussion, and Jack never knew that I had been a reader.)

During the mid-1970s, we became even closer as Jack visited the United States more regularly, and I spent the year 1975–6 at his old college in Oxford and at least part of almost every summer thereafter in London doing research. He often stopped by Baltimore as he was making his rounds of American archives, and I always made a point of seeing him for a few long visits when I was in the United Kingdom. Yet, our formal collaborations did not begin until 1979, just as he was moving to Oxford to take up his new chair.

Already by the early 1970s, the literature on colonial British American history had ballooned to such an extent that it was difficult for those in the field to stay on top of it, and with a large number of doctoral students at Johns Hopkins University, to which I moved in 1966, I made it a point of trying to do so. One always needs to be able to tell prospective historians in an era of prolific and exciting production in their field what they do *not* need to read, and I had been thinking for some years about organising a conference of experts among my peers, each of whom would take stock of where we had arrived in her or his individual area of expertise and make some suggestions about where we should go. While visiting my family and me at our house in the Aveyron in the summer of 1979, Jack talked at length about his plans to enhance American history study at Oxford by expanding its temporal range to include the colonial era and expressed his desire to do something dramatic that would direct attention to the growing significance of that area in American historical studies. When I outlined my idea for a small invitational conference on the state of the field, he immediately endorsed it.

Over the next two years, Jack and I proceeded to implement this idea. He got grants from the British Academy and Barclay's Bank International, and I got one from the National Endowment for the Humanities, and we recruited many of the leading scholars in the field to produce papers on the assigned topics. When it turned out that we needed a few thousand more dollars to pay the transportation and other costs for a week-long transatlantic conference, Jack, with his usual aplomb and without an appointment, walked into the Commonwealth Fund of New York, from which he had much earlier had a fellowship, and walked out of the door with a cheque for the sum required. Held at St Catherine's College in August 1981, this conference was memorable for those who attended, the papers being well-constructed and stimulating excellent discussions. Over the next few months, Jack and I edited these papers and published them with a joint introduction in a volume entitled *Colonial British America: Essays in the New History of the Early Modern Era* (Baltimore, MD, 1984). Having shared the editorial chores, we decided to divide the introduction into two distinct sections, one historiographical and the other theoretical, with each of us writing one. Jack took particular pleasure in thinking that no one would be able to tell which of us wrote which section; I don't think he ever told, and I never will. How much the conference and the book helped Jack in his successful campaign to extend the American history syllabus at Oxford is difficult to assess, but the book enjoyed a great success, many of the essays it contained being required reading in graduate seminars in colonial British American history for the next decade. More than once, Jack mused that this volume might well be the most successful book either of us would ever publish.

The success of this initial collaboration probably surprised us both equally. Only one of my few previous collaborations had turned out well, and Jack seems never even to have considered previously the possibility of collaborating on any project. But our collaboration rested on several important intellectual affinities. We were both transatlantic and comparative historians long before the concept of *Atlantic history* was invented. Although I had a deep interest in promoting transnational comparative studies of European colonies in the Americas, neither of us ever practised it in our empirical work. Nor did the fact that Jack's own empirical work focused on those colonies that would transform themselves into the United States prevent him from agreeing that it was anachronistic to study those colonies apart from the nineteen British American colonies in North America, the West Indies, and the Atlantic that did not separate from the British Empire in 1783 and that had formed part of the same political and cultural entity for the previous century and a half. Radical contextualists both, we inserted the words *British* and *Early Modern* into the title of our book to emphasise the situational and temporal divide before and after the imperial divorce that led to the creation of the United States.

Colonial British America would be the first of three collaborations. In response to an invitation from Blackwells, Jack and I edited *The Blackwell Encyclopedia of the American Revolution* (Oxford, 1991), which we designed in much the same manner as *Colonial British America*, dividing the subject to reflect the major areas of scholarly concern that had emerged in the previous forty years and making it as inclusive as space permitted. When Blackwells subsequently wanted to include this work in a new series, we took advantage of the opportunity to substitute a few newly authored entries for the weaker ones in the earlier version and to add several new ones. This new version was published as *The Blackwell Companion to the American Revolution* (Oxford, 2000). Our third collaboration was to serve as co-editors of a series of monographs published by Johns Hopkins University Press. Entitled *Early America: History, Context, and Culture*, this series produced ten substantial monographs between 1991 and 2005, when we both ceased our involvement in it. Although one reviewer naively condemned the *Blackwell Companion* because its many articles did not offer a coherent point of view, an objective neither possible nor desirable, Jack and I were satisfied that all of our collaborations had been useful contributions to the scholarship in our field.

Despite the emphasis in this memoir, it would be a grave mistake to measure Jack's contributions to historical study only in terms of his published work. Sequentially occupying key posts in London, Cambridge, and Oxford, he was particularly well-placed to promote and deepen the study of American history in the United Kingdom, and he certainly rose to the challenge. As his former Cambridge colleague Betty Wood observed in her remembrance of him, Jack 'did more, far more, than anyone else in the United Kingdom to ensure that early American history secured a firm foothold in British academe' and would go on 'to thrive during the 1980s and 1990s'.[26] As she pointed out, Jack's influence was critical in the establishment of the British Group in Early American History, an organisation founded in the early 1990s and now having an international membership running into the hundreds. At its annual meeting in 2010, this organisation organised a round table to commemorate his influence in early American history.

But Jack's influence also extended well into United States history. In May 1995, a two-day conference hosted by Anthony J. Badger and designed to honour Jack convened at Sidney Sussex College, Cambridge. Several of Jack's friends and former graduate students presented papers on the emergence of an American national political culture, a subject to which Jack had made many substantial contributions. The core of the audience and most of the presenters were drawn from the twenty-three doctoral students he had guided through their D.Phils., fifteen at Cambridge and eight at Oxford.[27] Many of them, in evidence of Jack's strong international reputation, had come from the United States specifically to study with him, and over half of them had written on nineteenth-century United States history. This conference also drew many friends and former colleagues at both Cambridge and Oxford, scholars who worked in Jack's field, and at least one of his former undergraduates. In his opening remarks, Badger stressed Jack's contribution as an exacting and caring teacher, who had, he said, been 'an inspiration and a role model to a new generation of American historians in Britain who endeavoured', like Jack, 'to write monographs as carefully researched as their counterparts in the United States, on topics in domestic United States history . . . and to be published in the United States'. As Badger pointed out, Jack established vigorous seminars at both Cambridge and Oxford in which he 'introduced British students of America . . . to the importance of careful and extensive archival research' and 'of getting known in the United States, attending conferences, and being networked to . . . leading American scholars'.[28]

Jack was indeed a model for such behaviour. His networking in the United States was legendary. Sometime in the 1950s, he met Richard Hofstadter, whom Jack regarded as the best American historian of his generation, and they formed a friendship that lasted until Hofstadter's

---

[26] B. Wood, 'A British colleague's memories of Jack Pole,' *Uncommon Sense* #128 (2010).
[27] For a complete list of Jack's completed doctoral students, see Starr, *Articulating America*, pp. 267–8.
[28] A. J. Badger, 'Preface', in ibid., p. x.

death in 1970, and this was not unusual. He established close relationships with many of the leading American historians of the last half of the twentieth century, often showing himself to be an exceptionally generous friend to his American associates when they came to the United Kingdom. Two of those associates, Joyce Appleby and J. G. A. Pocock, two other transatlantic historians, contributed essays to his Festschrift, which otherwise consisted of papers presented by Jack's former students and me at the Sidney Sussex College conference. Edited by Rebecca Starr, one of Jack's early doctoral students at Oxford, the volume, entitled *Articulating America: Fashioning a National Political Culture in Early America: Essays in Honor of J. R. Pole* (Lanham, MD, 2000), constituted a fitting tribute to Jack's career as an American historian.

My friendship with Jack did not extend far enough beyond our mutual professional interests to say much about his private side. Of course, no one could be around Jack for very long without discovering his obsession with cricket, including the avidity with which he followed Test matches and his role in co-founding, with David Cairns, the Trojan Wanderers, a cricket club for which he played well into his 70s and which survives him. But I never met any of his non-academic friends and met his wife Marilyn Mitchell only once, in the early 1960s, and possibly on the same occasion his son Nicholas and two daughters, Ilsa and Lucy. Ilsa has been especially helpful in constructing this memoir.[29] Sometime in the late 1990s, I began to notice that Jack seemed to have some slight physical—but absolutely no mental—impairment, but I never inquired why, and it was his friend Janet Wilson, not Jack, who first told me that he was suffering from Parkinson's Disease, almost a decade after he was diagnosed with it in the mid-1990s. By the middle of the last decade, this disease had stopped his annual pilgrimages to the United States and, as I was spending less time in the United Kingdom, I saw much less of him and was never in Oxford long enough to see more than a few of the paintings he produced in the years of his later retirement or to read any of the novel that he ultimately decided not to publish.

Jack's death on 31 January 2010, was followed by obituaries in *The Guardian* (4 March 2010), *The Daily Telegraph* (9 March 2010), *The Independent* (9 March 2010), and *The Times Higher Education Supplement* (8 April 2010). On 12 June 2010, his family and many of his friends and colleagues gathered at St Catherine's College for a memorial service, and

---

[29] Married in 1952 in the United States, Jack and Marilyn lived separately from the mid-1970s until their marriage was dissolved in 1988. Marilyn died in 2006.

several of them spoke eloquently and affectionately about him and his accomplishments over a long and productive life. Like them, I retain many fond memories of our long association and, with many of Jack's other American colleagues and intellectual protégés, a deep appreciation for his many profound contributions to the analysis of the American past.

JACK P. GREENE
Johns Hopkins University

Note.   I wish to thank Joyce O. Appleby, Ilsa Pole, Lucy Pole, Nicholas Pole, Rebecca Starr, Janet Wilson, and Betty Wood for help in constructing this memoir.

GRAHAM REYNOLDS

Arthur Graham Reynolds
1914–2013

GRAHAM REYNOLDS (the 'Arthur' was firmly suppressed from an early age) was born in Highgate on 10 January 1914. His father, Arthur T. Reynolds, a monumental mason, made the tombstones and crosses for Highgate cemetery, priding himself on his lettering. When Graham was about ten, his father died as the result of a war wound and his mother, Eva (née Mullins), daughter of a bank clerk, married Percy Hill, a property manager, who became mayor of Holborn in the 1930s. He was, according to Reynolds, a 'bad tempered brute', but he had the saving grace of having acquired a collection of mezzotints which provided the beginnings of a visual education in the home. Furthermore, the family's move to 82 Gower Street, so near to the British Museum, encouraged Graham's early interest in art.

From Grove House Lodge, a local preparatory school, he obtained a scholarship to Highgate School. The years there were largely unmemorable, except for the fact that one of the teachers was descended from Sir George Beaumont, Constable's patron. At school, as he later recollected, he did not suffer unduly from being known as 'the brain' and 'the swot'. In 1932, he went to Cambridge on a maths scholarship at Queens' College. After the first year he switched to English, but something of the mathematician's precision remained with him all his life. He used to say that if there had been a faculty of art history in Cambridge at the time, he would have joined that. In the event he was pleased he had chosen English, not least because he later heard that Eric Maclagan, Director of the Victoria and Albert Museum when he applied for a post there, would not allow any student from the Courtauld Institute—then offering the only art history degree course in England—to be placed on the short list for new appointments. A breakdown in 1934 led to a stay at the Maudsley Hospital, but did not

Biographical Memoirs of Fellows of the British Academy, XIII, 405–414. © The British Academy 2014.

prevent Graham achieving a first class degree in English in the following year. His interest in art was more fully aroused by the exhibition of British Art at the Royal Academy and by visits to the Fitzwilliam Museum where he came to admire the work of the director, C. R. Cockerell.

By this time he had formed the decision to try for a museum post and, while submitting job applications, he sought the advice of Arthur M. Hind, Keeper of Prints and Drawings at the British Museum. Hind's advice was simple: 'if you want to read the art historical literature, you must learn German', and so Reynolds spent the next six months as an exchange student with a German family in Cologne. It was, he recollected, an education not only in German but also in opera.

Career

His first employment was a nine months stint working on military range tables at Woolwich Arsenal, a post he obtained thanks to his Part I of the mathematics tripos. A breakthrough in attaining his chosen career followed in 1937 when he was successful in the competition for an Assistant Keepership in the Department of Engraving, Illustration and Design (EID) and Paintings at the Victoria and Albert Museum. The name EID served to distinguish the collection from the Prints and Drawings Department at the British Museum. There was no shortage of Rembrandt etchings and old master drawings, but the distinctive character of the department lay in its links with the decorative arts collections of the Museum. Ornament prints—which served as patterns for artists from the fifteenth to the nineteenth centuries—preparatory drawings for architecture and the decorative arts, and commercial graphics from posters and trade cards to Christmas cards and valentines formed the staple of the collection. The keeper of the whole department was James Laver, an authority on the history of fashion and then widely known as the author of the popular novel and success- ful musical *Nymph Errant*. In 1938, with the appointment of John Pope- Hennessy to the Paintings branch of the department, Reynolds did his apprenticeship on the Prints and Drawings side.

With war on the horizon in the summer of 1939, the staff turned to packing up the collections and Reynolds remembered the installation of cases in the vaults at Bradford on Avon and the bricking up of the Raphael cartoons in the area of the Poynter and Morris rooms on the ground floor of the Museum. Once the war started, he was seconded to the Ministry of Home Security, a branch of the Home Office. This work gave him an introduction to administra- tive competence. As he was later to put it: 'this experience taught me that there is no necessary conflict between the pursuit of art history and the ability to run a department'. He was also a member of the London Civil Defence Region (1939–45) and it was there that he met a teleprinter operator, Daphne, daughter of Thomas Dent a photographer in Huddersfield and herself a former student at the Huddersfield College of Art. They were married in 1943 and it is no exaggeration to say that Daphne remained a tower of strength for him throughout his life, until her death in 2002.

Back at the V&A, now under the directorship of Leigh Ashton, in late 1945, Reynolds was on hand for the re-installation of the collections at South Kensington, not least of the Raphael cartoons which were installed in their present spacious location. With the departure of Pope-Hennessy to the Sculpture Department and of Carl Winter, Deputy Keeper of the department, to be director of the Fitzwilliam Museum, Reynolds undertook the organisation of the Nicholas Hilliard and Isaac Oliver exhibition in 1947, one of the first major exhibitions after the Museum reopened. He took up the expertise on portrait miniatures from Carl Winter who had himself learnt from Basil Long, author of what has remained the basic reference work on the subject. It was a connoisseurial expertise based on a highly detailed study of stylistic character-istics, almost on lines propagated by Giovanni Morelli (1816–91) who had claimed that artists' treatment of anatomical details, such as hands or ears, could supply proof of authorship. Reynolds had his own exactitude of observa-tion: 'Look at the cross hatching behind the left ear; you can see that this miniature is by Bogle,' as he once explained to the present writer. For the 1947 exhibition, he was able to assemble 108 works attributed to Hilliard and 84 attributed to Oliver and it was a cause of satisfaction to him that these attribu-tions have remained generally accepted. Only occasionally was he called upon to defend his attributions. When, in a later exhibition, Roy Strong attributed Hilliard's *Young Man against a Background of Flames* (V&A) to Isaac Oliver, Reynolds described this as a 'most flagrant misjudgment' and his view has been widely accepted ('The English miniature of the renaissance: a "rediscovery" examined', *Apollo*, 118 (Oct. 1983), 308–11).

After Winter's departure in 1947, Reynolds was promoted to Deputy Keeper of Paintings and it was on the departmental collections that his expertise, his scholarship and his publications were based. The gift of John Sheepshanks in 1857 had founded a collection particularly strong in early Victorian painting which was first curated by Richard Redgrave, painter and historian. The scale and quality of the Sheepshanks gift led to other gifts and bequests, most notably that of Isabel Constable, Constable's youngest surviving daughter, in 1888. Indeed, until the foundation of the Tate Gallery in 1897, the South Kensington Museum held the national collection of British paintings and, although it ceased to acquire oil paintings after 1900, it remained the national collection of portrait miniatures and British watercolours. In due course, Reynolds became the internationally acknowledged expert in all these areas. Already in these early years, he was the principal contributor to the department's publication of its holdings, publishing small picture books on *Portrait Miniatures* (London, 1948), *Elizabethan Art* (London, 1948), *Victorian Painting* (London, 1948), *French Painting* (London, 1949) and *Constable* (London, 1950).

The post-war installation of the Museum under Leigh Ashton's inspiration had divided the display into 'Primary' galleries—a chronological arrangement of mixed media drawn from all departments—and 'Study' collections—in which displays remained by material. But it was only under Ashton's successor, Trenchard Cox (Director 1955–66), that a new home was found for the paintings. This was achieved by building over the south court and it was Reynolds's contribution to install the splendid display which opened in 1956. The new Paintings galleries (rooms 101–4) consisted of separate sections for Constable, eighteenth- to nineteenth-century British paintings, watercolours and the Constantine Alexander Ionides collection of old master paintings, which was shown as a separate unit in line with the terms of the bequest. Constable, of course, was everyone's favourite but, to a growing body of opinion, the early Victorian pictures—works by Mulready, Landseer, C. R. Leslie and William Collins, among others—after suffering decades of derision, were again seen as worthy of respect. Carel Weight, then Professor of Painting at the Royal College of Art, was said to have made a daily pilgrimage to the newly opened galleries, in particular to enjoy the nineteenth-century works.

With the retirement of James Laver in 1959, Reynolds was promoted Keeper of the Department of EID (changed to Prints & Drawings—P&D—in 1961) and Paintings, a post he held until the end of 1974. He had distinguished deputies in the two branches of the department—Brian Reade for P&D and Jonathan Mayne for Paintings—but it was Reynolds who provided the drive and the insistence on the maintenance of high standards of scholarship, curatorial practice and public service. Staff numbers were increased to allow for the cataloguing of some 2,000 new acquisitions a year, an essential task to give readers in the Print Room ready access to recently acquired material. The maintenance of the Print Room service was central to the department: entry was unrestricted and it served some 7,000 visitors a year.

Temporary exhibitions formed another key part of the departmental activity: the fragility of works on paper meant that these were newly installed three or four times a year. Reynolds himself was responsible for several of these, including those devoted to the work of two living artists, *The Engravings of S. W. Hayter* (London, 1967) and *The Etchings of Anthony Gross* (London,

1968), to which he wrote extensive monographs. Two departmental exhibitions in particular, both curated by Brian Reade, turned out to be trend setting for the taste of the 1960s: *Art Nouveau and Alphons Mucha* (1963) and *Aubrey Beardsley* (1966). Censorship was still in force and the Beardsley exhibition was vetted by the Metropolitan Police to ensure that no legal offence could be caused.

During the whole of his period as Keeper, Reynolds was assiduous in expanding the department's collections. Partly through the example of Daphne, herself a distinguished painter working in an abstract style in the 1960s, Graham evolved a lively interest in contemporary art and devoted his energies to making acquisitions in the fields of twentieth-century prints, drawings and watercolours. This became a commonplace in the 1970s but in the post-war period, when the Tate Gallery lacked a Print Room and the British Museum had little interest in contemporary material, only the V&A, among national museums, was active in this field. A modern print fund of £750 a year was set up for routine purchases; special funding had to be sought for acquisitions of prints by artists of the stature of Munch, Picasso and Matisse. Typical of many print lovers of his generation, he cared little for silkscreen prints and it was left to the Circulation Department to acquire most of these for the Museum in the 1960s. For watercolours and gouaches, the main acquisitions were of contemporary British artists from Nash and Burra to Hilton and Scott, while outstanding works by, for example, Nolde, Kokoschka and Klee were bought to provide an international context.

As Keeper of the department, Reynolds worked with great efficiency and dispatch. In his dealings with his staff, he maintained the fairly strict sense of hierarchy which he had inherited from the Civil Service tradition of his time. Members of grades junior to Assistant Keeper may have found him somewhat aloof, but this was due partly to his shyness and natural reserve and it was compensated by his absolute sense of fairness. There were definitely no favourites, and he was held in great respect by the whole department.

In 1967 he was invited by Robert L. Herbert to undertake a semester's teaching at Yale: a course on nineteenth-century British painting for undergraduates and a seminar on Constable for graduate students. It was not a happy experience: 'I have no talent for teaching and found the atmosphere at Yale stifling,' as he later said. The experience was made worse by the fact that Daphne took one look at New Haven and departed to Arizona and New Mexico to paint more exotic landscapes. Back at the V&A, Graham made another notable contribution to the Museum's major exhibitions: *Charles Dickens. An Exhibition to Commemorate the Centenary of his Death* (1970). It was centred on the bequest to the Museum in 1876 of John Forster, Dickens's friend and biographer, which included what is still the largest collection in the world of original Dickens manuscripts. Dickens specialists, headed by Kathleen Tillotson, were called in to advise, but the exhibition remained Reynolds's brain child, born, as he said, during his stay at New Haven in 1967 when re-reading Dickens provided a much needed leisure activity. The exhibition and the extensive catalogue represented a joint venture by the Museum Library and the Prints and Drawings Department under Reynolds's supervision.

During these years, he established a reasonably good working relation-ship with the new director, John Pope-Hennessy. The two had been colleagues since 1938 and he never allowed himself to be bullied by Pope-Hennessy's imperious ways. Relations with Roy Strong, director from January 1974, were less harmonious and Reynolds retired at the end of that year, just ahead of his sixty-first birthday. After retirement, he took on numerous honorary posts including the chairmanship of Gainsborough's House Society (1977–9), membership of the Advisory Council of the Paul Mellon Centre for Studies in British Art (1977–84) and of the Reviewing Committee on the Export of Works of Art (1984–90), and the Hon. Keepership of Portrait Miniatures at the Fitzwilliam Museum (1994–2013). He organised Constable exhibitions in Australia and New Zealand (1973), New York (1984) and Tokyo (1986) and he was advisor to David Thomson in the establishment of his Constable Archive in the 1990s. He was awarded an OBE in 1984 in recognition of a Constable exhibition he had organised in New York, a CVO in 2000 for his work on the royal collection of portrait miniatures, and he was elected to a Senior Fellowship of the British Academy in 1993.

Graham Reynolds's expertise over the whole range of his department's holdings has not been remotely rivalled before or since. Retirement allowed him more time for research and writing and, as will be seen in the discussion of his publications, the number of books published in the 1980s and 1990s was truly astonishing. Graham and Daphne lived at 24 Cheyne Walk in the 1940s, at The Logs Cottage, Well Road, Hampstead in the 1950s, and from about 1968 in Airlie Gardens, Notting Hill Gate. Upon retirement, they moved to a beautiful, if rather isolated, new home in Bradfield St George, near Bury St Edmunds, where they had had a week-end retreat since 1964. For a time they also had a pied-à-terre in London so that the move only briefly interfered with their busy social life.

Graham's natural shyness and reserve, modified doubtless under Daphne's influence, in no way prevented him from being a popular figure among a wide circle of friends. Apart from his V&A colleagues, these included, to name only a few, Denys Sutton, long time editor of *Apollo*; Eric and Stella Newton; Anthony Gross and Birgit Skiold among print makers; the painters Vera Cuningham,

Edward Wolfe, Adrian Heath and Patrick Heron; and, among other museum colleagues, John Gere, Carlos van Hasselt and Christopher White. Friendships were also formed with literary figures, for example, Sonia Orwell and, in particular, with Angus Wilson and his partner Tony Garrett who were near neighbours in Suffolk. Partly, perhaps, because they had no children, the Reynolds socialised a great deal. And if Daphne was known for her outspoken jollity and peals of laughter, Graham could display a sharp wit with stories that were often hilariously and wickedly funny. For friends in need, they showed a warmly compassionate and active regard which was deeply appreciated by those concerned.

Publications

His publications began with a popular introduction to *Twentieth Century Drawings* (London, 1946) followed by the catalogue of the exhibition *Nicholas Hilliard and Isaac Oliver* (London, 1947, 2nd edn. 1971) which has remained a standard work on the subject. His interest in portrait miniatures was maintained throughout his life; his concise account of the subject *English Portrait Miniatures* (London, 1952) was republished in a revised edition in 1988, a clear indication of its lasting value as an account of the life and work of the principal practitioners. After his retirement there followed the *Catalogue of Miniatures, Wallace Collection* (London, 1980), *European Miniatures in the Metropolitan Museum of Art* (New York, 1996), *British Portrait Miniatures, Fitzwilliam Museum* (Cambridge, 1998) and, finally, the catalogue of *The Sixteenth and Seventeenth Century Miniatures in the Collection of Her Majesty the Queen* (London, 1999) on which he had worked intermittently since the 1950s. It describes 447 miniatures, each reproduced in colour, and provides a splendid overview of the subject. British artists and Continental artists working in England, including Horenbout, Holbein, Hilliard, Oliver, Hoskins and Cooper, are particularly well represented, and there are also over fifty enamels by Jean Petitot, providing the largest group of colour reproductions of his work.

During the late 1940s he was still producing short popular surveys: *Van Gogh* (London, 1947) and *Nineteenth Century Drawings 1850–1950* (London, 1949), but there was also a more detailed study of the wood engraver *Thomas Bewick. A Resumé of his Life and Work* (London, 1949) and an *Introduction to English Water-Colour Painting* (London, 1950, rev. edn. 1988), based on his Ferens Fine Art lecture at the University of Hull, which indicated his increasing specialisation on late-eighteenth- and nineteenth-century British art. But it was his *Painters of the Victorian Scene* (London, 1953) which showed him to be a true pioneer. The revival of interest in Victorian painting may be traced back to the Robin Ironside and John Gere study of the *Pre-Raphaelite Painters* (1948) and to the W. P. Frith exhibition at the Whitechapel Gallery curated by Jonathan Mayne in 1951, but it did not take off until the V&A exhibition of Victorian art, organised by Peter Floud, Keeper of the Circulation Department, in 1959. At this early stage, Reynolds was at pains to explain that he was not writing a history of the subject. The purpose of the book, he explained, was 'to assemble and discuss a body of reproductions of pictures in which the contemporary Victorian scene is portrayed in recognizable exactness'. Among the social topics discussed were the depictions of order, self-control, material prosperity, graciousness and rigid class distinction.

This was followed by a fuller survey of the subject, *Victorian Painting* (London, 1966, 2nd edn. 1987). The general introduction was brief; the bulk of the text was contained in the detailed descriptive notes to the individual pictures reproduced. This survey of the different branches of Victorian art, principally genre and landscape, led to the conclusion that, at least before the last decades of the century, it was essentially insular, 'an indigenous, self propagating, ingrowing and original species'.

Reynolds continued to write widely on nineteenth-century British painting, with commissioned books on *Turner* (London, 1969) and a *Concise History of Watercolours* (London, 1971) which provided the subject with an international context; but it is for his work on Constable that his name will remain most closely associated. As with his other interests, the connection originated in the Museum's collection of paintings and drawings. This was founded by the gift of John Sheepshanks, who had known Constable from 1829, which included six paintings, most famously *Boat Building near Flatford Mill* (1815) and *Salisbury Cathedral from the Bishop's Grounds* (1823), and augmented by two key works, the full-scale sketches for the *Haywain* and the *Leaping Horse* from the collection of Henry Vaughan which were loaned in 1862 and bequeathed in 1900.

It was this core collection, together with her preference for rural South Kensington over the grime of Trafalgar Square, that persuaded Isabel Constable to make her munificent gift of the remaining contents of her father's studio to the Museum in 1888. It included oil paintings, sketches, watercolours, drawings and sketch books and accounted for 390 of the 418 entries in Graham Reynolds, *Victoria & Albert Museum, Catalogue of the Constable Collection* (London, 1960, 2nd edn. 1973). A model of museum cataloguing, this work formed the basis and set the standard of his future publications on the subject. It was followed by a narrative account *Constable the Natural Painter* (London, 1965) and it ultimately led to his contract with Yale University Press, acting for the Paul Mellon Centre for Studies in British Art, to write the second volume of the full oeuvre catalogue *The Later Paintings and Drawings of John Constable* (2 vols., New

Haven, CT, 1984) covering the years 1817 to 1837, for which he was awarded the Mitchell Prize. He acknowledged his debt to Leslie Parris, Ian Fleming-Williams and Conal Shields whose exhibition at the Tate Gallery celebrating the bicentenary of Constable's birth in 1976 was seen as the principal contribution to questions of attribution since his V&A catalogue. In particular, he mentioned their success in separating the works of his son Lionel from Constable's oeuvre. Volume I of the Yale catalogue was intended to be contributed by Charles Rhyne, professor at Reed College, Portland, Oregon. When he dropped out, Reynolds took on the task, aided by Rhyne's notes, and it was published as *The Earlier Paintings and Drawings of John Constable* (2 vols., New Haven, CT, 1996) covering the years 1790 to 1816.

These catalogues are awesome in their completeness. Close examination of the V&A collection had provided hitherto unnoticed dates which established a framework for the artist's career and a working method for the oeuvre catalogues. Exhaustive discussion of date, subject, versions, attribution and provenance, as well as links with Constable's correspondence and other contemporary sources, will render them standard works of reference for the foreseeable future. The editorial tasks for such a venture—the two catalogues had 1,087 and 1,465 illustrations respectively—were formidable and Reynolds always spoke warmly of the editorial team at the Yale Press, notably Faith Hart, Gillian Malpass and Guilland Sutherland. At the heart of these volumes was his own connoisseurial knowledge of the subject and his meticulous attention to detail in laying out the facts for his readers.

To quote from just one example, the entry for a small picture of Gillingham Mill, painted for John Fisher, Archdeacon of Salisbury, in the Fitzwilliam Museum (Vol. II, p. 135, No. 24.4), which is inscribed on the back, not in Constable's or Fisher's hand, 7 June 1824:

> In a letter which Constable received on 2 June 1824 Fisher told him that he planned to be in London on 14 June and would visit him. He accordingly determined to complete a small picture of Gillingham Mill for which Fisher had paid him when last in town (Corr., VI, p. 163). In spite of the date recorded on the back of No. 24.4 it was not entirely finished on 7 June, since Constable noted in his diary for 17 June: 'Came home and set to work on Fisher's picture—which I did very well' (Corr., VI, p. 165). It was ready the following Sunday when Constable wrote in his diary: 'Fisher took away his little picture of the Mill with a frame'. (Corr., VI, p. 166)

It is fair to say that, for good or ill, these great works do not take issue with the changing interests in the treatment of English landscape painting, particularly in the new emphasis on social concerns, which were coming to the fore in the 1970s to 1980s as Reynolds was writing his first volume. To take one example, Michael Rosenthal (*Constable: the Painter and his Landscape*, New Haven, CT,

1983) suggested that Constable's change of style in the mid-1820s was directly linked with his expressed concern at the riots of 1822 in East Anglia, caused by the continued agricultural depression. Reynolds could not have taken this on, as his book was published in the same year, but he remained adamant that there was insufficient evidence for such speculation: 'If Constable was influenced in his work by agricultural riots, he would have said so in his correspondence' was the curt end to any such discussion.

Yet Rosenthal was respected as a bona fide Constable specialist; Reynolds's real ire was reserved for the avowed practitioners of the 'new' art history. In his review of a book entitled *The New Art History*, edited by A. L. Rees and F. Borzello (*Apollo*, Oct. 1986, pp. 182–3), he turned savagely on those who claimed that 'words like connoisseurship, quality, style and genius have become taboo, utterable . . . only with scorn or mirth'. He took it as an attack on all that his work stood for, and he could not imagine that the subject could ultimately benefit from the questioning nature of these ideas. He was not alone in taking an uncompromising stand in the 1980s when the battle lines were firmly drawn; it was not until the following decade that there was more of an accommodation among the diverse practitioners of the subject.

Graham Reynolds was busy writing on portrait miniatures and on Constable well into his nineties. He contributed an essay for the catalogue of the exhibition of *Constable's Skies* in New York in 2004 and he remained an adviser to David Thomson both for his collection and his Constable Archive. His long term interest in both mathematics and English also survived into his last decade when he was writing, to quote his own words, 'fifty palindromes and fifty algorisms for my hundredth birthday'. In the event, a slim volume of his poems entitled *Symmetries* was published posthumously for private circulation in 2013. Meanwhile, both the Victoria and Albert Museum and the Royal Academy had been planning exhibitions of Constable's work in honour of Reynolds's centenary—a mark of distinction rarely achieved by a long retired museum curator. He died on 6 October 2013, just three months short of his hundredth birthday.

MICHAEL KAUFFMANN
Fellow of the Academy

Note. I am grateful to Christopher White for corrections and suggestions. For a recent interview with Graham Reynolds, see Felicity Owen, 'Art and Delight', *Apollo*, June 2005, pp. 78–81. Graham himself wrote an account of Daphne's work, *Daphne Reynolds. A Memoir* (Bradfield St George, 2007).

TOM TORRANCE

Thomas Forsyth Torrance
1913–2007

T. F. TORRANCE was one of the most capable and widely influential Scottish divines of the second half of the twentieth century. Possessed of seemingly limitless drive and industry, he deployed his energies over a long and remarkably full career in a number of spheres. He was an authoritative exponent of Christian doctrine, a pioneer in the conversation between theology and the natural sciences, a senior figure in the Church of Scotland and in the international ecumenical movement, and the *animateur* of all manner of scholarly and collaborative projects. To all his activities he brought the same qualities which characterise his prodigious literary output: concentration, seriousness of purpose, acute intelligence, decisiveness and vivid Christian conviction.

I

Torrance was born in China on 30 August 1913 to missionary parents working for the American Bible Society in Chengdu, the capital of Sichuan province. His father, Thomas senior (1871–1959), a Scottish Presbyterian from Lanark, went to China in 1896 under the auspices of the China Inland Mission, moving to Bible Society work after the 1910 Edinburgh Missionary Conference. In 1911 he married Annie Sharpe, an Anglican mission worker who had been in China since 1907. T. F. Torrance was their second child and first son; two more boys and two more girls were to follow, all the boys taking Presbyterian orders and all the girls marrying ministers.

Biographical Memoirs of Fellows of the British Academy, XIII, 417–436. © The British Academy 2014.

During the period of Thomas senior's service in China, foreign missionaries faced considerable hostility from the conservative element of the imperial regime and from other nationalists, and they and their converts were routinely subject to violence, of which the massacres by Boxer militants at the turn of the century were only the most extreme instance. Nevertheless, in later life Torrance looked back with gratitude to his early formation in a missionary household, with its warm biblical piety, the closeness of those who were foreigners in an exotic culture, the proximity of danger and the lived sense of the operations of providence, as well as the adventurousness and freedom from narrow suburban routine. More than anything, it made belief in God entirely natural, not something acquired by laborious dealing with doubt, and it bequeathed to Torrance a permanently missionary attitude and vocation.

Torrance received his early education at a Canadian Missionary School in Chengdu, but in 1927 the family returned to Scotland to improve the children's educational prospects. Torrance senior went back to China shortly afterwards for a last spell of missionary work, returning finally in 1934 just before the Maoist revolution swept away most of the work of Western missionaries (not all, however: when Torrance returned to China in old age, he found remnants of his father's activities). The family in Scotland was left in the hands of Torrance's mother, a purposeful and intelligent woman for whose virtues he had the highest esteem. At first they settled in Bellshill, a grim area in the depth of recession; Torrance attended Bellshill Academy, working hard to catch up on Latin and Greek. Then in 1931 they all moved to Edinburgh when Torrance began his studies at the University in classical languages and philosophy, registering for the ordinary degree to shorten his course and ease the family's financial burdens.

Torrance's intention was a first degree in Arts before proceeding to New College for Divinity studies in preparation for missionary work. He was a zealous undergraduate. Finding it hard to compete in Latin, Greek and Ancient History, he opted for courses in classical and modern philosophy under A. E. Taylor and Kemp Smith, began study of early church history and theology, and delved into the philosophy of science; a course in geography was later regretted. In an unpublished autobiographical account from his retirement years, Torrance presented his undergraduate self already assembling a set of philosophical and theological judgements and attitudes which would stay with him for the rest of his career: he never seriously qualified his early antipathy to Augustine and Schleiermacher, for example. Even when one allows for some retrospective simplification and imposition of order, the picture that emerges is one of remarkable intellectual energy, as well as of an early instinct for synthesis which became so strong in his published writings.

Torrance's sense of missionary vocation remained firm throughout his undergraduate career. Like other missionary children he was much involved in student mission work through the Evangelistic Association; the Torrance family flat in Edinburgh became a centre for student gatherings. He was awarded the MA in 1934, and moved to New College to study for the BD. Founded after the Disruption in 1843 as the college of the Free Church of Scotland, New College merged with the University Faculty of Divinity from 1929, when the United Free Church and the Church of Scotland became a single denomination, though the merger was not completed until 1935. Alongside institutional transformation, New College in the 1930s was a place where the theological shifts in Continental Protestantism associated with the Swiss theologian Karl Barth were being registered. Though Torrance specialised in systematic theology, he also immersed himself in biblical studies, warming to the theological and devotional exegesis of Norman Porteous in Old Testament and William Manson in New Testament. (Torrance would later edit a posthumous collection of Manson's writings.) He learned a good deal from Daniel Lamont, who taught apologetics and encouraged Torrance's nascent interest in thinking theologically about natural science. He was much less enthusiastic about John Baillie, Professor of Divinity and one of the last and most distinguished representatives of the moderate liberal Protestant trend in Scottish theology. Torrance thought Baillie's lectures marred by Kantianism and lacking in commitment to divine revelation.

Most of all, Torrance was captivated by the teaching and example of H. R. Mackintosh, Professor of Systematic Theology. Mackintosh knew liberal Protestantism from the inside: he had studied in Marburg with Wilhelm Herrmann (also Barth's revered teacher), and translated Schleiermacher and Ritschl. In lectures and writing, however, he espoused an *evangelisch* version of Christian doctrine increasingly at odds with his teachers, emphasising the primacy of divine revelation and the inseparability of teaching about incarnation and teaching about God. All this was calculated to attract Torrance's attention in a way which Baillie's patient correlations of Christian faith and theism were not able to do. In his closing years at New College, Mackintosh was strongly drawn to the work of Barth and communicated his enthusiasm to Torrance, thereby awakening a life-long dedication.

In 1936 Torrance was awarded the Blackie Travelling Fellowship for a term, enabling him to travel in the Middle East, determined to see and do everything. The trip proved adventurous in a rather John Buchan style (amongst other things, he was caught up in Arab–Jewish conflict in Palestine and arrested in Bosnia). While in Syria, Torrance heard the news of Mackintosh's sudden death. He returned to New College for a final year, graduating *summa cum laude* and receiving the Aitken Fellowship for postgraduate research. Henceforth his missionary vocation was to be enacted in academia, and he set off for Basle and doctoral studies under Barth, recently returned to his native city after expulsion from his post in Bonn.

II

Torrance spent only one year in Basle, but the impact of his time under Barth's supervision was immense. He heard Barth lecturing on the doctrine of God (the material would be published as *Church Dogmatics* II/1), attended Barth's seminar on the natural theology of Vatican I, and secured entry into Barth's smaller *Sozietät*, where the privileged group studied Wollebius's *Compendium* (a classic of early seventeenth-century Reformed scholastic theology). Torrance wanted to write a dissertation which would explicate the Trinitarian and Christological structure of Christian dogmatics in relation to the theology of grace; Barth wisely trimmed his ambitions and set him to work on the doctrine of grace in the apostolic fathers of the second century.

The period in Basle reinforced the theological convictions learned from Mackintosh and others, and deepened his admiration for Barth's theological achievement. After a year, however, his doctoral studies were interrupted when Auburn Seminary in upstate New York approached him to teach for a year (Baillie, who had taught at Auburn in the 1920s, had recommended him). The choice of teaching over continuing immersion in doctoral work is characteristic: he relished a busy, external vocation, even if it meant forgoing the opportunity to acquire advanced scholarly training. From the beginning, Torrance's intellectual powers were more those of the innovative thinker and advocate than those of the pure *Wissenschaftler*.

Torrance was not wholly at ease in the progressive ethos of Auburn. But it stimulated his evangelistic zeal as well as his limitless industry. He bore a heavy course load in doctrinal theology, studying and writing lectures at breakneck pace. The lectures, much influenced by Mackintosh and Barth, enabled Torrance to sketch out views on doctrinal topics which in later life he would amplify but not substantially revise. During the year, he was approached by other US institutions: McCormick Seminary in Chicago, and, more temptingly, the newly established Department of Religion at Princeton University, whose offer of a post was nevertheless declined. War was looming, and Torrance determined to return to Europe.

Back in Scotland, he applied for work as an army chaplain, but was told to wait a couple of years. He spent a year in Oxford working on his dissertation at Oriel, overseen by the Provost W. D. Ross and the epigraphist Marcus Tod (both unlikely mentors for a determinedly theological doctorate). But the shortage of parish ministers pulled him away from full-time studies once more: in March 1940 he was ordained to parish work in Alyth in Perthshire. With the interruption of war service, he was to remain in parish work for the next decade. Ministerial work brought him great happiness. He was conscientious in fulfilling his duties, and kept up theological interests by attending the Angus Theological Club and writing reviews and articles. In 1943 he again tried to enlist as an army chaplain, but was diverted to work in the Middle East with the Church of Scotland Huts and Canteens, providing pastoral and practical support to Scottish soldiers overseas. Subsequently he took up a gruelling post as chaplain to the 10th Indian Division in Italy; he was awarded the MBE for his war service.

When the war ended, Torrance returned to Alyth, picking up the threads both of parish work and of his still unfinished doctorate. He submitted the work in 1946, and spent a term in Basle preparing for what proved to be 'a fearful *rigorosum*'; he passed *magna cum laude*. The dissertation, published as *The Doctrine of Grace in the Apostolic Fathers* (Edinburgh, 1948), argues that New Testament teaching about the radical character of divine grace is fatally compromised in second-century Christianity by the incursion of moralism. It is not the work of one destined to become a front-rank patristic historian; though textually detailed, it lacks historical perspective, its argument is schematic and its judgements are at times peremptory. Its impact on the discipline of patristics was negligible. But it should be read for what it is: historical *theology*, extended consideration of a dogmatic topic through the medium of a body of texts. This genre was already losing favour when Torrance made use of it, but it was one to which he was often to have recourse, later examples achieving greater sophistication.

Shortly before his final term in Basle, Torrance became engaged to Margaret Edith Spear, an English woman whom he had come to know through one of his sisters. They married in October 1946, and enjoyed a long and happy marriage (Margaret survived her husband); Torrance's pursuit of his vocation would have been unthinkable without her presence. There were two sons, Thomas and Iain, and a daughter, Alison.

In late 1947, Torrance moved to become minister of Beechgrove Church in Aberdeen, a larger suburban parish where H. R. Mackintosh had ministered at the beginning of the century. The new parish gave him greater scope, as well as opportunities for contact with university staff, particularly Donald MacKinnon, recently arrived from Oxford to take up the Regius Chair of Moral Philosophy. Torrance was by now a rising star in church and theology. His enterprising side had already shown itself in his role in founding the Scottish Church Theology Society in 1945 (some of whose members like Ian Henderson and Ronald Gregor Smith became prominent in Scottish divinity) and, more importantly, in launching the *Scottish Journal of Theology* with J. K. S. Reid in 1948. The journal quickly established itself as a platform for the doctrinally serious, ecclesially and ecumenically engaged theology which was gathering momentum in the post-war period, and also provided an instrument for the dissemination of Barth's theology in Britain. It was destined to play a significant international role in theological publishing. From 1949 he participated in bi-lateral conversations between the Church of Scotland and the Church of England. And he continued to publish: in 1949 there appeared *Calvin's Doctrine of Man* (London), a detailed account of the Reformer's anthropology which contains early formulations of epistemological positions Torrance would later elaborate. It was becoming clear that a move to academic work would be a natural next step, and in 1950 he accepted the chair in Church History at New College, where he remained until retirement in 1979.

III

The merging of New College and the University Faculty of Divinity had resulted in two chairs of church history, the 'church' chair which Torrance assumed, and a 'university' chair occupied by J. H. S. Burleigh. Given Torrance's distinctly theological leanings, it was hardly an ideal appointment, but he worked hard in it, lecturing on topics in European Reformation and Scottish historical theology. Any chafing was short-lived. In 1952, G. T. Thomson, Mackintosh's successor, retired early, and the chair of Christian Dogmatics fell vacant. Torrance asked to be transferred; Baillie, Principal of New College at the time, was reluctant, but the transfer went ahead, and Torrance began his long tenure, teaching alongside Baillie in the Divinity chair and, from 1956, Baillie's successor, John McIntyre.

Once installed, Torrance's staple teaching was in the area of the theology of incarnation and atonement. Torrance sometimes regretted that the division of labour between the dogmatics and divinity chairs did not permit him to teach the doctrine of the Trinity. Reading the lecture texts—recently edited by a devoted former student (Robert Walker) and published in two volumes as *Incarnation* (2008) and *Atonement* (2010)—communicates something of his classroom presence and manner. They are didactic and polemical rather than exploratory, laying out a position and expecting assent rather than surveying possibilities, and their tone is intense, without a trace of detachment or irony. Some students found his teaching rather overwhelming: one had to be intellectually athletic to get the best from the lectures, and Torrance could be devastating in response to classroom questions he considered to indicate lack of engagement. Others were enthralled, exhilarated by the devotion, directness, clarity and comprehensiveness of his teaching, as well as by acts of kindness to students outside the classroom.

The scholarly and the ecclesial were never separate domains for Torrance, his choice of topics, his intellectual procedures and his rhetoric all shaped by a compelling sense of vocation as *doctor ecclesiae*. Especially in the 1950s, he directed the greater part of his ample energy to the theological renewal of the church—both the ecumenical church encountered in his participation in the post-war movement for church unity, and the domestic Reformed church in Scotland. Most of his writings from this decade were either occasional pieces or more substantial essays laying out principles of church reform; they were brought together in 1959–60 in a two-volume collection *Conflict and Agreement in the Church* (London). The dedications of the volumes speak of the world of Protestant ecumenism in which Torrance moved: the first was dedicated to Barth, the second to two leading Lutheran churchmen, the Swedish theologian and bishop Anders Nygren, and Edmund Schlink, the Heidelberg ecumenist. The collection shows Torrance at work on some of the chief topics of post-war ecumenical discussion: the apostolic character of the church in relation to ministerial order, intercommunion between separated denominations, and the nature of the sacraments. Torrance was committed to the ecumenical

fruitfulness of theological clarification, convinced that institutional reconciliation of the churches must derive from repentant affirmation of such
doctrinal principles as the priority of divine grace which both chastens
ecclesial self-assertion and establishes the church as the social coordinate
of the work of God.

His work from this period was animated by a variety of commitments.
He was persuaded of the value of what came to be known as 'biblical
theology', which used topical analysis to draw up a synthesis of biblical
patterns of thought, and which invested heavily in the distinctiveness of
biblical terminology and in its stability across the canon. To this were
added a particular reading of the Reformed tradition, in which Calvin's
vision of a renewed catholic church was set against later predestinarian
Calvinism, and a vivid sense of ecumenical opportunity.

Torrance's post at New College gave him responsibilities for theological
leadership in the Church of Scotland, and his co-editorship of the *Scottish
Journal of Theology* occasions for published commentary on its life. From
1954 to 1962 he was Convenor of the Church of Scotland Commission on
Baptism, established by General Assembly in 1953 to clarify the church's
baptismal theology and discipline. Its various reports and proposals
reflected his more sacramental perspective which allied him with those of
'Scoto-Catholic' persuasion (and also caused him to regret Barth's repudi-
ation of infant baptism in the mid-1960s). The Commission's eventual
proposals were largely ignored. A similar fate awaited the so-called
Bishops Report submitted to the General Assembly in 1957, which grew
out of bi-lateral conversations between the Church of England and the
Church of Scotland in which Torrance had been a representative. The
report proposed reunion of the two churches, but was vilified by a
campaign orchestrated by the *Scottish Daily Express* which regarded
episcopal government an offence to Scottish nationalist honour.

Torrance's efforts to shift the ethos of the Church of Scotland were
grounded in an interpretation of the Reformed tradition which did not
commend itself to the denomination as a whole. From H. R. Mackintosh,
he had learned disaffection for purely forensic and extrinsic accounts of
the relation of Christ and the believer, preferring a theology of union with
Christ. This, in turn, attracted him to a certain sacramental realism of
which Calvin, not Zwingli, was the exemplar, the attraction no doubt
reinforced by family connections to Anglicanism. A number of writings
from the 1950s stake out his position. In 1958 he edited and translated
from Scots the eucharistic sermons of Robert Bruce, preached at St Giles
in Edinburgh in 1589, a work of profound sacramental piety, and in the

same year contributed a substantial introduction and notes to a re-issue of an older translation of Calvin's *Tracts and Treatises*. A year later he published an edition of the catechisms of the Reformed churches, including Scottish domestic texts such as Craig's Catechism. A very lengthy introduction explained, *inter alia*, Torrance's preference for the sixteenth-century Reformed tradition over later high Calvinist scholasticism. Similarly, his 1960 revised and expanded edition of Wotherspoon and Kirkpatrick's *Manual of Church Doctrine According to the Church of Scotland* (his co-editor was Ronald Selby Wright, the liturgically minded minister of Canongate Kirk in Edinburgh) reinforced the high Genevan churchmanship of the original edition from earlier in the century.

Two longer pieces of ecclesiological writing from the mid-1950s gave more sustained expression to his amalgamation of evangelical and catholic sympathies. One, *Kingdom and Church* (Edinburgh, 1956), studied the relation of eschatology and ecclesiology by offering synthetic studies of Luther, Bucer and Calvin. The eschatology Torrance discovered in the Reformers is not apocalyptic or catastrophic so much as teleological: the new age inaugurated at the incarnation is at work in the temporal forms of the church, though such forms remain imperfect anticipations of the final end. Eschatology, in effect, both relativises and confirms visible order. A second piece, *Royal Priesthood*, published in 1955 as a *Scottish Journal of Theology* occasional paper, expounded what Torrance considered a biblical and ancient catholic account of the derivation of the church's ministry from the priestly ministry of Christ. The book is a minor classic of post-war ecumenical theology, rooting a high doctrine of ministry and sacraments in a vivid Christology, and resistant to the naturalisation of church order. The book was overshadowed by the remarkably hostile treatment given to it by Torrance's Edinburgh colleague James Barr in *The Semantics of Biblical Language* (London, 1961). Barr launched a vigorous attack on the biblical theology of the 1940s and 1950s, with its emphases on the coherence and distinctiveness of the biblical thought-world and on the way in which its 'Hebraic' character can be traced by etymological study of biblical language. In example after example, Barr sought to show that modern linguistic theory left no room for this style of theology; many of the examples were drawn from Torrance's work, which Barr clearly judged to be wholly without value. The rift which Barr's assault generated was lasting, the immediate tension somewhat eased by Barr's departure for Princeton Theological Seminary in the same year as the publication of his book. In later years, Torrance came to think that Barr's arguments expressed the 'phenomenalism' of modern biblical studies, which segregated biblical language from divine revelation. Torrance and Barr represented divergent theological cultures, one making its appeal to revelation and church, the other *wissenschaftlich*. Torrance was to devote much time over the next four decades to advancing reasons for the divergence and its effect on theological science and hermeneutics.

The latter part of Torrance's first decade at New College saw the appearance of the first fruits of two substantial editorial projects. One was a new translation of Calvin's New Testament commentaries (his brother David was also named as series editor), the initial volume of which in 1959 was the first half of the Gospel of John, translated by the Anglican Calvin scholar T. H. L. Parker, who shared Torrance's theological sympathies. But by far the most ambitious and influential editorial undertaking was the English translation of Barth's *Kirchliche Dogmatik*.[1] A number of Barth's writings were already available in English, including some collections of essays, some expositions of confessional texts, and Sir Edwyn Hoskyns's startling translation of the second edition of Barth's *Romans* commentary. But of Barth's huge *magnum opus* (by the mid-1950s Barth had published ten volumes) almost nothing had appeared in English. An abortive start had been made with G. T. Thomson's 1936 translation of the first part-volume, but his work was unsatisfactory. In the absence of a decent translation, Barth's mature work, easily the most eminent exercise in Protestant dogmatics for a century, remained almost wholly unknown to English readers, leaving reception (and rejection) of his work dependent on a limited selection of older occasional and polemical writings.

Torrance was ideally placed to remedy the situation. He knew Barth and Barth's writings, and his position in New College afforded a platform from which to promote Barth's ideas. From the early 1950s, Torrance began to plan a full translation of the *Kirchliche Dogmatik*, covering the volumes which had already appeared in German and those still in preparation. Torrance shared editorial oversight with Geoffrey Bromiley, at that time an Edinburgh Episcopalian clergyman; a translation team was established, and from 1956 the volumes appeared in rapid succession, so that by 1961 the English had caught up with the German. By this time, Barth had largely ceased to work on his *Dogmatik*; a final fragment was published in English in 1969 and in 1975 a re-translation of the first part-volume. completed the work

[1] G. W. Bromiley and T. F. Torrance (eds.), K. Barth, *Church Dogmatics* (13 vols., Edinburgh, 1956–75).

The impact of the translation is difficult to exaggerate: it opened up the full scope of Barth's mature thought, which as a result began to enter the mainstream of English-language theology, and to attract much better-informed and more sophisticated discussion than hitherto. Torrance's own interpretation of Barth did much to direct that discussion. A substantial study, *Karl Barth. An Introduction to his Early Theology 1910–1931* (London, 1962), was the leading account of Barth's earlier work for a quarter century; it was complemented by a large number of essays on Barth, collected after retirement as *Karl Barth. Biblical and Evangelical Theologian* (Edinburgh, 1990). Torrance held Barth in the highest esteem, ranking him alongside his other giants, Athanasius and Calvin. He brought his own interests to his reading of Barth. He was much pre-occupied by Barth's thinking about the nature of divine revelation and human knowledge of God, and was captivated by Barth's orientation of all Christian teaching towards the person and work of Christ, as well as by Barth's integration of the doctrines of the Trinity and the incarnation. Barth represented the contemporary possibility of uninhibited theology on the grand scale, all the more impressive when set alongside what Torrance regarded as the dreary sceptical revisions of Christian doctrine on offer in mainstream British theology in the 1960s and 1970s.

Aspects of Torrance's interpretation of Barth have not stood the test of time. Posthumous publication of a good deal more of Barth's early writing makes his account of Barth's development in the 1920s less secure. Moreover, Torrance's way of articulating the supremacy of divine grace made him insufficiently alert to Barth's abiding interest in moral theology as integral to dogmatics. Barth thought of the Reformed tradition as a kind of theocentric humanism, with a double theme of divine and human action; Torrance more naturally gravitated to the theology of human participation in Christ, leaving less space for ethical considerations. The difference emerged over Barth's late doctrine of baptism, which Torrance thought gave too much space to human agency. His puzzlement over what he took to be Barth's misstep indicates his unease with something deep in the fabric of Barth's thought. Such matters aside, Barth's secure place in the canon of modern theology for English readers would be unthinkable without Torrance's determined advocacy.

IV

By the end of the 1950s, Torrance was a considerable presence in theology in Scotland and beyond. His chair in Edinburgh provided access to a large company of ministerial candidates and graduate students eager to learn from him, as well as an abundance of external academic and ecclesial activities in Britain and abroad. He was able to appoint like-minded colleagues: his brother James, Alasdair Heron and John Zizioulas. Only once, in 1961, did he give serious consideration to moving (to Basle, as Barth's successor), but decided to stay the course at New College, partly for family reasons, partly because of the demands of operating in a very different academic culture. Long tenure at New College often entailed a spell as Principal, but Torrance's frank dislike of administrative and committee work, as well as his manifold outside engagements, relieved him of the prospect. There were, naturally, occasional frustrations or disagreements, but they did not extend beyond the usual differences of conviction and temperament. He did not always see eye to eye with John McIntyre on theological questions, and was unpersuaded by the broadening of the curriculum to include religious studies which McIntyre oversaw as Principal from 1968. But their differences lacked any trace of personal animosity, and Torrance remained content at New College for the rest of his teaching career.

Torrance's theological work over the next two decades until retirement, and on into the mid-1990s, ranged very widely: historical theology (especially patristic and Reformation), hermeneutics, the principles of theological rationality and the relation of theology and natural science, his inquiries into all these fields directed by a conviction that the chief articles of Christian dogma possess very substantial heuristic power. Despite this conviction, Torrance's published output in dogmatics remained relatively modest until retirement, mostly made up of journal articles and book chapters—some collected in two volumes of essays, *Theology in Reconstruction* (London, 1965) and *Theology in Reconciliation* (London, 1975)—along with a short book, *Space, Time and Incarnation* (Oxford, 1969), which brought together three lectures from different occasions, and, in 1976, a somewhat longer related work, *Space, Time and Resurrection* (Edinburgh). Often his thinking about dogmatic topics has to be gleaned from writing on related matters—the history of Christian thought, or the implications of Christian doctrine for the nature of reason. Moreover, the range of dogmatic topics treated in the 1960s and 1970s is fairly restricted: the doctrines of Christ and the Spirit, and some issues in ecclesiology and sacramental theology. Themes such as the divine attributes, creation and creatures, providence or sanctification rarely appear, and even the doctrine of the Trinity, in whose primacy Torrance was deeply invested, did not become a matter for extensive consideration in published work until the 1980s. Much of his most enduring dogmatic writing saw light after retirement, in a series of books which began with the published version of his 1981 Warfield Lectures at Princeton Theological Seminary (*The Trinitarian Faith*, Edinburgh, 1988) and was completed by *Trinitarian Perspectives* (Edinburgh, 1994), which assembled essays from the early 1990s, and by the monograph *The Christian Doctrine of God* (Edinburgh, 1996).

A good deal of British theological writing of the period around 1960 to 1990, especially the work of some distinguished patristic historians, was sceptical about the permanent validity of conciliar trinitarian and incarnational thought, its confidence eroded by biblical and doctrinal criticism and by a sometimes inchoate sense that the metaphysical principles assumed by classical Christian thought had been rendered untenable by modern philosophy. Torrance stood apart from that theological culture, and did not share its inhibitions; he criticised it variously as nominalist, dualist or phenomenalist, and considered the favoured alternatives—exemplarist Christology and non-trinitarian theism—wholly deficient. His intellect and imagination, as well as his religious affections, were profoundly stirred by the ideas of those theologians whose writings formed the canon out of which he generated his own understanding of Christian teaching, and by which he judged other accounts: Athanasius, the Cappadocians and Cyril of Alexandria among the fathers, Calvin among the Reformers, Barth among the moderns. Each afforded access to an immensely spacious and satisfying world of thought, free from the cramping effects of over-zealous attention to modern scruples, and provided a stock of concepts and patterns of argument which formed the matter of the extensive description of Christian doctrine to which some of his later writings were devoted.

Torrance's dogmatic writing commonly took the form of positive explication and commendation of the articles of the catholic creeds, and of some Reformation distinctives in the theology of grace and salvation. As he reached out to the great matters which seized his attention, his rhetoric often took on a measure of urgency, pressing the reader to share his sense of the spiritual import and explanatory power of a range of theological ideas and arguments. He wrote from within a set of traditions by which he was captivated; his texts are saturated with quotation and allusion. On occasions, analytical and logical order, as well as elegance and economy of phrasing, were compromised in the rush of ideas. The reader is persuaded by accumulation of concepts and description, with frequent restatement and amplification, the style bearing some resemblance to that of Barth, who also wrote *in extenso*, though usually less loosely than Torrance. The result is one of the most stirring, consistent and conceptually innovative bodies of theological writing in English from the last fifty years.

The cardinal, and inseparable, doctrines are those of incarnation and Trinity. Torrance considered Nicene teaching about the substantial unity (*homoousion*) of the incarnate Son and God the Father to be of limitless import. He did not think of the Council of Nicaea as a rather messy and indeterminate process of pastoral, political and doctrinal negotiation, but as a moment in which the mind and conceptuality of the church were stamped with divine truth. In its wake, resolution of all manner of theological questions may be effected by attention to the ontological and epistemological primacy of Christ's person and work. Christology is that from which other elements of Christian doctrine may be derived, and that in relation to which doctrinal authenticity is to be determined. Torrance often rehearsed the ancient and modern history of dogmatics as an intellectual and spiritual contest between affirmation of the *homoousion* and its entailments and refusal to acknowledge its constitutive place. On his account of the matter, the union of divine and human natures in the incarnation is such that the history of Jesus Christ is a double movement—of God to creatures in revelation and reconciliation, and of creatures to God in perfect actualisation of human relation to the creator. In descriptions of the first movement, Torrance wrote indefatigably of the ultimacy and unrestricted efficacy of the union of God and humanity in Christ: all history leads to and flows from this point, and in it all history finds its redemption. The second movement—that of Christ's 'vicarious humanity' which gathers all other human creatures into itself—was also much emphasised by Torrance, to forestall any idea that creatures complete their nature autonomously.

Torrance considered the doctrine of the Trinity a confession of the identity and nature of the one who works in the world in Christ and the Spirit. From this, much follows: the correspondence of God's inner being to God's external acts; the definition of each divine person by reference to that person's relations to the others (for which Torrance coined the term 'onto-relations'); the trinitarian order of divine action upon created things. Torrance was one of a number of theologians who contributed to the sea-change in English-language theology in the final two decades of the last century, by which trinitarian doctrine came to be considered not a problem but a resource.

Torrance's writings frequently address questions about the relation of material doctrine and the nature of created rationality. Of all those who operated within Barth's ambit, he was the most self-conscious and sophisticated in treating the nature of human intelligence, his work animated by belief that part of the apostolic vocation of theology is to expose the modern (and ancient) breach between mind and reality, and to display their proper kinship. He considered much modern biblical and dogmatic work to be constrained by conventions about reason and rational practice, and sought to show that, rightly conducted, theology can unmask and illuminate such conventions, as well as exemplify reason's proper exercise. Three related topics attracted his attention: biblical hermeneutics, theological rationality, and the relations of theology and the natural sciences.

His extensive writings on the nature and interpretation of Scripture have not found their way into the canon of modern literature on biblical hermeneutics. In part this is because a large-scale historical and constructive project on the theme was never brought to completion, though some of it appeared as journal articles, and in retirement Torrance published a short monograph on *The Hermeneutics of John Calvin* (Edinburgh, 1988) and a substantial collection of essays on patristic hermeneutics, *Divine Meaning* (Edinburgh, 1995). Moreover, Torrance did not engage with the key ideas and texts of Continental philosophy and literary theory which dominated the hermeneutical agenda from the 1970s: he had some familiarity with Heidegger, but Gadamer, Ricoeur and Derrida, for example, did not make an appearance in what he had to say. Further, most of his writing on hermeneutics took the form of *grandes lignes* readings of figures from the Christian past—the Alexandrians, Aquinas, Erasmus, Calvin, Reuchlin, Schleiermacher—in which his own proposals were often underexplored.

His chief concern was not with the detailed texture of Christian literary culture and its exegetical practices but with hermeneutical first principles, and with the pathology of what he judged to be modern hermeneutical defect. On his account, modern theological hermeneutics suffers from a dichotomy of linguistic-literary sign and thing signified, or an extrinsicist separation of divine communication and created media, of which the naturalism and nominalism of biblical studies is only the most telling example. To counter this, Torrance proposed a theological semantics in which human texts, along with the apostolic forms of ecclesial life in which they emerge, are fitting instruments of divine speech. The biblical writings are instrumental, and therefore possess a certain depth; they are constituted by their expressive or referential relation to the revelatory divine word, and properly to read such texts is to grasp their 'depth dimension'.

If Torrance's integration of biblical hermeneutics and doctrinally derived semantics, unique among his contemporaries, has largely been passed over, his writings on theological rationality and especially on theology and the natural sciences have evoked a good deal of attention.

Torrance found in Barth the consummate positive theologian of the modern era who pursued Protestant dogmatics free from the thrall of subjectivism and idealism, and operated under the conviction that the exercise of theological intelligence at full stretch requires eager assent to divine instruction. Like Barth, Torrance did not think this divine instruction limited to a sacred text; it is, rather, an act of self-communication, which it is the task of theology to indicate in language and concepts which are transparent to divine revelation. He wrote copiously on what he called the 'philosophy of theology' (reflection on the way in which theology's cognitive principles and procedures are shaped by its matter), presenting theological inquiry as inseparable from mortification of error, or as the mind's interrogation and formation by objective, self-bestowing divine reality. On this account, the intellectual virtues which Torrance prized in the theologians he most esteemed, and which he himself sought to exercise, are a certain adaptability and conceptual transparency to divine truth.

Similar themes recur in the substantial and strikingly original body of work on the relation of theology and natural science which some consider Torrance's most weighty intellectual achievement. He had lectured on the topic at Auburn in the late 1930s, but other tasks and preoccupations were such that it was only from the late 1950s that he was free to devote a great deal of intellectual and practical energy into shaping the nascent conversations between theologians and natural scientists; his contributions were recognised in 1978 by the award of the Templeton Prize for Progress in Religion. His published work in the field began with an authoritative text, *Theological Science* (London, 1969), followed by a host of articles and chapters and, after retirement, by a number of shorter monographs: *Christian Theology and Scientific Culture* (Belfast, 1980); *The Ground and Grammar of Theology* (Belfast, 1980); *Divine and Contingent Order* (Oxford, 1981); *Transformation and Convergence in the Frame of Knowledge* (Belfast, 1984); *The Christian Frame of Mind* (Edinburgh, 1985); and *Reality and Scientific Theology* (Edinburgh, 1985). His work gravitated to discussion of the first principles of inquiry, the 'frame of mind' which forms intellectual activity in theology and natural science. The history which Torrance offered is, doubtless, schematic; that aside, he was persuaded that the revolution in cosmology associated with Einstein (and, before him, with the Scottish physicist James Clerk Maxwell, whose

Dynamical Theory of the Electromagnetic Field was republished in 1982 under Torrance's editorship) presented unique opportunities to advance beyond the self-contained mechanistic physics of Copernicus and Newton which severely inhibited theological affirmations about natural reality. Torrance was quick to seize on the convergences between a theological metaphysics of nature and the new cosmology, and often frustrated by theologians who still undertook their work in captivity to an exhausted physics. He found in the new cosmology much that resonated with Barth's deep sense of the sheer givenness of divine revelation, most of all a coordination of acts of knowledge with the intelligibility of reality, reinforcing his conviction that, in natural science as in theology, thought is properly 'kataphysic', in accordance with the nature of its objects. Some of the most forceful passages in his published work describe progress in theology and science as conversion of the mind away from false representations by submission to the inherent order of reality, divine or contingent. Further, Torrance was attracted to a conception of a stratified universe in which lower-level natural phenomena refer to and are ordered by a higher purposive level, and so possess an intrinsic depth. The ideas were refined in conversation with the émigré Hungarian chemist and philosopher of science Michael Polanyi: Torrance promoted and wrote about his work and acted as his literary executor.

Torrance's interest in natural science—highly unusual for one so indebted to Barth—led him to distance himself from Barth's unqualified hostility to natural theology. Barth considered the modern project of natural theology and natural religion an assertion of the priority of human capacity over divine revelation which issued in idolatry. Torrance took a different tack, conceding Barth's worry about the independence of some natural theology, but maintaining that natural theology is not necessarily a bid for autonomy: it may be a subordinate extension of positive theology which traces the ways in which created reality, illuminated by divine revelation, may in turn illuminate its creator. If Barth's rejection of natural theology is the obverse of deist natural religion, Torrance's account of the matter recalls earlier theologies of nature in which 'positive' and 'natural' theologies are not competing but complementary.

In the midst of his professorial work in the 1960s and 1970s, Torrance's busyness as churchman and ecumenist showed no abatement. His stature in the Church of Scotland led to appointment as Moderator for the year 1976–7. He fulfilled the duties of the post—which is representative and ambassadorial rather than executive—with typical vigour, travelling widely within and outside Scotland, and promoting an elevated theological conception of the church's identity and mission. After demitting the office, he remained a figure of influence in the Church of Scotland General Assembly.

In ecumenical activity, he was much occupied with conversations between the Reformed and Orthodox churches. His knowledge of the Orthodox world was remarkably extensive. He pored over the classical texts of Eastern Christianity. Through involvement in the Faith and Order Commission in the 1950s he developed a host of friendships and working relationships with Orthodox theologians such as Georges Florovsky. He mentored Orthodox students in Edinburgh, including those like George Dragas and John Zizioulas who became interpreters of Orthodoxy in the West. He was associated with the Foundation for Hellenism in Great Britain, established by a leading Orthodox cleric, Methodios Fouyas. It was Fouyas who in 1973 arranged for Torrance to lecture in Addis Ababa on the 1,600th anniversary of the death of Athanasius; on this occasion, Torrance was consecrated an honorary protopresbyter of the Greek patri-archate of Alexandria. Torrance's first foreign tour as Moderator was to the Orthodox patriarchates of the East. These visits sowed the seed for the dialogue between the World Alliance of Reformed Churches and the Orthodox churches which, after initial consultations, began in 1988 and produced an agreed statement on the doctrine of the Trinity in 1991. Torrance was prominent in the discussions, and edited the papers which emerged from the dialogue. As with earlier ecumenical efforts in which Torrance was involved, however, the proposals failed to receive acceptance.

Torrance retired from his Edinburgh chair in 1979, widely esteemed and recognised by a string of honorary degrees and by his presidency of the Society for the Study of Theology and of the Académie Internationale des Sciences Religieuses. In his retirement year he was elected to a Fellowship of the Royal Society of Edinburgh, and in 1982 to the British Academy.

Until the mid-1990s, Torrance remained extraordinarily productive: a good deal of his most consequential writing appeared when retirement gave him greater freedom to set out at length ideas which had preoccupied him for decades. Between 1979 and 1996 he published sixteen books, edited a couple more, and wrote scores of shorter pieces. The topics are largely those which had engrossed him throughout his career (Christian doctrine, hermeneutics, the nature of scientific thought), though there were some new departures, including a charming, if somewhat partial, history of Scottish theology from John Knox to McLeod Campbell (*Scottish Theology*, 1996). Over the course of his professorship, he had toyed with summing up his thinking in a comprehensive dogmatic theology, but it did not make its appearance. Partly this was because the project was pushed aside by other writing tasks, but also partly because Torrance's intellectual urgency did not suit him for a large-scale systematic exercise in which proportion and a sense of the whole are of great consequence. Moreover, Barth's remarkable talent cast a long shadow: to those in his circle, the sheer scale of his achievement seemed such that any other Reformed dogmatics would be bound to appear feeble in comparison.

Alongside his writing, he continued to travel extensively. He lectured widely in Britain and North America in the 1970s and 1980s. He was deeply moved to return to the China of his childhood in the 1980s, to retrace his father's summer missionary trips to the upper Min valley, and to meet and take financial support to Xiang Christians descended from his father's converts.

In his final years he was confined to a nursing home, frustrated in some measure by the diminishment of his powers and activity but supported by his wife and family. He died on 2 December 2007; his funeral at St Mary's Whitekirk was attended by his extensive family and by colleagues and friends from around the world.

V

Torrance was a strenuous and decisive person, purposeful, frank, and, if the occasion required, able to mount a spirited challenge, though without any trace of vanity or desire for personal ascendancy. His resoluteness went along with warmth of pastoral concern. Beneath the external activity there was deep privacy: he was suspicious of introspection, and such autobiographical materials as remain are entirely concerned with external events and with the development of his thinking.

The character and measure of his achievements may be seen when he is set alongside two near-contemporary Scottish divines of similar distinction: John Macquarrie and Donald MacKinnon. All three were church theologians; all three possessed remarkable conceptual prowess; all three sought to pursue the tasks of Christian divinity with an eye to the changed cultural conditions of modernity, though they differed widely in their judgements about how those conditions were to be understood.[2] Torrance

[2] For the other two see Stewart Sutherland, 'Donald Mackenzie MacKinnon 1913–1994', *Proceedings of the British Academy*, 97 (London, 1998), pp. 381–9; and K. Ward, 'John Macquarrie 1919–2007', *Proceedings of the British Academy*, 161, *Biographical Memoirs of Fellows*, VIII (London, 2009), pp. 259–77.

found little to attract him in Macquarrie's correlation of existentialism and Anglican incarnational theology. Where Macquarrie learned much from Heidegger, Bultmann and Tillich, Torrance's mind was thoroughly catechised by the texts and ideas of the Greek patristic and Reformed theologians, believing them to outbid the claims of modern habits of thought. Macquarrie was by nature serene, even-tempered and attracted to synthesis; Torrance was an intense, and at times combative, thinker who treated intellectual problems as a summons to repentance and regarded compromise with distaste. Torrance found much more affinity with MacKinnon. Neither was pacific in temper or intellectual disposition; both were attracted to Barth as a vivid alternative to the buoyant liberal theologies of the pre-war years; both found in the doctrines of Trinity and incarnation the elements of a comprehensive metaphysics. But where MacKinnon's intelligence was agonised, endlessly self-interrogative and self-subversive, and frequently reduced to silence, Torrance, though no less averse to intellectual complacency, enjoyed far greater confidence and fluency: he thought by writing. Further, Torrance combined intellectual interiority with a busy external vocation as churchman, advocate and animator. In this, and in other ways, few contemporaries equalled him in range and scale of attainment.

JOHN WEBSTER
University of St Andrews

Note. My thanks to Professor Iain Torrance, Professor Alan Torrance and Professor David Fergusson for their assistance. A bibliography of Torrance's writings can be found in A. E. McGrath, *T. F. Torrance. An Intellectual Biography* (London, 1999); his voluminous papers are lodged in the library of Princeton Theological Seminary.

REG WARD

William Reginald Ward
1925–2010

WILLIAM REGINALD WARD, the scholar of British and European history, and especially religious history, was born on 23 March 1925 in Chesterfield, Derbyshire, into a family of Primitive Methodists. His paternal grandfather was a Primitive Methodist minister and missionary, who served for a time in Nigeria. His father was a local Primitive Methodist preacher who also worked for the Inland Revenue. Primitive Methodism, its religious practices and traditions, would have a profound and lasting influence on the historian's life and work. As his friend, the Oxford historian John Walsh, would later observe, Ward's Primitive Methodism instilled in him a dislike of hierarchy and pretension, a healthy distrust of authority, and a readiness to speak his mind.[1] He would also remain teetotal throughout his life. Ward's mother was the granddaughter of a Peak District quarryman and the daughter of a miner. She felt a certain pride in having married a civil servant, and was determined on making her only child into a proper 'gentleman', emphasising good manners and reminding him, even when he had reached the giddy heights of a professorship, that he take his hat off when indoors. The family moved from Chesterfield to Plymouth on account of his father's civil service job in about 1935. Reg (as he would be known throughout his life) attended Devonport High School for Boys, which at that time was very strict, with demanding academic standards. Here he studied Latin and developed the highly disciplined work habits that would stay with him throughout his life. Devonport

---

[1] J. Walsh, 'Profile: W. R. Ward: Methodist historian and historian of Methodism', *Epworth Review*, 22 (1995), p. 41.

Biographical Memoirs of Fellows of the British Academy, XIII, 439–462. © The British Academy 2014.

was heavily bombed during the Second World War, and the school was evacuated for a time to Penzance, Cornwall, which Reg had loved.

Defined as Medical Grade 4 on account of a bad ear, he was kept out of military service during the war. Instead, with the help of several scholarships, including a college open scholarship, he was able to matriculate at University College, Oxford, in 1943. He had intended to read Philosophy, Politics and Economics, but on the advice of his father (who was convinced there would be no post-war jobs for economists), Ward switched to Modern History, studying at the austere war-time Oxford with its depleted academic staff and a nearly empty Bodleian Library. He attended the Wesley Memorial Church under the ministry of Frederic Greeves. Ward graduated with a 'congratulated' First Class Honours in Modern History—the best in his year—in 1946. On the nomination of the future Labour prime minister, Harold Wilson, then a research fellow at University College, Ward was appointed as a tutor at Ruskin College, an independent adult education college in Oxford, where he taught for three years. While at Ruskin, he began working towards the Oxford D.Phil. with a thesis on the eighteenth-century English land tax. His supervisor was the distinguished historian of eighteenth-century Britain, Miss Lucy Sutherland, who had recently been appointed Principal of Lady Margaret Hall, Oxford. Sutherland, who later became Dame Lucy Sutherland, would have a major influence on all his subsequent work.[2]

At the end of the war, Ward met his future wife, Barbara, while they were both serving in a Christian harvest camp at Hove, organised by the evangelical Bishop of Rochester, Christopher Chavasse. The harvest camps brought together students and other young people to assist with bringing in the harvest while so many farm labourers were still away on military service. Barbara was helping as a cook, and Reg had the exalted title of 'quartermaster'. Their first romantic encounter took place while peeling potatoes. Barbara was a teacher, who had taught at a school for infants in Brighton and then at a school for physically disabled children in Sussex before meeting Reg. They shared a warm sense of humour and love of long country walks. Barbara would continue part-time teaching after her marriage. In their early years together, they would take a bus or train into the countryside on a Saturday, exploring much of the Peak

---

[2] W. R. Ward, 'Statement on Election as a Fellow of the British Academy' (2009), deposited with the Academy, available at <https://www.britac.ac.uk/fellowship/elections/ward.cfm> [accessed 3 April 2014].

District. Although raised an Anglican, she joined Reg in the Methodist Church. Theirs would be a long and happy marriage.

The University of Manchester and the political historian of institutions

In 1949, Ward was appointed to an assistant lectureship in the Department of History at the University of Manchester. The History Department was then under the formidable influence of Lewis Namier, who Ward later described as 'a presence equally instructive and perplexing'.[3] Barbara recalled needing to be 'very serious' in Namier's presence, but she also remembered that he was most supportive to Reg. Namier encouraged Ward's strict work habits, and under his influence Ward developed as an historian of eighteenth-century English politics and administration. Of Namier, Ward wrote in 1957 that 'his patience with young students grows no less with the years, and the archive of the *History of Parliament* has become a bottomless well of information'.[4] Ward's early work was greatly influenced by the Namierite approach, with its emphasis on detailed studies of human interactions, the importance of patronage and personal connections, and the role of institutions in elevating essentially venal human actors to achieve higher, collective aims. Ward completed his Oxford D.Phil. in 1951, and two years later he published a revised version of his thesis in the Oxford Historical Series, under the title of *The English Land Tax in the Eighteenth Century*.[5] The book provided a meticulous analysis of the local administration of the land tax, the difficulties in the assessment and collection of the tax, the administrative laxness and financial weakness of the mid-eighteenth-century state, and the role of debates over the land tax in sharpening party differences. It was, he argued, largely the ability of the British state to borrow so freely that allowed the increasingly inefficient land tax system, which had been formulated in the seventeenth century, to survive into the later eighteenth century. Only the acute financial pressures of the American war and the war with Revolutionary France finally forced significant fiscal reform. In what would be characteristic of all Ward's later scholarship, the book was based on extensive archival research, including work among the Treasury

[3] Ibid.
[4] W. R. Ward, *Georgian Oxford: University Politics in the Eighteenth Century* (Oxford, 1958), p. v.
[5] W. R. Ward, *The English Land Tax in the Eighteenth Century* (Oxford, 1953).

Records, minute books of the Land Tax Commissioners, and a number of collections of family papers.

For his second major project, Ward turned to the history of Oxford University during the eighteenth and nineteenth centuries. The first volume of this project, *Georgian Oxford: University Politics in the Eighteenth Century*, appeared in 1958, and reflected Ward's Namierite approach. It provided detailed accounts of the political manoeuvres among the Oxford dons, including their pursuit of patronage and favour from the Crown and political grandees, their interventions in the contests for the two university parliamentary seats, and their efforts to adjust their political positions to the political crises associated with the Revolution of 1688–9, the Hanoverian Succession, and the early years of George III's reign. The dons struggled to adjust to changing political realities, but on the whole they were loyal to the governments of the day (as reflected in the university sermons); indeed, Ward rejected the then prevalent notion that Oxford was a 'hotbed of Jacobitism for more than half a century after the Revolution'.[6] The book closed with a sustained discussion of religious movements, including the failed challenges to the orthodox Anglican hegemony in the 1770s associated with latitudinarianism and rational Dissent. There was an account of the failure of the Feathers Tavern Petition of 1771–2 to end the requirement of clerical subscription to the Thirty-Nine Articles of Faith in the Church of England, and of the unsuccessful movement in the 1770s to ease the terms of subscription to the Anglican articles required from Oxford dons, especially those not directly involved in theological teaching.

The second volume of his history of Oxford University, *Victorian Oxford*, appeared from Frank Cass publishers in 1965.[7] Again, the emphasis was on university politics, with accounts of the efforts of university dons to gain political patronage and support, and of the contests for the university's parliamentary seats, but now in the changing context of intensified religious beliefs, emerging liberal and democratic politics, and increased public calls for university reform. Moreover, while *Georgian Oxford* had focused on the role of the university in supporting the established order in Church and State, *Victorian Oxford* explored the development of Oxford University into a secular institution for promoting specialised research and educating a professional elite to serve the needs of an industrial, urban and imperial nation. It was the story of the

[6] Ward, *Georgian Oxford*, p. 55.
[7] W. R. Ward, *Victorian Oxford* (London, 1965).

intensified religious feeling during the Oxford Movement, followed by declining Anglican influence, liberal reforms, calls for increased efficiency in teaching and research, university commissions, and the waning political importance of the university. While *Georgian Oxford* closed with the debates over religious tests in the 1770s, *Victorian Oxford* ended with the reforms of the 1870s and early 1880s, including the repeal of most remaining religious tests. Both books were based on exhaustive research among a vast array of primary sources, and demonstrated an impressive grasp of historical detail. But the written style was dense, and one American reviewer of *Georgian Oxford* complained of feeling 'cast adrift on a sea of detail' and searching 'anxiously for a spot of synthesis from which he can observe what he has covered'.[8] Ward remained very much a disciple of Sutherland and Namier, and an historian's historian; he held the highest respect for the discipline and profession of history, and he could be as demanding on his readers as he was on himself.

During their early years in Manchester, Reg and Barbara shared a flat and then a small house, while Barbara did some teaching. Following the birth of their second child, they bought a house in Bramhall, to the south of the city, and Reg would commute to the university on a motor bike. By the end of the 1950s, there were three children, a daughter, Faith, and two sons, Aidan and Neil. Reg and Barbara travelled for Saturday excursions or holidays around Britain with the children in a sidecar attached to the motorbike; this included travel for holidays in Scotland, which they loved. Barbara recalls that the children were always well behaved in the sidecar, as they knew they would be going somewhere interesting. But Reg's daily commute from Bramhall to the university by motor bike was proving difficult, and there were financial pressures on the young family.

In 1959, Ward accepted the position of Warden of the newly built Needham Hall at the University of Manchester. The university had purchased a Victorian property off Spath Road in West Didsbury, and constructed three blocks of student residences. The family had a pleasant flat in one of the residences, which enabled them to sell the house in Bramhall. But the new position was not without its difficulties. As Warden, Ward was responsible for overseeing the buildings, student events and student behaviour, while he also spent long hours meeting with individual students and providing guidance. He ate his evening meals with the students in the hall, which was hard for his family. Endeavouring to

---

[8] L. L. Tucker, 'Review of W. R. Ward's *Georgian Oxford*', *William and Mary Quarterly*, 16 (1959), 271.

balance the demands of the Wardenship, his teaching, his research, and to
find time for his family, placed considerable strain on Reg. Although he
was promoted to Senior Lecturer, the financial pressures continued. It was
at this time that he and Barbara seriously considered moving with the
family to Australia, where there was a prospect of an academic appointment for Reg. Although the job prospect did not get as far as an interview,
there was an exchange of letters and Reg and Barbara were very serious
about the move although, as Barbara recalls, their parents were not at all
pleased about the prospect. Then came the offer of the Chair of Modern
History at the University of Durham and in 1965, the same year that saw
the publication of *Victorian Oxford*, Ward accepted the Professorship and
moved to Durham with his family. The years at Needham Hall had enabled
them to save for the purchase of a substantial house in Durham.

Ward's move to the history of Christianity

While he was working on his *Victorian Oxford* book, Ward had also grown
increasingly interested in religious history. This interest would, by the
mid-1960s, lead to a major shift in the direction in his work—with the
historian of the politics of national institutions (Parliament, the land tax,
Oxford University) becoming the historian of British, and then of
European Christianity. In part, this change was the result of Ward's
engagement with religious themes in writing his book on nineteenth-
century Oxford, and in part it reflected his involvement, as a committed
Methodist, in the controversies in the early 1960s concerning proposals
for the union of the Anglican and Methodist Churches. As he described
the transformation:

> It was impossible to write about nineteenth-century Oxford without paying
> heed to the religious stance of the parties involved; and in the later stages of that
> work [*Victorian Oxford*] another group of questions of religious belief and
> practice came rather closer home. The proposals for Anglican-Methodist union
> inevitably raised sharp differences of opinion on both sides, and on the
> Methodist side were marked by appeals to Methodist history which amply com-
> pensated in stridency what they lacked in illumination. But there was no mistak-
> ing the fact that what Methodism *had been* was part of the question of what
> Methodism was and ought to be. A situation characterized by so much heat and
> so little light almost required of a working Methodist historian that he examine
> some of the questions for himself.[9]

[9] W. R. Ward, 'Introduction', in *Faith and Faction* (London, 1993), p. viii.

There was probably another reason for Ward's move to religious history, and this was simply his appreciation, as a research historian, of the vital importance of religion for an understanding of British history, especially during the final decades of the eighteenth and first decades of the nine-teenth centuries. Britain was at this time experiencing the upheavals of early industrialisation and urbanisation, while the entire North Atlantic world was in the throes of what the American historian, Robert Palmer, described as 'The Age of the Democratic Revolution' in his influential two-volume work on this subject (the first volume was published in 1959 and reviewed by Ward in *Parliamentary Affairs* in 1960).[10] There was new interest in the role of popular religion in the political upheavals of these years—an interest sparked by one work in particular. In 1963, E. P. Thompson, the son of Methodist missionary parents, and a Marxist humanist who was then teaching at the University of Leeds, published *The Making of the English Working Class*, in which he explored the devel-opment of a political consciousness among the labouring orders between the 1790s and 1830s.[11] A key theme of Thompson's work was the crucial role of Evangelical Dissent, and especially Primitive Methodism, in shap-ing a working-class identity, and also in diverting the energies of the labouring orders from revolutionary activity in this world to striving for salvation in the next life. Thompson's work revived interest in the thesis of the French historian, Élie Halévy, who had famously argued in his *England in 1815* (published in French in 1913 and in English translation in 1924), that Evangelicalism in general, and Methodism in particular, had insu-lated Britain from revolution between the 1790s and 1820s.[12] The early 1960s witnessed, in short, a growing interest in both the revolutionary decades and the role of religion in popular politics.

Ward became active in the Ecclesiastical History Society from its foundation in 1961, publishing his first article on the history of Christianity, 'Oxford and the origins of Liberal Catholicism in the Church of England', in the Society's journal, *Studies in Church History*, in 1964. Through regular attendance of the meetings of the Ecclesiastical History Society, and later of the *Commission Internationale d'Histoire et d'Etudes du Christianisme*, or CIHEC (on which he served on the British

[10] R. R. Palmer, *The Age of the Democratic Revolution: a Political History of Europe and America, 1760–1800*, 2 vols. (Princeton, NJ, 1959 and 1964); W. R. Ward, 'Review of R. R. Palmer, *The Age of Democratic Revolution*, vol. I', *Parliamentary Affairs*, 13 (1960), 263–4.
[11] E. P. Thompson, *The Making of the English Working Class* (London, 1963).
[12] É. Halévy, *A History of the English People in the Nineteenth Century I: England in 1815*, trans. E. I. Watkin and D. A. Barker (London, 1924).

Sub-Commission) he developed an impressive knowledge of the history of Christianity since the Reformation.

He served as President of the Ecclesiastical History Society in 1970–1. He delivered a memorable presidential address to the annual meeting of the Society, speaking rather incongruously, as he later remembered, from the top of a pile of beer crates. Professor Hugh McLeod, FBA, recalled the powerful impact of the opening sentence of Ward's address on the audience, as he spoke of the generation of 1790–1830:

> The generation about which I wish to speak was, I make no doubt, the most important single generation in the modern history not merely of English religion but of the whole Christian world. For . . . there seems no doubt that the effectiveness of the Church throughout Western Europe was undermined by the same forces which were everywhere sapping the *Ancien Régime*, the whole institutional complex of which the religious establishments were part.[13]

Ward then proceeded in his address to develop a bold argument concerning English Christianity during this period. In the 1790s, he maintained, in response to the social upheavals of early industrialisation, the prospect of violent revolution, and the failings of the established Church to minister to a growing population, a wave of revivalist popular religion swept across much of England. This popular religion was largely non-denominational in character, rooted in cottage prayer meetings and itinerant lay preaching, reflecting a belief in the equality of souls and the moral capacities of common men and women, and including apocalyptic visions, exorcisms, and special gifts of the Spirit. Many labouring people deserted their parish churches or the staid chapels of old Dissent, and the traditional social order they represented. Instead, they hankered after visions of a new world to be born through the actions of the Spirit. 'The uninstitutional movements of God's grace so dear to the revivalists', Ward observed, 'evoked a powerful echo in men who were at the losing end of institutions and chilled the marrow of those with a stake in institutional stability.'[14] But the vision of a free, just and egalitarian society permeated by a genuine Christianity—and the dreams of a true people's Church, or *Volkskirche*, that would be popular, non-denominational, free of institutional constraints—did not long survive. The itinerant revivalist preachers began to long for family life, secure incomes and settled ministries; cottage meetings developed into institutional churches, and then into denominations. New clerical hierarchies emerged, with defined theological positions and the

---

[13] W. R. Ward, 'The religion of the people and the problems of control, 1790–1830', in Ward, *Faith and Faction*, p. 264.
[14] Ibid., p. 269.

imposition of authority. By the later 1840s, the *Volkskirche* ideal was fading, and, Ward suggested, Christianity began to lose much of its popular appeal.

Ward developed these arguments at greater length in his next book, *Religion and Society in England 1790–1850*, which was published in 1972 by Batsford, as part of its 'Fabric of British History' series.[15] In this book, he maintained that the weakness of the eighteenth-century British parliamentary state had left it unable to respond adequately to the popular radicalism of the 1790s. In response to its own weakness, the state looked to the established Church of England to help provide social control through the parish system, clerical influence in the old Poor Law, and a growing body of clerical magistrates. But this attempt to increase the authority of the established Church came at the same time as large numbers were being stirred up by revivalism and radical social visions, often rooted in apocalyptic and millenarian enthusiasms. Nonconformists, fired by revivalism, strenuously resisted the state's efforts to revive the established Church. Some, moreover, went on the offensive, attacking church rates and tithes, and calling for disestablishment. This warfare with the established Church, however, created divisions within the Nonconformist denominations, with some embracing the popular political agitation, and others insisting upon a more otherworldly spirituality. There was intense religious strife and instability during the 1830s and 1840s. In the event, the divisions within Nonconformity ensured that Nonconformists failed in their attempts to disestablish the Church of England. Moreover, the Nonconformist leadership, most notably the Methodist leader, Jabez Bunting, imposed order on the unruly elements within their denominations, often at the cost of schisms. Popular dreams of a new Christian social order of liberty and equality ended, and mid-nineteenth-century England settled into a denominationalism, dominated by institutional Churches, orthodox creeds, clerical elites and middle-class influence. The ideal of a popular, informal, non-institutional, non-denominational Church—a *Volkskirche*—faded, and with it, Ward suggested, the hopes of a Christian England. His account was based on extensive research among largely neglected Nonconformist primary sources, including Methodist Church archives and Nonconformist periodicals.

The book was on the whole well received. Sheridan Gilley, for example, was impressed with the power of Ward's historical thesis, and his achievement in evoking the rich diversity of religious and civic life in the urban

---

[15] W. R. Ward, *Religion and Society in England 1790–1850* (London, 1972).

Midlands, especially Manchester.[16] However, for Owen Chadwick, FBA, who had written so eloquently on the Victorian Church, Ward's book, though 'excellent', described only one aspect of the early nineteenth-century English religious life, that is, the Midland urban unrest set against 'the roll of drums and thunder of distant tumbrils'; while it ignored the more quiet devotion and respect for tradition that characterised religion in much of England. Chadwick was also unconvinced by Ward's efforts to show close connections between revivalism and urban radicalism. Nor did Chadwick agree with Ward that the failure of radicalism and the growth of denominationalism were 'bad things'. 'By reading Ward', he continued, 'the reader would hardly understand the "Halévy-truth", the civilizing order of Victorian society with the various churches as integral to the civilizing process.'[17] Some readers, meanwhile, continued to have difficulty with Ward's written style. 'His prose style', observed an American reviewer, 'is so dense and turgid as to make reading his book actually unpleasant.'[18] The distinguished historian of nineteenth-century Britain, Ursula Henriques, Sheridan Gilley later recalled, expressed to him 'her bafflement about *Religion and Society in England*'.[19]

Ward continued his work on early nineteenth-century Methodism with a two-volume edition of the correspondence of Jabez Bunting, the figure who had played the leading role in imposing denominational order on early nineteenth-century Methodism. *The Early Correspondence of Jabez Bunting 1820–1829* was published in 1972 by the Royal Historical Society, and *Early Victorian Methodism: the Correspondence of Jabez Bunting 1830–1858* was published in 1976 by Oxford University Press, with financial assistance from the Publications Board of the University of Durham.[20] 'Although', as Ward observed, 'Bunting was never a man to everyone's taste, and certainly not to every Methodist's taste,'[21] Ward none the less recognised the value of this large body of correspondence for an

---

[16] S. Gilley, 'Review of *Religion and Society in England 1790–1850*', *Catholic Historical Review*, 59 (1974), 698–700.

[17] O. Chadwick, 'Review of *Religion and Society in England 1790–1850*', *Historical Journal*, 16 (1973), 870–4, quotations on 873–4.

[18] L. F. Barmann, 'Review of *Religion and Society in England 1790–1850*', *Journal of Modern History*, 47 (1975), 556.

[19] Sheridan Gilley, letter to the author, 29 Sept. 2013.

[20] W. R. Ward (ed.), *The Early Correspondence of Jabez Bunting 1820–1829*, Camden Fourth Series, vol. 11 (London, 1972); W. R. Ward (ed.), *Early Victorian Methodism: the Correspondence of Jabez Bunting 1830–1858* (Oxford, 1976).

[21] Ward, 'Preface', *Early Victorian Methodism*, p. v.

understanding of the changes in early nineteenth-century British religious life.

Growing interest in German religious history

During the 1970s, Ward began receiving successive invitations to attend the *Deutscher Historikertag*, a major German national conference held every other year in historical studies, and also invitations to participate in workshops at the Georg Eckert Institute at Brunswick, a research institute specialising in the improvement of educational textbooks. He was initially invited to interpret English social Christianity to German and Continental scholars, but he soon developed an interest of his own in the history of German social Christianity. He began studying the German language at about the age of 50. While he did not master conversational German, he did learn to read the language to a sufficiently high level to be able to conduct manuscript research. Henceforth, he spent more and more time on the Continent, and Barbara recalled that they increasingly spent their holidays in Germany or the Low Countries, with Reg spending long hours in the archives.

Ward wrote his next book on German social Christianity in the late nineteenth and early twentieth centuries: *Theology, Sociology and Politics: the German Protestant Social Conscience 1890–1933* was published in 1979 by Peter Lang of Berne.[22] It was a study of Christian social engagement in industrialising and urbanising Germany. While Ward's work on English social Christianity had, up to this point in his career, focused on the social tensions resulting from early industrialisation, the French Revolution and Napoleonic Wars, his book on German social Christianity moved forward in time, exploring the social tensions of mature industrialisation, the First World War and the Russian Revolution. Following a review of the social Christian movement after the Revolutions of 1848, including the contributions of Johann Wichern and the Inner Mission, Ward focused on the challenges posed to the late nineteenth- and early twentieth-century social Christian movement by the German Social Democratic Party, which was then dominated by an atheistic, anti-religious Marxist ideology. The Social Democratic Party, with its vision of the coming classless society of justice and equality, held the high moral

---

[22] W. R. Ward, *Theology, Sociology and Politics: the German Protestant Social Conscience 1890–1933* (Berne, 1979).

ground for many German labouring people, while the Churches were viewed as overly connected to the governing elites in the Bismarckian state. The German Churches were thus placed in a difficult position. If they opposed the anti-religious Social Democratic Party, they would risk alienating further the labouring classes. But there seemed no way that Christian churches could establish a common ground with Marxism. In the German-speaking cantons of Switzerland, the Religious-Socialist Movement of Leonhard Ragaz, Herman Kutter and Karl Barth did attempt after 1906 to bring Christianity into alignment with Marxism but, despite some innovative writing in their journal *Neue Wege*, the movement became divided by the pressures of the Great War and Russian Revolution. Ragaz eventually left the Church for social and educational work in a working-class district of Zurich, while at the Tambach conference of 1919 Barth famously denounced efforts to 'secularise' Christianity by linking it to political movements. Another effort to define a social Christianity was that of Friedrich Naumann and Max Weber, who sought from the 1890s to gain working-class support by identifying Christianity with a German cultural nationalism. However, with the growing influence of extremist racial nationalism in the 1920s, this approach also foundered, as many German Christian cultural nationalists embraced the German Christian movement that would seek alignment with National Socialism after 1933.

This was the first English-language book on German social Christianity during this crucial period, and it was based on an impressive array of German primary sources. The book was, in many senses, an exploration of the idea of the *Volkskirche*, or non-denominational, non-institutional popular Church, now in the German context. Wichern had boldly proclaimed the ideal of the *Volkskirche* in a celebrated address to the first German Church congress, or *Kirchentag*, in late 1848. But, as Ward's historical account demonstrated, the *Volkskirche* ideal was no more successful in Germany at the end of the nineteenth century than it had been in England at the beginning of the century. Ward's scholarly connections with Germany and modern German religious history, meanwhile, would continue, and he became a member of the editorial board of the journal *Kirchliche Zeitgeschichte* from its founding in 1988.

Professor of Modern History at Durham

As Professor of Modern History at Durham University, Ward was a formidable intellectual presence, a highly committed academic leader and a supportive colleague, although to some he could also be at times perplexing, even acerbic. During his twenty-one years at Durham, he played an active role in the University Senate, served frequently as Head of the Department of History, and also served as Dean of Arts from 1972 to 1974. In the 1960s and 1970s, as one colleague recalled, being head of department was no 'dawdle', as there was no reduction in teaching load and very little secretarial support. By the 1980s, moreover, universities were experiencing cuts to their state funding, and were obliged to compete with one another for their share of the declining state resource. As a head of department, Ward stoutly defended the interests of History within the university. At the same time, he was concerned about what he believed were low levels of publication at Durham, and he felt that the department had to change its priorities and nurture more of a research culture. Nor was he wrong in his analysis. When he arrived at Durham, there was a sense in many quarters that it was a provincial university, which should be content to focus on teaching, and send those students wanting to do doctoral research to Oxford, Cambridge or London. Some lecturers were given to believe that research was a rather low-level adjunct to their undergraduate teaching. As a result of Durham curricular reforms in the 1960s, moreover, there was an attempt to combine an 'Oxbridge' tutorial system with a 'redbrick' system based on lecture courses. The result was a very heavy teaching load, with lecturers struggling to teach within both systems. Ward encouraged his colleagues to publish more, but he also understood the demands on their time. He became convinced that undergraduate students at Durham were being given too much attention in comparison with other universities, and he argued that Durham could 'no longer afford to give all students the Rolls-Royce treatment' and also be competitive as a research university.

He struggled personally to carve out time for his research on top of his heavy administrative and teaching loads or, as he once put it, to achieve research outputs in 'a life largely devoted to sustaining academic institutions placed under increasing strain, and to meeting the demands of students of various levels to be taught things of quite other sorts'.[23] To some junior colleagues, he could seem to be asserting his professorial

---

[23] Ward, 'Introduction', *Faith and Faction*, p. viii.

privilege, and they could resent what they suspected were attempts to min-imise his teaching. To be fair to Ward, they were not fully aware of the amount of time he gave to administration. His efforts to address all points of view in meetings, and his delight in detail, could lead to failures to communicate clearly with his colleagues. He sometimes made convoluted statements in departmental or Senate meetings, which few could under-stand or appreciate. His colleagues, one observed, 'used to joke about "Reg questions" at departmental seminars and job talks, which were often so long and syntactically and otherwise complex that he lost most people somewhere before he was half-way through'. Nor were his relations with colleagues helped by his waspish wit. He once described a rather self-important cleric and fellow historian as 'the stupidest man in the Church of England'. He had an appreciation for the absurd in life, enjoyed good-humoured banter and was in many respects modest about his own abilities but, as one colleague observed, he was 'sometimes not very thoughtful about the effect his words might have on somebody else'.

He could be demanding as a teacher and examiner, and he worked very hard at his teaching. In lecturing, he would usually take off his jacket, pace about a bit and try to create a relaxed mood. Yet, with his challeng-ing sentences, frequent allusions, assumptions of background knowledge and demanding standards, it is not clear how effective he was as a teacher of undergraduate students. Professor Jane Dawson recalled how as a second-year History undergraduate she had once asked Ward a point of clarification about the doctrine of predestination, and was directed to Karl Barth's *Church Dogmatics*! At the same time, however, he could exude great warmth, generosity of spirit, and lack of pretentiousness. Dawson also remembered coming by his office as an undergraduate to ask for some sort of permission from him as head of department. Arriving at his door, she was greeted by a 'Good, Jane, come and stir this and don't stop.' She was then 'handed the spoon for a pan of sauce cooking on the little double ring in his room', while Ward attended to another part of the cooking. 'After the initial surprise', she further recalled, 'it was nice to realise I was being treated as a person and not as a "student".'

This small two-burner stove in his room was entirely illicit, and would not have survived the tougher fire regulations of a later period. He enjoyed the daily ritual of cooking a hot lunch and sharing it with others. One of his academic colleagues recalls Ward's lunch-time culinary efforts:

> He invited colleagues to share with him, two by two, and we all meekly accepted. It was pure Austerity Cookbook. One colleague recalls repetitive . . . red kidney beans; my special memory is of stewed prunes. There was always a pudding, and

it was always stewed prunes. Took you straight back to the 1940s, even if you had never been there. He was such a generous man in many ways, but this was a form of hospitality you didn't want too often. The best thing about it was the washing-up.

In the mid-1970s, Ward contributed a recipe to a Methodist cookery book for a Chicken Curacao, which included the following guidance: 'Make up the white sauce (rich cooks may use a large can of evaporated milk; idle cooks may use a packet of savoury white sauce; the idle rich may use both).' 'West Indians and Dutch add curacao', he continued, 'sober Methodists achieve an acceptable result without injury to soul or body by adding a little rum flavour.' Ward certainly remained teetotal throughout his life. Although he was not evangelical about it, he did make it a point when he hosted departmental parties at his home, as one colleague recalled, to have 'lots and lots of different soft drinks' and no alcohol on offer, and then to encourage his guests to try different concoctions. (John Walsh recalls that at the bibulous dinner hosted by the dons for the under-graduates at Oxford University to celebrate VE Day in 1945, Reg was compelled to drink eight pints of orangeade: perhaps it was this memory that lay behind his determination to offer his guests a wide choice of soft drinks.)

During his Durham years, he strenuously opposed the union negotiations between the Methodist and Anglican Churches which had begun in the 1960s. He had a strong, almost visceral aversion both to the idea of an established Church and to bishops; and he viewed the proposal for union as an abandonment of Methodist principles. He joined with his fellow Methodist, Kingsley Barrett, Professor of Divinity at Durham University,[24] in resisting the union, objecting in particular to the notion of Methodists accepting the historic episcopate and the apostolic succession of bishops, which Barrett insisted was an idea based on 'very bad history and worse theology'.[25] Ward also harboured scepticism about the entire ecumenical movement, which he felt was dominated by church hierarchies and large institutional Churches. He personally believed that a revival of Christianity, were it to come, would emerge at the level of individual believers, and not through institutional unions and clerical hierarchies. There was, indeed, an anti-clerical tendency in Ward, and an abiding commitment to the Reformation ideal of the priesthood of all believers. Although he had

[24] On Barrett see J. D. G. Dunn, 'Charles Kingsley Barrett 1917–2011', *Biographical Memoirs of Fellows of the British Academy*, XII (2013), 3–21.
[25] 'The Reverend C. K. Barrett', *The Daily Telegraph*, 6 Sept. 2011.

Catholic friends, he harboured a prejudice against the Catholic Church, with its papacy, prelacy and magnificence.

In 1986, after forty years of teaching—at Ruskin College, the University of Manchester and Durham University—Ward retired from full-time teaching, and became a Professor Emeritus at Durham. He was only 61, so his retirement was a little early, though no one was surprised by the decision. He was experiencing arthritic pain in his knees—'bad enough', one colleague recalled, 'to make him grimace with pain at times'—though not so bad as to keep him from the country walks that he and Barbara loved. He was perhaps feeling a little out of tune with university life in the 1980s, and there were good retirement packages on offer. But probably most important was his commitment to research. He retired, as John Walsh has observed, in 'style, with a magnificent, symbolic celebration of his Nonconformist inheritance' held in the historic Elvet Methodist Church in central Durham. There was an evening of hymns, led by choirs and bands, with Ward interpreting the hymns from the pulpit with 'affection, eloquence and learning'.[26]

On his retirement, Reg and Barbara left Durham, and moved to Petersfield, an attractive market town in the south of England. The decision to move south was largely Barbara's. She knew that her husband tended to become absorbed in Durham University politics and she felt certain that he would continue to do so in his retirement. If he were really to have the time he craved for his research and writing, she felt there needed to be a complete break. She also wanted to move south, which would place her closer to her own roots in Brighton and Hove. In Petersfield, Reg could travel in an hour and a half to London for visits to the archives, lectures and seminars (and he regularly did so). They had a pleasant house, and enjoyed their walks in the surrounding countryside. Indeed, one colleague in Durham suspected that one of the attractions of the move for Reg was that he had exhausted all the country walks in the Durham area. He became active in the Petersfield Historical Society, and eventually became its President. He not only continued his historical research and writing, but became more productive than ever in his retirement.

[26] Walsh, 'Profile: W. R. Ward', p. 42.

The Protestant Evangelical awakening
and the 'Ward Thesis'

In 1992, six years after his retirement, he published what is arguably his most important work, the fruit of his years of research in the history of early modern politics and religion. *The Protestant Evangelical Awakening* was published by Cambridge University Press, and was almost immediately recognised as a seminal reinterpretation of the religious revival movement which transformed the North Atlantic world between the late-eighteenth and early-nineteenth centuries.[27] For the late Professor Jerald C. Brauer of the University of Chicago, a respected scholar of revivalism, Ward's book was 'the first comprehensive history of the rise, development, and spread of . . . what we call revivalism' and a 'superb history of the total picture of the evangelical awakening from central and eastern Europe, Scandinavia, Great Britain and North America'.[28] For another leading scholar of the history of modern Christianity, Professor David Hempton, now Dean of Havard Divinity School, the book was 'a display of quite breathtaking scholarship'.[29] The inspiration for the book, and what would become known as the 'Ward thesis' (as John Walsh has observed) came from Ward's reading of Will Herberg's *Protestant, Catholic, Jew* of 1955, a sociological account of immigration to the United States. Herberg had observed how religion served to preserve a sense of identity among vulnerable immigrant communities, in opposition to a dominant civic religion which made few demands but represented assimilation and conformity.[30] For Ward, Herberg's analysis helped him to reconceptualise the origins and nature of the Protestant Awakening.

In *The Protestant Evangelical Awakening* Ward located the beginnings of modern revivalism among vulnerable, displaced, powerless and often poor peoples in Central and Eastern Europe in the aftermath of the Wars of the Reformation, and especially the furious bloodletting of the Thirty Years' War of 1618–48. As he observed, the treaties making up the Peace of Westphalia that ended the Thirty Years' War in 1648 confirmed the

[27] W. R. Ward, *The Protestant Evangelical Awakening* (Cambridge, 1992).
[28] J. C. Brauer, 'Revivalism revisited', *The Journal of Religion*, 77 (1997), 272.
[29] D. Hempton, 'Review of *The Protestant Evangelical Awakening*', *The Linen Hall Review*, 10 (1993), 28.
[30] Walsh, 'Profile: W. R. Ward', p. 44; W. R. Ward, 'Will Herberg: an American hypothesis seen from Europe', in Ward, *Faith and Faction*, pp. 358–73.

principle that rulers were to determine the established form of Christianity—Lutheran, Reformed or Catholic—within their respective states, while certain guarantees were given to permit some religious minorities to worship in designated churches. However, there was no general religious toleration, and religious minorities were always vulnerable, distrusted and subject to the sudden withdrawal of even their limited ability to worship—while for decades after 1648 there was the constant danger that the fragile Westphalia Settlement would break down and there would be a renewal of religious warfare. According to Ward, it was among the threatened and marginalised Protestants in Central Europe, especially those who found themselves on the wrong side of the religious boundaries and subject to persecution by the civil and religious authorities—including being deprived of the ability to worship in church buildings—that people developed the practices that would become characteristic of revivalism. These practices included cottage meetings, prayer meetings, lay preaching, private Bible reading, the circulation of tracts, establishment of schools (to educate people to read their Bibles and tracts), fervent hymn singing, open-air meetings, and on occasion—especially during periods of acute danger—emotive, charismatic outbreaks, including convulsions, trances, visions, speaking in tongues, and apocalyptic dreams. Through the revivalist practices, minority Protestant communities in Central Europe resisted assimilation into the established religion, and preserved their identities.

Ward then traced the spread of revivalist beliefs and practices to poor or threatened minorities elsewhere in Europe, and then to Britain and its North American colonies. The beliefs and practices were communicated through the flow of religious refugees, itinerant preachers, private correspondence, the circulation of tracts, and concerts of prayer. As the movement spread, revivalist practices were formalised and networks were organised by a series of gifted leaders, including Spener in Frankfurt, Francke in Halle, Zinzendorf in Herrnhut, and the Wesleys and Whitefield in Britain and the North American colonies. The entire North Atlantic world was affected by what became known as the Protestant Evangelical Awakening. This movement, Ward insisted, must be understood as an international phenomenon, with its origins in popular resistance to assimilation into the religious establishments of the Westphalia Settlement and its support coming from common people determined to preserve their religious and cultural identities. 'Almost everywhere', he concluded, 'the revival began in resistance to a real or perceived threat of assimilation by the state in its modern shape, and the timetable of the revival, even in the

West, was set by the timetable of the Protestant crisis in Eastern and Central Europe where the threat was most raw and crude.'[31]

It was a work of monumental importance. Previous historians of modern revivalism tended to focus on the British and North American contexts. Ward was the first to develop a sustained account which traced the origins of the movement to central Europe, and demonstrated the causal connections between post-Westphalia political tensions, German Pietism, English Methodism, Scottish and Welsh revivalism, and the North American Great Awakening. While some might quibble with aspects of his account, or note omissions (for example, the lack of attention to Ireland), the 'Ward thesis' has become generally accepted. As the leading North American historians of modern evangelicalism, Mark Noll and Bruce Hindmarsh, later observed, 'Ward changed the historiography of early evangelicalism.' 'His scholarship', they continued, 'reconstituted 18th-century Anglo-American evangelical history in terms of 17th-century Central European history. This is one of the great contributions in all of modern historical scholarship.'[32] In 1990, meanwhile, Ward's contributions had been recognised with a Festschrift, *Protestant Evangelicalism: Britain, Ireland, Germany and American c.1750–c.1850*, which was edited by Keith Robbins and published under the auspices of the Ecclesiastical History Society. As well as contributions from fifteen leading scholars, the volume included a valuable bibliography of Ward's publications.[33] Then in 1992 he was further honoured with the award of the degree of Doctor of Theology *honoris causa* by the University of Basle in Switzerland.

Ward followed *The Protestant Evangelical Awakening* seven years later with a survey of European Christianity, *Christianity under the Ancien Régime 1648–1789*, published by Cambridge University Press as part of its 'New Approaches to European History' series.[34] While his book emphasised German and British Protestantism, especially Pietism, Methodism and revivalism, Ward also provided a sound discussion of Catholic Europe, and an excellent account of religion and the Enlightenment. The book suffered, as Ward explained to the author of this memoir, by needing to be cut by nearly a third to meet the required word limit for volumes in the series, and as a result the prose is probably

---

[31] Ward, *The Protestant Evangelical Awakening*, p. 353.
[32] M. Noll and B. Hindmarsh, 'Rewriting the history of Evangelicalism: W. R. Ward, 1925–2010', *Books and Culture* (March/April 2011), available at <http://booksandculture.com/articles/2011/marapr/historyevangelicalism.html?start=1> [accessed 11 November 2013].
[33] K. Robbins (ed.), *Protestant Evangelicalism: Britain, Ireland, Germany and America c.1750–c.1850*, *Studies in Church History*, *Subsidia* 7 (Oxford, 1990).
[34] W. R. Ward, *Christianity under the Ancien Régime 1648–1789* (Cambridge, 1999).

too dense for a survey text. The following year, he published another survey text, this time a study of the history of the Churches in Great Britain from 1660 to the present, which was translated and published in German.[35] The book is also valuable both for the breadth of its coverage and the balanced assessments of the different religious traditions. In 1993, moreover, he published a collection of twenty-two of his essays in religious history under the title *Faith and Faction*.

He was also active in editing work. Between 1988 and 2003, he co-edited (with Professor Richard P. Heitzenrater of Southern Methodist University in Dallas, Texas, and later of Duke Divinity School in North Carolina) John Wesley's *Journal* in seven volumes for the Bicentennial Edition of *The Works of John Wesley*, published by Abington Press in the United States.[36] Wesley's journal is nearly a million words in length, one of the longest printed sources of the eighteenth century, and editing the work was a mammoth task. The first volume included an Introduction of 119 pages, in which Ward explored the state of autobiographical religious writing in the late-seventeenth and early-eighteenth centuries, the nature and construction of Wesley's *Journal*, and then the nature of autobiographical writing in Wesley's later years. Among the delights of the volumes were Ward's extensive notes, which reflected his vast erudition, acerbic wit and sense of the absurd. One reviewer of the first volume applauded both Ward's 'elegant introduction' and 'meticulously edited text, with extensive biographical, topographical, biblical, and other notes'.[37] Ward also edited and published two volumes of the written replies of Church of England parish clergy in the diocese of Winchester to questions put to them by their bishops at Episcopal visitations.[38] During

[35] Reginald Ward, *Kirchengeschichte Großbritanniens vom 17. bis zum 20. Jahrhundert*, trans. Sabine Westermann (Leipzig, 2000).

[36] W. R. Ward and R. P. Heitzrater (eds.), *The Works of John Wesley, Vol. 18, Journals and Diaries I (1735–1738)* (Nashville, TN, 1988); *The Works of John Wesley, Vol. 19, Journals and Diaries II (1738–1743)* (Nashville, TN, 1990); *The Works of John Wesley, Vol. 20, Journals and Diaries III (1743–1754)* (Nashville, TN, 1991); *The Works of John Wesley, Vol. 21, Journals and Diaries IV (1755–1765)* (Nashville, TN, 1992); *The Works of John Wesley, Vol. 22, Journals and Diaries V (1765–1776)* (Nashville, TN, 1993); *The Works of John Wesley, Vol. 23, Journals and Diaries VI (1776–1786)* (Nashville, TN, 1995); *The Works of John Wesley, Vol. 24, Journals and Diaries VII (1787–1791)* (Nashville, TN, 2003).

[37] C. D. Field, 'Review of *The Works of John Wesley: Journals and Diaries I (1735–1738)*', *English Historical Review*, 109 (1994), 459.

[38] *Parson and Parish in Eighteenth-Century Surrey: Replies to Bishops' Visitations*, edited with an introduction by W. R. Ward (Guildford, 1994); *Parson and Parish in Eighteenth-Century Hampshire: Replies to Bishops' Visitations*, edited with an introduction by W. R. Ward (Winchester, 1995).

this time, he regularly attended seminars and conferences, wrote a steady stream of articles, contributed book chapters and book reviews, and was extremely generous in sharing insights, research and observations with his fellow historians.

In 2006, at the age of 81, Ward published with Cambridge University Press what would be his last book, *Early Evangelicalism: a Global Intellectual History, 1670–1789*.[39] It was in many respects a companion volume to his *Protestant Evangelical Awakening* of 1992. If his *Protestant Evangelical Awakening* had been primarily a study of the origins, development, and spread of the devotional practices associated with Protestant revivalism, in *Early Evangelicalism* he explored the theological and philosophical thought which informed the emergence of Evangelicalism in early modern Europe. According to Ward, amid the crisis of the seventeenth century many Protestants, especially the vulnerable minorities in Central Europe, rejected the dominant Aristotelian system and the theological systems that had been erected upon Aristotelian logic. For them, Aristotelian logic and theological creeds were bulwarks of powerful social hierarchies, absolutist states, and authoritative institutional Churches. In rejecting Aristotelianism and Orthodoxy, some, among them Johann Arndt, were drawn to mysticism, including the mysticism of the Jewish Cabbala teachings. Some embraced the vitalism of Paracelsus, with its beliefs in a basic life-force in all living things, in secret codes in nature, and in arcane cures for illnesses. Some were drawn to theosophy, or a belief in a hidden wisdom to be found in all ancient religious texts. Or they were drawn to prophecy, embracing Jakob Böhme's view of history as the cosmic struggle of love and wrath, shaped by the Paracelsian vital elements of salt, quicksilver and sulphur, and unfolding through the successive ages of the Father, the Son and the Spirit. Many searched the Scriptures for hidden messages and coded references to contemporary events, and were drawn to apocalyptic visions, including expectations of the Second Coming. Some, including Zinzendorf, believed in paranormal abilities, including telepathy and second sight, which they viewed as *charisma*, or gifts of the Spirit. This rich, strange and diverse collection of beliefs and ideas, Ward maintained, formed the intellectual content of early Evangelicalism.

Ward then proceeded to explore the development and influence of these radical mystical beliefs during the eighteenth century, giving

[39] W. R. Ward, *Early Evangelicalism: a Global Intellectual History, 1670–1789* (Cambridge, 2006).

particular emphasis to three figures: Count von Zinzendorf, John Wesley, and Jonathan Edwards. Zinzendorf, he argued, remained 'violently anti-system and anti-Aristotle' throughout his life, and held an eclectic set of beliefs.[40] In the case of Wesley and Edwards, however, Ward traced their growing discomfort with eclecticism and their efforts to impose 'systems' on the diverse beliefs within the evangelical movement, in the interests of bringing order to the movement. Wesley, in particular, although he had been greatly influenced by mysticism in his early years, came by the 1780s to downplay apocalyptic and millenarian enthusiasms. None the less, mystical and millenarian movements continued to surface, in the fervent piety of such figures as Swedenborg, Lavater, and Jung-Stilling, or in the popular evangelical enthusiasms that surrounded the French Revolution and Napoleonic Wars, or in the prophecies of Baroness von Krüdener, Edward Irving and the Albury circle. However, gradually the forces of order and rationality prevailed. By the 1850s, Ward concluded, with the development of denominationalism and the revival of Orthodox creeds, the radical mysticism of evangelicalism—like the ideal of the non-denominational, non-institutional, popular *Volkskirche* that he had explored in previous works—was largely marginalised.

Early Evangelicalism was extremely impressive for the wide range of its sources and coverage, although it lacked the analytical power of his *Protestant Evangelical Awakening*. As in most of his writings, there was a tendency to assume too much background knowledge on the part of his readers. He also described his varied collection of mystical, prophetic, charismatic and millenarian ideas without much effort to weigh and assess their relative importance within the larger evangelical movement. Indeed, he may have been unduly attracted by the strange and unusual in his account of influences. As the Reformed historical theologian, Kenneth Stewart, observed in reviewing the work, 'readers standing within even broad confessional Protestantism will have reason to wonder at the inclusivity of Ward's selection and treatment of leading persons'.[41] Certainly not all of the ideas discussed by Ward were of equal weight within the larger movement. None the less, *Early Evangelicalism* is a fascinating and evocative companion to the *Protestant Evangelical Awakening*, which fills out the larger 'Ward thesis' on the rise and diversification of evangelical

[40] W. R. Ward, *Early Evangelicalism: a Global Intellectual History, 1670–1789*, p. 118.
[41] K. Stewart, 'Review of *Early Evangelicalism*', *Calvin Theological Journal*, 44 (2009), 443–5.

piety in the North Atlantic world between the seventeenth and the mid-nineteenth centuries, and which is inspiring further work. In January 2008, the American Society of Church History held a special session at its annual conference in Washington, DC, honouring him as one of the most distinguished religious historians of the past half-century. It would be one of his last conference appearances and, with his 'droll sense of humour', 'vast erudition', and 'delight in the arcane', he was highly entertaining in his response to the panellists.[42]

Reg Ward died on 2 October 2010 in his home at Petersfield, after a nine-month struggle with cancer. He was working until nearly the end, latterly on a project involving Central European atheists. When he could no longer write, he worked on arranging his papers, so that others might carry on the work. He was survived by his wife, Barbara, his three children and his nine grandchildren. The year before his death, he was elected a Fellow of the British Academy. While some believed his election was long overdue, Ward was simply very pleased, and this is reflected in his warm personal statement on the occasion. This statement, significantly, highlighted the Primitive Methodist tradition and its 'long-term influences' on his life and work. For while Ward was a formidable European intellectual, he also remained firmly connected to his roots—Nonconformist, lower middle-class, teetotal, and provincial, with a strong Protestant work ethic and simple tastes. He was devoted to his family. He was kindly, well-intentioned and gentle in his manners. He also felt compelled to speak openly and candidly, and on occasion to play the 'Ranter'—in the Primitive Methodist belief that people are called to say honestly what they think and to correct one another, and sometimes simply to deflate pretensions. He had a sense of the absurd in life, and an ability to laugh at himself. His sympathies as an historian were with the poor and the marginalised, whether the embattled Protestants of seventeenth-century Central Europe or the struggling Methodist labourers in early nineteenth-century Manchester. He had a strong commitment to the historical profession, and was very much an 'historian's historian'—who had demanding standards in research and analysis, and who expected that his students, and his readers, should also work hard to follow his arguments. While the amount of work he produced is impressive, his greatest contribution was the 'Ward thesis' on the origins, development and diversification of Protestant revivalism and evangelicalism, from their origins

[42] Noll and Hindmarsh, 'Rewriting the history of Evangelicalism'.

in seventeenth-century German-speaking Central Europe to the larger North Atlantic world. It is a monumental achievement, which has reshaped our conceptions of the early modern history of European and North American Christianity.

STEWART J. BROWN
University of Edinburgh

Note. For advice and information in writing this memoir, I am grateful to David Bebbington, Arthur Burns, Jane Dawson, Sheridan Gilley, Howell Harris, Brian Harrison, Hugh McLeod, Mark Noll and Stella Fletcher, and especially to Barbara Ward and John Walsh.